STUDIES IN MODERN HISTORY
General Editor: L. B. NAMIER, F.B.A., Professor of Modern
History, University of Manchester

JENKINSON PAPERS

THE
JENKINSON PAPERS
1760–1766

EDITED
WITH AN INTRODUCTION BY

NINETTA S. JUCKER

LONDON
MACMILLAN & CO. LTD
1949

INTRODUCTION

CHARLES JENKINSON was born in Winchester, probably in 1727.[1] Both his parents came from well-established county families, but his father being a younger son and his mother the daughter of a cadet branch, neither of them had any fortune. The Jenkinson family, which claimed descent from Anthony Jenkinson, an Elizabethan explorer, settled in Oxfordshire early in the seventeenth century, became baronets at the Restoration, and represented the county in Parliament from 1705 to 1727. Charles's father, Colonel Charles Jenkinson of the Royal Horse Guards, was the youngest son of Sir Robert Jenkinson, 2nd Bart. of Walcot, M.P. for Oxfordshire from 1709 to 1717. His mother was the daughter of a naval captain, Wolfran Cornwall, whose family, long established in Hereford-shire, had a claim to the Barony of Burford in respect of their royal ancestor, Richard, Duke of Cornwall. Colonel Jenkinson and his wife Amarintha had four other children besides Charles who was the eldest. These were Robert who died in Hesse from " the fatigues of the war " in 1761, John who became a major in an Irish regiment, Elizabeth who in 1764 married her cousin, Charles Wolfran Cornwall, and Jane who was delicate and lived in Winchester with her mother after the Colonel's death in 1750.

Jenkinson was educated at Charterhouse and University College, Oxford, from where he graduated in 1752. There were then two lives between him and the baronetcy and little likelihood of its coming to him since his cousins Robert and Banks Jenkinson were young men, and Robert was married. He decided to go into the Church and a living was found for him in Oxfordshire through the influence of his connexions in the county. The living seems to have been in the gift of Sir Monnoux Cope of Hanwell, whose relation, Sir Jonathan Cope of Brewern, another Oxfordshire baronet, was Jenkinson's uncle by marriage. In the Liverpool Papers is a copy of a letter from Jenkinson to Edward Lockwood, Rector of Hanwell, dated from Oxford, May 16, 1753, in which

1. This seems a more likely date than 1729, since his baptism, though apparently registered May 16, 1729, appears in the parish register among the entries for the year 1727.

he writes: " Sir John [*sic*] Cope told me that you desired to know when I proposed taking the living of Hanwell; I imagine I shall get all my affairs settled for it by the middle of next month; so that, if you please we will agree on Midsummer Day for the delivery of it to me ".[1] But at the eleventh hour he changed his mind, and though a rumour persisted many years later that he had actually been ordained, he never again referred to his early intention of going into the Church, even in his correspondence with the Cope family and Edward Lockwood who was still Rector of Hanwell in 1781.

It seems likely that in 1753 Jenkinson had already come to the notice of Lord Harcourt, whose patronage helped him at the beginning of his political career. Harcourt was one of the leading Whigs in Oxfordshire, which at that time was ardently divided between the New and Old Interest in anticipation of the general election. Into this celebrated contest which ended with the return, on a vote of the House of Commons, of the Whig candidates, Sir Edward Turner and Lord Parker, Jenkinson threw himself with such vigour as a canvasser for the Whigs, that when in 1767, and again in 1768, he tried to stand for Oxford University, he found that his earlier activities, and particularly the writing of a popular election song, had fatally compromised him in the eyes of the Tories whose influence in the University was still preponderant.

There are scarcely any letters in the Liverpool Papers before 1760, and information about this period of Jenkinson's life is fragmentary and comes from other sources, notably the *Grenville Papers* and the Bute MSS. It seems probable, however, as Almon wrote in a *Letter to the Right Honourable Charles Jenkinson*, published in 1781, that between 1754 and 1756 he acted as a political amanuensis to Harcourt and that he wrote for him in the newspapers. Certainly in the summer of 1755 he drafted for Harcourt a paper in support of the militia, which he afterwards worked up into a pamphlet. In March 1756 he had begun to weary of this kind of service when he wrote, with a touch of the traditional arcadian affectation, to his friend Sanderson Miller, a Warwickshire squire:

1. Add. MS. 38580, f. 4. On January 2, 1857, Robert Henry Jenkinson, a son of Major John Jenkinson, wrote to his cousin, Lady Catherine Venables-Vernon Harcourt, who was Charles Jenkinson's granddaughter, returning her what seems to have been the original of this letter. See his covering letter, Add. MS. 38475, f. 408. The copy of the 1753 letter in the Liverpool Papers, which may have been made on this occasion though it is not in Robert Jenkinson's writing, is endorsed with some very inaccurate information about Jenkinson.

I have nothing to add than to tell you how much I envy you in your present employment in laying out your own domain amidst your hedges and ditches, and most sincerely wish that my present situation would let me leave the company of Dukes and Lords to attend them; among whom I have dug for these four years without once touching the ore they at first offered to my imagination.[1]

It does not appear from the *Grenville Papers* exactly when Harcourt introduced him to Lord Holdernesse,[2] but in November 1756 he had been working, possibly for several months, as a sort of apprentice Under-Secretary of State to Holdernesse " both at his own house and in the Secretary's office ". His position was unofficial and unpaid, but on the formation of the Devonshire-Pitt Administration he wrote to George Grenville with whom he was already acquainted :

It is commonly supposed that Mr. Pitt will dismiss Mr. Amien and Mr. Digby, who are Under-Secretaries in the Southern Province, and perhaps Mr. Rivers, who under the name of Interpreter of Southern Languages, has also acted as an Under-Secretary. I should think it a high honour to serve Mr. Pitt in either of these employments, and should be obliged to you, if you would only mention my name and situation to him, in case he should want anyone in those stations.[3]

Grenville, just reappointed Treasurer of the Navy in the new Administration, was on excellent terms with Pitt and Temple, but he had not enough interest in December 1756 to get Jenkinson a place, although he spoke for him and was thanked by Harcourt. The beginning of Jenkinson's career was not easy. He had already been seeking four years for opportunity and had to wait another five " serving as a volunteer " in the Secretary of State's office before he was given a place. During that time he lost a good deal of his confidence. Jenkinson's connexion with Grenville, which seems to have started in November 1756, was to last for ten years and pro-

1. Dickens and Stenton, *An Eighteenth-Century Correspondence*, p. 324.
2. See Jenkinson to George Grenville, November 15, 1756, in the *Grenville Papers*, i, 179-81. There is nothing in the Liverpool Papers to corroborate Almon's story that Jenkinson was presented to Holdernesse by his mother " who had been a domestic in his Lordship's family ". See a *Letter to the Rt. Hon. Charles Jenkinson* (1781). The only letter from Amarintha Jenkinson in this collection (p. 201) is homely but not more illiterate than those, for instance, of Mrs. Boothby Skrymsher, a lady of great social pretensions in Leicestershire.
3. *Grenv. Pps.* i, 179.

foundly to influence his political outlook. In 1756 he had not acquired any definite political connexion, though he would have called himself a Whig, and was being drawn by Grenville, and by the force of circumstances, into the orbit of Leicester House. He was anxious to please and to get on, and when Pitt came into office he bethought himself of the paper he had drawn up for Harcourt on the militia. The Militia Bill, introduced by George Townshend in December 1755 and thrown out by the House of Lords the following May, had been sponsored by Pitt and was still a subject of controversial interest. On November 30, Jenkinson sent his manuscripts to Grenville for an " opinion upon them, whether it may be of service at present to commit them to the press . . . or whether I should throw them wholly into the fire ".[1] Grenville's advice is not recorded but, as eventually published for Holdernesse in 1757, *A Discourse on the Establishment of a National and Constitutional Force in England* was scarcely polemical and any idea of working it up to please Pitt would seem to have been discarded.

Jenkinson, however, was always more interested in foreign than in home affairs, and in December 1758 he published with Holdernesse's consent *A Discourse on the Conduct of Great Britain with respect to Neutral Nations in the Present War*, in which he defended the British practice of seizing neutral vessels carrying enemy cargo. This practice, established by the so-called Rule of 1756, operated against the Dutch, who, with their great carrying trade, naturally maintained the thesis that the flag should cover the goods, and the frequent confiscation of Dutch ships had created such a state of tension between England and Holland that early in 1759 three Commissioners were sent over from the Netherlands to negotiate an agreement. Jenkinson, whose pamphlet, submitted to Grenville for advice and correction, went into a second edition in January 1759, threw himself hotly into the discussions, interviewed the Commissioners, and doubted whether " we shall be able to avoid coming to a rupture without giving up such of our rights as may be considered, perhaps, as too great a price for their friendship ".[2] James Marriott, a civilian, Fellow of Trinity Hall, Cambridge, whose own pamphlet on the same subject, *The Case of the Dutch Ships Considered*, brought him no substantial recognition, afterwards complained to

1. *Grenv. Pps.* i, 182.
2. Jenkinson to Grenville, December 26, 1758, in *Grenv. Pps.* i, 282.

Newcastle's agent, John Roberts, of the rewards heaped on Jenkinson for his slavish defence of measures which Government " had pursued but could not justify ".[1] No doubt Jenkinson hoped to please Newcastle to whom his friends were recommending him for a place, but his politics were honest. He was naturally doctrinaire and inclined to put law before policy, whether in dealing with the Dutch or the Americans. In any case he was soon to learn that it took more than a treatise on the ethics of captures to squeeze a pension from " a certain Minister who never does a favour with a good grace and must fairly be run down if you mean to have him accomplish any promise he had made to you ".[2]

In December 1758 he had been more than two years " about Lord Holdernesse ", still without a salary, and he thought it time that his services were recognised by a post abroad as " Secretaire d'Ambassade " or a " Commissioner of the Stamps or some such office ". On December 15 he wrote to Grenville that H. B. Legge had promised to speak on his behalf to Newcastle, and on the 26th that Newcastle himself said he would find him a place, but it was not until March 17, 1760, after sixteen months of persuasion, entailing " twenty-seven entries in Newcastle's memoranda, many letters " and " innumerable personal reminders ", that a pension of £250 a year was finally entered in Newcastle's notes. In the meantime Grenville, Harcourt, Lord Holdernesse, and Lord Portsmouth had enlisted on Jenkinson's side, Lady Yarmouth had been called to witness, and Holdernesse had quarrelled with Newcastle.[3]

Convinced by his dealings with Newcastle that " it is rather uncomfortable to depend upon such a man ", Jenkinson decided henceforth to pin his hopes to Grenville's interest at Leicester House. In the winter of 1759–60, when peace negotiations were in the air, he began a *Discourse on the Rights and Policy of Great Britain towards the Objects of Negotiation*. Obviously he hoped, in the event of an embassy being sent to Paris, that his *Treaty,* as he called it, would recommend him for the place of " Secretaire d'Ambassade ". On December 25, 1759, he wrote to Grenville suggesting that he should mention in the proper quarter " (if you have not done it already) that I am possessed of such materials, and have drawn up such a

---

1. See below, pp. 298, 349.
2. Jenkinson to Grenville, July 26, 1759, *Grenv. Pps.* i, 315.
3. See L. B. Namier, *England in the Age of the American Revolution*, pp. 85-6.

paper ", and added, " I am very much obliged to you for the kind offer of your service to make this affair turn to my advantage ".[1] But he was diffident about this essay and frequently wrote to Grenville of his doubts. " I shall lower every part of it where there is the least appearance of presumption ", he wrote in the same letter, " and to take off any objection which may after all appear in that respect, I shall alter its title, and call it no longer a *Memorial*, which implies its being written for a Minister, but a *Discourse*, which may be supposed to be written only for the perusal of friends ". Again on December 29 : " Modesty and firmness are the two points I shall have in view : I shall draw no conclusions myself, but shall do all I can to make others draw them ".[2] Eight months later he was still in the same vein : " The last fault I would willingly be thought guilty of is presumption, and I am apprehensive that my very attempt shall be thought presumptious, though the execution is (as it ought to be, and as I hope mine is) modest ".[3] It is not surprising to find after this that the essay itself lacked political courage and never once touched on the fundamental problems of colonial theory involved in the question of keeping Canada or the West Indies. An inherent reluctance to take responsibility for his opinions, due not so much to natural diffidence (like most doctrinaires he was often too certain of being in the right) as to a less creditable disposition to wait and see which way the cat will jump, seems to have been characteristic of Jenkinson, and it is easy to see how the evasive habit, developed during the long disappointing years of his early career, contributed later to the formation of popular misconceptions about him. In the end his essay on " The Objects of Negotiation " [4] was never published, perhaps because the negotiations themselves were so slow in getting under way. Almost two years before the peace was established he had received the promotion for which he had so long been waiting.

Having attached his fortunes to Grenville his chance came when the new reign began in earnest with the appointment of Bute as Secretary of State for the Northern Department in March 1761. Bute at this period treated Grenville with great familiarity and on his advice the King, in February 1761, had Grenville called to the Nominal Cabinet. When in March Bute became Secretary of State, Grenville persuaded him to take Jenkinson as Under-Secretary in his department. Jenkin-

1. *Grenv. Pps.* i, 333.   2. *Ibid.* 335.   3. *Ibid.* 353.
4. The MS. is now in the Liverpool Papers, Add. MS. 38336, ff. 1-154.

son was in ecstasies. " I am absolutely in love with Lord Bute," he wrote to Grenville on March 24, " his goodness shows itself to me more and more every day." [1] Bute was also pleased with the arrangement, and his brother James Stuart Mackenzie wrote to him three weeks later from Turin : " I am glad to hear that you have got two Under-Secretaries so much to your mind ".[2] Meanwhile, on April 3, Jenkinson was returned to Parliament for Cockermouth on the interest of Sir James Lowther, Bute's prospective son-in-law.

Although he was now an Under-Secretary of State and a member of Parliament, his relations with Bute were as personal as they had been with Holdernesse. He was given an apartment in " the great house in Cleveland Row " which Bute had taken for his office, " where I shall live and be always at hand ".[3] At this time the functions and loyalties of an Under-Secretary of State, even when a member of Parliament, were almost indistinguishable from those of a private secretary, and neither Jenkinson nor his friends thought it any degradation when, a year later, on Bute's becoming First Lord of the Treasury, he gave up the more official status of Under-Secretary to become his private secretary, with a salary provided out of the Treasurership of the Ordnance. In his joy at finding a career at last open before him, Jenkinson conceived a real personal loyalty for Bute which he never renounced in spite of the difficulties in which it later involved him.

The first document printed in this selection of Jenkinson's correspondence for the years 1761 to 1766 is a paper on *The Busyness of Secretary of State* which he probably drew up for Bute soon after his own appointment as Under-Secretary of State in March 1761. In it are described the domestic and the foreign side of the Secretary's work, the routine work of the Under-Secretaries, and the general running of the office. A good deal of responsibility was left to the Under-Secretaries. They opened the mail, circulated it among the ministers entitled to receive it, and sent it to the King, sometimes even before the Secretary of State himself had seen it. They also often drafted his replies, and it was their duty to " prepare materials and to get everything ready for the busyness they see likely to arise, and to get all inclosures, which are often-times much longer than the despatches, properly prepared against the time they are wanted ". Very little of this official

1. *Grenv. Pps.* i, 359.   2. Bute MSS.   3. *Grenv. Pps.* i, 361.

(xi)

side of Jenkinson's correspondence, most of which is preserved at the Record Office, has been included in the present selection, and all the foreign diplomatic letters have been omitted.

Jenkinson's private, or rather less official, correspondence during the two years that he was secretary to Bute, is principally concerned with patronage. His close connexion with " those who have it in their power to make so many people happy " brought him innumerable solicitations for " an introduction to Lord Bute sooner than a distant Levee Day ", and his interest was more sought during this time than it ever was again until the period of his supposed influence during the 'seventies.

The rest of his correspondence until April 1763 consists of letters from Grenville in reply to the news bulletins (printed in the *Grenville Papers*) which Jenkinson sent him according to an arrangement made by Bute, small jobs for Lord Harcourt and Sir James Lowther, a few requests for Parliamentary help in disputed elections, and a mass of letters from his friends at Oxford, principally concerned with the election of a Chancellor in 1762. To all these, except the letters from Grenville, Jenkinson's answers are not available.

While he was secretary to Bute, Jenkinson probably continued to dabble in journalism. Bute employed a number of pamphleteers and Jenkinson was the means of getting hold of such people as Roger Flaxman and Edward Richardson, who wrote in the *Gazette* as " Inquisitor ". On November 5, 1761, Ralph Griffiths, Jenkinson's publisher, for whom he had tried to obtain the printing of the Parliamentary votes, wrote to him suggesting that " opportunities may hereafter fall in your way of greatly serving me in my business, particularly if any publications of a more ordinary kind should occur ". Griffiths supposed that the Government would publish a reply to the French *Mémoire* on the negotiations of March to September 1761, and Jenkinson did actually draft an answer, but it was never published.

The bulk of the Treasury correspondence in 1762 naturally passed through the hands of the two Secretaries to the Treasury, Samuel Martin and Jeremiah Dyson, but Jenkinson formed a link between Bute and his agents in the City. On March 20, 1762, Edward Richardson applied to him to effect a meeting between Bute and Sir James Hodges, the Town Clerk, who shortly afterwards used his interest in the Corporation in defence of the Peace. Almon claims that Jenkinson played a confidential part in the negotiations with the City which were the immediate cause of Bute's decision to resign. According to *A History of the Late Minority*, it would seem that on March 28, 1763, while a committee of the Common Council were waiting in the lobby of the House of Lords with their petition against the Cider Bill, Sir John Phillips told Bute that they had another one ready to present to the King, whereupon Bute sent Phillips to the committee with his promise that if they refrained from petitioning he would use his influence to get the Act repealed next session. The same evening Jenkinson called on Sir James Hodges and brought him next day to see Bute, but the negotiations failed as Hodges was unable to persuade the Common Council to agree. There is nothing of this in the Liverpool Papers, but in the Bute MSS. is a remarkable letter from Jenkinson to Bute, dated March 28, 1763, congratulating him on his wisdom in not resisting the City's proceedings, for if he had resisted, wrote Jenkinson, everyone who now blamed his moderation would have supported the City against him. Whereas " Your Lordship may now hold out the appearance of supporting the cause of the two branches of the legislature while you are in fact promoting the King's interest and your own ".

A week later Bute resigned and was succeeded by Grenville at the Treasury, and on April 16 Jenkinson, in succession to Samuel Martin who resigned with his chief, became Joint Secretary to the Treasury with Jeremiah Dyson. Four months later Dyson was appointed to the Board of Trade and Jenkinson became senior Secretary to the Treasury. His colleague was Thomas Whately.

At the beginning of George III's reign the nucleus of what was eventually to evolve into our present Civil Service was still in process of crystallisation. Professor Namier writes in *The Structure of Politics* : " It was but very slowly that the Civil Service acquired its present corporate structure, independence, and aloofness. About 1760 the ' commis ' in the office of the Secretaries of State (who would now be Permanent Under-Secretaries) and the Secretaries to various Government departments were personal dependants of the Ministers, but at the same time frequently Members of Parliament. . . . The question in how far their allegiance was due to the person and how far to the office of the Minister was not solved as yet, and gave rise to conflicting loyalties and to bitter resentments." [1]

1. *Structure of Politics*, p. 47.

And in his Ford Lectures Professor Namier goes on to explain how economic pressure—many of these working politicians depended on their places for a livelihood — and a sense that efficiency was best served by continuity in administrative office, led them to seek to evade the consequences of personal allegiance by accepting each ministry in turn as the unquestioned expression of their Sovereign's choice. The unwillingness of ministers to retain them was the only effective check on their transcendent loyalty to the Crown, for it was often found "improper and disagreeable to give the entire confidence which Under-Secretaries must enjoy, to men who are known to be strongly attach'd or greatly obliged to other great personages ". On the other hand there was a natural affinity between the official and the Crown, the one seeking permanence, the other efficiency and fidelity. A succession of amateur administrations taught George III to appreciate the services of the well-informed, hard-working officials who, behind the façade of brilliant oratory from the front benches, carried on the real work of government; such men as Gilbert Elliot, James Oswald, Samuel Martin, Thomas Whately, Jenkinson, John Robinson, and Thomas Bradshaw of whom Walpole wrote in 1774: " He has since become a very active minister of the second or third class and more trusted perhaps than some of a higher class ".[1] In point of fact, as time went on, the King came to trust them more and more, in preference to others " though of birth yet not their superiors ". He interceded for them in his negotiations at every change of administration, and occasionally took care of them individually when ministers tried to get rid of them. They were in fact the only homogeneous element in the extremely heterogeneous collection of individuals known to contemporaries as the " King's Friends ", a name given loosely to anyone who practised independent loyalty to the Crown. Thus it was that the Civil Service, even at this early stage of its history, while lacking corporate structure, was yet not entirely unselfconscious, and its members maintained a degree of independence of ministerial patronage very irritating to the Party Leaders who could never entirely dispense with them because of " the penury there is of trained forces ".

For the " sub-ministers ", as Jenkinson called them, every change of administration was a test between loyalties — to their out-going chiefs, and to the King as permanent head of

1. Letter to Sir Horace Mann, November 14, 1774.

(xiv)

the executive — and it depended very much upon the personality of each man whether he chose the independent interpretation of his office, and how far he was successful in getting others to accept it.

On March 25, 1763, Bute asked Grenville to " take the assistance of all the King's friends that are determined to give it ",[1] and the employment of Jenkinson as Secretary to the Treasury was generally taken as a token of solidarity between them. Within a few weeks, however, Grenville had forgotten his " maker ", and by September 1763 was more or less openly hostile, to the intense embarrassment of the " King's Friends " who saw themselves in danger of being dropped if Grenville's quarrel with Bute were followed by a reconciliation with Pitt and Temple. Hence their unhappy efforts first to ignore the breach, and then to heal it. It was a hopeless task and Jenkinson was close enough to Grenville to know why. One of the most interesting documents in this collection is a memorandum on the relations between Bute and Grenville which Jenkinson seems to have written shortly after the fall of the Grenville Administration. No one was in a better position than he to know the ins and outs of Grenville's unreasonable suspicions of Bute and jealousy over patronage, and much of the material here corroborates the information in Grenville's diary.

As Secretary to the Treasury Jenkinson was even more embarrassed than most " King's Friends " by the cleavage between his former and his present chief, for though he in no sense continued to " belong " to Bute, he was loath to sever his connexion with the man whom he still believed to be the most influential in the kingdom. While Bute was in semi-retreat at Luton during the first months of the Grenville Administration, Jenkinson visited him frequently and tried to soothe his legitimate irritation at the way he was being treated by the ministers.

With regard to Grenville, Jenkinson, as Secretary to the Treasury, was in a more emancipated position than he had been under Bute, and he brought to it a measure of independence and reserve perhaps greater than most of his colleagues managed to maintain towards their chiefs. His attitude towards Grenville was perfectly correct, loyal, and, at first, ready to be friendly. He sincerely admired him as a statesman and worked for him with pleasure. Politically he was Grenville's disciple. But the letters to his chief, which are at first

1. *Grenv. Pps.* ii, 33.

almost intimate, grow more and more formal. There is evidence from Jenkinson's behaviour to Bute and from his lifelong correspondence with Harcourt, that it was his nature to be loyal and grateful. It was probably Grenville's fault that their relations deteriorated. Bute's peculiar reputation was such that none of his contemporaries could ever believe that anyone would maintain non-political relations with him. Even Gilbert Elliot did not wholly succeed in convincing people that by continuing to visit Bute he merely paid " what duty I can to private friendship ".[1] To Grenville, morbidly suspicious and in a violently irritated state of mind, Jenkinson's continued visits to Luton were little short of treason.

Smooth relations with Grenville were not facilitated by the fact that, as Secretary to the Treasury, Jenkinson's two principal correspondents on patronage matters were intimately connected with Bute. These were James Stuart Mackenzie and Sir James Lowther, respectively brother and son-in-law to Bute. On August 22, 1764, Jenkinson wrote to John Robinson of his doubts of being able to put through a job for Lowther : " I shall apply to Mr. Grenville and do all I can that everything may succeed as Sir James could wish. But alas ! my dear Sir, I have but little influence where I am always considered as a party. You must have observed this and the difficulties I have on that account been under." [2]

Jenkinson had no personal obligation to Mackenzie as he had to Lowther, but his sense of justice rebelled when Grenville included Mackenzie in his jealousy of Bute. In July 1764 Grenville interpreted an appointment made by Mackenzie, then patronage Minister for Scotland, as inimical to himself, and ordered Jenkinson to complain. " I always execute your commands with zeal and with pleasure," Jenkinson replied on July 5, " and I have more than once, as you may well know, spoke my sentiments with freedom against measures which I did not approve ; but I cannot, from myself, charge any man with an offence of which I have not reason to think him guilty ; and you would not, I am sure, wish that I should disoblige a friend by doing what could be of no use to you." [3]

It is scarcely possible to over-emphasise the importance of patronage, or " business ", as it was sometimes called, in eighteenth-century politics, or the part it played in the lives of politicians. England being an island, a large number of

1. See G. F. S. Elliot, *The Border Elliots*, p. 378.
2. See below, p. 326. 3. *Grenv. Pps.* ii, 382.

customs officers were necessary to check smuggling, and, as many old harbours were also Parliamentary boroughs, appointments in them were one of the principal means of obliging the voters. Similarly the Ordnance places in the little forts and castles on the coast were usually distributed with a view to their bearing on elections. Receiverships and collectors' places were among the plums which the Treasury had to bestow, but there were also smaller places such as surveyors of window lights, riding-officers, and tide-waiters, worth forty or fifty pounds a year, which were given to the dependants of influential voters or sometimes used to reward old servants of noblemen at the expense of the State.[1]

As senior Secretary to the Treasury Jenkinson dealt with the correspondence on this type of patronage, and though it does not appear that he had very great influence with Grenville in the disposal of places, it was this aspect of his work which made him most useful to his own borough patron, Sir James Lowther.

Like many other people in the eighteenth century, Lowther was a collector, but not being much interested in art, he collected constituencies, a passion he shared with the Duke of Newcastle, and from 1756 when the last accretion was added to his vast inheritance, he laid out his fortune and energies in the pursuit of them. He contested elections, and created interest in the borough corporations of the Border country, and bought up Haslemere in Surrey. At the climax of his career in 1782 he could return two members for Westmorland, one for Cumberland, two for Cockermouth, one each for Appleby and Carlisle, and two for Haslemere. They were known as Sir James's "nine-pins". So far as his early conquests had any reference to political issues they were undertaken in the interest of Bute and the Court, but it was not until many of the " King's Friends " found themselves in opposition to the Rockingham Government that he became drawn into their politics or bothered to give his members instructions about their behaviour in Parliament.

To look after his electoral interests Lowther employed a considerable staff of agents and " men of business ". One of these was John Robinson, his law agent and land steward, who learnt in his service the art of managing elections which he afterwards practised so successfully as Secretary to the Treasury during Lord North's Administration. The connexion between

1. See *Structure of Politics*.

Jenkinson and Robinson, so close during the 'seventies when for four years they practically ran the Treasury together, began in the years 1761 to 1764 when they were brought into almost daily correspondence over Sir James's incessant recommendations to places in the Customs and Excise. In those days Robinson managed the Lowther interest from the Westmorland end while Jenkinson was his principal agent in town. Ten years later they both freed themselves of the Lowther connexion by standing for a Treasury borough. Jenkinson was returned for Harwich in 1772, and Robinson in 1774.

It does not appear from Jenkinson's correspondence as Secretary to the Treasury that there was any clear division between the functions of patronage and financial secretary, though as senior Secretary from August 1763 he was probably more concerned than his colleague with the correspondence touching the management of the House of Commons. He corresponded officially with Mackenzie, and sent him regular news letters as well as dealing with appointments, and he had charge of the correspondence with some of Grenville's borough managers, notably with Griffith Davies at Harwich. As Professor Namier has dealt with this correspondence in *The Structure of Politics* in the chapter on Harwich and Oxford, it is omitted here. Between Jenkinson and Edward Kynaston, one of Grenville's Parliamentary managers and local manager for Shropshire, there is comparatively little intercourse, but he corresponded with Richard Webb on Cornish affairs and Tintagel in particular, and with Edward Wardroper on Rye and Winchelsea. He seems to have had charge of Bute's list of the House of Commons of 1761 which was still in use in November 1763, and in which Jenkinson himself entered the changes, and he received several voluntary and unofficial accounts of local politics with hints for the improvement of Government interest. The most interesting of these are James Marriott's account of Sudbury and John White's of the Isle of Wight boroughs. Jenkinson also corresponded with individual members on their claims to Treasury help in elections, and assured Bamber Gascoyne in April 1763 that the Customs officers at Malden would correctly interpret a leave of absence as an intimation from Government to support his election.

On the financial side Jenkinson's principal correspondent was Joseph Salvador, a Jewish merchant and financier, who was one of the chief City men consulted by the Grenville

Government. A good deal of his advice was taken and is embodied in the budgets of 1763 and 1764. In April 1764 Salvador played a part in furthering the support given by the Government to Clive to obtain an East India Direction favourable to him.

Another interesting Treasury correspondence is that between Jenkinson and R. Wolters, British Consul in Rotterdam and head of an elaborate system of secret agents on the Continent. Wolters's job was to keep the Treasury informed of the financial stability of the French Government and of the general fluctuations of credit in Western Europe. His agents claimed to report the secrets of French, Spanish, and Dutch finance, but their information seems to have been highly speculative and unreliable. Wolters wrote regularly to Jenkinson every week, and also to the Secretary of State. There are several volumes of his letters to Sandwich in the Record Office.

Jenkinson did not correspond directly with the merchants touching their contracts, but his papers contain a State of Contracts in 1764 and some correspondence with Messrs. Jones and Cust on the rate of exchange at which they were to supply moidores for the pay of the troops at Gibraltar.

Most of the financial matter in his papers consists of accounts and memoranda. The Secret Service accounts have been amply dealt with in *The Structure of Politics* and are consequently omitted here. Besides the Secret Service accounts his papers contain innumerable accounts, states, memoranda, and comparisons of the net and gross produce of the Customs and Excise, the produce of the Crown revenues, the extraordinary services on account of the Colonies, etc. etc.

Jenkinson was also the recipient of frequent reminders from private persons who enjoyed or expected pensions from the Treasury. Sir John Fielding applied to him for the money for his Horse Patrol and for his own pension. Doctor Johnson indirectly reminded him that his pension had fallen due. He corresponded with Feronce, the Duke of Brunswick's agent, on the subject of royal marriage portions and presents to ambassadors, and he dealt with the complaints of affronted diplomats who wished to circumvent the customs regulations. In addition there are many routine letters between him and Grenville and Grenville's private secretaries, Charles and Philip Lloyd. In short his correspondence touched every subject that was liable to interest the Treasury and presents in consequence a very varied appearance.

When Grenville left office on July 10, 1765, Jenkinson and Thomas Whately went with him. This gave them a chance of coming back later to better positions. In the eighteenth century the status of Secretary to the Treasury, even when he was a member of Parliament, hovered indecisively between Civil Service rank and political office, and it depended on the man himself whether he inclined more to the one or to the other. Many secretaries, like John Robinson, never passed on to higher office, but Jenkinson and his two successive colleagues, Dyson and Whately, all achieved a seat at the Treasury Board, and when in July 1765 the Grenvilles were forced out of office, it was to the advantage of the two secretaries to resign as politicians rather than wait to be turned out by the new Government as place-men.

Jenkinson seems to have left a good impression at the Treasury. On February 9, 1766, his friend Charles Lloyd, a clerk there and formerly Grenville's private secretary, wrote to him describing the behaviour of his successor: " Mr. Bradshaw's complaint is settled; I have owned his right which indeed I never disputed and he has said that he never intended to make use of the Imperial style. I am sure you do not approve of that imperative tone, because whenever your name is mentioned at the Treasury it is always with commendation for conduct the very reverse of it." [1]

The events of the last weeks of Grenville's Administration were set down in detail by Gilbert Elliot, and a copy of his diary for May and June 1765 is in these papers. It has not, however, been possible to compare it with the original which is at Minto House, from which short extracts have been published in the *Bedford Papers* and in G. F. S. Elliot's *The Border Elliots*.

Much more *esprit de corps* is noticeable among the " King's Friends " after Grenville's fall, and the letters describing their reactions to the Rockinghams and to Chatham are among the most entertaining in this collection. One of the most important documents is a paper describing a meeting of " King's Friends " in January 1766, when the fall of the Rockingham Administration seemed imminent and the " King's Friends " themselves were in search of a leader. Mackenzie and Sir James Lowther made some attempt to look after the corporate interests of the group, and Fletcher Norton wrote to Jenkinson on August 1, 1766: " It will not be my fault if

1. See below, p. 408.

(xx)

we do not all share one common lot ". But the lack of leadership and the hostility of the Rockinghams made it difficult for them to protect their own interests and the " independency " of the Crown, notwithstanding their weight in Parliament. It was a great disappointment when, on the fall of the Rockingham Government, Chatham, after restoring Mackenzie (without the patronage), failed to make any further concessions, and when in November 1766 there were some massed resignations especially from the Admiralty Board, Jenkinson in desperation begged Sir James to " send a servant to Lord B⟨ute⟩ and beg of him to come to town. . . . There are certainly the strongest symptoms that the Government is coming to a conclusion; and the King not knowing where to have recourse and complaining of his friends that they will not stand forward, may send for Lord Temple as he did for Mr. Pitt and put all into his hands, and we may be used as ill by the former, as we have been by the latter." [1]

Although on the formation of the Chatham Administration Bute did actually write a letter of reproach to the King " for not applying to me about my friends ", as nothing came of it his " friends " began to tire of such ineffective protection, and by July 1767 even Sir James Lowther had become " irritated by repeated violation of promises and by a total neglect ". Jenkinson himself was anxious to be free of the Lowther-Bute connexion and in May 1766 he first conceived the plan of standing for Oxford University. Had he been successful he might have made himself politically independent of the " King's Friends ", but his interest at Oxford was not sufficient. He had always closely followed University politics and had many friends there who kept him in touch with local affairs, but Government support in his election seems on the whole to have operated to his disadvantage, for as J. Tottie wrote to him from Christ Church on February 1, 1768: " There is not as yet such a change of sentiment in this University as to promise success to any political measure that is known to be set on foot and conducted by those that are called Whigs ".[2] At a by-election in January 1768 Jenkinson withdrew in favour of Sir William Dolben, but he stood again at the general election in March and was defeated by Sir Roger Newdigate and Francis Page. " I am more angry still," Nathaniel Wetherall wrote sympathetically on April 1, 1768, " to think that a poor fox-hunting squire is preferred

1. See below, p. 437.   2. Add. MS. 38457, f. 99.

(xxi)

before one of the greatest political characters in the king-dom." [1]

The "King's Friends", when they met in January 1766, discussed their attitude to the American problem and the repeal of the Stamp Act. Political convictions on the subject were conspicuously lacking, but it was comfortably decided that in such a divided House "wherever the Crown casts its influence there will be success and the measure is of that kind that Administration will have only to execute what the Parliament shall determine; and the Lawyers who must decide the question are almost all on the side of the Crown".[2] Like most of their contemporaries in England, "the gentlemen who could discourse together in confidence" regarded the whole American question as a law-suit between the Colonies and the Mother Country, to be determined in Parliament. Yet there is plenty of material in Jenkinson's papers to have broadened his views on America, if he had cared to digest it. Particularly interesting are the letters from Benjamin Hallo-well, Controller of Customs in Boston, who suffered in the riots against the Stamp Act. "The people here are so little acquainted with paying of duties," he wrote from Boston on November 10, 1764, "that they had rather be charged with a shilling on the exportation than ninepence on the importation here, they saying money is hard to be gott, and they can always find some kind of produce to send to market to be remitted to Great Britain, to pay for such goods as they import from thence. They also say that money will be scarce as that all duties to be collected for the Crown is to be remitted into the Ex-chequer."[3] John Temple shared this fear that the Colonies would be drained of their precious coin.

Jenkinson was unmoved. His attitude to the Americans was consistently doctrinaire. He had approved the Stamp Act and voted against its repeal as much from conviction as for party reasons, although Benjamin Hallowell wrote to him again from Boston on December 17, 1765, that the Americans " to a man seem resolved not to take them ⟨the stamps⟩, some people are determined to die rather than submit ".[4] Jenkinson always spoke in defence of the Act and of Grenville's memory, which he upheld in Parliament as late as 1774. After the war broke out his attitude was more rigid than ever. In 1777

1. Add. MS. 38457, f. 329.   2. See below, p. 407.
3. See below, p. 340.   4. See below, p. 402.

(xxii)

he was confident of victory and wrote a paper for Lord North on the proposed settlement of America after the war. "In my view nothing can be done with any prospect of success but to state to the Americans in plain and explicit terms, the conditions on which alone you will allow them to reserve a share in their own government, and in the mean time to govern them by powers vested in the Crown in the best and cheapest manner you can." [1]

By the end of 1766 Jenkinson's career had definitely taken the political rather than the Civil Service turn. He remained in opposition throughout the Rockingham Administration but accepted a seat at the Admiralty Board from Chatham in December 1766, and a year later was transferred to the Treasury where he remained until 1773. During these years he acquired considerable reputation as an expert on finance, and many of his contemporaries would have concurred in Horace Walpole's estimate of him as one of the ablest men in the House of Commons. Between November 1778 and October 1779 North four times considered appointing him Chancellor of the Exchequer, and in February 1779 described him to the King as "without exception by much the fittest person in England to have the direction of the finances of this country ".[2] On October 16, 1779, Sandwich wrote to the King that North " complained of not being supported in the House of Commons, and said that Mr. Jenkinson in the capacity of a Chancellor of the Exchequer would be of great use to him there, and very much so as a member of the Cabinet. Lord Sandwich thinks he ⟨North⟩ added that even if he ⟨Jenkinson⟩ was in the Cabinet as Mr. Fox was, being Secretary at War, it would have great advantages." [3] But George III was unwilling to allow North to resign, and he knew that if Jenkinson were in the Cabinet as Chancellor of the Exchequer, North would soon " hope for His Majesty's promise that he should quit the Treasury . . . because though the public affairs would be greatly benefited by it, Lord North would in a short time become a cypher at his Board ".

Only the King's reluctance to lose North and so fall into the hands of the Rockinghams once more, kept Jenkinson from a place for which he appeared singled out as much by

1. Add. MS. 38306, f. 71.
2. Fortescue, *Correspondence of George III*, iv, No. 2512.
3. *Corr. of George III*, iv, No. 2801.

his personal qualities as by his technical preparation and political antecedents. But his contemporaries, knowing him to enjoy North's confidence and the esteem of the King, could not easily understand how it was that he remained without a responsible office. (It is so natural to imagine that a Prime Minister enjoys being in office that probably few people besides the King believed in the sincerity of North's intention to resign.) For five years, from 1773 when Jenkinson left the Treasury to 1778 when, in the middle of the American conflict, he succeeded Lord Barrington as Secretary at War, he had no place of real political importance,[1] and spent a good deal of his time travelling abroad. It was during these years that the reputation of his supposed influence began to spread. Walpole affirms that in February 1773 he already " began to assume the airs of a minister ", and he was satirised by Mason in 1774:

> Let these prefer a Levee's harmless talk,
> Be asked how often and how far they walk,
> Proud of a single word, nor hope for more,
> Tho' Jenkinson is blessed with many a score.[2]

He was constantly obliged to assure his friends that " the world entertain an idea of my interest and power *very very* far beyond the truth ".[3] " I do assure you upon the word of an honest man, he wrote to John Scott, afterwards Lord Clonmel, on November 28, 1777, that my interest is not what the world supposes. It is but little, particularly with the Premier. It acts and operates only by fits, for reasons I could explain to you if we were together." [4] And on December 29 he wrote to the 2nd Earl Harcourt:

> The world are so obliging as to give me the credit of much more influence than I really have, and when I deny it I have seldom the good fortune to be believed. In the

1. In 1773 through the influence of Harcourt, then Lord Lieutenant of Ireland, Jenkinson was given an Irish Vice-Treasurership. His place at the Treasury Board went to Charles James Fox. In the same year he was appointed a Privy Councillor. In 1775 he resigned the Vice-Treasurership to become Clerk of the Pells in Ireland, a place of less consequence which he accepted to oblige Harcourt. Wraxall says he bought the Clerkship of the Pells from Fox (*Hist. and Posth. Mems.* ii, p. 8), but this does not appear from his correspondence. It was worth £2000 a year.

2. See *An Heroic Postscript to the Heroic Epistle to Sir William Chambers.*

3. Letter to Mrs. Weston, December 12, 1775, Add. MS. 38306, f. 11. Cf. his letter to Mrs. Pigot, January 15, 1777, *ibid.* f. 56.

4. *Ibid.* f. 78.

management of public affairs it is true that I sometimes have a share, I am always ready to give any assistance I am able, but I never intrude it, and to say the truth it is never called for but in emergencies when they cannot do without me.[1]

In March 1781 he was first openly attacked in the House of Commons on the charge of exerting secret influence, when Charles James Fox supposed that the Government's American policy was inspired by Jenkinson and accused North of accepting it " as the price of his place ". (Fox either did not know or did not believe that North always wanted to resign.) Between 1781 and 1787 Jenkinson was attacked in Parliament either directly or indirectly every year; four times by Fox, twice by Sheridan, once by Thomas Powis, and once by the Duke of Norfolk.

His reputation as an *éminence grise* would scarcely have gained so much credit without the precedent of Bute. In fact the legend of a " Minister behind the curtain " was never quite allowed to die out. Horace Walpole's romantic fancies contribute to keep it alive to this day, and even after 1765 when people began to pay less attention to the " Favourite ", Burke's *Thoughts on the Present Discontents*, published in 1770, kept the notion of secret influence before the public by attempting to make the " King's Friends " appear in the same mysterious and sinister light which had surrounded Bute. Today this mystery, a product of eighteenth-century romanticism, seems slightly absurd. Modern research, in particular Professor Namier's work on this period, has made clear the true nature and extent of George III's relations first with Bute and afterwards with his so-called friends. Even Burke himself admitted that his " Second Cabinet " might well appear " a vision of a distracted brain or the invention of a malicious heart " since the " King's Friends " often never saw the King except to kiss hands, and many of them had even less acquaintance with Bute. But the Rockinghams who were genuinely puzzled at remaining so long out of office, found it useful and consoling to suppose that their opponents exerted unconstitutional powers over the King, and encouraged by the literary element in their party, would not let the notion drop.

On the whole they found it easier and more convenient to picture George III under the personal ascendancy of a single

1. *Ibid.* ff. 78-9. Cf. his letter to Needham, April 4, 1777, *ibid.* f. 60.

individual rather than imagine him morally in the power of the somewhat nebulous group of his " Friends ", and when Jenkinson began to stand out from the others, they readily picked on him as the villain of the piece in lineal descent from Bute. Writing between 1783 and 1788,[1] Horace Walpole says :

> I have changed my opinion, I confess, various times on the subject of Lord Bute's favour with the King ; but this I take to have been the truth. . . . I believe that even before his accession the King was weary both of his mother and her favourite, and wanted to, and did, early shake off that influence. . . . Who then had real influence with the King, for his subsequent ministers indubitably had not ? — I should answer readily, Jenkinson. He was the sole confident of the King . . . and though the King's views and plans were commonly as pestilent to his own interest as to his people, yet as they were often artfully conducted, he and Bute were too ignorant and too incapable to have digested the measures ; and therefore, as nobody else enjoyed the royal confidence, there can be no doubt but Jenkinson was the director or agent of all his Majesty's secret counsels.

Fox and Sheridan were equally emphatic and publicly denounced the " system " (invented by Burke) of secret advisers to the Crown, but they were so easily carried away by their own rhetoric that it is difficult, at this distance of time, to guess how far they really believed what they said. The accusations against Jenkinson were a natural corollary to the political theory of the time. Opposition, in order to avoid the appearance of disloyalty to the Crown, was obliged to assume that Government was either coercing the King, or, if the harmony between Crown and Administration were manifest, that it had gained some sort of illegal ascendancy over him. Even in the interim between ministries political convention insisted, as Fox declared in 1783, that " he ⟨the King⟩ never can act wrong unless he is ill advised ".[2] If the evil counsellor did not exist he had to be invented.

Jenkinson appears on the whole to have been flattered by the suggestion of his influence which gave him considerable prestige both in and outside Parliament, and though he repeatedly declared that there was nothing illegal or unconstitutional in his relations with the King, and called on North

1. *Memoirs of the Reign of George III*, ed. G. F. Russell Barker (1894), iv, 88 n. 2. L. B. Namier dates this passage after 1783, from the handwriting possibly as late as 1788.

2. Wraxall, *Memoirs*, iii, 37.

to witness in 1783 " whether that pretended secret influence, so insidiously suggested, ever had any real existence ", yet he always managed to convey the impression that his advice carried weight and was frequently sought. In March 1783 he is reported to have answered Fox: " I stand up to refute the insinuation of being an evil adviser to his Majesty, and to deny the existence of secret influence behind the throne, in the unwarrantable sense of those expressions ". As a Privy Councillor, however, he had access to the King. " I confess that during the last five weeks I have been with him more than once. I never went except on official business; nor did I ever use any secret influence. That idea is only a trap for the credulous multitude." [1] But Fox was quick to seize the implication and answered promptly:

> The fact . . . at which, down to the present time, suspicion has only glanced, exultation has avowed. . . . I have learned that a Privy Councillor, though he is not a Minister, may offer his Sovereign advice, and not be accountable for its effects. Surely this House will never sanction a doctrine so replete with danger to the state.[2]

The self-confidence and satisfaction which Jenkinson had known during the years at the Treasury, seem partly to have deserted him after 1773 when something of his earlier evasiveness reappears with the unfortunate effect of seeming to corroborate the Rockinghams' suspicions. In 1785 Sheridan attacked him for deserting North. Jenkinson replied: " I by no means wish to deny that I supported many of Lord North's measures during his Administration, but in the office which I filled as Secretary at War, I was not responsible for the ministerial plans sent me from the Treasury ".[3] Yet he had always approved of the American war, believed it both just and necessary, and he had defended it in Parliament in 1782. Two years later when, as Baron Hawksbury, he defended the Government's proposed commercial treaty with France, he reminded the House of Lords that he was " no minister ". " I desire once for all . . . that it may not be supposed I either possess or claim any authority except the influence which my arguments give me." To which the Duke of Norfolk replied:

> as he is no minister, he cannot incur any responsibility. It is therefore the duty of ministers either to speak in their own persons or to place the noble Lord in a ministerial

1. *Ibid.* 39.   2. *Ibid.* 45.   3. *Ibid.* iv, 122.

situation so that he may be rendered responsible for his assertions respecting measures of Administration.[1]

It is easy to see why contemporaries were reminded of Bute. The Duke of Norfolk's words might have been spoken a quarter of a century earlier by Gilbert Elliot who wrote to Bute in 1761 :

> A just responsibility towards the publick ought ever in this country to be the inseperable concomitant of power and favour. It was for that reason that I ever heard you, with real satisfaction, reject the maxims of that false wisdom which I know has often been busy in painting to you the advantages of enjoying the latter, unexposed to the hazards of the former.[2]

It is reasonable to infer that Jenkinson, generally so positive in his opinions, had in fact no more taste than Bute for the hazards of responsibility, though it would be absurd to think of him as being in any sense " behind the curtain ". Such influence as he had, derived from his good sense and the un-common soundness of his training, a thing quite unusual in his time, and possibly one of the causes of the mystery which surrounded him. Yet his career was one of promise never quite fulfilled. In October 1779 North wanted him in the Cabinet either as Chancellor of the Exchequer or as Secretary at War ; in August 1786, shortly after he had been made a peer, Chancellor of the Duchy of Lancaster, and President of the Board of Trade, Shelburne, now Lord Lansdown, wrote of him to Francis Baring : " From this moment I put him down as minister under the King. It is a farce to talk of his not being of the Cabinet." [3] And in March 1787 the Duke of Norfolk, in his speech against the French commercial treaty, said of him : " I am aware that the noble Lord who has undertaken to support the treaty and to justify ministers has on his shoulders the principal burthen of government. He is a peer of great weight and authority." [4] Yet Jenkinson never was in the Cabinet and never rose to a ministerial office higher than the presidency of the Board of Trade, a place of less consequence in 1786 than it had been before the loss of the American Colonies.

There seems to be no reason other than temperamental inadequacy to have prevented him from reaching the top of

1. Wraxall, *Memoirs*, iv, 420.
2. See L. B. Namier, *England in the Age of the American Revolution*, p. 185. Gilbert Elliot's letter is in the Bute MSS.
3. Fitzmaurice, *Life of Shelburne*, ii, 294.   4. Wraxall, *Memoirs*, iv, 420.

the political ladder. In 1779 he had more than twenty years of vigorous life before him, and the disadvantages of his humble beginnings were removed by a peerage in 1786. Without possessing any electoral influence he carried considerable weight in the House of Commons where his reputation inspired awe as well as suspicion, and though Wraxall has tried to make fun of his education, the *Quarterly Review* in 1815 speaks of him as an " excellent classical scholar " possessing " as great a variety of reading as perhaps any of his contemporaries (except only Burke) ".[1] In any case he was probably unaware of his own " inelegancies of diction ", and would have taken it as a compliment to be told that in his speeches " all was fact and business ". He was not, however, a man of parts, and the array of wit and talent in the Opposition which included Fox, Burke, Sheridan, and the authors of the Rolliad, may possibly have had something to do with his aversion from open responsibility. But, after all, though his friends and enemies sometimes expected more of him than he actually achieved, he had no great cause to be dissatisfied with his career. From comparatively modest beginnings he rose, entirely through his own merit, to an earldom in 1796, and died, full of years and honour, in 1808, when his son, Robert Banks Jenkinson, better known as the Prime Minister Liverpool, was for the second time Secretary of State for Home Affairs.

In these papers of his Civil Service years he is seen rising, as he told Tommy Townshend in 1770, " by industry, by attention to duty and by every honourable means I could devise ".[2] The human and historical interest of these letters is not, however, to be measured merely by the light they throw upon Jenkinson's career (he was, after all, neither particularly remarkable as an individual nor representative of a class). Coming from so many and such diverse correspondents they open a window onto a panorama of everyday life in eighteenth-century England, showing the machinery of government at work, and its bearing upon the lives of hundreds of individuals either closely or remotely connected with it.

1. See Wraxall's *Answer to the Calumnious Misrepresentations of the Quarterly Review* (1815), pp. 17-18. Also *Memoirs*, i, 419-20 and note.
2. See *The Structure of Politics*, p. 15.

NINETTA S. JUCKER

98 Via di Priscilla
    Rome
    October 1947

ON March 25, 1761, Lord Bute took office as Secretary of State for the Northern Department with Jenkinson as his Under-Secretary of State. The next day Jenkinson wrote to Grenville, who since February 11 was a member of the Nominal Cabinet and therefore without the circulation of state papers : " His Lordship has also ordered me to communicate all things of importance to you, as between you and myself, though the circulation does not extend to you. When you come to town we will settle the nature of the correspondence." [1] In the Grenville papers for June and July 1761 there are fifteen letters from Jenkinson to Grenville giving accounts of the dispatches as they arrived at the Secretary of State's office. These related to the progress of the war and of the peace negotiations undertaken that summer.

On June 12 dispatches arrived from Hans Stanley, British Envoy in Paris, reporting Choiseul's readiness to conclude a separate treaty of peace with Britain on the basis of an *uti possidetis* as from May 1, July 1, and September 1, 1761, or from new dates to be proposed by England.[2] On June 13 news arrived of the surrender of Belleisle, and as Pitt had only been waiting for this event to fix the dates of the *uti possidetis*, it was decided at a meeting of the Effective Cabinet on June 16 to offer dates two months later than those proposed by France. A memorial of this offer was sent to Stanley on June 17.[3]

CHARLES JENKINSON TO GEORGE GRENVILLE [4]

St. James's, June 16, 1761.

Dear Sir,

I received yesterday the favour of your letter acknowledging the receipt of mine [5] by express, and I did not fail to acquaint Lord Bute with your congratulations on the occasion,[6] who expressed himself extremely obliged to you on that account.

I remember very well that you foresaw what appears by the dispatch of Mr. Stanley : I wish I could give you a more particular account of that dispatch, but, I know not for what reason, Mr. Pitt endeavours to keep from us here everything that he can, so that I have not read this dispatch, but only know the contents of it, from what I have been told. There

1. *Grenville Papers*, i, 361.
2. Stanley to Pitt, June 8, 1761, printed in Francis Thackeray, *Life of Chatham* (1827), i, 514-23. The dates refer to conquests in Europe, the West Indies and America, and the East Indies, respectively.
3. Thackeray, *op. cit.* ii, 523-4.
4. This letter is printed in the *Grenv. Pps.* i, 365-7.
5. Of June 13, *ibid.* 364-5.
6. The capture of Belleisle on June 12 by Admirals Hawke and Boscawen.

is, however, besides the letter on business, another giving an account of the state of the Court, which describes the King of France as melancholy and dejected ; the Dauphin as hated on account of his attachment to the Jesuits ; and the young Pretender (who appears, it seems, at length to be at Paris) to be always drunk. It mentions also that the Duke de Choiseul has obtained a degree of favour superior to Madame Pompadour, so as in fact to use her ill.

The same messenger who brought these dispatches from Mr. Stanley, brought others also from the Duke de Choiseul to Bussy,[1] and yet, notwithstanding this, and what Stanley has related, Bussy waited on Mr. Pitt on Sunday morning, and held the same language as before, and even added, that as Belleisle was now taken, he was to demand as a preliminary article, before they proceeded to treat on anything else, that that Island should be surrendered. He would not illuminate, as Choiseul says he had ordered him, and held a language very unfriendly and sour. This has surprised very much, as being diametrically opposite to all that Choiseul had said, but it seems to me to imply two things : the first is, that M. de Choiseul has a mind to draw the negociation to himself : the second is, that Bussy is personally indisposed to this country. This I have long thought, and I am now convinced of it. The Council sat to-day on the affairs of peace, etc. The next post I will let you know what they have determined.

You will receive at the same time with this the précis of the Dutch mail arrived to-day, but, as you will see, it contains nothing.[2]

I am obliged to you for the opinion you have sent me.[3]

I am, etc.

C. Jenkinson

1. François de Bussy, French Plenipotentiary for the peace negotiations. For an account of his embassy see W. Lawson Grant, " La Mission de M. de Bussy à Londres en 1761 ", in *Revue d'histoire diplomatique*, Paris, 1906. Bussy's truculent behaviour at St. James's cast doubts on Choiseul's sincerity, but W. L. Grant suggests that Choiseul, who meant to treat as far as possible directly with Pitt, paid very little attention to his ambassador whom he had chosen as a person weak enough to do no more than transmit Pitt's ideas to him. On June 9, and again on Sunday, June 14, Bussy, in the spirit of the French memorial of April 19, tried to convince Pitt that his non-acceptance of the dates proposed in the original French memorial of March 26, amounted to a rejection of the whole proposition. Thackeray, *op. cit.* i, 513, 534.

2. See Add. MS. 32924, f. 124 : " Précis of the Dutch Mail received, June 16, 1761 ".

3. On June 13 Jenkinson asked for Grenville's opinion on a Parliamentary case " that I may be sure in the advice I give Sir James Lowther who seems to rely very much on me in all his public concerns " (*Grenv. Pps.* i, 365).

The following paper in Jenkinson's handwriting on the functions of a Secretary of State and of his Under-Secretaries was presumably drawn up soon after his and Bute's initiation into the routine of the office, and is among the North papers in the Bodleian Library, Oxford.

MS. North, c. 3, ff. 284-6.

The busyness of Secretary of State consists of two parts :—

DOMESTIC	FOREIGN

The domestic busyness relates to instruments of various sorts for the King's signature, which are carried or sent by the Secretary of State to the King; These are all made out according to forms already established in the Office; or if any doubt arises, the members of the Office in such case represent the difficulty, and the Secretary of State then refers the case to the Attorney or Solicitour General, either to determine the ancient form, or to propose a new one.

Another part of the domestic busyness of a Secretary of State relates to his correspondence with the different Boards or with the several subordinate Ministers, for the King's information, either in matters of fact or of law; These are various according to the occasions, which give rise to them. The manner of doing this is settled according to forms preserved in the Office; a state of the case referred and the material relative to it are inclosed in the letter, which is signed by the Secretary of State; and there is not the least difficulty in the execution.

Another part of the domestic busyness of the Secretary of State is, when he acts as a Magistrate, being in right of his office a *Conservator of the Peace* and has thereby in many effects the same powers as a Justice of the Peace; In consequence of this he apprehends such criminals as are worthy the attention of Government, persons guilty of treason, spies etc. When these are apprehended by a warrant, directed to a Messenger, there is a Law Clerk belonging to the Office, to take their depositions; and they are disposed of according to the discretion of the Secretary of State, with the advice of His Majesty's Ministers, which belong to the law.

The other parts of the domestic busyness of the Secretary of State consist of such correspondence as may occasionally arise from domestic occurrences which in peaceable times are very few, and when they do arise, are of the nature of every other correspondence, where the King's commands are to be transmitted.

The foreign part of the busyness of Secretary of State relates to the different kind of correspondence, which he carries on with all, who bear His Majesty's commission in foreign parts, whether Ministers, Generals etc. The general intent of this is to convey the King's commands to them and to receive from them such intelligence as they can supply; it is impossible to describe particularly the nature of this, as it varies according to the different nature of the commissions, and the various occurrences of the times. All that can be done is to describe the mode or method, in which the busyness, relative to it, is transacted.

It consists of letters and instructions, *sent* or *received*.

Before any letter or instruction is read, the Secretary of State takes the commands of His Majesty, and consults upon it such of His Majesty's Confidential Ministers as he thinks proper. In consequence of this the draught of the letter is formed either by himself or by one of his Under-Secretaries. This should be done at least a day before the mail or messenger sets out; that is, on Monday for the mail of Tuesday and on Thursday for the mail of Friday. When the draught is settled in proportion to its importance it is circulated or not to any other of the Confidential Ministers; and after it has received their corrections, it is sent to the King; This is usually done early ⟨on⟩ the morning, on which it is to be dispatched and when that is done it is sent to the Office to be copied fair, or put into cypher; and being then transmitted to the Secretary of State for his signature, it is afterwards returned to the Office to be dispatched.

It is the duty of the Under Secretarys to prepare materials and to get every thing ready for the busyness they see likely to arise, and to get all inclosures, which are oftentimes much longer than the dispatches, properly prepared against the time they are wanted.

The letters received are brought always first to the Office; when they arrive either by mail or messenger, they are first opened by an Under Secretary, who dockets them; if the Secretary of State is in the way, he sends them first to him, who after having perused them, transmits them to the King; but if the Secretary of State is at the House of Lords or any otherwise engaged they are then sent immediately to the King, and after that they are put into a course of circulation as is agreed on among the Ministers. Each Secretary always sends his dispatches to the other Secretary, before he sends them to any other Minister; the dispatches out of cypher are always sent up from the Office first with a schedule of such as are in cypher; and as soon as these last can be dispatched, they are sent up also.

Besides all which thus relates to the different kinds of correspondence, the Secretary of State usually appoints one day in the week, when he sees all the foreign Ministers of course to discourse with them on the several points, which concern their respective Courts; he sees them also at all other times, when they have urgent busyness with him.

CHARLES JENKINSON TO GEORGE GRENVILLE [1]

St. James's, June 18, 1761.
Dear Sir,

Since I saw you I have perused Stanley's dispatch and shall be able to show you a copy of it when you come to town. It contains, however, nothing more than what I have already sent you. I think, indeed, that the abstract Lord Bute made of it was to Stanley's advantage; for in general the dispatch is very ill drawn, and though he has upon the whole acted properly, yet it is in a very odd manner. It is the first dispatch in which I ever saw metaphysical reasoning. I cannot help, however, observing one thing, which is that the Duke de Choiseul is a more sensible and able man than the world has generally represented him to be. He treats with a great degree of gaiety and laughter what is trifling in business, but whatever is of importance strikes him very strongly, and he immediately lays hold of it.

This appears very evidently upon the present occasion. He has a good deal of pride, and it is evident Mr. Pitt has not known how to treat that, but otherwise it is evident that he is agreeable and explicit in the manner of doing business.

Bussy holds still the same conduct as before: either he must be a very bad man and an enemy to this country, or the French Ministry use him very ill; both which are perhaps true in part.

After having given to you this preface of the general state of affairs, I will now acquaint you with what has been

1. In *Grenv. Pps.* i, 367-9.

determined by the Council upon them.[1] They were very fortunately unanimous and full of good humour, and the resolution they have taken has been a wise one. As the Duke de Choiseul has called upon us to propose new epochs, we have proposed them : for Europe, the 1st of July ; for the West Indies and America, the 1st of September ; for the East Indies, the 1st of November. You should observe that this is the same gradation which they observed in their epochs, so that the only difference is in the commencement between the 1st of May and the 1st of July. But we have added to this proposition these conditions, first, that the Peace, as it regards ourselves, shall be separate and distinct from whatever is concluded at Augsburg ; secondly, that there shall be something signed and agreed to before the 1st of August, otherwise we are to be no longer bound by these propositions ; thirdly, whatever captures are to be taken, are not to be comprehended in the general terms of the *uti possidetis* ; fourthly, to promote the work of peace, we propose at once to enter into compensation for the island of Belleisle ; and lastly to call upon them to propose whatever compensation, exclusive of all this, they may think necessary. This is the abstract of what will be sent to-morrow to Stanley, to propose to the Duke de Choiseul.

I will reserve what I have to say on these propositions, and on some private affairs, 'till the next post.

I am, etc., etc.

C. Jenkinson

GEORGE GRENVILLE TO CHARLES JENKINSON

Add. MS. 38191, ff. 70-71.

Wotton, June 21, 1761.

Dear Sir,

Though I was not at all surprized at the difference of language between that which M. Bussy first held, and that which Mr. Stanley reports from his conference with the Duc de Choiseul, yet I own M. Bussy's perseverance in it after having heard from M. de Choiseul does seem to me so extraordinary, that I cannot easily account for it, except in one of the ways that you mention, and yet there are great objections to both, as it is hard to believe that a man sent upon such a message would come so entirely ignorant of the views of his

1. Cf. Newcastle to Devonshire, June 18, 1761, Add. MS. 32924, ff. 158-9.

(6)

Court and of the Minister that sent him, or that knowing them he would venture to act so directly contrary to them. I think what you hinted in your first letter that M. de Choiseul has an intention to draw the negotiation to himself has a great appearance of truth, and goes farther towards reconciling these contradictions than any other supposition. Whatever the fact may be a little time will explain it, as it will be impossible to continue as it is after the Court of France has received the propositions sent from hence in answer to Mr. Stanleys dispatches, and grounded on them. I suppose the word *Captures* in the 3d proposition relates to the captures at sea which the Uti possidetis at the several epochs is not to extend to, and if the French captures upon us are (as it is said) as great at present if not greater than ours upon them the French will have no difficulty in complying with this article. The 4th proposition of entering into a compensation for Belleisle I take it for granted points to an exchange of it for Minorca, the only acquisition made by France upon the Crown of Great Brittain. What the 5th and last proposition [1] aims at I do not I own quite understand. We call upon them to know whether they wish to propose any *other compensation*. They have *no conquests upon the Crown of Great Brittain* (and *no other* has hitherto been admitted) to offer *in compensation* and I did not understand that any idea has yet been opened of their ceding the ancient rights and possessions of France to buy back any of *our conquests*, or whether our Government thinks that such a Treaty would turn out advantageous to us. I shall receive with the greatest pleasure your observations on these propositions. I still think it very desirable not to lose sight of the first overtures made from France, which from what you tell me of M. de Choiseul's character seems to me the likeliest as well as the best means of bringing these matters to a happy conclusion. Has M. de Choiseul's language to Mr. Stanley or any part of it been communicated to M. Bussy, and what does he say to it ? or what will M. de Choiseul say to Bussys language, when Mr. Stanley tells him of it as I

1. The fifth clause of Stanley's memorial was probably inserted to encourage France to make proposals of compensation in Germany. The position in Germany, which concerned the allies, was officially reserved for discussion at Augsburg, but England and France would both have been willing to consider it in their present discussions if either could have forced the other to introduce it. See Stanley to Pitt, June 12, where he says Choiseul has hinted that the German question cannot be a matter of indifference to George III personally, and the instructions sent to Stanley on June 19, bidding him on no account discard the British reserve as to further compensations. Thackeray, *op. cit.* i, 526, 535-6.

suppose he will ? [1] For surely it is both desireable and necessary to have this situation thoroughly explained and not to suffer it to remain upon such contradictory declarations. We propose being in town for a few days in a little more than a fortnight but we have not yet quite settled it, as soon as we have you shall know it. I am ever, my dear Sir, most faithfully and affectionately

Yours, etc.

George Grenville

On June 17, at an elaborately staged interview, Choiseul offered Stanley new and more conciliatory terms, including the evacuation of Wessel.[2] These were discussed at meetings of the Efficient Cabinet on June 24 and 26, when the English reply was agreed to.[3] On June 25 and 27 Jenkinson sent Grenville accounts of these meetings and of the Terms which were sent to Stanley on June 26.[4]

CHARLES JENKINSON TO GEORGE GRENVILLE [5]

St. James's, June 25, 1761.

Dear Sir,
    The negotiation between us and France grows so full of events and so embroiled, that it is difficult and even dangerous by letter to give any account of it. This makes me the more desirous that the time was come when we might converse together in town. It will be sufficient to say that Choiseul has transmitted conditions of peace under the greatest injunctions of secrecy, with which even Bussy is not to be acquainted, and none of our own ministers but those who are trusted in the utmost confidence. Upon these the Council sat yesterday, and determined that a counter project should be returned to it. They have not ultimately determined what it shall be, but they are to sit upon it again to-morrow.
    Thus far, however, I may now say for certain, that Canada is to be ours ; Choiseul has already consented to this. The

1. Jenkinson replied on June 23 : " Choiseul says that Bussy's instructions are conformable to what he says himself to Stanley, and that *Bussy is horrified with Mr. Pitt's presence*, which makes him act in the manner he does. This is *ridiculous* " (*Grenv. Pps.* i, 370–71 ; see also footnote on p. 371).
2. Thackeray, *op. cit.* i, 539–43.
3. See Add. MS. 32924, ff. 311–22, Newcastle to Devonshire, June 28, 1761.
4. See Thackeray, *op. cit.* i, 543–9.
5. In *Grenv. Pps.* i, 371–2.

fisheries are to be left to France,[1] but not Cape Breton. France is to evacuate Westphalia. Goree is to be restored. Senegal is to be ours. The other parts of the scheme are not ripe, but from all appearances we shall have a peace very soon ; I think a cessation of arms in less than a fortnight.

Pray take the utmost care of this letter. Lord Temple is in Town.

Stanley has sent the strangest dispatches that were ever seen.

I am, etc., etc.

C. Jenkinson

CHARLES JENKINSON TO GEORGE GRENVILLE [2]

St. James's, June 27, 1761.

Dear Sir,

Lord Bute asked me to-day when you would be in Town ; I told him in about ten days. He then answered, as that is the case, I will not send a messenger, otherwise I should, with an account of all that has passed in this memorable week ; he seemed unwilling to trust the post.

I will, however, just venture to say this, that there was a Council yesterday, which lasted as long as that on Wednesday, and to-day a courier is gone with a long dispatch to Mr. Stanley, containing our ideas on a Peace : we insist on all Canada, including Cape Breton, and the islands of Senegal and Goree ; Dunkirk to be destroyed ; Minorca to be restored ; the neutral islands to be left wholly neutral, or an equitable partition of them. These are sine quâ non. All the rest is left to Stanley to negotiate with. But in such case France is to evacuate all

1. Pitt preferred to continue the war rather than renew the clause of the Treaty of Utrecht which allowed the French to fish off Newfoundland. He was supported by Temple, but the rest of the Cabinet were against him. Grenville, Hardwicke, Bedford, Halifax, and Newcastle, were sure the French would never consent to give up the Fishery and they were anxious by all means to make peace at this opportunity. Bute was for an attempt to keep the Fishery but not to make it a *sine qua non*. " After this, the whole council *seem'd* to acquiesce in our measure ", Newcastle wrote when the Cabinet adjourned on Wednesday, June 26 (Add. MS. 32924, f. 316). In the draft of his letter to Stanley, which Pitt read to the Cabinet on June 26, the question of the Fishery was left to be discussed when the renewal of the Treaty of Utrecht should come under consideration, but Pitt made it clear to the Cabinet that this was not his own advice. Any attempt to keep the Fishery without making it a *sine qua non* he considered " puerile and illusory ". In the final draft an amendment by Bute was inserted to the effect that the Fishery would never be given back without " some great and important compensation " (*ibid.* f. 319).

2. In *Grenv. Pps.* i, 372-3.

the possessions of our allies in Westphalia and on the Rhine. This is the sum total of what is determined.

I shall long to talk with you upon it when you come to town.

I am, etc., etc.

C. J.

GEORGE GRENVILLE TO CHARLES JENKINSON

Add. MS. 38191, f. 72.

Wotton, June 28, 1761.

Dear Sir,

I write to you chiefly to acknowledge the receit of your letter by the last post, which you will be glad to know came safe to my hands in its proper time. The subject of it is in itself so extraordinary, and so delicate, that it would perhaps be difficult to form any judgement upon it even if all the particulars attending it were explained, but without knowing them it is quite impossible, especially as that very material article of Guadeloupe [1] which in the opinion of many is the most important of all does not yet appear to be at all settled. I heartily wish it may be so in a manner agreable to all our wishes, and I the rather hope it if the Fisheries are to be left to France as you mention. I shall wait to hear such farther particulars as may be proper to be sent in a letter by which we shall see how far the Project or the Counter Project [2] departs from the first terms offered by France which I have hitherto looked upon as the basis of this whole transaction.

My wife desires her compliments to you and I am with the greatest truth, dear Sir,

Your most obedient and faithful humble Servant,

George Grenville

1. There was much controversy at this time both in England and in France as to the relative values, strategic and economic, of Canada and Guadeloupe, one or other of which must be ceded at the peace. Grenville was in favour of keeping Guadeloupe, and a year later bore resentment against Bute for giving it up at a Cabinet meeting which he was too ill to attend (see *Grenv. Pps.* i, 450). On the question of Canada versus Guadeloupe, see C. W. Alvord, *The Mississippi Valley in British Politics* (1917) ; G. L. Beer, *British Colonial Policy* (1907), chapter viii ; Namier, *England in the Age of the American Revolution*, pp. 317-27. For an analysis of the pamphlet literature on the subject see W. L. Grant in the *American Historical Review* for July 1912.

2. The French project of June 17, sometimes called the " little leaf " of propositions, and the English counter-project of June 26, printed in Thackeray, *op. cit.* i, 543-9.

Add. MS. 38197, f. 220.

Anne, daughter of Sir Hugh Clopton, of Stratford-on-Avon, married July 17, 1720, Thomas Boothby Skrymsher of Norbury Manor, Stafford, and of Grosvenor Square, son and heir of Thomas Boothby of Tooly Park, Leicestershire, and M.P. for Leicester 1726–27. He died in 1751. Mrs. Boothby was a cousin of Horace Walpole's mother and was described by him as " not . . . the most amiable person in the world ".

Tooly Park, July 11, 1761.

Dear Jenkey,

We country gentlefolks are much alarmed at the sound of the coronation fixed for 22 of September ; some say October which I think more probable. This not being a secret I venture to beg you will set us right in this important affair as soon as your leisure permitts. And it is also said that a few days will show wether wee are ⟨to⟩ have a cessation of arms or continuance of the war ; when ever that account is to be published in the news papers be so good as to give me a line, that wee shall credit, for in this county the inhabitants are grown so bright that they scorn to put any faith in news papers, and I have improved my self much by hearing their wise opinions and consequently shall beleive nothing but from ministerial hands.

Mr. Boothby [1] desires his compliments to you, fears what with peace war and Royal Marriage settlements you will be fatigued to the injury of your health ; he says you talked of riding out in an evening, he hopes you do some times, for you may think of bussness on horse back and execute when you come home. Do take care of your health for according to the old proverb Good men are very scarce.

1. Charles Boothby Skrymsher, only son of Anne Boothby, took the name of Clopton in 1792. He attempted to stand for Parliament in 1761, when his mother wrote to assure the Duke of Newcastle " that her son has no relations to sollicit favors for, or any views further than an opinion that parliamentary business is a proper employment for the mind of a young man at his first entrance into life " (see L. B. Namier, *The Structure of Politics at the Accession of George III*, p. 30). Professor Namier writes : " Charles Boothby Skrymsher failed to obtain a seat in 1761 ; came forward as candidate for Leicestershire in March 1762, but withdrew from the contest (see Add. MSS. 32935 and 32936) and committed suicide in 1800, without ever having improved his mind in Parliament. Later in life his ambitions were social, and not political. The obituary note in the *Gentleman's Magazine* (1800, ii, 800) states that he was ' a very respectable gentleman and . . . in the habits of intimacy with the first noblemen in this country. . . . Mr. Boothby was the person supposed to be alluded to by Foote in one of his farces, as distinguished by his partiality to people of rank, and inclined to leave one acquaintance to walk with another of superior dignity. Hence arose his denomination of *Prince* Boothby ' " (*ibid.* 30 n. 2).

Mrs. Maria [1] desires her best regards and desires me to assure you that she is become a very good country Miss and intends to continue so the remainder of her life which she thinks you will approve off, but I fear the air of Grosvenor Square will again infect her. God bless you and forgive

Your sincere friend,

A. B. S.

The wedding [2] will I imagine be private and the coronation soon after ; you will be so good as to tell us as much as is fit for us to know of these matters.

JOHN ROBINSON TO CHARLES JENKINSON

Add. MS. 38198, ff. 5-6.

John Robinson (1727–1802) of Appleby, attorney ; law agent, land steward, and general man of business to Sir James Lowther; M.P. for Westmorland 1764–74, Harwich 1774–1802, was Secretary to the Treasury 1770–82. From 1770 to 1773 he and Jenkinson together ran the Treasury for Lord North. About him see *D.N.B.* Many of his letters, like the following, are rotted by damp along the margin so that the first word of each line is indecipherable. Wherever possible the most likely word has been inserted in angle brackets.

Appleby, October 4, 1761.

Dear Sir,

Your favour of the 29th past did not reach ⟨me ⟩ by being directed to Lowther [3] and as such ⟨ ⟩ then having to return, which, if you please ⟨ al⟩ways to me at Appleby, will be avoided, as proper ⟨direction ?⟩ is constantly left there how to forward the letters to ⟨me⟩ wherever I happen to be.

I am extremely obliged to you for the readiness with which you have applied for the discharge of the French prisoner and have no doubt it will be immediately done. Mr. Wilson [4] and the clergy at Carlisle have a very good

1. Maria, second daughter of Anne Boothby, married July 29, 1768, the Rev. Dr. Rowney Noel, D.D., afterwards Dean of Salisbury, a brother of Sir Edward Noel, 1st Lord Wentworth. He died in 1786.
2. The marriage of George III to Princess Charlotte of Mecklenburg-Strelitz took place quietly on September 8, and the Coronation was held on the 22nd.
3. The town of Lowther, not Sir James.
4. Probably Thomas Wilson, afterwards appointed Dean of Carlisle (July 1764) on the interest of Sir James Lowther. At this time England was full of French prisoners of war ; their release or exchange was obtained on application to the Commissioners of Sick and Wounded. The man referred to here was probably a civilian. It was not customary to intern them, and if occasionally one of them was imprisoned it was generally considered a great hardship. Cf. Holdernesse's letter, p. 19, and Ramsden's, December 9, pp. 20-22.

opinion of the poor man and will I am assure think themselves very fortunate ⟨in⟩ the favor of your assistance to him.

The Parliament I find sits for dispatch of ⟨business ?⟩ on the 3d of November. I have therefore taken the liberty ⟨to pr⟩ess Sir James earnestly thereon, and that he would consult Lord Bute and all his friends, as it is realy a ⟨point of⟩ great moment to him, but more so to his family ⟨who have not ?⟩ only the present time in view. There could not be do⟨ubt   ⟩ come in. But the doubt is, If so — How will that ⟨seat be⟩ recovered to the family.[1] It is most precarious, and at best ca⟨nnot be⟩ done, but by a contest, which in Cumberland is a terrible ⟨expence⟩. And there will be a wide difference, between defending the seats the family have, and attacking a popular Junto to gain them. These are the difficulties with me of which I have fully apprized Sir James. And happy should I be if any lucky measure could be thought of to obviate them, and settle this affair for the benefit of the family. In which I own myself totally in⟨capable⟩ of judging, and can only lay the state of things ⟨   ⟩ly before Sir James and his friends for more able persons to ⟨   ⟩ I fear I shall become very troublesome to ⟨you with my co⟩rrespondence, which I should be sorry to be and will conclude with assuring you that I ever am, dear Sir

      Your most obedient and most humble Servant,

                              J. Robinson

JOHN ROBINSON TO CHARLES JENKINSON

Add. MS. 38198, ff. 12-13.

                         Appleby, October 10th, 1761.

Dear Sir,

I had yesterday the favor of your letter ⟨of the   ins⟩tant and am obliged to you for your care of ⟨   ⟩ addresses.[2] Permit me now to trouble you with ⟨   fr⟩om the County least Sir James should have left town before they arrive. If he has I will take the first opportunity to acquaint you what

1. At the general election of 1761 Sir James was returned for Cumberland and Westmorland, but resigned the Cumberland seat, which had usually been held by a Lowther, to Sir Wilfrid Lawson, and himself sat for Westmorland, where his interest was less sure. The other member for Westmorland, John Upton, was friendly to the Lowther interest. On Lawson's death in December 1762, Sir James recovered the Cumberland seat without difficulty and brought in his brother, Robert Lowther, for Westmorland. See p. 119.

2. Westmorland may have addressed the King on his coronation.

he would have done with them, and I hope to send you the Cockermouth ones soon. I had wrote to Sir James at the request of some of our Militia Officers in regard to what I had heard about Major Wilson.[1] He takes great opportunities of saying strange things and doing every thing possible in his power to hurt Sir James interest in a low way behind backs, being the most inveterate of any one ⟨I kn⟩ow, under a specious shew of civility. But Sir James ⟨   ⟩ judge what is best when he talks to his friends. Though had there been a possibility of putting his dis⟨charge   Sir⟩ James receiving orders to reduce the number of officers ⟨   ⟩ that it would be agreeable, I should have thought it the best ⟨method that⟩ the renewal of commissions be postponed till something ⟨   ⟩ done this Sessions of Parliament in regard to the Militia Laws which most likely must be, as they are near expiring, perhaps the Parliament might, as a saving, order it. But the Secretary at War has twice wrote, directing an exact return of officers to be immediately made by Sir James.[2]

I am heartily glad to find Sir James is come to a resolution about his seat. We can now know how to act and I most sincerely hope it will hereafter turn out for the best.

Mr. Pitt's resignation[3] seems to alarm people a good de⟨al⟩ least the disagreements reported should be too true. But we⟨   ⟩ letters directed to me at Appleby will always be certain ⟨to find me⟩ wherever I am, as I constantly leave orders ⟨for them to be du⟩ly forwarded to me when I am from home.

I am with the greatest regard, dear Sir,

Your most obedient and most humble servant,

J. Robinson

RALPH GRIFFITHS TO CHARLES JENKINSON

Add. MS. 38198, f. 21.

Ralph Griffiths, LL.D. (1720–1803), was a publisher and the projector of the *Monthly Review*, a magazine of literary criticism which he started in 1749 because " the abuse of title-pages is obviously come to such a pass,

1. Roger Wilson, Major of the Westmorland Militia. He was possibly the Wilson who contested Westmorland against Sir James Lowther and John Upton at the general election in 1761 and secured enough votes to give the Lowther party a fright (see R. S. Ferguson, *Cumberland and Westmorland M.P.s* (1871), p. 128). This Wilson was not of Dallam, as Ferguson suggests, and if he was of the landed gentry, his family must have disappeared by the time the first edition of Burke's *Commoners* was published in 1833.

2. Sir James was Lord Lieutenant of Westmorland since 1758 and of Cumberland since 1759. He had trouble with another Militia officer in February 1763. See p. 130.   3. Pitt resigned on October 9.

that few readers care to take in a book, any more than a servant, without a character ". He continued to edit the *Review* for fifty-four years. In 1757 a famous quarrel occurred between him and Oliver Goldsmith, who had engaged to write for the *Review* on condition of receiving board and lodging with Griffiths and his wife (for a prejudiced account of their behaviour see John Forster, *Life of Goldsmith*, p. 120 *et seq.*). They were afterwards reconciled, and Griffiths's biographer, in the *European Magazine* for January 1804, speaks of the Dunciad in the Strand, " where we perfectly remember his shop to be a favourite lounge of the late Dr. Goldsmith ". See also Nichols, *Literary Anecdotes of the Eighteenth Century*, iii, 506-8, and *D.N.B.* Griffiths was Jenkinson's publisher. His two discourses were published in 1757 and 1758 from the Dunciad in Paternoster Row. In 1759 Griffiths carried his sign to the Strand.

November 5, 1761.

Sir !

Though the service you did me, in the affair of the *Votes*,[1] has been frustrated by the late unexpected changes, yet I cannot but retain the same warm sense of your kindness, as though everything had terminated just as you or I wished ; and I do therefore, Sir ! most heartily thank you for your good offices on that occasion. I should also incline to pay the same grateful acknowledgements to Mr. Grenville, for his favourable intentions towards me, on your account ; but that I dread nothing more than the taking any step which may in the least look like impertinence.

Were it not, too, that I am equally unwilling to presume too far on the kindness of my friends, I would take the liberty of here mentioning that, possibly, opportunities may hereafter fall in your way of greatly serving me, in my business : particularly if any *publications* of a more ordinary kind should occur. As I find I have inadvertently done the very thing I have been disclaiming, permit, Sir ! to explain myself. M. Bussy's negociations, for instance, printed at Paris,[2] have

1. In October 1761 Grenville wished to stand for the speaker's chair, but was dissuaded by Bute, who wanted him for leader of the House of Commons (see *Grenv. Pps.* i, 398). The printers of the House of Commons votes were appointed by the Speaker and Jenkinson had evidently used his influence to obtain a promise from Grenville to Griffiths.

2. *Mémoire historique sur la négociation de la France et de l'Angleterre, depuis le 26 mars 1761 jusqu'au 20 septembre de la même année, avec les pièces justificatives* (Paris, de l'imprimerie royale, 1761). It is not impossible that Jenkinson was responsible for the translation which is included in his *Collection of Treaties of Peace* (1785), iii, 80 (also in *Parliamentary History*, vol. xv, col. 1019 *et seq.*). The British Government did not publish an authorised reply to the French *Mémoire*, but Jenkinson prepared a lengthy answer (Add. MS. 38336, ff. 161-268) to show that France was the aggressor and to prove the fallacy of allowing her to compensate for British conquests in America by the restoration of her own conquests on Hanover and the German allies. Apparently no use was made of this essay, which was written before the end of the war.

suggested to me, that possibly our Government may be induced to offer something to the world : and should such a thing happen, it must prove advantageous to whoever is the bookseller. If any such occasion should fall in your way, and you should recollect your trusty operator in the Strand, it will be greatly adding to the obligations already conferred on, Sir !

Your most sincere and most respectful humble servant,

R. Griffiths

J. DYSON TO CHARLES JENKINSON

Add. MS. 38198, f. 23.

Jeremiah Dyson (1722–76), M.P. for Yarmouth (Isle of Wight) 1762–1768, Weymouth 1768–74, Horsham 1774–76. From 1753 to 1763 he was First Clerk of the House of Commons. In May 1762 he became joint Secretary to the Treasury, where he was Jenkinson's colleague from April 1763 to April 1764, when he became a Commissioner of the Board of Trade. He belonged to the group of Bute's friends and was supposed to have changed his politics at the beginning of the reign. He was an able Parliamentary lawyer described by Walpole as the Jesuit of the House. About him see *D.N.B.*

Old Palace Yard, November 18, 1761.

Dear Sir,

I was quite a stranger to what you mention concerning the Minutes. In general I did understand that they were usually sent to several of the Public Offices, and that some of the clerks had some advantage by sending them. However I think I may venture to answer for it that you shall not fail to receive them for the future.

As to taking a place for you in the House, I will give directions that it be done whenever the House is likely to be full ; and in general I trust it will not be neglected. If however by accident it should now and then be forgotten, you will be so good as to excuse it. And if in any more important point it should be in my power to contribute to your convenience or gratification, you will much oblige me by acquainting me with it, and thereby enabling me to convince you of the very sincere regard with which I am, dear Sir,

Your most faithful humble Servant,

J. Dyson

LORD NUNEHAM TO CHARLES JENKINSON

Add. MS. 38198, f. 57.

George Simon, Lord Nuneham, eldest son of Simon, 1st Earl Harcourt, by Rebecca, daughter of Charles Sanborne Le Bas, was returned M.P. for St. Albans in 1761 on the interest of Lord Spencer.[1] See a eulogy of him in Collins's *Peerage* (1812), iv, 449-52, " That tribute which truth owes to superior virtue ".

The following letter signed only with the initial " N." is undated but was written before the family came to town in 1761. As Lord Harcourt was in Cavendish Square on November 21 (see next letter), this letter is placed provisionally in November but the internal evidence is not sufficient to prove more than that it was written in 1761.

Monday, [? November 1761].

Dear Sir,

Though your letter gave me infinite pleasure, yet at the same time it caused me some uneasiness, for unfortunately the unbounded curiosity of a certain person was never at so great a height as on that day, I believe she gave me five hundred hints to see it, and repeated so often : Well what does Mr. Jenkinson say, it is very odd that he gives you no information about the dinner; what, does he send you no news ? that at last I was wearied to death with answering the same things over and over again, and very prudently retired out of the room, and tore your letter, lest she should ask for it without detours, and that I should then be obliged to tell a lye, to avoid shewing it to her.

We certainly leave this place on Monday, which I shall not regret, notwithstanding that if possible it looks more beautiful than ever ; Lady Harcourt is perfectly well and I hope as her spirits continue good, that she will not insist on his Lordship's remaining every year so improperly long in the country, contrary to the advice and opinion of all his friends, and what is still more surprizing, absolutely contrary to his own inclinations, as I heard he owned last winter, when he was a little angry with her, for persisting to stay here herself, and obliging him to stay here, so many months after the death of the late King.

I have received a letter since I last writ to you from the Dean of Canterbury,[2] who tells me, that poor Mr. Elers's [3]

1. See p. 82 and n. 1.
2. William Friend was Dean of Canterbury 1760–66.
3. Paul Elers, Clerk of the Peace for Oxford, died at Oxford in 1781, aged eighty-two. On January 5, 1763, he sent Jenkinson a scheme for taxing the

affairs are now come to that pitch of misery and distress, that unless a sum of money can be raised for him, he must be obliged to leave his family and go to jail, for which reason the Dean has very humanely undertaken a collection for him, and writes to me to acquaint Lord and Lady Harcourt and myself with it. I of course mentioned it to Her Ladyship, who received it as I expected, with anger, and coldness, and said sure he could not expect my Lord to do any more for him, for that it was entirely owing to himself that he was in want, I am sorry to say, that I never mentioned any affair of that kind to my good mother, that I had not the same answer given me ; Good God that any one can be so lost to all sense of humanity, as to have the power of dispensing happiness to others, and yet lose the benefit and pleasure of such an advantage by their absurd admiration and fondness for a few yellow counters. If you can find an opportunity of recommending poor Elers, to any of your acquaintance who can afford to ⟨lavish ?⟩ something on him, and are of that divine religion humanity, you will relieve the miseries of a very worthy unfortunate family, and much oblige him, who has the honour to be

Your affectionate humble servant,

N.

I need not desire you to destroy this letter immediately.

LORD HARCOURT TO CHARLES JENKINSON

Add. MS. 38198, ff. 24-5.

Cavendish Square, Saturday Morning.
Docketed in Jenkinson's writing : "November 21, 1761 8,
Lord Harcourt, C.J., Received do ".

Dear Sir,
    I have just wrote to the Duke of Marlborough [1] to let him know that Sir Edward Turner's [2] name is left out of the new

proceedings before J.P.s. It is docketed from " Mr. Elers, an old and experienced Justice of the Peace in Oxfordshire " (Add. MS. 38200, f. 217). His son William was a lieutenant in Harcourt's troop. In 1776 when Harcourt was leaving the Lord Lieutenancy of Ireland he acquired a pension of £150 a year for Elers. See Harcourt to North, May 4, 1776, in Colonel Blaquiere's Registers, P.R.O., S.P., Ireland, 63/438, p. 378, and T.14/15, p. 402.

1. On April 17, 1759, Jenkinson wrote to Grenville : " The young Duke of Marlborough is lately come to town, and by the advice of his mother has flung himself totally on Lord Harcourt to direct his conduct in the county of Oxford, and this with such circumstances as makes me think that Fox has no great influence over him " (*Grenv. Pps.* i, 297).

2. Sir Edward Turner of Ambrosden, 2nd Bart., M.P. for Penryn 1761-66, was one of the chief landowners in Oxfordshire and successfully contested the county for the new interest at the celebrated election of 1754. About him see Dickens and Stenton, *An Eighteenth-Century Correspondence* (1910).

(18)

Commission.[1] An omission that must give the greatest offense imaginable, as it must be considered as a design to affront a man of Sir Edward's rank and fortune. It must be an impertinence of Walker's,[2] at least it appears so to me by the very excuse that is made to palliate the omission. I hope the Duke will stop the new Commission, which I suppose may be done by an application to the Chancellor. If it is too late to insert Sir Edward's name, I am sure there ought to be a new Commission. If you will let me know next week, when the Queens jointure bill will be ready for the Royal Assent, I wont fail being in town to attend her Majesty to the house of Lords.[3] I should suppose it would scarce be ready before the middle of the week after next.

Yours, dear Sir, very sincerely,

Harcourt

LORD HOLDERNESSE TO CHARLES JENKINSON

Add. MS. 38198, f. 27.

Robert Darcy, 4th Earl of Holdernesse, was Secretary of State for the Northern Department from June 21, 1754, to March 12, 1761, when he resigned with a pension of £4000 a year to make way for Bute. For at least five years Jenkinson had worked under him in his office.

Bath, November 24, 1761.

Dear Sir,
  I trouble you with a few lines upon the following occasion. A person calling himself Comte de Choiseul, and brother to him that was Ambassador at Vienna and destined to be so at the congress, and now Ministre des affaires etrangeres,[4] came passenger to England with Captain Conningham [5] from St. Domingo by the way of New York with a passport, he landed at Falmouth, and took this place in his way to London, where

1. The Commission for Justices of the Peace.
2. Unidentified.
3. Harcourt was a member of the Queen's Household. In July 1761 he was sent as Ambassador to Mecklenburg-Strelitz to fetch her to England, and married her by proxy. On September 10 he was appointed her Master of the Horse.
4. César Gabriel (1712–85), Comte de Choiseul and Duc de Praslin (1762), cousin of the French Minister, Étienne François, Duc de Choiseul. In 1758 he succeeded his cousin as Ambassador to Vienna, and on October 12, 1761, Choiseul resigned to him the ministry of Foreign Affairs without giving up his control of French policy. Horace Walpole records a visit of his son, Renault César Louis, Vicomte de Choiseul, to England, in 1765 (Letters, vi, 216), but does not mention a brother.
5. ? James Cunningham, master of the Trial sloop, 14 guns.

I made a sort of *Bath* acquaintance with him. He interests himself for the release of the persons mentioned in the enclosure of his letter, allegding that they are not *gens de guerre* [1] but planters at St. Domingue and having occasion to go to France thought no other way secure than that they took, but being ignorant of the customs of war omitted aplying for a passport. Voilà mon histoire, you'll judge whether to trouble Lord Bute with it. This is the dullest place imaginable, except Lord Chesterfield who seldom appears there is not a sensible man to talk with or a girl to flirt with in the place, possibly the arrival of one of its representatives [2] may cause some motion, preparation, I hear is making for his entry, when any thing occurs possibly you may hear from me, en attendant je suis

tout à vous

Holdernesse

TOM RAMSDEN TO CHARLES JENKINSON

Add. MS. 38198, f. 36.

Tom Ramsden (1709–91 ?), fifth son of Sir William Ramsden, 2nd Bart. of Byram and Longley Hall, Yorkshire, was Latin Secretary to the King and consequently Jenkinson's colleague in the Northern Department of the Secretary of State's office. He was also Collector and Transmitter of State Papers. His mother, Elizabeth Lowther, was the daughter of John, 1st Viscount Lonsdale, and a sister of the 3rd Viscount from whom Sir James Lowther inherited estates and a baronetcy in 1750. Through this connexion Ramsden became one of Lowther's many political agents.

Byram, December 9, 1761.

It is so long since I wrote to you, My dear Jenkinson, that ⟨if my⟩ brother did not tell you how often he hears from me, ⟨you mig⟩ht justly think, that some accident had befallen ⟨me⟩. In other respects, you will not suspect me, though most ⟨   ⟩se their senses, and many do lose them, notwithstanding ⟨   ⟩ Statute taken out. I do not know, where ⟨   n⟩ext paragraph, after the above, least you ⟨should think th⟩ere was any connection. But as there is ⟨none I

---

1. Cf. p. 12, and Tom Ramsden to Jenkinson, October 17, 1761, enquiring after the two French prisoners Pierre Laporte and Pierre Simon Chollet who " are not yet set at liberty " and " were only passengers ". Ramsden supposed that the breaking-off of peace negotiations may have been the reason of their neglect, but " it is not a good reason, for they are an expence ⟨to the⟩ public and of no disservice to the enemy, and most of ⟨the⟩ prisoners in their circumstances have been discharged " (Add. MS. 38198, f. 15).
2. Pitt was M.P. for Bath 1757–66.

should⟩ be glad to learn from you, if you have heard it, ⟨what⟩ is the reason, that the Post Office money is not yet ⟨iss⟩ued. Potts [1] in a letter October 22d to me says, I shall next Tuesday receive the secret service money, and orders me to draw upon him ; but the money is not yet forthcoming.[2] Has not Todd [3] been with you on the subject ? I am sorry to see the stocks continue to fall, I am afraid that Spain does not quite satisfy us of their peaceable intentions ; and also that the great sum that must be wanted is not subscribed for. I like Mr. Speaker's speech.[4] There are some turns in it that ⟨mu⟩st, I

1. Henry Potts, one of the secretaries in the G.P.O., belonged to a Post Office dynasty. Samuel Potts, " one of the first clerks in the General Post Office ", died at Bath in 1752. Another Samuel Potts was Comptroller of the Inland Office at the G.P.O. at the same time as Henry Potts was Secretary. Both of them were turned out by Fox in December 1762 (see below), but were restored to their former places by the Rockingham Government in July 1765. Henry Potts was found dead in a hackney coach on January 1, 1768, while driving to a pastrycook's in Spring Gardens. Another Henry Potts, also of the Post Office, came to a violent death in 1787 when he was flung from his horse by a post-chaise.
2. Ramsden would seem to refer to the salary of £500 a year which he received as Collector and Transmitter of State Papers, and which, he wrote to Bute in April 1761, " by the report of the Attorney and Solicitor-General to the Treasury, cannot now be pay'd as it was in the late King's time ". Apparently the salary and extraordinaries of this place, £400 and £100 a year respectively, " were by the patent made payable out of the revenue of the Post Office. His Majesty having now given up that revenue to the public, all farther payment from thence is stopped." Ramsden was apprehensive that his salary would be transferred to the Treasury and begged that he might be " as little a sufferer, as the nature of the thing will allow, there being great difference in expence in fees etc. attending payments from the Treasury and the Exchequer from those at the Post Office " (Bute MSS.). Instead, however, he seems to have been transferred from the Post Office Revenue to the Post Office Secret Service, a change which must have happened very soon after his letter to Bute. See James Wallace to Bute, May 11, 1761 : " I am informed that the payments of the secret service branch of the Post Office, which have been suspended ever since His Majesty's accession by reason of the alteration made in the hereditary revenue of the Crown, are now about to be put in course again from the time of suspension " (Bute MSS. quoted in *Structure of Politics*, p. 241). At all events, by December 1761 Ramsden was receiving his salary from the Post Office Secret Service, and he is down for £500 on the list of disbursements from this fund for the year ending April 5, 1763, published in the *Grenv. Pps.* iii, 311. In addition to this salary he received £200 a year as Latin Secretary to the King.
3. Anthony Todd, son of Anthony Todd of Wolsingham, Durham, was at this time Secretary to the Foreign Office in the G.P.O., a place which he owed to the influence of his father-in-law Christopher Robinson, uncle of Jenkinson's friend, John Robinson, and Resident Surveyor in the Post Office. On December 1, 1762, Todd succeeded Henry Potts as Secretary to the Inland Office but lost the post again in July 1765 (see p. 378). He was reappointed shortly after Potts's death in 1768 and remained at the Post Office until his death in 1798, during which time he amassed a large fortune which he left to his daughter, Lady Lauderdale. The amount of this seems to have been exaggerated in the original obituary notice in the *Gentleman's Magazine*, 1798, p. 541. But see also pp. 622, 720, " It was always understood that Mr. Todd gave his daughter £50,000 three per cent annuities. He has left the chief part of his fortune to her Ladyship and her children, and to Lord Lauderdale £2000 and £120 a year." Herbert Joyce in his *History of the Post Office to 1863* (1893), p. 240, says that Todd entered the Post Office in 1738 and reckons his emoluments in 1787 at £3000 a year.
4. Sir John Cust, M.P. for Grantham, was Speaker 1761-70.

think, have come from under the old Great Wig. ⟨Sir⟩ James Lowther passed by without calling ; indeed I should not ⟨have se⟩en him, as I was then at Swillington, about 9 miles ⟨away⟩. We hear that he is to make his Election for ⟨Westmorland, Sir Wilfr⟩id Lawson [1] is to be chose for Cumberland and that he is expected back again in a fortnight ; I hope he will not bring Lady Mary [2] with him ; for I think such long ⟨journeys⟩ at this time of the year, is not reasonable. ⟨   ⟩ I have fixed no time for leaving this country ; I ⟨find it⟩ difficult to get away ; so many places ⟨to visit and people⟩ wanting company (though but stupid) preven⟨t   ⟩ I have not heard one syllable of my two Fren⟨ch prisoners [3]⟩ whether any relief can be had or not. I ask p⟨ardon for⟩ using that word, for I don't beleive they would live ⟨better⟩ at home. But why prisoners, that are not military either ⟨upon⟩ land or sea, should be kept at the expence of the public, I ca⟨nnot⟩ comprehend. I apply'd to Mr. Clevland [4] (by Mr. Fern [5] of the Admiralty) before I wrote to Lord Harcourt,[6] and perhaps he may not be pleased with a suit being made to any but himself.

I have not time to write to my brother, the Major,[7] this post, but if you should see him, be so good as to say, that I got his two last letters, and will write very soon. I hope all things go well with you, and that you keep your health and spirits all which I truly wish you. I beg my compliments to your Coll⟨eague⟩ Weston,[8] and family, whom I conclude you visit.

Ever y⟨ours⟩,

⟨T. R.⟩

1. Sir Wilfrid Lawson, 8th Bart., High Sheriff of Cumberland, and M.P. for the county December 1761 to his death on December 1, 1762. See pp. 13 n. 1, 108.
2. Lady Mary Stuart, eldest daughter of Lord Bute, married Sir James Lowther on September 7, 1761.
3. See p. 12 n. 4. On December 30, when war with Spain had become inevitable, Ramsden wrote again to Jenkinson : " The poor prisoners must now, I conclude, be content to stay, which I am sorry for on account of some " (Add. MS. 38198, f. 46).
4. John Clevland, Secretary to the Admiralty 1751 till his death on June 19, 1763. Before that he had been Second Secretary to the Admiralty 1746–51.
5. Charles Fearne, Clerk of the Admiralty and marine clerk. On June 28, 1764, he became Deputy Secretary to the Admiralty, a place which he retained till November 11, 1766.
6. Harcourt seems to have interested himself very much in the exchange and release of French prisoners. See Add. MS. 38198.
7. Frecheville Ramsden, sixth son of Sir William Ramsden. In 1761 he was a Major of the Earl of Effingham's troop, but the following year he became a Lieutenant-Colonel, Lieutenant-Governor of Carlisle, and equerry to the King. See p. 42.
8. Edward Weston, Under-Secretary of State in the Northern Department.

Pray remember me, to the good family in Cavendish Square,[1] and my Lord of Loudon.[2]

The following letter refers to the Durham election of December 1761 contested between Ralph Gowland and Major-General John Lambton. Ralph Gowland was a member of the old Durham family of Gowland and a field officer in the Durham Militia. At the general election of 1761 he contested Durham against the interest of the Lambtons who represented the city from 1734 to 1813, when they transferred themselves to the county. He was defeated, but the successful candidate, Henry Lambton, died shortly afterwards on June 26, 1761, whereupon Gowland again contested the borough against Major-General John Lambton, brother of the late member. This time Gowland was successful owing to the ingenious proceedings of the Mayor of Durham, who, having displaced sixteen members of the Common Council and " named others of inferior fortunes ", proceeded on October 21, 1761, to introduce a new by-law increasing the franchise " under the sanction whereof the Mayor etc., at several times swore two hundred and fifteen occasional freemen, who were fetched out of Yorkshire, Westmorland, Cumberland, Northumberland and the county of Durham in order to serve Mr. Gowland, then major of the Durham militia ".[3] The election lasted from December 7 to 12, when Gowland was returned with the help of his new supporters by a majority of 23. His friends anticipated a petition, and on October 23, while the Mayor of Durham was altering the franchise, Lord Darlington wrote to Newcastle to ask for Government support if the case should come before Parliament (Add. MS. 32929, f. 480).

RALPH GOWLAND TO CHARLES JENKINSON

Add. MS. 38458, f. 1.

Durham, December 18, 1761.

Sir,

Having the honour of being returned for this City against General Lambton after a poll of six days which ended last Saturday and finding a report prevails that the General intends to petition I entreat the favour of you to attend should it come before the House being very well assured you will not be prepossessed against me before you have heard the defence of, Sir,

Your most obedient humble Servant,

Ralph Gowland

1. The Harcourts.
2. John Campbell, 4th Earl of Loudoun.
3. Hutchinson, *History of Durham*, ii, 46. The rightful freemen were so incensed at this depreciation of their privileges that they refused to act under their charter, which consequently lapsed. The story is told in detail, *ibid.* 36-47.

On December 23 Lambton appealed to Newcastle [1] whose approbation he had sought before the election,[2] but Newcastle remained neutral and when Lambton's petition came before the House on May 11, 1762, "no one of the Treasury voted".[3] The petition was successful and Gowland did not sit in Parliament until 1775, when he was returned for Cockermouth on the interest of Sir James Lowther.

Copy in the handwriting of Jaspar Mauduit of Sir Jeffery Amherst's Certificate of the Number of Troops furnished by the Provinces in North America for the Publick Service in the Year 1762

Add. MS. 38334, ff. 250-51.

Jaspar Mauduit, brother of Israel Mauduit about whom see *D.N.B.*, was Agent for Massachusetts, though Israel did the work of the agency. Both the Mauduits were dissenters and members of the Society for propagating the Gospel in Foreign Parts. They were linen drapers by trade.

RETURN OF THE TROOPS FURNISHED BY THE SEVERAL PROVINCES IN
NORTH AMERICA FOR THE PUBLICK SERVICE FOR THE YEAR 1762 *

Provinces or Colonies	Number of Men voted to be levied cloathed and paid including those that remain'd last winter who were to be reinlisted	Number of Men actually raised and took the field	Of which there are to remain during the winter
Newhampshire †	534	534	51
Massachusetts Bay ‡ . .	3220	2991	591
Rhode Island .	666	653	64
Connecticut .	2300	2300	323
New York . .	1787	1474	173
New Jersey § .	666	595	64
Pensylvania ‖ . .	——	——	——
Maryland . .	——	——	——
Virginia ¶ . .	1000	657	——
North Carolina	——	——	——
South Carolina **	——	——	——

[*See notes to table on following page*

These are to certify the Right Honourable the Lords Commissioners of his Majesty's Treasury that the above is a true state of the respective quotas of men raised by the several Provinces on the Continent of North America in consequence of his Majesty's requisition for the service of the year 1762 as nearly as the numbers can be ascertained from the straggling manner on which the Provincialls generally take the field.

Jeff: Amherst

1. Add. MS. 32932, f. 314.   2. *Ibid.* 32925, f. 32.
3. James West to Newcastle, *ibid.* 32938, f. 166.

LAURENCE SULIVAN TO CHARLES JENKINSON

in Cleveland Row

Add. MS. 38458, f. 2.

Laurence Sulivan, M.P. for Taunton 1762–68, was a Director of the East India Company and leader of the majority in the Court of Proprietors, where he opposed the influence of Clive. From 1741 to 1752 he was a Company's factor in Bombay, became a Director in 1755 and was Chairman of the Company in 1758, 1760, and 1761, and Deputy Chairman 1763–64, when he carried the election of his list of Directors against the interest of Clive.[1] In 1762 he was out of the Direction by rotation though still

1. See p. 270.

Notes to table]

* For an analysis of the support given by the various colonies throughout the war see S. L. Beer, *British Colonial Policy*, pp. 52-71. This list should be compared with Amherst's list of 1761, a copy of which, also by Jaspar Mauduit, is in the Liverpool Papers, Add. MS. 38334, f. 68 (partially reproduced in Beer, *op. cit.* p. 67, from the correspondence of the Colonial Governors of Rhode Island, II, p. 349). After the fall of Montreal, the colonies were asked to raise only two-thirds of their previous levies, but Amherst's list of 1760 (printed in *Minutes of the Provincial Council of Pennsylvania*, IX, p. 48) and the account sent by Loudoun to Holdernesse in August 1757 (P.R.O., C.O. 5/48), show that even before this event the colonies responded in more or less the same proportion.

† In 1761 New Hampshire voted 534, but raised only 438 men. According to Loudoun, this colony, though fairly populous, was poor.

‡ In 1761 Massachusetts raised only 2637 men, and Connecticut fell short by 300 of the number voted. But New York did better in 1761 than in 1762, raising 1547 of the 1787 voted. Throughout the war these three colonies offered the most vigorous co-operation, and together furnished nearly seven-tenths of all the colonial troops, though their population only amounted to one-third of the total white population of the continental colonies, and though Massachusetts was suffering at the time from a trade depression (Beer, *op. cit.* p. 68).

§ In 1761 New Jersey voted only 600 troops and raised only 554. The strong Quaker influence here made it particularly difficult to get support (see Beer, *op. cit.* p. 59).

‖ In Maryland and Pennsylvania, the two rich proprietary colonies, the granting of effective support was hampered by local disputes, fostered, according to their Governors, with a view to evading the requisitions (see *ibid.* p. 69). In 1762 Maryland, Pennsylvania, and North Carolina were especially rebuked for their complete failure to respond (Egremont to Amherst, July 10 and September 11, P.R.O., C.O. 5/62), and the following year Pennsylvania received an intimation of the King's " surprise and displeasure " when, notwithstanding the Pontiac rising and the laudable example of Virginia, who sent Amherst 1000 militia, she still refused to contribute anything (Halifax to Governor Penn, October 19, 1763; Minutes of the Provincial Council of Pennsylvania, IX, p. 114).

¶ In 1761 Virginia mustered her full thousand.

** In 1761 South Carolina had been unable to raise troops for service under Amherst because she was engaged in a conflict with the Cherokees (see Beer, *op. cit.* p. 66). But Amherst wrote in his certificate for that year that she made provision for raising 1000 men to serve against the Cherokees under Colonel Grant " of which there were upwards of 500 raised and actually took the field " ; exclusive of the Corps of Rangers kept in the pay of the Province, and principally employed in escorting provincials, etc., to the army and the ports. See a copy of Amherst's Certificate for 1761, Add. MS. 38334, f. 68. As usual, North and South Carolina were rebuked this year for their lack of zeal. See Egremont to Amherst, July 10 and September 11, 1762, and Egremont to the Colonial Governors, December 12, 1761, and Pitt to Amherst, December 17, 1760. C.O. 5/60, 61.

retaining his influence over the Directors. In 1768 he suffered heavily in the fall of India stock but continued to play a part in the Direction until his death in 1786. See his letters and an account of his career by H. O. Love in H.M.C., *Palk MSS.* p. 30 n. 2. Sometime, probably as early as 1761, he became associated with John Dunning, afterwards Lord Ashburton, and through him with Shelburne, who supported him in opposition to Clive's policy of territorial aggrandisement. (See Miss L. Stuart Sutherland's essay in the *English Historical Review*, July 1934 : " Lord Shelburne and East India Company Politics, 1766–69 ".) He was also an intimate friend of Robert Palk of Ashburton, sometime Governor of Madras, from whom he received frequent financial assistance. To these friends he was indebted for his seat at Ashburton, which he represented from 1768 to 1774 and which he unsuccessfully contested in 1761 against Thomas Walpole and the hereditary Tuckfield interest of the Orford family. (See Namier, *Structure of Politics*, p. 375.) Ashburton was a cloth-manufacturing borough amenable to merchant representation. Before 1761 Lord Orford seems to have returned both members, but in 1760 Nathaniel Newnham, an East India Director, started a new interest there which, however, he abandoned when he found that Newcastle supported Walpole. He was disgusted by the appearance of Sulivan in January 1761 as a candidate " upon the interest, that I had, though not near so strong as mine would have been " (Add. MS. 32917, f. 222). Apparently both Newnham and Sulivan cultivated the manufacturing interest, the one by promoting their exports (see *Structure of Politics*, p. 157) and the other through the India Company's judicious purchase of " Ashburton long ells " (see *A History of the Administration of the Leader in the India Direction* (1764), p. 15) ; in spite of which Thomas Walpole was returned on April 20, 1761.

Mile End Green,[1] January 4, 1762.

Sir,

My Petition together with that of the Freeholders of Ashburton complaining of an undue return for that borough being appointed to be heard at the Bar of the House of Commons the ninth of February next : I take the liberty to acquaint you that the merits of that election will certainly be brought before the House, and to request the favour of your attendance.

I should not have presumed to have troubled you with such application at this time, nor should I have known I was at liberty to do it, if I had not seen several of the Circular Letters dispatched by my opponent, wherein he even affects to doubt whether I am serious in my appeal to the justice of the House. I am with great regard, Sir,

Your most humble servant,
Lau. Sulivan

1. The parish of Stepney had associations with the East India Company. Their principal docks were at Blackwall, and at Poplar they ran a hospital and alms-house and a school for seamen's children. Mile End was not a residential quarter for Directors ; one other Director, George Stevens, lived at Poplar in 1762 and Sulivan himself only stayed there from 1762 to 1763.

Sulivan apparently had the goodwill of Fox when he stood for Ashburton (see Horace Walpole to Fox, November 21, 1762), but early in February 1762 Bute for some reason decided to join Newcastle in support of Thomas Walpole, possibly in an attempt to woo Lord Orford, who had a considerable Parliamentary interest.[1] Pressure was put on Sulivan to renounce his petition. On February 18 he wrote to Newcastle : " I solemnly declare that I never made a proposition to your Grace, the Duke of Devonshire, Lord Anson, or any other person concerning my election for Ashburton and therefore the letter your Grace has favoured me with I cannot comprehend ; that overtures have been made to me through Lord Hertford I acknowledge, but it's as true that I determined not to attend to them " (Add. MS. 32934, f. 425). The same day Devonshire wrote to Newcastle : " Mr. Sulivan told Lord Bute he would give up the election and my brother George was sent from Court to settle it with him at the House. When he came there Mr. Sulivan had changed his mind " (Add. MS. 32934, f. 421). A fortnight later Sulivan gave in, but pointedly declined an offer of support elsewhere from Newcastle, " as my future expectations are from Lord Bute alone at whose desire I gave up the contest " (Add. MS. 32935, f. 158). In March 1762 he was returned for Taunton on the interest of Lord Egremont,[2] but in November 1767, on the death of John Harris, the other member for Ashburton, Horace Walpole wrote : " Lord Orford I hear has compromised Ashburton. Palk is to come in for this session and Sullivan and Charles Boone [3] next Parliament " (Horace Walpole to Thomas Walpole, November 4, 1767). The interest for one seat at Ashburton remained in the Palk family till 1831.

DR. JOSEPH BETTS TO CHARLES JENKINSON

Add. MS. 38198, f. 72.

Joseph Betts, M.A., Fellow of University College, Oxford, was an astronomer and mathematician. In July 1762 he applied to succeed Bradley as Astronomer Royal and Savilian Professor of Astronomy, and in September 1764 to succeed Bliss as Astronomer Royal and Savilian Professor of Geometry. After much soliciting he was given the Chair of Geometry in January 1765 but died the following year on January 7, 1766. He corresponded frequently with Jenkinson, principally about his own preferment.

1. In November 1762 Fox tried through Horace Walpole to win Orford's support by offering him a place. See Fox to Walpole, November 21, 1762, in *Memoirs*, i, 168, and Walpole's answer of the same date in the *Letters*. Bute may have had the same hope in February or he may have seriously hoped to gain Thomas Walpole or his father-in-law, Sir Joshua Vanneck, who had been useful in the peace negotiations of 1761. In any case there was a short truce between Bute and Newcastle in January.
2. In a list of " the nobility " with " Their independant interest in Boroughs ", in the Liverpool MSS., Minehead and Taunton are ascribed to Lord Egremont with a note : " N.B. These boroughs being Scot and Lot are uncertain and Mr. Sulivan's opinion was he owed his success to having no opponent " (Add. MS. 38334, ff. 271-2).
3. About him see L. B. Namier, " Charles Garth and his Connexions ", *English Historical Review*, July 1939.

Dear Sir,

Our College is at this time petitioning His Majestie to get our Licence of Mortmain enlarged. I am told the Secretaries of State have it much in their power to procure a grant of this favour : if so, your assistance herein will be thankfully acknowledged ; and I beg you to lend it.

Our motives for applying are wholly these. We have been assured that the present Master intends to leave us an estate for good purposes : which in our present circumstances, we can neither accept or enjoy.

You'll believe me that I was much affected with the news of the Bishop of London's [1] death. I should have esteemed it a great honour, had Providence permitted it, to have deserved the notice and patronage of so excellent a Prelate : But though that is now a vain wish, I shall never forget your friendly intentions to serve me, or the obliging manner you were pleased to signify them in. I am glad to hear of my friend Hoare's [2] success. Would you save yourself and me trouble, " I mention this as you were so good to think of me unasked and without solicitation " ? recommend me to your good Lord Bute, or His Majestie, " Whom you are frequently with as I am told ", for the next Stall to Hoare's ; and you'll not be tormented with future applications. You have heard no doubt of Dr. Bradley's [3] illness : but I find his Professorship is engaged to Mr. Williamson of Baliol : [4] I was told of this some months ago, or had applied for it. Had Dr. Bradley the nomination of his successor, and he seems to be a good judge of the science, if the testimony of all Europe has weight I flatter myself I should have been the person, he might have recommended : But Providence I trust will provide for me. I am, dear Sir,

Your obliged humble Servant,

J. Betts

1. Dr. Hayter died on January 9, 1762. He was Bishop of London from September 1761.
2. Joseph Hoare, B.D., was appointed Prebendary of Westminster on January 19, 1762. He was afterwards Principal of Jesus College 1768–1802. The prebends of Westminster were Crown patronage worth £300 a year. They were considered by Newcastle as the form of preferment " first and most eligible next to deaneries and bishoprics and sometimes more difficult to be had than a deanery ". See Norman Sykes, *Church and State in England in the Eighteenth Century* (1934), p. 149.
3. James Bradley, D.D. (1693–1762, see *D.N.B.*), F.R.S., Savilian Professor of Astronomy at Oxford and Astronomer Royal, died on July 13, 1762.
4. John Williamson of Dumbarton, M.A. (Balliol).

JOHN BINDLEY TO CHARLES JENKINSON

Add. MS. 38198, f. 77.

John Bindley junior was a distiller like his father before him, but left trade shortly before February 1762 to become Secretary of the Excise. In February 1763 he was promoted to be a Commissioner of Excise but resigned in January 1765, with a view to standing for Parliament. The interest he boasted in Malmesbury, Rochester, and Liverpool did not avail him, but in December 1766 he was returned for Dover. His Parliamentary career ended in 1768 when he left politics to become a wine merchant. In 1762 he was ambitious of becoming a "King's Friend" and tried to work up a connexion with Bute through Jenkinson, but any political consideration he enjoyed during Grenville's ministry was spurious and rested only on his connexion with Charles Townshend, whose death in 1767 may possibly have determined Bindley's return to trade. He died at Bath on February 18, 1786, and is described in the obituary notice in the *Gentleman's Magazine* as " a gentleman to whose abilities the revenue of this country is considerably indebted as well for its augmentation as improvement in several capital branches ". His creed was, " a man's ideas are as much his property as the guinea in his pocket ", and he was given a pension by North in consideration of his innumerable schemes for raising revenue.[1]

Excise Office, February 13, 1762.

Dear Sir,

The intimacy that subsisted between us in our early days makes me take the liberty of asking your assistance towards procuring an honor, I have long wished (and had some reason to expect long ago by means of another person high in Government) of an introduction to Lord Bute.

When you recollect that I was taken out of trade in which I had a prospect of getting a prodigious fortune, by gentlemen in the first rank in the Revenue, and appointed to a place of the consequence of Secretary to the Excise at the first step, and recollect that the acquaintance with these gentlemen and indeed every man that I know in power, arise from the service I had actually done Revenue on two or three considerable occasions, it will I believe speak in favour of my abilities on one hand and my readiness on the other to devote my self and services to the business of the public and Government (for my friends all know that my goal is only to rise from Secretary to Commissioner of Excise on a vacancy, and that the profit of my business which I left was between 2 and 3000£ per ann.).

1. Some of these are in the Liverpool Papers (Add. MS. 38335, ff. 310-11); others are referred to in Bindley's letters to Jenkinson (*e.g.* 38216, f. 129; 38204, ff. 7, 172; 38206, f. 230; 38210, f. 62).

But as I had done service already to my country and the Revenue by furnishing a new branch of commerce to the former (viz. the exportation of British spirits) and considerable funds to the latter and as I have also two or three considerable improvements ready to produce of the like nature, and foresee a large field open for more, I have chosen to enter into a plan of life wherein I hope to make my self serviceable, and do credit to those who think me fit for the plan which they themselves chalked out for me, rather than to continue in trade under the alluring and almost certain prospect of doubling my fortune which is not inconsiderable in ten or twelve years.

Being engaged therefore in the service of the Crown and the public, you will not wonder at my desire to be known to the Minister who from all accounts is said, to deserve that confidence which he possesses in so distinguished a manner of both the one and the other. And I do flatter my self likewise that under his Lordships permission I can produce a plan, extreamly wished for by gentlemen of landed estates in Scotland which shall entirely prevent the smuggling of French brandy into Scotland, and institute in its place brandy made from corn of its growth. Government wont be less benefited by this than the country as I expect an additional revenue will hence arise of £30,000 per ann.

I leave it Dear Sir to you, mention what you please to procure me the honor I wish of paying my duty to his Lordship, which I am offered by several different hands another way, but which I should wish to be done only through you. I am Dear Sir,

Very truly yours,

Ino. Bindley

MRS. BOOTHBY SKRYMSHER TO CHARLES JENKINSON
at the Earl of Bute's office

Add. MS. 38458, f. 6.

Thursday morning.
Docketed "February 25, 1762".

Dear Sir,

Perhaps you have heard that your friend Charles Boothby stands for the county of Leicester [1] in the room of Mr.

---

1. On Charles Boothby's candidature see Add. MSS. 32935, ff. 200, 285, 287, 316, 374, 382, 495 ; ibid. 32936, ff. 40, 54, 56. He had already attempted to

Smith,[1] Lord Denbigh[2] has an estate in that county and interest; and he writes me word that he will not declare until next Thursday when the gentlemen of the county meet. His Lordship's ancestors and Mr. Boothby's have for many generations acted in conjunction at all elections in that county as I did say unto him in my letter. And as they are now both united in loyal affection to our good King I hoped that might induce his Lordship to assist my son. I wish you would speak to Lord Bute upon this point. One word from his Lordship to Lord Denbigh would have great weight. You know Mr. Boothby's principles for the support of the Kings measures are firm and as I have not the honor to be at all known to Lord Bute it would be presuming too far to write to him my self therefore leave this affair to your better judgement, Lord Granby[3] supports Mr. Boothbys intrest, and the turn and disposition of the County of Leicester runs greatly in favor of Mr. Boothby. An opposition is talked of but no certain person named, and Sir Thomas Palmer[4] the other Member tells me he does not know that any is intended, but I am sensible that there are some gentlemen that will endeavour to raise one if they can. But if Lord Bute will countenance Mr. Boothby so far as to speak to the Earl of Denbigh the effect will be great. One thing is certain who ever is chose in opposition to Mr. Boothby their only merit will be to oppose the Kings measures, and to please those that chuse them, they must do so, or for ever lose their favor. Mr. Boothby has been down and well received and is going again this instant, I am

Your obliged humble servant,
A. Boothby Skrymsher

stand for Leicestershire at the general election (see p. 11 n. 1). In 1762 he was supported by Newcastle, who wrote to his " stewards and agents in Nottinghamshire, to do their utmost to serve Mr. Boothby, for the County of Leicester " (*ibid.* 32935, f. 285).

    1. Edward Smith of Edmondthorpe, Leicestershire, M.P. for the county from 1741 to his death on February 15, 1762.

    2. Basil Fielding, 6th Earl of Denbigh. His estate was Newnham Paddox, near Lutterworth.

    3. The Manners were a Leicestershire family; the Duke of Rutland was Lord Lieutenant of the county. Newcastle had great hopes of Granby's interest prevailing, but Granby himself was less sanguine and eventually advised Boothby to withdraw rather than force a poll.

    4. Sir Thomas Palmer, 4th Bart., M.P. for Leicestershire from 1754 to his death in 1765, when he was succeeded in his seat by his son, Sir John Palmer. The successful candidate for Smith's seat was Sir Thomas Cave, 5th Bart., of Stamford Hall, M.P. for Leicestershire 1741–47, 1762–74. He was of a very old Leicestershire family and his father had represented the county in all the Parliaments of Queen Anne's reign.

MRS. BOOTHBY SKRYMSHER TO CHARLES JENKINSON
Add. MS. 38458, f. 8.

Upper Grosvenor Street. February 26. 1762.

Dear Sir,

This post has brought great accession of intrest Lord Stamfords [1] which is very considerable Lord Exeters [2] and Lord Willoughby De Broke,[3] but I have not heard a word from Denbigh indeed I think I shall not, and yet he will do right, if he could put it upon the footing at the meeting of the gentlemen next Thursday that the peace of the county will be preserved by accepting of your friend that our opponents would be glad to come into, and save appearances, where they are convinced that a poll would be against their intrest as well as pocket. The only person that they have hopes of standing is a young gentleman of eight hundred pound a year all he can do if he is so ill advized is to create trouble and charge for Mr. Boothby's freinds are so superior to all that these people can get together that it will be quite disproportionate, a word to the wise is enough. The world is still upside down for Maria was out of bed this morning soon after nine.

Your obliged

A. B. S.

JOHN ROBINSON TO CHARLES JENKINSON

Add. MS. 38198, f. 95.

Appleby, March 13, 1762.

Dear Sir,

I am just now favoured with your letter ⟨   ⟩ truly congratulate you on the good ⟨news you were⟩ so obliging as send me. I purpose to leave this place on Monday and make what haste I can to town, as the weather and waters will permit me, the one being at present very bad, and the others very high. It give⟨s⟩ me pain to press you too much on Captain

---

1. Harry Grey, 4th Earl of Stamford, formerly M.P. for Leicestershire 1737–1739.
2. Brownlow Cecil, 9th Earl of Exeter, formerly M.P. for Rutland 1747–54, Lord Lieutenant of Rutland and Recorder of Stamford.
3. John Verney, 14th Baron Willoughby de Broke.

Deane's [1] account situated as you acquaint me you are at the Admiralty [2] but merit alone will not do, though I hear from all hands Lord Anson continues to speak of him with great regard and warmth of friendship. A little application therefore I hope may do him effectual service. I dare say the ⟨people at White⟩haven think themselves under great obligations for the Artillery and stores, but I have ⟨not heard from   ⟩ since the order was sent them. I am with ⟨great regard⟩, Dear Sir

                    Your most obedient and most humble Servant,
                                                        Jo Robinson

The letters in the *Grenville Papers* from Jenkinson to Grenville on foreign affairs continue at intervals of three or four days from June to October 1761. The last answer to these reports in the Liverpool MSS. is dated June 28, 1761.[3] In the middle of October Grenville became leader of the House of Commons and therefore a member of the Effective Cabinet in receipt of the circulation of papers and no longer dependent on Bute for information. Jenkinson and he were, however, corresponding in the spring of 1762, and when Grenville stayed at Wotton in April Jenkinson renewed his news bulletin.[4]

GEORGE GRENVILLE TO CHARLES JENKINSON

Add. MS. 38191, f. 73.

Great George Street, March 22, 1762.

My dear Sir,
        You will certainly meet Lord Bute at Court at 12 o'clock as he desires and therefore will not trouble him with my

1. Joseph Deane, Captain in the R.N. from October 17, 1758, distinguished himself on the St. Lawrence in 1760, when he was in command of the expedition from Quebec to Montreal, and was mentioned in *An Account of General Amherst's Expedition* as "strongly recommended in Lord Colville's letter" (*Gent. Mag.*, 1760, p. 462). See also *ibid.* p. 485, October 4, "This day Major Barré and Capt. Deane arrived express in the *Vengeance* frigate from Quebec . . . with the news of the surrender of Montreal and all Canada". He was one of the family of Deane of Appleby to which Hannah Deane, Robinson's mother, belonged, but the exact relationship is not stated in C. B. Norcliffe, *Some Account of the Family of Robinson of the White House, Appleby*, which seems to be the only genealogical work in which this family is mentioned. He died at Whitehaven in 1780. In spite of Colville's recommendation, Robinson was obliged to solicit many times in his behalf.

2. Grenville was Treasurer of the Navy until May 1762, when he became Secretary of State.

3. See p. 10.

4. See p. 36, and *Grenv. Pps.* i, 420, 439.

congratulations in writing upon an event [1] so highly interesting and so critical in every respect. May the consequences of it be answerable to the joy it must give to every good Englishman, and the honour derived from it be equal to my warmest zeal for the Kings glory and my affectionate wishes for Lord Bute. I am ever

Most faithfully and most truely yours etc,

George Grenville

JOHN ROBINSON TO CHARLES JENKINSON

Add. MS. 38198, ff. 105-7.

Charles Street, 27 March 1762.

Dear Sir,

I was favoured with your letter to me last night and am much concerned the application we have made with regard to coals is likely to fail,[2] but realy after the Commissioners stated to me the difficulties that attended it, and what they had before reported in regard to it, though I wish it so much, I could not even expect they would or ought to act otherwise, than I apprehend they will. Mr. Hooper [3] was most obligingly civil on the occasion, as indeed was the Board in general, but I found that a president [4] of this kind, and the danger of frauds on the revenue, were such obstacles, as could not be got over, and as they seemed to think no means ⟨   ⟩ be prescribed effectually to prevent ⟨   ⟩ could not strenuously press gentlemen instrusted with ⟨   ⟩ management of the revenue, to report in favour of a measure which they apprehended prejudicial to it. In their former

1. News of the taking of Martinique by Admiral Rodney and General Monckton reached London about March 22. See letter of John Clevland, Secretary to the Admiralty, to the Duke of Newcastle, March 22, 1762, Add. MS. 32936, f. 34.
2. Sir James Lowther had inherited extensive collieries in Whitehaven (together with a fortune of two million pounds) from his third cousin, James Lowther of Whitehaven, who died in January 1755. No details of Lowther's memorial to the Commissioners of Customs are given in the Treasury Minute Book, but it was read to the Treasury Board on February 4, referred to the Attorney-General at Lowther's expense, and agreed to on April 28. See P.R.O., T. 29/34.
3. Edward Hooper, Commissioner of Customs 1748–93, formerly M.P. for Christchurch 1734–47. In 1761 the two members for that borough were returned on his interest (see *Structure of Politics*, p. 180). He came from an old Dorsetshire family. (See *ibid*. p. 198, and *Letters of the First Earl of Malmsbury*, 1870, vol. i *passim*.)
4. *I.e.* precedent.

reports, they have been so good as state the exemption allowed in 1721,[1] and do not absolutely report against the Petition, only submit the consequences to the Treasury from a precedent of this kind, and from an opportunity, given by this indulgence of frauds. I hope they will be no more strenuous against it in their present report, and that also they may report the small annual product ⟨   ⟩ of the Treasury, which may be leaving it to their favor ⟨   ⟩ my acquainting the Commissioner that their form [2] ⟨   ⟩ were not only Treasury they were so good as say they would send them again, that the Treasury might have the whole before them — As the Commissioners thought no methods could be fixed to prevent frauds, it did not occurr to me then, but I have since thought, that if the duty was to be paid down, subject to a Drawback on a Certificate from the Coast Officer of the Customs, that the coals were actually landed within the port of Carlisle, no detriment could arise to the revenue. As I caught cold by going to the Custom House yesterday and am unable to wait on you to day, I desired, Mr. Garforth [3] to mention this to you, though in hopes then, I might wait on you ; But as I can't, I take the liberty to trouble you with this letter ⟨   ⟩ if you approve of what is proposed ⟨   ⟩ to communicate it to Mr. Hooper [4] or some of your friends at the Board of Customs, as I am assured Sir James will be ready to comply with every restriction that may be thought requisite to prevent frauds in the revenue — I was with Sir James a little while this morning, but he is not so well, as he can be troubled with much business yet ; but I am certain he will think himself much obliged to you for the great

1. Robinson evidently refers to the Act 9 Anne, c. 6 "for raising and appropriating certain duties . . . upon coals to be water born and carried coast-wise". See particularly § 8, which declares a duty of 2 shillings the chalder and $4\frac{8}{16}$d. the culm to be paid on coals imported from any place in Great Britain and charged on the owner. This Act was perpetuated by 5 George I, c. 19.

2. L.c. 19.

3. John Baines assumed the name of Garforth on succeeding to the estates of his uncle, the last of the old Yorkshire family of Garforth of Steeton Hall in Craven. He was a solicitor in London and a steward and agent of Sir James Lowther, to whom he acted as man of business, though less successfully than Robinson. He was Clerk of the Peace in Cumberland, and in June 1762 applied for the place of Assistant Clerk to the House of Commons, for which he had the interest of Sir James. In 1779 he was elected M.P. for Cockermouth on Sir James's interest, and again in 1789. From 1783 to 1789 he sat for Haslemere, another pocket borough of Sir James. He is mentioned in Hutchinson's *History of Cumberland*, vol. ii, p. 111, as a capital burgess of Cockermouth.

4. Hooper replied to Jenkinson saying he would lay Robinson's suggestion before his Board. Add. MS. 38198, f. 104.

pains you have taken, when he can be acquainted with the whole.

I am with great regard, dear Sir
your most obedient and
most humble servant

John Robinson

I find Lord Anson [1] is now so well as to do business — He will ⟨   ⟩ vacant ships — If therefore you could apply to his Lordship by letter for the *Bedford* [2] for Captain Deane it would be the highest obligation. If Sir James could write I am sure he would —

Ever yours

J. R.

After the entry of Spain into the war in January 1762 the question arose of withdrawing the British troops from Germany and confining our offensive to a single front in Portugal, in which case it was contended that the vote of credit could be reduced from two millions to one. The policy of abandoning Germany was pleasing to the King and hateful to Newcastle for sentimental reasons,[3] and it was strenuously upheld by Grenville on grounds of economy. Bute was sympathetic to Grenville's policy and was secretly enquiring into Treasury accounts to prove the necessity of withdrawing from Germany, but the issue was really personal between Grenville and Newcastle, who was indignant at the prospect of being overruled in his own department. Both he and George III believed that Grenville had designs on the Treasury. On April 8 there was a stormy Cabinet meeting when Grenville " arraign'd the German War " and " the Duke of Newcastle defy'd him upon every article ".[4] The next day Grenville withdrew to Wotton to await events. While he was there Jenkinson sent him news bulletins.

CHARLES JENKINSON TO GEORGE GRENVILLE [5]

St. James's, April 10, 1762.

Dear Sir,

When my servant returned yesterday I was surprised to hear that you was getting into your coach to go out of town. It gave me, however, pleasure in this respect, that it was a

1. Lord Anson was First Lord of the Admiralty. Robinson wrote to Jenkinson on February 9, recommending Captain Deane for a line-of-battle ship and hoping that Bute could be got to speak for him to Lord Anson (Add. MS. 38198, f. 75).

2. The *Bedford* was a third-rate ship with 64 guns. William Martin was her Master in 1763.

3. See Professor Namier's analysis of George III's and Newcastle's attitude towards Germany in *England etc.* pp. 354-5.

4. See *England etc.* p. 365. For an account of the crisis which ended in Newcastle's resignation on May 25 see *ibid.* pp. 353-80.

5. In *Grenv. Pps.* i, 420-22.

proof your health was better than it had been for two or three days before. I meant to have called on you that morning, but was prevented by a mail and messenger that arrived. The despatches from Petersburg carry a bad aspect with them in two respects. 1st, It appears that the Emperor [1] is totally Prussian, and is absolutely in the power of the Court of Berlin, so that we shall have no more influence with him than what will arise from our connection with His Prussian Majesty, and in proportion as we are friends to him. On the other hand, the Emperor stands alone in this opinion : the Empress and the Chancellor, and not only they, but even the Mistress and the Favourites, are of different opinion, and though not Austrians, they are not so warm friends of His Prussian Majesty as the Emperor.

The Emperor has refused to let Wroughton [2] be presented to him, or to accept his credentials.

Wroughton charges Keith [3] with being the cause of this, who abides by the Emperor's clique, and seems too ready to support the Prussian system.

Keith has asked leave to come home. The King of Prussia is more angry with us than ever, and he abuses his Ministers here in the grossest terms, saying they have betrayed him, and sold himself to England. There is no Treaty as yet signed between him and the Emperor. France is very much affected with the news of the loss of Martinique. This is in general the whole of the news we have received by this mail. The letters from Lisbon of the 29th, which were received yesterday, represent that the Spaniards will soon begin to act. Tyrawly [4]

1. Peter III had succeeded to the throne on the death of his aunt, the Empress Elizabeth, who died on January 5. After a reign of about six months he was dethroned and murdered. His wife became Empress as Catherine II.

2. Thomas Wroughton, Minister Resident at St. Petersburg, where he had previously been Consul-General 1759–61. He arrived under his new appointment on March 12, 1762, but was not received by the Emperor who, from admiration for Frederick the Great, had become an Anglophobe. Wroughton returned to England in May and accused Keith, the British Envoy Extraordinary in St. Petersburg, of machinations against him. A recriminatory correspondence passed between them. P.R.O., S.P. Russia, xci, 69. See D. B. Horn, *British Diplomatic Representatives*, Camden Series (1932), pp. 115-16.

3. Robert Keith, Minister at Vienna 1748–57, Envoy Extraordinary at St. Petersburg 1757–62. He returned to England early in October 1762. The account of his recall in *D.N.B.* is inaccurate. See D. B. Horn, *op. cit.* p. 115.

4. James O'Hara, 2nd Baron Tyrawley (1690–1773, see *D.N.B.*), Ambassador to Lisbon and commander of the British troops in Portugal, was supposed to be piqued at not receiving the supreme command of the joint forces, and affected to believe that the Spaniards would never attack. See his letter to Pitt, April 15, 1762 : " I believe that ten thousand well disciplined troops upon the frontiers of either might take their choice whether they would come to Lisbon or march to Madrid ; but I am also of opinion, that neither army will give themselves

has as much mauvaise plaisanterie as ever ; he thinks himself there in a very awkward situation.

I saw Lord Egremont this evening, who looks very well. Lord Bute desires me to present his compliments to you.

I am, etc., etc.

C. Jenkinson

CHARLES JENKINSON TO GEORGE GRENVILLE [1]

St. James's, April 13, 1762.

Dear Sir,

Though the news we have received since I wrote last is not of any great importance, I cannot help troubling you with this letter.

We received our Dutch mail on Monday.

The first accounts that were received in France of the loss of Martinique was by the garrison of Fort Royal, which some of our ships landed at Rochelle, the latter end of last month. All their trading towns are in the greatest alarm and consternation upon it : but what is unfortunate, they have accounts that Mons. Blenac's squadron, hearing at sea that Martinique was gone, had changed its course and was gone for St. Domingue.

A great many private accounts from Ireland give the same intelligence of the riots that have happened there, as you will see in the newspapers. It is, however, singular, that Lord Halifax has not as yet mentioned anything about them. The King, however, has ordered Lord Egremont to write to him to-night upon that subject.

I think when you return to town you will find a change of sentiment with respect to continental measures, and I think we begin to turn our thoughts seriously towards putting an end to that burthen.

I am, etc., etc.

C. Jenkinson

the trouble of so long a march, for I am much mistaken if all this does not end in a cup of mild beer " (*Chatham Correspondence*, ii, 175). See also Walpole, *Memoirs*, i, 114 ; and his letter to Mann, August 29, 1762 : " Lord Tyrawly is returned, and as they were not pleased to see him and English troops in Portugal . . . he now will not allow there is any war there, calls it a combination to get our money, and says he will eat every man that is killed, if the Portuguese will engage to roast him ".

1. In *Grenv. Pps.* i, 439-40.

Add. MS. 38191, ff. 75-6.

Wotton, April 14, 1762.

Your two letters, my dear Jenkinson, of the 10th and 13th of this month were extremely welcome to me, not merely from the love of news (however incident that disease may be in general to those that are in the country) but from a better motive than any political one, the pleasure I shall allways feel from every mark of your attention and friendship. I have been perfectly well ever since I got here ; and have had leisure to look back upon the scene that has pass'd, and to consider of that which is likely to open : both furnish ample matter for reflexion and may such reflexions as are necessary for our honour and our safety occur in time to those upon whose determination they must depend ! if I mistake not there never was a crisis in which the publick busyness so evidently required to be touched in *all respects* with a *firm* hand, and in some with a *gentle* one. The account your first letter gives me of the state of things in the north is certainly an unpleasing and precarious one in both the lights in which you consider it, and therefore calls for the utmost dexterity and temper in the conduct of our affairs at that Court, and with those two necessary ingredients I should flatter myself from the union of our interests that our views at that Court are still likely to succeed. I am not surpriz'd at what you tell me of the *plaisanterie* being still continued from Lisbon. I expected that, and that is all I expected from the beginning ; but I must say that if my house was on fire and any one sent to assist me in putting it out should so grossly mistake as to think that the season to laugh at me instead of helping me I should be strongly tempted to knock his brains out. If the alarm and consternation are so great and universal in France upon the loss of Martinique as it is represented, those dispositions are happy omens of an honorable issue to us if they are not counterbalanced by a persuasion that we are neither in a condition or temper to avail ourselves of our advantages. This seems therefore to me to be the first point, and essentially necessary to be obviated, and if this proposition is true, nothing can contribute so effectually to peace as to convince France

(39)

by a great reduction of our expences that it is in our power though not in our wish to continue the war, as nothing but the contrary persuasion can induce France and Spain in their present circumstances to go on under such heavy and repeated blows. I am so full of these thoughts that I cannot write upon this subject without giving vent to them otherwise I should not have troubled you with reading what you have so often heard ; but you will consider that your letter has given occasion to it by the paragraph relative to this subject, which I most ardently wish may be well founded, from a conviction that it is the likeliest means to bring honour and safety to my King, peace to my country, and reputation and good will to my friends. I desire the favour of you to return my kindest compliments to Lord Bute. I propose to be in town on Monday next if nothing happens to prevent to me, and am, my dear Sir, most truely and affectionately

Your most obedient and faithfull humble servant,

George Grenville

JOHN BINDLEY TO CHARLES JENKINSON

Add. MS. 38198, f. 194.

Southampton Street, Bloomsbury Square, Tuesday Evening.
Docketed " May 18, 1762 ".

Dear Sir,

Our early acquaintance in a time of life (when sincere friendship is most prevailing) assures me you will, if in your power, assist me at present. Mr. Earle [1] is dead, who was a Commissioner of Excise. I was promised the vacancy. I desired it, having proposed the funds which raised 1 million the two past years. I can now put a plan into the hands of Government which will raise 5 or 600,000£ the succeeding year, provided I am only removed from the post of Secretary to the Excise to Commissioner. The difference in point of profit is not more than 100£ a year. I find I am not to succeed by the assistance of those who promised me and tempted me out of trade. Your advice and assistance on the present occasion will lay me under a lasting obligation and

1. Augustus Earle, Commissioner of Excise from November 1740 to his death on May 17, 1762. His place was given to Thomas Bowlby, who was gazetted on June 19. Bindley, in spite of his timely application, had to wait till February 1763, when he and Henry Vernon were made Commissioners of Excise *vice* Frederick Frankland and Henry Poole. See p. 85.

will be the means of pointing out some plans which will be of considerable advantage and from which some reputation will accrue to the proposers. I am, dear Sir,

Your devoted and faithful humble servant,

Ino: Bindley

LORD HARCOURT TO CHARLES JENKINSON

Add. MS. 5726 D, f. 94.[1]

Newnham, June 18th, 1762.

Dear Sir,

Lady Harcourt's illness confined me so much at home, before I left London, that I had no opportunity of paying my respects to Lord Bute, or of begging the favour of his Lordship to bestow some little employment of fifty or sixty pounds a year upon Bowley,[2] who has served me upwards of thirty years, with great integrity. As my own situation, does not afford me the means of making any provision for this old servant, I would beg the favour of you to present my respects to Lord Bute, and to mention the affair to him, making no doubt from what I have already experienced of his Lordship's goodness, that Bowley will be provided for, and in such a manner, as may permit him, to continue still in my service.

Lord Bute I am sure will excuse my not writing to him upon this occasion, because he knows it cannot proceed from want of respect, but from a desire to give him as little trouble as possible. I am dear Sir most sincerely yours,

Harcourt

JOHN ROBINSON TO CHARLES JENKINSON

Add. MS. 38199, ff. 5-6.

Lowther, July 7, 1762.

Dear Sir,

After sealing up the packet the inclosed letter and paper came to me from Mr. Howard ;[3] you will see from them how

1. This letter is not in the Liverpool MSS., but in a miscellaneous collection of fragments of letters ; the last three words and the signature are cut off and pasted into 5726 B, f. 41.

2. In November Harcourt was still soliciting for his servant Bowley (see p. 81). It was quite usual in the eighteenth century for anyone connected with Administration to expect the Government to provide old-age pensions for personal retainers.

3. Unidentified.

they treat the lady, and what distress she must be reduced to, I dare say therefore, I need not add any thing to urge your assistance to obtain the redress the law of her country has given her. However in obedience to Sir James commands I must say, that he desires you'll be so good as forward what you have already begun, and get Mr. Grenville to send orders to Mr. Keith [1] to compel Mr. Towell's [2] performance of the verdict.

You will also with this receive several letters which for dispatch are sent with the pacquet and which you'll please to forward. Those to Lord Halifax and Lord Ligonier if convenient Sir James would be glad you could deliver and solicit, and I hope you'll meet with success. [3] These have delayed your return [4] being sent as soon as intended, but I hope that is not of consequence. When I was at Whitehaven, I consulted the gentlemen about the stores required by the Ordnance for the Artillery sent, they will immediately provide 70 or 100 barrells of powder, or if that is not satisfactory the whole 140 barrells, but are desirous of having it come down by the same ship which brings the Artillery as the securest conveyance, and would also be extremely glad to ship 300 barrells more, as store for the town and use of the shipping. They will also directly set about the works after they have the advice and opinion of the Engineer, and being anxious to compleat them, would be glad the Engineer was ordered as soon as possible. Mr. Wooller I believe, on the East Coast, who I mentioned to you when in town, is the nearest and most capable. Some accounts to Whitehaven say the ship for the Artillery is taken up and that it will be shipped very soon. Your assistance therefore as soon as convenient to you will much oblige them.

When you may be at the Board about these matters, it would oblige Sir James if you would enquire what has been done about the encroachments on the fortifications of Carlisle, which Colonel Ramsden hath spoke to Sir Charles Frederick [5] about, and whether any return hath been made to the Orders given by the Board. Should any further ⟨account⟩ of the matter be wanted from us, I will send it to you.

The practice of smuggling hath been very long complained

1. Robert Keith?   2. Unidentified.
3. This sentence has been crossed out.
4. The writ for Jenkinson's return for Cockermouth is dated June 30. He was re-elected on his appointment as Treasurer of the Ordnance.
5. Sir Charles Frederick, 3rd Bart., K.B., M.P., was connected with the Ordnance from 1746, when he became Clerk of Deliveries. In 1750 he was made Surveyor and Assistant to the Master General of the Ordnance.

of as the ruin of our country, and the Isle of Man as the support of that destructive trade. It hath continued so long and the representations made have had so little effect, that it is become a doubt whether the Government realy desires to crush it. If they do wish to prevent it, from the present situation of persons and things, I will send you up some accounts of that trade, that may assist, but otherwise I would not trouble either you or myself about it — though it is beyond a doubt the prevention of it would be of the greatest use to the publick and the fair trader. I fear I shall weary you with so many things therefore shall only assure you that I am with great regard, dear Sir,

Your most obedient and most humble servant,

J. Robinson

Lady Mary and Sir James are both well.

On July 13, 1762, the places of Astronomer Royal and Savilian Professor of Astronomy fell vacant by the death of James Bradley, the famous astronomer. The appointment to the first place lay with the King, and to the second with nine electors all in public offices,[1] and it was therefore essential for the candidate to have some interest with Administration. As Bute's secretary Jenkinson was the natural channel of approach for applicants, while his University connexions enabled him to gain and pass on information about the academic and other qualifications of the candidates. In 1762 the favourite for the post of Astronomer Royal was Nathaniel Bliss, who had been Bradley's assistant at Greenwich, but Jenkinson's old friend, Joseph Betts,[2] also applied.

JOSEPH BETTS TO CHARLES JENKINSON

Add. MS. 38199, f. 40

University College, Oxford, July 20, 1762.

Dear Sir,

Some time ago I mentioned Dr Bradley's illness to you, who is now dead. You are not a stranger to the general turn of my studies, and particular application to astronomy. In the year 1744 I determined the orbit of a very remarkable comet and published my numbers in the Philosophical Transactions, which though it did me credit with many lovers of astronomy, I must own displeased Dr Bradley, who at that time thought he was the only person in the world, that could

---

1. See a list of the electors at the end of this letter.   2. See p. 27.

solve that problem, allowed by Sir Isaac Newton to be the most difficult one in that science. Since that time I have occasionally solved two not inconsiderable problems relating to navigation ; the numerical solution of one was some years since obtained from me for the use of Captain Cambel,[1] a friend of Dr Bradley, by Mr Bliss ; but whether the Captain knew to whom he was obliged for it is more than I can say. The problem is now in print and of great use towards determining the latitude at sea with peculiar advantages. Since that time a problem of the same nature was put into my hands by Dr Bradley without the demonstration, when I obliged with one ; but for whom I know not. Dr Pemberton [2] has since wrote a long comment on this problem in the last vol. of the Philosophical Transactions, page 910.

That I have given no other specimens of my abilities in this long interval, you who know me cannot be surprised at. Dr Bradley used me coldly at my first setting out in those studies ; my engagements with my pupils have since taken up great part of my time ; and I thought it labour thrown away to engage in difficult researches which could not entitle me to the slender return of thankful acknowledgements, especially from persons, who I thought should have paid them, were it only for encouragement.

Had the late Martin Folkes Esq.[3] or Mr Graham [4] been alive, there would have been less necessity for my speaking so much of myself, which I could wish to have avoided. They both however when alive honoured me with their friendship, and when at Oxford very obligingly visited me, tho' personally a stranger to them before. And give me leave to add that Monsieur Clairant,[5] a professor at Paris, by the direction of Lord Cavendish to whom I have not the honour to be personally known, paid me a visit a few years since. And I think it can be no disservice to me when it's known that I was a long time a correspondent with the late Mr Simpson of Woolwich,[6] on

1. Stuart Campbell ? Captain R.N., died May 10, 1792.
2. Henry Pemberton (1694–1771, see *D.N.B.*), F.R.C.P., F.R.S., Gresham Professor of Physics. He was employed by Newton to edit the third edition of the *Principia* in 1726.
3. Martin Folkes of Clare Hall, Cambridge, President of the Royal Society (1741), numismatist and antiquary. He died in 1754.
4. Possibly George Graham, F.R.S., a watchmaker who died in 1751, or Richard Graham, F.R.S., Controller of Westminster Bridge, died 1749.
5. Alexis-Claude Clairant (1713–65) mathematician, member of the Académie des Sciences.
6. Thomas Simpson, F.R.S., Master of the Royal Academy at Woolwich, died on May 22, 1761.

whose wife and daughter I find his Majesty has been graciously pleased to settle a pension purely in consideration of the merit of that great man.

There are three candidates I hear for the Professorship and all of Oxford.[1] One I know nothing of, another is my senior and has spent a good deal of time in historical enquiries relating to astronomy. The third I shall not mention, tho' I do him no injustice to observe, that he declares publickly he would not have offered himself a candidate for the place, had he thought I would have accepted it, while at the same time I have sufficient grounds to believe his friends have been recommending him for it a long time — at least a great while before he spoke to me about it.

But to detain you no longer, give me leave to observe that I desire nothing here said may have the least weight with you unless I produce proper credentials of my abilities should they be called in question. If not let me hope for your recommendation to Lord Bute, whose impartial disposal of preferment encourages me to hope for his favour. You'll excuse me when I add farther that unless I could succeed Dr Bradley at Oxford as well as at Greenwich I should be a sufferer. The professorship here is sunk considerably and is not more than £135 a year and the Professor by statute is rendered incapable of holding any Church preferment or place in a College ; and the salary at Greenwich is but £100 yearly, subject as I presume to some deductions. Greenwich is my native air, there I went to school, which makes me reflect on a comfortable situation there with additional pleasure.

Do you know Lord Litchfield?[2] I am perswaded he remembers my hearty endeavours to have served him on a late occasion. Possible a sight of this letter might incline him to recommend me to his Majesty : but I trust I am speaking to a friend who can and will supply what may be wanting on my part. You'll be pleased to favour me with a line. The electors for the professorship are on the other side. I am with great truth

Your obliged humble servant,

Jo. Betts

1. These were presumably John Williamson of whom Betts wrote to Jenkinson in January 1762 (see p. 28) ; Thomas Hornsby, who got it (see p. 46) ; and John Smith of Balliol, who succeeded Betts as Savilian Professor of Geometry in 1766. Of these Williamson was the only M.A. senior to Betts.

2. George Henry Lee, 3rd Earl of Litchfield, was High Steward of Oxford University in July 1762.

Electors to the Professorship :
> The Archbishop of Canterbury
> Lord Chancellor
> Chancellor of the University
> Bishop of London
> Principal Secretary of State
> Chief Justice of the King's Bench
> Chief Justice of Common Pleas
> Chief Baron of the Exchequer
> Dean of the Arches.

NATHANIEL BLISS TO CHARLES JENKINSON
Add. MS. 38199, f. 42.

Nathaniel Bliss (1700–1769, see *D.N.B.*), F.R.S., and Savilian Professor of Geometry from 1742, had collaborated with Bradley in his observations at Greenwich and expected to succeed him.

Oxford, July 20, 1762.

Sir,

The place of his Majesty's astronomical observator being now vacant by the death of my worthy colleague, Dr. Bradley ; Lord Macclesfield [1] and some other friends have been so good as to think me a proper person to succeed him and are I believe making interest for me. If it should lie in your way to second any application of theirs in my favour, I flatter myself that I may expect it from the friendship and regard you have always shown to

Your most obedient humble servant,

Nathl. Bliss

A few days later Bliss was appointed Astronomer Royal, but as he was already Savilian Professor of Geometry, the chair of Astronomy still remained open. About one of the candidates, Thomas Hornsby (1738–1810), Jenkinson made discreet enquiries. On July 25 Shute Barrington wrote to him from Oxford : " In answer to your quaere concerning Hornsby ; his abilities in the practical part of astronomy are highly thought of by the learned in that science ; and with regard to his moral character, I speak knowingly, he is a man of worth and integrity ".[2] Early in 1763

1. George Parker, 2nd Earl of Macclesfield, was a celebrated amateur astronomer and President of the Royal Society from 1752. In 1739 he and James Bradley erected an observatory in his grounds at Shirburn Castle, Oxfordshire, where Bliss also worked with them. Macclesfield was mainly instrumental in procuring the change of style in 1752–53. See *D.N.B.*

2. Add MS. 38469, f. 33.

(46)

Hornsby was appointed to the chair, but in the meantime Joseph Betts again applied for Jenkinson's goodwill.[1]

In August 1762 John Fane, 7th Earl of Westmorland, was dying. On August 29 Horace Walpole wrote to Mann : " His Chancellorship of Oxford will be an object of contention. Lord Litchfield will have the interest of the court which now has some influence there : yet, perhaps, those who would have voted for him formerly may not now be his heartiest friends." In a footnote Walpole explained that he meant the Jacobites. Jacobitism, which had once flourished at Oxford, was now extinct and by 1760 the term had a purely retrospective application, but the University was at least predominantly Tory, and the Whigs, who in the past had been subjected to a certain amount of academical persecution, were still traditionally excluded from the office of Vice-Chancellor and were in a minority among the Heads of Houses.[2] But on the vacancy of a Chancellor in 1762 a group of men at Oxford [3] turned, in the spirit of the new reign, to the Court, inviting Bute's Government to step in between parties, instate the Whigs on an equality with the Tories, and complete the University's reconciliation to the House of Brunswick. Jenkinson's friends, Shute Barrington and Thomas Bray, were particularly active in an attempt to induce Bute to stand for Chancellor and so play at Oxford the part which Newcastle had played at Cambridge. The opportunity did not appeal to Bute but he gave his interest to Lord Litchfield, who was then High Steward of the University. The other candidates were Lord Aylesford, Lord Suffolk, and Lord Foley, each of whom had a personal interest at Oxford. From the point of view of the " King's Friends ", Litchfield was a poor substitute for Bute, and almost to the last Barrington, Harcourt, and Bray continued to hope that a powerful opposition might induce him to withdraw in Bute's favour. It was Jenkinson's task to convince them of " the necessity of Lord L⟨itchfield⟩'s being supported by government with the exertion of all its influence ".

It was clear at an early stage of the canvassing, which characteristically began a month before Lord Westmorland's death, that the support of Government was not enough to ensure victory and that the balance between factions was held by the independent Whigs, who were ready to support whichever party would better their condition. But the confusion of parties and of political terminology was considerable. In the middle of the campaign some of Litchfield's Tory supporters nearly spoiled his chances by proclaiming that he would make no concessions to the Whigs, and it was only after this that Bray and Barrington, who, like Jenkinson, would have called themselves Whigs, considered the advisability, as a diplomatic measure, of Lord Litchfield's giving " some assurance to the great men who apply to the Whiggs that he will nominate Vice Chancellors out of their Heads of Houses in their turns and proportionably to their numbers ". The advice was acted upon, and Litchfield was elected Chancellor on September 23 by 370 votes to 167,[4] his majority being almost entirely due to the last-minute accession of the Whigs.

1. See pp. 62, 103.
2. See J. R. Green, *Oxford in the Last Century*, London, 1859.
3. Not, of course, the undergraduates, who had no say in the election of a Chancellor.
4. " He had many more to vote but the majority being so great the poll closed " (Bishop of Oxford to Newcastle, September 27, 1762 ; Add. MS. 32942, f. 368).

THOMAS BRAY TO CHARLES JENKINSON

Add. MS. 38469, ff. 35-6.

Thomas Bray (1706–85), son of Nicholas Bray of Stratton, Cornwall, M.A. Exeter College 1732, D.D. 1758, Dean of Raphoe 1776–85, Canon of Windsor 1776, Rector of Lincoln College 1771–85. He seems to have had many influential connexions in Oxfordshire including the Harcourts, the Spencer Churchills, Lord Parker, and of the humbler kind, Jenkinson, and Charles and Philip Lloyd.

Exeter College, August 1, 1762.

Dear Sir,

So much secrecy hath been observed in the canvass for Chancellor that nothing material came to my knowledge till last night. I find Lord Litchfields strength is in Queens, Brazen-Nose, Trinity, with some scattered votes in other Colleges ; that the accession of Christ Church and the Whiggs is expected. In some instances I know Lord Litchfield's friends depend upon some of the scattered votes which will fail [sic] them. As things appear to me, Lord Litchfield can succeed but in one of these two ways ; either first by an accession of Lord Suffolk's [1] party, in confidence of Lord Suffolk's being appointed High Steward. Or secondly by the accession of the Whiggs. How far the first expedient is practicable I know not. You know there are two candidates besides Lord Litchfield : Lord Suffolk, and Lord Aylesford ; [2] the former supported by Magdalen ; the latter by New College. I think it more likely that the friends to the Lords Aylesford and Suffolk should unite ; than that the friends of either should accede to Lord Litchfield. Supposing this to be the case, and that the accession of Christ Church, Merton, Exeter, St. Johns, Wadham, and the Whigg part of Jesus should be necessary ; you are then to consider how these Colleges might be put in motion. The Dean and Canons [3] can influence Christ Church effectually. Dr. Hay [4] can influence St. John's. At Merton they are independent one of another ; but the List

1. In 1762 Henry Howard, 12th Earl of Suffolk, M.A., D.C.L. (1761), was in his twenty-third year.
2. Heneage Finch, 3rd Earl of Aylesford, M.A., D.C.L. (1761), was Lord Suffolk's maternal uncle.
3. David Gregory, D.D., was Dean of Christ Church 1756–67. He was formerly Regius Professor of Modern History and Languages at Oxford 1724–36, and a Prebendary of Oxford 1736–56. He and Shute Barrington were two of the eight canons.
4. George, afterwards Sir George Hay (1715–78), D.C.L. (St. John's). In 1762 he was Chancellor of Worcester, King's Advocate and vicar-general to the Archbishop of Canterbury, M.P. for Sandwich, and a Lord of the Admiralty. About him see D.N.B.

for making interest for Fellows, will show how they may be applied to. Our Rector [1] is at Hereford. I have wrote to him two or three times on this subject, and he is as willing as I am to do his best for the person recommended by the Government. We have many voters, at least 30 in our books. But our votes lye at a great distance in Devonshire and Cornwall, and would not easily be prevailed on to come. But if a proper letter was sent from some great man, suppose from Lord Talbot [2] who was of Exeter, recommending the candidate that is agreeable to the Government, I believe upwards of twenty might be brought together. Such letter might be sent to our Rector Dr. Webber at Hereford who would immediately send it to me. Or the letter may be sent to College directed to the Rector or in his absence to the Subrector, then I should open it and make the proper use of it. Mr. Hoare [3] is keeping residence at Westminster and could give the best directions about Jesus. I do not know the most proper application to the Warden of Wadham ; [4] but Mr. Stone [5] of Chippen Norton hath great influence over the Warden and you know how Mr. Stone might be engaged to act. Unless the cause is supported vigorously, I fear it would not succeed. For the other side have in general their votes lying near ; and being used to victory, would make the utmost push. Having now given my sentiments freely, I am ready to receive instructions, and am

Your affectionate friend and obedient servant,

Thomas Bray

LORD HARCOURT TO CHARLES JENKINSON

Add MS. 38469, ff. 38-9.

Newnham, August 19, 1762.
1/4 past 10 o'clock.

I am much obliged for the account you sent me, which gives room to hope that our troops were in possession of the Havannah very early in July.[6] Without being too sanguine we may expect an account from Lord Albemarle every moment,

1. Francis Webber, M.A., D.D., Fellow of Exeter College and Rector 1750–71.
2. William Talbot, 1st Earl Talbot (1761), D.C.L. (Exeter College), was Steward of the Household.
3. Joseph Hoare, recently appointed Prebendary of Westminster. See p. 28 n. 2.
4. George Wyndham, LL.D., was Warden of Wadham 1744–77.
5. Unidentified.
6. Havanna was not taken till August 12, and the news reached England on September 29.

as the wind has been very fair to bring the ships up the Channel. I have heard that Lord Westmoreland was given over by his physicians the day before yesterday. Paralytic strokes are terrible to people much younger than his Lordship, who I conclude is dead by this time.[1] I wish Lord Bute was Chancellor, because I think he is in every respect the properest person, and the most likely to be serviceable to the Crown and to the publick in that important station, which I am confident he would fill with real dignity and honor. I have little [2] interest in the University and therefore it is not in my power to promote this measure, but shall most readily exert the little influence I have, in case it shall be thought proper to pursue the design.

The only delicacy I have in the affair, is my regard for Lord Litchfield, who most undoubtedly has been a candidate for the Chancellorship. I know him so well, that I really believe his friendship and obligations to Lord Bute, would induce him to wave this or any other advantage to serve Lord Bute. The difficulty consists in mentioning the affair to him. Lord Talbot who lives in great intimacy with Lord Litchfield would be the properest person to sound his Lordship. But whatever is done must be done immediately. The whole depends upon dispatch. If the Tories and the most violent people of Lord Westmorelands party should out of resentment to Lord Litchfield, whom they dont like [3] set up any body in opposition to Lord Litchfield, that I think would afford the fairest opportunity of proposing Lord Bute who would be sure of Lord Litchfield's friends, he would certainly have the Whiggs, and to my knowledge he would break into the other interest. I shall write to Lord Litchfield, who I believe is at Ditchley [4] to know what step he proposes to take, and I wish most earnestly for an opportunity of promoting a measure which would be for the service of his Majesty, very beneficial to the publick, and honourable with regard to Lord Bute. I am Dear Sir,

Most sincerely yours,

Harcourt

The ladies [5] present their compliments.

1. He died on August 26.
2. Harcourt first wrote " no " then " little " above the line.
3. Lord Litchfield was descended from Charles II and the Duchess of Cleveland, had been a Jacobite, and must be reckoned a Tory in 1762. Harcourt's calculations on his lack of interest at Oxford are absurd.
4. His seat in Oxfordshire.
5. Lady Harcourt and her daughter Lady Betty Harcourt who on June 30, 1763, married Sir William Lee of Hartwell. See p. 222.

Christ Church, August 20, 1762.

Dear Sir !

I returned hither yesterday, and on my arrival found such authentic intelligence of Lord Westmoreland's actual, or approaching death ; that I immediately determined to seize the opportunity of testifying the grateful sense I entertain of the favour [1] conferred upon me by Lord Bute by exerting my utmost endeavours to promote his succession to the vacant Chancellorship. I feel my situation dogged with great and various difficulties ; my youth, the unwillingness which older men have to adopt plans of action chalked out by younger ones ; the absence of the Dean ; the few of my own brethren [2] who are upon the spot, and the fewer still of the Whig heads, are so many impediments in my way. I have already however sounded those to whom it was proper to communicate this scheme and find them disposed to forward it ; but as I cannot *declare* Lord B.'s approbation, I wish to know from you his sentiments ; without that authority nothing can be done. I conceive that Lord Litchfield, the only formidable candidate who at present occurs to my mind, must relinquish his pretensions, and that Blackston [3] must concur and cooperate. The state of this society is such that no vigour can be exerted in a step of moment without the presence of the Dean who is at his house near Durham ; when I know any thing authentic from you, which I beg may be as early as possible, I will write to him, and press his return ; tho' that might be more

1. Barrington presumably referred to his appointment on May 22, 1762, to a Prebend of Hereford. Other " favours " he had received were a prebend of Pratum Majus in Hereford and a canonry of Christ Church in September and October 1761, but these came from Newcastle. See an amusing account of his promotion in Norman Sykes, *Church and State in England in the Eighteenth Century*, pp. 158-9.
2. The Canons of Christ Church.
3. Sir William Blackstone (1723–80, see *D.N.B.*), barrister, Vinerian Professor of English Law and Principal of New Inn Hall. The first volume of his *Commentaries* appeared in 1765, but his interest at Oxford was already formidable in 1762. He had recently entered into a political alliance with Lord Suffolk. He was brought into Parliament for Hindon in 1761 by Fox and Shelburne, who believed him to be devoted to Bute (see *England etc.* p. 198 and n. 2), but at the election of a Chancellor in September 1762 he was one of the two Heads of Houses who voted against Litchfield. See Add. MS. 32942, f. 368. He had a legal practice in Westminster where he spent a good deal of his time.

effectually done perhaps by the *grandis epistola — a Capreis*. I am, Dear Sir, with unfeigned regard and esteem,

Your most sincere and faithful servant,

S. Barrington

Harcourt wrote again to Jenkinson on August 22 and 25.[1] He had meant to meet Litchfield at Oxford races and discuss his withdrawal in favour of Bute but the meeting did not take place. Harcourt thought it odd that no one had proposed Bute for Chancellor, but finding that " the person from whom such a compliment might be expected " had no intention of making it, he began to minimise Litchfield's interest in the University. " Lord Litchfield's success ", he wrote on August 25, " will in my opinion depend much more upon the difficulty of finding a proper person to oppose him, than upon his own interest. I am informed that many even of his old friends don't mention him with the cordiality and warmth they used to do. Many of Lord W⟨estmorland⟩'s party are still very averse to him, and the Whigs at best are but luke warm in support of him."

LORD HARCOURT TO CHARLES JENKINSON

Add. MS. 38469, ff. 46-7.

Newnham, August 30, 1762.

Dear Sir,

By last nights papers, I find Lord Westmoreland is dead. I saw a person yesterday who came from Oxford, where I hear several candidates are mentioned, for the Chancellorship. The Bishops of Durham,[2] and Winchester,[3] Lord Foley, Lord Suffolk, Lord Oxford, and Lord Aylesford. Several that I have mentioned, have I dare say no thoughts of courting the honor of the Chancellorship, but I think it shews a sort of unsteadyness in the members of the University, and forebodes no good to Lord Litchfield : I may be out in my conjectures, but am still of opinion that there may be room from this jumbled state of things, to bring the University to chuse Lord Bute. Though I most heartily wish Lord Litchfield success, in case Lord Bute absolutely declines all thoughts of having it himself, yet I am sure he ought to be the man. If Lord Litchfield should be pushed hard, sure he would be glad of so fair an opportunity of paying Lord Bute the compliment of making over his interest to him. The great and only point is,

1. Add. MS. 38469, ff. 42, 44.
2. Richard Trevor was Bishop of Durham 1752–77.
3. Thomas Balguy was Bishop of Winchester 1759–95.

(52)

that Lord Bute's name ought most certainly not to be made use of unless there was a moral certainty of success : for I would not upon any consideration have him miscarry in an attempt of this nature. Bray I suppose is still in town. If any thing is to be done he must be consulted, for he is more capable, and more desirous of conducting such an affair, than any body I know. Yours dear Sir

Most sincerely,

Harcourt

We are just setting out for Cockthrop — where the family will stay till the beginning of October : But I shall be in town about the 7th of September.

Jenkinson's correspondents at Oxford wrote almost every day, and sometimes twice a day, to keep him informed of the state of parties. Barrington wrote on August 31 [1] to say that New College had nominated Lord Aylesford. On September 3 Harcourt acknowledged a letter from Jenkinson informing him that Bute would not stand for Chancellor, but Harcourt still hoped that Litchfield " might be prevailed upon to decline in time if there should be the least prospect of getting Lord Bute chose ".[2]

SHUTE BARRINGTON TO CHARLES JENKINSON

Add. MS. 38469, f. 52.

Christ Church, September 7, 1762.

Dear Sir !

On my arrival here last night I found your letter ; I am solicitous to inform you of my private sentiments from what I have been able to collect tho' I have not time to write an ostensible letter : The Whiggs by the confession of both parties have it now in their power to give the election to either of the candidates. Lord S⟨uffolk⟩'s youth, and his connection with Blackstone, are the objections under which he labours; and I think he will not long continue the candidate of that faction ; they must nominate another against whom neither of these lies. Lord L. from the best advices is in the minority at present, tho' his friends much puff his strength ; his adversaries are virulent, and their enmity is not so much in favour of Lord S. as in opposition to him. There never was so favourable a conjunction for a third person ; and I am persuaded that if

1. Add. MS. 38469, f. 48.   2. *Ibid.* f. 50.

B.[1] could be completely gained, and Lord L. convinced that he cannot obtain his point, that Lord B. might be elected. If the latter has any thoughts of this honour he must not push Lord L., that will ruin him with the friends of Lord S. through whom he must be chosen. Our Dean unfortunately does not return till Saturday ; when he does I will suggest any measures you shall propose. I most anxiously wish that you could be here at that time and continue till Monday. The election is fixed for the 23d. Adieu in haste and with real regard and esteem,

Most sincerely and faithfully yours,

S. Barrington

Secret and Confidential.

I am extremely obliged to you for your kind inquiries after Lady Di ; [2] she is astonishingly recovered.

THOMAS BRAY TO CHARLES JENKINSON

Add. MS. 38469, ff. 54-5.

Exeter College, September 7, 1762.

Dear Sir,

I received the favour of yours last Saturday. On the day I wrote to you last there was a meeting of the Heads of Houses ; the little that was done did not come to my knowledge, till after I had wrote my letter, and it was no more than this. The Vice Chancellor [3] asked whether there was any form of putting persons in nomination ? For his part he would take that opportunity of nominating Lord Litchfield as a candidate, a noble man of great honour, and a friend to the University, who had behaved himself in a most obliging manner when they made the late Address,[4] and he must add that Lord Litchfield was a person most agreeable to his Majesty. The President of Magdalen [5] said that he was obliged to vote with his College for Lord Suffolk. The Vice Chancellor said that Lord Suffolk would be a good candidate 20 years hence, and

1. Blackstone.
2. Barrington married on February 2, 1761, Lady Diana Beauclerk, daughter of Charles, 2nd Duke of St. Albans.
3. Joseph Browne, D.D., Provost of Queen's College, was Vice-Chancellor 1759–65.
4. The University's Address to George III on the birth on August 12 of the Prince of Wales.
5. Thomas Jenner was President of Magdalen 1745–68.

(54)

the person who gave me information thinks the Vice Chancellor said he did not like the persons he was set up by, which was understood to mean Dr. Winchester [1] and Dr. Blackston : though perhaps he might be mistaken with respect to Dr. Blackston. Since that time the Vice Chancellor and others in connexion with him have been incredibly active, and it is said have made considerable progress, particularly by insisting that Lord Suffolk was too young to be Chancellor. The Vice Chancellor said yesterday that they had gained ground in New College, All Souls, and Lincoln. I hear they are sure of six in Corpus, and that if Lord Aylesford declines, most of University have promised to be for Lord Litchfield. I cant positively answer for every thing I mention. Intelligence is difficult to be come at, there are so few people here. The opposite side to Lord Litchfield lose ground ; and I hear to day from a pretty intelligent man on the Tory side, that he apprehends it will end in Lord Litchfield's being Chancellor and Lord Suffolk High Steward. Dr. Barrington came here last night, and this day desired a conference with me. He is in hopes that Lord Suffolk's party finding themselves hard set, would make an offer for a third person, and might be induced to come in to Lord Bute. I am not wanting in inclination or zeal but cannot think as Dr. Barrington does. I think that if the object is changed, a compromise will in some shape take place between the parties now at variance. At present a decent, though not the most eligible advancement, is made towards the Court by Lord Litchfield's friends. If this over-ture was closed with, they would hardly go back, but the same motives that brought them so far, would carry them on to all due respect for the Government. Whereas should this scheme be disconcerted, or compleated by a compromise with Lord Suffolks party (for Lord Aylesfords party is next to nothing) I am afraid things would run back into the old channel. While I deliver my opinion, I am apprehensive that there may be other lights concerning this subject, unknown to me, and therefore I shall keep my self, and all I can, on the reserve till directed by you to the contrary. And preparing for all events I have wrote to our Rector to press his being in College a week before the election. That in case any service of the Government should require our joint endeavours, we may do our best. This day the Vice Chancellor gave public notice that the election will be on the 23d. instant. I wait

1. Thomas Winchester, D.D., Vice-President of Magdalen 1754–80.

with impatience to see Dr. Atwell.[1] Certain it is that as things stand at present, Christ Church,[2] and the disengaged Whiggs can turn the election in favour of either of the parties engaged. But every day now may make an alteration. I am with sincere respect

> Your affectionate friend and obedient Servant,
>
> Thomas Bray

Barrington wrote twice on September 8, an " ostensible letter " (Add. MS. 38469, f. 56), and the following :

SHUTE BARRINGTON TO CHARLES JENKINSON

Add. MS. 38469, f. 58.

Christ Church, September 8, 1762.

Dear Sir !

I was so cramped in time yesterday that I was equally incapable of giving a minute answer to the secret articles of your letter or of writing the ostensible one you requested. The latter I enclose to you herewith. Dr. King [3] is not yet arrived, which somewhat surprises me considering the zeal he expressed. If he will enter zealously into the interests of Lord B. his zeal may be of service ; for how much soever his popularity is diminished he still retains a certain degree of influence, and if Lord L. could be prevailed upon to relinquish his pretensions he might be very useful in talking to those heads who have supported him. With relation to Blackstone he holds a language at London which does not correspond with his activity here by his emissaries ; for his personal appearance would be detrimental to the cause he wishes well to. Why should not he be sounded, and as he declares neutrality and consequently cannot plead pre-engagements, why should he not be pushed by Lord B. if things can be brought to bear in his favour ? Might not King feel the pulse of those he is connected with ? For I could wish to have the

1. Joseph Atwell, D.D., formerly Rector of Exeter College 1732–37, and now Prebendary of Westminster 1759–68.

2. At the election Christ Church gave 59 votes to Litchfield, more than any other College. See a letter from the Bishop of Oxford to Newcastle, Add. MS. 32942, f. 368.

3. William King was Principal of St. Mary Hall, 1719, to his death on December 30, 1763. His epitaph, written by himself six months before he died, is printed in the *Gent. Mag.* xxxiv, 139.

nomination come from that quarter, unless it should be thought more advisable to have the offer made by the Whigs. If you incline to that sentiment I will propose the measure to the Dean when he comes ; who by what I can learn may possibly be here earlier than Saturday. It is no easy task to keep the Whigs much longer in suspence ; they want their directions and murmer at their being deferred, it cannot therefore but be necessary to take as quick and as decisive steps as the delicate circumstances Lord B. is placed in will admit of. Dr. Atwell was not arrived yesterday. Whither is the intrepid spirit of Talbot fled ? I am, dear Sir, with real regard and esteem,

Your most sincere and faithful servant,

S. Barrington

Bray also wrote on September 8 and Barrington wrote again on September 9 (Add. MS. 38469, ff. 60, 62). Since it was now clear from Jenkinson's last letter that Bute himself would not enter the contest, Barrington temporarily lost interest in the election and discovered an unforeseen obligation " not . . . to act beyond my own vote " against Lord Suffolk, " whom every member of the University knows I love and esteem ". He predicted a union between Suffolk and Foley and lamented the indiscretion of some of Lord Litchfield's " warmest adherents who declare that tho' the Whigs should join him yet they will ever be considered as entitled to no merit with him nor partake of his favour ".

SHUTE BARRINGTON TO CHARLES JENKINSON

Add. MS. 38469, ff. 64-5.

Christ Church, September 10, 1762.

Dear Sir !

The additional weight which the Whigs are to throw into Lord Litchfield's scale, (considering the certain advantages which the Heads forego, when by uniting with the other party, from the paucity of competitors the Vice Chancellorship would be insured to them) merits some assurances that the proscription, which has been so long held up against them will now be removed, and that they will injoy their share of academical honours. I cannot but be of opinion that some declaration should be obtained upon this point ; and if Lord L. could be prevailed upon to promise the nomination of the High Stewardship to the Duke of Marlborough, Lord Harcourt, or some other unexceptionable Whig, it would be a cogent motive to unite the party more closely ; which with-

(57)

out these preliminaries it never cordially will. No reasonable objection can be urged against these stipulations, and I most earnestly intreat you to put them en train ; for the propositions must come from those who can with propriety and firmness insist upon the performance of them ; and rest assured that these steps can alone produce a real zeal in the minds of a party, which by the absurd and indiscreet declarations of the most active and most contemptible of Lord L.'s canvassers is somewhat alienated and cooled. The Dean is not yet returned, and probably will not be till Sunday. His absence must prove detrimental to Lord L. as many individuals of the society by the most pressing solicitations from friends and relations were daily engaging on the other side till the sentiments of Government were known, which will retain the free in their *allegiance* ; but this division will invalidate a strength otherwise formidable. Let not however the body be charged hereafter, should Lord L. be vanquished, with intentional want of vigour and unanimity, when the genuine cause is the remote distance of its head, and the impossibility of preventing the force of private applications where no preengagements can be urged. Do not forget what I have so repeatedly inculcated that the virulence of the opposition is pointed more against the managers than the person of Lord L. I am dear Sir ! with the [*sic*] real regard and esteem

Your most sincere and faithful servant,

S. Barrington

THOMAS BRAY TO CHARLES JENKINSON

Add. MS. 38469, f. 66.

Exeter College, September 10, 1762.

Dear Sir,
    The Governments approbation of Lord Litchfield shall engage my most active endeavours. I have not lost time, since the vacancy, in applying to the voters of Exeter College, desiring in general that they would be here at the election and vote with the College. Some answers I have already received which are favourable. I dont doubt but we shall make a creditable appearance. Notwithstanding what I wrote last, I have had an opportunity this day of being fully and finally convinced by a pressing application, that Lord Suffolk is the grand object of those who oppose Lord Litchfield. The

Master of Balliol,[1] I believe, would be very happy, if he was to receive a line from the Marquis of Carnarvon [2] recommending Lord Litchfield. The cause might be four or five votes the better for him. As Lord Litchfield will be obliged to the Whiggs, in some measure for his success, would it not be reasonable that his Lordship should give some assurance to the great men who apply to the Whiggs that he will nominate Vice Chancellors out of their Heads of Houses, in their turns, and proportionably to their numbers ? The exclusive appropriation of that office to the Tories, is a most invidious distinction ; whereas equal respect from the future Chancellor would compleat a desirable coalition, and best promote his Majesties service. But this is not my business, though the suggestion may not be unseasonable. Whatever further instructions you are pleased to give me, shall meet with a most chearful compliance. I am

Your affectionate friend and obedient Servant,

Thomas Bray

Jenkinson acted on Barrington's advice and took steps in the matter of offering concessions to the Whigs.[3] On September 13 Barrington wrote : " I admit in its fullest extent the force of your reasoning with regard to the necessity of Lord L⟨itchfield⟩'s being supported by government with the exertion of all its influence ; and I am convinced that the Whiggs will cordially strengthen its hands . . . when the preliminaries I suggested to you are secured ". When the Dean returned to Christ Church Barrington would hint " the propriety of his representing to Lord B⟨ute⟩ the necessity of Lord L⟨itchfield⟩'s being explicit with regard to the High Stewardship and the Vice Chancellor ".[4] By September 14 the accession of the Whigs was apparently secure [5] and on September 19 Barrington wrote to Jenkinson, " I most sincerely congratulate you upon the moral certainty of success in an event which as Lord B had engaged in we both should have been mortified had he been vanquished ".[6]

THOMAS BRAY TO CHARLES JENKINSON

Add. MS. 38469, f. 78.

Exeter College, September 19, 1762.

Dear Sir,

Since my last nothing material hath happen'd. The list I sent you will be justified by speedy experience. Tis com-

1. Theophilus Leigh was Master of Balliol 1726–85.
2. Henry Brydges, Marquis of Carnarvon, afterwards 2nd Duke of Chandos.
3. See Barrington to Jenkinson, September 12, Add. MS. 38469, f. 68.
4. *Ibid.* ff. 70–71.
5. See Bray to Jenkinson, September 14, *ibid.* f. 72.
6. *Ibid.* f. 76.

monly imagined that Lord Suffolk's and Lord Foley's friends are so much at variance that they will both stand the poll. But nothing depends on their agreement or disagreement. I verily believe that the good temper that subsists between Lord Litchfield's friends will continue, and that there will not be hereafter in this place a majority of persons disrespectful to the government. I observe with inexpressible pleasure an earnest desire of doing what is known to be agreeable to his Majesty. I am

Your affectionate friend and obedient servant,
Thomas Bray

JOSEPH BETTS TO CHARLES JENKINSON

Add. MS. 38469, ff. 74-5.

September 19, 1762.

Dear Sir,

As the friends of Lord Litchfield were to have a meeting yesterday, I delayed writing till I could give an account of our affairs that might be depended on ; especially as I was in hopes the friends of Lord Suffolk would have given up by this time : but they begin to be heated exceedingly, and so do Lord Foley's too, and declare positively they will stand the poll, be their numbers what they will. However I was well informed last Friday night, that one of Lord Suffolk's managers had been with the President of Magdalen and pressed him to come into Lord Foley ; but was told, if Lord Suffolk gave up, he should be for our friend ; and he did not doubt but great part of this College [1] would too. We had a meeting the Tuesday before, and then the numbers for Lord Litchfield were 237 before Christ Church or Merton had declared : but yesterday we had a promise from Christ Church of 50 votes at least ; and from Merton of 18. And examining our numbers again with all possible care, we found we had 328 for Lord Litchfield, some votes, doubted of before, having come in ; and that every possible allowance being made in favour of Lord Suffolk and Lord Foley's forces they could not jointly amount to above 190. Near 200 voters have refused coming up, and several are abroad : but you will be careful not to mention the numbers unless to sure

1. University College.

friends — no good can come off too great security. The opposition will have up every man they can, and of course we must. Our College is pretty unanimous.

Thus much for Lord Litchfield. Give me leave now to tell you that I am not quite satisfyed with your reasons for not being of that service to me you could wish in respect to the Professorship.[1] If either of the candidates had ten times the philosophical merit they can pretend to : its possible it might not be known to statesmen, Arch-Bishops and Lord Chancellors, without the recommendation of friends. For this reason I referred you to the transactions for the solution of a problem done by me 18 years ago, declared by Sir Isaac to be of the greatest difficulty. And if either of the candidates on a late occasion,[2] or for the Savilian Professorship can solve that problem, I desire to be mentioned no more. Whiston [3] declared to me at Oxford before Mr. Bliss that he had attempted it several times in vain : and what Keil [4] thought of it, may be collected from his 17th. Lecture, when he speaks of our most skilful astronomer and geometer, Dr. Halley : [5] but leaves the solution of the problem quite untouched himself. But if my qualifications are still doubted of, and you do me the honour to call on me next Thursday, you shall have satisfaction enough, and some respecting one of the candidates that perhaps you may think not a little curious.

You are pleased to observe farther that you are personally acquainted with very few of the electors ; [6] and that your Master and friend has very little connexion with them. I wish only for half as much. But though he should be busy about the Peace, and no doubt much engaged with the Duke Nivernois,[7] you may possibly find a leisure moment, just to remind him that Lord Mansfield his countryman is one of the

1. The choice of Nathaniel Bliss for Astronomer Royal in July 1762 (see p. 46) still left open the place of Savilian Professor of Astronomy which Betts had originally considered inadequate alone, but on September 12, 1762, he reopened the question to Jenkinson, having in the meantime apparently learned that a pension (of £250) went with the place of Astronomer Royal, and also hoping to be allowed to keep his fellowship, which was not normally tenable with the chair (Add. MS. 38199, ff. 233-4.
  2. *Ibid.*
  3. William Whiston, sometime Lucasian Professor of Mathematics and Boyle Lecturer at Cambridge, whence he was expelled in 1710 for suspected Arianism. See *D.N.B.*
  4. John Keill, Savilian Professor of Astronomy, died 1721.
  5. Edmund Halley (1656–1742, see *D.N.B.*), famous astronomer and Savilian Professor of Geometry. He succeeded Flamsteed as the second Astronomer Royal.
  6. See a list of the electors on p. 46.
  7. Louis-Jules Mancini, Duc de Nivernais (1716–98), French Ambassador to England, arrived here for the peace negotiations on September 12, 1762.

electors — that the principal Secretary of State [1] is another — that the Lord Chancellor [2] is a 3d ; and the Bishop of London a 4th, a prelate you are certainly known to.[3] Lord Litchfield will not want much application — fix the rest and the thing is done. The Archbishop [4] has declared against me, though I was warmly recommended to him by Mr. Forster,[5] a favour I shall never forget. What Forster's motive could be for doing it unasked, considering I voted against him when he stood for the Headship, I will leave you to determine. I have been moreover recommended to him by several others ; but it is to be feared he has not forgot the affair about Testimoniums : and till that slips his memory, I make no doubt he will be always ready not to recommend any Fellow of University College. The Dean of the Arches [6] will I presume go with him. What has been done for me with the Lord Chief Justice of the Common Pleas,[7] or Chief Baron of the Exchequer [8] I cannot say ; but can easily foresee if I have no friends, they may do wrong, and yet act according to the best of their knowledge.

I am very glad you have such plenty of philosophical men in town. Lord Macclesfield and Dr. Watson [9] were the chief I believe that recommended Mr. Bliss and I trust I am not unknown to them, though I have grounds to conclude, that neither of them will recommend me for obvious reasons, unless their opinions are asked. It's my own fault that I have not been many years a F.R.S. I have been often sollicited to take that honour : but the expence was certain, and I seldom in town to attend their meetings : and till Lord Macclesfield took the chair, and new regulations were made, it was not much worth a philosopher's while if truth may be spoken. But I now see my mistake ; had I spent my time in philo-

1. Lord Egremont was Secretary of State for the Southern Department.
2. Robert Henley, 1st Baron Henley, afterwards 1st Earl of Northington (1764).
3. Richard Osbaldeston, formerly Bishop of Carlisle, was elected Bishop of London on February 8, 1762. He may have known Jenkinson through Sir James Lowther.
4. Thomas Secker, Archbishop of Canterbury 1758–68.
5. Probably Nathaniel Forster, Fellow of Balliol, or his brother, Samuel, Fellow of Wadham College, Registrar of the University from 1761 to 1797. The reference to his election is obscure. There does not seem to have been a Forster among the Fellows of University College and Betts would scarcely have had a voice in the election of a Head of any other college.
6. Sir Edward Simpson, M.P. for Dover, Master of Trinity Hall, Judge of the Prerogative Court and Dean of the Arches. See p. 296.
7. Charles Pratt, afterwards Lord Camden (1765).
8. Sir Thomas Parker.
9. Richard Watson, F.R.S., died 1769 ?

sophical shops amongst opticians, and mathematical instrument makers during my stay occasionally at London, I might possibly have been talked of as much as other great men : but for my comfort I have the honour to be mentioned in the writings of some great men both at home and abroad, a testimony which the most quick-sighted of my ~~rivals~~ friends will be distressed to discover in support of their pretensions. If Hoare [1] was applied to I believe he could say nothing against me, possibly something for me, which Lord Harcourt who loves to encourage merit might attend to, but you are now weary and so am I.   I am dear Sir,

Your obliged humble servant,

Jo. Betts,

Thomas Hornsby was elected in January 1763, but two years later Betts's prospects were again revived by the death of Bliss.[2]

SHUTE BARRINGTON TO CHARLES JENKINSON

Add. MS. 38200, f. 1.

Christ Church, October 1, 1762.

Dear Sir !

I am this instant returned from Beckett ; [3] at which place I received your letter of the 28th. I saw Mr. Flexman [4] yesterday, and found him extremely ready to undertake the employment. I made no conditions, but informed him that he should hear from me. I am convinced that you can procure no person better, probably few so well, qualified for the province you mean to assign him. You will let me know your final determination, which I will take care to communicate to him. I most sincerely and heartily felicitate you upon the surrender of the Havannah. The conquest important in itself, is made more so by the juncture at which the intelligence arrives. Spain must now come into the terms prescribed ; and Lord B. will have the peculiar good fortune of finishing the war with eclat, and establishing *soon* the peace upon the

1. Joseph Hoare. See p. 28.   2. See p. 341.
3. Lord Barrington's seat in Berkshire.
4. Roger Flexman, D.D. (1708–95), political and historical pamphleteer. In 1752 he published *Critical, Historical and Political Miscellanies*, which went into a second edition in 1762. This may have suggested him to Barrington as a useful scribbler, but the only other works ascribed to him seem to be of a religious character. His pamphlet is not in the catalogue of the British Museum. About him see *D.N.B.*

basis he would wish. I rejoice at Lord L's [1] sense of the obligations he owes the Whigs : I hope he will regulate his conduct accordingly. I feel myself much flattered by the kindness of your expressions ; and beg that you will rest convinced that I shall always think myself happy in seizing every opportunity of testifying the real regard and esteem with which I am, Dear Sir

Your most sincere and faithful servant,
S. Barrington

MRS. BANKES TO CHARLES JENKINSON

Add. MS. 38200, ff. 5-6.

Margaret, daughter of John Wynne, Bishop of Bath and Wells, married, May 1753, Henry Bankes, M.P. for Corfe Castle.[2] The Bankes were an old Dorsetshire family who had represented Corfe since 1660. They were connected with the Jenkinsons four generations back. Charles Jenkinson's great-grandmother, Mary, wife of Sir Robert Jenkinson, 1st Bart. of Walcot,[3] was a daughter of Sir John Bankes (died 1677). She brought the name of Bankes into the family.[4] In 1760 relations between the two families were still very close and in 1768 the brothers John and Henry Bankes used their interest at Corfe to return Jenkinson's brother, Captain John Jenkinson.

Duke Street, Westminster, October 8 ⟨1762⟩.

Sir,

Mr. Bankes being gone into Dorsetshire I hope you will excuse the liberty I presume to take of troubling you on account of his relation Mr. Robert Coker,[5] whom my Lord Bute by your obliging recommendation was pleased to prefer to the office of a Kings Waiter. Mr. Bankes saw the patent pass'd and all fees paid before he went out of town but found it was necessary for Mr. Coker to come to town to be sworn into his office. his father being too infirm for such a journey his mother [6] brought him to town, and he went on Wednesday

1. Probably Lord Litchfield.
2. See p. 89.   3. See p. v.
4. See, e.g., Robert Bankes Jenkinson, 2nd Earl of Liverpool, the Prime Minister.
5. Robert Coker and Henry Bankes were connected through their ancestress Mary Hooper (died 1688), who married, first, John Brune of Athelhampston by whom she had a daughter Mary, who married Sir Ralph Bankes of Kingston Hall, grandfather of the John and Henry Bankes of these letters ; and secondly, in 1654, her first husband's cousin, Robert Coker of Mapouder (1617–97), by whom she was the great-grandmother of the boy Robert Coker.
6. Susanna, daughter of Laurence St. Lo, D.D., Canon of Wells, married William Coker of Mapouder.

(64)

before the Commissioners of the Customs to be sworn, when they objected to his age for being incapable of knowing the obligation of an oath he being in his eleventh year, but a stout boy, and his uncle [1] (who went with him) not knowing what his age was and thinking it of advantage to make him appear as old as possible, answered he was under fourteen which was also the answer that Mr. Coker made after his uncle, on being afterwards asked the same question. As you Sir may probably be acquainted with some of the gentlemen who are Commissioners if you would be pleased to send a line in his favour it might perhaps get the affair immediately dispatched, it being of some consequence to the family on account of inconvenience and expence to make their stay in town as short as possible and Mr. Coker is appointed to attend the Commissioners again this day between the hours of twelve and two. If Sir you do not think proper to interfere in it I have only to beg you will pardon this trouble from Sir

Your most obedient humble servant,

M. Bankes

Mrs. Bankes's application was successful. Robert Coker's name appears as a King's Waiter in London, patent dated September 7, 1762, in a list of " appointments in the Customs ",[2] and on January 24, 1763, John Bankes expressed his thanks to Jenkinson in a present of a hamper.[3]

RALPH GRIFFITHS TO MR. JENKINSON

Add. MS. 38469, f. 80.

Turnham Green, October 15 ⟨1762⟩.

R. Griffiths presents his best respects to Mr. Jenkinson, Ordered his binder to send on Wednesday for the journals.[4] His name is Lacy, in St. Martins Lane, the corner of St. Martin's Court. In future commands of *that nature* may, if Mr. Jenkinson pleases, be sent to him to save loss of time.

As to the *books* not yet sent in, there is at present but one

1. His only paternal uncle was Thomas Coker, Rector of Mapouder, who died in 1790.
2. Add. MS. 38335, f. 79.
3. See p. 123.
4. The journals of the House of Commons? Cf. p. 15. The printing of the House of Commons votes had apparently been promised him by Grenville in October 1761, but the promise was not fulfilled.

set of Parliamentary History [1] to be had in the whole trade ;
and they cannot be had for less than £8 or 9.* Chandler's
Debates,[2] complete are also very scarce and dear. A good sett
will cost about six guineas.

Hales [3] and Hawkins's [4] Pleas of the Crown were sent in
some time ago ; also Rapin.[5]

* A new edition is expected very soon — at the first price.
The original price being but £7. 4. 0.

LIEUT.-COL. BRUDENELL TO CHARLES JENKINSON
Add. MS. 38200, f. 43.

Lieutenant-Colonel Robert Brudenell, third son of George, 3rd Earl
of Cardigan, M.P. for Great Bedwin 1756–61, and for Marlborough
1761 to his death on October 19, 1768, was Vice-Chamberlain to the
Queen and Lieutenant-Governor of Windsor Castle.

Taplow, Sunday, October 17, 1762.

Sir,
    I have just seen Mr. Hamilton [6] who thinks himself
obliged to you, for your polite reception of him, I am sorry to
find that his unlucky stars still persevere in their attendance
on him, his birth and character intitle him to a better lot :
I wish he had been fortunate enough to have seen Lord Bute

1. *The Parliamentary or Constitutional History of England from the Earliest Times to
1660*, 24 vols., published 1751–61 ; a second edition appeared in 1762.
2. *The History and Proceedings of the House of Commons from the Restoration to the
Present Time, containing the most remarkable motions, speeches, resolves, etc., etc.*, printed
for Richard Chandler, 1742.
3. Sir Mathew Hale's *Pleas of the Crown*, first published in 1678, went into seven
editions, the last in 1773.
4. William Hawkins's *Treatise on the Pleas of the Crown*, first published in 1716,
appeared in a fourth edition in 1762, but Griffiths's name is not among the booksellers for whom it was printed.
5. N. Tindal's continuation of Rapin de Thoyras's *History of England* appeared
1757–63. But there are also other editions, 1744–45, 1745–47, 1751, 1757–59.
Griffiths was not one of the booksellers for whom it was printed.
6. Probably James Hamilton of Suffolk Street, a poor relation of the 6th
Duke of Hamilton. Professor Namier writes of him in *The Structure of Politics*
(p. 285) : " The Duke of Hamilton had a poor cousin, James Hamilton, and
asked Henry Pelham to give him a consulship in the Mediterranean, or a place
in the Customs or the Excise ; Pelham promised to do so and in the meantime,
as an earnest of his goodwill, gave him an annuity of £200 from secret service
funds. When Pelham died, the Duke of Hamilton, in his letter of condolence to
Newcastle, asked that the pension be continued — ' this is all the young gentleman has at present to subsist upon '. The ' young gentleman ' occasionally
raised again the question of a place, but meantime subsisted on his ' retaining
fee ', which was still paid when Newcastle left the Treasury in 1762 and in his
secret service accounts is responsible for a total of £1400." The last half-yearly
payment in Newcastle's accounts was in April 1762 (*ibid.* p. 575) ; if the pension
was continued another payment was due in October.

who I am well convinc'd, can feel for the distress of others, and knows how to reward merit.

Pardon this intrusion on you, I would not have presumed to have troubled you with my last, but under the hopes of procuring for Mr. Hamilton, by your means, an interview with Lord Bute, sooner than a distant Levee Day, which I imagine is open to any person of his rank, I could not deny him the satisfaction, at least, of being known to you, who have so close a connection, with those who have it in their power, to make so many people happy, and are yourself ever so ready to promote every good cause. If I have presumed too far, I hope you will be kind enough to forgive it, from the principle, on which I have proceeded, that of serving, an unfortunate, worthy man. I am

Your obliged friend and very humble servant,

Robert Brudenell

SHUTE BARRINGTON TO CHARLES JENKINSON

Add. MS. 38200, f. 51.

Christ Church, October 19, 1762.

Dear Sir !

I have been prevented hitherto by various avocations from informing you that I have wrote to Flexman to attend you any morning by eight o'clock, an hour at which I should not have directed any body to be waited upon in London but a Minister, or a Minister's right hand. I flatter myself that upon conversing with him you will find him excellently adapted to your purpose. I most sincerely rejoice at Keppel's [1] promotion ; it will make him happy and give an honest and deserving man to the bench. His diploma has passed the Convocation this afternoon, and I will transmit it to him immediately. I am, dear Sir, with unfeigned regard and esteem

your most sincere and faithful servant,

S. Barrington

1. Frederick Keppel (1729–77), fourth son of William Anne Keppel, 2nd Earl of Albemarle, King's Chaplain and Canon of Windsor, was preferred to the bishopric of Exeter on November 7, 1762. It was thought that his preferment was due to the capture of Havanna on August 12 by his brother, Lord Albemarle, news of which reached England on September 29, but Walpole, whose niece Keppel had married, wrote to Conway on October 29 : " My nephew Keppel is Bishop of Exeter, not of the Havannah, as you may imagine, for his mitre was promised the day before the news came ".

GREGORY SHARPE TO CHARLES JENKINSON

Add. MS. 38200, f. 52.

Gregory Sharpe (1713–71), F.R.S., D.D., Fellow of Trinity, Cambridge (see *D.N.B.*), was the eldest of a Yorkshire family of six brothers, two of whom, John, M.P. for Callington, 1754–56, solicitor to the Treasury (died 1756), and William, keeper of the Council records, acted as guardians to the 6th Lord Baltimore, hereditary proprietor of Maryland, while Horatio, the second brother, was Governor of Maryland from 1752 to 1769.[1] Gregory Sharpe was Prebendary of Salisbury from 1757 and chaplain to George III. In 1761, despairing of substantial preferment, he had thoughts of joining his brother in Maryland, where Horatio promised him á rich living on the interest of Lord Baltimore ;[2] but in the same year Lord Shaftesbury appointed him to the living of Purton in Wiltshire, and in November 1763 he was elected Master of the Temple.

October 20, 1762.
Purton, near Wootton Basset, Wiltshire.

Dear Sir,

In the absence of my brother,[3] who is at Bath, I have no friend to apply to but yourself : in his name as well as my own I beg leave to trouble you with this letter.

Unsuccessful in my profession, and infirm, and lame, I am compelled to sollicit for some addition to my present income ; and the regard you have been pleased to express for me encourages me to hope that you will be so good to mention me to the Earl of Bute, and with my most dutiful respects to his Lordship, prevail upon him to be intreated to recommend me to his Majesty that I may succeed Mr. Turner[4] as Professor of Modern History in the University of Cambridge, which Professorship, as I am informed, is now vacant by the death of that gentleman.

I shall only add at present, that if, in consequence of his

1. See Lady Edgar, *A Colonial Governor in Maryland* (1912).
2. See letters from Horatio Sharpe to Lord Baltimore and C. Calvert, March 4, 1761, in Maryland Hist. Soc. Publications, *Archives of Maryland*, ix, 491-2.
3. William Sharpe, Clerk of the Council, who died in 1767.
4. Shallet Turner, Fellow of Peterhouse and Regius Professor of Modern History, 1741–62. His neglect of his professorial duties was considered scandalous even for those days when the Chair of Modern History and Languages had become virtually a sinecure. See D. A. Winstanley, *Unreformed Cambridge* (1935), pp. 156-7. Turner is stated in Venn, *Alumni Cantab.*, to have died on November 13, but there is a letter from Sir Harry Erskine to Jenkinson in the Bute MSS. dated October 16, 1762, in which he says that Thomas Gray, the poet, is applying in the room of Turner " who died about three months ago ". Gray himself speaks of his application as " rather of the latest " (Egerton MS. 2400, f. 153). Neither Gray nor Sharpe succeeded to the chair, which was given to Lawrence Brocket, a friend of Sandwich and Sir James Lowther. On his death in 1768, Gray succeeded him.

(68)

Lordship's recommendation I have the honor to succeed in this or any other promotion, I shall ever retain the most gratefull sense of his Lordship's goodness and of the many favors you have conferred on, Dear Sir,

Your most faithfull and obliged, humble Servant,

Greg: Sharpe

EDWARD RICHARDSON TO CHARLES JENKINSON

Add. MS. 38200, ff. 53-4.

During the autumn of 1762 Bute was exerting himself to create an interest in the City where his projected peace terms were not likely to be well received. In order to undermine Pitt's influence with the merchants he made use of coffee-house spies and scribblers " who every day filled the public papers with scurrility and invective against that Minister ".[1] Edward Richardson was one of these. He contributed to the *Gazetteer* as " Inquisitor ", and on September 11, 1762, he wrote to Bute : " Avarice constitutes no single part of my passion . . . if any assistance should be wanted by any visiting the print shops I could delight in that service ".[2] Although he does not appear to have been in trade, Richardson had connexions among the merchants and was under the protection of Sir Matthew Blackiston, Lord Mayor of London 1762-63. In 1762 there was a minority in the Common Council favourable to Bute and under the leadership of Sir James Hodges, the Town Clerk, to whom Richardson acted as agent in his dealings with the Government. Between May 1762 and August 1763 Richardson appears to have enjoyed a Secret Service pension of £50 a year,[3] and in October 1762 he was appointed controller of the Pepper Warehouse. In 1767 he was instrumental in detecting a fraud in the Customs for which he claimed a fantastic reward and afterwards petitioned Parliament.[4] Some of the last years of his life were spent in the King's Bench prison, for debt, but he was free in March 1782 when he asked Jenkinson for " a sketch though ever so faintly of the recommendation which first introduced me to Lord Bute's and your attention ".[5]

October 20, 1762.

Sir,

After returning you my warmest thanks for your having so kindly condescended to make my little concerns a part of yours, I beg leave to transmit to you the compliments of Sir Mathew Blackiston who desires you to thank my Lord Bute

1. Almon, *History of the Late Minority* (1766), p. 15 ; the passage refers to 1761, but Bute's tactics were the same in 1762.
2. Bute MSS.
3. This appears from the Bute MSS. See two lists of Secret Service pensions in the Windsor Archives. He may possibly have been the Mr. Richardson who was receiving a Secret Service pension of £50 a year in 1779 and whose name was passed on to Rockingham and to Shelburne in 1782. See Windsor MSS., Secret Service Pension Books, and a list of pensions dated April 21, 1782 in *George III Calendar, February to June 1782*.
4. Add. MS. 38342, f. 97.   5. *Ibid.* 38218, f. 33.

for his munificence to me,[1] at the same time am directed to acquaint you that he intends to present you with four tickets for the ensuing City Feast in complasance to those you may esteem his Lordship's friends.

This morning have had another conference with Sir James Hodges.[2] This gentleman gives me leave to assure you, he is so much at my Lord Bute's service, that if you should think it in his power to do his Lordship any kind ⟨   m⟩easure with the citizens with respect to the public good, he shall be very ready at any time to meet and consult with you on that point. I am also directed to assure you that you may, if ever you should think fit, enter into any converse with him with the utmost safety and honour. Sir when you please to see me, have some what to suggest I can not commit to paper: am with the most profound respect and humility,

Yours,

Ed: Richardson

FREDERICK STUART TO CHARLES JENKINSON

in Parliament Street, Westminster

Add. MS. 38469, f. 86.

Frederick Stuart, Bute's third son, was born in September 1751, and in 1762 was at school at Winchester where he often visited Jenkinson's mother. He was afterwards M.P. for Rothesay 1776–80, and Buteshire 1796–1801, and died unmarried in 1802. In 1768 he ran away from Oxford to Paris and was sent home by Sir John Lambton. On September 19, 1768, J. S. Mackenzie wrote to Jenkinson " about that worthless boy Frederick. . . . My brother desires me to send him off forthwith to the East Indies . . . and if he will not go, my brother says he will positively hear no more of him." [3]

Winchester, October 20, 1762.

Dear Sir,

I received your letter a long time ago and I beg pardon for not writing before. But was prevented. The election week [4]

1. Richardson's patent as controller of the Pepper Warehouse is dated October 22, 1762. Add. MS. 38335, f. 78.
2. Sir James Hodges, Town Clerk, formerly a tradesman on London Bridge, was knighted in June 1759 and died at Bath on October 19, 1774. In 1770 he read a remonstrance to the King for ignoring the City's petition against the repeal of the Townshend duties. On his activities over the Cider Bill see p. xii.
3. Add. MS. 38469, f. 181.
4. The so-called " Election " of scholars of Winchester College to New College, Oxford, took place at Winchester, usually in the week following July 7, St. Thomas à Becket's day. During " Election Week " the Warden and two Fellows of New College were received with ceremony and entertained by Winchester College. See A. K. Cook, *About Winchester College* (1917), pp. 390 *seqq.*

coming on I was so taken up with going out and all that that I could not write before. I heard from Mrs. Jinkinson [*sic*] that papa had bought a very fine estate at *luton* in *bedfordshire*.[1] She said she thought it worth three thousand pounds a year. We have no news here at all, tell when the Parliament and if the Cyder Ackt will be reprieved. The people rail at it here particularly them in the Close. Dr. Buller [2] Mr. Sturges [3] and them. I beg you will excuse my not writing more.

Ever yours affectionately,
F. Stuart

EDWARD RICHARDSON TO CHARLES JENKINSON

Add. MS. 38200, f. 55.

October 22, 1762.

Sir,

Your message to Sir James Hodges proved a most agreable one. But having had a fall from his horse about a fortnight ago has not since that time been out of his house. I am commanded to assure you of his first visit, that is, the day he is able to go abroad you will see him at South Street — in the meanwhile I am to give you an invitation to his ⟨rooms⟩ at Guild Hall. Sir James appears to me very desirous of a speedy interview with you. My good Sir, I am and ever shall be

your most obedient and faithfull humble servant,

Edward Richardson

MRS. BOOTHBY SKRYMSHER TO CHARLES JENKINSON

Add. MS. 38200, ff. 56-7.

Tooly Park, October 23, 1762.

Dear Jenky,

Do not be dismayd at the sight of a letter from me and fancy I want to ask you questions touching State affairs, no, wee country country [*sic*] gentry have not that wicked curiosity ; wee content ourselves with lighting bonfires and

---

1. Bute bought Luton Hoo in Bedfordshire in 1763.
2. William Buller, Prebendary of Winchester August 1763, afterwards Bishop of Exeter 1792 to his death in 1796.
3. John Sturges, Chancellor of the diocese and Prebendary of Winchester 1759. He died in 1807.

tapping our beer barrells when wee hear of a conquest or a retakeing, and firmly believe you politicians are pretty fellows, very pretty pretty fellows.

Now to my business, your freind George Grenville being at the head of the Admiralty has the power of disposeing of the commissions of the marine officers and I do intreat you to obtain of him a company of marines for Mr. Onesipherus Swann [1] who has been many years in the service and is a first Lieutenant, I need not say more to recommend him than that he was a great favourite of Admiral Boscawen's who recommended him strongly to Lord Temple when he was at the head of the Admiralty and his Lordship did promise to give him a company, but it slipped his memory which occasioned such a fracas betwixt that earl and admiral that the admiral never fully forgave Lord Temple but often mentioned it and constantly said Swann was one of the best marine officers he ever saw for he was intrepid decent and alert, and if he had lived would have taken care of him — He has been unlucky, was in a 20 gun ship in the West Indies at the beginning of this war, and taken prisoner by the French, and tumbled about till at last he was in the custody of Don Velasco that died so nobly at the Havanah, who sent him and other English prisoners to Jamaica when Admiral Cotes commanded upon that station, who knows him very well and will inform you that he merits what I ask for him. Perhaps you may not know that I am very delicate upon these occasions and have no notion of troubling my friends in the behalf of worthless undeserving persons, I think it a sin against the publick, and a scandal to my self.

Wee were all very happy to hear by Mrs. Fitzroy that you are very well. They have been so obligeing to pass two days with us and said they had seen you before they left London and that you was in perfect beauty and health. You know Charles Boothby often told you that he feared your close attention to busyness might hurt you, he desires his affectionate compliments to you as does also Sir William who is become a marine himself, Mrs. Maria loves you much, I think she is ever most fond of you at a distance. I am sorry to hear our old freind Lord Portsmouth is in so bad a way.[2] That the

1. His commission as 1st Lieutenant of Marines is dated September 22, 1759, and on February 6, 1762, he wrote to Mrs. Boothby for her interest to prevent his being reduced to half-pay. He was given a company on June 6, 1772.
2. He died on November 22, 1763.

ways of pleasantness and the paths of peace may ever be your lot is the sincere wish of your humble etc., etc.

A. Boothby Skrymsher

Not haveing the honor of being known to Mr. Grenville I have no right to trouble him with any compliment upon this occasion but leave it to you to say what is proper from me if any is [*sic*] thing is proper to be said. Mr. Swann is in the regiment commanded by Colonel Bendish [1] now at Chatham.

GREGORY SHARPE TO CHARLES JENKINSON

Add. MS. 38200, f. 71.

Purton, October 26, 1762.

Dear Sir,

The laying my letter before the Earl of Bute is an act of real friendship, which I shall ever acknowledge with the utmost gratitude ; and though I am not so fortunate as to succeed in what I directly applied for, having at the same time intreated his Lordship's recommendation for some preferment, I shall still hope, by means of your kind interposition, for success some other way, which will greatly contribute to the happiness of him, who is, with the most perfect regard and esteem, dear Sir,

Your most faithful and obliged, humble servant,

Greg: Sharpe

LORD HARCOURT TO CHARLES JENKINSON

Add. MS. 38200, ff. 75-6.

Newnham, October 29, 1762.

Dear Sir,

Since Mr. Keppel's appointment to the Bishoprick of Exeter, I received a sort of a joint letter from Dr. Barnard,[2] the Master of Eton School, and from Dr. John Burton,[3] de-

1. Lieutenant-Colonel Richard Bendish.
2. Edward Barnard, D.D., Fellow of St. John's, Cambridge. He was Headmaster of Eton 1754–64, Canon of Windsor 1760, Provost of Eton 1764. About him see *D.N.B.*
3. John Burton, D.D., of Corpus Christi, Oxford. Fellow of Eton 1733 ; died February 11, 1771. He was nominated one of the first trustees of the Settlement of Georgia. See a memoir of him in the *Gent. Mag.*, 1771, pp. 305-7, and also in 1781, p. 120. See also *D.N.B.*

siring me to assist them in obtaining the living (which Keppel held with his Cannonry) for a person who has many years been Chaplain to Eton College, a worthy man with a very small income. The living is in the gift of the Crown in consequence of Keppels preferment. The value of it they call about £140. I should be glad to know whether there has been any application yet made for the living, for if there has been none, I should be glad to give them some little help, without applying for it in such a manner, as might weaken any future application I may make for Bray, who to the immortal scandal of our friends in Oxfordshire, has obtained no favour for all the services he has done the Government.

I shall see the Duke of Marlborough in a few days, and will see whether Bray has anything to expect from that quarter. I have not yet heard whether any steps have been taken with regard to the City of Oxford, nor do I foresee any possibility of transacting that affair successfully : For what security can be given by the Chamber [1] for any sum of money, as the right of election is in the Freemen, who are very numerous, and by no means likely to be any longer under the influence of the magistrates. [2]

I shall go to Burford on Tuesday next, and return on Thursday. If you should have occasion to write to me on Tuesday, your letter will find me at Mr. Lenthal's. [3]

The approach of the Session of Parliament makes me very anxious to hear that matters are likely to go well. I wrote to

1. Here the word " magistrates " has been written and crossed out. In the eighteenth century the word " Chamber " was synonymous with " Corporation ". See, e.g., a letter from Charles Lyttelton to Sanderson Miller in *An Eighteenth-Century Correspondence*, p. 421 : " The Corporation or Chamber of Exon have a very good estate ", etc.

2. On March 24, 1766, the Corporation of Oxford was £5670 in debt. In this extremity, on May 12, the Mayor and Aldermen wrote " in the first instance " to their member, Robert Lee, offering to get him and his colleague, Sir Thomas Stapleton, re-elected if they would discharge the city's debt. Otherwise, " the whole council are determined to apply to some other person or persons in the county to do it ". It appears from Harcourt's letter that, in 1762 at least, the Corporation were by no means certain of returning their candidates, and, possibly for this reason, the offer in 1766 was refused. But shortly before vacating their seats, on January 26, 1768, Lee and Stapleton complained to the House of Commons of attempted bribery and later produced the letter from the Corporation. The case caused a scandal, but the House, though shocked, preserved a sense of proportion — after all, much larger sums were sometimes spent on elections — and on February 10 the Oxford magistrates were dismissed with a rebuke from the Speaker after spending five days in Newgate in great fear for their lives and property (see *Parliamentary History*, xvi, 397-402). It is clear from Harcourt's letter that as early as 1762 the Corporation was seeking a way out of its embarrassments.

3. William Lenthall of Burford Priory, an Oxfordshire Whig. He supported the New interest at the election of 1754 and died in October 1781.

Lord Bute the day I came out of town, and I hope he received my letter. It related to what had passed between us, concerning Lord L⟨incoln⟩ [1] who was not at the drawing room on Monday last.

Yours, dear Sir, most sincerely,

Harcourt

WILLIAM SHARPE [2] TO CHARLES JENKINSON

Add. MS. 38200, ff. 77-8.

Bath, October 30, 1762.

Dear Sir,

I should not have given you the trouble of a letter from this place had it not been in regard to my brother the Doctor who informed me of the application he had made to you for the Professorship of modern History in room of Mr. Turner. Permit me therefore just to say, that he has lived almost all his days without any preferment 'till very lately, and what he now possesses is likely to prove much less than was imagined, the Lectureship of St. Georges,[3] and the living Lord Shaftesbury has given him in Wiltshire (which is only a vicarage [4]) not producing together more than about £300 clear, after paying Curates and a Collector to gather the Tythes, etc. and it unluckily happens that the Parsonage House is in so bad a condition as to call for more than one year's income to make it habitable. As these are facts, I flatter myself you will agree with me, that this is but a poor provision for one who is infirm and lame, and whose expences are on that account the greater, and will therefore more readily afford him your kind assistance

1. In October 1762 Lincoln, Newcastle's nephew and heir, created a sensation by deserting his uncle for the Court. On Monday, October 25, Harcourt wrote to Bute : " Lord Lincoln was not at Court to-day, a slight disorder of one of his children hurried him back to Oatlands yesterday. Whatever promises and assurances he may have made to the King, or whatever engagements he may have entered into with your Lordship may be relied upon for I take him to be a man of strict honour. The part he has to act must certainly give him some uneasiness but . . . I am sure he won't hesitate one moment about the measures he has to persue " (Bute MSS.). Lincoln was summoned to an audience on October 24 and, according to the King's version of the interview, forswore acting with the Duke of Newcastle, though he told another story to his uncle. See Namier, *England etc.* pp. 427-8, and below, p. 82.

2. See p. 68 n. 3.

3. In February 1762 Gregory Sharpe was appointed to the lectureship of St. George's, Hanover Square, on the interest of Lord Hardwicke. See Add. MS. 35596, f. 369 ; *ibid.* 35597, ff. 7, 26.

4. Gregory Sharpe was Vicar of Purton in Wiltshire 1761-71.

(75)

to obtain this Professorship, or else any Prebendary or Cannonry that may hereafter happen to become vacant ; this will lay the Doctor under the most lasting obligation as well as him who is, with the greatest truth and regard, dear Sir

Your much obliged and most obedient servant,

W. Sharpe

P.S.   The Duke of Devonshire went from hence a few days since, intending as I was informed to proceed to Chatsworth till the meeting of the Parliament, but makes London in his way.

SHUTE BARRINGTON TO CHARLES JENKINSON

Add. M.S. 38200, f. 85.

Christ Church, October 31, 1762.

Dear Sir !

I very sincerely congratulate you on your having closed with Flexman, as I am convinced you will find his abilities adequate to any task you will assign him ; and I believe his fidelity may be depended upon.   The late step of the Duke of Devonshire [1] occasioned rather concern than surprize ; for after the first instances of imprudence one's wonder ceases at the last.   His Grace does not seem to have attended to the very obvious and essential difference which results from the two characters of the present King and his Grandfather ; and that it is of more permanent bad consequence for a great temporal peer to ⟨have⟩ incurred the displeasure of the one than the other.   I am much hurt at the idea however that this conduct may be productive of disagreeable effects to Lord Bute since the defection and ill humour of such a man though not to be dreaded is not at the same time to be wished. I most ardently hope to hear from you soon that a peace is

1. After Newcastle's resignation in May, Devonshire withdrew from the Cabinet Council though still retaining his place of Chamberlain of the Household, a half-measure which drew on him " the irritation which during four months of anxious embarrassed discussions about the peace treaty had gathered against the ' non-coöperators ' " (Namier, *England etc.* p. 430).   On October 3 he received at Bath an *office* letter from Lord Egremont summoning him to attend the Cabinet, " as the final decision of the peace was now to be taken ".   To this he replied the same day, excusing himself on the grounds of his " uninformed situation " (Add. MS. 32943, ff. 48-9, and *England etc.* p. 431).   This was " the late step " which so infuriated the King that he caused Devonshire to be removed from his office on October 28 under humiliating circumstances.   For a full account of these events see *England etc.* pp. 430-36.

concluded ; I have myself no doubts of the terms. I am, dear Sir, in haste, but with unfeigned regard and esteem

Your most sincere and faithful servant,

S. Barrington

On November 3, 1762, George III caused the Duke of Devonshire's name to be struck from the Privy Council Book, a procedure for which Jenkinson afterwards compiled the following list of precedents.

*List of Privy Councillors struck off the Council List
from the Restoration to the present time — 1762*

Add. MS. 38334, f. 194.

19 May 1674. His Majesty in Council this day declaring his displeasure against the Earl of Shaftesbury commanded the Clerk of the Council that his name be left out of the number of Privy Councillors.

7 January 1675/6. It was this day ordered by His Majesty in Council that the names of the Lord Viscount Halifax, and the Lord Holles be struck out of the List of Privy Councillors.

4 August 1676. His Majesty having dismissed the Earl of Kincardin from his Council in Scotland, is pleased to discharge him from this Board.

12 June 1678. This day His Majesty in Council ordered that the name of Sir Robert Carr Chancellor of the Dutchy of Lancaster should be struck out of the Council Books.

12 July 1678. His Majesty was this day pleased to order and command that Mr. Montagu's name be erased out of the List of Privy Councillors.

15 October 1679. It was this day ordered by His Majesty in Council that the Earl of Shaftesbury's name be struck out of the List of His Privy Council, he having discharged him from being President thereof.

18 January 1680. This day His Majesty was pleased to command in Council, that the name of James Earl of Salisbury be struck out of the List of the names of the Lords of His Majesty's most Honourable Privy Council ; Registered in the Book of Council Causes, which was done accordingly.

24 January 1680/1. This day His Majesty was pleased to command in Council, that the names of Robert Earl of Sunderland, Arthur Earl of Essex, and Sir William Temple

be struck out of the List of His Majesty's most Honourable Privy Council, registered in the Book of Council Causes, which was done accordingly.

24 October 1683. It was this day ordered by His Majesty in Council, that Sir Francis Pembertons name be struck out of the list of Privy Councillors.

21 October 1685. His Majesty was this day pleased to command that the Lord Marquis of Halifax be struck out of the List of Privy Councillors. [N.B. His Lordship was at that time Lord President.]

23 December 1685. His Majesty acquaints the Lords, that for reasons best known to himself, he hath thought fit to leave the Bishop of London out of the Council, and ordered his name to be struck out of the Council Book.

29 October 1688. His Majesty was pleased this day in Council to order and command, that Robert Earl of Sunderland, Lord President of the Council and Principal Secretary of State be struck out of the list of Privy Councillors.

   Memorandum. Sir Thomas Chichely was removed from the Council by King James and said in a Marginal Note in the list to be 2 March 1686/7.

23 June 1692. It is this day ordered by Her Majesty in Council, that the names of George Marquess of Halifax, Charles Earl of Shrewsbury, John Earl of Marlborough, and Arthur Earl of Torrington be struck out of the List of the Lords of their Majesties most Honourable Privy Council.

12 March 1695. This day His Majesty in Council called for the Council Book and struck out the names of the Marquess of Normanby, the Earl of Nottingham and Sir Edward Seymour.

21 January 1696. His Majesty in Council was this day pleased to strike the Earl of Monmouths name out of the Council Book.

About 1720 or 1721. John Aislabie Esq. was struck out of the List of the Council by His Majesty in Council.

7 November 1724. It was this day ordered by His Majesty in Council, that the name of Thomas Earl Coningsby, be left out of the List of the Lords of His Majesty's most Honourable Privy Council.

31 May 1725. It was this day ordered by His Majesty in Council, that the name of Thomas Earl of Macclesfield be left out of the List of the Lords of His Majesty's most Honourable Privy Council.

1 July 1731. This day His Majesty in Council called for the
Council Book, and ordered the name of William Pulteney
Esq to be struck out of the List of Privy Councillors.
25 April 1760. This day His Majesty in Council called for the
Council Book, and ordered the name of Lord George Sackville to be struck out of the List of Privy Councillors.
3 November 1762. This day His Majesty in Council called for
the Council Book and struck the name of William Duke
of Devonshire out of the List of Privy Councillors.

COLONEL ROBERT BOYD TO CHARLES JENKINSON

Add. MS. 38200, f. 91.

Lieutenant-Colonel, afterwards Major-General, Sir Robert Boyd
(1710–94) was in Germany in 1752 on the staff of the Marquis of Granby.
His regiment was the 1st Foot Guards. In 1766 he became Colonel of
the 39th Foot ; in May 1768 he was appointed Lieutenant-Governor of
Gibraltar and became Governor in May 1790. He died on the Rock in
1794, and is buried in a bastion of the fortress. See *D.N.B.*

Head Quarters at Kirchain, November 3, 1762.
Dear Sir,
    As by the surrender of Cassell, there is a prospect of the
Army's going soon into winter quarters, I have wrote to my
Lord Halifax, by this opportunity, to beg he would apply to
the King for leave to let me come home, when the campaign
is over. I am very little known to his Lordship and therefore
entreat your good offices on this occasion, and I should be
very glad to have this leave, as soon as possible, that I may
make use of, at a proper time.
    I had apply'd to Mr. Grenville, just before he was removed
to the Admiralty, upon this subject, and I added that I hoped
His Majesty, would be graciously pleased to continue my
appointment, as Commissary of the Hessians, even although a
peace should take place, untill the expiration of our treaty
with them, which is in June next. This douceur, to a man
who has a new house to furnish, would be very convenient
for my finances.
    I flatter myself that my Lord Bute, will not only patronize
this request, but will continue his goodness to me, by some
other provision, when my employment of Commissary ceases.
    It will be a singular case if after having served all this

war, I should be set down at the end of it, with a less income than I had, when it begun.

Yet singular as it is, that will be my lot, when I have no other provision from government, but a Company of Guards.

After thirty two years service abroad, I most heartily wish to pass the evening of my life at home, which I could do comfortably, if I had the same income as before the war. A government [1] added to my Company would almost be the thing and I hope I shall not be thought unreasonable for proposing this. Your assistance, my Dear Sir, would be of great service and I am persuaded it will not be wanting to

Your much obliged humble Servant,

Robert Boyd

In November 1762, while Fox was engaged in recruiting a majority to defend the Preliminaries in Parliament, others of Bute's friends were expected to help in the work of talking to members on " their several claims and pretensions ", *e.g.* regiments and governments for army officers, contracts for the merchants, etc.

LORD HARCOURT TO CHARLES JENKINSON

Add. MS. 38200, ff. 95-6.

Newnham, November 5, 1762.

Dear Sir,

Colonel Evelyn [2] who came here last Tuesday tells me that General Acourt who is Lieutenant Colonel of the Coldstream Regiment is supposed to be so much displeased and disappointed in not getting the Regiment that Gansell [3] had, that it is thought he will go into Opposition. You know that there are two brothers in Parliament,[4] and I should imagine it might be no difficult matter to secure them.

1. The value of a governorship of a home garrison varied from £1289 : 2 : 6 a year, which was the income for Plymouth, to £182 : 10s. for North Yarmouth or Carlisle. The average was about £300 a year. Boyd did not secure a home government. The Lieutenant-Governorship of Gibraltar, which he was given in 1768, was worth £730 a year.

2. William Evelyn (1723–83), sixth son of Sir John Evelyn, 1st Bart., and great-grandson of the diarist ; Colonel of the 29th Foot and M.P. for Helston. He was first cousin to Harcourt, whose father, Simon Harcourt, married Elizabeth, sister of Sir John Evelyn.

3. Lieutenant-General William Gansell was appointed Colonel of the 55th Foot on August 20, 1762. He had previously been Lieutenant-Colonel of the 2nd Foot Guards.

4. William and Pierce Ashe A'Court, M.P.s for Heytesbury, their pocket borough. In 1754 and again in 1759 Major-General William A'Court applied

Since you received Mr. Westons letter, we find that great pains have been taken to bring Sir Samuel to a right way of thinking, every kind of civility and complaisance has been exerted by a great man whose Lady is related to Lady Floodyer.[1] I need say nothing more, you will know who I mean and I fancy it will have its effect. Notwithstanding which I hope your Lord will have an opportunity of explaining matters to him, which will set every thing right. I came from Burford[2] yesterday, and shall continue here some time longer. My curiosity would almost carry me to town, if I did not think it would have the appearance of running for the Plate,[3] which I have no thoughts of doing.

Yours Dear Sir most sincerely,

Harcourt

If any thing should offer for Bowley,[4] you wont forget him.

Pressure was successfully brought to bear on Sir Samuel, either through Jenkinson's mediation with Bute or by the " great man " himself. An inducement to right thinking may have been the contract for victualling troops in America which Fludyer and his partner Adam Drummond were given in 1763, in preference to Messrs. Colebrooke and Nesbitt.[5]

In October 1762 Newcastle needed a rallying-point for his fast-disintegrating party. Convinced that " We shall never have so proper an occasion as this of the ill usage of the Duke of Devonshire ", he began to canvass for sympathetic resignations, which, however, he meant to restrict, lest they should become " a burthen, and give the Ministers places to dispose of to encrease their party immediately ".[6] The decisive action of the Court in dismissing Devonshire was the signal for a general clarification of allegiances.

to Newcastle to be made a Colonel. From 1754 Pierce Ashe was in receipt of a Secret Service pension of £500 a year, but this ceased in 1762 when he and his brother remained with Newcastle in opposition (*Structure of Politics*, pp. 35, 531, etc.).

1. Lady Fludyer was Caroline Brudenell, a cousin of Lady Caroline Lennox, wife of Henry Fox. Her sister, Louisa Brydges Brudenell, married Richard Weston, who thus became connected with one of the leading Government contractors. On November 2, 1762, Weston wrote to Jenkinson from Newnham that he had been warned that Sir Samuel Fludyer meant to go into opposition, because a certain victualling contract which Bute had promised him had been given to another firm. Bute MSS.

2. Weston wrote : " Lord H. is gone to Burford races and returns to-morrow or Thursday ".

3. Harcourt was anxious to avoid the appearance of competing for any of the places vacated by the friends of the Dukes of Devonshire and Newcastle.

4. See p. 41.

5. See p. 239 and n. 2.

6. See Namier, *England etc.* p. 434.

LORD HARCOURT TO CHARLES JENKINSON

Add. MS. 38200, ff. 99–100.

Newnham, November 7, 1762.

Dear Sir,

I have wrote to Lord Bute about Lord Newnham but my letter to his Lordship is far from being pressing. I have expressed my desire to see Lord Newnham in his Majesty's service but I have left it entirely at large, to take place now, or hereafter, whichever may be most convenient to his Majesty and his Administration, which I am sure I dont mean to distress, but to support with as unfeigned a zeal as any man in the Kingdom.

Lord Newnham will write to Lord Spencer [1] to sound his disposition and to know his opinion of men and measures. He will do it under pretence of knowing his Lordships pleasure if any thing should offer to make a re-election at St. Albans necessary. Lord Newnham has not lately seen Lord Spencer, but it is imagined that his attachment if he has any, is to Mr. Pitt. But I dont find that he has any particular regard for his Grace of Newcastle. I suppose we shall have more resignations,[2] those who have allready resigned dont surprize me, nor do I think his Majestys affairs will receive any great detriment from the steps they have taken. I hope and really believe that Lord L⟨incoln⟩ will continue firm and steady to his engagement,[3] which will be of as much service to Lord Bute, as disservice to the Duke. The world allready begins to smoke the affair, for a letter which I received last night from London hinted at it, as a most extraordinary event.

When you see Mr. Grenville I wish you would present my humble respects to him, and beg the favour of him, in my name, to appoint one Mr. Robert Twycross a Lieutenant in

1. John Spencer, 1st Baron Spencer, a cousin of the Duke of Marlborough, had inherited an electoral interest at St. Albans from Sarah, Duchess of Marlborough (see Namier, *Structure of Politics*, p. 130 and n. 4). In 1761 Lord Nuneham was returned on his interest. On the running of " a third man " for the election see *ibid.* p. 133.

2. So far the principal resignations were those of Lord George Cavendish, Controller of the Household, on October 29, and Lord Rockingham on November 3. For an analysis of the resignations which Newcastle eventually secured see Namier, *England etc.* pp. 445-9.

3. See p. 75 n. 1. Lincoln was at pains to make it clear that he was not joining opposition, though no one but Newcastle believed that he was. See *England etc.* p. 443.

the Navy, for which he is properly qualified, as he has gone through the necessary examinations. If you will give him a memorandum of this request, I flatter myself it will be granted. But if I write it may lay him under the difficulty of a letter, which trouble, I could wish to save.

Lady Harcourt Lady Betty and Lord Newnham desire their compliments.

Yours, dear Sir, most sincerely,

Harcourt

Professor Namier writes in *England in the Age of the American Revolution* : [1] " When Newcastle planned to ' strike terror ' through resignations he was thinking of ' persons of high rank or great distinction ', not of minor followers who, if unprovided for, would become a ' burthen ' on him, while their places would furnish the Court with additional patronage. But no Government could be expected willingly to provide for the servants, political or domestic, of the Opposition, and Newcastle vainly flattered himself that it would be left to him to decide who was, or was not, to relinquish his place." On November 24 Fox recommended " a thorough rout " of Newcastle's dependants, but the massacre of the Pelhamite innocents was deferred till after the voting on the Preliminaries.

TOM RAMSDEN TO CHARLES JENKINSON

Add. MS. 38200, f. 101.

Swillington, November 8, 1762.

Though I know nothing but the news papers say, I cannot ⟨but be⟩ uneasy at what I see in them. The resignations ⟨are ver⟩y surprising, and can tend to nothing but bringing ⟨conf⟩usion at home. I don't expect to see the ⟨   ⟩ *good* ones can be assigned.

⟨   ⟩ Dear Jenkinson, to have some good account ⟨from the⟩nce, without entering into secrets, which I do not ⟨desire⟩ besides it is not safe writing any thing by the post. ⟨You⟩ may depend upon it, that your letters will not pass without being seen ; and therefore may say nothing but what is actually done. Do you intend to let these good people resign only what they chuse, and leave them in possession of what gives them power in the country ? [2] It greives me to know, what

1. P. 470.
2. When it came to the point Ramsden was quite ready to plead mercy for some of the victims. See p. 119.

J.P. (83) H

distress this behaviour must cause to our truely good and gracious King.

⟨I sen⟩d this under cover to Mr. Morin,[1] as being a more safe ⟨address⟩ Thank you once more on Popplewell's [2] account; you have made ⟨his fam⟩ily very happy. My best wishes attend you and yours.

Adieu.

JOHN BINDLEY TO CHARLES JENKINSON

Add. MS. 5726 C, f. 45.

This memorial is undated, but obviously comes before the next letter. In Jenkinson's *List of the Principal Officers of Excise with Observations* (after February 1763) Dudley Baxter is described as "recommended by Sir Dudley Rider whose niece he married. Salary £610 a year. Supposed to be worth by bills for law suits not less than £3,000. Appointed by patent during pleasure in Mr. Pelham's time" (Add. MS. 38335, f. 52). Sir Dudley Ryder was Chief Justice of the King's Bench 1754–56, and father of the 1st Earl of Harrowby. Dudley Baxter married Elizabeth, daughter of William Ryder, a younger brother. He apparently expected to lose his place in the "massacre of the Pelhamite innocents", but possibly through the good offices of Bindley and Jenkinson he retained it till his death on December 10, 1766.

Dear Sir,

I must trespass so far on our former friendship to acquaint you that Dudley Baxter Sollicitor to the Commissioners of Excise is a man whom I have known for 14 years to have been a most industrious and intelligent Officer. He has many good plans for the improvement of the Revenue, and he and I have long flattered ourselves that our joint labours would produce many good things for the Revenue. I must only further add that his bread actually depends on his place, and that he has no profession in the world to get a shilling by having entirely neglected the Law. I leave it to you to [*sic*] whether tis in your power or whether tis prudent to give any hint in his favour. But I could deny [*sic*] in justice to my friend Baxter to give you these hints on his situation.

1. Peter Michael Morin, Under-Secretary of State 1760, and again 1765–68. He was in receipt of a Post Office Secret Service pension of £250 per annum. See *Structure of Politics*, pp. 239–40; *Grenv. Pps.* iii, 311; and p. 244 below.
2. Ramsden wrote to Jenkinson on July 25, 1762, recommending Popplewell, "a young man who has been some time in the Custom House, in the Jerkers Plantation Office, at a small salary", and on October 17 he wrote again to thank him for securing Popplewell's promotion (Bute MSS.).

JOHN BINDLEY TO CHARLES JENKINSON

Add. MS. 38200, f. 103.

Excise Office, November 12, 1762.

Dear Sir,

My good friend Dudley Baxter Esq. Sollicitor to this board desires the honor of paying his duty to Lord Bute next Wednesday which he has been prevented from doing before by indisposition a great part of the summer, and by a great deal of business that he is generally engaged in on account of this Office. And as next Wednesday is an holiday and himself an entire stranger to you I intend myself the honor of introducing him to you and can recommend him as a very honest clever and industrious man in his office.

I am infinitely obliged to yourself and many other good friends who have been so kind to represent me in that favourable light, as I am sure they have done to Lord Bute, as induced his Lordship to speak and behave to me in the very gracious manner he was pleased to do on Wednesday. My utmost endeavours shall always be employed to merit his Lordships protection, and do some justice to my friends recommendation. And I remain Dear Sir with the greatest truth and respect

Your devoted and obliged humble servant

Ino: Bindley
in Southampton Street, Bloomsbury.

We will be at his Lordships between 9 and 10.

LORD HARCOURT TO CHARLES JENKINSON

Add. MS. 38200, ff. 106-7.

Newnham, November 16, 1762.

Dear Sir,

I saw a letter yesterday from town that mentioned Lord Kinnouls [1] resignation, and that Lord Lincoln intended to resign. If by such a step his Lordship means to pay a com-

---

1. Thomas Hay, 8th Earl of Kinnoul. According to Walpole he was Newcastle's " bosom confidant, dwelling in his very house " (*Memoirs*, i, 164). He was Chancellor of the Duchy of Lancaster but resigned in November 1762, though " not at all in the manner which I had reason to expect . . . by his declarations " (Newcastle to Hardwicke, November 13, Add. MS. 32944, ff. 352-3). See Namier, *England etc.* p. 441.

pliment to his uncle at the expense of his employment, as Lord of the Bedchamber, there may be no impropriety in it, provided he supports his Majesty's measures. You know where the shoe pinches, his Lordships antipathy to a certain person is very violent,[1] but I hope and still believe that neither that or any thing else, will make him do a wrong thing. His resentment may be great : but his duty and respect ought to get the better of all other considerations. When he was last at St. James's, he knew that Mr. F⟨ox⟩ was to be employed, and therefore I dont foresee any thing that can induce him to depart from his engagements, or to act contrary to the assurances he then gave. I shall be in town to morrow seven'ight, time enough to attend Lord Bute in the evening. The letter which I saw yesterday came from a very humble servant of his Grace's,[2] one very much attached to him, a man of honor and principle ; but he writes in so desponding a stile, that I allmost flatter myself, that his Grace despairs of success in his opposition.

Yours, dear Sir, most sincerely

Harcourt

The preliminaries of peace signed in Paris on November 8, 1762, were to be laid before both Houses on December 2. This was the test case of Bute's Administration.

LORD BUTE TO SIR JAMES LOWTHER[3]

Add. MS. 38200, f. 112.

London, November 17, 1762.

My dear Sir James,

I am extremely obliged to you for your kind and friendly letter, the Peace is at last signed, and such a one as this nation never saw before, but war seems to be declared at home with the utmost virulence. I am the mark for the party watch word, but the whole is in reality aimed at the King himself

1. The King wrote to Bute of an interview with Lincoln which took place on October 24 : ". . . as to the speaking to his friends, he has great difficulties owing to his attachment to the Pelhams and his great aversion to Mr. Fox " (*ibid.* p. 427). Lincoln eventually resigned on November 19.

2. Newcastle.

3. This letter is a copy. The original is in the *Lonsdale MSS.* and an extract from it is printed in H.M.C., *Lonsdale MSS.* p. 131 ; it is also quoted in Professor Namier's essay on " Circular Letters " in the *English Historical Review* for October 1929.

whose liberty is now to be decided on, liberty that his poorest subject enjoys of choosing his own menial servants. The happy conclusion of the Peace, has however drawn the teeth of faction, but they have made themselves desperate and must persist in their presumptuous folly. I hardly know how to desire you to take so long a journey at such a season, and yet the presence of a person of your character and great consideration joined to the relation we stand in cannot fail to have the best effects, and be in a peculiar manner acceptable to me. I am sorry to hear Lord Darlington [1] does not come up, but have no pretence to desire it of him if inconvenient. My friends tell me the House of Lords is to be the principal scene of action, where I am to be arraigned, for the King's preferring the Duke of Marlborough a Tory [2] to the Duke of Devonshire, a Whig, for making the Peace and being an anti-German⟨y⟩.[3] Adieu, my dear Sir James. My most affectionate compliments attend my daughter. I am with the greatest truth and regard most sincerely yours.

LORD HARCOURT TO CHARLES JENKINSON

Add. MS. 38200, ff. 116-17.

Newnham, November 17, 1762.

Dear Sir,

When I was last in town I heard that Lord Bath, had interested himself so far for Mr. Byde's brother,[4] as to recommend him to Lord Bute. I don't know what favour Lord Bath has asked for him, but if Lord Bute is disposed to do any thing for him, the affair which I am going to mention, may possibly afford his Lordship the means of paying a compliment to Lord Bath, of obliging Mr. Byde, and of accommodating Sir John Evelyn [5] who has been a Commissioner of the Customs

1. Henry Vane, 2nd Earl of Darlington, brother-in-law to Sir James Lowther, whose sister Margaret he married in 1757. He had extensive Parliamentary interest in Durham, and was Governor of Carlisle Castle.

2. Anyone connected with Bute at this period was liable to be branded a Tory. The Spencer-Churchills were the leading Whig family in Oxfordshire, and, as son-in-law to the Duke of Bedford, Marlborough was connected with another great Whig family.

3. The copy has a " y " which is not in the text in the *Lonsdale MSS*.

4. John Byde, younger son of Thomas Byde of Ware and brother of Thomas Plumer Byde, M.P. for Hertfordshire, about whom see Namier, *England etc.* p. 13 and n. 2. John Byde was a director of the South Sea Company and a Portugal merchant who had suffered through the Lisbon earthquake of 1755.

5. Sir John Evelyn, 1st Bart., Harcourt's uncle by marriage (see p. 80), was Commissioner of Customs since 1721. He was removed from his place on March

near forty years. I have the honor of being nearly related to Sir John Evelyn, and though I have not had the pleasure of seeing him lately, yet as he is advanced in years, I believe I could undertake to prevail upon him to give up his place as Commissioner in favour of Mr. Byde's brother, for one may reasonably conclude, that he would be glad to pass the remainder of his life out of the hurry and bustle of the world, Mr Byde paying him part of the salary as an annuity. If this proposal meets with Lord Bute's approbation, I shall very ⟨   ⟩ mention it. Sir John, who as an ⟨old⟩ Servant of the Crown, and one who ⟨has⟩ been diligent and attentive to his duty, may very justly be entitled to some degree of indulgence, after so many years service, and I dont see how that can be done any other way at so easy a rate, as by the method proposed.

Yours, dear Sir, most sincerely,

Harcourt

JOHN POWNALL TO CHARLES JENKINSON

Add. MS. 38200, f. 118.

John Pownall, brother of Thomas Pownall, Governor of Massachusetts, was Secretary to the Board of Trade 1753–68 ; Under-Secretary of State for America 1768–76. He was M.P. for Saint Germans 1775–76 when he was appointed Commissioner of Excise.

Plantation Office, November 18, 1762.

Dear Sir,

I am sorry it has not been in my power sooner to obey the commands I had last the honor of receiving from you ; but more so, that the inclosed account does not contain a more perfect and satisfactory answer to the question concerning the African trade.

The materials of this office are very imperfect with respect to this branch of commerce ; but what facts I have put down may I believe be depended upon, and I shall be happy if they are of any use, for I am with the greatest regard and respect, dear Sir,

Your most obedient and most faithfull humble Servant,

J. Pownall

15, 1763, and given a pension of £550 a year, but died the following July. His place was not given to John Byde, who had, however, been appointed cashier of the Salt Office on January 24, 1763, in place of Newcastle's friend, William Mitchell. See Add. MS. 32946, f. 228.

The nomination to the two seats at Corfe Castle was a working partnership between the families of Bankes and Bond who together had represented the borough for a century, the Bankes since 1660 and the Bonds since 1676. In 1761 the members were Henry Bankes and George Cholmondeley, Viscount Malpas. In November 1762 Henry Bankes, who was about to vacate his seat in order to become a Commissioner of Customs, put his interest at the disposal of Government, who recommended John Campbell of Calder for the seat.

HENRY BANKES TO CHARLES JENKINSON

Add. MS. 38200, f. 123.

Docketed " November 20, 1762 ".

Dear Sir,

I am this moment returned from my brother [1] out of Dorsetshire, having consulted him upon the business lately mentioned to me by Mr. C. ; [2] and with which I take it for granted, that you are not only acquainted, but that I am extreamly obliged to you therein. Untill I see you, I cannot conclude this affair to my own satisfaction, nor consistent with the regard in justice due to you from me. I am made to understand, this affair requires dispatch and secrecy, and therefore beg the favour to see you here at your own house immediately. I am just got out of my post chaise, and cannot wait upon you at Lord B. ; and besides, it would otherwise be very improper for me to do it now, in my present situation of affairs. I am Dear Sir

Your most obliged humble servant,

H. Bankes

Your own house. Noon. I am much disappointed in not seeing you ; and should have that pleasure as soon as possible ; and therefore beg that you would let me know at my house in Duke Street Westminster the moment you come home and I will immediately come to you.

It was customary at this time for the leader of the House of Commons to hold a meeting of the friends of Administration at the Cockpit on the night before the opening of the session. Members were summoned by

1. John Bankes of Kingston Hall, M.P. for Corfe Castle 1722–41. He died without issue in 1772, when the estates went to his brother Henry.
2. John Calcraft, the Army agent and Fox's friend, had an estate at Rempston, near Corfe Castle.

circular letters sent into the country some weeks before the opening, and by a second whip circulated in London by the Treasury on the day before the Cockpit meeting. See Professor Namier's essay on "Circular Letters", in *E.H.R.*, October 1929.

TOM RAMSDEN TO CHARLES JENKINSON

Add. MS. 38200, f. 121.

Swillington, November 20, 1762.
Saturday Night.

My dear Jenkinson,

I was this morning at Temple Newsam and found Mr. Ingram [1] at home. He intends to set out on Monday to be present at the ⟨open⟩ing of the Parliament ; and I find himself so perfectly well ⟨inclined⟩ to support the cause that we wish well to, and particularly ⟨   ⟩ [2] that I resolved to give you this hint that he may be ⟨summoned⟩ to the usual meeting the night before, as I conclude ⟨that custom ?⟩ will be observed. He intends to go directly to Lord Irwin's ⟨house⟩ in the Cloysters, Westminster, where the letter may be left. If you should have a moment to spare, I should be very glad to know the names of the Opposers (if any) the first day : as to what they may say, I care not, and I hope nobody else will.

Lord Rock⟨ingham⟩ is gone for London ; I find he was at Court the day after his resignation, and seemed much pleased with the notice that the K⟨ing⟩ took of him.[3] I have not seen him since I came into the country. How is opposition (which I suppose is to be the consequence of resignation) to be reconciled with that duty and respect which is due ? For it will be impossible in reality to separate the K⟨ing's⟩ actions from his ministers.

I know you have little time to spare, and therefore I do

1. Charles Ingram, junior, son of Colonel Charles Ingram and nephew of George, 8th Viscount Irwin of Horsham and Temple Newsam in Yorkshire, was M.P. for Horsham, their pocket borough, 1747–63, when he succeeded his uncle as 9th Viscount Irwin. The Ingrams had hitherto supported Newcastle, but left him at the crisis in December 1762, and in November 1763 Charles Ingram, then Viscount Irwin, asked Pitt to name a friend for the vacant seat at Horsham. *Chatham Corr.* ii, 266. See Albery, *Parliamentary History of Horsham* (1927). Ingram's sister, Isabella, married Colonel Frecheville Ramsden of Swillington, Tom Ramsden's brother, on March 17, 1761.

2. A portion of this letter is torn away here. The missing words presumably referred to peace preliminaries or foreign measures.

3. Rockingham resigned his lordship of the Bedchamber on November 3. According to Walpole and Albemarle, the King was haughty towards him when he came to resign. Walpole, *Memoirs*, i, 160 ; Albemarle, *Memoirs*, i, 143.

not expect much writing from you, my dear Jenkinson. You need not answer my ⟨last ?⟩ being satisfied : but should be glad to know whether Lords Lincoln and Ashburnham [1] ⟨have actua⟩lly resigned. Adieu.

Ever yours,

T. R.

P.S. Sunday morning. A thousand thanks for yours of the 13th, which sets me quite at ease and answers every thing I want to know. It came very safe and sound with an admirable direction. Adieu.

HENRY BANKES TO CHARLES JENKINSON

Add. MS. 38200, f. 125.

Duke Street, Westminster, Sunday night 11.
Docketed " November 21, 1762 ".

Dear Sir,

I am this instant favoured with your obliging and friendly letter ; and shall wait on my Lord, Tuesday morning at the appointed time. This morning I saw Mr. C⟨alcraft⟩ ; and told him in the very words of your letter, what my brother's answer was. But added, what is really and sincerely true, that the agreement and ingagement my brother and Mr. Bond's [2] family had entered into, and ever since strictly adhered to, was, that neither was at liberty absolutely to promise or give their interest to any other person, without the concurrence of the other party ; but, that my brother would upon all future occasions use his best endeavours with Mr. Bond, for his concurrence to the gentleman recommended by the King. This answer Mr. C. said he would to-morrow morning report to Mr. Fox. I am dear Sir,

Your most obliged humble servant,

H. Bankes

1. Lords Lincoln and Ashburnham reluctantly resigned their places of Lord of the Bedchamber and Ranger of St. James's Park respectively on November 19. See Namier, *England etc.* p. 444.

2. John Bond of Grange, nephew and heir of Denis Bond, M.P. for Corfe Castle 1722–27, and son of John Bond, M.P. for Corfe Castle 1727–44. John Bond junior was M.P. for Corfe 1747–80. He died in 1784.

Add. MS. 38200, ff. 127-30.

Newnham, November 21, 1762.

Dear Sir,

To morrow I intend to write to the Duke of Marlborough about Bray who has a very good claim to his Grace's favour.[1] It may be of advantage to get him appointed one of the Kings Chaplains, but unless his Grace will do more for him, that empty honor, will do him very little service. In the late Kings time it was a necessary step towards preferment, but of late it has not been so.[2] To Mr. Lloyd [3] I don't think a Chaplainship would be of much consequence, as he has so near a prospect of being provided for. No man would be readier to serve Mr. Lloyd than I should be, whenever it may be in my power, for no man can entertain a higher opinion of him.

I am glad to hear that Lord Egmont [4] has got the Post Office. I know very little of his Lordship. He may be a serviceable man in the House of Lords, if that place should become the scene of busyness. But I cannot conceive how it should unless Lord Hardwicke and Lord Mansfield should carry their complaisance to the Duke of Newcastle so far as to oppose. But I should not suspect either of them of carrying their complaisance so far, or more properly speaking, of being guilty of so much imprudence. I am vastly pleased to hear

1. Cf. p. 74. The claim may have been for services in the election of Lord Charles Spencer for Oxfordshire in 1761.

2. This seems to have been a tradition at least as early as 1700 and George II looked on the royal prebends as the particular province of his chaplains. See Norman Sykes, *Church and State in England in the Eighteenth Century*, pp. 151, 155. The King's chaplains had no salary but were exempted from the act restricting plurality of benefices, and under George II constituted a waiting list for preferment. In 1760 George III created over twenty new ones, but both Bray and Philip Lloyd received higher preferment without first being appointed chaplains.

3. Philip Lloyd (1729–90), son of Philip Lloyd of Greenwich and brother of Charles Lloyd, Grenville's private secretary, was a friend of Jenkinson from their student days, having graduated B.A. at Christ Church, Oxford, in 1750, D.D. in 1763. He was tutor to Grenville's sons and a hack writer for Grenville. The provision expected for him in November 1762 was a prebend of Westminster which Grenville obtained for him in April 1763, and which had evidently been promised since October 1761. See *Grenv. Pps.* ii, 213. Lloyd kept the prebend until February 1765, when he was presented by Lord Huntington to the living of Peddleton in Dorset and at the same time became Dean of Norwich.

4. John Perceval, 2nd Earl of Egmont (Irish) (1711–70), M.P. for Bridgwater till May 1762, when he was raised to the English Peerage as Baron Lovel and Holland. He became Joint Postmaster-General on November 27, 1762, two days after he had moved the Address in the House of Lords at the opening of the session.

that Lord Strange [1] is to be Chancellor of the Dutchy, for he is the properest man in England for that employment. His Parliamentary credit stands very high, the world entertains a good opinion of his integrity, and the Whigs in general will be pleased. His employment will give him great credit in the Northern Parts, and will prevent or at least put a check to any ill impressions that other people may endeavour to make in those parts.

I know very little of Mr. Byde's brother [2] for the affair I mentioned took its rise from an accident; Colonel Evelyn [3] while he was last here, was talking of a proposal that had been made to Sir John by a Mr. Goodscall [4] of Surrey, who by Lord Bingley's,[5] or more properly, by Lord Chancellor's means had hopes of getting leave for Sir John to resign to him. After some letters had passed about it, the Chancellor declined giving his assistance, and the thing dropped of course. As I knew that Lord Bath had been asking a favour for Mr. Byde, and had recommended him to Lord Bute, it occurred to me that a fairer opportunity or an easier method could never offer of assisting Mr. Byde, of paying his brother a compliment and of indulging an old Servant of the Crown, by allowing Sir John Evelyn to resign to Mr. Byde.

I knew very little of Mr. Byde,[6] his son was recommended to me by Colonel Evelyn, and I appointed him one of his Majesty's Pages, more with a view of paying a compliment to his uncle, than from any other consideration. I have cultivated an acquaintance with Mr. Byde [7] because he is a worthy man, and because I wished to see him act with Lord Bute. There was something so singularly honourable in the manner of his election, that I thought him worth attending to. I brought him to Lord Bute's Levée, the only one he was ever at without being absolutely listed on any side. His general principle seems to be the support of the Crown, and as far as I can judge he is well disposed towards Lord Bute. His brother was settled at Lisbon, and was a considerable sufferer by the calamity that ruined so many of the British merchants.

1. James Stanley, eldest son of Edward, 11th Earl of Derby, usually called Lord Strange, though that title, which was a barony in fee, had in fact descended to the Duke of Atholl as heir-general of James, 7th Earl of Derby. Lord Strange was M.P. for Lancashire 1741–71, and Chancellor of the Duchy 1762–71. He died in 1771 in his father's lifetime.
2. See p. 87.   3. See p. 80 and n. 2.
4. William Godscall of Albury, Surrey.
5. George Fox Lane, created Lord Bingley of Bingley in Yorkshire May 4, 1762.
6. John Byde.   7. T. P. Byde. See p. 87 and n. 4.

After the earthquake he returned to England, and now lives upon a fortune of five or six hundred a year that an uncle left to him. He is also in the South Sea Direction, which circumstance I mention to shew that he is at least in some estimation among men of busyness, and I suppose he is very capable of the employment. In point of birth [1] he is certainly superior to several who sit at the Custom house board. When I get to town I shall make further enquiries about him.

Before I finish my letter I must throw out a thing that may be of service, if attended to in time. As soon as the Preliminaries are ratified I suppose the first care will be to get the troops home. The charge of bringing them home will be great, but the expense may in some degree be lessened by care and attention. For instance instead of bringing Burgoyn's horses from Portugal, why should not the men have leave to dispose of their horses there. If the regiment is to be reduced I am sure it will be a saving in that article only of five or six thousand pounds, and perhaps more, for the hire and victualling of transports to carry between six and seven hundred horse, must amount to a large sum. Was the regiment even to be kept up, I am very clear in my own opinion, that it might be remounted for less money than the expense of bringing them home. When a regiment is reduced, I apprehend that the men are entitled to the horses, or to a certain sum of money. All which purposes would be answered by what I have proposed, and the dismounted Dragoons might be brought over directly as easily and as cheaply as a Regiment of Foot, without waiting whole months for horse transports. What I have said with regard to Portugal will in a great degree hold good with regard to the German Army. If the three Regiments of Horse and ten of Dragoons are to be embarked at Bremen-See you won't get them home in six months, because they will require such a number of transports, but if an order was sent for an exact return to be made of such horses only as are in their prime, and really worth bringing home, I am convinced that a very great saving to the publick might be made, if the old and blemished horses were ordered to be disposed of. It would make such a difference, that perhaps two thirds of the transports might be sufficient for that service. The Artillery horses I apprehend are furnished abroad by contract, therefore no saving can be made upon

1. The words *rank and* are written before *birth*, but appear to have been crossed out.

(94)

that article ; but it might be recommended to all the foot officers to bring home as few as possible, or it might be worth while to allow them half as much as the charge of bringing home their horses, and to oblige them to dispose of them abroad. As I consider the Captains and Subalterns of Foot, as the sinews of the Army, it might be a little hard to oblige them to part with their horses abroad, without some consideration. When I see you in town I will explain what I mean more fully. I shall be in town on Wednesday. I bring the Tormentor [1] up with me, and shall dine with her father in Stratton Street, and attend Lord Bute in the evening.

Yours Dear Sir most sincerely,

Harcourt

LORD HARCOURT TO CHARLES JENKINSON

Add. MS. 38200, ff. 135-6.

Sunday morning near 9 o'clock.

Docketed " November 28, 1762 ".

Dear Sir,

Lord Chedworth [2] is come to town, but I have not yet been so fortunate as to meet him. I shall endeavour to see him after Court, and hope to find him very well disposed. He has a very great estate, with a very small income. His estate is upwards of 9000£ per Annum, but out of it he pays 4800£ Penny Rent in jointures to his mother and brothers widow. These incumbrances together with sums, which his affection and good nature have engaged him to pay for his brother, leave his Lordship so streightened in point of circumstances, that I am persuaded some *Bienfait de la Cour* might be very acceptable. As I have no authority to give the most distant hint to his Lordship, that some favour might possibly be obtained from the Crown, I desire you would endeavour to lay this letter before Lord Bute to know his sentiments as soon as possible, and I will follow his directions in this and in every thing else, that may be for the service of his Majesty, or for his Lordships credit.

The narrowness of Lord Chedworths circumstances have

1. His wife ? See p. 17.
2. Henry Frederick Howe, 3rd Baron Chedworth, succeeded his brother May 9, 1762. His estates were Stowell and Compton in Gloucestershire and Wishford in Wiltshire ; they must have swallowed up his sister-in-law's jointure, for the 2nd Baron Chedworth married the daughter and co-heir of Sir Philip Parker-a-Morley-Long, possessed of a fortune of £40,000. She died in 1775.

hitherto kept him more out of the world than he desired to be ; and a hesitation to his speech makes him appear to a disadvantage. He is by no means deficient in point of abilities, and I have great reason to believe he is a man of honor. His estate gives him great interest in Glocestershire, and I think he is likely enough to improve it.

Yours, dear Sir, most sincerely,

Harcourt

SHUTE BARRINGTON TO CHARLES JENKINSON

Add. MS. 38458, f. 10.

Christ Church, November 30, 1762.

Dear Sir !

The intelligence of Mr. Palmer's [1] death has this instant reached me ; the vacancy occasioned by it I could wish to see supplied by a whig of character, moderation, and attachment to a Minister, whom not less from inclination than gratitude, I respect, and whose interests I am solicitous to promote. Such a person as I have described does not at present occur to me ; and if he did, he must possess a farther requisite of not being obnoxious to the tories. The Chancellor [2] must be immediately gained for fear of applications, with which he may comply, from other quarters. I need not suggest to you the necessity of dispatch in the nomination of the candidate. You are sufficiently acquainted with the temper of the place to give advice, and Lloyd [3] has ample materials to furnish you with. Our Dean [4] who is in Abingdon buildings in Westminster should be easily consulted. I am compelled to write in haste, but you will believe me with real regard and esteem

Your most sincere and faithful servant,

S. Barrington

THOMAS BRAY TO CHARLES JENKINSON

Add. MS. 38458, f. 12.

Exeter College, November 30, 1762.

Dear Sir,

You will hear by the time this can reach you that Mr. Palmer our University representative is dead. There are

---

1. Peregrine Palmer, of Fairfield, Somerset, M.P. for Oxford University 1741–62.   2. Lord Lichfield.   3. Philip Lloyd ?
4. David Gregory, about whom see p. 48 and n. 3.

letters here giving an unquestionable account that he died last Saturday.[1] I represented to you the importance of conducting this particular election well. It will be proper to consult with our Chancellor about a candidate. When any person is fixt upon, or you have any thing to communicate on that subject, your favouring me with a line will be a sincere pleasure to

Your affectionate friend and obedient servant,

Thomas Bray

SHUTE BARRINGTON TO CHARLES JENKINSON

Add. MS. 38458, f. 14.

Friday, December 3, 1762.

Dear Sir !

An express was dispatched to Sir W. Bagot[2] from hence during the course of the week charged with an offer from the Tory heads of support ; what reply he has sent I know not : but I differ in my opinion from the Chancellor as I conceive he will never decline a proposal which may be productive ultimately of such advantage to his son now at Venice.[3] If Lord Beauchamp[4] had been of age I think he would have succeeded ; and the character of Sir James Macdonald[5] is such that were he of more consequence, and born on this side of the Tweed he might probably have been elected. If the Staffordshire Baronet becomes the candidate, he will set out with such advantage from starting early, that it will be next to impossible to prevent his being chosen. I most heartily congratulate you on your victory,[6] and though I collect from

1. According to *Gent. Mag.* (1762, p. 600), he died on Tuesday November 30.
2. Sir Walter Wagstaff Bagot, 5th Bart. of Blithfield, Staffordshire ; M.P. for Newcastle-under-Lyme 1724-27, Staffordshire 1727-54, and Oxford University December 1762 to his death in January 1768. He was a member of Magdalen College and matriculated in 1720 ; D.C.L. by diploma July 1754.
3. Richard Bagot, one of Sir Walter Bagot's five sons, was Secretary to the Embassy to the Republic of Venice from 1760 to 1764. In the Civil List accounts of 1762-63, £1030 are entered to him. In January 1765 he was appointed a Commissioner of Excise.
4. Francis Seymour Conway, eldest son of the 1st Earl of Hertford, was born in 1743. He was returned to the Irish Parliament for Lisburn in 1761 ; M.P. for Lostwithiel 1766-68, and for Orford 1768-94, when he succeeded to the peerage.
5. Sir James Macdonald, 8th Bart. of Sleat in the Isle of Skye. Horace Walpole wrote of him : " He is a particular friend of Lord Beauchamp, and a very extraordinary young man for variety of learning. He is rather too wise for his age and too fond of showing it, but when he has seen more of the world he will choose to know less." He died at Rome in 1766, aged twenty-four.
6. On Wednesday December 1, the Opposition moved to defer considering the Preliminaries for a fortnight as Pitt was unable to attend, but Administration defeated the motion by 213 to 74. See Walpole, *Memoirs*, i, 175.

the numbers that the whole of either strength was not exerted, yet I hope that whenever it is it will be in the same proportion. I am, Dear Sir, with unfeigned regard and esteem

Your most sincere and faithful servant,

S. Barrington

TOM RAMSDEN TO CHARLES JENKINSON

Add. MS. 38200, ff. 143-4.

Pontefract, December 4, 1762.

I take the first opportunity, My Dear Jenkinson, to thank ⟨you⟩ for your letter of the 30th November. I am truely concerned at ⟨what⟩ you say of your own health in the present great hurry, ⟨which m⟩ust affect you the more, knowing how anxious you are at present. Pray take care of yourself, as much as you ⟨ca⟩n. I thank you for the printed paper, which I have ⟨received. It⟩ is wonderful to me, how so good a peace could have ⟨been m⟩ade, in our present weak condition, wherein both the ⟨sine⟩ws of war are very much wanted, money and men. It can not surely be found the least fault with : even the King of ⟨Prussi⟩a, however unreasonable he may be, cannot but be satisfied, having left him only one enemy to fight, and having supported him when he had three of the great Powers together to engage ; but I hope he will make peace in the course of the winter.

What you tell me of Sir James Lowther's behaviour to my Lord Bute, gives me the greatest pleasure. I assure you, that I would most willingly undertake to attempt the reconciliation of the two brothers,[1] ⟨and⟩ had resolved to use my endeavours, as soon as I got to ⟨tow⟩n, for that purpose. And what you tell me of Lady Bute's wish will not make me less desirous to bring it about. But by a letter received the last post, I understand, that the two brothers have met at Mrs. Bab Lowther's [2] house, when Sir James had behaved so

1. See p. 119. These letters from Ramsden contain all the information in the Liverpool Papers about the quarrel between Sir James and his brother. Robert Lowther (1741–77) is a dim figure and does not seem to have taken much interest in his brother's political schemes. He sat for Westmorland from June 14, 1759, to the dissolution, and again from March to December 1763 (see p. 122 n. 2). These were his only excursions into politics.

2. Barbara Lowther, second daughter of Governor Robert Lowther and sister of Sir James.

well, and had as ⟨　⟩ the next day at Mr. Lowther's lodgings, That I fla⟨tter myself⟩ that every thing is settled and
done, and are made friends I shall therefore be glad to hear
from you, that it is so. ⟨Tell⟩ me (if you can) whether Sir
James intends to return into ⟨Cumberland ?⟩ to fetch Lady
Mary, and when ; or whether he will come to London ? I
was very glad, she had Lady Darlington [1] with her.

I feel your concern for the duel you mention ; your good
nature is too sensible ; for the case is very distant from you.
Whether the man deserves to die or not, I don't know, but I
am very sure he deserves to suffer a great deal. I remember
to have seen some account of the affair in the papers, without
naming the parties.[2]

I wrote to you the last post on Thursday.[3] Pray don't let
the contents give you any trouble, for the affair, I fancy, does
not press for immediate dispatch.

I have been told here, that my Lord Mayor was very
violent the first ⟨day⟩ in his speech, abusing the Preliminaries
most grossly.[4] I hope it is not true. My brother the Colonel
sends his best wishes, and I am

Most truely yours,
Thomas Ramsden

I am very glad the family in Upper Grosvenor Street [5]
are out of town ⟨for⟩ I cannot but suspect, that the head of
that house has not done ⟨her⟩ duty to reconcile, but has rather
blown the coals ; her pride and ⟨love of⟩ governing being
disappointed by the Knight, she has secured the ⟨　⟩
by any means.

1. Margaret, another sister of Sir James Lowther, married Henry Vane, 3rd
Earl of Darlington, in 1757.
2. According to *Gent. Mag.* (1762, p. 500), a duel was fought on October 5
" between a noble lord and a Member of Parliament ", when neither was killed
and the commoner had the advantage.
3. Ramsden wrote to Jenkinson on December 2 recommending Lieutenant
William Smith of the *Shannon* for a guardship at Portsmouth. " He has been a
lieutenant some years and about 30 in the navy " (Add. MS. 38200, f. 141).
4. William Beckford, M.P. for the City, was Lord Mayor of London 1762-63.
In the first debate on Preliminaries on November 25 he compared Florida for
barrenness to Bagshot Heath. Cf. Walpole, *Memoirs*, i, 174.
5. Mrs. Bab Lowther's ?

SHUTE BARRINGTON TO CHARLES JENKINSON
in South Street, Grosvenor Square
Add. MS. 38458, f. 16.

Christ Church, December 5, 1762.

Dear Sir !

The messenger dispatched by the heads of houses to Sir Walter Bagot with offers of assistance returned last night with intelligence of his acceptance. I am glad that government is not interested in the success of any other candidate ; a *Staffordshire baronet* on such ground and with such advantages must be invincible. I am, Dear Sir, with real regard and esteem

Your most sincere and faithful servant,

S. Barrington

I wish you as complete a victory on Thursday as you gained on Wednesday.[1]

THOMAS BRAY TO CHARLES JENKINSON
Add. MS. 38458, ff. 20-21.

Exeter College, December 6, 1762.

Dear Sir,

Having been absent yesterday I am a day behind others in intelligence. Last Saturday night,[2] (two days later than expected) returned the President of Magdalen's express from Sir Walter Baggot, who accepts the overture of representing the University. I apprehend that the general inclination to avoid a contest at this time, will induce such a majority to acquiesce in Sir Walter as will make any other scheme impracticable. Should things take a different turn, you shall hear from me.

I must now apply to you upon my own account. Just before Lord Harcourt went to London I put his Lordship in mind of a request I had formerly made, that Lord Newnham would second Lord Parker [3] in moving the House for me to

---

1. See p. 97 n. 6. The Preliminaries were to come before both Houses on Thursday, December 9.
2. December 4.
3. Thomas, Viscount Parker, eldest son of the Earl of Macclesfield, M.P. for Newcastle-under-Lyme 1747-54, Oxfordshire 1754, when he was returned on the

preach the 30th of January Sermon.[1] Lord Harcourt told me in a few words, that Lord Newnham did not open his mouth in the House, and that he would speak to you to second Lord Parker, which I presume his Lordship has done. I now desire that favour of you. Last night Lord Parker did me the honour to acquaint me by letter, that the Speaker remembered his promise of appointing me to preach the next turn, and that his Lordship would move the House. I shall by this post acquaint Lord Parker with my request to you, and hope you will take an opportunity to speak to my Lord on the subject within a few days. I should be glad to know your opinion about Sir Walter Baggot. I am

Your affectionate and obedient servant,

Thomas Bray

DAVID GREGORY TO CHARLES JENKINSON

Add. MS. 38458, f. 18.

David Gregory (died 1767) was Regius Professor of Modern History at Oxford 1724–36, a Canon of Christ Church 1736–56, and Dean of Christ Church 1756–67.

Christ Church, December 6, 1762.

Dear Sir,

I rejoice with the friends to the University that Sir Walter Bagot is so far from declining at this critical time the offer it has made him of electing him its representative, that he has sent word, he with great thanks accepts the honour intended him. This was communicated to me in form this day from Magdalen College, of which Sir Walter was formerly a very responsible member. We have thus very luckily escaped a contest, which probably might have occasioned great heats and animosities among the younger part of the University, who are made of very combustible stuff.

I have the honour to be with great regard, dear Sir,

Your most obedient and most humble servant,

D. Gregory

vote of the House of Commons, to 1761, Rochester 1761, to March 26, 1764, when he succeeded his father as 2nd Earl. He was one of Jenkinson's earliest connexions.

1. The annual sermon in commemoration of the execution of Charles I preached to members of the House of Commons in St. Margaret's, Westminster. On December 15 the House of Commons ordered Bray to preach this sermon on Monday, January 31, " and that the Lord Parker and Mr. Jenkinson do acquaint him therewith ". *Commons Journals.*

JOHN BANKES TO CHARLES JENKINSON
at his house in South Street in the new buildings
Add. MS. 38458, f. 22.

Corfe Castle, December 8, 1762.

Dear Sir,

The necessary hurry of the election for this borough, on 6th instant, obliged me to defer my letters to you, and Mr. Campbell,[1] till this post. But that the earliest notice thereof might reach London, my sincere friend and trusty nephew Mr. Thomas Bankes J'anson, (eldest son of Sir Thomas J'anson and my sister, of New Bounds near Tunbridge in Kent, an old friend and acquaintance of yours at University College in Oxford [2]) found time to inform my brother of our success, and desired him to acquaint you and Mr. Campbell therewith, as I doubt not he did, on the receipt of his letter. I have now the pleasure to inform you, that I arrived here Saturday 4th, and by the conversations that I had with several of my principal friends, before we proceeded to the Election, found them all to a man so inclinable to accept of the gentleman whom I should recommend, that we were unanimous in our choice of John Campbell of Calder, Esq. for our representative in this present Parliament, in the room of my brother. As he was a stranger to the electors, it was necessary for me to account for his nonattendance, and to apprise them of his good character, qualifications, estate, and employments, wherein I endeavoured to do him no more justice than I thought he deserved, knowing it to be unnecessary. Herein, and also in the choice of Mr. Campbell, I was very sincerely seconded and assisted by my good and faithfull friend John Bond Esq, the late Member for this borough. I know not why, nor by what means it happened, that for some time past it has been reported by certain people here, that there was going to be a new Election, and that a stranger was to be chosen. They soon took the alarm, and formed themselves into parties against the stranger ; but by the circumspection and prudent conduct of

1. John Campbell of Calder was returned for Corfe Castle on December 6, 1762. He was M.P. for Corfe Castle 1762–68 and had previously sat for Pembroke, Nairnshire, and Inverness Burghs, 1734–61.
2. Mary, daughter of John Bankes of Kingston Hall and sister of John and Henry Bankes, married Sir Thomas I'Anson, 4th Bart., in 1724. T. B. I'Anson succeeded his father as 5th Bart. in June 1764. He graduated B.C.L. (University College) in 1748 and was Rector of Corfe Castle 1748–99.

my nephew J'anson, who frequently entertained them at his house, they were reduced to a better way of thinking, and readily concurred in the person whom I recommended to them. As I presented him to the Rectory of Corfe Castle fourteen years ago, and he lives in great esteem with his parishioners, I have always found him very usefull, and fit to be trusted in all my concerns here ; for he has always executed them faithfully and in the most judicious manner. He desires me to assure you of his best respects, and readiness to serve you at all times either in Dorsetshire or elsewhere. Having used my utmost endeavours for the credit and benefit of Mr. Campbell, and almost completed the payment of all his election expences, agreably to the directions which he has given, and reduced them to a very moderate sum, I propose to return home to Kingston Hall near Winburne in Dorsetshire this afternoon, where I shall be proud to receive you whenever anything leads you that way, and in the mean time any commands that you may have for me. I am truly sensible of the late favours to a friend of mine, for which you will be pleased to accept my best thanks, which I shall likewise return to one of your's in a few days ; and am with the great sincerity, dear Sir,

Your ever affectionate kinsman and most obedient servant,

John Bankes

JOSEPH BETTS TO CHARLES JENKINSON

Add. MS. 38200, f. 147.

December 8, 1762.

Dear Sir,

In a letter written by Dr. Vansittart [1] to me by the last post, there is the following paragraph. " I called by accident at Lord Litchfield's to day, from whom I learned that the Election you have such chance of gaining is to be brought on very soon : [2] his Lordship seemed much desirous of your success : he wishes to convince the rest of the electors of your superior qualifications of which himself is persuaded : he would be pleased to produce some *testimonium* to show his approbation not to be the effect of private friendship or partiality."

1. Robert Vansittart, Fellow of All Souls College, Regius Professor of Civil Law 1767–89 ; Barrister-at-Law in the Inner Temple and Recorder of Windsor.
2. See pp. 43, 63.

You may remember my good Sir, that in my last letter I informed you, Lord Macclesfield would not recommend any one for the Professorship, having served Mr. Bliss so lately, but that I had reason to believe he would be ready to give his opinion of the candidates, were he applyed to ; and if I don't forget you said he should be applyed to. Mr. Bliss to my knowledge has spoken of me very respectfully to his Lordship, and you see of what consequence his Lordship's testimony may be of to me, and I am sensible you are well enough known to his Lordship to obtain it. I must beg of you therefore to wait on him, and to signify to my good Lord Litchfield what he shall please to say of me. I am with hearty thanks for all favours,

Your obliged humble servant,

Jo. Betts

P.S. The Vice Chancellor will write to Lord Litchfield.

TOM RAMSDEN TO CHARLES JENKINSON

Add. MS. 38200, f. 152.

Pontefract, Monday, December 13, 1762.

I cannot, my dear Jenkinson, defer till to morrow ⟨   ⟩ of a letter from [sic] you this night, congratulating you on ⟨the su⟩ccess and victory obtained on Thursday. The Colonel[1] ⟨arrived (?) last⟩ night, with an account of the Numbers on the Division.[2] ⟨   ⟩ Pitt spoke for 3½ hours. Surely never man ⟨   ⟩ disgrace, than after talking so long, to find ⟨the minority dimin⟩ished since the former division : What ⟨   ⟩sh resigners do now ? What a s— figure ⟨they⟩ must make. I assure you this news gave us here ⟨the⟩ most sincere joy and satisfaction. Charles Townshend[3] is said to have been one of the Majority. He is an unaccountable man

---

1. F. Ramsden.

2. For lists of the Minority on December 9 and 10 see Add. MSS. 33035, ff. 50-51 ; 33000, ff. 232-5 ; 32946, ff. 273-7 ; 33002, ff. 476-8 ; and also Wilkie's list published in *History of the late Minority* (1766), pp. 85-8, and *Parl. Hist.* xv, 1272–74. For an analysis of the divisions see Namier's *England etc.* pp. 461-6.

3. Charles Townshend was expected to vote with the Minority, but lost faith in them and joined the Majority when Pitt declared his independence, and left the House without voting. See Lady Temple to her husband, December 17, *Grenv. Pps.* ii, 22 ; and Walpole, *Memoirs*, i, 183.

⟨   ⟩ Poor Offley.[1] I see the two Potts [2] are broke : not for their being sound, I believe. The Newcastle coals seem to have lost their caking quality ; they are run to dust.

Thank you for your last letter, and am much obliged to you for your intention of speaking for Smith.[3] I have not been out of this house since Saturday sennight. The gout seized my foot, and has kept me a prisoner. It is on the retreat, and I *hope* to get out one day this week. Adieu.

Most truely yours.

SHUTE BARRINGTON TO CHARLES JENKINSON

Add. MS. 38458, f. 23.

Christ Church, December 16, 1762.

Dear Sir !

Sir Walter Bagot was elected this morning without opposi-tion. As I conclude that he will continue to act with the Tories whose principles he adopted early, I congratulate you on having gained an additional vote ; which though not necessary, will yet render future victories more complete. His private character is unexceptionable but I confess I cannot but lament the hard fate of this university ; which is doomed to be represented by men incapable of protecting its honour if it should ever be attacked. If you should chance to hear that the only copy of verse in our Collection [4] addressed to Lord B. has been rejected ; do not conceive that it arose from any dislike to him ; but from a contrary motive of re-spect, and good opinion. I will explain this hint when I see you. I am, Dear Sir, with real regard and esteem,

Your most sincere and faithful servant,

S. Barrington

The following letter refers to the petition of Samuel Touchet to the Treasury for an exclusive grant to trade on the river Senegal. Samuel Touchet, M.P. for Shaftesbury 1761–68, merchant, financier, and Govern-

1. John Offley, M.P. for Orford 1754–68, remained faithful to Newcastle, for whom he resigned his place of Groom of the Bedchamber and lost a Secret Service pension of £400 a year. See *Structure of Politics*, pp. 272-3 ; *England etc.* p. 429 n. 2.

2. Henry Potts, Secretary to the General Post Office, and Samuel Potts, Comptroller of the Inland Office at the G.P.O. They were restored to their places by the Rockingham Government in July 1765. See p. 379 and n. 1.

3. See p. 99 n. 3.

4. Oxford verses on the Peace. One of them is printed in *Gent. Mag.* xxxiii, 40.

ment contractor, came from a Manchester firm of cotton manufacturers, and during the 'fifties was the leading Lancashire merchant in London.[1] In 1756 he joined Thomas Cumming, a merchant alleged to have been employed in Africa by an English company in the African gum trade, in a scheme for the capture of Senegal, then a French trading centre exporting slaves and gum Senegal used in linen and calico printing. In return for fitting out an expedition and using his boasted influence with the native chiefs, Cumming asked the British Government, in the event of success, for a monopoly of the trade to Senegal, and actually secured a letter from Pitt dated February 9, 1757, promising his interest " in obtaining an exclusive charter in your favour for a limited term of years with regard to that vein of trade, which your industry and risque shall have opened to your country ".[2] In fact it was Touchet who fitted out five ships at a cost of " upwards of six thousand pounds " [3] for which Cumming mortgaged to him a half share in the promised charter.[4] The expedition was successful. Fort Senegal capitulated on May 1, 1758, and Cumming was received by Pitt on his return " with the utmost demonstrations of joy and congratulations on the success ", but as the granting a monopoly proved exceedingly unpopular and was found to be incompatible with the African Company's charter, he was given a pension instead. As secrecy had been considered vital to the success of the expedition, Touchet failed to apply, " in the manner prescribed in the prize-act, for a grant of his expected conquest ", and therefore received no compensation beyond his share of the prize money. Meanwhile he suffered heavily during the crisis of 1761 and temporarily stopped payments.[5] On recovering in 1762 he once more pressed his claims on Government. On July 23 Lord Egremont forwarded his petition to the Board of Trade for comment,[6] and in December it was known that Touchet meant to bring his case into the House of Commons. The old feeling against monopolies was again aroused. Touchet's scheme affected the cotton manufacturers, whose case was put in a vigorous pamphlet from " a merchant in London " : [7] gum Senegal, wrote the merchant, was used in printing linens and calicoes, " a trade in which we are yet unrivalled by our neighbours "; to increase the price of gum by granting a monopoly would raise the price of printed textiles and drive foreign importers to manufacture their own. In fact, English manufacturers would rather see the gum trade in the hands of the French Senegal Company than in those of a British monopolist. The economic argument was reinforced by a personal one. Touchet, wrote the pamphleteer, had done no more than any other contractor in supplying the sinews of war and might consider himself amply rewarded by his Government contracts. The proposed monopoly touched the shippers as well as the manufacturers, and in fact all the merchants of the west coast ports concerned in the African trade joined in petitioning against it.

1. See *The Cotton Trade and Industrial Lancashire*, by A. P. Wadsworth and Julia de Lacy Mann (1931), p. 241 and *passim*.
2. See Touchet's petition to Parliament printed in *A Letter to a Merchant in Bristol from a Merchant in London*, 1762.
3. *Ibid*. Wadsworth and Mann say £10,223. *Op. cit*. p. 246.
4. This was probably Touchet's third attempt to secure a monopoly. See *ibid*. pp. 244-6.   5. See *Structure of Politics*, p. 211.
6. P.R.O., Board of Trade Entry Books, C.O. 389/31, f. 181, and see *Board of Trade Journals 1759-63* (1935), p. 291.
7. *A Letter to a Merchant in Bristol etc.*, 1762.

THE MERCHANTS OF WHITEHAVEN TO CHARLES JENKINSON

Add. MS. 38200, f. 161.

Whitehaven, December 23, 1762.

Having been certainly informed that Mr. Samuel Touchet intends to move for an exclusive Grant or Charter to monopolize to himself for a certain time the whole trade of the River Senegal we have petitioned the Lords of Trade that they would oppose this unreasonable attempt. An attempt so contrary to the laws now in being, so injurious to the free and open trade now carried on to the coast of Africa and so prejudicial to the trading interest of Great Britain you may be assured is very alarming to us. Therefore we humbly desire that you would use your best endeavours to overthrow so distructive a scheme.

We have also (in conjunction with our neighbouring ports) petitioned the Earl of Egremont that the Island of Granada now ceded to England, may under proper restrictions and regulations, be made a free port — a proposal in our opinion so highly advantageous to the general and commercial interest of these Kingdoms — that we cannot foresee any objections that can reasonably be offered against it.

We therefore once more earnestly request that you will to the utmost of your power and interest, promote a work of such great and general utility which will be the greatest obligation to, Sir,

Your most obliged and most humble servants,

	Peter How [1]
Edwd. Fletcher	John Senhouse
Wm. Fletcher	Rob. Watters
Isaac Stephenson	Wm. Hicks
Isaac Kelscity	John Coupland
Glb. Griffith	John Wilkinson [1]
Joseph White	Jam: Martin
John Hartley	Heny. Ellison
John Dixon	John Younger [1]
Wm. Gilpin	John Ponsonby
	Edwd. Fletcher
	Thom. Lutwidge

1. See pp. 277-8 for the case of How, Younger, and Wilkinson.

Touchet's claim was turned down by the House of Commons in March 1764, and Senegal was invested in the African Company. Meanwhile in October 1763 Touchet once more went bankrupt, this time finally. See Wadsworth and Mann, *op. cit.* p. 247.

On the death of Sir Wilfrid Lawson, M.P. for Cumberland, on December 1, 1762, Sir James Lowther vacated his seat for Westmorland, to stand for Cumberland.

CHARLES JENKINSON TO SIR JAMES LOWTHER

Add. MS. 38458, ff. 25-8.

London, December 27, 1762.

Dear Sir James,

Your express arrived yesterday a quarter before three in the afternoon. I immediately set to work to get you appointed to the Stewardship of the Chiltern Hundreds. Unfortunately Sir Francis Dashwood, who must sign the instrument was out of town ; I found out however a clerk that could prepare it, and I sent it down by a messenger to Sir Francis, who properly executed it about twelve last night, and I have the honour to transmit it to you herewith inclosed. I approve of the resolution you have come to, as I think it, indeed, the only step you had to take. The only danger you have now to encounter, is an opposition in Westmoreland, and what gives the more reason to apprehend this, is, the great distance of time before the election can come on.[1] You act very nobly in again forgiving your brother [2] and shewing your affection to him by making him an offer to choose him for Westmoreland ; I suppose if he would stand, no one would pretend to oppose him, but from his former conduct I cannot suppose that he will act so wise a part ; and that being the case, you certainly act wisely in taking Mr. Robinson in his stead ; one, whose excellent character is so well known, as he is, in the county, must go down better than any one else, who is not immediately of your own family. But there is one thing you should look forward to, which is a new election for West-

1. Owing to the adjournment of the House of Commons from December 21 to January 20, the Westmorland election did not come on till February, when Robert Lowther was elected in place of his brother. He sat for Westmorland from March to December 1763, when he accepted the Stewardship of the Chiltern Hundreds and his seat was given to John Robinson.
2. See p. 98.

moreland, in case of Mr. Upton's death [1] which does not appear to be very distant ; I fear you would be very much distressed to find a person to supply his place. Lord Bute directs me to present his affectionate compliments to you ; he is extremely sensible of your kind attention to his interests, and is happy, I am sure, on every occasion to give you proofs of his very great regard for you. I send enclosed two letters for Lady Mary. Lady Jane,[2] who was once very much out of order, is now quite recovered.

With respect to publick affairs I think our enemies are totally at present discomfitted ; the firmness of the King, and the executions that have been made, have thrown them into the greatest alarm, and unless the Yorkes will take a part, and the Attorney General [3] puts himself at the head of the Opposition, I should question, whether they will long remain in a body together. The Duke of Newcastle is turned out of all his Lieutenancies ; Lord Northumberland succeeds to him in Middlesex, the Duke of Kingstone [sic] in Nottingham, and Sherwood Forest ; and Lord Egremont in Sussex. Lord Holdernesse succeeds Lord Rockingham, as Custos Rotulorum of the North Riding of Yorkshire, and Admiral of the Coast, and Lord Huntindon succeeds him as Lord Lieutenant and Custos of the West Riding of Yorkshire. The Duke of Devonshire continues in his Lieutenancy.[4]

By the last account we have from Lord Granby,[5] there appear but little hopes of his recovery. This will make a great change in the political world ; for as the Duke of Rutland cannot long survive his son, the family of Manners will be lost to the world, till Lord Rous [6] comes of age.

My best respects attend Lady Mary, and I have the honour to be with the greatest truth and the most sincere regard, dear Sir,

Your faithfull humble servant,
C. Jenkinson

1. John Upton junior of Middleton, M.P. for Westmorland 1761–68. He did not die as Jenkinson expected, and retained his seat till the dissolution of Parliament. He contested it at the next election, but was defeated, although supported by the Lowther interest.
2. Lady Jane Stuart, Bute's second daughter. In February 1768 she married Sir George Macartney, afterwards 1st Baron Macartney.
3. Charles Yorke.
4. Of Derbyshire.
5. Granby fell dangerously ill of a fever at Warburg in the winter of 1762–63. He recovered, however, and returned to England early in 1763.
6. Charles Manners, Lord Roos (afterwards 4th Duke of Rutland), eldest surviving son of Lord Granby.

INSTRUCTIVE RELATION IN REGARD TO THE
BOROUGH OF SUDBURY

The following letter is docketed " Instructive Relation in regard to the Borough of Sudbury in Dr. Marriotts of December 28th, 1762 ". Add. MS. 38200, ff. 197-200.

James Marriott (1730 ?–1803), knighted 1778, on whose career as a lawyer see *D.N.B.*, was M.P. for Sudbury 1781–84 and 1796–1802. He was a Fellow, and after 1764 Master of Trinity Hall, and Vice-Chancellor of Cambridge 1767–68. At the beginning of his career he " belonged " to Newcastle, wrote pamphlets for him, acted as his agent in the University, and attempted to manage the borough of Sudbury for him. But in 1761 he became jealous of Jenkinson, who had been rewarded by Administration for his treatise on *Neutral Nations*, and decided to write for Bute. In 1762 he published *Political Considerations*, a futile plea for reconciliation between Bute and Newcastle. He lived at Twinstead Hall, near Sudbury.

In 1761 Sudbury had the reputation of being one of the most corrupt boroughs in England and was certainly one of the most expensive.[1] Having upwards of 800 voters, its electorate was too large to be tackled individually by the Treasury, and came under the category of constituencies undertaken for the Treasury by merchants in return for Government contracts.[2] In 1761 the members were Thomas Fonnereau and John Henniker, merchants and Government contractors. Fonnereau was the senior member and had represented Sudbury since 1741 on the interest of his father, Claude Fonnereau of Christ Church Park, Ipswich, son of a Huguenot refugee. Thomas Fonnereau also commanded the entire interest at Aldborough, which was represented by his brother and nephew. Thus in December 1762 he was an influential man with three seats at his disposal. Hitherto he had supported Newcastle and voted with the minority on the Peace, though his allegiance was then wearing thin. But he had a grievance against the Treasury. In the preceding Parliament, Thomas Walpole, who sat with him for Sudbury, and was associated with him in his contracts, had worked against his interest by corrupting the Receiver-General, one Thomas Fenn, a man originally recommended by Fonnereau. In 1761 Walpole left Sudbury for Ashburton and the new member was friendly to the Fonnereau interest, but the offending Receiver still remained in office. On May 1, 1762, James Marriott advised Newcastle that Fonnereau believed he had received a " clear promise " from the Treasury that Fenn should be removed " *this year* ", and someone in his own interest appointed. " The confusion of interests in that borough ", wrote Marriott, " will be inevitable and beyond conception if the old member is not obliged in this point. It is the single favour. The minister can grant no other favour for any principal person in the borough to the representative of 800 constituents " (Add. MS. 32938, f. 16). To save himself Fenn adopted re-

---

1. In March 1761 Horace Walpole wrote of the general election : "Venality is grosser than ever ! the borough of Sudbury has gone so far as to advertise for a chapman ". On the abuse which some historians have made of this statement, see Namier, *Structure of Politics*, p. 195.

2. See *ibid.* p. 62.

insurance tactics not uncommon in the eighteenth century. "Mr. Fenn," wrote Marriott, "if removed, cannot complain that he is turned out 'merely because he voted for Mr. Gordon, *a person not recommended by your Grace'*, for he was polled the last man, and voted for Fonnereau and Henniker after doing all he could against them so that by his own artifice he has deprived himself of all the advantage of this sort of complaint. If Mr. Fonnereau does not charge the present Receiver-General with faults more than usual among his brethren I understand that he thinks himself entitled to the power of changing the person in this place *as the right of the old member of the borough in the interest of the first lord of the Treasury* — a plea that has cost him in three elections terribly dear" (*ibid.* f. 16). Fenn, however, had interest with the Administration and was not removed. But in December 1762 the Fonnereaus were ready to sell themselves to the Court, and Marriott, being as keen to manage Sudbury for Bute as he had been for Newcastle, applied to Jenkinson in the following letter on Fonnereau's behalf. The Fonnereau brothers were eventually bought, not by Fenn's removal, but by an increased share in the contract for victualling Gibraltar — the share in fact which had been Thomas Walpole's.[1]

THOMAS FONNEREAU AND JOHN HENNIKER [2] ESQUIRES

Borough of Sudbury.

Mr. Thomas Fonnereau has represented this Borough in four Parliaments, before which period it was extremely unsettled, and the interest of the common people, which was the predominant one, and also violent against Government, carried all before it. It consists of 800 voters or more ; who are a great incumbrance upon the representative because it is not in the power of Government to do the freemen of the borough in general any favour ; but it has been usual to give the place of Receiver General of the County of Suffolk to some person belonging to and residing in this borough at the recommendation of the representative.

Mr. Thomas Fonnereau recommended the present Receiver General, Thomas Fenn,[3] a manufacturer, to this place which he obtained.

Mr. Thomas Walpole [4] being chosen for Sudbury in the

1. See n. 4 below, and p. 213.
2. John Henniker, F.R.S., merchant and shipbuilder, M.P. for Sudbury 1761–68, Dover 1774–84, New Romney 1785–90. He was afterwards knighted, and in 1800 was created Lord Henniker of Stratford-upon-Slaney in the Irish peerage. Like the Fonnereaus, he deserted Newcastle for Bute at this crisis.
3. See Add. MS. 38334, f. 206, for a list of Receivers-General of the Customs "when and by whom appointed, as imagined". Thomas Fenn appears as Receiver-General for Suffolk from 1753, together with Michael Thirkle from 1742, but no patron is assigned to them.
4. Thomas Walpole, merchant and banker, second son of Horatio Walpole and first cousin of Horace Walpole. In 1761 he was returned for Ashburton (see

last Parliament affected a distinct interest from Mr. Thomas Fonnereau and his friends, and he attached to himself the Receiver General Fenn, who from that time, notwithstanding his obligations to Mr. Fonnereau became an opposer of his interests and those of the Corporation of which he was not then a member ; and has failed in his attempts since to be elected into it. But being a Dissenter he affected an appearance of being at the head of the people of that denomination who are numerous in Sudbury.

This conduct of the Receiver General occasioned violent resentments on the part of the Capital Dissenters who are men of the best fortunes in the place, well knowing his late low condition in life. And more especially the advantages taken by Fenn to strengthen his influence by means of the large sums of public money in his hands were thought very oppressive and unjustifiable.

Mr. Fonnereau very much pressed the late first Lord of the Treasury for the removal of Fenn and that the place might be put under new regulations.

This removal was *the less objectionable* because from the nature of the Land Tax, which is voted only from one year to another, the office of receiving such a tax of course follows the nature of the tax received, and therefore the Receiver General is only an annual officer ; and besides there are many very strong and obvious reasons to any Administration why they should not suffer this office to remain in any one person's hands too long : and more especially so as almost to retain by a prescription a place of such great profit and influence as if it was really upon the footing of a Patent Office.

Mr. Fenn had held this place about ten years ; and the plan proposed was to curtail the profits made to a vast amount of the public money and to settle the rest of the profits in such a moderate and equitable way as should prevent animosities and disturbances for the future in the Borough ; and to lessen the great weight of expence of bearing public offices in that Corporation, and above all to ensure an earlier payment of the public money for the benefit of Government.

The Duke of N⟨ewcastle⟩ promised, and Mr. Fonnereau

p. 26). He sat for Sudbury 1754–61 with Thomas Fonnereau, with whom he was associated in business. In 1756 the Government contracts for victualling Gibraltar were given to Messrs. Walpole, Fonnereau, and Burrell, but as Walpole remained faithful to Newcastle, he was removed from his contracts in the general proscription of December 1762, and his share of the Gibraltar contract was used to buy the Fonnereaus (see *Structure of Politics*, p. 63).

received a letter from Mr. West by his Grace's order fully to that effect; which letter I have seen. But the D. of N. being desirous to oblige the D. of Grafton, Lord Lieutenant of the County, who had applied to him on Fenn's behalf, and above all desirous to keep the Borough always open for Mr. Thomas Walpole's interest in the person of Fenn, broke his promise with Mr. Fonnereau.

Dr. Marriott having an estate in the neighbourhood and having built a house near Sudbury and spent about £1000 among the people in the town and neighbourhood, and being well acquainted with the principal inhabitants was thought of by them, at the end of the last Parliament as a proper person to be joined with Mr. Fonnereau to represent the Borough.

In consequence of this resolution 500 voters signed a paper at the motion of the principal inhabitants in which they referred themselves to Mr. Fonnereau's nomination publicly. A Committee was appointed to receive the nomination, a List of Candidates was made by Mr. Fonnereau : and on its being reduced by two, the Committee were to have pitched upon Dr. Marriott ; if he thought proper to accept.

Dr. Marriott acquainted the D. of N. with the exact state of the Borough two months before the Committee came to town : [1] but the D. referred all the papers to Mr. W⟨alpole⟩. The consequence was that neither Dr. Marriott nor Mr. Fonnereau could obtain any answer from the D. of N. (who was attentive to no persons or things but Mr. Walpole's accomodation only) till the very day the committee were to receive in a few hours the final nomination of a member to be joined with Mr. Fonnereau.

The new settling the place of Receiver General was expected, and was mentioned then to the D. of N. as a preliminary to his recommendation of any representative : but the Duke insisted upon the necessity of his cultivating the D. of Grafton. Dr. Marriott thinking himself distrusted and neglected in these particulars and having received no favour from the D. of N. of any kind, although he had been employed about six years before as the D.'s domestic librarian, without the common civilities due to a gentleman ; now absolutely refused the repeated instances and even prayers of the D. of N. to offer himself as a candidate, so late, at a now more uncertain, enhanced, and prodigious expence, and under a

1. Possibly Add. MS. 32916, f. 352, Marriott to Newcastle, December 27, 1760.

patron who in this instance itself showed that he was not to be depended upon.[1] This conduct of the D. of N. — not leaving Dr. M. three hours to deliberate — deprived him not only of standing himself *with advantage* but also of the opportunity of recommending a friend to the Committee.

Mr. Heneker then was named, and the Receiver General inviting and abetting an opposition Mr. Heneker was chosen with great difficulty and at an enormous expence.

From that period to this the Borough has remained in the utmost confusion. The Capital Dissenters are so irritated with the Receiver General Fenn and his abettors that their clergyman is driven out and their meeting house shut up.

From having given out that his cause was the cause of the whole dissenting body, Dr. Marriott was prevailed upon by some of the principal people among them in the beginning of last summer to use his interest with Dr. Avery [2] who manages the temporal affairs of the general body of dissenters, to know whether any application in this light and by this channel had been made to the D. of N. Dr. Avery was pleased to say that he knew of no such application : that he was well acquainted with the characters and tempers of Fenn's opposers, and farther that no such application should be made without his first acquainting Dr. Marriott.

Besides the D. of Grafton Mr. Fenn had secured the interest of the D. of Devonshire, and the D. of G. was sufficiently imposed upon so as to be induced to acquaint the D. of N. upon Fenn's assertions that he, Fenn, had on his being recommended by Mr. Fonnereau paid the sum of £400 to Mr. Fonnereau's nominee : insinuating thereby that it was for Mr. Fonnereau's own use. This insinuation publicly thrown out irritated Mr. Fonnereau very justly.

The fact was that one Mr. Searling, since dead, a very honest man who had been security for the former Receiver General Mr. Voyce, waved his own pretensions to Mr. Fonnereau's recommendation on Voyce's death, by an agreement made with Fenn, without Mr. Fonnereau's privity when made, and Mr. Searling then accepted £400 from Fenn at Fenn's own motion, as a consideration for Searling's relinquishing his

---

1. See Add. MS. 32916, f. 352. Sudbury was at this time too expensive for Marriott, who asked Newcastle to support him instead of Philip Fonnereau at Aldborough (*ibid.* 32917, f. 447). Newcastle refused, and on February 28, 1761, Marriott abandoned hopes of coming into Parliament under his patronage and decided to write for Administration instead (*ibid.* 32919, f. 342).

2. Dr. Benjamin Avery, Treasurer of Guy's Hospital, died September 1764.

own claim upon Mr. Fonnereau's promise, now relinquished in favour of Fenn.

The profits made by the Receiver General who was prior to Fenn were so very moderate, that Searling was easily induced upon that account to part with his pretensions. Whereas the case since has been greatly altered and Mr. Fonnereau, Mr. Heneker, and their friends undertake to prove that the present Receiver General in the course of 10 years has made enormous profits of the public money, and in one year only has had in his hands or employed for his own private use £38,000 or thereabouts.

Upon the whole as the case now stands if Mr. Fonnereau and Mr. Heneker and the principal people of the Dissenting interest, and of the rest of the Capital inhabitants of the Borough of Sudbury are not obliged in removing the present Receiver General, as they desire, there will be hereafter not any stability of interest or any peace in the Borough : and unless they are obliged, by a person agreeable to them in a borough being nominated, it would really seem more eligible, that this place of Receiver General should be intirely removed from the hands of any person living in or connected with that Borough.

In the present state of things the heats are so great, that the leading people in the Borough are at this time making friends, and it is said have made them, to render the conduct of this Receiver General an object of Parliament, for which purpose they have used very uncommon industry to procure documents of all sorts, and the charges laid are very heavy. It should seem that if this plan goes on, so as to bring these charges and proofs before the House, there is no knowing where it will stop nor whom it will affect, as it will probably bring on an inquiry into the conduct of all the Receivers General in England and may lay a foundation for divisions in the House.

Mr. Thomas Fonnereau in the late Division was in the Minority although he resents the behaviour of the D. of N. and has not visited him since May last.[1]

The obliging Mr. Thomas Fonnereau and Mr. Heneker, on his application, in the affair as mentioned will also attach Mr. Fonnereau's brother Mr. Philip Fonnereau [2] and his

1. See *England etc.* pp. 463-4. In one of Newcastle's lists of the Minority (Add. MS. 33002, ff. 476-8) ten names are marked with an X as doubtful. Two of these were the Fonnereaus.
2. Zachary Philip Fonnereau of St. Antholm's, London, M.P. for Aldborough 1747-74. "When in December 1762 the Fonnereaus . . . were on the point of

son,[1] who have great expectations from Mr. Thomas Fonnereau and owe to him their seats in Parliament for Alborough and it will also oblige Mr. Heneker's father in law Mr. Major, Member for Scarborough [2] who, in case of the death of Mr. Osbaldiston,[3] as I am well informed, has in himself the whole interest in that place ; so that by the present Receiver General's removal no less than 5 or 6 members would be greatly obliged and firmly attached to the interests of first Lord of the Treasury and the Crown.

There is no other Lord of the Treasury has or can have any weight or secure a single vote fairly in the Borough of Sudbury otherwise than any one may chance to affect to acquire an interest for himself in the person of Fenn ; of which Borough I perfectly know the interior.

In representing the above facts to the best of my knowledge as a collateral information, I mean to open to the Earl of Bute with your permission through your channel an opportunity of determining with facility how far his interest and his Majesty's is concerned or not in obliging readily all persons desirous of the above mentioned removal and change in the Borough of Sudbury.

I understand that Mr. Heneker with Mr. Fonnereau's approbation has already made or will certainly make very soon pressing instances to his Lordship upon this head.

Mr. Fonnereau too has authorised me to say that if this favour is granted to Mr. Heneker's application he will take the earliest opportunity to wait on the Earl of Bute to express his thankfulness in the most effectual manner.

It is pretty extraordinary that when the present Receiver General was continued in May last Mr. West gave Mr. Fonnereau to understand, that the *only* obstacle to this business

deserting Newcastle for Bute, and Newcastle reminded Zachary Fonnereau of the assurances he had given, ' he owned very plainly that it was interest ; that he had a family ; his brother and he had spent thirty thousand pounds in elections ; that he had got but little from my brother and me, and that he must look out to his interest. I suppose his price is some valuable remittances to Minorca etc. ; when a man knows himself that he is bought, one has nothing to say to him.' " See *Structure of Politics*, p. 63. The letter quoted is from Newcastle to T. Walpole.

1. Philip Fonnereau, M.P. for Aldborough 1761–68, the only Parliament in which he sat. In 1761 he was an undergraduate of Trinity Hall. See Add. MS. 32917, f. 447.

2. John Major, M.P. for Scarborough 1761–68, Director of the South Sea Company, and High Sheriff of Sussex. In 1765 he was created a baronet with remainder to his son-in-law, John Henniker, with whom he was in partnership in Government contracts.

3. William Osbaldeston, M.P. for Scarborough 1735–47, 1754 to his death in 1766.

was the influence of his Lordship at the Board of Treasury.

If there can be any opening between his Lordship and Mr. Fonnereau, I should be very happy to be in any degree the means of affecting it, and to endeavour to merit that patronage with which I am honoured by every attention in my power.

Fonnereau was not successful in his application.[1] He presented memorials of his own to Bute and Fox, and on February 5, 1763, Marriott wrote to Bute (Bute MSS.) : " I am sorry to hear that Mr. Fox's taking up the affair of the Receiver General at Sudbury in consequence I imagine of Mr. Sam Touchet's application, who I am informed is deeply concerned with almost all the Receivers General in Great Britain, adds to the difficulties your Lordship is under at present in regard to the request of Mr. Thomas Fonnereau and Mr. Henniker (the latter of whom was in the majority). I well know the borough and the truth of the observation may be experienced next Parliament, that the influence of the present Receiver if continued till then is such only . . . as not to avail against the general disgust of his powerful opposers, but is only sufficient to render a vain expense more enormous to the person who so ever shall lean upon him for any interest in the place, and that venal as this borough has got the name of being since Mr. Rigby's[2] excess of liberality in it, yet if the Receiver General was a person agreeable to the general body of Dissenters and Freemen, I am much disposed to believe that to a candidate who in that case should not be opposed, £1500 would be all the expense of the election." On the same day he wrote to Jenkinson : " Upon a full conversation with Thomas Fonnereau and some of his friends I am sorry to find that a middle way to be taken with the present Receiver General (of which you dropped a wish) will not be satisfactory in the least . . ." (Bute MSS.).

SIR GEORGE DALSTON TO TOM RAMSDEN

Add. MS. 38200, f. 213.

Sir George Dalston of Dalston, Cumberland, is described in Burke's *Extinct Baronetage* as 4th and last Baronet, his only child, a daughter, having married a Frenchman named Dillon ; in Wotton's *English Baronetage* (1771), i, 351, however, a son is mentioned, " Sir William Dalston . . . the present baronet ", of whom, according to G. E. C., nothing is known.[3] In 1752 Dalston was Sheriff of Cumberland, and in 1759 Lieutenant-Colonel of the Yorkshire Militia. He had been a Volunteer in Haddock's Squadron

1. Cf. Walpole, *Memoirs*, iii, 112 n. 2.
2. Richard Rigby, the Duke of Bedford's " man of business ", was M.P. for Sudbury 1747-54.
3. This Sir William Dalston may have been confused with Sir William Dalston of Milrigge, Sheriff of Cumberland, knight ; or with William Dalston of Acorn Bank, Westmorland, wrongly described in the *Annual Register* (1771, p. 180) as Sir William Dalton [sic], Bart.

in 1740. He was related to the Ramsdens, his grandfather, Sir John Dalston, 2nd Bart., having married a daughter of William Ramsden of Byram and Longley Hall (wrongly described in Wotton as Sir William Ramsden), great-grandfather of Tom Ramsden of these letters. Dalston was one of the Lowther group and a friend of John Robinson, with whom he canvassed for Sir James in 1757 when he gave a ball at Carlisle and another one " for the ladies at Whitehaven " before the election. In 1761 he was in financial difficulties and sold the Dalston estate.

York, December 30, 1762.

My dear Ramsden,

Was I a stranger to your good⟨ness⟩ I might attempt to apologize for the ⟨presumption⟩ in giving you this trouble. There is an oth⟨er reason⟩ I must declare, that is : I know none but your selfe ⟨who⟩ can give me any asistance or any information, in what light I stand with regard, to a small annuity of £200 a year, the which I have received since Xmass 1761 by two payments of 100 pounds each ; [1] how this arrises, or out of what it is paid I am an intire stranger ; and small as it is, I should be very sorrey to loose it ; and more so at this time when I have lost by the Militia been disembodied the pay, which was pretty considerable, as I had the honor to be a Lieutenant Colonel. My Lord Rockingham stood my friend through whome I received the above pension. I have heard it is a quartring ⟨   ⟩ out of some place ; and that Mr. Winne [2] had it paid to him. I cannot but say how anxious I am to know the event of this inquiry ; I can have but little hopes of success. I am not in the least known. This house has been for some ⟨time⟩ a house of invalids, but is now pretty free. ⟨   de⟩sire I would join with my best respects theirs ⟨to all⟩ where you are and the rest of the family of the ⟨Ramsde⟩ns. Am dear Sir,

Your most obliged and sincere friend,

G. Dalston

1. Cf. Rockingham to Newcastle, May 15, 1762 : " What will become of poor Sir George Dalston's £200 pr. ann ? " (Add. MS. 32938, f. 291). Professor Namier has tentatively suggested Dalston for one of " Lord Rockingham's two friends " mentioned in a list of Secret Service pensions for 1761 (*Structure of Politics*, p. 536 n. 4). But of these pensions the first, of £150, dated from 1756, and the second was added at Christmas 1759 (*ibid.* pp. 536, 557), whereas Dalston's £200 a year started in 1761. It probably came, as Dalston supposed, from some place and not from the Secret Service funds.

2. Presumably one of the Yorkshire Winns of Nostel Priory.

TOM RAMSDEN TO CHARLES JENKINSON

Add. MS. 38200, ff. 211-12.

Pontefract, January 3, 1763.

I have not wrote to you, my Dear Jenkinson, of a long time but I think it is always to give you some trouble, ⟨I write⟩ now to send you a letter, which I received on Saturday ⟨last ?⟩ from Sir George Dalston, to desire I would enquire after ⟨the money which⟩ was paid him one year, though as you will see ⟨   ⟩ that his name may not be mentioned ⟨   ⟩ But of this you will be informed.

What he wants to know is, whether it is to be continued to him ; and indeed a most material question it is to him to be answered in the affirmative ; for I fear his finances are greatly delabré. You will see, who his patron to the Duke of Newcastle was ; who no doubt has now, very justly, no power. But if any thing can be done to help this *poor* man, I should be glad of it. His loosing the pay of Lieutenant Colonel in the Militia, and this 200 at the same time, will totally break his back I fear. You know, the man, I believe ; and therefore should be glad of your advice. I wish you would speak to my brother, and shew him the letter, as he is now in Charles Street, if Sir George ⟨is in⟩ your list.

I was very glad to see in the news paper, that Mr. Lowther is elected for the County of Cumberland ; and hope that every thing is settled between the two brothers to their mutual satisfaction. And then I believe the quarrel, according to Lilly's Gram⟨mar⟩ will be the renewing of their love, which with⟨out the⟩ coup d'eclat could never have been ; for I ⟨very much fear⟩ that a certain person (who ought rather to have ⟨mended⟩ matters) blew the coals : I am not the only person ⟨who⟩ thinks so. But this entre nous. I was very glad to hear of Lord Darlington [1] getting a place ; it would please the King vastly.

What a fine kettle of fish have these wise opposers made : Cloe would have made a better. May not more than one be pleased by the Lieutenancy and the Custos. I have not had any letter, that has mentioned any news from London ; the

1. Henry Vane, 2nd Earl of Darlington, was appointed, in January 1763, Governor of Carlisle and Master of the Jewel Office, the first worth £182 : 10s. a year and the second £450.

Colonel wrote to me on the day of his arrival there, but he had not seen any body. I long to hear, that Granby has determined to act a right part, and what we wish ; for it is a numerous family of one sort or other.[1] Pray tell me, that your health is better ; it being so material to me. The gout will not get out of my foot, though better ; but the weather is severely cold, that I fancy ⟨is what⟩ prevents its going entirely. I have been confined upwards of four weeks.

⟨A l⟩etter to an acquaintance here brought us last post an ⟨account⟩ of the great loss the French have sustained by their ⟨   ⟩ Fleet being taken by Kepple. It is great ⟨   . I⟩ will not detain you longer with reading my ⟨   ⟩ so Adieu.

Most truely yours,

T. R.

WILLIAM YOUNG TO CHARLES JENKINSON

Add. MS. 38200, ff. 215-16.

William, afterwards Sir William Young, 1st Bart. (1769), was Lieutenant-Governor of Dominica from its cession to Great Britain in 1763 till 1770. He was a native of the West Indies, his father having apparently emigrated there from Scotland after the rising of 1715. In 1775 he accompanied Robert Melville on a mission to France to obtain indulgence for the British settlers in Tobago. He died in the island of St. Vincent in 1788.

Docketed January 3rd, 1763.
Tuesday Night.
New Bond Street
near Maddox Street.

Sir

As Mr. Grenville was pleased to signify his desire, that I shou'd be permitted to see the Report of the Board of Trade relative to our new West India Colonies, I take the liberty of reminding you of it, conceiving that it may have escaped your memory, from the multiplicity of business that you are constantly engaged in. If it shou'd be agreeable to you I will do myself the honor of waiting upon you, and perusing it, when and where it may be convenient to you to appoint. Mr. Grenville has this day signified to me his wishes that I

1. John, 2nd Duke of Rutland, who died in his forty-fifth year in 1720, had nine children by his first wife and eight by his second. His son, the 3rd Duke, father of Lord Granby, had eleven children. Of this family four were in Parliament in 1762 ; Granby was M.P. for Cambridge, his brother Lord George for Grantham, his cousin John for Newark-on-Trent, and his uncle Lord Robert for Kingston-upon-Hull. There was also Thomas Thoroton, M.P. for Newark, their " man of business ". See Namier, *Structure of Politics*, p. 134.

should discourse with Governor Dalrymple,[1] on some certain points connected with this business; but as I am not yet fully appriz'd, what the plan recommended by the Board of Trade may be, it is impossible for me, to explain what my sentiments may happen to be on this subject. I flatter myself you will do me the justice to believe that this request does not arise from any impertinent curiosity, and that I have the honor to be, with esteem

Sir,
your most obedient and most humble servant,
William Young

P.S. The observations I have had the honor of communicating to Mr. Grenville, were thro' the hands of my particular friend Mr. Harris,[2] who deliver'd them at the Treasury. If they are return'd to me, I will furnish a better copy.

LORD DARLINGTON TO CHARLES JENKINSON

Add. MS. 38200, f. 219.

Raby Castle, January 7, 1763.

Dear Sir,

Having desired a person in town to enquire into the nature and income of the office,[3] I had the honor of kissing hands for the day I left it ; I received the enclosed, which I take for granted is by no means a true state, as you will perceive this only makes the annual salary 9 instead of 1300. Now my Dear Sir, as you have always been very obliging to me, I am induced to believe you will forgive my requesting you to be so freindly, to take the trouble of gaining a real knowledge of this affair, and informing me thereof, for I literaly know no person I can apply to, either so capable of attaining it, or so likely to come at the means of finding it out, as I am told the Patent grants only a mighty small salary, and that the remainder was always given by the Treasury. Let me once more entreat your forgiveness, and am dear Sir,

Your obedient humble servant,
Darlington

1. Campbell Dalrymple, Governor of Guadeloupe since 1762.
2. Presumably James Harris, M.P. for Christchurch, 1761–81, about whom see *D.N.B.* He was appointed a Commissioner of the Treasury on April 23, 1763. The plan was probably Thomas Curlett and Alexander Clunie's plan for the settlement of Dominica, St. Vincent, and Tobago. See *Commons Journals*, C. 391/70.
3. Master of the Jewel Office. See p. 119.

JOHN ROBINSON TO CHARLES JENKINSON

Add. MS. 38200, ff. 226-7.

Appleby, January 15, 1763.

Dear Sir,

Being confined by a severe cold, I have not ⟨seen Sir⟩ James since the Sessions at this place on Monday last, ⟨and⟩ have been prevented meeting him at Kendal yesterday ⟨as⟩ I fully intended, but I hear he is well, and Lady Mary also at Whitehaven. An address [1] was agreed to at the Sessions here, prepared, and signed, as it would also be by the gentlemen at Kendal. I have to day received an account of the death of a Mr. Lawrence Harrison an Officer in the Salt Duty stationed at Brampton in Cumberland. As it will be for Sir James interest to fix another friend there in his room, I take the liberty to mention his death to you and to add also, that the Commissioner of that branch of the Revenue being very quick in disposing of all those places, if it is not thought improper ⟨   ⟩ the present, though common in the former Administration, I wish ⟨that mea⟩ns could be taken to prevent the place being disposed of till Sir James can apply properly for it. The place I apprehend can't exceed £50 a year, but for ⟨   ⟩ Sir James hath many applications, and therefore I hope this step taken by me will not be thought wrong. As to Election matters here, they go on very well. I have canvassed every place in the Division of the County, where Lord Thanet's [2] interest and several of the other opposite ones lay, and find Sir James's much increased since the last Election, so much that I think there is little left for an opponent to hurt him in that part whoever it is. Accounts from other parts are also favourable, and whoever is the person to stand, I hope there is no doubt but that every thing will go as Sir James desires, which alone is ⟨   ⟩ I am, dear Sir,

Your most obedient humble servant,

J. Robinson

1. On the Peace.
2. Sackville Tufton, 8th Earl of Thanet. The Earls of Thanet were hereditary sheriffs of Westmorland and possessed estates in the county and in Yorkshire. From 1754, by a compromise between Lowther and Thanet, each recommended one member for Appleby (see R. S. Ferguson, *Cumberland and Westmorland M.P.s*). In 1761 Sir James secured a seat at Westmorland (see p. 13 n. 1), but owing to the death, on December 1, 1762, of Sir Wilfrid Lawson, M.P. for Cumberland, he was now making interest in both counties. He got himself returned for Cumberland on December 28, and brought in his brother for Westmorland on March 3, 1763. See p. 108.

Kingston Hall, near Winburne
in Dorsetshire, January 24, 1763.

Dear Sir,

I return you a thousand thanks for the favour of your letter, and your most obliging offer of further services to my family, who have the honour and happiness of being related to you. Your kindness to Mr. Coker and my brother will never be forgotten by either of us.[1] And whenever an opportunity offers of giving you a proof of the sincerity of my gratitude and personal regard for you, I shall execute it with the greatest pleasure. I hope you will forgive the delay of my acknowledgements, which was occasioned by a desire of begging your acceptance of a basket of provision, which I intend to send next Wednesday morning to Blandford 26th instant, and put it into Iliffs Flying Waggon there, which will be in London the Friday evening after, and stops either at the White Horse, or Black Bear, or both, in Piccadilly, and afterwards puts up at the One Bell in Friday Street. But I take it for granted, if the Waggoner makes no mistake, it will be left for you at one of the former places. And for the greater certainty your servant may give previous notice of leaving it at one of those Cellars ; or may call for it about the time of the return of the Waggon. You will be sure of receiving a turkey, a goose, and two brace of mewed partridges ; all which I shall order to be killed to-morrow morning. Some addition will be made to them, if my people have luck in shooting to morrow. In the basket, I will put a note of its contents, and hope, in this frosty season, you will have it fresh and good, carriage paid. It is greatly at your service ; and as I am certain that you are too much hurried with business, I beg to know nothing of it's safe arrival, till you have a quarter of an hour's leisure, and then only by two lines. I was exceedingly pleased to hear of your good success, and wish for a long continuance of it. You will be very kind in making my most humble respects and best wishes acceptable to your great friend. Mr. J'anson [2] was lately here, with his brother Henry,[3]

1. See p. 64.   2. See p. 102.
3. Henry I'Anson, fourth son of Sir Thomas I'Anson, 4th Bart., born 1734, was afterwards commander of the *Mecklenburgh* cutter.

who is Captain Barrington's first Lieutenant of the *Hero* Man of War, and returned with him to Corfe Castle. I communicated your letter to Mr. J'anson, who thinks himself greatly obliged to you for your favourable sentiments of him. He has frequently mentioned the pleasure he received in being honoured with a good share of your friendship at University College in Oxford. And begged me not to forget to return you his thanks, and to assure you of his sincerest respects and wishes of success in all your undertakings. And as to what has lately happened, he most heartily rejoiced with dear Sir,

Your ever affectionate kinsman and most obedient servant,

John Bankes

JOHN BARRELL TO CHARLES JENKINSON

Add. MS. 38200, f. 230.

The following letter is addressed to " the honourable John Jenkinson ", but was obviously meant for Charles and not for his brother Captain John Jenkinson. John Barrell is unidentified.

January 26, 1763.

Dear Sir,

I am extremely unhappy in your displeasure at any part of my letter, and solemnly declare nothing was more remote from my thoughts, than a supposition that you could be influenced by any other motive than the publick service and the duty you owe your Noble Patron.

All that I meant was to shew the distress of the daughter of Sir George Hamilton [1] and to acquaint you that she had invested me with a power to forego any part of her claim to any one that would reach a friendly hand to help her in her distress.

These Sir were the sentiments of my heart. As such I beseech you accept them in excuse for any unguarded expression of mine, and let the deplorable state of an aged good woman blot them out of your memory, and be so kind as to favour me with the honour of waiting on you for I have the

1. From the description of his daughter's age and distress this appears to be Sir George Hamilton of Barnton, who died in great poverty in 1726. G. E. C.'s *Complete Baronetage* says little is known of him except that he was a grandson of the house of Binning, that he married one Helen Balfour, and was created a baronet in 1692. " It is presumed that he died s.p.m. and that the Barony on his death became extinct." G. E. C. quotes two remarks from Robert Mylne, the antiquary, who wrote that Hamilton " before his death, which happened 26 October 1726, was a common beggar in the streets of Edinburgh ", and that " After his death, his Lady, who was as proud as Lucifer himself, and a great phanatick, turned Papist for bread ".

(124)

sincerest esteem for Mr. Jenkinson and am with real regard dear Sir,

Your most obliged and most humble servant,

John Barrell

LORD HARCOURT TO CHARLES JENKINSON

Add. MS. 38200, ff. 236-7.

Cavendish Square, January 31, 1763.
Monday Evening.

Dear Sir,

I was just sitting down to write to you to beg the favour of you to let me know whether there was an intention to remove Mr. Boothby from the Comptrollership of the Ports of Swansea and Cardiff : when I received a letter from Lord Vernon, who as a very old and intimate friend and neighbour of Mr. Boothby's, interests himself extreamly in every thing that concerns his wellfare. I was told yesterday at Court, that Mr. Boothby's name was in a List that was handed about, of persons intended to be dismissed,[1] but as such Lists are frequently produced, without the least authority, I ventured to contradict the report, as I knew that Mr. Boothby's place was obtained (by the Duke of Devonshire) but at the request of Lord Vernon.

This employment was held by Mr. Cope, after whose death it was given to Mr. Boothby.

I shall be greatly obliged to you, if you will let me know how this affair is determined : that in case the report is groundless, I may have it in my power to send Lord Vernon an account which I am sure will be most acceptable to him, and to every one who is acquainted with Mr. Boothby.

Yours dear Sir, most sincerely,

Harcourt

I have troubled you with Lord Vernon's letter, which I received about an hour ago.

1. Brooke Boothby, afterwards 6th Bart. of Bradshaw, Ashe, was appointed Controller of Cardiff and Swansea on June 7, 1757. He is mentioned in Newcastle's list of expected removals (Add. MS. 32946, f. 180) of January 23, 1763, as to be replaced by George Whately and a warrant for Whately's appointment was actually made out on January 26, 1763, but afterwards cancelled. See P.R.O. Treasury Letters to Customs and Excise, T. 11/27, p. 262. Newcastle did not know who Boothby was but thought " he belonged to the Duke of Devonshire in Ireland, but I don't know it " (letter to Hardwicke, January 24, 1763, Add. MS. 32946, f. 196). Boothby was still Controller of Cardiff in 1779 (see *Parliamentary Register*, 1st series, vol. 16, p. 443). George Whately was appointed Warehouse-keeper to the Stamp Duties in April 1763.

TOM RAMSDEN TO CHARLES JENKINSON

Add. MS. 38458, f. 29.

Charles Street, 3 o'clock.
[Marked in pencil " January 31, 1763 ".] [1]

Since I was with you I have seen Mr. Lowther. ⟨He⟩ has not yet heard from Sir James which gives him ⟨great u⟩neasiness ; and, I am sorry to say, with too much ⟨reason as⟩ he has had some applications from gentle⟨men of the⟩ County to know whether he proposes to stand, ⟨ ⟩ you know, he could give no positive answer ; [to]day there is a publick advertisement of a meeting of the gentlemen of the County, and inviting him to declare himself. I find in him the greatest inclination to do everything that is agreable to his brother, I therefore leave you to guess how much he must be distressed to know how to act. If he takes no notice of the gentlemen they will have too much reason to be offended ; and, if he does —— for God's sake use all the means ⟨in your⟩ power to remedy these difficulties, and don't let ⟨our fri⟩end put himself so egregiously in the wrong, ⟨if you can⟩ possibly help it.

DOCKETED " MR. JOHN WHITE TO SIR H. ERSKINE, BOROUGHS OF THE ISLE OF WIGHT "

Add. MS. 38458, ff. 32-3.

The following letter refers to the management of the Isle of Wight constituencies, which were of the mixed type where Government and private interest overlapped. The Treasury had partial control of the Island through the Ordnance Office because places in the little forts and castles on the coast were Ordnance sinecures. While Newcastle was at the Treasury, Lord Holmes acted as Government manager for five seats in the three Island boroughs, for which he received an allowance of £600 a year

1. In Add. MS. 38458, f. 31, appears the following newspaper cutting (name of paper unidentified) marked : " London, January 31, 1763. A numerous Meeting of the Gentlemen of the County of Westmoreland being expected this evening at the Half-Moon Tavern, in Cheapside, it is hoped that, if Mr. Lowther intends to be a candidate for that County, he will favour them with his company, and take that opportunity of declaring his intention." From this notice the British Museum cataloguer derived the date of Ramsden's letter and marked it in pencil. There is, however, another letter from Ramsden from Pontefract dated by him January 31, 1763 (Add. MS. 38200, f. 238). The letter printed here must have been written very soon after.

out of the Secret Service money (see Namier, *Structure of Politics*, p. 255 and *passim*). Thomas Holmes, 1st Baron Holmes, was M.P. for Yarmouth, Isle of Wight, 1747–64. His father, Henry Holmes, and his maternal grandfather, Sir Robert Holmes, had been Governors of the Island, and he himself had considerable influence there, though not enough to enable him to control elections without Government support. When on May 23, 1760, he asked Newcastle for a peerage, he declared that " every one knows I have a greater weight in the Island of Wight than any Governor or any other person ever had " (Add. MS. 32906, f. 241). Three families had a hereditary interest in the Isle of Wight boroughs, the Holmeses, the Worsleys, and the Dummers, but the six members for the Island frequently exchanged seats. In 1761 Lord Holmes and his brother Henry sat for Yarmouth, and a third brother, Charles, was M.P. for Newport. Admiral Charles Holmes died on November 21, 1761, and the seat was given on Newcastle's recommendation, and somewhat against Lord Holmes's wishes, to William Rawlinson Earle of the Ordnance Office. General Henry Holmes died on December 28, 1762, and his seat was acquired by the Government for Jeremiah Dyson, Clerk of the House. In December 1762 the Holmes members supported Government, but their strong family interest was considered dangerous by John White, an unidentified correspondent of Sir Harry Erskine. The death on November 22, 1762, of John Wallop, 1st Earl of Portsmouth, Governor and Vice-Admiral of the Island, seemed an opportunity for Government to recover the interest which it was losing to Lord Holmes.

Bloomsbury Square, February 1, 1763.

Sir,

The measure observed with Lord Holmes in regard to the political affairs of the Isle of Wight appears to me very prudent. The returning Mr. Dyson for Yarmouth will in some degree lessen the weight of Lord Holmes, who intended that seat for his nephew.[1] For although it does not take from his power of directing a future election for that borough, if he should live to see it, yet it keeps out of the House a man, who upon his death must succeed to his estate, interest, and views, and who, had he filled that seat, must have been subservient to the will and controul of his Lordship. By referring to my letter to Mr. Webb,[2] you will see the state of the Borough of Yarmouth, and how only it is possible to get possession of it hereafter. You will there too find an account of the Borough of Newtown.[3] What I have to add now is regarding the

1. Lieutenant-Colonel Thomas Troughear, Deputy Governor of the Isle of Wight, died on January 31, 1763, the day before this letter was written.
2. P. C. Webb, Solicitor to the Treasury ? About him see p. 192.
3. Yarmouth was temporarily weaned from the Holmes's influence. Lord Holmes, who died on July 21, 1764, was succeeded in his seat by John Eames, a Master in Chancery, who gave information about the boroughs to Jenkinson. See Add. MS. 38204, f. 203, and below, p. 313. This seat returned to the Holmes family for one year in 1780, when it was held by Edward Rushworth, son-in-law of Leonard, 2nd Baron Holmes. Newtown was represented from 1754 to 1775 by Newcastle's friends Sir John Barrington, 7th Bart., and Harcourt Powell.

Borough of Newport, the constitution of which and its present situation I likewise gave to Mr. Webb. Lord Holmes ever since he had the management of affairs in that corner of the Kingdom, has followed the same sure policy at Newport which secured him Yarmouth. Upon every vacancy of a Burgess he filled his place with a relation of his own ; at this time his relations make a very considerable body in the Corporation, and if he continues this practice two or three years longer (as there are several very old Burgesses) he will have such a determined majority in his own family, that he may return such Members as are agreeable to himself only.[1] I should apprehend this to be a shackle which he ought not to put upon this borough. And as it may be improper to break with him, a method may be found, which possibly may prevent it. The Governor always had the care of these boroughs recommended to him ; and till the late Lord Portsmouth, he directed the return of the Members. Lord Portsmouth was told to leave this to Lord Holmes, which has subjected us to the present difficulty. Whoever is made Governour will, nay must be desirous of regaining the influence which his predecessors enjoyed. My Lord Holmes must expect this, and consequently can't entertain any jealousy of those who appoint him. May it not therefore be proper to give the Governour insights into the state of the boroughs, and recommend it to him to endeavour to fill up the vacant Burgess's places with inhabitants of the town who are not related to Lord Holmes ? The inhabitants hate his Lordship ; and they are always controuled by the little emoluments which they receive from being gunners etc. of the little forts round the Island. The Governour can never possess himself of the same power which Lord Holmes enjoys or may soon enjoy, and whenever it should be found necessary, such Governour is removeable ; which being done puts an end to his influence there. By this means only, it seems to me, that this borough can be preserved. The Governour should take this difficulty upon himself which I can't help supposing, he will readily do, and if any rupture should ensue, it must be between Lord Holmes and the Governour.

Men have been mentioned as likely to succeed to this place.

1. The growth of family interest in a corporation was a recognised danger. Cf. Griffith Davies's warning to Grenville about Harwich, and Jenkinson's instructions " to give you one caution, which is, that for the future, not above two of any one family be elected into the Corporation " (Add. MS. 38305, f. 5). See Namier, *Structure of Politics*, pp. 466-7.

One who is agreeable to His Majesty, to the gentlemen and inhabitants of the Island, I flatter myself, would easily accomplish this affair. In conversation with my friends there, I have heard the Marquis of Carnarvon [1] mentioned with great respect, and as a man beloved by the people in general. I beg pardon for inserting this circumstance, I only intend it for better and wiser consideration. I am with great respect, Sir,

Your most humble servant,

John White

I am this instant informed that Colonel Troughear, Lord Holmes's nephew is dead. His next heir is a clergyman. [2]

CHARLES JENKINSON TO SIR JAMES LOWTHER

Add. MS. 38200, ff. 239-42.

South Audley Street, February 2, 1763.

Dear Sir,

I have just had the favour of your letter by express ; it gave me the greatest pleasure to see by it in how noble a manner you can sacrifice your own resentment for the service and ease of Lord Bute, and it is an additional proof of your great readiness in this respect, when even a suggestion of mine could induce you to it ; this suggestion was indeed totally my own ; and Lord Bute, who knew nothing of it at the time I wrote to you, became afterwards accidentally acquainted with the state of the affair, and without regarding any prudential consideration undertook at once with the warmth of a relation the support of your interest and honour, determining to carry the point whatever might be the consequence of it. This he did, before he even knew of your application, and he has fortunately succeeded in obtaining what you desire, without being obliged to take any violent measure or incurring the inconvenience, which I thought there was reason to apprehend. One of the persons whom you named will be appointed Sheriff : Lord Bute, who intends to write to you, will probably inform you how all this was brought about, and

1. James Brydges, afterwards 3rd Duke of Chandos, at this time Lord Lieutenant of Hampshire.
2. The Rev. Leonard Troughear, son of Thomas Troughear of Northwood, Isle of Wight, and of Elizabeth, sister of Lord Holmes, took the name of Holmes and was created Baron Holmes in 1798. He was a member of each corporation in the Island. See Add. MS. 32935, f. 336.

it will be matter of conversation, when we meet. I cannot help however observing that the affair has ended in such a manner, that with some precautions which may be suggested, you may, I hope, avoid any of these difficulties for the future.

I will take care that the Westmoreland address shall be properly presented, and it shall be inserted in the Gazette, as having been transmitted by you.[1]

Your opinion concerning Lord Hallifax's conduct with respect to your letters is certainly right. The Secretary at War thought, as you did, and therefore sent back the affair to his Lordship, who has now referred the whole to the Attorney and Sollicitor General, for their opinion on the manner in which he ought to proceed ; as this is a new case, some delay will be unavoidable, but I will endeavour to expedite matters as much as possible.[2]

It is not yet I believe determined, who is to be the Deputy Governor of the Isle of Wight. If Stanwix[3] is the man I will not fail to let you know ; but I am confident, that in that case Lord Bute will not be unmindfull how important it is to your interest to have a friend at Carlisle.

You mention nothing of your Election, but I hear from all hands, that you are not likely to meet with any difficulty. I hope your brother's conduct has been such as to give you satisfaction. As I hear nothing from you concerning the motion for the writ I suppose you have some reason to delay it.

1. An address to the King of congratulation on the Peace, from " the Lord Lieutenant and Custos Rotulorum, Justices of the Peace, Grand Jury, Clergy and Freeholders of the County of Westmoreland ", transmitted by Sir James Lowther to the Earl of Halifax, is reported at length in the *London Gazette* of February 5, 1763.

2. Lowther wrote to Halifax on December 28, 1762, complaining of an act of disrespect on the part of Henry Curwen, M.P. for Carlisle 1761–68, Major of the Cumberland militia. Curwen had illegally discharged the militia without informing Sir James, who as Lord Lieutenant of Cumberland was preparing to disembody them. Lowther asked for an enquiry into the Major's conduct and wrote again to Halifax on January 16. His letters were forwarded to the War Office, who returned them to the Secretary of State, and on February 17 the Attorney- and Solicitor-General submitted a report to Halifax to the effect that Curwen's action was irregular but neither illegal nor void, and probably arose from a misconstruction of his orders from the War Office. They recommended a public explanation and " proper excuses and full declarations . . . both as an officer and a gentleman, to the Lord Lieutenant ". See *Calendar of Home Office Papers, 1760–65*, Nos. 783, 792, 793, 807, 812, 930. Curwen was afterwards M.P. for Cumberland 1768–74. About him see Ferguson, *Cumberland and Westmorland M.P.s*, p. 345.

3. Major-General John Stanwix, M.P. for Appleby, had sat for Carlisle from 1746 to 1761. He was just returned from active service in America, and was appointed Deputy Governor (not Governor, as stated in the *D.N.B.*) of the Isle of Wight in May 1763. He was lost at sea in 1766. See an obituary notice of him in *Gent. Mag.*, 1767, p. 164.

I am only sorry that by these means we should be so much longer deprived of your company in town.

Nothing of any importance has passed in Parliament ; we had yesterday some little talk on the abolishing of the thirtieth of January ; [1] we came however to no resolution ; and it seemed to be the general opinion of the House to let this cerimony subsist, as it had hitherto done, as there might otherwise be disturbances among the lower kind of people. Nicholson Calvert afterwards made a speech, that had neither sense nor witt, but was full of wretched and low allusions, with a view to satirize the most respectful characters in this country.[2]

My best respects attend Lady Mary, and I am with the greatest truth and respect, dear Sir,

Your faithfull humble servant,

C. Jenkinson

Lord Bute has just given me this letter, so I send it you enclosed.

LORD DARLINGTON TO LORD BUTE

Add. MS. 38200, f. 244.

Raby Castle, February 6, 1763.

My dear Lord,

Mr. Staunton,[3] an uncle of mine informs me, he purposes paying his respects to your Lordship, and not having the honor of being known to you, begs I will give him this letter, as an introduction. He realy is a worthy good man, represents the Borough of Ipswich, and is most sincerely attached to His Majesty's interest ; he has been kind enough to say, my opinion in political affairs, he shall always desire to have. I do assure you my Lord, I am happy to be instrumental, in adding a friend more to your knowledge, although I flatter

1. The anniversary of the execution of Charles I.
2. Cf. Walpole, *Memoirs*, i, 191. Nicolson Calvert, a London brewer, was M.P. for Tewkesbury 1754–74. (On his election in 1754 see Namier, *Structure of Politics*, p. 160.) In the debate on the January 30 ceremony he referred metaphorically to the Royal family as *the Steadys*, a family living in Surrey, where young *Steady's* mother carried on an intrigue with a Scotch gardener ; he hoped the true friends of young *Steady* would advise him to recall his old friends and turn away the gardener. Walpole thought this " a very bold and extraordinary speech ".
3. Thomas Staunton of Stockgrove, Bucks, M.P. for Ipswich 1757–84, married Jane, third daughter of Gilbert, 2nd Baron Barnard, and sister of the 1st Earl of Darlington.

myself, your Lordship now finds no need of any *new* acquisitions, and that every thing goes on, as your most sanguine friends could wish. I am at present detained here upon real business of my own, yet if your Lordship has any commands for me, believe me, they will be instantly obeyed with pleasure, by

Your Lordships sincere friend and obliged humble servant,

Darlington

JOHN ROBINSON TO CHARLES JENKINSON

Add. MS. 38200, f. 247.

Appleby, February 6, 1763.

Dear Sir,

I sent the letter you favoured me with lately ⟨to Sir James⟩ at Whitehaven, relating the salt officer,[1] which ⟨you have⟩ been so kind as prevent filling up for Sir James's ⟨recommen⟩-dation, and conclude you will soon hear from him who he would wish should be appointed. We remain perfectly quiet in Westmorland, though our accounts from town inform us of two or three turbulent spirits who would make mischief if they could. You will have heard almost by this time from Sir James about the Writ, which it is much [*sic*] none of the opponents moved for before ; as it will be here by Wednesday night, I apprehend nothing will prevent the Election being on the 17th instant. ⟨   ⟩ I had the pleasure of seeing Lady Mary or Sir James ⟨though⟩ they have been at Whitehaven, but I hear they are well⟨. I am dear⟩ Sir with great truth,

Your most obedient and most faithful servant,

J. Robinson

CHARLES JENKINSON TO SIR JAMES LOWTHER

Add. MS. 38200, ff. 257-8.

February 22, 1763.

Dear Sir,

Lord Halifax called yesterday on Lord Bute, and acquainted him in what manner, he intended to treat the complaint that you made against Major Curwen ; he will

1. For an account of the Salt Office see Edward Hughes, *Studies in Administration and Finance* (1934), particularly pp. 209-19.

(132)

write to him by this post a severe letter of reprimand, and tell him that he must make the proper submission to you, if he expects to escape the punishment, which is due to his irregular conduct ; his Lordship intends at the same time to write to you, recommending it to you, to accept of Mr. Curwen's submission ;[1] Lord Bute, when he informed me of this, ordered me to write to you, and to desire you in his name to be satisfied with it, as he hoped you would find your honour and reputation fully saved by it.

I am just come from the House of Commons where we have at last had a long day. Sir J. Philips moved that we should appoint a *Commission of accounts*[2] to examine into the receipts and disbursements of the money that had been raised since the commencement of the war ; we have had a long and vague debate upon it, almost every body has been against a Commission of accounts ; Government was of the same opinion ; but as they were unwilling to appear against an enquiry in general, which is considered as a very popular measure, they have moved that a Select Committee of the House of Commons should be appointed for that purpose, and this measure will be pursued.

Lord Albemarle is just arrived in town from the Havannah.

I have the honour to be with the greatest respect, dear Sir,

Your faithful humble servant,

C. Jenkinson

LORD HARCOURT TO CHARLES JENKINSON

Add. MS. 38200, ff. 286-7.

Newnham, April 4, 1763.

Dear Sir,

Out of regard for Mr. Elliot,[3] I cannot avoid mentioning to you the general uneasyness that his son's commission[4] has

1. Halifax wrote to Lowther on February 22 that Curwen had been ordered to make proper excuses either in person or by letter for his neglect of the Lord Lieutenant. See above, p. 130 n. 2. Lowther was evidently unwilling to let the matter drop, for on June 15, 1763, Halifax wrote to him once more that the Cumberland Militia was considered disembodied and not entitled to any further pay notwithstanding the informality of its dismissal.

2. Cf. Walpole, *Memoirs*, i, 191.

3. Gilbert Elliot of Minto (1722-77), afterwards Sir Gilbert Elliot, 3rd Bart. (1766), M.P. for Selkirkshire 1753-65, Roxburghshire 1765-77, Treasurer of the Chambers May 1762-70. As a Scotsman he was an adherent of Bute and a " King's Friend ". See G. F. S. Elliot, *The Border Elliots* (1897), and *D.N.B.*

4. Cf. Gilbert Elliot to his father, May 20, 1762, quoted in G. F. S. Elliot, *op. cit.* p. 373. Hughe Elliot was ten years old when he received his commission

occasioned, and had I the honor of being acquainted with him, half so well as you are, I should most undoubtedly take the liberty to advise him to resign the Commission, as well on account of Lord Bute, on whom great part of the abuse falls, as for his own sake, and even for the young gentleman's sake, who will scarce be able to reap any other advantage from it, but the half pay, and of that even he may be disappointed, by some ill-natured vote in Parliament. I hope Lord Bute wont carry his resolution [1] into execution, till he sees what turn Lord Waldegrave's illness takes. Such a disorder as the small pox at his time of day, may very probably be attended with fatal consequences : which may enable Lord Bute to make an ample provision for one of his sons.[2] I am Dear Sir,

Very sincerely yours,
Harcourt

On April 8, 1763, Bute put into effect his long-standing intention of resigning the Treasury, to the dismay of his followers, who had seen themselves provided for indefinitely under the protection of the " Favourite ". To the Grenville–Halifax–Egremont Administration who succeeded him, he bequeathed his friends. Jenkinson, who had been his private secretary, while enjoying the place of Treasurer of the Ordnance, was handed over to Grenville on April 16 as Joint-Secretary to the Treasury, and at the same time Grenville was asked " to take the assistance of all the King's friends that are determined to give it ".[3] The transference of " King's Friends ", however, gave a false impression of the solidarity of Bute and Grenville. In reality the members of this group knew very little of the motives and intentions of their patron ; believing implicitly in his continued influence, their instinct was to rally round him, but not understanding either his panic or the conditions of the new Administration founded on a half-promise of his withdrawal, they were puzzled to find him more elusive than ever.

as Lieutenant in an Irish regiment, a job which was apparently done without his father's knowledge. " It is a thing I would not have done nor asked myself ; however it is very lucky for him, and if properly supported will give him an early chance for a company." Unfortunately it was taken up by Wilkes, who tried to make a scandal of it in his *North Briton*, Nos. 42 and 45. When Hughe Elliot came of age he was not allowed to take up his commission and instead entered the Diplomatic Service. See *D.N.B.*

1. Of retiring?
2. James, 2nd Earl of Waldegrave, died on April 10. He was Lord Steward of Cornwall, Lord Warden of the Stannaries, and a Teller of the Exchequer ; none of these places was given to any of Bute's sons, nor to either of the young Elliots. It is not clear from the text whether Harcourt refers to Bute's sons or to Elliot's.
3. Bute to Grenville, March 25, 1763, *Grenv. Pps.* ii, 33.

JOHN BINDLEY TO CHARLES JENKINSON

Add. MS. 38200, ff. 293-4.

6 o'clock, April 8, 1763.
Southampton Street.

My dear Friend,

I have been in the City since I saw you and can inform you that all the friends of my Lord most sincerely lament the cause of his resignation [1] and as sincerely wish the recovery of his health. Not an unprejudiced man in the Kingdom but laments the insolent opposition and the cruelty of quarrelling with a Minister because he happened to profess himself a friend to a virtuous Administration. The reflection is miserable that even after such a declaration a deluded people could not have patience to wait the result. However the most glorious point for this country he has attained, Peace, and which having attaind will forever endear him to the friends of this almost ruind country, and I am sure all his friends commend him that having finished this great and good work he risques no further the loss of his health and peace of mind. Pardon me if I venture to recommend one thing which is that his Lordship will give his friends a day to wait on him and shew their respect. I heard this much hinted from his friends, and I heard those who are not his friends declare he would not see them. Other lies they propagate are that Lord Hardwick and Charles York [2] have been offered President of the Council and Chancellorship and refused both. That the Cocoa Tree [3] members are all dissatisfied with my Lord's retirement and are gone to the Opposition, that the D. of Bedford is to succeed immediately

1. Bindley wrote to Jenkinson on April 7 (Bute MSS.), expressing concern at Bute's intended resignation. He had a scheme to mitigate the rigour of the Excise laws, but supposed he must give it now to Grenville.
2. There is no evidence of such an offer at this time.
3. In the *History of the Late Minority* (p. 61) Bute was accused of having " collected the refuse of a despicable party, who had for some years, formed a club at a coffee house, who, having no name of their own, assumed that of the house and were called the Cocoa Tree Club ". Gibbon, who was a member and considered the Cocoa Tree a very respectable institution, wrote of it in his journal for November 1762 : " at present we are full of Privy Counsellors and Lords of the Bedchamber ; who, having jumped into the Ministry, make a very singular medley of their old principles and language with their modern ones " (Gibbon's *Journal*, ed. D. M. Low, 1929, p. 185). As Tories, the Cocoa Tree were accused of Jacobitism, though they held themselves identical with the Country Gentlemen. See *A Letter from the Cocoa Tree to the Country Gentlemen*, 1762.

at the Treasury,[1] that my Lord and Mr. F.[2] have quarrelld and that Lord B. does not care about the success of the present administration, they have even the insolence to insinuate His Majesty is displeased with his resignation. All these things considered I most earnestly hope his Lordship will see all his friends.

Mr. T.[3] is to be at Mr. Burrell's[4] at seven who will most strongly enforce his steady attachment to the Administration. The world say he will not accept. I am pretty confident he will. I shall call at seven at Burrell's and if anything occurs you shall hear from me. If my Lord approves seeing his friends pray let me know this evening, and make it public. I pray to God to preserve his health and happiness and I beg you to assure his Lordship that, independent of obligations I have the strongest personal attachment to and reverence for him and that I will remain inviolably his dutiful and devoted Servant

And your faithful and sincere friend,

J. Bindley

DR. WILLIAM ROBERTSON TO LORD BUTE

Add. MS. 38200, ff. 295-7.

William Robertson, D.D. (1721–93), author of the *History of Scotland* (1759), was appointed Principal of Edinburgh University in 1762 through the influence of Bute, in order that he might have means and leisure to write a History of England to be dedicated to his patron. See Bute to Baron Mure, February 27, 1762, in *Caldwell Papers*, ii, 146. For the same purpose in August 1763 the office of King's Historiographer for Scotland was revived in his favour with a salary of £200 a year. At the time Robertson was working on his *History of Charles V*, but he had contemplated writing a History of England at different times since 1759. See Dugald Stewart's Life of Robertson prefixed to his *Works* (1817), pp. 44-50.

1. Cf. Walpole, *Memoirs*, i, 206. It seems to have been generally believed that Bedford had resigned the Privy Seal with a view to coming in at the head of the Treasury.

2. It was with Shelburne that Fox quarrelled seriously because Shelburne allowed Bute to believe that Fox would resign the Paymastership on receiving a peerage as a reward for leading the House of Commons through the crisis. See Fitzmaurice, *Shelburne*, ch. iii. Fox and Bute remained on good terms.

3. Charles Townshend had been President of the Board of Trade since March, but the ministers were so much afraid of his deserting them for Pitt that they offered him the place of First Lord of the Admiralty in the hope of more firmly securing his allegiance. See p. 140.

4. Peter Burrel junior, M.P. for Launceston, Surveyor-General of the land revenues of the Crown 1769–75. He was a Director of the South Sea Company and an intimate friend of Townshend and Bindley.

College of Edinburgh, April 9, 1763.

My Lord,

I had this day the honour of your Lordships letter of the fourth, and as you are of opinion that I have not fully explained myself in my last, I shall in obedience to your desire, lay open to your Lordship every thing that is my thoughts with regard to the affair about which you have gotten so much trouble. At the same time I can scarce conceive any task more difficult than for one who is about to receive favours beyond what he ever expected, to undertake to define what should be the mode or extent of conferring them. But as it is in this uncommon method that my Lord Bute's generosity has prompted him to treat me, I shall go on without farther apology, to write with the same freedom I have hitherto been allowed to take.

When I mentioned £200 as an adequate ⟨salary⟩ to be annexed to the office of Historiographer, I ⟨spoke⟩ according to my own ideas of the matter at that time. But upon receiving your Lordship's letter of ⟨   ⟩ I communicated the matter to a friend whom I often consult in my private affairs both as a man of business, and of prudence. He viewed the subject with ⟨as⟩ minute attention to the articles of profit and loss that I had done and the sum of what he suggested proceeded upon these principles

    I possess at present

as Minister of Edinburgh . . .	£138 . 17 . [2]
as Principal	111 . 2
as Kings Chaplain . . .	49 . –
	£298 . 19 . 2 [1]

Besides this I have ex officio a free house in the College. I propose to resign my stipend, and if I shall receive, in lieu of it, a salary of £200, an addition of £61 is made to my income. But in pros⟨ecuting⟩ my intended work I shall be obliged to reside four or five months in London every second year, and I can⟨not⟩ compute the expence of my journeys up and down and resi⟨dence⟩ there at less than £100. This your Lordship will ⟨per⟩ceive is no extravagant calculation and exhausts

1. Cf. a curious article on Robertson's pecuniary achievement as an historian in the *Scots Magazine* for April 1772 (xxxiv, 196) : " The Principal of the College of Edinburgh has a house allowed him and £100 per ann.". In spite of his plea for £250 a year, Robertson's stipend as Historiographer was fixed in July 1763 at £200 (*Scots Mag.*, 1763, p. 416).

nearly the whole additional salary. I took notice that ⟨there⟩ is a process now depending for the augmentation ⟨of the⟩ stipends of the Ministers in Edinburgh, and if by ⟨that⟩ they shall gain (as they flatter themselves) an addition of about £30 per annum, this makes a considerable alteration in the calculation. What I ⟨stated⟩ with regard to the expence of purchasing the books ⟨necess⟩ary towards carrying on the work was first mentioned in a letter to Mr. Baron Mure [1] which he transmitted to my Lord Bute. As I intend to apply my whole force, and devote my whole time to my task, and shall aim at rendering it not only a composition of some elegance, but a work of such accuracy and research as may in some degree be worthy of the patronage with which it is to be honoured, there will on this account, be such a large collection of ⟨books⟩ necessary as would be very inconvenient and imprudent for me to purchase out of my private funds.

These are all the facts which I think it necessary to mention to your Lordship, and if I must now say what I think would be a sum sufficient to indemnify me, I shall endeavour to judge in my own case as if I were determining it for a stranger. I think that a salary of £250 per annum should be annexed to the office of Historiographer. With regard to the sum requisite for books, and for copying papers and Mss. in the publick offices, it must be more a matter of conjecture. I should think four or five hundred pounds no extravagant sum. Lord Royston has made such a large collection of books relative to the English History as will be necessary for me, and if it be thought proper to mention it to him he can say whether I have exceeded or fallen short of what is requisite. I do not wish to gain upon this article of books, and shall be most pleased if the sum allotted me for that purpose were granted on condition that the books should ⟨be⟩ given to the College Library here at my death.

After having said all this with great pain to myself, lest I should be suspected of claiming too much, or presuming too far I again conclude with assuring you that I shall be entirely satisfied with the manner in which my Lord Bute shall see proper to determine the matter, as I have the best reason

1. William Mure of Caldwell, formerly M.P. for Renfrewshire, since 1761 a Baron of the Scots Exchequer. He was a friend of Bute and helped to manage the Bute estates when Bute himself was absent from Scotland. He had great influence on local affairs, particularly on the patronage in Scotland. See his correspondence with Stuart Mackenzie in the *Caldwell Papers*, edited by W. Mure for the Maitland Club, 1854.

from what is past to confide in his generosity for what is to come. I am with great regard, my Lord,
Your Lordships most obedient and most faithfull servant,
William Robertson

Robertson neither received the money for his books nor left them to the University. On March 19, 1765, he wrote to Will Mure : " You know that when I was made His Majesty's Historiographer for Scotland, a proposal (which carried with it the force of a command) accompanied that grant. In consequence of it I am under an engagement, as soon as my present work is published, to attempt the History of England. This engagement I am bound by every tie to fulfill, and it will require the whole of my time and all my attention during the rest of my life " (*Caldwell Papers*, Part II, ii, 23). In 1769 the *History of Charles V* was sold to the bookseller for £4500, and in 1772 Robertson was working on a history of the discovery and conquest of America which was published in 1777 (see *Scots Mag.* xxxiv, 196). In 1786 he sold his Spanish library, and in 1791 he published a *History of India in Antiquity*. The History of England seems to have suffered the same eclipse as its patron.

WILLIAM HAMILTON TO CHARLES JENKINSON

Add. MS. 38200, f. 299.

William, afterwards Sir William Hamilton (1730–1803), M.P. for Midhurst 1761–64, son of Lord Archibald Hamilton and grandson of William Douglas, 3rd Duke of Hamilton. In July 1764 he was appointed ambassador to Naples. See *D.N.B.* In 1791 he married his mistress, Emma Hart, afterwards Nelson's Emma.

Kings Mews,[1] April 11, 1763.
Dear Sir,
The last time I took the liberty of troubling Lord Bute about an affair that I have very much at heart, both on account of Mrs. Hamilton's [2] ill state of health, and my own situation, his Lordship was so good as to say, that he would turn it in his mind and do the best for me that he could. I was, and am still thoroughly satisfied as to Lord Butes kind intentions towards me and therefore did, and do rely solely upon his Lordships goodness. Will you then be so kind as to let Lord Bute know from me that as I understand Sir James Grey [3] will be at home very soon, and have reason to believe

1. Hamilton was one of the King's Equerries.
2. Hamilton's first wife was Catherine Barlow, daughter of Hughe Barlow of Lawrenny Hall, Pembrokeshire, who brought him an estate of £5000 a year. She died in 1782.
3. Sir James Gray, K.B., Ambassador at Naples from 1758. He was transferred to Madrid in 1764, when William Hamilton succeeded him.

that he does not mean to return to Naples, I shall esteem
myself for ever under the greatest obligation to his Lordship,
if he would procure me the promise of succeeding Sir James in
case he should not return. I most heartily wish Lord Bute a
speedy recovery of his health and am, dear Sir, with great
regard,

Your most obedient humble servant,

Wm. Hamilton

JOHN BINDLEY TO CHARLES JENKINSON

Add. MS. 38200, ff. 300-301.

Monday Night, 10 o'clock.
Docketed " April 12, 1763 ".

My dear Mr. Jenkinson,

I thank you for your note. My friend I find is much
puzzled. He has many advisers and all flatter him with the
confirmation of his own ideas — that his abilities will command
anything from any Administration.[1] A peerage for his son [2]
and fuller power for himself, in his present situation,[3] or the
peerage with what he is now offered, would certainly fix him,
for the present, and would forever damn him with the Opposition, who would then see plainly he had deserted them, though
I believe they are pretty well convinced of that already ; but

1. Charles Townshend was so full of confidence that when on April 15 he
decided to accept the Admiralty he took Peter Burrell with him to kiss hands
as one of the Commissioners, " as if the seats of his colleagues at that board were
in the nomination of the first commissioner " (Walpole, *Memoirs*, i, 209). As he
refused to accept unless Burrell were appointed, the Admiralty was given to
Sandwich instead. Townshend's place at the head of the Board of Trade, which
he had occupied for a month, was given to Shelburne.
2. The peerage was not obtained until a few days before Townshend's death,
and was never enjoyed by either of his sons. On August 28, 1767, Lady Dalkeith
was created Baroness Greenwich with remainder to her heirs male, but her two
sons, Charles and William John Townshend, died unmarried in 1782 and 1789
respectively, and the title became extinct at her death in 1794.
3. The Board of Trade at this time was only an advisory body, and its Presidents were constantly seeking to give it political authority. Halifax, during his
long tenure of the Presidency (1751–61), improved its status. He had the monopoly
of colonial patronage and was a member of the nominal Cabinet. But under
Townshend's immediate predecessor, Lord Sandys, the Board reverted to its
former footing. Townshend during the month that he was President, March–
April 1763, enjoyed the same power as Halifax had done, with a nominal rank
of Cabinet Counsellor, but without permission to go into the King with State
papers, except those relating to the Board of Trade. See Walpole, *Memoirs*, i, 193.
On the Board of Trade see A. H. Basye, *The Lords Commissioners of Trade and
Plantations, 1748–82* (1925), and O. M. Dickerson, *American Colonial Government,
1696–1765* (1912).

yet, they are tampering. There are those about him who tell him he has a right to these things and a certain person whom I have mentioned to you I believe to be the only man who advises him honestly.

I am exceedingly concerned, (for I have the tenderest feelings for my Lord Bute) to hear the insolent lies that are thrown out and not only thrown out but asserted in print, that his Lordship advised the Beer Tax.[1] Surely it ought to be contradicted and proved as I can do, that that Tax was approved, enforced, and espoused by the Duke of Newcastle, Mr. Legge and Mr. C. T. and at a time when Mr. Pitt was in Administration, and at the time that my Lord was known only as a private nobleman to thousands, amongst whom I declare myself to be one. When it was mentioned to Mr. G. Grenville he disapprovd it, and he of all men I conversed with alone disapproved it. At the same time this falsehood is contradicted why not a truth asserted, viz. that Lord Bute advised the taking it off this year, that Lord Bute was laying a foundation to take it off. And this I would most readily agree to make public on my own affidavit, however unpopular or distinguished it would make me appear, as I am a witness to the truth of it, rather than to see and hear a man so unjustly, so villainously abused, for the very thing that he was striving and desirous to remedy. Perhaps as my Lord is determined to be quite a private man, it is not worth his while to bestow a thought on what ill nature and envy may invent. However wherever I converse I have, and will endeavour so to do for the future, asserted all that I knew about the Beer Tax etc. I am dear Sir,

Your faithful friend,
John Bindley

1. See Owen Ruffhead's pamphlet, *Considerations on the Present Dangerous Crisis* (1763), the gist of which appears in *Gent. Mag.* for May 1763 (p. 211). Bute seems to have been cleared of responsibility for the beer tax, an additional duty of three shillings the barrel laid on December 24, 1760 (1 George III, c. 3), and was even attacked for wishing to take it off. See an answer to Ruffhead's *Considerations* in *Gent. Mag.*, June 1763, pp. 269-73, where the beer tax is described as the best that could be devised. " It is therefore unfaithful and unkind to government in a servant of the crown (who to purchase popularity had thoughts of sacrificing this piece of national strength, but wanted skill to effect it) to declaim against this method of collecting . . . the revenue." Whether Bindley had a hand in clearing Bute does not appear.

SHUTE BARRINGTON TO CHARLES JENKINSON

Add. MS. 38200, ff. 306-7.

Christ Church, April 13, 1763.

Dear Sir !

Your letter of the 11th instant relieved me from an anxiety, which the unaffected esteem and regard I bear you, had created. Sensible of what your services intitled you to, yet not ignorant of the difficulties which impede the good intentions even of such a Minister and patron as Lord Bute and prevent their being carried into execution, I could not but be very uneasy during the suspense, and cannot but felicitate you now, in the warmest sincerity of my heart, on his having so properly rewarded you in one of the last acts of his administration.[1] I lament, and may now do it without the imputation of flattery, his having quitted the helm of government. I am convinced that he was defective neither in the good qualities of the heart nor head ; and however his conduct may have been calumniated by malice and detraction, that when the period in which he presided over the councils of this country comes hereafter to be reviewed with that dispassionate judgment which men are at present incapable of, and all the various difficulties with which he had to struggle are calmly weighed, he will be regarded as an able and honest Minister. I feel much for the King who must be deeply affected with the loss he has sustained. The virtues of Lord Bute's successor in the Treasury we neither of us are strangers to ; and I have no doubt from his love of financing and his having peculiarly applied himself to that branch of politics that he will succeed.

The only literary intelligence which this place affords is the approaching publication of Lord Clarendon's papers in 2 Vol. quarto.[2] The Editor was induced by a letter of Archbishop Sancrofts [3] in his possession to make inquiry concerning

1. Cf. Walpole, *Memoirs*, i, 210. Before leaving office, Bute gave Jenkinson the reversion of Sir Edward Walpole's place of Collector of the Customs, to the annoyance of Horace Walpole, who enjoyed the stipend and had hoped to obtain the continuance of the place to himself. In one of Newcastle's lists of expected removals (Add. MS. 32946, f. 177) is a note : " Mr. Charles Jenkinson, reversion of Sir Edward Walpole's place in the Customs held by Mr. Mann. N.B. Robert Jenkinson is to hold it." Robert is probably a mistake of Newcastle's for John, Jenkinson's only surviving brother.

2. *The State Letters of Henry Earl of Clarendon*, published by Millar and other booksellers in December 1763, price £1 : 11 : 6.

3. Archbishop of Canterbury 1678-91, when he was deprived for refusing to take the oaths to William and Mary.

a very singular entry in our Chapter Book, which is so extraordinary that I am amazed it has till now remained unknown. The instrument of James the 2d nominating one Massy a notorious papist to the deanery of Christ Church in 1686 contains a dispensation to him from attending prayers, from administering the sacrament according to the rites of the church of England, and from subscribing to the 39 Articles, and from taking the oaths of adjuration and supremacy. This flagrant violation of the ecclesiastical constitution was not inferior to any breach of the civil, and the only difference between that Prince's conduct here and at Magdalen is that the preferment in the former instance is indubitably vested in the crown ; in the latter it is elective.

Some of the younger masters opposed to day the Chancellor's letter recommending dispensing with an act, but it was carried by a great majority. You make me happy by talking of coming here at the Commemoration ; and I flatter myself that you need no assurance from me that when you have a vacant week or longer period you will confer an obligation on me by permitting me to see you. I am, dear Sir, with the truest regard,

Your most affectionate and faithful servant,
S. Barrington

EDWARD RICHARDSON TO CHARLES JENKINSON

Add. MS. 38200, f. 308.

Wednesday, April 13, 1763.

Sir,

I am very sorry to have incurred your displeasure, and that you should think me overrating that little merit I claim on the State,[1] under favour of my noble freind and patron the Earl of Bute. Truly warmed with every sentiment of gratitude to his Lordship for his condescension and unparalelled hospitality to me, who ⟨could⟩ but so slenderly deserve, you will please to receive this my acknowledgement in littera scripta. And as to the concern I felt from the little rebuff lately received from blind Mother Fortune, who pushes me from her

1. Richardson was probably concerned in the negotiation with Sir James Hodges, to whom, as spokesman of the City, Bute was alleged to have offered to get the Cider Act repealed if the Corporation would refrain from presenting their petition. See p. 69.

wheel, I now drive a far off — I hope I know enough never to be wiser than my superiors ; if they think me so worn out and shattered as to order me into port, there I must lay — but please to remember, the condition of a hulk is not my choice, and though I am unworthy to be trusted with the footiest commission the State can bestow, yet I shall continue to make it my first and greatest duty to defend its friends, to the last drop of my blood, against the devices of its enemies. You must indeed pardon me for adopting a little of the Ajacian sullenness, since *si parvis componere*, like him I lose the contended prize, that is, for want of artfull pleading. The race ⟨we⟩ learn, is not always to the swift, the battle to the strong nor favour to men of skill ; hence I hope for my advantage one day or other, I mean whenever it may suit Time, Chance and you. After all give me leave to repeat my earnest desires, that you would commend me to my Lord and pray say all the good you can of me, and believe me, it shall never give you reproach. I am now preparing a little summer furniture, if you would please to favour me with the remainder of my Lord's kind order [1] of Xmas last you will add another obligation to the many great ones already conferred on, Sir,

Your ever steady, faithfull and most obedient servant,

Ed: Richardson

JOHN ROBINSON TO CHARLES JENKINSON

Add. MS. 38200, f. 305.

April 13, 1763.

Dear Sir,

You were so good some time ago as take ⟨a n⟩umber of receipts for the subscription to Dr Burn's book.[2] He is now ready with it for publishing, and wants the subscriber's names

---

1. Richardson was Comptroller of the Pepper Warehouse since October 22, 1762 (Add. MS. 38335, f. 78). He also appears to have enjoyed a pension of £50 a year out of the Secret Service money. See p. 69 n. 3.

2. *Ecclesiastical Law* (2 vols., London, 1763), by Richard Burn, LL.D. (1709–1785), legal writer and topographer. He was for fifty years Vicar of Orton in Westmorland (see *D.N.B.*). His book on ecclesiastical law is a classic and went into nine editions. It is wrongly described in the *D.N.B.* as having appeared in 1760. Burn was a protégé of Sir James Lowther, whose name appears in the list of subscribers for twenty-five sets. The list is distinctly representative of the Lowther interest, territorial, political, and family. It includes three Robinsons besides John Robinson ; two other subscribers from Appleby ; Dr. Vane, the Prebendary of Durham, and Peter Bowlby, Registrar of the Dean and Chapter of Durham ; also Jenkinson, Ramsden, and Fletcher Norton, Lowther's Member

to print off. If you will be so good therefore as favour me with an account of those you have taken and the number of receipts you have disposed of, it will oblige the Doctor, and dear Sir

Your most obedient humble servant,
J. Robinson

EDWARD RICHARDSON TO CHARLES JENKINSON

Add. MS. 38200, f. 311.

Sunday noon, April 17, 1763.

Sir,

The present, disloyal, malignant mood of the citizens of London,[1] those, I mean, who call themselves the Corporation, however trifling and insignificant many of them appear as individuals, yet are they, at this time, of consequence enough in their united capacity to give some challenge to ministerial attention. Corruption begets corruption, and where the little toe of a state should be infected, the cautious head would surely direct a cure. But if it be objected, as I fear it may be, but with too much truth, that these gentry, the common council chaps, are become incorrigible, yet somewhat might be done to prevent the spreading of their poyson. *Ense residendum est, ne pars sincera trahatur.* The chance trade of the City may be very easily and very considerably too, curtailed this approaching season, for whilst I imagine His Majesty may proceed with a superior dignity to the Abby[2] than to St. Pauls, I do, at the same time, believe the lottery may be drawn with more safety within the Guild Hall of Westminster, than of London. You will believe so too, the difference of the Corps of Guards that waite round those different places duly consider'd. I shall conclude these little, but well meaning hints with one very general one, that is, the grievous Tax laid upon coals coming into the Port of London, a Tax partially imposed

for Wigan ; Lord Bute, Lord Darlington, and Robert Lowther are also included. Subscribers of Jenkinson's circle were John Bindley, Anthony Todd, Philip Carteret Webb, Edward Weston, Richard Phelps, Charles Cornwall, Jeremiah Dyson, William Dowdeswell, Welbore Ellis, Sir Edward Turner, and Lord Harcourt.

   1. The Corporation of London was devoted to Pitt and refused to address the King on the Peace. In March 1763 they united with the Western counties in petitioning against the Cider Bill.

   2. Probably for the Thanksgiving Service for the Peace which was held on May 5.

for the emolument and interest of an incorporated set of City sharpers who under constant dissimulation of making good the orphans fund,[1] plundered by their fathers a hundred years since, have received great sums annually without accounting, or applying those sums for the uses for which they have been as impudently asked as indeed they have been ignorantly ⟨given?⟩. But my good Sir more of this hereafter, that is when His Majesty shall have withdrawn the ray of his royal countenance from that climate of contention, envy, malice, madness, meaness and all uncharitableness. Oh Heaven! how much have I to thank my Lord and you who have helped the once wretched me out of this stye of nastiness and of pride. I am afraid you will say I give to my expression too great a latitude, but pardon me, for I can not utter my sentiments lukewarmly upon the present posture of public affairs, nor will my zeal for so just a cause, my affection for so great a master suffer me to be silent or deny, though in my ears a cock should crow a thousand times thrice. I finish with that most manly motto of Father Pauls — *Esto Perpetuus!* it is a short lesson, but I hope so deeply engraven on my heart, that no time, no difficulty, no danger, no distress, (I trust in God) shall ever raze or deface. As I was in the beginning with you so I am now, and ever shall be, that is most heartily and most humbly

Yours,

Ed. Richardson

BAMBER GASCOYNE TO CHARLES JENKINSON

Add. MS. 38200, f. 312.

Bamber Gascoyne, M.P. for Maldon 1761–63, eldest son of Sir Crisp Gascoyne (1700–1761), Lord Mayor of London (about whom see *D.N.B.*), was appointed Commissioner of the Board of Trade on April 20, 1763. The appointment gave him anxiety on account of the necessary by-election at which he was to be opposed by John Huske, a London merchant of American extraction.[2] Many of the freeholders of Maldon were revenue officers whose recalcitrance was all the more disturbing because there was

1. Towards the end of the seventeenth century the Corporation of London was heavily in debt to the Orphans' Fund deposited in their Chamber, and in 1691 an Act was passed (5 & 6 William and Mary, c. 10) " for the relief of the orphans and other creditors of the City of London ", by which an additional duty of sixpence a chaldron was added to the existing charge of metage on coals coming into the Port of London.
2. About him see p. 149 n. 1.

an Act forbidding interference with them in elections. In December 1762 Gascoyne had voted with the minority, but he was now on good terms with Administration and was supported by the Treasury at this election. See *Structure of Politics*, p. 137, where part of the following letter is quoted. Nevertheless he was defeated by Huske and left without a seat until January 16, 1765, when he was returned for Midhurst in the place of William Hamilton, who vacated his seat to go as British Envoy to Naples.[1] In the obituary notice in the *Gentleman's Magazine* (1791, p. 1066) Gascoyne is wrongly described as M.P. for Liverpool. After Midhurst he sat successively for Weobly, Truro, and Bossiney; from 1779 to 1782 he was a Lord of the Admiralty. It was his son Bamber Gascoyne the younger[2] who sat for Liverpool.

Maldon, April 21, 1763.

I have herewith sent you a list of the Freemen of Maldon who are in office under the Government to desire an immediate conveyance to them that they are to assist me, for I am sorry to tell you that they are to a man almost against me. The opposition to me is carried on with great violence and open bribery. Ribbons with Liberty, Property, and no *Excise* are the ornaments of my opponents horses and carriages and some other devices of this sort which I do not choose to mention. Guineas and scraps of North Britons are scattered all over the town and I can assure you that the opposition is founded by that ingenious gentleman Mr. Wilkes and his crew and is more immediately at Government than me, therefore if not strongly and cheerfully supported by Government I must fall a victim to their resentments. They have received great life from the event of the Gloucestershire opposition[3] and declare their intention of following this amusement wherever there is an opening. Mr. Clamptrot who has lately been appointed Surveyor of the riding officers by Lord Bute has an interest here, he lives at Colchester. The Searcher under him is John Draper of this place, a Freeman; I must therefore desire you to write to him to enforce his Searcher to vote for me or discharge him. I ⟨   ⟩ fixed for Tuesday ⟨   ⟩ and must see you before I return. I therefore beg you will send a line to my house where and when I may have the pleasure of seeing you, and am Sir,

Your most obedient humble servant,
Bamber Gascoyne

1. See p. 139.
2. Through his daughter, who married the 2nd Marquis of Salisbury, the younger Gascoyne was grandfather of the great statesman, Lord Salisbury.
3. On April 27, 1763, Thomas Tracy of Sandywell was returned for Gloucestershire in the place of Norborne Berkeley.

I have herewith sent you a letter from the Adjutant of the Eastern Battalion of Militia, who is under Colonel Rebow,[1] who is obliged to Lord Holland for his seat in Parliament. All the officers are under the influence of Lord Rochford.[2]

JOHN BINDLEY TO CHARLES JENKINSON

Add. MS. 38200, f. 314.

Professor Namier writes in reference to the preceding and the following letters : " The same day John Bindley, a Commissioner of the Excise, thus explained to Jenkinson the way of dealing with subordinate officials of his own office, in view of the Act forbidding interference with them in elections " (*Structure of Politics*, p. 138). Excise officers were forbidden to intermeddle in elections (by canvassing, soliciting, writing, etc.) on pain of a penalty of £100 and disqualification, under three Acts of William and Mary. They were also forbidden to do so by departmental orders since Queen Anne's reign. See Edward Hughes, *Studies in Administration and Finance*, pp. 281, 284, 311. These orders covered excise, malt, leather, salt officers, etc., but not customs officials.

11 O'clock, Excise Office or Southampton Street.
Docketed " April 21, 1763 ".

My dear Sir,
    Brooksbank [3] intimated to the Board what you mentioned yesterday and the affair being of the most delicate nature, I can foresee no way of serving Mr. G⟨ascoyne⟩ but by his application in person or by letter, to those who have votes, in which case leave of absence may be given to the officer who will then understand what is meant. You know I am at your service and shall always be ready to do anything to serve you and your friends.

I am very sincerely yours,

John Bindley

N.B. The method proposed above is the only one used here in former cases.

1. Isaac Martin Rebow, M.P. for Colchester 1754 till his death in 1781.
2. Rochford was Lord Lieutenant of Essex 1756–81 and naturally had great influence in the county. See *England etc.* p. 224. In 1764 he was appointed High Steward of Colchester.
3. Stamp Brooksbank, a clerk in the Excise who eventually became a Commissioner 1776–92. In one of Newcastle's lists of expected removals, dated January 23, 1763, he is marked as Bindley's probable successor as Secretary to the Excise (Add. MS. 33001, f. 175).

H⟨uske [1]⟩ wrote to me yesterday which I thought very extraordinary to assist him with the votes here.

WILLIAM HUNTER TO CHARLES JENKINSON

Add. MS. 38200, f. 321.

William Hunter was a Custom House official, sent to Maldon in April 1763 to work for Gascoyne. On May 12 he wrote to Jenkinson asking to be appointed " to a small collection in an outport " in consideration for his services (Add. MS. 38200, f. 331). A portion of the following letter is printed in Namier's *Structure of Politics*, pp. 138-9.

Tuesday Evening, April 26, 1763.

Sir

I am sorry to acquaint you the bad success Mr. Gascoigne has met with in carrying his election at Malden, an incident I am confident could not have happened, but from (I must say) the ungenerous behaviour and proceedings of the Officers of the Customs etc. freemen of that Borough, a circumstance too tender for me to be more explicit in this manner. I likewise Sir should be very unjust to Mr. Gascoigne should I not presume to inform you, that the most principal gentlemen of the County were nervous in his interest, and his very genteel and polite carriage towards the electors, had they a due sense of loyalty to one of the best of Kings in whose service they are and respect to his Minister's high station and their dependance on his pleasure either to reward or punish, ought to have produced the most cheerful complience and concurrence with every request from him to support his election.

I do not take upon me positively to assert, but only suggest there has been transactions little distant from brib—y and cor—n and very detrimental to Mr. Gascoigne, on this occasion, of which more may come to your knowledge.

It now remains only for me to beg leave further to acquaint

1. John Huske, returned for Maldon April 26, was a son of Ellis Huske, Councillor of the province of New Hampshire. He had been a merchant in Boston but was now living in England, and died here in 1773. He was accused in America of being the author of the Stamp Act, and a poem, " Oppression ", was written against him and published in America and in London in 1765. See *Notes and Queries*, 12th Series, viii, 217, 335. He was connected with Charles Townshend, to whom he had been deputy in the office of Treasurer of the Chambers about 1760. The connexion of both with Charles Townshend may account for Huske's application to Bindley in the Maldon election. See Namier, *Structure of Politics*, p. 138 n. 2, and below, p. 162.

you I have been upon a visit to the several and respective Officers of the Customs, freemen of the Corporation on behalf of Mr. Gascoigne, in the course of which I trust and am willing to hope, nothing has been wanting on my part to declare how necessary it was to compliment him with their votes and interest, and I am ready to afirm, that not any the least intimations consequent thereon has been delivered to those officers or their friends from me, but what has been strictly upright and consistent with the freedom of elections, however warm in His Majestys service and the honour of the honourable House of Commons I have expressed myself, but by what authority I set out from London on Saturday morning last, upon the account you will pardon me mentioning at this time. I have the honour to be Sir,

Your most obedient and most faithful humble servant,

Wm. Hunter

JOHN OLLIVANT COLSWORTHY TO CHARLES JENKINSON
at the Treasury Chambers, Whitehall
Add. MS. 38200, f. 326.

John Ollivant Colsworthy was one of the Commissaries in the Control Department of the Commissariat in Germany. In March 1763 the British troops in Germany were ordered home, but as the Commissariat supplied the whole allied army, it took some time to wind up their affairs, especially as new contracts had been entered into practically up to the time of the cessation of hostilities.[1] Instructions for the return of officers and commissaries were issued from the Treasury on June 17,[2] and the Commissariat was finally dissolved in July, but the affairs of the Control Department were in such disorder that the Commission of Enquiry to examine into German accounts which had been established at the end of 1761, was revived by Grenville in September 1763,[3] in order to settle them, and on November 5, 1763, Colsworthy, who was back in England, applied for an appointment under this Commission.[4]

Bremen, May 4, 1763.

Sir,

I should not have delay'd so long the pleasure of sending you this private letter, to express my remembrance of your former favors, had not the continual hurry of business, which occasion'd frequent removals prevented me.

1. See *State of the Commissariat during the late War in Germany*, Add. MS. 38335, f. 174; and Colonel Pownall's letter to the Treasury Board, June 24, 1763, *ibid.* f. 106.   2. *Ibid.* f. 106.

3. P.R.O., T. 29/35, p. 105. See p. 157.   4. Add MS. 38201, f. 221.

Colonel Pownall [1] writ me an official letter, sometime ago, which he concludes in this manner, " I cannot dismiss this letter without marking to you with great pleasure, the accurate and distinct manner in which it appears to me that you have executed this your commission : and in a manner that promises service to the public ".

I am willing to present you with this little testimonial of my having exerted my best endeavours in the execution of my office.

Since I brought my papers down here from Stolbzenau the Commissioners of Enquiry [2] have been directed to lodge a large parcel of magazine accounts with me ; which I have receiv'd, and am now busy in preparing a book with specifications of my office, by which any particular account may be immediately referr'd to, without difficulty, and which book I hope to have the honor of presenting to you when I return to England, by which you will be much better capable of judging, than I am now of explaining, how I have been employed in Germany.

Colonel Pownall acquaints me he has propos'd a department for me to the Lords of the Treasury, and that he waits their answer.

1. Colonel Thomas Pownall (1722–1805 : about whom see *D.N.B.*) was a brother of John Pownall, Secretary to the Board of Trade, and had been Governor of Massachusetts 1757–59. In 1761 he was sent to Germany as one of three extra Commissaries to control the conduct of the Army contractors and check mismanagement and frauds by the officers of the magazines. (See two letters from him in Liverpool MSS. : Add. MSS. 38198, f. 28 ; 38199, f. 99.) As the result of his reports a Commission of Enquiry was set up at the end of 1761 to re-examine contractors' accounts. In May 1762 he was put in charge of the Control Department of the Commissariat, which was then divided into the two branches of supply and control. The whole department was ordered home in July 1763 although the work on the 1762 accounts was by no means finished. (See *State of the Commissariat* and Pownall's letter to the Lords of the Treasury giving details of his career in Germany. See also their report, Add. MS. 38338, f. 168.) The Commissariat's last business in Germany was the sale of the King's property in magazines, which was left under Pownall's direction, and, according to the *State of the Commissariat*, which was written to the glorification of the Intendant, General Hunter, and to the discredit of his successors, " the net amount of the sale does no honour to the management of this business, which, if conducted with prudence and fidelity, is unfortunate to those who were concerned in it ". Add. MS. 38335, f. 182.

2. A Commission of Enquiry consisting of three Commissaries was originally set up towards the end of 1761 and was revived specifically from time to time. On March 30, 1764, Lord Barrington wrote to Newcastle : " An address was this day moved . . . to thank the King for appointing Commissioners to examine the German accounts and to desire that examination might be continued. This gave me an opportunity to mention the care your Grace had taken (by appointing similar enquiries) to cheque German expences : that two out of three of the present commissioners had been appointed by you " (Add. MS. 32957, f. 305). The commission which Barrington referred to was that which Grenville set up in September 1763. See p. 201.

I am the only Commissary that is now at Bremen [1] and if it were their Lordships pleasure, that the papers belonging to the Public Offices should from time to time be lodg'd with me towards their being transported to England, I can register the specifications of each department and lay, at one view, the whole of the accounts before my superiors : my present plan being only my own office, which does not consist of above thirty chests.

If I could send you any particular information relating to things here, that would be acceptable to you, I should think myself happy to receive the honor of your commands, which I would execute with the utmost care and dispatch. There are some things which I hope to represent to you when I return to England. For my own part I do assure you I have not reap'd the least benefit or advantage whatsoever, from my employ, except my allowance from the King. The calamities of the Warr, and the manner people in our station are oblig'd to live, has occasion'd me to spend fifty pounds more than my pay of two pounds per day, from the 21st of July to the 21st of April, which is a little severe, to a person who has but indifferent health and many fatigues to combat with. But I hope, and make no doubt, it will be properly considered when I return home.

I beg to have the honor of hearing from you, and that you will believe me at all times with great truth

Your most faithfull and most obedient servant,

John Ollivant Colsworthy,
Commissary of Controle

SIR EDMOND THOMAS TO CHARLES JENKINSON

Add. MS. 38458, f. 34.

Sir Edmond Thomas, 3rd Bart. of Wenvoe Castle, Glamorgan, M.P. for the County 1761–67, was re-elected on May 11, 1763, on being appointed Surveyor-General of Woods North and South of Trent.

Wenvoe Castle, Glamorgan, May 6, 1763.

Dear Sir,

I have the satisfaction to acquaint you that there appeared so great a concurrence of interests in my favor, that at the

1. On the evacuation of the British troops from Germany in March 1763, the Commissariat moved its headquarters to Hanover.

meeting held according to an advertisement intended against me, it was unanimously resolved to give me no further opposition, so that I hope to be re-elected on Wednesday next without any more trouble. You will be so good as to make my grateful acknowledgments where I shall ever retain a just sense of the kindness I have been honoured with on this and every other occasion. I hope to be in London in a few days and to have the pleasure of assuring you in person how much I am Sir,

Your sincere friend and humble servant
Edmond Thomas

Lord Talbot has been now in this neighbourhood for some days.

J. S. MACKENZIE TO CHARLES JENKINSON

Add. MS. 38200, ff. 332-3.

James Stuart Mackenzie, M.P. for Ross-shire 1761–80, younger brother of Lord Bute, took the name of Mackenzie on succeeding to the estates of his grandfather, Sir George Mackenzie of Rosehaugh. He was British Minister in Turin 1758–61, but returned to England on the death of the Duke of Argyll in 1761 when he was given the management of the patronage in Scotland. In April 1763, on the death of the Duke of Athol, he was appointed Keeper of the Privy Seal in Scotland. At the time he was on good terms with Grenville, and continued, by mutual agreement, to manage affairs in Scotland, but later jealousies arose over the patronage, and in May 1765 the ministers became so incensed against Bute that they obliged the King to deprive Mackenzie of the Privy Seal which had been promised him for life.

Knaresborough, May 15, 1763.

I thank you my dear Sir for the trouble you have taken in executing the commissions I troubled you with before I left London. I beg you will let Mr. Udny [1] know that he should acquaint Mr. Smith [2] of Venice, that (in consequence of the

1. John Udny (1720–1800), son of Robert Udny of Auchterelon, was a dealer in pictures and antiquities and lived in Italy, where he acted as British Consul in Leghorn, and in succession to Joseph Smith in Venice. He and his wife were friends of Horace Walpole.
2. Joseph Smith (1682–1770), "the merchant of Venice", a well-known collector of books, MSS., paintings, coins, etc., was British Consul in Venice 1740–60, and was apparently engaged in commerce there. In July 1762 he agreed to sell his collection of art treasures to George III for £20,000, "half whereof to be paid forthwith and the other half in three years by three equal payments with 5 per cent of interest for what shall remain due" (Smith to Mackenzie, printed

(153)

letter he (Smith) wrote to *me* lately about the security to be given him for the payment of the remaining £10,000, with interest at 5 per Cent from the 5th January 1763) the Treasury had granted that Warrant, and that such a Warrant is the security given in like cases, you might instance Sir Charles Sheffield's and any others that occur to you.

I wish you would write a line to Udny to the above mentioned purpose as he would then communicate it to Smith, and by that means I should stand clear with the old gentleman, who, I am afraid, suspects that I have not done all I could to hasten the payments to him.

As to Mr. Brown's [1] leave of absence from Utrecht, if you will obtain it for him from the Treasury, I fancy that will do the business ; or, a word drop'd to Baron *Ber* the Hanoverian Minister will certainly compleat it ; favour me with a line when this is done.

I think my brother better in every respect since he has been here, except as to his sleeping in which article he does not find any amendment as yet, though I hope he will soon ; his appetite and his spirits are much better.[2] Hume [3] joined our Colony this morning from Scotland, Mr. Worseley [4] will be here this evening from his house about 30 miles off ; Elliot has been here about a week, but continues his journey northward in a day or two, Sir Harry and Lady Erskine [5] are both here. We rise very early, ride and walk a good deal, dispute frequently and laugh heartily. *So* we go on, free from all business and plague. Adieu my dear Sir.

in Fortescue, *Correspondence of George III*, i, 30, and see L. B. Namier, *Additions and Corrections*, 1937, pp. 12-13). In 1765 his library was sold *en bloc* to George III for £10,000 and forms the nucleus of the King's Library at the British Museum. See *D.N.B.* and E. Edwards, *Lives of the Founders of the British Museum, 1520–1870*, ii, 469.

1. ? Brown, British resident at Utrecht.
2. On the formation of the Grenville Ministry, Bute, whose health was impaired, retired for several weeks to Yorkshire to drink the waters of Harrogate and enjoy the society of his circle of Scottish literati.
3. David Hume the historian, or John Hume.
4. Thomas Worsley of Hovingham, M.P. for Orford and Surveyor-General of the Board of Works. He was " a kind of riding-master to the King " and an old friend of George III and Bute, who brought him into Parliament in 1761. See Namier, *England etc.* p. 176 and n. 3.
5. Sir Harry Erskine, 5th Bart. of Alva, M.P. for Anstruther, 1754–65, Lieutenant-General and Colonel of the 1st Royal Scots. He had literary pretensions and was one of Bute's circle of " silly authors and flatterers ". In 1761 he married Janet, sister of Alexander Wedderburn, afterwards Lord Chancellor and 1st Earl of Rosslyn.

JOHN BINDLEY TO CHARLES JENKINSON

Add. MS. 38200, f. 355.

Southampton Street, Saturday Evening.
Docketed "June 3, 1763".[1]

My dear Friend,

I am going out of town this evening and return on Tuesday morning before which time I expect to have some matters relative to *Clermont* [2] which I wish you to know. I must only desire you and my Lord will draw the inferences agreeably to your superior judgements : and whatever you may hear from me you may assure yourself is never suspected by the parties who talk to me to be told to you ; *they* conceive they may go to Grosvenor Square,[3] but they never suspect me of consequence enough to convey any thing to his *Lordship*.[4] I never mention anything to *them* but my apprehensions of losing my place (which thank God I little fear). They know Mr. T⟨ownshen⟩d loves me and I conceive all is designed for him and they keep telling me he *only* can preserve me or push my future fortune. But my obligations are due only to my Lord and my affection and duty to his Lordship will never be diminished.

Pray send me a line into Southampton Street, advising me what time I may call upon you on Tuesday between 11 and 1 or on Wednesday before one. Having several engagements makes me so precise. In the mean time I remain dear Sir,

Your very sincere friend,

John Bindley

LORD GEORGE SACKVILLE TO CHARLES JENKINSON

Add. MS. 38200, f. 358.

Pall Mall, June 14, 1763.

Sir,

The Duke of Dorset has sent me the enclosed application to Mr. Grenville, which I beg the favour of you to lay before him.

1. June 3, 1763, was a Friday.
2. Newcastle's country seat. After his resignation Newcastle wished all his friends to visit him at Claremont. See Namier, *England etc.* pp. 380-401.
3. Charles Townshend lived in Grosvenor Square. 4. Bute.

(155)

The Duke of Dorset has long cultivated an interest in the borough of Hythe, and has always been indulged by the Lords of the Treasury in having his recommendations accepted of, for the few offices in that port.[1]

I have some reason to hope that the Commissioners of the Customs will present the two persons to the Treasury named in the enclosed paper, but at all events the Duke of Dorset flatters himself that Mr. Grenville will be so good as to comply with his request.[2]   I am Sir, with great reguard

Your most obedient, humble Servant,

Geo: Sackville

SAMUEL MARTIN TO CHARLES JENKINSON

Add. MS. 38200, f. 359.

Samuel Martin (1714–88), M.P. for Camelford, a West Indian and brother of Joseph Martin, Governor of North Carolina, was Jenkinson's predecessor as Joint Secretary to the Treasury, an office into which he was brought by Pitt in 1756.   On the formation of the coalition Government in 1757 he refused an offer of a pension of £1500 a year instead of his place (see Namier, *England etc.* p. 371).   He served at the Treasury successively under three chiefs, but as a member of the Leicester House group his only attachment was to Bute with whom he retired in April 1763, when he was given the reversion of Horace Walpole's sinecure of Usher to the Exchequer.   Unknown to Newcastle, in May 1762, he furnished Bute with information from the Treasury (see *ibid.* pp. 366–71).   About him see *D.N.B.*

Wednesday, June 15, 1763.

Dear Jenkinson,

As to the Abbess of Herevorde, I declare to God I never had any communication with her directly or indirectly : nor

1. Lionel Cranfield Sackville, 1st Duke of Dorset, was Lord Warden of the Cinque Ports 1708–12, 1714–17, and 1728 to his death in 1765. During that time he tried to convert the Lord Warden's Parliamentary interest at Hythe into a family concern. His son, Lord George Sackville, was M.P. for Dover 1741–61 and Hythe 1761–68. In 1767 Lord Holdernesse, who succeeded the Duke of Dorset as Lord Warden, attempted to destroy the Sackville interest at Hythe in a preliminary contest for the election of a mayor, but he was defeated, and Sackville wrote on February 13 : " my friends would not forsake me . . . and I had the pleasure of seeing most of those in Custom House employments vote with me, and all of those who were under the Lord Warden, though they were assured in the most positive manner that they would be immediately dismissed from their offices " (H.M.C., 9th Report, Part III, *Stopford-Sackville MSS.* i, 118). But at the general election in the following year Sackville was heavily defeated. See correspondence in G. Wilks, *The Barons of the Cinque Ports* (1892), pp. 99–116. Sackville, known after 1770 as Lord George Germain, sat for the family borough of East Grinstead 1768–82, when he was created 1st Viscount Sackville.

2. He did so. On June 19 Sackville wrote to thank Jenkinson for his interest on this occasion (Add. MS. 38201, f. 2).

do I know one syllable of any claims sett up by the Abbey of that name.

I have long agoe apprized both Mr. Grenville and you, that you must expect claims from individuals of Germany for years to come. I suppose the Abbess may be the leader of the procession of claimants, and I presume you will find it necessary to turn her, and the whole train who will follow her over to the office of German reference, which Mr. Grenville resolved to erect.[1]

I have mentioned what occurred to me upon Monsieur Alt's [2] papers at the foot of his letter 7th of June and am dear Jenkinson

Sincerely yours,

Saml. Martin

Endorsed : " Inform Mr. Weston of this ".

GEORGE JOHNSTONE TO LORD BUTE

Add. MS. 38200, ff. 361-2.

Governor Johnstone (1730–87), third son of Sir James Johnstone, 3rd Bart. of Westerhall, Dumfriesshire, had been a captain in command of the *Hornet* sloop. In November 1763 he was appointed Governor of West Florida. He remained in the province from 1764 to 1767, when he returned to England and stood for Cockermouth at the general election of 1768, under the patronage of Sir James Lowther. For a florid account of his career see *D.N.B.*

London, June 16, 1763.

My Lord !

After retiring from the greatest concerns of the nation, in order to enjoy that tranquility which your health required, and your disposition leads to ; it may appear very impertinent in me to break in on your hours of rest by any weak concern of mine.

It is indeed my Lord extremely irksome to my self, and if I could meditate any means of avoiding it, I would not trouble your Lordship.

---

1. In June 1763 the Commissariat in Germany was in process of liquidation, and the final orders for its recall were issued on July 7, but as there were still a great many unsatisfied claims from German creditors, Grenville decided to set up a Commission to deal with them, which was done in September 1763. See p. 201.

2. Monsieur Alt, the Resident from Hesse Cassel.

It is needless for me to recapitulate the many instances of your Lordship's favor to me, and in particular by recommending me at different times to Lord Egremont for the Government of Florida.

I shall only say when I went for Scotland with my friend Mr. Home, that I understood as positively as a man can believe in the Political Creed, that I was to go Governour of that division of Florida bordering on the Mississipi and extending eastward along the Bay of Mexico to where ever the division should be fixed (for it was then uncertain) or by what ever name it might afterwards be called.[1]

But I am informed this morning by Lord Egremont that he intends me for the other division of Florida comprehending the Peninsula of Islands, against which I guarded by a minute I delivered your Lordship, at your friendly desire, and likewise pointed out on the map the distinction.

I am very sensible either the one, or the other is superior to my desert : but as the first is infinitely more advantageous, it becomes extremely difficult to lower our views after such assured expectations.

My Lord Egremont informs me that the person who is a competitor for the western Division of Florida, is not yet named ; from whence I suppose some check of mind has naturally occurred in this transaction, but that he is intended to be nominated in a day or two. May I then once more request your Lordship's interposition before such final decision?

Though my Lord Egremont has ever behaved to me with the greatest civility, yet from his total silence concerning the place he intended to send me to, which was the object of my solicitation, I guessed there was something misterious in his views and in case he could send me to any corner of that

---

1. Florida was one of the three provinces ceded to England by the Peace of Paris and was divided by the British Government into East and West Florida, separated by the Appalidricola river. It was the least known of the new acquisitions, and there was some doubt as to its boundaries. In March 1764 the Board of Trade, on the advice of Johnstone, settled the northern boundary of West Florida considerably further north than was agreed at the treaty. Johnstone appears to have misrepresented the facts in connivance with the land speculators, who wished to settle along the Mississippi in the territory belonging to the Indians. See Alvord, *The Mississippi Valley in British Politics*, i, 204 n. An article in the *Gent. Mag.* (1763, p. 552) on the relative merits of East and West Florida considered West Florida healthier and likely to be more prosperous because of its outlet on the Gulf of Mexico. It was thought that the private commerce of the West Indian islanders could be drawn to Pensacola and would bring in a flood of silver coin. In spite of these advantages, West Florida proved a disappointment, as it gained a reputation for unhealthiness. By 1770 settlers and land speculators had ceased to come there, and Governor Chester described the colony as " little more at this day than the garrison town of Pensacola " (Alvord, *op. cit.* ii, 166).

Cession which should retain the name of Florida, he might alledge that he had then fullfild your Lordships request.

It was this suspicion which made me trouble your Lordship oftner than my own sensations could well vindicate, and I am sure much oftner, than your honourable nature required, untill I thought it fixed beyond a doubt with any man : This was likewise the occasion of my writing to your Lordship at a time, which hurt my own delicacy, in order to be at a certainty, that I might not be obliged to trouble your Lordship as at present, when your interfering might not be so agreeable to your generous plan of life.

I explained these things to Lord Egremont with as much assurance as a man of any modesty can press towards a point which he finds is disagreeable to the person from whom he is immediately to obtain it ; and where the discussion of that point must involve the question of his own merit, first as to the office, and 2dly in competition with another.

His Lordship rested upon never having given me any promise, of which I acquit him ; and secondly that I had been recommended as a man fit to find out harbours amongst dangerous rocks and shoals and so he has been pleased to cut off a corner to work on.

Wherever I am employed, I shall endeavour to exert myself to the utmost of my abilitys for the public good, and in honour to your Lordship's recommendation, But the Western Part of Florida, is as much a maritime Province, as the other, more especially as it is now divided, being left a long stripe of land running along a navigable river and a vast extent of sea coast, so that the principal success of the Colony will depend on proper naval establishments ; and besides that in case no harbor is found on the Peninsula, *Pensecola* must then be made the receptacle for our fleet and the key to the Spanish West Indies.

I will not offer to make this letter longer by an apology : I hope your Lordship will feel for my situation ; and I would rather be prolix on the occasion, than not perfectly understood. I am My Lord

Your Lordship's most obedient and devoted servant,
Geo: Johnstone

Add. MS. 38201, ff. 6-7.

Christ Church, June 23, 1763.

Dear Sir !

On the notification which your letter conveyed to me of the arrival of Monsieur de la Condamine [1] at this place, I made it my immediate business to inquire at what inn he took up his quarters ; and finding that he was lodged at the Bear, I went thither to execute the commands with which you favoured me, meaning to ask him to my house, and shew him every mark of civility which his own established character as a sçavant, and your recommendation, intitled him to. He informed me that he had during the course of that day seen every thing remarkable in the University, and that he was then ready to set out for Blenheim,[2] and from thence he meant to pursue his tour to Stowe ; [3] and that he purposed returning to London to day. I used every argument to induce him to prolong his stay here, that I might shew him the literary treasures which our public library contained, and those other curiosities which as a man of science and of taste he might wish to examine leisurely, and which I was apprehensive had been but cursorily and imperfectly pointed out to him, and that I would introduce some men of knowledge to him. He expressed himself sensible of my intentions towards him, and intimated a wish that his time would allow him to continue here ; but his arrangement was made.

You flatter me by intimating that it is long since you heard from me ; if any thing had arisen here either in politics or

1. Charles Marie de la Condamine (1701–74), traveller, mathematician, and member of the French Academy, was lately arrived in England. On June 5 Walpole wrote to Sir Horace Mann : " I have told you of our French : we have got another curious one, La Condamine, qui se donne pour philosophe. He walks about the streets, with his trumpet and a map, his spectacles on, and hat under his arm." He became embroiled in a ridiculous quarrel with his landlady who turned him out, whereupon he published an indignant letter to the people of England telling them, wrote Walpole on June 20, " that he has travelled in the most barbarous countries, and never met with such savages as we are — pretty near truth ; and yet I would never have abused the Iroquois to their faces in one of their own gazettes ". La Condamine's letter is in *Gent. Mag.* for 1763, p. 304, together with an answer vindicating English manners on the grounds that " M. Condamine . . . was found amusing himself with the philosophical society of two fair nymphs, who with more propriety might be styled two Graces rather than two Virtues ".
2. The Duke of Marlborough's seat in Oxfordshire.
3. Lord Temple's seat in Buckinghamshire.

literature worthy your attention I should have written to you ; on any other foot I shall not think of interrupting you. Lloyd [1] went from hence this morning ; he will communicate to you a conversation which passed relative to myself ; I shall esteem it as an act of friendship if you will let me know your sentiments on the subject. I am most sincerely solicitous to see you ; and hope that the load of business may grow lighter as the fifth of July approaches ; I shall keep a bed for you ; which implies no more than that I would not have you relinquish all thoughts of coming till the last day of the celebrity. I am, dear Sir with unfeigned regard and esteem

Your very sincere and faithful servant,

S. Barrington

ROBERT NUGENT TO CHARLES JENKINSON

Add. MS. 38201, f. 8.

Robert Nugent (1702–88) of Carlanstown, County Westmeath, afterwards 1st Viscount Clare (1767) and 1st Earl Nugent (1776) in the Irish peerage, was a notorious turncoat and opportunist. Lord George Sackville wrote of him in September 1764 : ". . . upon the least appearance of ministerial jumbles he is in violent agitation till he has found a safe harbour to protect him against the impending storm ".[2] He was M.P. for Bristol 1754–74, where " he was intrusted with the nomination to every place and employment in the disposal of Government ".[3] On January 5, 1763, he was appointed Joint Vice-Treasurer of Ireland. About him see *D.N.B.*, and Claud Nugent, *Memoir of Robert, Earl Nugent* (1898).

Dublin, June 26, [1763].

Dear Sir,

I received a note from Mr. Grenville, some days since, informing me that he had complied with my request in favour of Bristol ; and I returned him my thanks, as I now do to you for your kind attention. Oswald [4] set out with

1. Philip Lloyd.
2. Lord George Sackville to General Irwin, September 5, 1764, H.M.C., 9th Report, Part III, *Stopford-Sackville MSS.* p. 191. See also Namier, *England etc.* p. 426 n. 4.
3. Josiah Tucker, *Review of Lord Clare's Conduct* (1775), p. 16. On Nugent's interest at Bristol see Namier, *Structure of Politics*, pp. 110–14.
4. James Oswald (1715–69) of Dunnikier, M.P. for Kirkcaldy Burghs. On May 4, 1763, he was appointed Joint Vice-Treasurer of Ireland. Like Gilbert Elliot, he was a Scottish barrister who made a name for himself as one of " the ablest men in the House of Commons ", where he " was master of a quickness and strength of argument, not inferior to Fox " (Walpole, *Memoirs of George II*, i, 59). One of the Edinburgh intelligentsia, he was a friend of Adam Smith, was interested in

Rigby[1] on Sunday morning in the Packet, replete with Irish wine and politicks. He may possibly get rid of both in his passage to the opposite shore. He has been very hospitably treated and very much liked here. Happily for me I was indisposed some part of the time, with a sore throat — a less evil than a fever, which would certainly be the consequence, in my constitution, of unceasing nocturnal compotations. I am now stepping into my post-chaise to visit the wildest part of Ireland, where I have an estate great in bulk and small in revenue.[2] I hope to render the one a little more proportionable to the other and then revisit old England where you have not a friend more sincerely than I am, dear Sir,

Your faithful humble servant,

R. Nugent

EDWARD RICHARDSON TO CHARLES JENKINSON

Add. MS. 38201, ff. 11-12.

Marked in Pencil by the British Museum Cataloguer :
"June 1763".

Sir,

Mr. Husk, since Sunday last is entirely freed from those surmises I spoke to you off when I last had the honour to see you. Reports had been artfully spread, which, indeed, would have led him into error, but through your candour I was enabled to set ⟨him⟩ right. He is much obliged to you, yet I dare not let him ⟨   ⟩ however it is at present sufficient, that he has found ⟨it was ?⟩ all Gasconade.[3] Had the pleasure yesterday to dine with him and another of your hearty freinds Sir Henry Cheir[4] where we toasted very frankly my Lord

economics, and was, like Elliot, a first-class financial expert. Before his appointment in May 1763 he had been a Commissioner of the Treasury. As a Scot he was naturally a follower of Bute. Some of his letters are published in *Memorials of the Public Life and Character of James Oswald of Dunnikier*, 1825. About him see *D.N.B.*

1. Richard Rigby (1722–88), M.P. for Tavistock, the Duke of Bedford's man of business. He made the third in this crew of Joint Vice-Treasurers. He was also Master of the Rolls in Ireland and had been there before in 1760 as secretary to Bedford, then Lord Lieutenant. See *D.N.B.*

2. Carlanstown, near Castlepollard. See C. Nugent, *op. cit.* p. 6.

3. See p. 149, and *Structure of Politics*, p. 139. It seems to have been a peculiarity of Maldon for its members to come in against the Government interest, and then to veer round and make their peace.

4. Sir Henry Cheer, Deputy Lieutenant of Middlesex and Justice of the Peace, was knighted on December 10, 1760.

Butes and yours, and next week meet again for the same good purpose. Beleive me I could write a whole ream in commendation of these new acquisitions, but forbear, for you shall see and prove their works. On the other hand am concerned to hear the wig or rump interest are making opposition to Mr. Conyers [1] in Essex. Their progress in favour of Luther [2] is very rapid, of which shall say no more, supposing your earlier intelligence and the readiness of your friends to frustration. Our new Member has already been canvassing for that purpose. Dr. Demainbray [3] presents his most respectful regard and wishes to learn whether Lord Warwick's letter reached Mr. Grenville's hand, being under a doubt. What say ⟨you⟩ my good Sir? May I withdraw a little from the town this burning weather and seek repose *sub tegmine fagi*, and am I to sing *Mellibee Deus*, or *Dominus, haec otia fecit*. In the mean time begin to fear I shall never see his Lordship again, so strict is he in his present state of seclusion. How⟨ever⟩ hope I yet exist in his Lordship's memory, as most cert⟨ainly he⟩ ever shall in mine. Pray when you see opportunity ⟨be so⟩ kind to rehearse a few of Virgil's lines for me to his Lordship, they are really very apposite to the case of your humble servant. If I recollect right, the lines I mean begin with " In freta dum Flavii ", and end with the following " Semper honos, nomenque, tuum laudesque manebunt, me quaecunque vocant terrae ". Hold, I beg your pardon, I am taking up your time as tho' it were your own, I forget I am robbing the publick, conclude therefore with very humble haste. My good and honoured freind

Your most obedient and most obliged servant,

Edward Richardson

1. John Conyers, of Copt Hall, was not elected for Essex till February 25, 1772, when he succeeded Sir William Maynard. He was returned again at the general election of 1774 but died the following year.

2. John Luther was returned for Essex on December 13, 1763, on the death of William Harvey. He continued to sit for the County until 1784. He was the Whig candidate and was supported by Newcastle in this election (see Add. MS. 32950, f. 35). On December 16, 1763, Horace Walpole wrote to Lord Hertford: " The Court have lost the Essex election, merely from Lord Sandwich interfering in it, and from the Duke of Bedford's speech; a great number of votes going from the City on that account to vote for Luther. Sir John Griffin, who was disobliged by Sandwich's espousing Conyers, went to Chelmsford at the head of five hundred voters."

3. Dr. Demainbray, experimental philosopher, Principal Surveyor of the Customs and inspector of the East India Company's warehouses. Some letters from him are in the Bute MSS.

SHUTE BARRINGTON TO CHARLES JENKINSON

Add. MS. 38201, f. 13.

Christ Church, July 3, 1763.

Dear Sir !

An opinion of yours upon the question Lloyd proposed to you is to me almost decisive ; and yet I think that there are arguments which might be urged on the opposite side which you would allow to have some weight. I wish you could permit me to have some conversation with you on the subject during this week. I need not suggest to you the light in which Lord L⟨itchfield⟩ would take your appearance only on one day ; and the real solid service you might do the Whig and Government cause by your interposition at this juncture more particularly. Unless you, who are perhaps one of the only persons who can, intervene, I am apprehensive that Lord L⟨itchfield⟩ will pursue measures which must hurt his own character and interests, and prove detrimental to the Whigs of this place ; whose conduct at his election merits a better return than I am afraid it will receive. It is confidently whispered, and I believe on good grounds that Lord Northampton is to be nominated High Steward during the Encaenia.[1] I am, dear Sir, with real regard and esteem,

Your sincere and faithful servant,

S. Barrington

T. RAMSDEN TO CHARLES JENKINSON

Add. MS. 38201, f. 18.

Pontefract, July 9, 1763.

My dear Jenkinson,

I should have wrote to you before this time, and hope you will excuse my idleness. Spent a week with my brother Robert[2] in Nottinghamshire, and have been here one week ;

1. On July 5. Charles Compton, 7th Earl of Northampton, was Ambassador to Venice 1761–63. He died at Lyons on October 18, 1763, aged twenty-six. He matriculated at Christ Church ; D.C.L., 1759.
2. Robert Ramsden of Osberton, Nottinghamshire, fourth son of Sir William Ramsden. He had been an Army officer.

and found my friends at both places ⟨pre⟩tty well. I shall be very glad to hear that you are perfectly recovered, and have a little leisure to see the country for some days. We have the greatest appearance of plenty in these parts ; have been blessed with rain, which makes it pleasant, and has not yet done any damage to hay, with which all are very busy. Politicks are very much subsided in these parts, at least where I have been. No coal.[1] I hope, with a certain sett. I hear (though without good authority) that H.R.H. the Duke of Cumberland is to come to Wentworth House.[2] It is a long journey for any body, that is not very well in health, to stay only for a few days, and therefore can scarce credit it.

I have heard from my brother since the last Review. The Duke of Aquitain had a narrow escape, and if the accident has hurt the beauty of his face, it will be very mortifying, to him. The Colonel is now, I conclude at Cambridge, and will go this day to Sir William Maynard in Essex.[3] I have not had the pleasure of seeing his son, but am just going to Swillingdon to dine ; but hear the dear little fellow is very well.[4] I shall be very glad to hear from you, that all the Harcourt family are well. Sir John Evelyn,[5] I fear, is not alive ; for by my brother he was ill, and it is not likely, that so old and worn a person can stand any fresh attack.

Pray assure your sister and brother of my best wishes and believe me, my dear Jenkinson

Most affectionately yours,

T. R.

1. There was a contemporary joke " whether the King shall use Scotch coal, Newcastle coal or Pitt coal ". See Horace Walpole to Horace Mann, December 5, 1760.
2. Lord Rockingham's seat in Yorkshire.
3. Sir William Maynard, 8th Bart. of Walthamstow, M.P. for Essex 1759–72.
4. F. Ramsden married on March 17, 1761, Isabella, sister of Charles, 9th Viscount Irwin. She died the same year in childbed, leaving issue George Ramsden, afterwards Captain of the 15th Hussars.
5. Sir John Evelyn, 1st Bart., died on July 14.

LORD SANDWICH TO CHARLES JENKINSON

Add. MS. 38201, ff. 25-6.

Admiralty, July [1] 15, 1763.

Sir,

Having received a letter from Mr. John Harrison,[2] desiring, that another Board of Longitude may be summoned (before his son proceeds to make a second trial of his time keeper) to take into consideration, what sort, and what number of observations, are really necessary for ⟨a co⟩nclusive trial thereof, and that the correctness and propriety of the instruments intended to be made use of for making such observations, may be carefully exam⟨ined⟩ I am to desire you will please to g⟨ive⟩ me, and the rest of the Commission⟨ers⟩ a meeting, at this place, on Thursday the 4th of next month, at 11 o'clock in the forenoon, to determine upon these matters ; and, at the same time, to take into consideration a Memorial from the University of Gottingen, and a letter from Mr. Michaelis, Director of the Royal Society there,[3] in behalf of the widow and chil⟨dren⟩ of the late Professor Meyer, whose ⟨   ⟩ invented tables of the moon's moti⟨on⟩ and some other papers relative ⟨to⟩ the method of finding the longitu⟨de⟩ were

1. Sandwich omitted the month, which can be supplied from internal evidence. Lower down he refers to " Thursday, the 4th of next month ", and since he was First Lord of the Admiralty from April 18 to September 9, 1763, during which time August was the only month of which the 4th fell on a Thursday, it follows that this letter was written in July.

2. John " Longitude " Harrison (1693–1776), mechanic and inventor of a time-piece to discover the longitude at sea. With the pocket time-keeper he perfected in 1759 he applied for the £20,000 reward offered by an Act of Parliament of 1713 to anyone who should discover a method of determining the longitude at sea. With this instrument his son, William Harrison, made two successful experimental voyages, the first to Jamaica and back, from November 18, 1761, to March 26, 1762, and the second to Barbados in 1764. But it was not without infinite trouble that Harrison eventually recovered the whole of his £20,000 reward. See *D.N.B.* and correspondence in the *Scots Magazine*, xxvii, 457-63 ; and in *Gent. Mag.* see Index under " Longitude ". See also *Gent. Mag.*, 1763, September 28 (p. 462) : " The Rev. Mr. Nevil Maskelyne, fellow of Trinity College, Cambridge, and Mr. Charles Green, of the Observatory at Greenwich, are appointed by the Commissioners of Longitude, to make observations in a voyage to Barbadoes, for the trial of Mr. Harrison's watch, Mr. Irwin's marine chair, and Mr. Meyer's method of finding the longitude by the distances of the moon from the sun and fixed stars ". Harrison afterwards accused Maskelyne of preferring Meyer's method of finding the longitude and suggested that the Astronomer Royal had not paid sufficient attention to his own invention. See *D.N.B.*, Harrison.

3. Johann David Michaelis (1717–91), celebrated Professor of Hebrew studies in the University of Göttingen. He was also interested in geography and natural science.

formerly laid before the Commissioners and some trials and experiments were afterwards made, on shipboard, to determine their accuracy, upon which no resolutions have, as yet, been taken. I am, Sir,

Your most humble servant,
Sandwich

On April 23 Wilkes published the *North Briton*, No. 45, attacking the Ministry for the Speech from the Throne in defence of the Peace. The Government retaliated by issuing a General Warrant for the arrest of " the authors printers and publishers ", under which forty-nine persons were arrested. Many of these afterwards brought successful actions against the Secretaries of State and their servants, from whose office the Warrant was issued. The Government's instructions were very clumsily carried out, for most of the defendants were awarded damages, not on account of the illegality of General Warrants, a point which was never determined, but because they proved themselves innocent of any connexion with the *North Briton*.

J. S. MACKENZIE TO CHARLES JENKINSON

Add. MS. 38201, ff. 27-8.

Edinburgh, July 16, 1763.

A thousand thanks to you, my dear Sir, for your letter of the 8th instant giving me an account of the issue of the cause between the printers and the messengers.[1] I observe by the relation of that affair in the newspapers, that the printers seized by the messengers were not found by the Jury to have been the printers of that No. 45 of the North-Briton for which they were apprehended ; and upon that account obtained damages ; this alters the case greatly from the light in which we saw it here at first, for we thought that the printers had been acquitted by the Jury of having committed any crime in printing that infamous paper, and in this light I dare say many people at a distance will understand it, if pains be not taken to explain it to the publick, as was done after Wilkes's

1. An action for false imprisonment brought by Huckwell, a journeyman to Dryden Leach, printer, against the Secretary of State's messenger, who had arrested him on suspicion of being concerned in printing the *North Briton*, No. 45. The case was heard on July 6 and 7, the messenger being defended principally by Charles Yorke, the Attorney-General. Though there was only one plaintiff and one defendant, the case was referred to loosely as the case of the printers against the messengers, as a number of others who had been arrested also brought successful actions.

being set at liberty by the Chief Justice Pratt ; for you may remember the Faction at that time endeavoured to make the world believe that he obtained his liberty from an illegality in the Warrant granted by the Secretary of State and not upon account of his privilege as was really the case.[1] I am very much concerned however, that the Jury have given damages against the messengers whatever were their reasons for doing so, as I am sure it will hurt Government and tend to animate that cursed spirit of Faction which prevails so much at present in the southern part of the Kingdom. I say, the southern part, because I would fain hope that it is confined to London, its environs and the cyder counties ; as to this part of the United Kingdom, I am happy to find the greatest unanimity among all descriptions of men here ; all express the strongest sense of duty and affection to the King's person, and the warmest desire to support his Government with dignity ; they feel with indignation the insults offered to their Sovereign, and they trust that the next Session of Parliament will take up this business with the utmost vigor ; they think that if Parliament does not interpose with a very high hand, there will very soon be an end of Government, and that anarchy must take place ; these are the sentiments of many sensible cool men here, who view what is now passing with very serious concern.

I thank you for the care you have taken of my commissions ; I wish you would get the order sent down to the Excise here, directing them to treat with Mr. Forbes [2] of Culloden about the purchase of his exemption from paying duty in a certain Barony (or Lordship) in his estate here ; Mr. Dyson knows how this affair stands, and I spoke to him about it the day before I left London ; the distinguished merit and services to the Crown of the late Lord President Forbes (this gentleman's father) ought to entitle the latter to every sort of indulgence which can with propriety be shown him by Government in the purchase of this exemption.

1. " It is not true that the legality of the warrant ever came in question in Guildhall on the trial of the actions brought by the journeymen printers " (extract from the *Gazetteer* for July 16, printed in *Gent. Mag.*, 1763, p. 346). Huckwell was awarded £300 damages, though " he was detained but a few hours at a messenger's house where he had a very good dinner " (*ibid.* p. 342).

2. John Forbes of Culloden, son of the famous Duncan Forbes, President of the Court of Session, who died in 1747. The family estates suffered severely in the rebellion of 1745, when Duncan Forbes spent £30,000, or several years' rents, in the King's cause, for which he never received any compensation. John Forbes, " by economy and judicious management ", succeeded in retrieving the fortunes of his family (Burke's *Commoners*, 1833). On Duncan Forbes see C. de B. Murray, *Duncan Forbes of Culloden* (1936).

I shall expect to hear soon again from you about what Government thinks of these late trials, and how they intend to proceed in consequence of what has passed ; mean while I remain my dear Jenkinson most sincerely

Your faithfull humble servant

J. Mackenzie

J. S. MACKENZIE TO CHARLES JENKINSON

Add. MS. 38201 ff. 31-2.

Edinburgh, July 21, 1763.

I am much obliged to you, My dear Sir, for the very distinct minutes you sent me in your letter of the 12th instant, of the Attorney-General's pleading in the case of the Messengers and Printers, and I beg you'll continue to send me everything of that kind as it is most interesting to me, as well as to every mortal I converse with here. Did the Chief Justice tell the Jury that they were to determine the law part as well as the fact in question ? [1] There has been a letter received here from a very sensible man who was present at Guildhall and who mentions that circumstance, which greatly surprises all the Judges and the Lawyers here.

I am not sure whether or not I asked the favor of Mr. Grenville the last time I had the honour to be with him, to name Mr. Robert Stewart Collector of the Customs at Tobago to be one of the Commissioners for the Division of Lands in that island, if I did not mention it, I meant to have done it, and therefore wish you would say a word to Mr. Grenville on the subject. This Mr. Stewart is very knowing in that part of the world having resided in the West Indies for several years. The sallary he has as Collector is very small, and the perquisites can amount to nothing for a long while to come, as there are I believe at present few or no inhabitants in that Island.

I beg you will remember to send me an express when the

1. " His Lordship . . . said they [the jury] had a right to know his opinion in point of law . . . and then went on to tell them that, as at present advised, he was inclined to think so and so, whereupon the jury found their verdict for the plaintiffs. This goes a good way upon the principle of the jury being judges of law as well as of fact, which if it comes to be established, will have extraordinary consequences " (Hardwicke to Newcastle, July 9, 1763 ; P. C. Yorke, *Life of Hardwicke*, iii, 511).

Queen is delivered. I purpose leaving this to morrow, but you will continue to direct to me at Edinburgh, if you please ; except when you send an express, and then orders should be transmitted from the General Post Office at London to the Post Office here to forward it to me by express wherever I may happen to be at the time. I believe, however, that that is a thing of course, whenever an express is sent.

As I wrote to you on the 16. instant I have nothing further to trouble you with at present but to assure you My dear Sir, that I am

Most sincerely yours

THE ARCHBISHOP OF CANTERBURY TO CHARLES JENKINSON

Add. MS. 38201, f. 35.

Thomas Secker was Archbishop of Canterbury 1758–68.

Lambeth, July 21, 1763.

⟨Si⟩r,

I am afraid M. Gibert [1] gives you a great ⟨deal of trou⟩ble : and indeed he gives me some. But I ⟨   ⟩rsons in his situation, and that of his flock, ⟨   ⟩ anxious and inquisitive, and apt to make ⟨   ⟩ if not complaints. One should be so ones self ⟨in that⟩ condition. And therefore I exercise my patience ⟨   ⟩ recommend him to yours. He wants to know, ⟨what⟩ I cannot tell him, whether any of the money, which the King had given, may be applied to purchase here such utensils for the ⟨si⟩lk-worm business, as they will want in

1. The Rev. H. Gibert, for fifty years Rector of Rolton in Lincolnshire. The *Gent. Mag.*, 1770, p. 279, says " he was a French Protestant and left his country for his religion ". His application to the Treasury for a " grant of lands in North America in favour of himself and certain French Protestants " was read on July 6, 1763 (P.R.O., T. 29/35). The Society of French Protestants, who were waiting at Plymouth to embark for America in 1763 under the leadership of Gibert, were under the protection of the Archbishop of Canterbury, who wrote to Halifax on October 21 urging that their departure be speeded up. Their secretary had written to him complaining that they were little guarded against the rigours of the climate and had buried three children in six days. (In *Cal. H.O. Papers, 1760–65*, No. 1046.) They were still awaiting embarkation on December 29 when Sandwich wrote to the Lords of Trade that " Mr. Wolters, His Majesty's agent at Rotterdam, has informed me of a very disagreeable report being industriously spread in Holland, that the French settlers who have been engaged in London for the King's American dominions, are kept in jaol at Plymouth till the time of their departure and that one Gibert, their chief, has spread this rumour in France " (P.R.O., S.P. 44, 139, f. 266). Gibert died in England in 1770.

America, and not be able to get there, or at least not so cheap, nor possibly so good. I asked Mr. Grenville at Court yesterday concerning this : but just as he had begun to explain himself to me upon it, the King called for him. Be so good as to learn his thoughts and acquaint M. Gibert with them, when he ⟨wai⟩ts on you. He hath remonstrated to me also, that some ⟨   ⟩ who was to have carried him and his people over, ⟨now refuse⟩ to take them : and that he knows not how or when ⟨   u⟩nless the King will allow them a ship : which, he saith, they can navigate themselves. I am totally ig⟨nora⟩nt of all matters of this sort. If you will hear him at your ⟨leisur⟩e, and assist him, or set him right as you see occasion, you wi⟨ll do⟩ an a⟨ct⟩ of great humanity, and oblige

Your faithful servant,

T⟨ho. Cant.⟩ [1]

J. S. MACKENZIE TO CHARLES JENKINSON

Add. MS. 38201, f. 43.

July 30, 1763.

Many thanks to you my dear Sir, for your letter of the 21st instant, though I am heartily sorry to learn by it, the turn of the D. of Bedford's conversation at present,[2] as well as some other hints you drop'd to me ; where will all this frenzy end ? I beg however you'll continue to let me hear constantly from you, and remember that to a man at a distance, many things are interesting news, which appear nothing to those who are on the spot.

The principal reason for my writing to you at present is to mention an affair to you, concerning which Mr. Elliot may possible speak to you. You know his father is the Lord Justice Clerk [3] here and in that quality, is the principal official corre-

1. The signature is missing, but Secker usually signed himself in this way.
2. This appears to be the only reference to Bedford's conversation in July, but it is safe to assume that Mackenzie objected to it as being hostile to Bute, whom Bedford had never forgiven for curtailing his powers as ambassador to negotiate the Peace of Paris. He afterwards refused to join Administration so long as Bute remained at Court. See *Bedford Corr.* iii, 114-37 *passim* ; Fitzmaurice, *Shelburne*, i, 203.
3. Sir Gilbert Elliot of Minto was Lord Justice Clerk of Scotland from April 1763, when he succeeded Charles Erskine of Tindwald.

spondent of the Secretary of State ; the late Lord Justice Clerk who died last April enjoyed a small pension of £100 a year which the late Duke of Argyll procured for him in the name of his son in law, one Mr. Kilpatrick ; this pension was given upon account of the Lord Justice Clerk's having been, (or pretending to have been) at some extraordinary expences in procuring intelligence etc. to transmitt to the Secretary of State soon after the last rebellion ; so instead of obtaining a sum of money to reimburse him, he got this pension of £100 a year ; and I am informed that the Duke of Argyll had it put in another person's name, in order that a succeeding Justice Clerk might not claim any right of it ; this being the state of the case, I never intended that the present Justice Clerk should have it, but that it should be suppressed, or if it was to be continued as a pension, God knows ! I have many sollicitors, who stand in much greater need of it, than the Lord Justice Clerk ; however he now claims it, and spoke to me about it before I left Edinburgh, I told him upon what footing his predecessor had obtained it, but he alledged that by his commission he was to have all his predecessor had had, and that though he had not this £100 in his own name, yet he enjoyed the benefit of it, I thereupon told him that I could say nothing to it, till I had talked to Mr. Grenville upon the subject ; and in the mean while I desired that Mr. Kilpatrick might leave the money lying in the Exchequer, till the point was finally settled. Now, in case Elliot speaks to you on the subject (which, were I in his place, I should be ashamed to do) you might tell him, as from yourself, that the matter will be settled when I return to London, and have talked to Mr. Grenville about it, and if you please, you may at the same time acquaint Mr. Grenville how the affair really stands, for the fact is, that the present Justice Clerk has no more right to that £100 than I have, but if he and his son will condescend so far as to make a point of it, to be sure it is not worth disobliging them for such a trivial matter.[1]

I inclose a paper of recommendations to offices here, which you'll be so good as to have carried through the Treasury.

Adieu my dear Jenkinson. I am

Yours most sincerely,

J. Mackenzie

Direct to me, as usual, at Edinburgh.

1. See Elliot's letter, p. 200.

The following letter refers to the management of the borough of Rye. Edwin Wardroper had been Newcastle's local manager for the borough of Winchelsea, but when Newcastle left the Treasury, Wardroper remained a " zealous and active " friend of Government — or deserted his chief; the eighteenth century was not sure which way to take it. At the same time he extended his activities on behalf of the Treasury to the neighbouring boroughs of Rye and Hastings,[1] where Edward Milward, formerly Newcastle's agent, also found himself obliged to cleave to the Treasury.[2] Rye was one of the three Sussex boroughs which Newcastle during the years he had nursed them from the Treasury had come to look on as his own allodial property and the only one in which, thanks to the loyalty of his agent, Thomas Lamb, he was able to maintain his interest against the Government.[3]

EDWIN WARDROPER TO CHARLES JENKINSON

Add. MS. 38201, f. 52.

Rye, August 1, 1763.

Sir,

The Freemen met to day according to annual custom for the nomination of a Mayor (the Election being this day month). Mr. George Onslow [4] our late Member came down on purpose and attended on behalf of the Duke of Newcastle and in his name proposed and urged the choosing Mr. Procter in opposition to Captain Pigram,[5] Mr. Norris [6] our present Member likewise was present, and the Placemen being told that not one of them would be removed on their voting for Procter nor for any other reason with an assurance that they had authority from the Ministry for saying so, some of those who had before promised me and Pigram were by that means and some threats if they acted otherwise, induced to change their minds so that Procter had a majority of hands. I can hardly believe they had such an authority as they pretended and if it be so should not think of contending with them.

1. On October 29, 1763, Thomas Lamb wrote to Newcastle about some impending changes at Hastings: " The Hastingers . . . are . . . to remove Mr. Ashburnham, and to choose Mr. Luke Nicoll in his stead, this is your Grace's friend Mr. Wardroper's scheme, who labours most incessantly both here and elsewhere against your interest " (Add. MS. 32952, f. 139).
2. See p. 249.
3. See Namier, *Structure of Politics*, p. 170.
4. George Onslow, afterwards 1st Earl of Onslow, M.P. for Rye 1754–61, Surrey 1761–74. He was the son of Speaker Onslow and married a niece of Newcastle's. See *England etc.* p. 449 n. 2.
5. N. Pigram, Captain in the Revenue service at Rye.
6. John Norris, M.P. for Rye 1762–74, was in opposition with Newcastle and voted against the Preliminaries in December 1762.

You very well know the advantage of having a Mayor that may be depended upon, if the Ministry still think of takeing the town out of the hands of the Duke of Newcastle as was Lord Bute's resolution that is the first step to be taken and would not be very difficult when the Placemen are convinced which way their interest leads, but in order thereto some removes are absolutely necessary. You'll be so good to lay this before Mr. Grenville and to lett me know his sentiments if it be necessary I would come up and wait on him and receive his commands or if he inclines to let the matter rest shall act accordingly. I shall hope to hear from you soon and am Sir
Your most obedient servant,
E. Wardroper

I hope Mr. Prosser [1] will not be forgott.

The election of a mayor was to take place on August 29, and on August 16 Lamb wrote to Newcastle congratulating him on the state of his interest : " I'm persuaded that at present things will go agreeable to your Grace's warmest wishes, and (as Wardroper and Pigram declare they will stand a poll) I may I hope affirm we shall be more than two to one, this besides the Bench and we are there for your Grace, seven out of eight ; these have no votes for mayor but have for members so that your Grace sees we are strong indeed should anything be wanted that way ".[2] Thanks to Thomas Lamb, Newcastle's party carried the day, and on April 6, 1764, Newcastle wrote to the mayor, jurats, and freemen of Rye thanking them for " the continuance of your goodness and friendship to me ".[3]

The following letter refers to the Parliamentary management of Tintagel. John Richmond Webb of Lincoln's Inn, M.P. for Tintagel, also called Bossiney, 1761–66, was Grenville's election manager at Fowey and Tintagel. In January 1765 he was appointed one of the Welsh judges. He died on January 15, 1766.

The principal interest at Tintagel had descended to Bute from his father-in-law, Edward Wortley Montagu, but Lord Edgcumbe, a local landowner and one of the principal election managers in Cornwall, also had influence there, though not enough to secure him a seat in 1761. In 1758 and again in 1760, some local government appointments were in dispute between the burgesses of Camelford and Tintagel, and Edgcumbe used his influence for the Tintagel men in the hope of winning a seat there. See Namier, *Structure of Politics*, pp. 375, 418-20.

1. On July 6, 1763, Wardroper wrote to Jenkinson asking that one Prosser, a surveyor at Rye ,should not be kept long from starting his duties by the routine instructions to newly appointed officers. Add. MS. 38201, f. 15.
2. Add. MS. 32950, f. 148 ; see also f. 198.
3. Add. MS. 32958, f. 27.

JOHN RICHMOND WEBB TO CHARLES JENKINSON

Add. MS. 38201, ff. 53-4.

Camelford, Thursday Morning, August 4, 1763.

Dear Sir,

You know the situation of the borough of Tintagell, and that all attempts have been made by the friends of Lord Edgecombe to gain the Mayor from us : one of which has been to promise a nephew of his to make him an alderman at Lostwithiel. What I have to beg you to contrive is, there is now a vacancy of the Surveyorship of the Window Lights in, I take it, the middle division of the county of Cornwall, upon the late Surveyor, one Elliot's being superannuated ; that this vacancy may not be filled up till you hear farther from me, let who will have made application, for the fate of the borough may in all probability depend upon it.

I beg when you see Lord B. you will present my respects, and let him know that Mr. Mayne [1] and I are setting out this morning for Tintagell, where I shall do him all the service in my power : and that after I have seen the Mayor a second time (for I have seen him once to no effect already) I will do myself the honour of acquainting him with the state of things. I am, dear Sir,

Your very obliged and obedient servant,

J. R. Webb

GEORGE GRENVILLE TO CHARLES JENKINSON

Add. MS. 38191, ff. 78-9.

Wotton, August 5, 1763.

Dear Jenkinson,

The Treasury messenger brought me your packet yesterday at dinner time, and as you tell me in it there is no occasion to send him back till to morrow morning, I shall keep him till then accordingly. I find by Mr. Wood's [2] answer that there

1. Possibly one of the brothers of Sir William Mayne, afterwards Lord New-haven ; Edward Mayne who died 1777, or Robert, M.P. for Gatton 1774-82.
2. Robert Wood, M.P. for Brackley, Under-Secretary of State in Lord Halifax's department. He was a distinguished Homeric scholar and was well known as the explorer of Palmyra and Baalbek. See *D.N.B.* ; Namier, *Structure of Politics*, pp. 50-51.

is no objection to Lord Rochfords [1] coach and wine being transhipped in order to go to Spain ; I therefore desire you will inform Lord Rochford of the answer, and give orders accordingly if no farther objection is made to it. I have complyed with the desire in favor of Mr. Price and have signed that appointment as well as the other papers you sent to me. I am very glad that you have satisfied Wood and Rivers [2] about the Agencys to the new Colonies.[3] I will speak to Lord Egremont upon this subject when I see him here, which if nothing particular prevents it I hope to do in a few days. There was a letter to me from Lord *Montacute* signed *Montagu* [4] about some wine or brandy seized for not paying the London duty. It was referred to the Commissioners of the Customs who I think have reported strongly against it, and I desired Charles Loyd [5] (whose health you know has obliged him to go for a little while into the country) to write a very civil letter to Lord Montagu for me to sign, and to send him the report inclosed. I do not remember that this was done. I wish therefore that you would ask Mr. Broughton [6] who can inform

1. William Henry Nassau Zulestein, 4th Earl of Rochford, was appointed Ambassador to Madrid on June 8, 1763.
2. James Rivers, appointed Clerk of the Signet on January 4, 1763, was Robert Wood's colleague in the Southern Department, where since 1756, or earlier, he had acted as Under-Secretary " under the name of Interpreter of Southern Languages " (see *Grenv. Pps.* i, 181). He never sat in Parliament and belonged to the type of civil servant who was more clerk than official.
3. The colonies ceded to Great Britain by the Peace of Paris, viz. Canada, East and West Florida, Grenada. Grenville presumably refers to the Government agencies, which were more or less sinecures ; the colonial agents were appointed by the colonial assemblies.
4. Anthony Browne, 6th Viscount Montagu (1686–1767), a Roman Catholic. He nominated two members for Midhurst. See *Structure of Politics*, p. 178.
5. Charles Lloyd (died 1773), brother of Philip Lloyd, Dean of Norwich (see p. 92 n. 3), was Grenville's private secretary. He was Receiver-General for Gibraltar, February 1763 till the fall of Grenville's Government (see *Grenv. Pps.* iii, 86), and first clerk and deputy teller in the Exchequer. He lived with his mother, who was housekeeper at the Salt Office (see E. Hughes, *Studies in Administration and Finance*, pp. 219, 278). He was a capital burgess of Orford (see Add. MS. 38477, f. 37), and seems to have been brought in by Grenville, who meant him to manage the borough for the Treasury; but when Grenville left office in July 1765 Lloyd apparently attempted " to set up for a personal interest in the borough " and " has built a fine house and assembly room at Orford " (see *Structure of Politics*, pp. 482-3). In June 1765 Grenville attempted to get Lloyd into the Corporation of Harwich, intending him to manage the Treasury boroughs for him as John Roberts had done for Newcastle, but Lloyd's career as a borough manager and his hopes of representing a Treasury borough were cut short by Grenville's going out of office in July 1765 (*ibid.* p. 468, and Add. MS. 38305, f. 8). Lloyd was also a pamphleteer on behalf of the Grenville Ministry and co-operated with Thomas Whately, Secretary to the Treasury 1764-65. In June 1766 Grenville apparently ordered Lloyd not to be concerned in any more publications (see *Grenv. Pps.* iii, 251), but this did not stop his literary output. See pamphlets attributed to him in the Catalogue of the British Museum and E. H. Barker, *An Enquiry into Charles Lloyd's Claims to be Junius*, 1828.
6. R. Broughton, clerk in the Secretary of State's office, Southern Department.

you, and if nothing has been done, I desire you will send a note to Lord Montagu inclosing the report and telling him that I am gone out of town, and had left directions before I went to have it sent to him as soon as received, and that I had ordered his request to be complyed with if it could be done. Mr. Broughton will shew you Lord Montagu's letter. The intelligence I received of Sir Edward Deering [1] being absent from the Assizes seems so well founded that I doubt of the truth of the report that he refused to sign the Address, but I have directed a particular enquiry to be made into it. I am apt to believe that it was once mentioned by the Sheriff and dropped without farther notice, at least it has been so stated to me. I have heard again from Mr. Norris [2] about John Lamb,[3] the man dismissed at Rye whom I promised to provide for in some other place of like value, and very much wish to have it performed as soon as may be. I think his place was no more than £50 or £60 a year, and therefore desire you will look out and enquire if there is any thing vacant that will do for him. Does Mr. Palmer [4] accept of his appointment? I do not mean by that question to give it to Mr. J. Lamb, because it is too much for him but merely to know if Mr. Palmer is provided for. I am, with great truth, dear Jenkinson,

Your faithfull humble servant,

George Grenville

J. R. WEBB TO CHARLES JENKINSON

at his house in Parliament Street, Westminster

Add. MS. 38201, f. 57.

Wells, Sunday, August 7, 1763.

Dear Sir,

I had the honour of writing to you on Thursday last from Camelford, which I hope you have received : I find since I have been at the borough, the necessity of repeating the request I made to you in my last. I find also that the Collector

---

1. Sir Edward Deering, 6th Bart., M.P. for New Romney 1761–87, a Tory.
2. John Norris, M.P. for Rye. See p. 173.
3. Probably a relation of Thomas Lamb, Newcastle's agent at Rye (see p. 173). A John Lamb was appointed Surveyor of the Customs at Rye by a warrant dated April 6, 1762. See P.R.O., T. 11/27, where however there is no record of his dismissal.
4. See *Gent. Mag.* xxxiii, 466, list of promotions for September 1763, " Mr. Palmer, Surveyor of Deptford Yard, in the room of Mr. Pomeroy ".

of Padstow had not then received the order you was so good to say should be sent for William Avery's being superannuated : It is owing I dare say to some neglect at the Custom house, but it was the ⟨more⟩ a mortification to me, as the opposite party had the impudence to give out that the letter, which I had sent to our friends at the borough, upon your telling me that the thing was done, was a mere forgery of our friends ; for that nobody but Lord Edgecombe could now procure such a favour.

I must beg you to let the inclosed be delivered as soon as may be, and to be assured that I am dear Sir,

Your most obliged and obedient servant,

J. R. Webb

LORD LE DESPENSER TO CHARLES JENKINSON

Add. MS. 38201, f. 59.

August 10, 1763.

Dear Sir,

Many thanks for your kind enquiries, so I find I must eat my own venison at last, I will tell you what I will not eat,— my fingers ends nor my words. I regretted your departure I assure you, that worthy family has engaged my respect and affection so much that I never feel happyer than in their companys, I will not say anything about you or Mackye [1] lest I should offend your modesty, or raise his choler. I received this day the news of my friend Doctor Thompsons [2] death, I think him a great loss, being so able and integer in his profession, I am most sincerely concerned, to you it may be indifferent, Martin [3] will laugh, but his death is of serious consequence to me and mine. I shall be in town to morrow to attend the Birthdays. Adieu dear Sir, many thanks for your friendly visit and believe me with great truth and cordiality.

Your most faithfull and obedient servant,

Le Despenser

1. John Ross Mackye, M.P. for Kirkcudbright, was Jenkinson's successor as Treasurer of the Ordnance. His claim to have secured " above one hundred and twenty votes " for the Peace of Paris, reported in Wraxall's *Historical Memoirs* (iv, 671), is dealt with in *The Structure of Politics*, p. 228.

2. Thomas Thompson, M.D., of Pall Mall, died on August 5, 1763. There is a memorial statue to him in the garden of Dashwood's house at West Wycombe.

3. Samuel Martin ?

(178)

J. S. MACKENZIE TO CHARLES JENKINSON

Add. MS. 38201, f. 64.

August 17, 1763.

Since my last to you, my dear Sir, I have received the favor of your letters of the 26th past and 11th instant for which I give you many thanks.

The activity of opposition, and the languor on the part of Government, was what I saw too much of before I left London, not to apprehend that each would daily increase ; and I am much concerned to find, by the sketch you give me of things in your last, that my conjectures on that head are but too likely to prove well founded. I have had hints given me by some of my correspondents of a tendency towards a Coalition ; and for the sake of the King's affairs, I most ardently wish that something of that kind may be soon brought to a proper consistency ! What I have been able to collect from my letters seems to point only at the *Yorks* ; [1] I wish you had thrown out to me something more than you did, relating to your suspicions on that very interesting point. Do let me hear soon again from you.

I have had but one recommendation to transmit to you at present, so shall insert it at the bottom of my letter : Adieu My dear Sir I am most sincerely

Your faithful humble servant,

J. Mackenzie

Lady Betty [2] desires her compliments to you and begs you'll take the trouble to forward the inclosed to Spa.

Recommendation.

David Cleghorne to be a Tidesman at Thurso in the room of George Gunn deceased.

1. Cf. Hardwicke to Royston, August 5 (P. C. Yorke, *op. cit.* iii, 513). For a rumour that Sir Joseph Yorke was to succeed Egremont as Secretary of State, see a letter to him from Sir James Porter, November 21, 1763, in H.M.C., 12th Report, App. IX, p. 337. It is not clear from Porter's letter whether the rumour was current before Egremont's death or after. Mackenzie was probably referring only to the current belief that Hardwicke would be taken into Administration and Charles Yorke made Lord Chancellor.

2. His wife and cousin, Lady Elizabeth Campbell, daughter of John, 3rd Duke of Argyll.

Add. MS. 38201, ff. 74-5.

Newnham, August 26, 1763.

Dear Sir,

I was not surprized to hear of poor Lord Egremonts death,[1] or of the manner he was seized. Uninformed as I am, I should suppose Lord Egmont [2] likelier to succeed him, than any of the others that are mentioned. Lord Egmont is a speaker, and on that account perhaps more desirable than some others of equall, if not of superior abilities, though there is a certain address that might not be agreeable to foreign Ministers, and others that may have occasion to transact busyness with him.

I should be glad to know whether Lord Bute has taken a view of Luton Park,[3] and whether he likes it. I am so selfish, that I wish, he may disapprove of it, and that he may be under the necessity of purchasing Wittenham.[4]

I intend to write to Mr. Grenville to sollicite something for poor Bowley,[5] who has really been unlucky. My idea is to ask something of Mr. Grenville, without specifying any thing in particular, which might leave Mr. Grenville a greater latitude, if he is disposed to grant the request. But as you are a better judge, and can see things through their proper medium, I shall most readily acquiesce to your opinion, and am dear Sir,

Most sincerely yours,

Harcourt

1. Egremont died on August 21 of an apoplectic fit. His death, by vacating the office of Secretary of State, reopened the negotiations for a change of ministry.

2. John Perceval, 2nd Earl of Egmont, was Postmaster-General in August 1763. On the conclusion of the new arrangements he became First Lord of the Admiralty *vice* Sandwich, who succeeded Egremont. Horace Walpole also thought that Egmont was in the running for Secretary of State. On September 1 he wrote to Mann : " It seemed to lie between your old friend Lord Sandwich, and Lord Egmont ". Two years later, during the Rockingham Ministry, Egmont ingratiated himself into the King's favour and played an important part in the relations of the Rockinghams to the King, but in 1763 he was not seriously considered for high office.

3. Bute bought Luton Park in Bedfordshire in September and retired there for the winter of 1763–64. See below.

4. Presumably the manor of Little Wittenham, near Abingdon in Berkshire, which stood within a few miles of Nuneham. This manor belonged to the two daughters of Edmund Dunch, one of whom had married Sir George Oxenden 5th Bart., and the other the 3rd Duke of Manchester. In 1765–66 Lord Charles Grenville Montagu, second son of Harriet Dunch, conveyed a moiety of the manor to Sir George Oxenden, who thus came into possession of the whole.

5. See pp. 41, 81.

J. S. MACKENZIE TO CHARLES JENKINSON

Add. MS. 38201, f. 73.

August 26, 1763.

Many thanks to you my dear Sir ⟨for⟩ transmitting to me the welcome news ⟨of⟩ the Queens safe delivery of a Prince [1] ⟨upon⟩ which I most heartily congratulate you, and all, who love and honor our excellent Master.

By your not sending an express directly ⟨to⟩ myself, I did not receive your letter till two days after the Common Post brought ⟨us⟩ the joyfull tydings; Lord Hallifax wrote ⟨offi⟩cially to the Lord Justice Clerk, and by the express which carried him that letter, ⟨your⟩ letter came to me; but what vexed ⟨me⟩ most, was, that they stupidly inclosed ⟨my⟩ letter in the packet to the Justice Clerk, ⟨he⟩ being at that time in some remote ⟨par⟩t from Edinburgh, his packet with my letter in it, was forwarded to him from Edinburgh ⟨so⟩ that he had to return it thither, and then from thence it was conveyed to me here. I wish you would rub their heads well who were the occasion of all these fracass ⟨   ⟩ and another time pray let the express c⟨ome⟩ directly to myself.

The Indians have openly revolted, it is ⟨said⟩ in North America; [2] we are fitting out ag⟨   ⟩ Fleet; the Cyder Counties are so turbulent that an appearance of troops among⟨st⟩ them is become necessary; [3] all these things are said; do tell me with what foundation. Adieu My dear Sir, I am

Most sincerely yo⟨urs⟩

If Mr. Grenville should be spoke to ⟨about⟩ the £100

1. Prince Frederick was born on August 17.
2. After the French were driven out of North America, the British Government put a stop to its customary gifts to the Indians, who, pending a settlement of their territorial claims, found themselves unprotected from the frauds and violence of unscrupulous and uncontrolled fur traders and land speculators. The result was the rebellion of Pontiac, which broke out in Detroit on May 9, 1763, and spread over the whole of the West. News of the Indian war in Amherst's dispatches of June 11 and 27 did not reach London till shortly before August 5, when the Board of Trade reported to the Ministers their suggestion that Government should prepare a proclamation of the Indian boundary. See Alvord, *Mississippi Valley*, i, pp. 187-8 and n. 334; Parkman, *The Conspiracy of Pontiac*; and L. S. Mayo, *Jeffrey Amherst* (1913), ch. xi. The Government's reactions to the rebellion, culminating in the proclamation of October 7, are described in Alvord, *op. cit.* i, ch. vii.
3. Cf. Walpole, *Memoirs*, i, 222. The cider counties voted instructions to their members to get the Act repealed.

pension to the Lord Justice Clerk (concerning which I formerly wrote to you) might he not say, that when I came to London he would talk to me about it, or something to that purpose?

JOHN ROBINSON TO CHARLES JENKINSON
Add. MS. 38201, f. 78.

Whitehaven, August 27, 1763.
near 8 at night.

Dear Sir,

I wrote to you from Carlisle which I hope you will duly receive. Having just then heard of Lord Egremont's death I took the liberty to mention to you my hopes that notwithstanding Sir James's absence, the office of Custos Rotulorum of this County would be secured for him.[1] Lord Egremont also was Vice-Admiral of the County, an office that was in Sir James's family before, equally with the Custos, and considering Sir James's large property on the sea coast and his concern with maritime affairs, it is no less desirable to him than the Custos. You will know how extremely anxious he was about the Custos, perhaps rather too much so at the time, and therefore I dare say if the doing Sir James this service hath not already occurred to you, yet when you are informed of the consequence to him, you will not omit a moment to do all you can. Perhaps Lord B⟨ute⟩, as Sir James I apprehend talked with his Lordship fully about the Custos, may in this situation of things in Sir James's absence, undertake to mention this business to His Majesty. You will say I am anxious about this, and indeed I am, for I think nothing at this juncture could happen more fortunate for Sir James's interest. The Vice Admiral of Westmorland has rested ever since Lord Egremont got Cumberland as Sir James would not accept that office, as the Duke of Newcastle gave the other for this County from the family. I am just arrived here and have only time to write this in great haste to save the post, but with great truth and regard am ever

Most faithfully yours,
whilst J. Robinson

1. Sir James Lowther was appointed Custos Rotulorum of Cumberland in October 1763. He was made Vice-Admiral of Cumberland and Westmorland in April 1765.

TOM RAMSDEN TO CHARLES JENKINSON

Add. MS. 38201, f. 83.

Pontefract, August 31, 1763.

I should not have thanked you, my dear Jenkinson, for your last letter, by this post ; but that I have something to say, and something to trouble you with. I have not any body to fly to but yourself when I want any thing for my friends, (for as to myself, I thank God, have no wants,) And therefore hope you will forgive me. I have had a letter from my relation Major Agnew,[1] to entreat me to help his son, Lieutenant Alexander Agnew, to be employed at sea. He says, that he hears a squadron is going to the E. Indies, which he thinks might give room for admitting a young Lieutenant into business. He says, *he is an honest, open hearted, spirited fellow, (no great economist) and thinks he shall have no dishonor from him.* If you can help me on this occasion, *without much solicitation*, shall be much obliged to you. It is with regret, that I ask of you knowing how many solicitations you must be troubled with. I think, that there is not one at the Admiralty Board of my acquaintance : The 1st[2] I knew once ; But that drop'd soon after the year 1748. Old Buss [3] and he not being very good friends.

Lord Rock⟨ingham⟩ is gone for London this morning ; He called at Byram [4] in his way from York races, and intended to have stayd a few days, but an express arrived yesterday noon, upon which he went home immediately, and designed to go for London this morning ; and I understand (for I have not seen him) that he said he should stay only two days. My Lady is left at Byram till Friday. What the meaning of this sudden flight is, I know not ; but you prob⟨ably do.⟩

I have never heard any thing of what passed, when the Duke of Cumb⟨erland⟩ was at Wentworth : and I do believe, it was more talked of, at a distance. But probably will make the world imagine something.

1. James Agnew of Bishop Auckland, Major of the 7th Dragoons, was fourth son of Sir James Agnew, 4th Bart. of Lochnaw. He died on October 21, 1770. His son was Captain R.N. and was probably the Captain Agnew of the *Fury*, sloop of war, who died at Durham on February 23, 1792.
2. Lord Sandwich.
3. Unidentified.
4. The Yorkshire home of Sir John Ramsden, 3rd Bart., Tom's brother.

I have time for no more, for I am just going (8 o clock in the morning) with some company to Swillington [1] about 8 miles. The weather now very fine, and not hot. I [sic] best wishes attend you and *yours*, and am with the greatest truth,

Your very affectionate,

Thos. Ramsden

CHARLES LLOYD TO CHARLES JENKINSON

Add. MS. 38458, f. 37.

[? August 31, 1763.]

Dear Sir,

I am really ashamed knowing as I do the many matters of consequence that engage your attention to trouble you on an occasion which scarcely deserves your notice. But your kind attention to me on all occasions encourages me to hope that you will give directions that I should have the seat intended for me by Mr. G⟨renville⟩, that which was Mr. Fane's. [2] I see the intention of the inferior people is to put a slight on my nomination and reduce me to the necessity of seeking out a place where I can get it. The detail of this matter I will not enter into. I am very clear that Mr. G. designed I should have Mr. Fane's seat and with your permission I never will depart from my pretensions. I beg you will spare me the mortification of a defeat in a point really of no other consequence than to shew that you think me not unworthy of your countenance. I am dear Sir,

Your most obedient humble servant,

Chas. Lloyd

1. F. Ramsden's home.
2. Henry Fane, M.P. for Lyme Regis 1757–77, younger brother of Thomas Fane, 8th Earl of Westmorland, was a nephew of John Scrope, the celebrated Secretary to the Treasury. His place was an under-clerkship in the Treasury. It was given to Lloyd on August 29 (Treasury Minute Book T. 29/35, p. 56). This letter is marked in pencil August 31. If the date is correct Lloyd must have been still in the country (see p. 176), otherwise he would have heard of his appointment by then.

MRS. BOOTHBY SKRYMSHER TO CHARLES JENKINSON

Add. MS. 38201, f. 91.

Tooly park. fryday evening six o clock.
September 2, 1763.

Dear Jenkey,

Securiety of one thousand pound will be given for John Smith alias Douglas,[1] his future good behaviour, by several gentlemen and trades men in the Town and County of Leicester ; one of which is Charles Boothby who has sub-scribed one hundred pounds towards that sum. The papers are now before Lord Mansfeld who thinks it not unreasonable that he should be pardoned upon those terms. His repreive expires next Monday. Lord Denbigh told the Goaler of Leicester that he knew the King intended to pardon Douglass but that there was now such a hurry of bussness in regard to publick affairs of State that without a further respite the man might be hanged before the pardon could pass through the offices. The Sheriff will wee hope give him a day or 2 longer till an answer can arrive to this which comes to you by express. I am ashamed to trouble you but I am worryd continualy about this man who by all report of his neighbours deserves a better fate. If you get him another repreive I shall thank you as long as I live for upon my honor hear is such a desire to save him that is astonishing. One of the Aldermen of Leicester has come running seven mile on foot in a heavey rain to desire me to write to you again and it will be excessive hard if the man should be hanged and a pardon given after his execution. The affection of this house attends all the Jenkeys. I am

Your obliged,
A. Boothby Skrymsher

1. John Smith, alias Douglas, " who lately kept the Blue Bell at Leicester ", was convicted of forgery on July 31 at Leicester assizes. On August 31 Halifax wrote to Mansfield that the King had considered his reasons for a reprieve but had ordered the sentence to be carried out. Similar letters were sent to Lord Warwick and Lord Denbigh (*Cal. H.O. Papers*, 1760–65, No. 979). The *Gent. Mag.* (1763, p. 410) says Smith was charged with returning from transportation, but the charge is stated as forgery in the *Cal. H.O. Papers*.

J. S. MACKENZIE TO CHARLES JENKINSON

Add. MS. 38201, ff. 97-8.

September 3, 1763.

I have the favor of your letters of the 25. and 27. past; you will easily guess that the latter has greatly rous'd my curiosity, and I wait with impatience for the arrival of next Post, when you are so obliging as to promise me, that I shall have a long letter from you, with as full a detail as you can procure of the important subject now in question. By a letter which I received from another person last Post, I was inform'd that Mr. Pitt had been three hours that morning with the King; May all this turn out to the advantage of the good King, and to the tranquillity of his Government, I most ardently pray! Meanwhile I am much obliged to you, my dear Sir, for giving me early notice of what has past, and I earnestly entreat you to continue the like speedy communication to me of every thing that occurs worth transmitting.

As I purpose going to Bute the beginning of next week, I shall hardly have an opportunity for some days to acknowledge the reception of your next letter; but all letters directed to me at Edinburgh will be constantly forwarded to me wherever I shall happen to be.

There is a thing I meant to have mentioned to you before, but forgot it; from the time I was appointed Privy Seal of Scotland till I came to this country I called myself by my own name, and not by that of my office, but on my arrival at Edinburgh, happening to dine with the Duke of Queensberry where the whole body of the Judges of this country, the Lord Advocate [1] and Sollicitor General [2] were assembled, they came upon the subject of the office I hold, and were of opinion that I should always call myself Lord Privy Seal of Scotland, while I had the honor to hold that office, as it had been the practice of this country to do so, when a commoner held it; in consequence of this everybody in this country calls me, and I call myself, by the name of my office. Mr. Hume Campbell [3]

1. Thomas Miller of Glencoe.
2. James Montgomerie and Francis Garden were joint Solicitors-General, April 30, 1760, to June 12, 1764, when Garden was promoted to the bench and Montgomerie became sole Solicitor-General.
3. The Hon. Alexander Hume Campbell, Lord Clerk Register of Scotland 1756-61.

when he was made Lord Register of Scotland in the year 1756 (an office much inferior in point of dignity to that of the Privy Seal) always called himself by the name of his office, the late Speaker said that he ought to do it ; the Lord Advocate is likewise called always by the name of his office. Now what I wish to know before I return to London is, what I should call myself on *that side* of Tweed ; God knows ! I have not the smallest desire to be a *real* Lord, and much less to be a *nominal* one, but as it is the practice here to give that appellation to the Second Great Officer of the Crown as well as to several offices inferior to him, it will be somewhat aukward to be called by one appellation in one part of the Kingdom, and by another in the other part. However, be that as it may, all I wish to know is, what I am to call myself, *south of Tweed* ? could not you talk to the Speaker about this, and get it settled for me one way or other before I return to London ? For I dare say you will feel for me how auckward it would be for me to have that point to discuss myself. Forgive me, My dear Friend, for troubling you so long about so trivial an affair, but as I mentioned it I thought it necessary to explain the thing fully to you.

I am most sincerely yours etc., etc., etc.

Lady Betty desires her compliments to you and returns you many thanks for taking care of her letter.

LORD THOMOND TO CHARLES JENKINSON

Add. MS. 38201, f. 105.

Percy Wyndham O'Brien, 1st Earl of Thomond, younger brother of Charles, 2nd Earl of Egremont, and brother-in-law of George Grenville. In this Parliament he was M.P. for Minehead.

Dover Street, September 7, 1763.

Sir,

I had the favour of your letter yesterday, when I was with Mr. Grenville, upon which we immediately sent for Mr. Charles Lloyd and explained it once more to him.

The puzzle seems to be in Mr. Henry Manley [1] being

1. Henry Manly, Mayor of Taunton and formerly Newcastle's election agent in the town, for the management of which he received £70 a year Secret Service money (*Structure of Politics*, p. 256 and *passim*). He was Mayor continually from 1755 to 1762 (*ibid.* entries in Secret Service accounts, pp. 531-75).

Mayor, at the time this was granted.

Now I beg you will understand it was given to Mr. *Henry Manley*, and not to the Mayor of the town, and the arrear is to be paid to Mr. Henry Manley, which I hope you will be so good as to do, next Friday morning, when his daughter will call again at your house.

I am sorry you have so much trouble, and am Sir

Your most humble servant,

Thomond

JOHN BINDLEY TO CHARLES JENKINSON

Add. MS. 38201, f. 107.

Excise Office, September 9, 1763.

My dear Friend,

I had not the pleasure of seeing you after Mr. Grenville did me the honor to see me. I found he had not read my papers about Cyder but bid me remind you of them. I wish him to see them immediately as I think every thing that can be said on that head is contained in them.

Mr. G. did not say any thing to me relative to my own affair but I only wish to have it remembred that I am ready to the utmost of my abilities to serve my friends in whatever capacity they choose to recommend.

One Grosvenor Bedford [1] a very honest fellow is under an apprehension that his place in Philadelphia which he had held 30 years may be taken away in case of any new arrangement there. He therefore entreated me to mention him as my friend to you and as a man I beleive deserving of protection.

I am dear Sir on all occasions

Your faithful friend,

J. Bindley

Horace Walpole wrote to Grenville on Bedford's behalf on September 7, and received an explanation of the Government's colonial policy in reply (*Memoirs*, ii, 4 ; *Grenv. Pps.* ii, 113-15). Contraband trade with the enemy in America during the war and the need to raise a revenue for colonial defence had directed the attention of Government to abuses in the financial administration of the colonies where the revenue derived from customs duties amounted to barely a quarter of the cost of collection. On July 22, 1763, the Board of Trade reported to the Treasury that one of the principal

1. Grosvenor Bedford was Collector of Customs in Philadelphia, but lived in London, where he was confidential agent to Horace Walpole and his deputy in the sinecure of Usher of the Exchequer.

causes of this deficiency was the absence of the collectors whose functions were performed by deputies working for very little money but what they made in bribes (Add. MS. 38335, ff. 144-7; Beer, *British Colonial Policy*, pp. 231-2 and note 1). The Board made various other recommendations which eventually led to the revival of the Molasses Act and the passing of the Stamp Act in 1764, but the abolition of sinecures being a measure which the Treasury could undertake without waiting for further legislation, Grenville acted on their advice forthwith and ordered all customs officers to proceed to their posts in America (Add. MS. 38335, f. 155).

On this occasion an exception was made for Grosvenor Bedford, although a few months later Henry M'Culloh, Clerk of the Crown for North Carolina, applied for the place and undertook to fulfil the duties on the spot.[1] Bedford kept it precariously until his death on November 5, 1771. A few months before he died Walpole once more interceded to save it for him. See Walpole to Bedford, June 27, 1771.

SIR WILLIAM MEREDITH TO CHARLES JENKINSON

Add. MS. 38201, f. 110.

Sir William Meredith, 3rd and last Bart. of Henbury, Cheshire, M.P. for Liverpool 1761–80, was a Tory under George II and a Radical under George III; he was returned in 1761 as a Tory. See Namier, *England etc.* pp. 60, 213, 243, etc. He belonged to the Newcastle-Rockingham party and championed American rights against the Stamp Act. His brother-in-law was Barlow Trecothick, the American merchant and M.P. for the City 1768–74. Meredith was a Lord of the Admiralty from August 1765 to November 1766, and afterwards tried to unite the Grenvilles and the Rockinghams when both were in opposition. He often spoke in debate and wrote several pamphlets, including an answer to Charles Lloyd's *Defence of the Majority* in 1764, and *Historical Remarks on the Taxation of Free States*, 1778. He died at Lyons on January 2, 1790. About him see *D.N.B.*

Henbury, September 14, 1763.

Dear Sir,

I beg you to accept my sincerest thanks for the favor of your letter, and your kindness in sending a leave of absence to *Arthur Lord*.[2]

My situation, you know, compels to trouble you very often; and I am now oblidged to recommend to your protection a Memorial, which an owner of the *Britannia* will deliver to you.

I presume, it is the principle of the Custom house never to depart from the letter of the law, to the prejudice of the revenue. But, in this instance, they seem to make a distinction

1. See p. 231.   2. A Land-waiter at Liverpool. See p. 208.

where there is no difference in reason or in equity ; but, to exact the payment of the duty in this case may have fatal consequences ; for, had it not been for making property of the wreck, the Dutch seamen perhaps might not have been saved ; and if it ⟨be⟩ known that such property is liable to be diminished by a heavy duty, the crews of many another vessel that is wrecked may be left to perish. And the words of the Act being *caught and taken by the crew of such vessels only* there would be the same loss for saving the wreck of an English as of a Dutch ship.[1]

He will lay before you the fact, as reported to the Commissioners of the Customs with their opinion, which, I presume, may save the delay of any further reference to their Board.

I think myself extremely obligded to you for the news, you was so kind as to send me, and am, with the greatest regard, dear Sir,

Your faithful, humble servant,

Wm. Meredith

I go to Liverpool next week, and will send the Memorial about Irish provisions after knowing the sense of the merchants fully upon it.

JAMES HARRIS TO CHARLES JENKINSON

Add. MS. 38201, f. 111.

James Harris of the Close, Salisbury, M.P. for Christchurch 1761–81, had been a Lord of the Admiralty since December 1762, but removed with Grenville to the Treasury in April 1763. He resigned with the rest of the Treasury Board on the fall of the Grenville Ministry in July 1765. He was the father of the 1st Earl of Malmsbury. See his correspondence with his cousin Edward Hooper in the *Letters of the First Earl of Malmsbury* (1870), vol. i.

Salisbury, September 15, 1763.

Dear Sir,

An ale-house keeper in my neighbourhood had his house burnt down some months ago, by which, among other things,

1. In April 1762 Charles Yorke as Attorney-General gave an opinion for Sir James Lowther that by an Act of 12 Charles II wrecked goods do not count as imported goods and are therefore duty free, but by 12 Anne, c. 18, and 5 George I, c. 11, goods " except wrecked goods or jetsam ", salved out of any stranded ship are liable to the same duties as if regularly imported. See P.R.O., T. 11/27, ff. 172-3. The law recommended anyone " who shall save any ship or effects and cause them to be carried into port or to any Custom House near " to be rewarded, but to obstruct the escape from wrecks or plunder them was a felony. 26 George II, c. 19, § 1, 5.

he lost more than two hogsheads of strong beer, and a hogshead of small.

You can be so good to resolve me the following questions.

Is it proper in such incidents to apply to the Treasury on account of the duty ?

In what manner must a person apply, with what affidavits, what certificates ?

Will not the expence of carrying such a matter through office exceed the loss, which is far from being considerable, it being no more than the duty on the quality above specified ?

Pardon the trouble of this letter, and believe me to be with great truth, Dear Sir

Your most obedient humble servant,

James Harris

MR. JACKSON TO CHARLES JENKINSON
in Parliament Street
Add. MS. 38201, f. 114.

Richard Jackson (died 1787), about whom see *D.N.B.*, was a barrister, known to contemporaries as " Omniscient Jackson ". He was M.P. for Weymouth and Melcombe Regis 1762–68, New Romney 1768–84. Politically he was a follower of Shelburne except during the years 1763–65 when he supported Grenville. In 1765 he appears to have been one of Grenville's private secretaries, though there is not a single letter from him printed in the *Grenville Papers*, but on January 12, 1765, Joseph Harris, an American who was afterwards assistant to Edmund Burke as secretary to Rockingham, wrote to John Temple in America : " Mr. Jackson has lately been made private secretary to Mr. Grenville and generally supposed to have considerable influence with him " (*The Bowdoin and Temple Papers*, Mass. Hist. Soc. Coll., 6th series, ix, 43). Lord Fitzmaurice in his *Life of Shelburne* (i, 224) also refers to him as Grenville's private secretary. Notwithstanding this connexion, in 1765 he was one of the 49 members who voted against the Stamp Act and he supported its repeal in 1766, when he resumed his former connexion with Shelburne, who made him a Lord of the Treasury in July 1782. He was agent for the province of Connecticut and an intimate friend of Benjamin Franklin, with whom he co-operated in the production of several pamphlets, notably *The Interest of Great Britain Considered* (1760).

Paris, September 18, 1763.

Dear Sir,

Mr. Grenville told me a few days before I left London that he should have occasion to talk to me on some American subjects respecting the Customs, when he had procured the requisite materials from ⟨the⟩ Customhouse, which Mr.

(191)

Hooper [1] was then eng⟨aged in⟩ collecting. I asked him whether those mater⟨ials were⟩ likely to be immediately ready or whether I shou⟨ld have⟩ time to go into Burgundy, where I had a desire to see a friend ; a journey which I then computed at little more than a fortnight, he told me there was no doubt there would. I am now returned hither after having been delayed by every impediment that can arise from bad weather bad roads and short days, the pavées are everywhere broke up, and from thence it becomes necessary to turn out into mud sometimes above the axle tree. The last is no small impediment among fortified towns. I propose to stay here 10 days perhaps 12, but if you inform me by letter that my presence is necessary I shall set out the day after I receive it. I have nothing particular to detain me here, and have been here before, so that my chief desire of staying arises from what principally carried me into Burgundy the want of a little dissipation and absence from ⟨business⟩. My apprehension that I may be wanted ⟨is the⟩ less, as I know that business seldom moves ⟨fa⟩st at this time of year. I would not trouble you to write unless my immediate return will be of any use, in which case please to direct to me chez Messrs. Dufour Mallon & Roger, Banquièrs, Rue Grenier à Paris for I have got no lodging and know not where I shall be. I ⟨beg⟩ leave to trouble you with my respects to Mr. Grenville and that you would believe me to be with the most sincere regard dear Sir

Your most obedient faithfull humble servant,

Rd. Jackson

PHILIP CARTERET WEBB TO GEORGE GRENVILLE

Add. MS. 38201, f. 116.

Philip Carteret Webb, Solicitor to the Treasury, was M.P. for Haselmere 1754–68. In April 1763 he was present with Robert Wood, the Under-Secretary of State, when Wilkes's papers were seized by Lord Halifax's orders. Immediately afterwards Lord Temple brought actions in Wilkes's name against Wood and Halifax. The case of Wilkes v. Wood was heard in the Common Pleas on December 6, 1763, and resulted in £1000 damages for Wilkes. Webb gave evidence for the defendant and was subsequently indicted for perjury. He was tried and acquitted on May 21, 1764. The

1. Edward Hooper, Commissioner of Customs 1748–93. He came from an old Dorset family, was M.P. for Christchurch 1734–47 where he had interest for two seats. See *Structure of Politics*, pp. 180, 198, also W. T. Laprade, *Parliamentary Papers of John Robinson*, pp. 90, 107.

case of Wilkes *v.* Lord Halifax was not heard until November 10, 1769, as Halifax was so adroit in pleading privilege. Wilkes recovered £4000 damages. In both cases the damages were defrayed by the Crown, the money being issued to Webb.

Busbridge, September 18, 1763.

Sir,

I have made the inquiry you directed, concerning Mr. Balfe the printer of the N.B. No. 45, and find he follows his trade of a printer in the Old Bailey in the same *low* way he did, and I have no reason to believe he is more under Mr. Wilkes' influence than he originally was.

Inclosed you will receive copies of the Lord Ch⟨ief⟩ Justice Lord Wills [1] sittings for the years 1761 and 1762. There is reason to beleive the tryal may be prevented from being brought on within the Term, but that cannot be said with certainty ; as to the tryals against the Earl of Halifax they cannot be brought on till after the Term, probably not till Hilary Term.

I am preparing the breifs you directed, with all the dispatch in my power, and I remain

Your most oblidged and most obedient servant,

Philip Carteret Webb

JOHN BINDLEY TO CHARLES JENKINSON

Add. MS. 38458, f. 39.

The following letter refers to the state of the borough of Honiton. In November 1763 Anthony Bacon, the merchant, unsuccessfully contested it at a by-election against Sir George Yonge who had " a traditional and very expensive interest " there (see Namier, *Structure of Politics*, pp. 130, 202, 247). Honiton had a large electorate, between 500 and 1000, and ranked as one of the most costly and corrupt in England. Sir George Yonge " is reported to have said in his old age that he had inherited £80,000 from his father, his wife brought him a like amount, the Government paid him £80,000, but Honiton swallowed it all " (see *ibid.* p. 202). It is therefore surprising that a person of comparatively small fortune like John Bindley should have hoped for Government support in attacking it. In previous elections Sir George Yonge had been subsidised by Newcastle, so that Bacon may have been an acceptable candidate to Government in 1763. His influence at Honiton had permanency, although he never again contested it. In December 1783 friends of the younger Pitt drew up a paper in anticipation of a general election and placed the following note against Honiton : " Send Mr. Robinson to see Mr. Bacon . . . for on Mr.

1. Add. MS. 38201, f. 117. Sir John Willes was Chief Justice of the Court of Common Pleas 1737–62.

Bacon's sending for the proper person *in due time* . . . will depend our bringing in a friend not in opposition to but with Sir George Yonge and make both come easy " (W. T. Laprade, *Parliamentary Papers of John Robinson*, p. 112).

West Hatch, 9 o'clock Monday Night.
Docketed " September 19, 1763 ".

My dear Sir,

A very particular friend of mine and a very eminent banker of the City, has been with me this evening and hath shewn me a letter from the principle man in the borough of Honiton, representing that Anthony Bacon [1] of the City, is come there to canvass, and observing to my friend that he would give no countenance to him or any other person till he knew his sentiments either as to Bacon or any other he might choose to wish well to. My friend, a staunch supporter of Administration knowing my idea as to Parliament wishes me to offer myself there provided Bacon is not a friend to Administration and provided my friends choose to have me in Parliament ; and other things prove convenient. As I have before mentiond to you my desire on this head I should be much obliged to you, if you judge it proper, to represent this matter to Mr. Grenville ; if however Bacon is agreeable to Government my friend will do him all the service in his power and which he would wish to know as soon as possible. I am going into Kent to morrow at one o'clock from the office but will call upon you before ten on Wednesday and I remain, dear Sir,

Yours sincerely,
John Bindley

GEORGE MIDDLETON TO CHARLES JENKINSON

Add. MS. 38201, ff. 122-3.

George Middleton, Inspector of Custom House Seizures in Scotland, was a would-be hanger-on of Bute. Like Bindley, he was full of uncalled-for suggestions, including one that Jenkinson should tour Scotland as Bute's political agent. He had a grant from the Crown of the revenue

1. Anthony Bacon, " a Manxman who started his business career in the Maryland trade, subsequently became a Government contractor for the victualling of troops in the West Indies and Africa, a mine-owner and the founder of important iron works in Glamorganshire, a mining adventurer in Cape Breton and one of the greatest manufacturers of munitions during the American Revolution " (Namier, *Structure of Politics*, p. 72 ; see also his essay " Anthony Bacon " in the *Journal of Economic and Business History*, Boston, Mass., November 1929). In 1764 Bacon was returned for Aylesbury. See p. 259.

(194)

of Holy Island, near Berwick, and died " at his house of Seton near Old Aberdeen " on August 11, 1772.

Seaton, September 24, 1763.

My dear Sir,

I pray you to believe that a plain country gentleman may have nervous sentiments of gratitude without possessing pompous words to express it. This is my case on receiving a kindness from your hand though in such busy resort, and that of a nature which releives my mind from an anxiety which nobody else would do, and vexation hung about me while print and people asserted a resolution of his [1] to cross the water — which at this immediate juncture looked like furnishing envy and vice with a handle to call it fugitation and timidity. He has proved himself a great man ; I am sure he is a good one. May a little moving about and country excursion ascertain him a happy man. For his anxiety and agitation of mind these two years past are enough to sap a much stronger constitution.

If real danger could exist in speculation, we seem in a crisis that needs a speedy meeting of Legislature and the Kings Civil List being settled, it will be then, and then only known, how far His Majesty can ascertain and protect his chosen servants in the quiet administration of Government, and whether murder and assassination, as well as dissunion between the two Kingdoms can be legally exhorted in print. Assuredly by that time Mr. Grenville's seconds and supporters in House of Commons will be of try'd elocution and fidelity.

I shall in a very particular manner rejoice in every personal honor and advantage you obtain, I am sure you deserve them ; and though I do not wish you joy of your augmented labor and trust in present office, it is because I know not whether the fatigue does not too much diminish the enjoyment. For though I hope and beleive your constitution and spirits are firm and equal, yet I scarce conceive them of the athletic kind. I likewise waved any mention of my late application, I know when convenient you'll expedite that business, which Mr. Nelthorpe [2] about six weeks ago told me would probably be done by Treasury Warrant appointing me to allow £50 to Mr. Isaac Grant,[3] Sir Harry Innes's [4] Dep⟨uty (?)⟩, as the sum

1. Bute's.
2. James Nelthorpe, died October 4, 1767 ?
3. Isaac Grant, Writer to the Signet at Edinburgh.
4. Sir Harry Innes, 5th Bart. of Innes, father of the 5th Duke of Roxburgh, Inspector of Seizures 1748–62. He died on October 2, 1762.

adjudged due him by Commissioners of Customs off the moiety accruing to my office between October and Lady Day last.

I beg to be esteemed with perfect regard and truth, dear Sir,
Your faithfull humble servant,
Geo: Middleton

R. WOLTERS TO CHARLES JENKINSON

Add. MS. 38201, ff. 126-7.

R. Wolters was British Consul in Rotterdam, which was then the centre of an organisation of secret agents on the Continent. Wolters's function was to collect and transmit information to the Treasury on such various subjects as the state of French finances, the strengths of the French and Spanish navies, the reactions of the Dutch market, and the recruiting of foreign immigrants for the British American colonies. See his letter books of which there are 24 in P.R.O., S.P. Holland, 84, Nos. 415-532 *passim*. These letters are addressed directly to the Secretary of State, but he also corresponded with the Treasury through Jenkinson, to whom he wrote as often as once a week, and whom he supplied with lists of new foreign books on finance, commerce, and history. In the Liverpool MSS. (Add. MS. 38468) is a collection of eight tracts on French finances, none of them in Jenkinson's own hand, dating from about 1757 to 1766. Wolters died in 1770. He was probably a Hanoverian. In 1809 complaints were raised in the House of Commons against a Mr. Wolters being Ordnance Storekeeper in Hyde Park, when it appeared that he was " a Hanoverian who had been thirty seven years in England and recommended by Lord Chatham " (Add. MS. 34713, f. 238). As Wolters had a numerous family, this may have been one of his sons.

Rotterdam, September 25, 1763.
Dear Sir,
The inclosed is all that I can hitherto gett upon the finances of France, my correspondent [1] in a private letter promises to keep his word.

As I know that this person has some connections att the Hague and elsewhere, if the same advices should come to you from other quarters you will please to let me know that I may stop my hand with him.

It seems that the commercial diffidence att Amsterdam is in some degree subsided, att least more business has been

1. Iacottet, his agent in Paris. See p. 219. There are several letters from him in French in the Liverpool MSS. including three apparently enclosed in this from Wolters. Add. MSS. 38201, ff. 128-30.

done upon the exchange for a week or ten days, than had been transacted for six weeks before. Measures are, it is said, taken to support some houses that would have given way.

Notwithstanding all this several of the more knowing merchants are in great anxieties for the course of this week, in which it is known that bills to the amount of a considerable summ become due.

It is a great happiness that these misfortunes have hitherto had so little influence upon the merchants of London ; nay even some of the merchants of Amsterdam speak of the great comfort and support they have received from their friends in England.

I have the honour to be most truely dear Sir,
Your most humble and most obedient servant,
R. Wolters

SHUTE BARRINGTON TO CHARLES JENKINSON

Add. MS. 38201, f. 134.

Christ Church, September 28, 1763.

Dear Sir !

I am just informed that the Dean of Windsor [1] has received a fall which he is not likely to survive. Should that event happen, of which you will probably receive the earliest intimation, you will be so good as to deliver the inclosed letter to Mr. Grenville. After so recent a conversation as has passed between us on this subject it would be superfluous to add any arguments but one, which I then omitted ; that my having married the only sister of the Duke of St. Albans [2] whose seat is in the place, and whose family has maintained so ancient an interest in it, gives some propriety to this request. I am convinced that I shall want in this application no good offices

---

1. Dr. Penyston Booth was Dean of Windsor from 1729. His accident was not fatal, and he did not die until September 21, 1765, aged eighty-four. When, in January 1764, Bedford and Grenville were quarrelling over patronage, Bedford recommended " Sir Richard Wrottesley to the Deanery of Windsor whenever that should be vacant. His Majesty . . . told the Duke that Windsor was promised to Dr. Barrington, at which the Duke seemed displeased. This had been settled by Mr. Grenville for Dr. Barrington some time ago " (Grenville's Diary, *Grenv. Pps.* ii, 486). In the end, however, it was not Grenville who disposed of the Deanery, which was given to Frederick Keppel, Bishop of Exeter, on October 15, 1765. See p. 392 and n. 3.
2. See p. 54 n. 3.

which it is in your [sic] to interpose on my behalf. I am, dear Sir ! with real esteem and regard

Your most sincere and faithful servant,
S: Barrington

If you are of opinion that the immediate delivery of my letter will be of more service than the postponing it you will be so kind as to do so.

JOHN BINDLEY TO CHARLES JENKINSON

Add. MS. 38201, f. 135.

Excise Office, September 28, 1763.

My dear Sir,

I have sent you a Compare of the gross produce of the duties under the management of our Board, for the years 1762 and 1763.[1] By which you will find an amazing deficiency in the malt and in the beer ale and spirits &c in the country. These deficiencies are accounted for by the scarcity of barley, the great quantities of cyder last year, the diminution of our people by the war and the encrease of smuggling since the peace. All these inconveniences except smuggling will cure themselves, and that is to be cured when the times and dispositions of men are in an humour more enclined to approbation and reformation. I hope those times are not far off, and I shall always be ready to communicate my ideas on the subject when Government please to call upon me. I must desire you to deliver one of the papers to Mr. Grenville with my duty, and I hope you will make me happy by letting me know you intend sleeping at my farm three or four days this week and the next in expectation of which I remain

Very truly yours at command,
John Bindley

1. Add. MS. 38335, f. 140. In this document the collections from low wines and spirits show a decrease of £64,015 : 3 : 8½ from the £1,330,482 : 16 : 1½ at which they stood in 1762. The old duty on malt showed a decrease of £157,418 : 18 : 3¾, and the additional duty had decreased by £82,538 : 8 : 8¾. The total decrease on the year 1762 was £212,793 : 8 : 9½.

JOSEPH CAWTHORNE TO CHARLES JENKINSON

Add. MS. 38201, ff. 140-41.

" Joseph Cawthorne, late of Madeira, merchant " was gazetted bankrupt in December 1764. Four pamphlets attributed to him are in the British Museum, but the earliest of these was written in 1768. In 1782, under the pseudonyms of Coriolanus and Cincinnatus, he published two pamphlets in defence of Lord North's Administration. In 1782 he received a pension of £100 a year and sums varying from £10 to £25 were given him in 1779 and 1780 as bounties or " for a pamphlet ". See Secret Service Books in Windsor Archives.

Rawthmells Coffee House, Henrietta Street,
Covent Garden, September 30, 1763.

Sir,

That politeness and benignity of disposition which are known to be so characteristical to Mr. Jenkinson will plead more effectually my excuse than any apology I can make for writing to you.

You will probably recollect Sir that, I had once or twice the pleasure of waiting on you by orders, and how I acquainted you that exclusive of the great expence I had been at by writing and causing others to write in support of the just cause of my Lord Bute, I had also sustained a loss of some hundreds by a disappointment concerning the new Loan.

This, I represented to my Lord who was lately pleased to say, he was sorry that his resignation had put it out of his power to oblige me ; upon which I patiently submitted, and sat down with what I had lost by my zeal, and did not intend to give my Lord farther trouble ; but, it happens that a relation of mine of the age of 15, a very promising youth for drawing, is desirous of completing himself in the Drawing room of the Tour, and as I have not the honour of being known to my Lord Granby, or any of the gentlemen in the direction of the civil branch of Ordnance, I found myself under the necessity of applying to Lord Bute, hoping that, in consideration of my efforts in his Lordship's service, and of my loss he would be pleased to grant my small request, to procure admittance for the boy into the Drawing Room ; but, as I am afraid of incurring my Lords displeasure by being too troublesome, I have been prevailed upon by the advice of some gentlemen who are acquainted with the goodness of your disposition, to write to you Sir upon the subject, humbly requesting that, though I have not the honor of being known to you, that you will either be pleased to prevail on his Lordship to give me a letter to, some one of the gentlemen of the civil branch of Ordnance, or to put me in the way *yourself* how to get the youth admitted. But, if instead of either of these acts of politeness, you should condescend to attend to the request of a stranger, and with *your own* interest get him admitted, it would be an act of generosity worthy of Mr. Jenkinson, and it would engrave the deepest sense of gratitude upon the breast of, Sir,

Your most humble and most devoted servant,

Joseph Cawthorne

GILBERT ELLIOT TO CHARLES JENKINSON

Add. MS. 38201, ff. 138-9.

Treasury Office, Friday noon.
Docketed " September 30, 1763 ".

You will ⟨remember⟩ you have in your hands a letter from Mr. William Kilpatrick Clerk of Session about £100 payable to the Justice Clerk,[1] he only wants to know that it will be agreeable that he should pay it now as formerly. I mentioned this matter to Mr. Grenville, a considerable time ago, but it has probably been forgot. Not finding him here this day, and being obliged to go out of town till Wednesday, I have left the inclosed letter for him on that subject, as I find my answer about this ⟨   ⟩ being now above one ⟨   ⟩ that allowance in Mr. Kilpatricks hands. I must therefore beg that favour of you to look out Mr. Kilpatricks letter as Mr. Grenville will probably call for it, and if he direct you to acquaint Mr. Kilpatrick to continue to pay as usual, you will be so good as to enclose your letter for Mr. Kilpatrick to me at my house in town, and I will forward it as I ever am Dear Sir

Yours etc.

Gilb. Elliot

1. See p. 172.

AMARINTHA JENKINSON TO CHARLES JENKINSON
Add. MS. 38469, f. 88.

October 2, 1763.

Dear Charles,
I should last post have returned you my thanks for the kind entertainment I met with in Parliament Street, but was prevented by company. Fred [1] was at my dore to receive me, and never misses a day enquireing after my health. He makes great enquires as to the forwardness of the house, and if tis true about the estate being bought, in Bedfordshire, what it bring in, &c. and thinks Mr. Cornwall [2] and my self very stuped not to bring him more particulars. The Sessions does not end till Wednesday noon, but Mr. Cornwall is ready to atend the moment he is summoned. I hope you are quite free of your cold. When ever tis convenient or agreable to you to let me see you, at my little habitation, it will give me great pleasure and you will meet though not a grand table, a sincear and harte wellcome. All here joyn with me in complyments as due. I will not forgett porke meate and hoggs pudings when in season. I am dear Charles
Your most affectionate mother,
A. Jenkinson

COLONEL THOMAS POWNALL TO CHARLES JENKINSON
Add. MS. 38201, f. 149.

On September 2, 1763, Colonel Thomas Pownall, David Cuthbert, and Charles Wolfran Cornwall were appointed Commissioners " for inspecting into, examining and stating the accounts and such demands as are still unsatisfied on the head of extraordinary services, alleged to have been performed during the late war in Germany " (Treasury Minute Book, August 31 and September 2, 1763, P.R.O., T. 29/35. On the constitution of the office see the Minutes for October 10, *ibid*. f. 185). This was all that remained of the Commissariat which had been recalled in July. On March 30, 1764, Parliament moved that the Commission for examining German accounts might be continued, and it was still in existence when the Grenville Ministry fell. On July 25, 1765, Pownall wrote to Newcastle : " Having begun under your Grace the line of business in which I am at present engaged, the controle of the German affairs, I hope that I shall

1. Frederick Stuart. See p. 70.   2. Charles Wolfran Cornwall. See p. 257.

have the satisfaction to finish them under the same patronage. There have been now four different Treasuries since I began. I have had the satisfaction to act under each with that degree of approbation that I had and have every reason to expect the reward of my services " (Add. MS. 32968, f. 258).

Golden Square,
October 4, 1763, ½ past nine.

Dear Sir,

Mr. Cuthbert and myself have mett this evening agreeable to the idea of last night and have prepared a report thereupon which we shall be ready to present to the Board to-morrow.[1] Can you tell me whether Mr. Cornwall be come to town, that if he be, I may send to him to see it and form his judgement thereon before we present it. I am obliged to be at Lincoln's Inn early to-morrow morning or I would call upon you to show you the report, but I have ordered Mr. Boyve [2] to make a copy of it and wait upon you with it. I am dear Sir,

Your most obedient servant
T. Pownall

JOSEPH SALVADOR TO GEORGE GRENVILLE

Add. MS. 38201, f. 151.

Joseph Jeshurum Rodrigues, better known as Joseph Salvador, was a member of a wealthy Portuguese Jewish family who came over from Holland at the beginning of the century. He was a partner in the firm of Francis and Joseph Salvador, who, after the death of Sampson Gideon, negotiated loans for the Government. He was president of the Portuguese Jewish congregation and a great philanthropist. He built a house in White Hart Court and owned an estate in Tooting. He was a considerable proprietor of East India stock and the first Jew to be a Director of the Company. He was also a member of the Dutch East India Company. In the great credit crisis of 1772–73, he lost everything that he owned in Europe but managed to save his American property and retired to North Carolina, where he died, " at an advanced age ", in 1787. His nephew, Francis Salvador, who emigrated to South Carolina in 1773 and became a member of the first Provincial Congress, was killed in action when the Indians attacked South Carolina in 1776. See James Picciotto, *Sketches of Anglo-Jewish History* (1875), pp. 162-3. Salvador's letters have no punctuation. This has been supplied to make them intelligible.

1. P.R.O., T. 29/35, f. 185.
2. Jerome Boyve was appointed first clerk to the Commissioners of German Accounts, at ten shillings a day. See P.R.O., T. 29/35, f. 185.

Sir,

The transaction I acquainted you of last Friday is certain (as I am assured), but I am likewise informed that it will have no bad effect and merely arises from private affairs ; the discredit of stocks continues though it seems to day as if something in the wane ; [1] a proper assistance and of a private nature might set everything right again and enable you to pursue a plan in Parliament that might do the Ministry great honour. If you choose to appear the restorer of credit, I am ready to do my part among the friends of the Ministry, if not perhaps things may mend themselves, perhaps grow much worse. As Mr. Jenkinson has appointed me to wait on him on Monday I don't apprehend you will have any commands for me till after that time, but I ever am at your commands and beg leave to subscribe my self, Sir,

Your most obedient humble servant,
Joseph Salvador

The following letter appears to refer to Jenkinson's " Papers concerning the late negotiations for the Peace " which were sent to Dr. Johnson in 1763 and which he returned unread two years later.[2] The papers were a treatise on the peace terms which Jenkinson, under Grenville's protection, prepared in the winter of 1759–60, and which was sent to Johnson presumably as material for a pamphlet. Boswell afterwards assiduously reported that the £300 annuity which Johnson received in July 1762, and which he had difficulties in accepting on account of his improvident definition of pensions and pensioners in the *Dictionary*, was granted to him " solely as the reward of his literary merit, without any stipulation whatever, or even tacit understanding, that he should write for administration ". Robert Yeates was one of the Chief Clerks in the Treasury.

ROBERT YEATES TO CHARLES JENKINSON

Add. MS. 38201, f. 157.

Abingdon Buildings, October 5 [1763].
Sir,

Mr. Samuel Johnson will wait on you at any time you please to appoint. If you think proper to make the appoint-

1. Stocks fell slowly at the end of September and beginning of October. East India stock dropped from 159 on September 28 to 153 on October 4, but the discount on Navy Bills rose from 7¾ on September 20 to 10 and 11 on October 4.
2. See p. 391.

ment by a Note addressed to him I will take care to have it conveyed by the person who talked with him on the matter I mentioned to you. I am Sir

Your most obedient humble servant,

R. Yeates

MR. KLUFT TO CHARLES JENKINSON

Add. MS. 38201, f. 167.

J. D. Kluft was a clerk in the Secretary of State's office for the Northern Department. His name only appears in the Court and City Register for the year 1762, but a Mr. Kluft, probably the same person, was Secretary to the Princess Dowager of Wales (see Fortescue, *Corr. of George III*, ii, p. 321), and in the Windsor Secret Service Accounts a Mr. Kluft received £200 a year between 1779 and 1782.

Little Dean Street, South Audley Street,
October 7, 1763.

Mr. Kluft presents his compliments to Mr. Jenkinson.

He did not receive Mr. Jenkinson's note of Wednesday till yesterday in the afternoon ; and is very sorry not to be able to comply with Mr. Jenkinson's wishes of calling of [*sic*] him this morning. He has moreover some motives to wish, that Mr. Jenkinson would favour him in writing, with what he has to say to him from Lord Bute. As to my Lord's private Letter Book,[1] Mr. Kluft has long ago endeavoured to obtain an opportunity of delivering it, together with his Lordship's seal, into his own hands ; and is still very desirous of the honor to do so ; or otherwise to resign the one and the other into the hands of any person authorised to the reception of them by a written order from his Lordship. For as Mr. Kluft is quite ignorant of Mr. Jenkinson's belonging any more to my Lord Bute, either in a public or private capacity, he thinks himself not at liberty to deliver them in any other manner.

1. Lord Bute's private letter book in the British Museum (Add. MSS. 36797), acquired at the sale of the Harrowby MSS. in 1903. The first 86 ff. are copies of private letters from Bute to various correspondents in chronological order, dating from July 12, 1761, to April 8, 1763, the day on which he resigned the Treasury. They are all in the same handwriting, which could be Kluft's, though it is difficult to be certain of such a formal, clerkish hand. The best evidence that this is the book which Kluft refers to is the fact that the correspondence ceases on April 8, 1763. The entries which follow that date are in a different hand ; they are copies of miscellaneous letters from 1756 to 1765, and do not represent a continuous correspondence.

ANTHONY TODD TO CHARLES JENKINSON

Add. MS. 38201, f. 166.

General Post Office, October 7, 1763.

Dear Sir,

I just now recollect that when I wrote to you last night, in relation to the New York mails, I forgot to mention that no packet boats are now sent to His Majesty's Islands in the West Indies, all the letters go by occasional merchant ships which may be heard of and from whence and when they sail at all times at Lloyds Coffee House.

I am glad we are to have the pleasure of your company on Sunday being with true respect and esteem

Yours most sincerely,

Anth: Todd

JOSEPH SALVADOR TO CHARLES JENKINSON
in Parliament Street

Add. MS. 38201, f. 174.

Tooting, October 10, 1763.

Sir,

I have revised the state you mentioned to me to day of the publick want. They seem to amount to about £8,700,000 but think many articles are rated full high. I therefore in what I propose laying before Mr. Grenville I [sic] state them att £8,500,000.

There seems to me to be a very capital difference from this calculation which will make it much less and seems to bring the whole nearer to Mr. Grenville's ideas. I will endeavour to explain it.

We have allowed for the Extraordinary Naval Services transports etc. 2,000,000 founded on there being due in the first 6 months about £1,400,000, the remainder you thought would be incurred. Now on consideration I apprehend great part of the above sum may have become due under the estimates voted last year as no navy Bills have been paid ; if so this sum must be lessened all that, which will make a very considerable difference. I beg pardon if I enquire into this as I apprehend there must be something in it and should be sorry to give crude ideas for facts after having examined them. I beg your answer and am Sir

Your most obedient servant,

Joseph Salvador

R. WOLTERS TO CHARLES JENKINSON

Add. MS. 38201, ff. 179-80.

Rotterdam, October 11, 1763.

Dear Sir,

I have to acknowledge the honour of your's of the 4th.

The inclosed [1] will show you that my friend has not yet been able to procure what we want, if he comes to me before the departure of the post you will have what he brings me, but I hardly expect it as the French mail arrived late this morning.

If his friends are as willing as they are able to give us a state of the finances we shall soon have full satisfaction. I judge that nothing has been finally determined before the departure of the Court for Fontainebleau, as my usual correspondent takes no manner of notice of it.

This mail has brought us the news that the Chancellor is dismissed and replaced with the title of Vice Chancellor by M. de Maupeou, late first president of the Parliament of Paris, who declining to take this place without the Seals, these have been taken from M. de Brou.[2] It was expected that Mr. Bertin [3] would soon fall.

By my Madrid letters of the 19th of September, the money intended for France was reduced to under the half, and that even not remitted, the Marquis de Squilau was bent upon nothing but saving, he is to have the department of the finances above the load which he allready had.

1. Add. MS. 38201, f. 181. An unsigned letter addressed " à M. Wolters, Agent de Sa Majesté Brittanique, logé sur les Bambijes à Rotterdam ".
2. Guillaume de Lamoignon (1683–1772), the father of Malesherbes, was Chancellor from 1750. In 1763 Louis XV made him the scapegoat in his quarrel with the Parlements. He was exiled from Court in October 1763 but refused to resign the Chancellorship until 1768. In the meantime Maupeou, formerly President of the Parlement of Paris, succeeded him with the title of Vice-Chancellor which the Parlement refused to recognise. Feydeau le Brou, Garde des Sceaux, resigned the seals to Maupeou on October 11, 1763.
3. Bertin, whose financial measures of April 1763 had brought about the quarrel between Louis XV and the Parlements, was dismissed from the Contrôle Général on December 13, after the Government had compromised with the Parlements on November 21, by a modification of the taxes.

I know no farther anecdotes about the causes of the failures att Amsterdam than what I told you, but your hint will make me attentive to collect them.   Credit revives more and more there and elsewhere, but the affairs of the Neuville's who made the first link of that chain are desperately bad, their books are brought to the Chamber of Insolvency, and found so bad that the creditors have little to expect.

It is surprising and not to be accounted for that notwithstanding the fall in England the stocks advanced yesterday att Amsterdam 3 per cent.

I send to morrow by a Trader the negociations of the Noailles in England in the 16th century, allso a sequel to Voltaire's universal history, his history of Peter the Great I am told you have in England.

I have the honour to be most truely dear Sir
   Your most humble and most obedient servant,
         R. Wolters

P.S.   as I am sealing my letter my friend is now arrived ; I have absolutely declined his scheme of going to Paris, as besides the uncertainty of its usefulness, it would be attended with much greater expence, than I should care to throw the public into without particular orders.

When Lord Hertford was appointed British Ambassador to France after the conclusion of the Peace, he invited David Hume to be his acting secretary, as the official Secretary to the Embassy, Charles Bunbury, was obnoxious to him.   Hume was given a Secret Service pension of £200 a year instead of salary.   He arrived in Paris on October 14, 1763, and remained there till the fall of the Rockingham Ministry in July 1766. In June 1765 he was appointed official Secretary with a salary of £1200, and shortly after, when Hertford was sent to Ireland, he remained in Paris as Chargé d'Affaires until the arrival of the new Ambassador.

DAVID HUME TO CHARLES JENKINSON

Add. MS. 38201, f. 185.

London, October 12, 1763.

Sir,
I have been told by Lord Hertford, that the King has been graciously pleased to favour me with a pension of two hundred pounds a year without deductions.   I set out for Paris with his Lordship to morrow ; and I desire you will be

so good as to pay the money, as it becomes due, to Messrs Coutts and Company, Bankers in the Strand. I am Sir

Your most obedient humble servant,

David Hume

SIR WILLIAM MEREDITH TO CHARLES JENKINSON

Add. MS. 38201, ff. 186-7.

Henbury, October 12, 1763.

Dear Sir,

⟨The⟩ leave of absence, that you had the kindness to obtain for one *Arthur Lord*, a Landwaiter at Liverpool, has, I am afraid proved fatal to him ; for, the vessel, in which he sailed is reported to be shipwrecked in Beaumarris bay with 150 passengers on board and a rich cargo ; though I have just now heard, that she is safe at Milford haven, but so many circumstances, with so strong a probability of her loss are handed about, that my fears outweigh every hope that she has escaped.

⟨If⟩ the ship is lost, I must intreat you to present my respects to Mr. Grenville with my earnest request that Richard Whiteside may succeed him ; who is the very person, for whom you have heard me express so much anxiety, and who is, I am persuaded, the worthiest of ⟨pre⟩ferment of any officer in the port ; having done the business ⟨of⟩ Landwaiter occasionally, above twenty years, and been ⟨de⟩luded with constant promises as long. This ⟨is⟩ the first place of valu, that has become vacant, since the Duke of Newcastle left the Treasury. Sir Ellis Cunliffe [1] had the nomination of three Landwaiters at once, the very week the Duke retired ; and rejected this *Whiteside*, though he voted for him and was recommended by all his own friends.

I hear, that Gascoin is making interest at Liverpool, [2] whe⟨re⟩ he is sure to be joined by a great part of the Corpora-

1. Sir Ellis Cunliffe, 1st Bart., M.P. for Liverpool 1755-67.
2. In 1780 Bamber Gascoyne brought in his son for Liverpool at an alleged cost of £8000. See a *Letter to the Earl of Sefton* by Ignotus (1806), p. 8 : " For many years previous to 1780 owing to our then representatives, Sir William Meredith and Mr. Pennant (now Lord Penrynn) having been wholly anti-ministerial, the late Bamber Gascoyne was uniformly applied to on all public matters, and . . . was of infinite service to the town, and procured himself an interest with the leaders of the corporation, which has since been gratefully exerted in favour of his

tion, a majority of which consists of one family (the Gildarts') [1] their relations and friends. It is said likewise, that Sir Ellis Cunliffe has declared his intentions to resign. But, without a Mayor, the rest of the Corporation are insignificant ; and a Mr. Campbell, a friend of our's, is in nomination, and I don't find, they will oppose him : if they do, we shall strug⟨gle⟩ for it. And, if he is elected, we have enough to keep up the succession, as the measure of adopting Gascoin has thrown two or three at least of the Corporation into our party. But, if we dont get a Mayor now, Gascoin or the devil may come in for *me*.

I go to Liverpool to morrow. When I have seen the turn of things, and the temper of the people, I will take the liberty of writing to you, and telling my sentiments fully and freely, as I did last Session of Parliament ⟨   ⟩, though, the part, I take, is very immaterial ; yet I will ⟨pre⟩serve my own faith and integrity to those, with whom ⟨I m⟩ake engagements. At the same time, I will not give up my own independency, and shall very unwillingly ⟨par⟩t with the goodwill of my constituents.

The resolution of writing a long letter to you after my visit to Liverpool has prevented me from thanking you sooner for your last good offices, and begging you to present my grateful and respectful acknowledgments to Mr. Greenville. I am, dear Sir

Your most obliged, faithful servant,

Wm. Meredith

JOSEPH SALVADOR TO CHARLES JENKINSON

Add. MS. 38397, f. 72.

White Hart Court, October 21, 1763.

Sir,

I congratulate you on Mr. Grenville's success in reconciling the East India Company with the Bank.[2] 'Tis the

descendants ". Bamber Gascoyne, the younger, was M.P. for Liverpool 1780–96. See W. D. Pink and A. B. Beavan, *The Parliamentary Representation of Lancashire* (1889), p. 201.

1. One of this family, Francis Gildart (died May 25, 1780), was Town Clerk for Liverpool, and three of them are in the list of freemen who voted at the general election of 1784. Richard Gildart, who died in 1770 aged ninety-nine, was Senior Alderman, and M.P. for Liverpool 1734–54.

2. The East India Company were negotiating a loan from the Bank. See p. 221.

greatest point that could have been gained. This, seconded by some other resolute step at a proper time will put the rating the publick levies of this year in Mr. Grenville's power and will enable him to execute the most sanguine of my wishes. Some small clouds yet hang over the City should they burst they will not now have the effect they would have had in past. I am with great regard Sir

Your most obedient servant

Joseph Salvador

SIR WILLIAM MEREDITH TO CHARLES JENKINSON

Add. MS. 38201, f. 205.

Henbury, October 25, 1763.

Dear Sir,

Being just returned from Liverpool, I was followed by an express to acquaint me with the death of *Arthur Lord*, who was put on shore at Milford and died immediately. I am earnestly desired to send an express, so that Mr. Greenville will be troubled with a new application, before he has my letter of thanks by this day's post.

Every thing turned out at Liverpool beyond my hopes. My friend was elected Mayor ;[1] and the division among the gentlemen, who opposed me, so much greater than I expected, especially in the Corporation, that no acts of power *can* be effected now ; and the interest of my friends has now some reality and foundation, and I hope, all divisions will cease. There is an idea of Sir Ellis Cunliffe resigning his seat in parliament ; but I know no other presumtion for it, than his state of health, which is miserable. Though, it is often mentioned, who is *not*, I can't guess who *is* likely to succeed him ; nor shall I (seem at least) to interfere ; but, have hinted a person to my particular acquaintance, that, I think, may, if he pleases be chosen.

As I hope to see you in a few days, I will trouble you no more than to assure you that I am, most respectfully, dear Sir,

Your oblidged, faithful servant

Wm. Meredith

1. See p. 209.

JOSEPH SALVADOR TO CHARLES JENKINSON

Add. MS. 38397, f. 73.

Tooting, October 25, 1763.

Sir,

I wish the difficulty relative to the East India Company may be totally removed by the step taken. It always was judicious, it was but part of what I thought right. I fear the rest may become absolutely necessary.

T'would have been lucky had Mr. Touchet's [1] affair broke out att a less interesting time. I am alarmed to day with many bad consequences already flowing from it. Should I on coming to town find but a small part of what is reported true, although not sent for I must beg one serious audience of Mr. Grenville ; too much is depending for me to wait ceremonies and I fear you have not att present the full information of the City that the times demand. I propose going to court where I hope to see you when I may receive your further commands. I foresaw much. I dread more if not timely and prudently stopped. I am with great regard, Sir,

Your most obedient humble servant,

Joseph Salvador

JONATHAN SCOTT TO CHARLES JENKINSON

Add. MS. 38201, ff. 208-9.

Jonathan Scott, according to Almon, the author of *Anti-Sejanus*, was a printer and publisher, associated with John Entick, Arthur Beardmore, and Edward Shebbeare in the publication of *The Monitor*, which was William Beckford's paper, conducted by Entick and speaking for the City groups who were interested in the Seven Years' War. See W. T. Laprade, " The Power of the English Press in the Eighteenth Century ", in the *South Atlantic Quarterly*, October 1928. *The Monitor* was founded in 1755, and its profits were to go to Scott. Shebbeare dropped out after receiving the first quarter of his stipend and Scott was later imprisoned for debt. On October 11, 1762, he gave information against Entick which led to his arrest on a charge of sedition. See *State Trials*, xix, 1030 *seqq.*, where Scott publishes his " voluntary information ". In November 1763 he gave evidence against Wilkes in the proceedings on the *Essay on Woman*.

1. Samuel Touchet (see pp. 105-6) went bankrupt in October 1763. See Wadsworth and Mann, *The Cotton Trade and Industrial Lancashire*, p. 247.

October 25, 1763.

Honoured Sir,

I have this day delivered a Memorial, concerning the Monitor, (of which I was the publisher for many years) to my Lord Halifax and am emboldened to hope you will be pleased to back the representation thereof, with your good offices on my behalf ; my imprisonment and sufferings have been without an equal, and the more surprizing still the suffering in behalf of the Government. I have long bore the enemy's triumph, over the greatest distress and misery ; But with your assistance, knowing so well the merits of the case, I doubt not the getting the better of them in my turn, and do my country signal service. I am, honoured Sir !

Your most obedient servant,

Jonathan Scott

JOSEPH SALVADOR TO CHARLES JENKINSON
in Parliament Street
Add. MS. 38397, f. 74.

White Hart Court, October 31, 1763.

Sir,

On my arrival in the City and meeting the Directors of the East India Company I found a happy change in their affairs many of their bonds having come in and made it as we hope unnecessary to take any further steps concerning them. This is a very happy circumstance and I hope a prelude to a change all through our affairs.

I am informed there is a derangement in the City ; it may seem very considerable to you but I flatter myself will prove nothing of importance. I am Sir,

Your most obedient servant,

Joseph Salvador

JOSEPH SALVADOR TO CHARLES JENKINSON
in Parliament Street
Add. MS. 38201, f. 216.

White Hart Court, November 1, 1763.

Sir,

Although we have got rid of the India Company, private credit is in so bad a state that the thoughts of it affects me

(212)

greatly, I fear I must represent as the only means the bold stroke of paying the Navy ; [1] it seems impossible to do without it and small inconveniences must give way to great evils. Reflecting with regard to the issuing, I am clear you can do it for the Exchequer Bills may be issued to any service, so near 4 millions may be issued on it ; you know what has been, yet ere I press I shall remember your words and bring some proof it can do no mischief there ; I hope to see the Governor of the Bank to morrow and to find his views and dispositions.

As you promise to favour me with your company on Saturday I will endeavour to get Mr. Oswald [2] to meet you. I think his advice may be of infinite service. I don't know a gentleman who understands those affairs better. If improper we will only meet. I wish we were safe through these times as I fear what I dare not mention unless some bold steps retrieve us. I beg your answer and am, Sir,

Your most obedient servant,

Joseph Salvador

PEREGRINE CUST AND ROBERT JONES
TO CHARLES JENKINSON

Add. MS. 38201, f. 218.

Peregrine Cust, M.P. for various constituencies 1761–75 and 1776–85, and brother of Sir John Cust the Speaker, was a merchant and Government contractor. When in the winter of 1762–63 Newcastle's friends were deprived of their contracts, part of the contract for remitting the money to pay the troops at Gibraltar was given to Cust and his partner, Robert Jones, instead of John Bristow (see Add. MSS. 38338, ff. 109-11, " State of Contracts in 1764 "). The rest of the contract went to Burrell and Fonnereau (see above, p. 111 n. 4). Robert Jones, M.P. for Huntingdon 1754–74, was Sandwich's " man of business ". See Namier, *Structure of Politics*, pp. 352-3. For a short account of Cust and his family see *ibid*. pp. 307-8 ; and *Records of the Cust Family* compiled by Lady Elizabeth Cust (1909), vol. ii *passim*.

November 2, 1763.

Sir,

Upon application at the Pay Office to day for the money ordered for the pay of the troops at Gibraltar, we were told they could not issue it unless we would give our Bill at sight upon our Agent at Gibraltar in dollars estimating the dollar

1. *I.e.* the Navy Bills.   2. James Oswald ? See p. 161 n. 4.

$52\frac{1}{2}$ cant be paid or remitted to Gibraltar under near 60 ⟨moidores⟩. We are willing to remit moidores according to our agreement, if we are permitted to give our Bills in that specie and not in dollars. We beg the favour of your interest with their Lordships for this liberty and that we may be permitted to draw our Bill at 2 months instead of sight it being impossible to send it in by time to Gibraltar after we receive it from the Treasury.[1] We are Sir,

Your most humble ⟨servants⟩,

Pere: Cust
Rob. Jones

SIR WILLIAM MEREDITH TO CHARLES JENKINSON

Add. MS. 38201, f. 224.

Henbury, November 5, 1763.

Dear Sir,

Nothing ever struck me more than the very kind manner, in which you told me of Lord's[2] employment being given to Williamson.

There are times and circumstances that render such a disappointment irreparable. And on my naming a few incidents, you will see what I feel. After my election the Duke of Newcastle gave the disposal of every thing to Sir Ellis Cunliffe, on this express condition, that, he should recommend none of my f⟨riends.⟩ Three vacancys of Landwaiters happening at once, they were all filled by Sir Ellis, who soon after took out instructions for this Williamson in order to keep up a succession in his own party. Williamson is appointed and my friend kept out. So that, in fact the persecution of the old Ministry attends me still, but with consequences much more injurious ; For, I might have supported, as I gained, my interest, without ministerial favor ; but to let me give away two or three low, mean offices, and take the very first reputable one, that becomes vacant, out of my hands, is indeed exposing me to all possible contempt and ridicule.

There is another consideration that aggravates my disappointment ; for it has long been my study to put an end to those divisions, that my election occasioned ; had I succeeded

---

1. The Treasury agreed to these terms. See Treasury Minutes for December 8, 1763, P.R.O., T. 29/35, ff. 225-6. On October 5 Jones and Cust contracted to pay their remittances to Gibraltar in moidores. *Ibid.* f. 175.

2. See p. 208.

(214)

for Whiteside,[1] it was my intention to have offered my assistance to Williamson in hopes of reconciling some persons who retain a bitter remembrance of my prevailing against their inclinations ; but as they have found a new channel through which they can supersede me still, their insolence will be increased, and the breach wider than ever.

Sir Ellis Cunliffe was applied to before Lord Strange,[2] but (I hear) excused himself with some handsome expressions, from interfering against Whiteside, but they found Lord Strange very ready to *interfere* ; though I am pretty sure he does not know (I question, if he ever *saw*) this Williamson (whom Mr. Greenville calls a *friend of his*) and very little of those who recommended him.

These, t'is true, are local circumstances, unknown at the Treasury, and Lord Strange wrote before I did ; but, I could have no idea, that it was necessary to get start at the post office ; since, for these last 40 years, the Members have recommended to certain (not all) vacant offices within the port as uniformly as the great officers of State nominate the inferior ones of their own departments. And it ought to be ascertained always what they have to depend on ; for, to leave these places open to the sollicitation of third persons would involve whoever represents Liverpool in endless difficulties, and sometimes perhaps make the Minister himself uneasy ; though, not in the case of so disregarded an individual as myself. But having acted with Administration without a thought for myself, against the sense of my constituents, (at a time, when the very people, for whom I am now given up, were acting the part of incendiaries against Government) I own I did hope to have been allowed the same degree of credit, as my predecessors did (as they ought to) enjoy ; especially after Lord Bute had told me " *I might command* (I repeat his words) as much regard from him, as was ever shewn to a Member for Liverpool " : When I had the honor to wait on Mr. Greenville I asked nothing, but the next vacancy for *Whiteside*, and though his answer (which I recollect exactly) did not *specify*, yet it *implied* a promise so much that I took it as one. And, if he is ever pleased to shew him the kindness, he intends, he will do an act of charity and justice very worthy of himself ; but, I cannot presume to sollicit him ; for, as I can never forgive myself

1. Richard Whiteside, whom Meredith recommended to succeed Arthur Lord as a Land-waiter at Liverpool.
2. Lord Strange was Chancellor of the Duchy of Lancaster.

for having once deluded the poor man (his heart being almost broken with former disappointments) I will not incur a possibility of deluding him again.

There is nothing so immaterial as the part I am to take ; yet, I cannot disown those feelings, that spirit and sense (if there's a grain of either) must raise in a heart, impressed as mine is ; but, into whatever situation I am thrown, I shall preserve a grateful and respectful remembrance of your kindness, and shall esteem the continuance of your friendship, as a real honor and happiness to my life.

I leave home to morrow, but shall not reach London, till we meet at Philippi. I am, my dear Sir,

Your faithful, humble servant,

Wm. Meredith

By February 1764 Newcastle counted Meredith as a friend. See his list of " Original Tories who voted with us " [on General Warrants, February 17], dated February 26. Add. MS. 32956, f. 116. See also f. 187 for another list dated March 2.

LORD SANDWICH TO CHARLES JENKINSON
in Parliament Street

Add. MS. 38201, f. 222.

Whitehall, November 5, 1763.

Dear Sir,

You promised to return my list of the House of Commons [1] with such alterations in it as had come to your knowledge, be so good as to send it me, if you can, by the bearer.

I have some small arrears due to me as Ambassador to Spain which stop somewhere in the Treasury, I believe for want of your letter to the Auditor of the Exchequer. Be so good as to let me know how that matter stands, and if it depends upon you to dispatch it I flatter myself you will.[2] I am

Your most obedient and most humble servant,

Sandwich

1. Add. MS. 38333, ff. 74-106. Cf. Namier, *England etc.* p. 203. This is the original list of the House of Commons which was compiled for Bute in the middle of December 1761. It had been subjected to many revisions since then. The last corrections were made before the opening of the session on November 15, 1763. Professor Namier suggests that it was on the receipt of this letter from Sandwich that Jenkinson made his last notes on the list.

2. As Ambassador to Spain between February and September 1763, Sandwich drew £3200 from the Civil List, and Richard Phelps, his secretary, £582, though the embassy never took place.

CHARLES JENKINSON TO SIR JAMES LOWTHER

Add. MS. 38201, f. 230.

London, November 8, 1763.

Dear Sir,

I have the honour to write to you by Mr. Grenville's directions, who desires me to express to you his wishes that you would second Lord Charles Spenser in the compliment that is to be made the Queen at the opening of the Session on the birth of her second son ; to have a person of your fortune, family and importance concerned in this proposition will add very much to the compliment, and you will exceedingly oblige Mr. Grenville by complying with his request.[1] We have no news. Mr. Mackenzie who came yesterday from Luton assures me that Lord Bute and all the family are well. I have the honour to be with great respect dear Sir,

Your faithful humble servant,

C. Jenkinson

GEORGE MIDDLETON TO CHARLES JENKINSON

Add. MS. 38201, f. 234.

Seaton, Tuesday, November 8, 1763.

Dear Sir,

I presume your hurry is somewhat abated and I may now remind you of your intentions of 28th July, of bringing my request through your Board,[2] as the Commissioners of Customs had transmitted their Report, Mr. Nelthorpe concluded it would be closed by Warrant from the Lords of Treasury ordering the sum accrued during the vacancy burthened with the payment to Mr. Isaac Grant which by the Commissioners Report it seems is to be £50. I will therefore beg your answer when convenient not only to this but to a point I anxiously wish, a firm majority of Parliament ascertaining the Kings measures ; and a permanent Administration. Here we begin very feelingly to wish there could troops enough

1. Grenville, having successfully got rid of Bute, wanted Lowther, Bute's son-in-law, to show himself a supporter of Administration in an expression of loyalty to the Crown.
2. See p. 195.

be spared to enforce the revenue raising, and free good subjects of sollicitation, which really is not the case, as the reduction upon peace seems exceeding great. Our Members are all hastening to Cockpit, except Lord Macduff [1] now E. of Fife by father's death. Jokers say he latently belongs to E. of T.[2] and waits till the candles are lighted up. Lord Adam Gordon [3] passed Saturday.

I am very happy in receiving a few lines from our friend [4] in perfect spirits and tranquillity and so fond of his new rural residence. I am one of those superficial phylosophers who brace myself up to an enthusiastic faith that all will be for the best, though I am not without hearty wishes that your unaldermanlike body may escape colds and coughs with late sittings, for I suppose there will be a deal of tongue fighting before Xmas. Adieu my dear Sir and be assured you have the affectionate good wishes of

Your obliged humble servant,

Geo. Middleton

LORD SANDWICH TO CHARLES JENKINSON

Add. MS. 38201, f. 232.

Tuesday morning.
[" November 8, 1763."]

Dear Sir,

I wish you would send me a list of all the vacant seats in Parliament at this time, as I cannot compleat my number without it, I make out but 555 Members.[5]

You may put Conolly [6] and Mackworth [7] both present and friends. I am

Very sincerely yours,

Sandwich

1. James Duff, 2nd Earl Fife in the Irish Peerage, afterwards (1790) raised to the English Peerage as Baron Fife, succeeded his father on September 30, 1763. He was styled Viscount MacDuff from 1759, when his father was created 1st Earl Fife. At this time he was M.P. for Banffshire. About him see also below, p. 312.   2. Temple ?
3. Lord Adam Gordon, M.P. for Aberdeenshire 1754–68, fourth son of Alexander, 2nd Duke of Gordon.
4. Bute.   5. See p. 216.
6. Thomas Conolly, M.P. for Malmesbury 1759–68, Chichester 1768–80.
7. Herbert Mackworth the elder, of Gnoll, Glamorganshire ; M.P. for Cardiff 1738–66.

R. WOLTERS TO CHARLES JENKINSON
Add. MS. 38201, ff. 226-7.

Rotterdam, November 8, 1763.

Dear Sir,

By my correspondent's unluckily mistaking an article of my letter, the inclosed[1] did not come to my hands in time for last Friday's mail.

You will see that it contains vast projections which however fine in theory may be found very difficult in practice.

By what you have allready had, you will now be able to judge, if it is worth while to encourage the continuance of this correspondance or to put a stop to it ; the correspondent thinks what he has allready done great, and I shall be at a loss how to deal with him, unless you will please let me know your intentions.

I have absolutely declined proposing to you a favourite project of his, which was a journey to Paris, and his going before hand to London ⟨to⟩ convince you that by his connections att the French court he might be of the greatest use there ; but to this was tacked his desire of having a caracter, or being one of the British Embassador's family : he is out of humour with me that I did not greedily enter into his views.

The continuance of this correspondance will depend upon your decision ; and I should be glad to know att the same time if you would have me make him an offer for what he has done, or ask him what he expects.

I cannot promise that this person will be able to perform the great things which he says he can, as he has not yet been able to procure what I so earnestly pressed for, viz, the present state of the French finances.

As this correspondant thinks that he has the honour to be known to Mr. Grenville, I must tell you that it is Mr. Iacottet late Collonel of the Duke of Modena's Guards. It was att Lausanne that he thinks that he knew Mr. Grenville about 30 years agone when Lord Weymouth was there. ⟨The⟩ history of his adventures would make a volume, ⟨and⟩ particularly

1. Add. MS. 38201, ff. 228-9, copy of a letter in French, received by Iacottet from a correspondent in Paris, dated October 27, 1763, and transmitted to Wolters on November 1. It contains a forecast of French taxation. Cf. also Wolters' Letter Book, P.R.O., S.P. Holland, 84, 503, Wolters to Sandwich, November 8, with enclosures from Paris.

what brought him hither, and some part of his memoirs would look suspicious, allthough my doubts have been fully cleared up by a friend, professor att Leyden. I have the honour to be most truely, dear Sir,

Your most humble and most obedient servant,

R. Wolters

JOSEPH CAWTHORNE [1] TO CHARLES JENKINSON
Add. MS. 38201, f. 254.

Salopian Coffee house,
Charing Cross, November 21, 1763.

Sir,

I had once occasion to acquaint you that I was soliciting Lord Bute for the reversion of an Office abroad. His Lordship's answer was that with his Office he had resignd all connection with the affairs of the nation. However as there is reason to think he has sufficient interest to procure a thing he might chuse to solicit for, if you Sir will be pleased to use your good offices with his Lordship so as to procure me the said reversion I will pay you *one thousand pounds* which is an object worth some notice. As no body will ever know from me any thing about this offer I hope you will see no offence or even impropriety in the proposal since you very well know 'tis natural to and incumbent on all to endeavour to promote their own happiness, adhering at the same time to the strictest and nicest rules of honor, which you may depend on from me. In the mean time I have one advantage by this address, and that is of having the honor to profess myself, Sir,

Your most humble and most devoted servant,

Joseph Cawthorne

JOSEPH SALVADOR TO CHARLES JENKINSON
Add. MS. 38397, f. 75.

White Hart Court, November 22, 1763.

Dear Sir,

Tis with pleasure that I can inform you that in the final determination of the East India Company's affair regarding

1. See p. 199.

(220)

their bonds, the measures taken have had the full effect and they assured me that they no longer wanted any assistance, that even that from the Bank would not be fully employed, and that even that sum would become unnecessary after January.

The decisive week with regard to the support of the funds is this. It seems to promise passing off much better than could be expected considering how ill the Dutch have kept their mighty promises. Were you apprised of the state of foreign property as I hinted I should wish Mr. Grenville when rid of the arduous affairs now before him would settle some plan for proceeding in the money'd operations of the season. I think the prospect will mend daily if somewhat is done. I don't mean concluding, but doing something towards it. I am always att command and beg leave to subscribe myself, Sir,

Your most obedient humble servant,

Joseph Salvador

R. WOLTERS TO CHARLES JENKINSON

Add. MS. 38201, ff. 259-60.

Rotterdam, November 22, 1763.

Dear Sir,

I have to acknowledge the honour of your's of the 15th instant.

I have in consequence of its contents wrote fully to the friend who had recommended M. Iacottet to me to know his thoughts, for M. Iacottet's thoughts of what he has done are so different from my own that I can not well sett a price to the value of his services. In the mean time he has promised to procure something worth your notice, of which we shall only be able to judge when we have it.

If you can contribute to bring the allowance of £100 per annum to the widow Gentil upon a stable footing you will do a very charitable act ; as she is ruined and undone if this is not effected before January next. All these uncertainties proceed from a very well intended step of Mr. Richardson, which was to have her pension kept from the List of pensions to save deductions.

Not onely I judge as you do that the overturning a whole system of finances is next to impracti⟨cable⟩ but we have had in this country an instance of the danger of these methods in *1748* : the farms were abolished, and after trying for a whole year a thousand methods to serve in lieu of them, they were, seeing before their eyes the ruin of the publick, obliged to come to the old taxes with the difference onely of collecting them for the publick instead of by farmers : none of the methods attempted by head money etc. produced the half of what they were sett down for.[1]

However in the present situation and discredit of France they must do something ; and to know what that is to be I believe that I may more safely rely upon my usual correspondents than upon other means.

It is confirmed from different quarters that the Directors of the French East India Company refuse to serve under the immediate direction of the King, and that M. La Borde finds very few people that care to contribute to his scheme of a new company.[2] I have the honour to be most truely, dear Sir,

Your most humble and most obedient servant

R. Wolters

The expulsion of Wilkes from the House of Commons on December 24, 1763, occasioned a by-election at Aylesbury, where Anthony Bacon was returned on January 25, 1764.

LORD HARCOURT TO CHARLES JENKINSON

Add. MS. 38458, ff. 41-2.

Cavendish Square, Friday Night,
November 25 [1763].

Dear Sir,

I received a letter this evening from Sir William Lee [3] which I have sent you, that Mr. Grenville may see (if you have a mind to shew it to him) Sir William's opinions of Aylesbury. The chief point to be considered, is the proper time of naming the candidate, for till that is done, no essential

1. Bertin's taxes were modified on November 21, 1763 (see p. 206 n. 3), and the Parlements were invited to present memorials on the best means of simplifying taxation.
2. The French East India Company was practically ruined by the war, and though it began to recover after the lottery of 1765, it had become the object of attack by the economists Gournay and Movellet. In 1769 it was deprived of its privileges and the shareholders sold out their rights to the Crown.
3. Sir William Lee was Harcourt's son-in-law. He married Lady Betty Harcourt on June 20, 1763.

steps, can be taken. Whether Mr. Childs [1] name, can be made use of, before Mr. Wilkes is actually expelled the House of Commons, must be submitted to Mr. Grenville's better judgment : But whatever commands Mr. Grenville may have, I shall most readily transmit them to Sir William who I am sure will do every thing in his power to assist any gentleman recommended by Mr. Grenville. I am, dear Sir,

Yours most sincerely,

Harcourt

EDWARD KYNASTON TO CHARLES JENKINSON
in Parliament Street
Add. MS. 38201, f. 266.

Edward Kynaston, M.P. for Montgomeryshire 1747–72, a Tory, was one of Grenville's Parliamentary managers.

Saturday evening, November 26, 1763.

Sir,
      After Mr. Lowndes's [2] return from Mr. Grenville he desired me to send to Mr. Devon [3] Mr. Child's partner, to meet us this evening ; instead of coming he sent me the inclosed. If therefore by this post a letter must be sent relating to the Aylesbury Election, I should imagine, that an other person must be thought of. I heartily wish that you may have success in recommending a proper person, and am Sir,

Your most obedient humble servant,

Edward Kynaston

LORD HARCOURT TO CHARLES JENKINSON
Add. MS. 38201, f. 270.

Cavendish Square, November 30, 1763.

Dear Sir,
      I did not get to Lord Vernons [4] time enough to send a letter by last nights post, and as I have no servant in town but

1. Robert Child, the banker. He seems to have withdrawn as candidate for Aylesbury and was returned for Wells on December 26, 1765.
2. Richard Lowndes, M.P. for Buckinghamshire 1741–74, another Tory.
3. Thomas Devon, banker, died April 16, 1767.
4. George Venables-Vernon, 1st Baron Vernon, married as his third wife, in April 1744, Martha, daughter of Simon Harcourt and sister to the Lord Harcourt of these letters.

a valet de chambre, I have no means of conveying a letter to Sir William Lee sooner than by tomorrow nights post, a loss of time that might be prejudicial to Mr. Child. I therefore beg the favour of you to let the enclosed letter be conveyed to Sir William by one of your messengers, that he may have it this evening, as he lives but a mile and a half beyond Aylesbury.

Yours, dear Sir, most sincerely,

Harcourt

I set out for Oxfordshire to morrow morning.

R. WOLTERS TO CHARLES JENKINSON

Add. MS. 38201, f. 272.

Rotterdam, November 30, 1763.[1]

Dear Sir,

I send the inclosed in hopes of its coming (as the wind is), in time at Harwich to go with the mail of yesterday, and I write to Mr. Iacottet to inform me of the sequel of this intended pecuniary transaction, whilst I shall make it my business to know what advices our merchants, who are engaged in the French stocks, receive from their Bankers att Paris.

What security the French Court can give in its present contest with the Parliaments, I do not well see ; and without it I may judge that they will not draw much money out of this country, although 5 per cent is a great inticement to a nation which loves money.

My advice, sent yesterday to the Earl of Sandwich will have informed you that the whole Parliament of Rouen has resigned.[2] I have the honour to be most truely dear Sir,

Your most humble and most obedient servant,

R. Wolters

1. An almost identical letter from Wolters to Sandwich of November 30 is in Wolters' Letter Book (P.R.O., S.P. Holland, 84, 503) in which he says his information comes from " a person whom I have employed at Mr. Jenkinson's desire ". On November 29 Wolters sent Sandwich a printed account of the transactions in the Parlement of Rouen. *Ibid.*

2. Bertin's fiscal edict of May 31, 1763, aroused violent opposition in the French Parlements. On August 5 Rouen addressed a particularly bold remonstrance to the King, and when on August 18 the Duc d'Harcourt, as Provincial Governor, was sent down to register the edict, the president of the Parlement told him his action was illegal. On November 16 the magistrates passed an *arrêt* declaring the edict void. This *arrêt* Harcourt caused to be erased from their books, whereupon the whole Parlement resigned.

Add. MS. 38201, ff. 282-3.

Rotterdam, December 2, 1763.

Dear Sir,

As it is not possible to bring M. Iacottet to come in to terms reasonable and equitable, I have wrote to the friend who had recommended him to me ; you will see his thoughts in the inclosed.[1] You will please to lett me know if you approve my giving him 100 ducats, and to have done with him.

As to M. Iacottet's abusive language, I do not mind it, as I never gave him reason to expect the great things which he seems to have in view. You will please to lett me know if I am to draw upon you for the amount of the 100 ducats. I am sorry that an affair of which I had reason to have great expectations turns out so ill.

I had the honour to write to you the 30 past. One of our merchants has a letter from France this day, in which his correspondent surmises ⟨that⟩ a tax of 5 per cent may be thought on to be laid upon all the publick stocks, but I can hardly think that the French Ministry would do a thing that must inevitably knock up the credit of the nation. I have the honour to be most truely dear Sir,

Your most humble and most obedient

R. Wolters

P.S. After finishing this letter I receive my French letters. You have inclosed what my Paris correspondent sends me.

ARCHBISHOP OF YORK TO CHARLES JENKINSON

Add. MS. 38201, f. 287.

Robert Drummond (1711–76), second son of George Hay, 7th Earl of Kinnoull, was Archbishop of York 1761–76, and Lord High Almoner to the King. See *D.N.B.*

1. Add. MS. 38201, f. 284. Wolters's anonymous correspondent, who writes from The Hague, thought Iacottet had acted in good faith and might still be useful in the future, and that he should be given at least enough to pay his agents, but did not know if 100 ducats was too much. See also *ibid*. f. 285, Iacottet to Wolters, complaining of his treatment : " Ce n'est pas votre amy qui doit décider de cette recompense mais bien son supérier, de l'équité duquel j'augure trop pour penser un instant qu'il exige qu'on le serve pour la gloire ".

Dartmouth Street, December 3, 1763.
Saturday night.

Sir,

You'll excuse my troubling you with this letter, as I imagine there has been some mistake in the delay of issuing from the Treasury the money for the Almoner's Office. His Majesty's bounty from this Office is given to a variety of persons, in small sums, and at stated times : so that the Treasury have always accelerated the issues to this office, whatever other delays there have been.

The two quarters of pensions due at Michaelmas last are payable now by the course of the Office : I sent to the Pension Office,[1] and I am told that there is no order from the Treasury. I apprehend these two quarters amount only to £500 : but the Almonry cannot at present get any money, as in usual course, from the Pension Office, and the fact is, that to prevent the course of his Majesty's bounty being stopt towards these poor objects I have thrown in my own money. I shall be obliged to you, if you will take this into consideration, as soon as you can : and I am with true regard Sir,

Your most obedient humble servant,
R. Ebor

CHAUNCY TOWNSEND TO CHARLES JENKINSON

Add. MS. 38201, f. 310.

Chauncy Townsend, M.P. for Westbury 1747–68, and Wigtown Burghs 1768–70, was a merchant, Government contractor, and mine owner. About him see Namier, *England etc.* pp. 284-5.

Bath, December 10, 1763.

Sir,

I have been confined here with illness for some time which has prevented my looking after mony affairs, but being now in reall want, must desire the favor of your orders to pay my warrants (near £12,000) having received none near 8 months,

1. The Pension Office, under the Paymaster of Pensions, dealt with annuities, etc. on the Civil List. In an account for 1754 (Add. MS. 33044, f. 11) is an entry : " The Lord Almoner for Private Pensions, £800 ". Details of payments made by the Pension Office are not always given in the Civil List accounts at the Record Office, but there are also the yearly lists of Pensions and Bounties from the Audit Office between 1759 and 1782 (A.O. 3/791). About the Pension Office see *Structure of Politics*, pp. 230-32.

I hope this will be no inconveniency ; if it should, the half will do for me.

I expect to be able by the time the House meets after Xmas to attend my friends, the prevention of doing it last month made me very unhappy which I flatter my self they will beleive. I am Sir,

Your most obedient humble servant,

Chauncy Townsend

TOM RAMSDEN TO CHARLES JENKINSON

Add. MS. 38201, f. 312.

Pontefract, December 11, 1763.

I give you many thanks, my dear Jenkinson, for your letter ; I held you excused for not writing oftener. I have been in the oven. Thought you under the same harrow.

Much obliged to you for speaking for Agnew ; who will hold himself in readiness to set out when sent for, having wrote to his father for that purpose, this day.[1]

I am heartily sorry, though not surprised, for what has passed in the Court of Common Pleas.[2] Liberty and lycentiousness seem to be united ; and I think mobs seem to be encouraged to govern us. But I hope you will be able to convict some, and to treat them with a little hemp. It is a pitty that squinting rascal[3] can't yet be produced. I suspect he will be gone before you meet again after the Holydays. I shall begin to fall in love with Jurys of all sorts. I see a list of them. Only one amongst them that I know. His losing the being Banker to the Jewel Office, did not please him. Ask Todd[4] about it.

You will have seen my brother the Colonel from whom I heard the same day as yours is dated. I am surprised at some

1. See p. 183.
2. On December 6 Wilkes obtained £1000 damages against the Under-Secretary, Wood, and about the same time the printers of the *North Briton* obtained £400 damages against the messengers of the Secretary of State's office.
3. Wilkes was severely wounded in his duel with Samuel Martin on November 16, and was unable to attend the House on the question of privilege. He ran away to France on December 26, and was outlawed during his absence.
4. Anthony Todd, Secretary to the Post Office from December 1762. The reference is possibly to an intercepted letter.

people particularly Lord Shelburne.[1] Why should *one* Agent[2] have more than 5 Regiments to his share. Such orders might be given. And £1000 p. Ann. which they would at the least produce, is fully sufficient for any Agent. One or two Agents might possibly be angry, but many others would be pleased. I heartily wish you all imaginable success. Have time for no more. Adieu.

HENRY McCULLOH'S MEMORANDUM TO CHARLES JENKINSON

Add. MS. 38201, f. 315.

Henry McCulloh was Secretary and Clerk of the Crown for North Carolina. In 1761 he addressed a memorial to Bute entitled *Miscellaneous Representations relative to our Concerns in America* (edited by W. H. Shaw and printed in London, 1905), in which he pointed out the advantages of turning the French out of Louisiana rather than Canada (see Alvord, *Mississippi Valley*, i, 62). W. J. Smith, editor of the *Grenville Papers*, says (ii, 373 n.) that among Grenville's papers was a letter from Henry McCulloh to Jenkinson, dated Turnham Green, July 5, 1763, which contained a state of taxes usually raised in Pennsylvania and the Southern Colonies and estimated that £60,000 a year might be raised from a stamp duty in America. The letter was accompanied by two draughts addressed to Grenville, one of *Proposals with respect to a Stamp Duty in America,* and another *For creating and issuing Bills of Credit, under the Denomination of Exchequer Bills of Union for the general Use of His Majesty's Colonies in America.* Mr. Smith assumed from his signature that McCulloh was an old man.

December 12, 1763.

Mr. McCulloh humbly prays that the Right Honourable George ⟨Grenville⟩ Esq. will be pleased to appoint his son Henry Eustace McCulloh ⟨who is⟩ now Collector of Benfort and Currituck in North Carolina, Collector of ⟨   ⟩e in place of the aforesaid Collection.

1. In the debate on Parliamentary privilege, which took place on November 24, " the three people supposed to be influenced by Lord Shelburne, viz., Mr. Fitzmaurice, Colonel Barré, and Mr. Calcraft, were in the minority " (*Grenv. Pps.* ii, 229), and on November 29, when the same resolution came on in the House of Lords, Shelburne spoke against it and voted with the minority. At Grenville's instigation he was dismissed from his office of Aide-de-Camp to the King on December 7 (*ibid.* pp. 230, 236).

2. John Calcraft, the Army agent and former friend of Fox, was deprived of " some little places, which served to provoke more than to hurt him ". Horace Walpole was shocked by " the vast number of regiments to which he was agent, and the outrageous plurality of places he held " (*Memoirs*, i, 208, 264). He was agent to 49 regiments. See Namier, *Structure of Politics*, p. 36. An agency was worth about £200 a year.

North Carolina did not agree with Mr. McCulloh's health when ⟨he w⟩as there, he therefore chuses to decline going to that Colony. But if he ⟨be⟩ appointed Register of Licences and Bonds given for the liberty of importing ffrench rum, sugar and molasses into America he apprehends he could be of great use in that particular. Or if a Stamp duty takes place the appointing him supervisor and comptroller of the distributers accounts might be of service, particularly in those affairs which are of a new nature and require great application to bring them into a regular course.

The following "Remarks" were presumably inclosed in Henry McCulloh's letter of December 12, 1763.

Add. MS. 38201, f. 316.

Remarks with respect to the Collectors of the Customs in North America

Mr. Bedford has been several years appointed Collector of Philadelphia without having resided there, the said Bedford is also Stationer to the Excise Office in London which is a place of great value.[1]

Mr. Kennedy is Collector of New York worth upwards of £600 per annum he has resided there for several years, but has not regularly transmitted his accounts.[2]

Mr. Cliffe has been for many years appointed Collector of Rhode Island without residing there, Mr. Wanton acts as his Deputy.

In Connecticut Government the Collections are from £100 to £250 per annum, as informed most of the Collectors there and in the other Charter Governments are concerned in trade.

Boston is the best Collection on the Continent of America. Mr. Hale was appointed about two or three years ago Collector there, but by what interest is not known.

1. On Grosvenor Bedford see p. 188. In addition to his other places he was storekeeper to the Excise at £120 a year.
2. Archibald Kennedy (1685–1763) was descended from a younger branch of the Earls of Cassilis, and his son, Captain Archibald Kennedy, R.N., succeeded as 11th Earl in 1792. Kennedy was appointed Collector of Customs and Receiver-General of New York in 1722 and became a member of the Council in 1727. He speculated in land and wrote pamphlets on the colonies. See *Dictionary of American Biography*. If McCulloh's "Remarks" were written in December 1763, he seems to have been unaware that Kennedy died on June 14.

The Collections in New Hampshire and Nova Scotia are not of any great value.

Mr. Temple [1] is Surveyor General of the Northern District in America.

In Maryland the Collections in the several districts are valued at from £100 to £300 per annum.

Hampton the lower District of James River in Virginia is reckoned worth from £450 to £500 per annum, Mr. Carey Mitchell is appointed Collector of said port.

The Collection of the upper District of James River in Virginia is worth £300 per annum, but is executed by deputy.

The Collection of York River in Virginia £400 per annum.

The Collection of Rappahanoch about £200 per annum.

In North Carolina there are 4 Ports viz. Cape Fear worth about £250 per annum, Newbern £90 per annum, Bath Town £70 per annum, Edenton £250 per annum.

Charles Town in South Carolina is a Collection reckoned worth upwards of £600 sterling per annum.

Whyniah and Port Royal are small Collections.

The Collections in Georgia are very inconsiderable.

Mr. Randolph [2] is Surveyor General of the Southern District in America.

If any regulations are made with respect to Coast Cockits in America, the appointment of an Officer as Supervisor and Comptroller of the Entry's and Coast Cockits in the Charter Governments might be a good and effectual means of obstructing the clandestine trade. And Mr. M'Culloh humbly apprehends, that from the knowledge and experience he has had in business he could (if appointed in that character) be

---

1. John Temple was appointed Surveyor-General of the Customs in North America in 1760. He was distantly related to the Grenville family and in 1786 succeeded Sir Richard Temple of Stowe as 8th Bart. On his claim to the title see *G.E.C.* In 1767 the office of Surveyor-General was merged in the newly created Board of Customs for North America and Temple became one of the original five Commissioners, but was removed in 1770 and returned to England, where he became Surveyor-General of the Customs 1772–74. In 1785 he was appointed Consul-General to the United States. In 1767 he married a daughter of James Bowdoin of Boston, afterwards Governor of Massachusetts 1785–87, about whom see *D.N.B.* About John Temple see the preface to *The Bowdoin and Temple Papers* in the Collections of the Mass. Hist. Soc., 6th series, vol. ix. A copy of a letter from the Commissioners of Customs to Temple, dated March 28, 1764, ordering him to proceed to Canada and report on the port officers in Quebec and Montreal, is in the Liverpool Papers, Add. MS. 38337, f. 324.

2. Peter Randolph was one of the Randolphs of Virginia, descended from William Randolph (1651–1711) of Turkey Island, about whom see *D.A.B.* See a copy of a letter from the Commissioners of Customs to Peter Randolph, March 9, 1764, ordering him to proceed on a survey of all the ports in his district, and his reply of May 20 suggesting that the Commissioners can have no idea of the distance — 1800 miles — which would have to be covered. Add. MSS. 38337, ff. 324, 325.

of great use to the Crown and to the public. But if no such regulations are made Mr. M'Culloh hopes to be appointed Collector of Philadelphia or any other Collection now executed by Deputy, which as conceived is contrary to law.[1]

The appointment of a Treasury Remembrancer in America will likewise be of great use in bringing all the accounts of the revenue there before the Right Honourable the Lords of the Treasury.

J. GUNTER TO ALEXANDER HUME
Enclosed in Hume's letter of December 16

Add. MS. 38201, f. 330.

The acquisition of Canada in 1763 gave Great Britain a virtual monopoly of the fur trade which during the last decade had become more and more concentrated on Quebec (see G. L. Beer, *British Colonial Policy*, pp. 213-14). At this period the most important skin in the trade was beaver, which was used in hat-making. Beaver was an enumerated commodity with a drawback on re-exportation, which meant that foreign hatters importing skins from England could get them as cheaply as the British manufacturers (*ibid.* p. 215). Hence in March 1763 the feltmakers petitioned Bute, through James Oswald, to get the drawback abolished and have an export duty imposed instead. (See a letter from George Prescott, M.P. for Stockbridge, to Oswald, March 9, 1763, saying he has been applied to by the hatters' company and has drawn up a case of their proposals for Oswald to lay before the Treasury, in *Memorials of the Life and Character of the Rt. Hon. James Oswald* (1825), p. 225.) In December 1763 the feltmakers again petitioned the Treasury, this time successfully. After some opposition from the Hudson's Bay Company, who thought an export duty would lower their prices, an Act was passed on April 5, 1764 (4 George III, c. 9), abolishing the old duties, except for a nominal import duty of a penny a skin, and imposing an export duty of sevenpence.

John Gunter was clerk or secretary of the Feltmakers' Company, also called the Company of Hatters. Alexander Hume, M.P. for Southwark, was a merchant and East India Company Director. Before George III's accession he had been one of the Leicester House connexion. See Namier, *England etc.* p. 205.

December 10, 1763.
Docketed "J. Gunter in behalfe of the Feltmakers".

Sir,

The Master and Wardens of the Feltmakers Company have ordered me to wait on you in their names and to beg your advice and assistance once more relating to an alteration of the duty upon beaver skins.

If your health should be too much impaired to give them

1. See p. 188.

any active personal assistance they hope you will advise them what is the most proper method for them to take in order to obtain the desired relief. I am Sir,

Your greatly obliged humble servant,
J. Gunter

J. GUNTER TO ALEXANDER HUME
Enclosed in Hume's letter of December 16

Add. MS. 38201, f. 331.

December 14, 1763.

Sir,

    The Feltmakers company order me to present their thanks to you for the assistance you have undertaken to give them and entreat the favor of you to apply in their behalf to Mr. Jenkinson in such manner as you think will conduce most to their interest and whenever any personal attendance is necessary on their part they will be ready to act according to your instructions. I have inclosed their Memorial and the paper of calculations [1] which they had the honor by your means to lay before my Lord Bute, the contents of which they will be ready to make good upon the shortest notice. I am Sir

Your most obliged humble servant,
J. Gunter

ALEXANDER HUME TO CHARLES JENKINSON

Add. MS. 38201, f. 329.

Hill Street, December 16, 1763.

Sir :

    I endeavour [*sic*] to see you at the Treasury on Wednesday to let ⟨you⟩ know the Company of Hatters íntend to apply to the Treasury on the same as they did last. You may remember

---

1. See Add. MSS. 38377, ff. 227-33. The memorial is addressed to the Lords of the Treasury. Two printed " cases of the manufacturers and others concerned in the making and vending of beaver hats " are in the Liverpool Papers, Add. MSS. 38337, ff. 228, 229-30. See also Treasury Minute Book, January 12, 1764 : " Read a memorial of several persons employed in selling . . . beaver hats . . . Mr. Rossiter and several other persons concerned in the same trade are called in " (P.R.O., T. 29/35). On April 9 the feltmakers returned thanks to the Treasury for their help. *Ibid.*

what past between Lord Bute and them. As I did not meet with you I told my business with Mr. Bradshaw [1] and left with him a letter I had from the clerk of that Company desiring him to give it to you, on my coming home I found a second letter from the Clerk with a Memorial and Calculations all which I inclose and desire you'l communicate them to Mr. Grenville for his consideration and he chuses to permit the principals of that Society to wait on him and will appoint a time on your letting me know it, I will communicate it to them. I am Sir

Your most obedient humble servant,
Alexander Hume

In his various official capacities, first as secretary to Lord Bute, then as Secretary to the Treasury and later as Secretary at War, Jenkinson received a number of letters from his friend Sir John Fielding, the famous Bow Street magistrate and brother of Henry Fielding, the novelist. Some of these letters are in the Bute MSS., two are in the *Grenville Papers*,[2] and five are in the Liverpool MSS.,[3] where there is also an " Abstract of Sir John Fielding's Plan of Police ".[4] This document has been printed in its entirety in Mr. R. Leslie Melville's *Life and Work of Sir John Fielding* (1934), pp. 137-40, and is therefore not reproduced here.

On April 10, 1761, Fielding wrote to Newcastle that he had " drawn out so simple and yet so unexceptionable a plan of police, as must infallibly secure peace and good order to this metropolis, and do immortal honour to your Grace ",[5] and this plan is probably the same which came into Jenkinson's hands and was presumably seen by Grenville some time in 1763. In that year two of the provisions of the plan were given effect. Fielding received a grant of £20 a year from the Treasury towards keeping records of deserters at Bow Street, whose descriptions were to be furnished by the War Office,[6] and in the same year improvements were made in street lighting which were supplemented on April 29, 1764, by a Treasury grant of £10,000 for paving and lighting Westminster.[7] But the two main provisions of the plan were ignored. The first of these was the establishment of regular police courts presided over by stipendiary magistrates, a project which was only carried out in 1792, though the Middlesex and Westminster Justices instituted a system of rotation officers in April and October 1763.[8]

1. From 1763 to 1766 Thomas Bradshaw was one of the principal clerks in the Treasury. See his letters below, p. 412 etc.
2. *Grenv. Pps.* ii, 363, 366-7.
3. See p. 260 and Add. MSS. 38211, ff. 4, 74.
4. Add. MS. 38334, ff. 75-9.
5. Add. MS. 32921, f. 404. Mr. Melville thinks this is the plan referred to in the first edition of Fielding's *Extracts from the Penal Laws*, apparently published in April 1761. See *Scots Magazine*, p. 200, and Melville, *op. cit.* pp. 133, 136. There is no copy of the first edition in the British Museum, and Mr. Melville, who possesses a copy, does not give its date.   6. *Ibid.* p. 147.
7. P.R.O., T. 38/715 ; Melville, *op. cit.* pp. 149-50.   8. *Ibid.* p. 141.

The second point was the use of cavalry to watch turnpikes and pursue felons. Fielding complained that his police methods were cramped by Grenville's illiberality, but a military police even if intended " to co-operate with and act under the civil power " was a thing which no British government in the eighteenth century would have touched. At that time the standing army was small, the London mob was a real and alarming factor in politics, and the Opposition were always on the lookout to make capital of any apparent despotic tendencies on the part of Government. In these circumstances the efficiency of the police as a detective force had to be subordinated to the major purpose of keeping peace in the metropolis.

If Grenville ever saw the plan, there is apparently no correspondence between him and Jenkinson about it ; but in October 1763 Fielding was allowed to experiment with a civil horse patrol ; possibly as an alternative to his projected use of the cavalry. On October 17 eight horsemen supplemented by " a private Foot Patrole consisting chiefly of Peace Officers " took the road, and it appears, from a letter from Fielding of November 1, that Grenville had allowed him to send out two extra horsemen.[1] He was to draw the money for the horse patrol from P. C. Webb, solicitor to the Treasury, but he had difficulty in getting it, which involved him in correspondence with Jenkinson. So did his application for an extension of the time limit to the experiment, which, in spite of all his endeavours, was stopped in October 1764.[2]

SIR JOHN FIELDING TO CHARLES JENKINSON [3]

Add. MS. 38201, f. 328.

Bow Street, December 16, 1763.

Sir John Fielding presents his respectful compliments to Mr. Jenkinson, begs leave to acquaint him, that, notwithstanding the dispatch which Mr. Grenville so obligingly gave to the affairs of the police, I have still got by me their Lordships Order on Mr. Webb for the £600. I have sent message on message to him but in vain, he now says he has not got the money to pay it, and as this delay in some measure defeats his Majesty's kind intentions to the public in this behalf, stops the payment of the printers and other bills usually paid at this season and obliges me to advance money for the current and necessary expences, I should take it as a particular favour,

1. Melville, *op. cit.* pp. 150-54.
2. See *Grenv. Pps.* ii, 363, 366-7, 369, 385, and Melville, *op. cit.* p. 163. Mr. Melville is mistaken in assuming from the tone of Fielding's letter of June 28 (*Grenv. Pps.* ii, 367) that he found Jenkinson " an unpleasant fellow ". His letters to Jenkinson in the Bute MSS. which cover the years 1761-63 are almost all signed " your affectionate friend ", as are also the majority of his letters in the Liverpool MSS., including the last two for 1779 (Add. MS. 38211, ff. 4, 74).
3. This letter is printed, with an error in transcription, in Melville, *op. cit.* p. 158. In the fourth line Mr. Melville reads : " I have *not* still got by me, etc."

if you could by any means forward this matter. Agreeable to your request I sent proper persons to the places you pointed out, but as nothing happened worthy notice, did not trouble you on that head.[1] I am with all due respect Sir

Your respectful friend and obedient humble servant,

J. Fielding

E. WESTON TO CHARLES JENKINSON

Add. MS. 38201, f. 325.

St. James's, December 16, 1763.

Dear Sir,

If you have any entry in your office of presents made by the late King to the Dutch, Orange, Hessian, and Danish Ministers, upon the conclusion of the marriages of the late Princess Royal, Princess Mary, and late Princess Louise, in 1733, 1739, and 1743 : I beg you will let me know the particular sums given, for Lord Halifax's information who has His Majesty's command to make enquiry.[2] I am very sincerely, dear Sir,

Your affectionate humble servant,

E. Weston

Jenkinson replied on December 20 : " I can assure you that there is no charge of this kind entered in any of our Books ; and if there were any such presents, they were of a private nature and not known to the Treasury " (Add. MS. 38304, f. 4).

ANTHONY TODD TO CHARLES JENKINSON

Add. MS. 38201, f. 336.

General Post Office, December 17, 1763.

Dear Sir,

I left my name with you last week along with Sir Thomas Stanhope,[3] when you were so very busy that I could not think of desiring to see you, even though my business was of great

1. Government may have anticipated a fresh outbreak of the riots which took place on December 3, on the occasion of the burning of the *North Briton*.
2. The marriage arranged between Princess Augusta, eldest sister of George III and Prince Ferdinand of Brunswick, took place on January 16, 1764. See p. 258.
3. Sir Thomas Stanhope, Colonel of Marines, died March 7, 1770.

consequence to my wife and me, for I had her commands to ask if you could not in the holydays come to see us at Walthamstow, and in the course of next week will endeavour to call and perswade you, as there will be some of your friends with us, Mr. Stanhope [1] having promised and I believe also Potenger. [2] The inclosed contains an abstract of Mr. Allen's [3] account of Bye and Cross Road Letters for a year to Midsummer last, which as usual you will be pleased to lay before their Lordships. I am with true respect, dear Sir,

Your most obliged and obedient servant,

Anthony Todd

LORD EGLINTON TO CHARLES JENKINSON

Add. MS. 38201, ff. 337-8.

Alexander Montgomerie, 10th Earl of Eglinton, a Lord of the Bedchamber, was one of the representative peers of Scotland from 1761 to 1769.

Piccadilly, Sunday morning, 7 o'clock.
Docketed " December 18, 1763 ".

Dear Jenkinson,

I return you a thousand thanks for your kind and obliging note. I really feel my self doubly indebted to you for your attention, as I have not of late met with so much where I thought I was better intitled to it.

I was with Mr. Mackenzie a few days ago and have no reason to think he would not endeavour *to have justice done me* if he was at liberty, I say justice because it is unjust to prefer a new connection to an old friend.

I took the liberty to write to my Lord Bute and just mentioned to his Lordship that it was 15 years since his Lordship had first done me the honor to introduce me to the late Prince of Waleses private partys, that I had ever since made it my study to deserve the protection of that branch of the Royal Family, and had (by his Lordships good offices) so far succeeded,

1. Probably Lovel Stanhope, Under-Secretary of State with Edward Sedgwick in Halifax's department. He lost his place at the change of Government in 1765, but was restored in 1771. From 1774 to his death in 1783 he sat in Parliament for Winchester.
2. Richard Pottinger, Under-Secretary of State from 1754 to 1760.
3. Philip Allen, Comptroller of the Bye and Cross Road Letter Office and nephew of the celebrated Ralph Allen of Bath, " who first established cross posts ". See Philip Allen's obituary in the *Gent. Mag.* for 1785, p. 666.

that I was well received at Leicester house, when Lord Marchmont [1] was not known there but from his connection with
Lord Hardwick, nor Lord Cathcart [2] but from his attachment
to the Duke of Cumberland.

That my Lord Marchmont should be preferd to me I dont
pretend to complain of, but why Lord Cathcart should, I own
I am at a loss to guess unless it is that he cannot well be suspected *guilty of an attachment to Lord Bute* a crime which I should
hope might now be pardoned, but I believe never will.

I aske a thousand pardons for troubling you with all this
stuff, but you know every thing is taxed in this country, and
to hear the grievances of ones friend, is a tax due to humanity.
I know your disposition too well to think you unwilling to pay
every duty of that kind, so (without supposing you are growling
at me like a surly porter who is paying the additional halfpenny
on the pot), I shall end without making any apology.

Your sincere friend,

Eglinton

EDWARD WESTON TO CHARLES JENKINSON

Add. MS. 38201, f. 345.

St. James's, December 20, 1763.

Dear Sir,

I thank you for your answer to my inquiry of the 16th,
since writing which I have obtained some information about
the presents from the Master of the Ceremonies, and send you
a copy of his letter inclosed, by which you will see that those
gratifications to the Foreign Ministers concerned in the Marriage
Treaties, were given by the then head of the Treasury, under
a warrant or letter from the Lord Chamberlain. I am ever,
dear Sir,

Most affectionately yours,

E. Weston

To this letter Jenkinson added the following note which was presumably
addressed to Grenville : " I trouble you with the inclosed that you may be
apprized of what I dare say you will hear more of ".

1. Hugh Hume-Campbell, 3rd Earl of Marchmont, appointed January 1763,
on the death of the Duke of Athol, Keeper of the Great Seal in Scotland.
2. Charles Schaw, 9th Baron Cathcart, formerly Aide-de-Camp to the Duke
of Cumberland, appointed, January 1763, First Commissioner of Police in place
of Lord Marchmont.

COPY OF A LETTER FROM SIR CHARLES COTTRELL DORMER TO EDWARD WESTON INCLOSED IN WESTON'S LETTER

Add. MS. 38201, ff. 346-7.

Sir Charles Cottrell Dormer, Knight, was Master of Ceremonies to George II and George III, in which office he succeeded his father in 1758. The office was quasi-hereditary and, with a short gap, remained in his family for nearly a hundred and seventy years. It had been held by his great-grandfather, Sir Charles Cottrell, M.P. for Cardigan, Ambassador to The Hague, and Master of Ceremonies to King Charles I, Charles II, and James II. Missing a generation, it passed to Sir Charles's father, Sir Clement Cottrell, who took the name of Dormer, and finally to his son, Sir Clement Cottrell Dormer, who gave it up in 1796.

Chesterfield Street, December 16, 1763.

Dear Sir,

I have examined this morning upon the receipt of your letter, all my notes very carefully, and send you the following extracts for my Lord Halifax's information.

Mr. Duncan, employed in the negotiation for the Prince of Orange's wedding, had through my father's hand £300, who complains that the said Mr. Duncan, Monsieur Du Park Grand Maître, and Monsieur d'Aylva Grand Ecuyer, had each £300 apeice carried them by another person, to the prejudice of his office and just right.

Upon the marriage of the Princess of Hesse, my father remembering what had passed before, and hearing the Lords Justices had ordered £1200, complained to the Duke of Grafton, Lord Chamberlayn who immediately signed another letter ⟨and⟩ sent him to the Treasury with it; but was there told the money was already issued : upon which he went directly to Sir Robert Walpole, produced my Lord Chamberlayn's letter, and made his complaint. Sir Robert answered he was totally ignorant that he was concerned, and that, never designing to do him a prejudice, he would rectify it directly. So upon Mr. Tilson's arrival with the money (whom he had sent to the Bank, it not being a Treasury day) gave it directly into my father's hand, who carried it as ordered.

To Colonel Baron Donorop	600
To Monsieur Alt	300
To Monsieur Schermfield	300
	£1200

The first was sent to negotiate the marriage ; the second was, and still is, the Minister here ; the third was the young Prince's Secretary.

I should not have mentioned what concerns myself but for this reason, that though my father had justice done him both by my Lord Chamberlayn and Sir Robert Walpole, he never could get it altered, and the right letter entered at the Treasury, where it remains wrong to this day. You see therefore the late King's gratuitys were the same at both weddings, £1200.

As to the Queen of Denmark's wedding, I have no mention made of it. Baron Solenthal was, upon that occasion, from Envoy made Ambassador Extraordinary. He had £1000 as Ambassador, and I don't believe any other gratuitys were given.

I am etc.,

Charles Cottrell Dor⟨mer⟩

J. S. MACKENZIE TO CHARLES JENKINSON

Add. MS. 38201, f. 348.

Burlington Street, Wednesday Evening.
Docketed " December 21, 1763 ".

I have several little things to say to you, and I have not set eyes on you for some days ; will you dine with me to-morrow (Thursday), if you will, a few minutes before, or after dinner will discuss our business. I understand that nothing is yet settled about the contract in which Mr. Drummond ¹ and Sir Samuel Fludyer ² are concerned, and that the latter is to

1. Adam Drummond of Meggins, M.P. for Lymington 1761–68 ; St. Ives 1768–78 ; merchant and Government contractor. In 1755 he married Catherine Paulett, daughter of Harry, 4th Duke of Bolton, and widow of William Ashe, M.P. for Heytesbury. Drummond had been to America as an officer in the Seven Years' War. See Namier, *England etc.* pp. 282-3 and n. 1.
2. Sir Samuel Fludyer, M.P. for Chippenham, about whom see p. 81. See Newcastle's list of removals from Treasury appointments, Add. MS. 33001, ff. 23-4, and Grenville's *State of Contracts in 1764*, Add. MS. 38338, ff. 109-11. When those merchant M.P.'s who had voted against the Preliminaries in December 1762 were deprived of the renewal of their contracts, the contract for victualling the troops in North America was taken from Sir George Colebrooke and Arnold Nesbit and given to Messrs. Drummond and Fludyer, while Moses Franks, the American partner in the first contract, was continued in the second. See Namier, *Structure of Politics*, p. 66. See also Sir George Colebrooke to Newcastle, July 15, 1765, on the matter of the contracts " in which I was engaged with the Treasury, before Mr. Grenville gave me notice to quit ". " The contract for victualling

be with Mr. Grenville to-morrow morning about it ; my only concern in it, is about Drummond, whom I wish Mr. Grenville would pay some attention to, as he is extreamly well inclined to support Government, notwithstanding the powerfull draw-back he has, to divert him from it, in his brother in law, the Duke of Bolton,[1] and who (I will be answerable for it even to the King himself) will have no influence on Drummond, if Mr. Grenville will take the least pains to prevent it, for I know him to be a most honest worthy man. If you could drop a hint of this, before Sir Samuel Fludyer comes to Mr. Grenville to morrow morning, it might be of service ; if not, there is no help for it.

If Sir Samuel should refuse the contract on the footing Mr. Grenville offers it, I wish Drummond were immediately talked to about it.

ROBERT MELVILL TO GEORGE GRENVILLE

Add. MS. 38201, f. 350.

General Robert Melvill (1723–1809) was in command of the regiment at the reduction of Guadeloupe in 1759, and became Lieutenant-Governor of the island (not Governor as stated in *D.N.B.*). In October 1763 he was made Governor of the ceded islands (Grenada, the Grenadines, St. Vincent, Dominica, and Tobago) and retained the post till 1770. In 1782 he accompanied Sir William Younge on a special mission to France to obtain indulgences from the French Government for British settlers in Tobago, which was recaptured by the French during the War of American Independence. Although appointed to the ceded islands in October 1763, he was still in London on April 10, 1764, and had contracted debts in consequence of his appointment which obliged him to write to Jenkinson for an advance on his salary (Add. MS. 38202, f. 234).

was given by Mr. Grenville to Sir Samuel Fludyer, Mr. Drummond and Mr. Franks. The two former had signed a contract for Pensicola, but they gave up that to Mr. Henniker, in order to come into the places of Mr. Nesbit and myself " (Add. MS. 32967, f. 434). In Grenville's *State of Contracts* there is some attempt to show that the removals were not purely political. Apparently Colebrooke and Nesbit had contracted for North America (exclusive of Quebec) at 4¾d. per man a day, while Fludyer and Drummond undertook this contract " at the rate of 4d. a day which compared with the former contract is a saving to the public of 15 3/4 per cent ". Similarly for Quebec the old contract was " at 5½d. a day for each man victualled ", and the new one at 4¾d., a saving of 13⅝ per cent. It should be remembered, however, that the old contracts were made during the war when insurance rates were higher.

1. Charles Poulett, 5th Duke of Bolton. His influence saved Drummond from the consequences of his attachment to Grenville. In July 1765, on the formation of the Rockingham Government, Newcastle was anxious to restore the sufferers, and offered Sir George Colebrooke the renewal of his old contract, but

Derby Street, December 21, 1763.

Sir,

In consequence of what you was pleased to say to me, on the head of my appointments, I intended to have had the honour of waiting on you yesterday and offering my thoughts in person ; but reflecting on the hurry you might be in, and being also desirous, to avoid troubling you with conversation on so indelicate a subject, I have judged it best, as well as most respectfull, to submit them in writing, and shall be ready to attend you Sir, whenever you are pleased to desire it.

I should have been much happier Sir, to have avoided giving you this interruption but trust you will be so kind as to excuse it, and will be pleased to bestow some attention on my letter, as soon as leisure will permit.

I shall only add here, that the sum allowed for outset to the Governor of Guadeloupe, when he went out, was only £600, but he received abroad, near £700 more, as a necessary sum to enable him to purchase slaves ; and when I have the honour of seeing you Sir, I will shew, that such a help may be equally given to me, without occasioning any real loss of money to the publick. For I protest Sir, however desirous I am of being put on a *proper* footing to undertake this Government, I'm no less intent to save every unnecessary charge to the publick which I must think highly the duty of every conscientious man employd, on this occasion.

I have the honour to be with great respect and esteem Sir,
Your most faithfull and obedient humble servant,
Robert Melvill

Melvill enclosed a schedule of " First Expences necessary at the outset for a Governor going to command in the Ceded Islands on a moderate computation ". The expenses amounted to £2120. (*Ibid.* f. 351.)

Colebrooke, who seems to have preferred remitting to victualling as more " consistent with my business as a banker ", replied, in the letter quoted above, that " Drummond is brother in law to the Duke of Bolton and though Sir Samuel Fludyer has no pretensions to be well considered by the present Administration, yet Mr. Drummond, I doubt not, will have the protection of the noble Duke above mentioned, who will expect to see him continued in this thing, or that he should be considered in something else ". Bolton had hitherto supported Pitt and Temple, but in July 1765 found it inconsistent with the dignity of a Peer of England " to be dragged along in the suite of any private man or set of men whatever ", and assured Lord Egmont of his attachment solely to the Crown. See Egmont to the King, July 13, 1765, in Fortescue, *Corr. of George III*, No. 134.

WILLIAM GUTHRIE TO CHARLES JENKINSON

Add. MS. 38201, ff. 358-9.

William Guthrie (1708–70), journalist and historian, wrote for Chesterfield in the *Broadbottom Journal* in which Chesterfield fought Carteret. See W. T. Laprade, *The English Press in the Eighteenth Century*. His reports of Parliamentary debates for the *Gentleman's Magazine* were revised by Dr. Johnson. In 1745 he received a Secret Service pension of £200 a year from the Pelham Government, continued to him by Bute in 1762. See *Structure of Politics*, pp. 283-4. About him see *D.N.B.*

Great Titchfield Street, December 22, 1763.

Sir,

I chuse to trouble you during this Recess, as you may have a minute or two to throw away.

Since seeing you, I have been able to get only one letter into the Gazeteer, and that too, under pretext of rendering it more decent, was robbd by the printer of all its virility. I have sent another which I think is of consequence ; and therefor I hope it will not be emasculated likewise.

I cannot help repeating, that if the Government had a weekly paper of its own, it would be attended with many public advantages. The success of the late trials have made unfavourable impressions, but they are not uneffaceable after the people begin to cool.

The illegality of the forms of the Warrants from the Secretary of States office for apprehending printers etc. has been long suspected under former Administrations, and I cannot but think that it would have been much more for the ease and popularity, not to mention the dignity of Government, if prosecution for Libels, not amounting to Treason or not attended with extraordinary circumstances, had always been left to a Justice of the Peace, or to a regular presentation, by which they may be punished equally as if both Houses of Parliament were the prosecutors.

Without some new Act of Parliament, it possibly may be found impracticable to proceed against Libels but in the way here mentioned, and a regular method of proceeding may certainly be chalked out, without adding to the powers of subordinate Magistrates, which might remedy the evil (now growing more alarming from the events of the late Tryals) and free the great Officers of State from the trouble and often unpopularity of judicial proceedings, besides the expence to the Government which attends them.

I am very ready to communicate all the lights I have to this proposal, the utility of which I am so much convinced of, that I think the more it is considered it will be the more approved of. I have the honour to be with great esteem, Sir,

Your faithful and most obedient humble servant,

Wil Guthrie

CHARLES JENKINSON TO SIR JAMES LOWTHER

Add. MS. 38458, ff. 44-5.

London, December 24, 1763.

Dear Sir,

The Petition of the inhabitants of Cockermouth will be complied with in the manner you desired ; the Treasury will not fail to come to a decision upon it on Monday. Mr. Grenville directs me to acquaint you that he will at the same time appoint the two persons you recommend to be receivers of the Land Tax for the counties of Cumberland and Westmoreland in the room of Mr. How.[1] The receipt of the Excise is not in the disposal of every Department of Government ; the collectors are at liberty to employ whom they please to remit their money, being otherwise responsible for its being properly done.

We are informed here that the Attorney General is to have a very vigorous opposition at Wigan, and that persons are gone down with a great sum for that purpose.[2] It would be a very distressing circumstance if a person in so high a station of the law, and one so necessary for the conduct of the Kings busyness in Parliament particularly in the present conjuncture should be out of Parliament. It has been said that you had some thoughts of chusing him for Westmoreland ;[3] if this

1. On January 9, 1764, the Treasury appointed Receivers-General of Land and House Taxes in Cumberland and Westmorland, but there is no mention in the Treasury Minutes of a petition from Cockermouth.

2. Sir Fletcher Norton, M.P. for Wigan 1761–68, was re-elected on December 24, 1763, on becoming Attorney-General. The contest in 1761 cost his opponent, George Byng, £20,000. See Ferguson, *Cumberland and Westmorland M.P.s*, p. 424. Norton came from Westmorland, was a protégé of Sir James Lowther and a "King's Friend". He sat for Appleby 1754–61, Wigan 1761–68 on Lowther's interest, and was afterwards M.P. for Guildford 1768–82, when he was created Baron Grantley.

3. Sir James's brother, Robert Lowther, M.P. for Westmorland 1761–64, was the pawn in Sir James's election manœuvres, who might have been removed to make way for Norton.

should be your intention it would be very fortunate for him and fortunate for Government too, in case it should turn out that he should be disappointed at Wigan. When your election is over, will you do me the favour to let me have a short note with an account of it. We have no news. Wilkes is getting well again. My respects attend Lady Mary. I have the honour to be with great truth and regard, dear Sir,

Your faithfull humble servant,

C. Jenkinson

CHARLES JENKINSON TO EDWARD WESTON

Add. MS. 38304, f. 4.

December 24, 1763.

Dear Sir,

I can speak with confidence that Lord Bute always had the best disposition towards Mr. Morin ;[1] but I do not recollect that his Lordship made any particular engagement either in his own name or the King's. This however is no proof that no such engagement was made, but only that I was not privy to it. As to writing to Lord Bute on this subject I have been obliged to make it a rule ever since his Lordship quitted business not to trouble him concerning any application whatsoever, and I know I act hereby conformably to his Lordship's intentions. As no man is better acquainted with Mr. Morin's services, or has personally a higher regard for him than myself, I shall rejoice most sincerely to hear of his success on this and every other occasion. I will call on you soon.

I am etc.,

C. Jenkinson

1. Peter Michael Morin, Under-Secretary of State. On December 23 Weston wrote to ask Jenkinson if he knew anything about a promise from Bute or from the King to increase Morin's pension of £250 a year as Morin had applied to Halifax for a rise. See Add. MS. 38201, f. 360. Shelburne wrote of him in his *Autobiography*: "There was an old man in the Secretary of State's office, Mr. Morin, afterwards my secretary, who was clerk in the Duke of Newcastle's time and appointed to attend at his house. He told me that it was a great pity that the Duke of Newcastle should do Mr. Stone's business and Mr. Stone the Duke of Newcastle's ; that he used to attend at Newcastle House till twelve at night doing nothing, and then the Duke would sit down to write despatches and cut out work for him to copy the whole night " (Fitzmaurice, *Life of Shelburne*, i, 43).

ROBERT YEATES TO CHARLES JENKINSON

Add. MS. 38201, f. 376.

Robert Yeates was one of the four principal clerks in the Treasury.

Abingdon Buildings, December 29, 1763.

Sir,

I have the pleasure to acquaint you that Mr. Tod [1] has been with me this morning and that I find he was the person who was privately consulted by Mr. Oswald [2] before he made the proposal respecting the Russia Linens to Lord Bute. Mr. Tod told me the papers relating to this matter are in the hands of Mr. Touchet [3] from whom he will procure them, and as soon as he has digested the contents which he thinks will be in about a day or two he will give me notice and will be ready to wait on you at any time you shall think proper to appoint, when I am perswaded he will give you very satisfactory information.

I have just now finished with Mr. Tyton [4] the Plantation Bill [5] and will send a fair copy of it to Mr. Whateley this evening.

I have not yet received a draught of the Warrant for the Princess's annuity when it comes to my hands I will dispatch it immediately. I am Sir,

Your most obedient humble servant,

R. Yeates

EDWARD RICHARDSON TO CHARLES JENKINSON

Add. MS. 38201, f. 386.

The City's hostility to Government did not diminish after Bute's resignation. On every issue which arose in that year the Common Council opposed Administration, until Walpole believed they were setting themselves up

1. William Tod was interested in the linen trade. There was at this time a scheme to take off the drawbacks on foreign linens exported to the Colonies. Tod wrote about this to Jenkinson on March 13, 1764, referring him to a pamphlet on the linen industry written twenty-five years ago, and which he had caused to be reprinted in 1753 (Add. MS. 38202, f. 156).
2. James Oswald, about whom see p. 161 n. 4.
3. Samuel Touchet, merchant and M.P. for Shaftesbury. See p. 105.
4. John Tyton, Solicitor to the Customs, " eminent for his skill in drawing all the Acts of Parliament relative to the revenue " (obituary notice in *Gent. Mag.*, 1790, p. 186).
5. See p. 251.

against Parliament. Bute's vacillations over the Cider Bill in March 1763 were interpreted as " a contempt of both Houses of Parliament and pre-ferring the Common Council to them ", but Grenville, who knew "the manner of dealing with the moneyed people and the merchants ", was not afraid of their supposed corporate aspirations. Nevertheless the London mob, who followed the City's lead and had taken Wilkes to its bosom, was a force in politics, and, being under the jurisdiction of the City magistrates, its weight on the side of " liberty " gave the Corporation an advantage over Government. When riots broke out over the burning of the *North Briton* on December 3, it was generally believed that the magis-trates had countenanced them. An enquiry was held in the House of Lords on December 6, and Bedford, " spluttering with zeal and indis-cretion ", accused the Lord Mayor, William Beckford, and other officers of taking no steps to suppress the mob, " but on reflection the Ministers chose to pass over the insult, rather than quarrel seriously with the City of London ", and thanks were voted to the sheriffs for their zeal on this occasion (Walpole, *Memoirs*, i, 263). Three days later the Common Council met to vote for returning thanks to the sheriffs. " The numbers were even and the Mayor gave the casting vote in the negative ", alleging " amongst other reasons against the returning thanks, that he should look upon it as prejudging Mr. Wilkes's cause " (*Grenv. Pps.* ii, 237). In these circumstances Grenville still found use for Bute's coffee-house spies.

Tuesday night.
Docketed " December 1763 ".

My good Sir,

Subsequent to the many motions that have been lately made in our various Assembly's my time has been a good deal taken up in sounding the opinions of the citizens. Among the cooler and more discerning part I plainly descry an honest willingness to lend a helping hand to extinguish those flames that I fear are growing too prevalent for the stoutest party wall to withstand. Sir James Hodges [1] who I accidentally met with last week at Mr. Pitt's and upon whom I waited this morning at Guild Hall, I am strictly positive is a well wisher to the Administration and has enjoyned me to assure you of his readiness to assist in every measure that might tend to their service, prescribed within his little sphear, whensoever you shall think fit to communicate as heretofore. If the Ministry imagine themselves able to bring over the citizens to the Court by the merit of their own administration, depend upon it they are deceived ; they are as wide of the mark as cancer from capricorn. Our Senatus Concillium must be stroaked on the head, and have their gingerbread too as well as yours, all then would soon be as well of this as the other side Temple

1. Sir James Hodges was the leader of a minority in the Common Council who were friendly to Government. See p. 70.

Bar. Happy, thrice happy me, who content my self with the crumbs that have fallen from my Lord's table, content I say, for I would feign have you convinced of my disinterested firmness whensoever I address you on subjects of policy. And I am now certain you would do well to send for Sir James, no man knows the present trim of the citty better nor can any man there give you better advice in this reigning fit of madness. Your friends have hitherto indeed, my dear Sir, but too much contemned popularity, which you know in this free country has ever been the scaffolding to ministerial buildings. We have seen a fair lay'd foundation but shall never behold its progress without the aid of your citizens poles, scurvy as they are, to raise it. In the mean while if I can go any where or do any thing that may produce to you either a pleasure or service, you know me always ready, who am Sir,

Your most obedient servant,

Ed. Richardson

JOSEPH SALVADOR TO CHARLES JENKINSON
Add. MS. 38202, f. 2.

White Hart Court, January 3, 1764.

Dear Sir,

I beg you would acquaint me when I shall have the pleasure of seeing you that I may not be absent or employed. I want to see you as much as you can desire it. I think you will see it necessary from the discourse we had to day for I am in haste that all your business be put in form. I know if not done before Parliament meets we shall be diverted with Mr. Wilkes and Cyder Bills etc. without end which will compleat the ruin of my projects for the reduction of any stocks. For God's sake let a hand be had to that.

You heard my sentiments of to day ; might I advise nothing further than the necessary occurrences should be tried this year but ⟨if⟩ anything, it should be something bold and large which may vindicate ⟨our⟩ trying it, the other way will give a mean opinion. Pray reflect ⟨on⟩ the largeness of the debt [1] and that an alteration att the pace pro⟨posed⟩ would

1. The debt was 140 millions. To discharge it Grenville took £2,000,000 out of the Sinking Fund ; he also found £1,800,000 Exchequer Bills " at such a discount as to weigh down with them the whole building of the public credit "

take up 210 years, the duration of the world is hardly ⟨suffic⟩ient to finish it. On the other side, should you succeed, a savi⟨ng of⟩ £30,000 per annum will be a great stroke, nor can it, if it fail, ⟨bring⟩ any reproach, as had I the honour of advising Mr. Grenville ⟨I⟩ would, in what is called opening the Budget, throw it out in this manner; I would acquaint Parliament with the measures for the navy supplies that no more was wanted, that I presumed the certain knowledge of this fact might have some good effect on publick securities, that I saw with concern the low state of Navy Bills and the Navy Annuities in particular and would willingly co-operate in giving them relief, provided the publick did not suffer; [1] that in such desire it must be a general satisfaction to the whole, as you could admit of no future claims; that perhaps a lottery offered them with some compensation to bring their Stock to 3 per cent might be found useful to the publick and them; that Mr. Grenville had seen some proposals for that purpose which if met with approbation might answer the end and if he found any disposition in the proprietors he would reconsider it carefully and if proper, adopt it, that the success as far as it might take must be useful but that he reserved to himself the providing next year for what might not succeed in this. By this means the tempers might be tried, the thing thrown out and only executed if likely to be attended with success. Above all things we want money before any thing can be done with success, and tis my opinion that tis only by large lotteries that the publick debt can be brought into shape; the question is whether to attempt it now or hereafter. If you drop into little Lotterys my best hopes are lost. [2]

No doubt you are informed what passes in France, tis little less than an open rebellion. [3] I am, Sir,

Your most obedient servant,

Joseph Salvador

(*Annual Register*, 1764, p. 30), and made a contract with the Bank for the renewal of their Charter, the Bank to take a million of these Exchequer bills for two years at 3 per cent interest and to pay a fine of £100,000 (*Annual Register*). See also *The Budget*, by David Hartley, and Grenville's replies in *The Wallet ; An Answer to the Budget*, etc. See p. 308 n. 2.

1. Cf. Hartley's pamphlet suggesting that Grenville blackmailed the subscribers to renew their annuities. *The Budget*, pp. 20-21.

2. Grenville refused to hold a lottery. See a Government advertisement quoted by Hartley in *The Budget*, pp. 5-7.

3. See pp. 206, 224.

EDWIN WARDROPER [1] TO CHARLES JENKINSON

Add. MS. 38202, f. 9.

January 7, 1764.

Sir,

The bearer Thomas Pollard is a ⟨   ⟩man in Sheerness yard and as his brother ⟨is a⟩ freeman here [2] and a very good friend and ⟨we⟩ll wisher to the present Ministry and not ⟨at⟩ all engaged to the Duke of Newcastle I ⟨should⟩ take it as a particular favour if you ⟨would⟩ be so good to give him a recommendation ⟨to⟩ Lord Egmont [3] to be advanced according to his merit upon the first vacancy. He will bring a strong recommendation from his superior officers in the Yard and I believe is really deserving. Mr. Milward of Hasting [4] will speak to you in his favour the first opportunity, his father and family being much connected with him. I am Sir,

Your most obedient servant,

E. Wardroper

On January 22 Jenkinson replied that he had forwarded this recommendation to the Admiralty (Add. MS. 38304, f. 8). It was unsuccessful, as was also a second one made on October 9, 1764 (*ibid.* f. 83), although Wardroper had now constituted himself Grenville's manager for Rye in opposition to Thomas Lamb.

JOSEPH SALVADOR TO CHARLES JENKINSON

Add. MS. 38202, f. 13.

White Hart Court, January 8, 1764.

Dear Sir,

I flattered myself that I should not soon ⟨have⟩ had occasion to trouble you but I am obliged to do it by the ⟨Bank's⟩ opening of the transfer Books of the 3 per cent Annuities yesterday. Whatever is the cause nothing operated but to lower the stocks. The few who wish to hinder the bad consequences thereof oppose ⟨in⟩ vain ; opinion prevails, should it get master I can't tell where ⟨it will⟩ stop. 'Tis long since that I have told you an issue on the Na⟨vy is⟩ necessary. I see it

1. About him see p. 173.   2. Rye ?
3. As First Lord of the Admiralty.   4. See pp. 173, 283.

still continue so, I beg you would for ⟨   ⟩ by all possible means ; 'tis unreasonable the whole sistem of ⟨   ⟩ funds should suffer for the few Navy Bills that stick out.

I hope Mr. Grenville will begin the meeting of Pa⟨rliament⟩ by explaining fully his determination on the moneyed affairs, otherwise I fear the consequences. I know no other method to ⟨raise up⟩ spirits. I know we drop greatly, I can't tell the reason.

I could not refuse sending you the inclosed wh⟨ich I⟩ beg you would lay before Mr. Grenville. I have known Mr. ⟨Wynne [1]⟩ many years a regular bred attorney in good practice and a ⟨   ⟩ character, his assiduity makes me no way doubt of the good educ⟨ation his⟩ son has had ; as such persons are rare in the Islands, Mr. Wy⟨nne⟩ may be worthy the Government's attention. Mr. Long and Mr. Dor ⟨   ⟩ known to you can best inform his character if worthy tis ⟨   ⟩ Mr. Wynne should not be named to Mr. Grenville. I beg you ⟨   ⟩ excuse this.

⟨I p⟩ropose waiting on Mr. Grenville Tuesday or Wednesday, ⟨I be⟩g to press some resolution in our money affairs. I am ⟨with⟩ great regard Sir, your most obedient humble servant

Joseph Salvador

CHARLES JENKINSON TO JOSEPH SALVADOR

Add. MS. 38304, f. 6.

January 9, 1764.

Dear Sir,

I had this morning the favor of your letter. The opening of the Transfer Books of the 3 per Cent Annuities was unknown to us ; It is in the power of the Bank to open or shut the Books just when they please ; and the Treasury never give any orders about it ; I will talk on the other points of finance with you when I see you ; I have laid your request in favor of Mr. Wynne before Mr. Grenville, and he directs me in answer to assure that he will pay very particular attention to your recommendation.

I am, etc.

C. Jenkinson

1. A. Wynne, Attorney at Law, died in Basing Lane on February 14, 1784, aged seventy-two.

On the conclusion of the Peace of Paris in February 1763 the Government was confronted with the problem of justifying their choice by developing the territories they had acquired ; at the same time, the relative unpopularity of the Peace made it incumbent on them to render their American policy as little burdensome as possible to the country. Although the question of Canada versus Guadeloupe was eventually settled in favour of Canada, the restoration of the French West Indies was generally regarded as a sacrifice of British commercial interests. To meet this criticism, Grenville, who had opposed the cession of St. Lucia and Guadeloupe and the proposed renunciation of Havana, was determined not only to prove the value of the new continental colonies, but also to stimulate the development of the remaining British West Indies, and, if possible, to injure French commerce in order to compensate for the loss to British trade. Hence on the one hand the tightening-up of customs regulations in America and the attempt to make the colonies pay for their own defence, and on the other the revival of the spirit of the navigation laws, embodied in the Plantation Act of 1764. The Plantation Act had also a fiscal aspect. The failure of the requisition system in America during the war [1] had rendered necessary the establishment of a standing army in the colonies, and early in 1763 it was determined to maintain there a permanent force of 10,000 men at a yearly cost of approximately £320,000, that is, £220,000 more than had hitherto been spent on the upkeep of garrisons in America.[2] But the war had been a strain on British financial resources, and there was a strong feeling in England, with which even some sections of American opinion concurred,[3] that the colonies should at least contribute to the expenses of their own defence. Mr. G. L. Beer, in his *British Colonial Policy* (pp. 269-70), writes : " The difficulty in securing adequate support from the colonies during the war with France and subsequently thereto during the Pontiac conspiracy convinced the British government that parliamentary taxation was the sole and only means of obtaining from the Colonies their just share of the cost of their own defence ". The measures which followed, the Plantation Act and the Stamp Act, were among the great contributory causes of the American Revolution, yet neither in 1764, nor again in 1765 when these measures came before Parliament, did anyone foresee their consequences, and this, though notice had been given of them more than a year beforehand and considerable correspondence had passed between England and America on the subject.[4]

The Plantation Act, also called the Sugar Act, was moved in March 1763 but deferred till this session, when the old duties were due to expire.[5]

1. See p. 24.
2. G. L. Beer, *British Colonial Policy*, p. 267. The figures quoted by Beer are from the *Commons Journal*, xxix, 681 ; xxx, 470-71.
3. See Beer, *op. cit.* p. 268 n. 2.
4. For an account of Grenville's fiscal and commercial measures and their influence on the American Revolution, see G. L. Beer, *British Colonial Policy*, and *The Old Colonial System*, ii, 269 ; Van Tyne, *Causes of the War of Independence* (1922), 125-282 *passim*; Schlesinger, *Colonial Merchants and the American Revolution* (1917) ; W. S. M'Clellan, *Smuggling in the American Colonies* (1912) ; Alvord, *The Mississippi Valley in British Politics*.
5. Strictly speaking neither the Stamp Act nor the Plantation Act originated with Grenville. The Plantation Act was moved by Lord Sandys in 1763, but at whose instance is not known (see Jaspar Mauduit to the Speaker of the

On December 30, 1763, Jaspar Mauduit, the agent for Massachusetts, wrote to the Speaker of the Assembly : " I am now to inform the General Court that this scheme is resumed, and the quantum of the duty is to be one of the first things considered immediately after the meeting of Parliament" (Mass. Hist. Soc. Coll., 1st series, vi, 193).

WILLIAM WOOD TO CHARLES JENKINSON

Add. MS. 38202, f. 18.

William Wood was Secretary to the Board of Customs. He died on March 25, 1765, aged eighty-six.

Tower Hill, January 9, 1764.

Sir,

I received the favour of your letter of the 14th November, soon after which I was taken ill, and have ever since been confined to my house. I now send you an account of the money paid into the Exchequer by the Receiver General for three years past, by which you will observe that the year 1763 is more than the year 1762 by £391,186 : 18 : 1, and exceeds the year 1761 by £383,451 : 19 : 10.[1] I hope to be able very soon to shew you the cause of this great increase of the year 1763, and at the same time that the Customs will not diminish (as you say some people imagine) in future, under a carefull and frugal management. Nor our commerce decline in any articles. And for the East India Company, I am willing to hope their commerce, will increase but not the customs arising from it, it being the interest of the nation, that the goods (unless the tea's) should be re-exported to the foreign countries, even exclusive of our own Plantations : Though I really wish the continuance of the tea, for the sake of paying the annuities of the Public Debt — the monies arising from the duties for the consumption of tea's only in this Kingdom, having for some years, amounted to about £500,000 per Annum. My journey to Bath, was of considerable service to me, for my long complaint of indigestion, but a great cold, attended with a fever, attacked me soon after my return from thence, and

Massachusetts Assembly, December 30, 1763 : Mass. Hist. Soc. Coll., 1st series, vi, 193). But Grenville has rightly been identified with them both, for he willingly sponsored them and made them an integral part of his imperial policy.

1. Add. MS. 38335, f. 312 : " An account of the money paid by the Receiver General into the Exchequer for the three following years, viz. 1761, £1,866,151 . 18 . 11 3/4; 1762, £1,858,417 . 0 . 8 3/4; 1763, £2,249,603 . 18 . 9 3/4 ".

brought me so low that my spirits were almost sunk. I have in some measure recovered them, and am extreamly obliged to you for your kind wishes, who am with great truth, and respect, Sir

Your most humble servant,

Wm. Wood

CHARLES JENKINSON TO WILLIAM WOOD

Add. MS. 38304, f. 6.

Parliament Street, January 9, 1764.

Sir,

I have had the favor of your letters of the 5 and 7th instant, and am much obliged to you for the information you have sent me, I should be further obliged to you for an account of enumerated duties from 1710 ; [1] it will be necessary to call for an account of these duties and of the duties of the 6th of George 2d [2] to be laid before Parliament ; I wish you would turn in your thoughts at what time it may be proper to have these accounts commence.

I am etc.,

C. Jenkinson

I am glad to hear that your health is mended.

1. The "enumerated" duties were on those colonial products which, in accordance with mercantilist policy, could only be exported to Great Britain or to some other British colony. At the beginning of 1764 Grenville was contemplating an addition to the enumerated list, and during this session, by the Act of 4 George III, c. 15 (the revised Molasses Act, sometimes called the Plantation Act), coffee, pimento, coconuts, hides, whale fins, raw silk, potashes, and pearlashes were added to the list. See Beer, *British Colonial Policy*, pp. 221-2. At the same time colonial iron and lumber were enumerated but were allowed to be exported direct to Africa, America, and Asia (*ibid.* pp. 223-5). See also two pamphlets, *The Regulations lately made* (1765) and *The late Regulations respecting the British Colonies considered* (1765), by John Dickinson.

2. The Act of 6 George II, c. 13, "for the better securing and encouraging the trade of His Majesty's sugar colonies in America ", was the famous Molasses Act of 1733, many times renewed since then and due to expire at the end of this session. If properly enforced, this Act, which placed a duty of 9d. a gallon on foreign molasses imported into America, would have been ruinous to the prosperity of the Continental colonies, for their trade with the Spanish, French, and Dutch West Indies provided the balance in gold and silver with which they paid their English creditors. See Van Tyne, *Causes of the War of Independence*, i, 47, 128. Smuggling and the corruption of British customs officials in America had hitherto succeeded in neutralising the effects of the law, but it was on this Act that Grenville now based his Plantation Bill and the administrative reforms which had already, in part, taken effect.

WILLIAM WOOD TO CHARLES JENKINSON

Add. MS. 38202, f. 23.

Tower Hill, January 10, 1764.

Sir,

I had the favour of yours last night, acknowledging mine of the 5th and 7th and hope you have received mine of yesterday. Herewith you have an account ⟨of⟩ the Enumerated Duties from 1710, with my thoughts ⟨on⟩ what time it may be proper to have the account ⟨of⟩ the enumerated duties, and the duties of the 6th ⟨Ge⟩orge 2nd commence : however I wish that every ⟨th⟩ing which may have been thought of respecting the Plantations, may be defered to another year, except continuing the Act of the 6th of George 2nd for a year, or longer. For if what I have occasionally heard mentioned be true, I conceive you want information of several things from the Plantations, especially an " Account what Duties are payable by any Act of Assembly, in any of the British Plantations, in America, on the importation, and exportation of negroes, wines, rum, or other liquors ; or on any goods, or merchandize, and shipping ". Pray excuse this liberty, I have taken which I should not presume to have done, was not I very well acquainted with the former disputes, and debates that have happened, whenever matters relating to the Colonies, came before Parliament, and had not given not a little attention in the course of my life, to the better settling trade, and navigation of the Plantations. I was once young but am now old ; yet as they are of such advantage to their Mother Country, their welfare is still uppermost in my thoughts. I am with great truth and respect Sir,

Your most humble servant,

Wm. Wood

P.S. I sent to be laid this morning before the Commissioners your letter to them relating to the Morocco Ambassador,[1] and your letter to me, relating to Mr. Grenville's case.

1. The Morocco Ambassador's baggage had been detained at the Customs.

THE EARL OF SANDWICH TO CHARLES JENKINSON

in Parliament Street

Add. MS. 38202, f. 24.

On November 22, 1763, Lord Sandwich announced his intention of standing for High Steward of Cambridge University in the event of Hardwicke's approaching death. Hardwicke's son, Lord Royston, the other candidate, was supported by Newcastle. For sixteen years Newcastle as Chancellor of Cambridge had commanded a following there, but his influence was now on the wane ; a minister as High Steward with control of Crown and Government patronage, could overshadow him. Sandwich and Halifax were the only Cambridge men in the Cabinet, and as they had come to a private agreement " that the first should be Steward and the last Chancellor " (*Grenv. Pps.* ii, 228), the King was obliged, though most unwillingly, to support Sandwich or forgo the opportunity of hurting Newcastle. Sandwich had just earned the name of " Jemmy Twitcher " for his attack on Wilkes, and his nomination was very unpopular. For eight weeks the King and Grenville tried in vain to dissuade him from standing or make Halifax stand in his place.[1] At last on January 24, the King informed Sir James Lowther that Sandwich had his goodwill (Add. MS. 32955, f. 259), but Sandwich did not wait for this intimation to enlist the help of the Treasury.

January 11, 1764.

Dear Sir,

Pray remember that you have long promised me an answer from Mr. Pelham,[2] and some other Members of the University of Cambridge ; Mr. Jackson [3] was allso so good as to say he would apply to Mr. Stevens of St. Johns College.[4]

I am very sincerely yours,

Sandwich

JOSEPH SALVADOR TO CHARLES JENKINSON

Add. MS. 38202, f. 42.

White Hart Court, January 20, 1764.
4 o'clock.

Dear Sir,

I heartily congratulate you on the completion of the Bank Bargain which the Governor has been so kind to inform

1. Professor Winstanley suggests that Halifax was unwilling to oppose Newcastle, with whom he had been on friendly terms. See D. A. Winstanley, *Cambridge in the Eighteenth Century* (1922), p. 59 n. 1.
2. Probably Henry Pelham, son of Thomas Pelham of Lewis, Fellow of Peterhouse, formerly M.P. for Bramber 1751–54, Tiverton 1754–58, now Commissioner of Customs.
3. There are at least six possible Jacksons including Richard Jackson.
4. William Stevens, Fellow of St. John's 1756–77.

me he looks upon as compleated and calls a General Court on Wednesday to give the necessary and proper information to them.[1] I don't doubt that measures so properly taken will be attended with the desired success. Now don't let the little ardour that will be revived by this arduous affair be lost but complete with all speed the business of the year. If the Bank could be induced to begin to take in a part of the Exchequer Bills it will do greatly or to give money for those you may be obliged to issue for the payment of the Navy ; when you are ready I am ready att minute's warning and ever devoted to the service I am with the greatest regard Sir,

Your most Obedient humble servant,

Joseph Salvador

CHASE PRICE TO CHARLES JENKINSON

Add. MS. 38202, f. 48.

January 21, 1764.

Dear Sir,

If the hint I threw out yesterday to you is worth attending to, I fancy I can procure you facts sufficient for the purpose. I find Lord Egmont has got the Island of St. Johns and intends proceeding towards Dominica.[2] This does not interfere with my little object in those parts of the world ; and I should be

1. Cf. announcement in *Gent. Mag.*, January 25, 1764 (p. 45) : "At a general court of the Governors of the Bank, it appeared that the renewal of their charter for 21 years, from 1765, had cost £110,000 and that they had likewise agreed to lend the government a million on Exchequer bills, to the year 1766, at 3 per cent and then to be paid off ". The Government announced this contract to be the most beneficial ever made with the Bank. See *Annual Register*, 1764, p. 31, and Hartley's pamphlet *The Budget*, where he gives an extract from a Government advertisement.

2. Lord Egmont was among the first of those who developed vast schemes for land settlement in America on the conclusion of peace. His application for a grant-in-fee of the island of St. Johns " on behalf of himself and his nine children, and a great number of land and sea officers " was refused by the Board of Trade, who disliked such extensive grants and did not see " that any advantage whatever can arise to the public, or to the several adventurers, by leaving the parcelling out of the lands to the said Earl . . ." (Acts of the Privy Council (Colonial), 1745–66, iv, 654, quoted in Namier, *England etc.* p. 315). Two other joint applications for similar grants were refused, and the island was not parcelled out until July 23, 1767, when " 66 grants were made to private individuals, or groups of individuals, each grant comprising about 20,000 acres " (*ibid.*). Lord Egmont had medieval leanings, and his application for the grant included a scheme to organise the island on the feudal system. Egmont's memorial was presented to the King in December 1763, and Chase Price's letter shows that he was believed to have succeeded in his application, which was not the case.

glad to speak a word to you upon that head between this and Monday one o'clock.

I find on all sides opposition gathering to your American Bill, but more of this when I have the honour of seeing you. I am dear Sir,

Your most obedient humble servant,
Chase Price

CHARLES JENKINSON TO C. W. CORNWALL

Add. MS. 38304, f. 7.

Charles Wolfran Cornwall (1735–89) of Berrington, Herefordshire (a cider county), was a first cousin of Charles Jenkinson. In 1763 he was appointed Commissioner for examining German accounts and, on the conclusion of his commission, received a bonus of £3000, not a pension of £1500 a year as stated in *D.N.B.*[1] See below, p. 415. In August 1764 he married Jenkinson's sister, Elizabeth, and attached himself politically to his brother-in-law. In 1768 he was returned for Grampound and afterwards sat for the Treasury boroughs of Winchelsea and Rye. In 1780 he became Speaker of the House of Commons. See *D.N.B.*

January 22, 1764.

Mr. Jenkinson presents his compliments to Mr. Cornwall, and is exceedingly obliged to him for the information he sent him last night ; upon conversation with Mr. Grenville he finds that he will have no objection to go into a committee provided it be fully understood that it be not done with a view to repeal the Cyder Act, but only to amend and explain it.[2] As to the Bill which was drawn, it is laid aside as being no longer of any use : if the gentlemen of the Cyder Counties should hereafter find themselves at liberty to agree to the

1. The mistake in *D.N.B.* is copied from Manning's *Lives of the Speakers.* Actually in 1773 Cornwall was granted a yearly pension ostensibly for his work as Commissioner of German Accounts, but it was of £500 not £1500. The patent is in P.R.O. Treasury Patent Books, T. 64/216, p. 239. Most likely the pension was given him as a *douceur* on his leaving Opposition for North's Government.

2. Cf. Walpole, *Memoirs*, i, 443 ; also Walpole to Hertford, January 22, 1764, and *Chatham Corr.* ii, 279, 281. On January 24 Dowdeswell proposed a Committee of the whole House to consider the Cider Bill. Grenville opposed the motion but agreed to a committee to consider grievances and suggest amendments, though not with power to repeal the Bill. This was carried by 167 to 125. Bute in his panic had promised to repeal the Bill if the City would refrain from petitioning against it, and Government was hard pressed when the question was reopened. On a question against Excise proposed in the Committee by Dowdeswell the Government majority was only 20. On February 7 the Bill was compromised, two shillings being imposed instead of five.

principles on which it was drawn, and which are the same as were suggested at the meeting with Mr. Grenville the Bill may then be recalled and the consideration of it resumed. Mr. Jenkinson is sorry that he has it not in his power therefore to send the Bill to Mr. Cornwall, whom as his friend and relation he shall always esteem and be happy to obey his commands, and to whom Mr. Grenville will at all times be ready to give every mark of his attention and regard.

Mr. Jenkinson begs his compliments to Mrs. and Miss Cornwall.[1]

On Friday, January 13, 1764, Prince Ferdinand of Brunswick arrived in London for his marriage to Princess Augusta, eldest sister of George III. The wedding took place on the 16th, and on the 25th the Prince left England with his bride after a visit of less than a fortnight. As the hero of the English campaigns in Germany he was greeted with enthusiasm by the London mob, but his reception from the Government that had let him down was naturally less cordial, while the meagre hospitality of the Court provoked the ridicule of Opposition. The Prince himself delighted them by his behaviour " so much à la minorité ", particularly his visits to Newcastle, Pitt, and Cumberland, for an account of which see Horace Walpole to Mann, January 18, and to Hertford, January 22.

ALEXANDER FALL TO CHARLES JENKINSON

Add. MS. 38202, f. 67.

Alexander Fall was a merchant. In December 1763 he was called as a witness in the proceedings in the House of Lords on the riots over the burning of the *North Briton*. See *Parliamentary History*, xv, col. 1383. The punctuation in the following letter has been added, as there is none in the original.

January 29, 1764.

This week past I have been in every publick place, and the faction which decrease in number, as many of them are ashamed of their champion,[2] yet keep up the spirit of their party by notorious lies such as the Hereditary Prince's visiting Mr. Pitt, Lord Temple, Devonshire, dining twice with Newcastle and when he dined with Cumberland which they say he did three times there was no company but men of his party,[3] and further say he was hurryd out of the Kingdom in

1. His mother and sister.   2. Wilkes.

3. Prince Ferdinand's visit to Pitt on January 22 is mentioned in the " Historical Chronicle " in the *Gent. Mag.* (p. 45), as also that he dined with Cumberland on the 20th (p. 44). See also Walpole to Hertford, January 22 : " He not only wrote to the Duke of Newcastle and Mr. Pitt but has been at Hayes to see the

order to prevent the state of the nation coming to his ears, which he would on that give His Majesty his best advice ; they likewise say the Princess is gone abroad without the least acquaintance with the Queen owing to the intrigues of the Princess Dowager and Lady Bute.[1] The friends of Government answer by giving them flatly the lie and say the Prince never visited Pitt Devonshire and Temple, and offer to lay, which the others are wise anuff to decline and observe that as His Majesty and Ministry are throughly sensible that as the debt of the nation is great it is absolutely necessary that there should be an example of frugality from the Throne and as it was impossible to keep the Prince and his retinue here without a great expence which was of no real service to the Prince, it was wisdome to let him go home as soon as he wanted to be gone. They likewise say that Wilks visited Lord Hertford att Paris who returned his visit (this I believe is truth [2]) ; they likewise say that Bacon [3] was obliged to get member coast what it would other ways he could not pass his accompts as contractor ; he pay'd 5 guineas a man att Ailsbury and £8,000 it coast him oposeing Young att Honneton.[4] They had got me a candidate for that Borrough ; the grounds they had some of my friends that thought they had interest there proposed a subscription in some of the Clubbs unknowen to me to support me in the election. I believe some trifle might have been subscribed but when it came to my knowledge I stopt it. On the whole notwithstanding the low attempts of the party all goes well, the people in general begin to be very well satisfied and Government will soon be as well established without doors as within.

A. Fall

A scheme to supply London with fish by waggon trains was promoted in March 1762 by John Blake and the Society of Arts on a capital of £3500,

latter, and has dined twice with the Duke of Cumberland . . .", etc. Cf. *Chatham Papers*, ii, 271, 277, 283 ; and *Grenv. Pps.* ii, 487.

1. Cf. Walpole, *Memoirs*, i, 275.
2. Cf. Walpole to Hertford, January 22.
3. Anthony Bacon, merchant, about whom see p. 194 n. 1, succeeded Wilkes as M.P. for Aylesbury on January 25, 1764. With regard to this passage Professor Namier writes in *The Structure of Politics*, pp. 72-3 : " Whether the reason for his first entry into Parliament is correctly stated in the letter quoted above, I cannot say ; but in principle it was plausible. Twenty years later it was to be the regular practice of nabobs returning ' from India's plundered land ', to insure against inquiries into the origin of their fortunes by providing themselves with seats in Parliament." Bacon was M.P. for Aylesbury 1764–84.
4. See pp. 193-4.

£2000 of which were advanced by the Society and the rest borrowed from them by Blake " on his pledged security ".[1] By December 1763 the scheme had failed owing to the opposition of the fishmongers, who owned the fleet and tried to keep prices up by limiting supplies (see R. Leslie-Melville, *Life and Work of Sir John Fielding*, pp. 129-30, where the following letter is transcribed), and Blake's accounts showed a loss of £3502 : 10 : 9.[2] On February 1, 1764, the Society of Arts " almost unanimously " released him from his obligations, but on March 1 Parliament voted him £2500 to carry on his scheme.[3] The *Gentleman's Magazine* was somewhat inconsistent in its comments on it. In March 1763 when Blake presented an optimistic report, it declared that " the price of fish is not reduced so low as the nature of the thing will admit. . . . It is from a rivalship that the public can expect benefit." [4] But when in March 1764 the company was again doing badly, it complained that " the prices at which they [soles] have been sold in London have been so moderate that unless greater encouragement be given to the new undertaking, the Town can no longer be supplied with fish by land-carriage ; the consequence of which will be, a renewal of the exorbitant prices by the fishmongers ".[5] Even with the help of a grant from Parliament the scheme was once more a failure. On May 13, 1765, Blake declined an invitation from the Society of Arts to revive the project and on June 12 they accepted his offer to hand over the money and stocks remaining on his hands. Later he was involved in disputes over the accounts, but on January 21, 1767, " the question so long agitated by the Society of Arts in relation to the land carriage fishery, was finally determined in favour of Mr. Blake ".[6]

Both John and Henry Fielding were interested in the fishery from a philanthropic point of view. In 1756 Henry Fielding lamented in the *Journal of a Voyage to Lisbon* that fish, so plentiful on the coast, should be so dear in London that poor people never tasted any but sprats, and as a remedy suggested " the absolute necessity of immediately hanging all the fishmongers within the bills of mortality ".[7] As a magistrate Sir John Fielding must have been familiar with the " near a hundred acts of Parliament for preserving the small fry of the river Thames ".[8]

SIR JOHN FIELDING TO CHARLES JENKINSON

Add. MS. 38202, f. 68.

Bow Street, January 30, 1764.

Sir John Fielding presents his respectful compliments to Mr. Jenkinson, being informed that there either has or is to be some plan for supplying London with fish to be laid before

1. See an article in the *Gent. Mag.*, March 1762, p. 99, and the first report of the undertaking, *ibid.* p. 537.
2. *Gent. Mag.*, 1763, p. 617.
3. *Annual Register*, 1764, p. 49, and *Gent. Mag.*, 1764, p. 142.
4. P. 143.   5. P. 393.
6. *Gent. Mag.*, 1767, p. 45.
7. *Journal of a Voyage to Lisbon* (ed. J. H. Dent, 1932), pp. 264-5, quoted by Melville, p. 129.   8. *Ibid.* p. 265.

Mr. Grenville, I have sent you the enclosed, which, when thoroughly considered will I am persuaded, fully answer the purpose and at the same time re-imburse the original subscribers to that stock. But, as from that enquiry which I was obliged to make, relative to those fisheries that supply the London markets, when I first took up and promoted the land-carriage fishery by recommending the same, not only to Mr. Blake,[1] but to the Society, I am so much master of the whole fisheries that I hope Mr. Grenville will not come to any resolution in this matter without giving me an opportunity of explaining myself on this subject, which I will do to you at any time. I am sure I should not mention this if I did not know I could be extremely useful, and I am your affectionate friend and obedient humble servant

J. Fielding

JOSEPH SALVADOR TO CHARLES JENKINSON

Add. MS. 38202, ff. 72-3.

February 1, 1764.

Dear Sir,

When I had last the pleasure of seeing you I explained my sentiments concerning what was still wanting by means of the Supply this year to re-establish our sinking credit and gain the moneys wanted by the Government. I think the last done, if the first view is not obtained, much will still be wanting to the great work, and that a reestablishment of publick credit will be as essential to the glory of the Ministry as the having gone successfully through the Supply.

The Bank Contract, the getting the unsubscribed Navy in, and the other measures pursued have brought us on far in our way but there is much to do yet, there is no doubt that all may be done.

I observed to you the different situation the nation is in from what it was last year, tis on this great principle the remedying the present disorders lyes. We last year owed much abroad and were exhausted of cash ; we this year owe little

1. John Blake of Parliament Street, " many years an East India captain, the proprietor and conductor of the scheme for supplying the London markets with fish by land carriage ", died " advanced in years " on February 24, 1790. His son, John Blake, East India captain and naturalist, is noticed in the *D.N.B.*

abroad, our cash is in great part replenished but a much more alarming danger nods over us, our credit is hurt, our paper wants circulation ; tis not a superabundant cash that will relieve this evil.

The conduct of postponing part of our foreign demands last year was necessary, we could not pay more. The paying or making every just claim we can current is essential now, it will aid circulation.

It would be happy could the whole publick debt be brought into that state without any moneys being raised but tis impossible from the situation of the supply, tis plain the Navy course must be stopped some time this year or Exchequer Bills must be circulated or some other method taken to raise money.

While the Navy debt does not keep its regular course publick credit can never be restored it being a debt without a fund allotted, although a Parliamentary debt, will ever sell with discredit and its bad influence must operate on the whole as it must on all contracts the Navy have to make which must likewise be a considerable loss to the Government.

Exchequer Bills will as soon as new ones are issued sell att a considerable discount, they will depreciate all the other annual funds, ruin East India Bonds, and by employing the moneys wanted most on circulation they will lay a dead load on credit.

There is no way essentially to serve publick credit but by a declaration that the course of the Navy will be kept up and I fear I should add that no new Exchequer Bills may be issued.

An argument may be made, this is not to be done but by raising new monies, which must hurt. I answer tis no new money raised but the same debt formed into a different manner. The circulation will be rendered easier and therefore publick credit will be raised for the debts now to be paid are among ourselves.[1]

Another argument is, it must then be charged on the Sinking Fund. My answer is it lies already there. The Navy debt has a right of satisfaction or payment on the whole nation. I dread the thought of the first expence necessary for the safety of the Kingdoms not having a right of payment or satisfaction from all its revenues. The placing it therefore on the Sinking Fund is only appropriating it.

1. Grenville proposed to pay off the debt by taking £2,000,000 from the Sinking Fund. He boasted that he would not open a new loan or accept a lottery. Hartley accused him of merely postponing the debt, not paying it, and declared that this was the reason the stocks would not revive.

I hope you are persuaded of the propriety of making this circulation if the means can be found, we must not stop att trifles. The funds may be found at 3 per cent or with more advantage, can it then be a doubt when it is not only useful but profitable to Government and necessary to publick credit tis equal to me whether profitable to a contributor or not, but be sure our ends are answered.

Another demonstrative advantage will accrue to Government, tis that next year their hands may be clear and they may attend to the great object of reduction. This they must lose the view of if they leave the work undone and Navy Bills to run without payment.

I think it my duty to communicate my sentiments in which I am clear and that such a spirited conduct will greatly conduce to retrieve our affairs while the languid postponing to another year must be attended att best with a slow return of our credit.

I beg to take this method to communicate my thoughts to Mr. Grenville, as I may have omitted something I think essential which I remarked in discourse to you. I shall ever further his views but must humbly lay my sentiments before him. I am with great regard dear Sir

Your most obedient humble servant,

Joseph Salvador

COLONEL THOMAS POWNALL TO CHARLES JENKINSON

Add. MS. 38202, f. 79.

Scotland Yard, February 3, 1764.

⟨Dear⟩ Sir,

I have some points to mention to you and some proposals to make thereupon ⟨relating⟩ to the affair of the accounts which I apprehend wou'd be agreeable to you and the spirit ⟨of the⟩ Treasury Administration. I have suggested them to my colleagues who approve my ⟨plan⟩ and I wish before 'tis proposed in form ⟨to⟩ have half an hour's conversation with you or if not convenient to you with Mr. Grenville ; and I beg I may have an hour ⟨appo⟩inted me which I will have the honour to attend. I am Sir,

Your obliged servant,

T. Pownall

GEORGE SPENCER TO CHARLES JENKINSON

Add. MS. 38202, f. 92.

George Spencer wrote to Bute on March 29, 1763, enclosing a list of 46 vessels trading from New York, against whose owners he claimed to have evidence of smuggling during the war. An action which he had started against some of them in the Admiralty Court at New York had been dismissed and he petitioned to have it reopened (Add. MS. 38200, f. 281). On July 4, 1763, he repeated this petition to Grenville (Add. MS. 38201, f. 14).

My lodgings at Mr. Cooper's,
Hat and Feather on Snow Hill,
Saturday, February 11, 1764.

As Sir Jeffery Amherst, a few days ago, was pleased to tell me that he had given the Lords of the Treasury an account of my affair, and that their Lordships had it also from him in writing, and did not doubt but they would take the matter ⟨into⟩ consideration ; I presumed to prefer a Petition on that occasion, humbly praying ⟨their⟩ Lordships that they would be pleased not only to consider me for that important ⟨dis⟩-covery I made of the designs of the French against New-York, etc. as set forth in that Petition, but that they would also be pleased to grant me a special authority to prosecute those persons only at New-York, though at my own expence, against whom I had commenced actions, as mentioned in the said Petition, for the recovery of the penalties, etc. on the provisions they have exported contrary to the Act of Parliament ; of which actions I was denied prosecution, as you will find by the proofs which I must take the liberty to deliver you for your perusal. And as ⟨there⟩ is now in London one Mr. James Searle,[1] who intends to embark for New-York ⟨and⟩ Philadelphia very soon, that can prove the particular quantities of provisions contained in eight cargoes, the penalties thereof may easily be recovered ; and in which, the revenue of the Crown is greatly interested. And as 'tis a matter that now requires dispatch, if 'tis agreeable to you, Sir, to be my friend therein, permit me liberty, most humbly, to make you an offer of two thousand guineas ; which sum shall be punctually paid you out of the moiety I may receive. As to the reward for that intelligence I gave the Ministry of the designs of the French, I hope their Lordships will be pleased to grant me a small

1. Unidentified.

(264)

pension, with which I shall be satisfied. I presume, Sir, the Petition was delivered to you on Monday last, by Mr. Barnesly;[1] and most humbly pray, that you'll be pleased to present it to the Lords as addressed ; and if, Sir, you are favourably pleased to use your interest in my behalf, you may rely on my performance as above, and the greatest secresy therein ; and that, if 'tis agreeable, I will transmit you the proceedings, from time to time, in the affair. I hope, Sir, you'll be pleased to pardon the disagreeable necessity of my giving you this trouble, and permit me the honour to be Sir,

Your most devoted, and most obedient servant,

George Spencer

On February 14, 1764, the House of Commons sat on the legality of General Warrants, a question which nearly succeeded in overturning the Government. In the first division the ministry were so hard pressed that they carried their motion for adjournment by a bare majority of 10, and in the second division their majority was only 24. The question was to come on again on the 17th, and in the interval strenuous efforts were made to whip in every possible adherent, in spite of which the Government majority on that day was only 14.

EDWARD KYNASTON TO CHARLES JENKINSON

Add. MS. 38202, f. 97.

Edward Kynaston was one of Grenville's Parliamentary managers. See p. 223.

See p. 223.

Pall Mall, Thursday morn.
Docketed " February 15, 1764 ".

Dear Sir,

Knowing that the Opposition sent for a person out of bed to attend the last long day,[2] I take the liberty just to mention the names of some gentlemen, that perhaps a line from you or Mr. Grenville may engage their attendance to morrow.

1. There were three Barnesleys in the Treasury : William Barnesley, messenger of the chambers at 6s. 8d. a day, and deputy messengers Samuel Barnesley senior and junior. Samuel Barnesley senior, who died in 1794 aged ninety-five, is described in the obituary notice in the *Gent. Mag.* (p. 768) as " of the Treasury Office where he had been employed almost from his infancy and had acquired an ample fortune ".
2. Cf. Horace Walpole to Lord Hertford, February 19, 1764 : " You would have almost laughed to see the spectres produced by both sides ; one would have thought that they had sent a search-warrant for Members of Parliament into every hospital. Votes were brought down in flannels and blankets till the floor of the House looked like the pool of Bethesda."

Mr. Hill [1] and Mr. Hern [2] very seldom stay out a long day. Mr. Gulston [3] is infirm, but perhaps may come down, and take somebody off. I hear that Mr. Vaughan [4] is to go into the country next week, I leave it to you whether it will not be proper to keep him in town a little longer, as the coterie boast that the Ministry must soon be overturned. I hear that Lord Percival [5] is in Essex a sporting, should not he be desired to attend to morrow? I did not see Mr. Myddleton [6] last Tuesday in the House, a line from Mr. Grenville may be proper to be sent to him. I beg, that you will excuse this impertinence, and believe me with true esteem dear Sir,

Your very obedient humble servant,

Edd. Kynaston

LORD HARCOURT TO CHARLES JENKINSON

Add. MS. 38202, ff. 105-6.

Lord Newnham voted with the minority on February 17 and, as Walpole wrote to Hertford, " is likely to be turned out of doors for it ".

Saturday ¾ Past One o'clock.[7]
Docketed " February 19, 1764 ".

Dear Sir,

The enclosed copy of a letter which I have just wrote to his Majesty, will give you some idea of my distress. I wish you would take an opportunity of shewing it to Mr. Grenville, to whom I have not spirits enough to write. I hope this untoward affair will not be attended with all the bad consequences which the friends of faction expect. I shall be very cautious for the future, of answering for any man's behaviour, but I

1. Thomas Hill, uncle of Edward Kynaston and M.P. for Shrewsbury 1748–68, was the son of Thomas Harwood, a Shrewsbury draper, but took the name of Hill on succeeding to the estates of his maternal uncle, Richard Hill, in 1727. See a short biography of him in *Structure of Politics*, p. 300.

2. Francis Herne, M.P. for Bedford 1754–68. He was of a London merchant family. See *ibid.* p. 134.

3. Joseph Gulston senior, merchant and M.P. for Poole 1741–65, when he retired in favour of his son. His father was " Rio " Gulston, a Brazil merchant. See John Nichols, *Illustrations of the Literary History of the Eighteenth Century*, v, 1-60 : " The Gulston Family ".

4. William Vaughan of Corsy Gedol, M.P. for Merioneth County 1734–68.

5. John James Percival, afterwards 2nd Baron Lovell and Holland, and 3rd Earl of Egmont, was M.P. for Bridgwater 1762–68.

6. Richard Myddleton, M.P. for Denbigh Borough 1747–88.

7. Saturday was February 18. See note to next letter.

think I can give the strongest assurances of my own unalterable zeal for His Majesty's Government, and for the support of Mr. Grenville's administration.

Yours, dear Sir, most sincerely,

Harcourt

COPY OF A LETTER FROM LORD HARCOURT TO THE KING[1]

Add. MS. 38202, ff. 107-8.

Cavendish Square, Saturday ½ past one.
[February 18, 1764.]

Sir,

I am under such perturbation of mind, and so completely unhappy on account of Lord Newnham who (I find) has taken a part in the last question, so contrary to your Majesty's interest, so contrary to the wellbeing of this country, and so diametrically opposite to my own principles, that I think myself called upon in duty and honour, to declare my disapprobation of it.

Lord Newnham has hitherto attended so little to affairs of Government, that I fear he has allowed himself to be imposed upon by those, who have but too well succeeded, in making him, and other unweary people, the dupes of faction, and the tools of ambition.

That I might not suffer in Your Majesty's good opinion, which I value above all things in this world, I have presumed Sir, to trouble you with my sentiments on this occasion.

The goodness and sensibility of Your Majesty's heart will suggest better excuses for the great liberty, which I have presumed to take, than any that can be urged by Sir

Your Majesty's most dutyfull and faithfull servant,

Harcourt

1. An undated copy of this letter differing slightly in the text (it gives unwary for unweary) is in the *Harcourt Papers*, iii, 99 (1880–1905), together with the King's reply dated from the Queen's House, February 18, acknowledging Harcourt's dutiful affection and assuring him that Newnham's conduct has done Harcourt no prejudice with the King.

Add. MS. 38469, f. 93.

Winton, February 26, 1764.

Dear Sir,

I expected a letter from you a long time ago, but as I had not the happiness of hearing from you I thought of writing to you to put you in mind ; if you will send an answer as soon as you receive this I shall be obliged to you. I desire you will send me 4 or 5 dozen of franks for I have promised as many as ever the *Duke* of *Newcastle* did places. If you will let me hear from you and tell me all the news you have which is a great deal I am sure, if you will tell it all to me. Give my compliments to Miss Jenkinson.

I am ever yours,

F. Stuart

HENRY WILMOT TO CHARLES JENKINSON

Add. MS. 38202, f. 140.

Henry Wilmot was Agent for the Leeward Islands.

Lincolns Inn Fields, March 3, 1764.

Sir,

The same reason which prevented me from waiting upon you on the Land Tax Bill, now prevents my waiting upon you on another occasion. For though I am much amended, yet I cannot walk without crutches. There is a Bill I understand to be brought into the House, about Certificates and Stamp dutys abroad, and lowering the duty on sugar etc. imported into North America.[2] This Bill as I understand extends to sugar, rum and molasses. Now as I am Agent for the Leward Islands I think it my duty to acquaint you, that if the Bill stands thus, the Duty will in a great measure be lost. Where

1. Bute's son, aged ten. About him see p. 70.
2. The Plantation Bill was introduced by Grenville on March 9, 1764, after opening the Budget. It comprised various resolutions, of which the fifteenth was in effect the Stamp Act. This was deferred for further reference for a year, and in the meantime the various Colonial Agents were instructed to enquire of their respective Assemblies whether they preferred any other method of taxing themselves (see below, Israel Mauduit's account of the Optional Offer about the Stamp Act, p. 306).

ever sugar is mentioned, the words *or paneels* should be added, rum, *or spirit*, molasses *or syrup*. For paneels are not called sugar in the *Book of Rates* ; There is a spirit from sugar, not called rum, and a syrup from the canes, not called molasses. And all the sugar rum and molasses will go by the names of paneels, spirit, and syrup, and be run into North America as such, and without this door to fraud, all paneels, spirit and syrup (which by the Bill are intended to be included) will escape. For no North American jury will find paneels spirit or syrup, to be sugar rum or molasses.

There is one word I would say for the Island of Antigua which I wish might be considered. They have been at several thousand pounds expence in building barracks etc. and pay considerably for the subsistence of the Regiment there. And none of the other Islands have contributed. I think therefore they ought to be exempted from the Stamp Duty. And I do verily believe if they are not they will withdraw their subsistence.[1]

I begg your pardon for being thus troublesome to you and am Sir,

Your most obedient and most faithfull humble servant,

Hen: Wilmot

JOSEPH SALVADOR TO CHARLES JENKINSON

Add. MS. 38202, f. 147.

In January 1764 the proprietors of East India stock were alarmed by news from Bengal, where Governor Vansittart's revolution in favour of Cossim Ali Khan had ended disastrously in the outbreak of hostilities between the new Nabob and the Company, culminating in the murder of the Company's agent and the massacre of 150 Englishmen at Patna. When the *Lapwing*, which brought this news, left Calcutta, Meer Jaffeir, the old Nabob, had been restored by the Governing Council, but " an action must decide whether Jaffeir is Nabob or the English driven out of the Country " (article in *Gentleman's Magazine*, February 1764, p. 54). At the same

1. Cf. Governor Lyttelton to William Knox, July 22, 1764 (Knox MSS., Hist. MSS. Com., *Various Collections*, vi, 89). Apparently it was at the instance of the Colonial Agents that Grenville was persuaded to defer the Stamp Act. Lyttelton wrote from Jamaica : " I think that the part you took in conjunction with your brother agents was a very judicious one ; and considering how much one American colony differs from another in the frame of its government, temper of the people and capacity of bearing particular taxes, had a Stamp Duty been imposed the last session of Parliament to take place in all alike without previous information of the local circumstances attending each, it might have proved in some efficacious and in others have been productive of greater discontents than the object was worth ".

time reports reached England of the cleavage of parties in the Calcutta Council and of the general demoralisation of the Company's servants in Bengal. To consider these problems a General Court of Proprietors met on February 27 and March 1, when it was suggested, but not finally determined, to appoint John Spencer President in place of Vansittart, and make other alterations on the Calcutta Council. Dissatisfied with these measures, which represented the policy of the Directors, Sir Francis Gosling, Joseph Salvador, Clive himself and six other proprietors, called a General Court on March 12, at which the Directors were urged to send Clive immediately to Bengal with full powers as President of the Council and Commander-in-chief.

Since Clive's return from India in 1760 his quarrel with Sulivan was the main preoccupation of "Leadenhall politics". At the East India elections of April 1763 Sulivan and his friends were returned and in that month instructions were sent to the Calcutta Council to withhold payment on Clive's jagghire. On April 28, 1763, Clive filed a suit against the Directors, which was still pending a year later when the question of his commission coincided with the annual elections. On March 27, 1764, he wrote to the Directors refusing to go to India if Sulivan continued at their head. "At the same time," he wrote, "I never desired or even wished to name a direction" (Court Book 73, ff. 35-40). The stock ledgers and transfer books of the Company, however, bear witness that he and his agents were "splitting" votes for this election, and in fact in December 1763 he used the threat to do so, in an attempt to induce the Directors to sanction his jagghire.[1]

Clive at this time could influence six Shropshire votes in the House of Commons (see Namier, *Structure of Politics*, pp. 352-6). In December 1762 these were used against the Preliminaries, and at the ensuing East India elections Fox mobilised the resources of the Pay Office against him in an unparalleled example of direct Government interference in East India elections. Even while this was happening Clive was in correspondence with Grenville, and fear for his threatened jagghire soon induced him to make peace with the Administration. (See Miss L. Stuart Sutherland's article in *E.H.R.*, July 1934, "Lord Shelburne and East India Company Politics, 1766-69"). About December 1763 he temporarily discontinued his connexion with Newcastle and transferred his allegiance to Grenville, who was mediating between him and the Directors, and in March 1764 all Government officials who were stockholders in the Company had instructions to vote for Clive's list of Directors.

White Hart Court, March 6, 1764.
Dear Sir,
I thought the plan I followed sure of success vizt. that of getting Lord Clive to go to Bengal and Mr. Amyand [2] to head

1. See Court Book 72, f. 238, December 14, 1763 : " That if this agreement takes place Lord Clive then promises upon his honour to give the present Court of Directors no trouble at any future election ". On December 16 the Chair reported that this condition was not meant to appear but arose in conversation only. Cf. Clive's promise to Grenville on November 7, 1763, *Grenv. Pps.* ii, 161.

2. George Amyand, merchant, M.P. for Barnstaple 1754-66, was created a baronet in August 1764. From 1763 to 1764 he was a member of Sulivan's Direction but was not re-elected in April 1764.

the direction. My hopes are suspended by Mr. Amyand's informing me that he has definitively agreed with Mr. Grenville not to stand. If Mr. Grenville had suspended this matter till Friday I think I should have fixed Mr. Amyand. I now doubt of it much yet shall try and still hope for Mr. Grenville's protection.

I hope you will continue qualifying.[1] I wish Mr. Glover [2] and the Governor of the Bank [3] were spoke to and that I knew your sentiments who to put in this affair if Mr. Amyand will not. May Mr. Jones [4] or Mr. Cust [5] be proper? And shall we then have full support? Your immediate sentiments hereon will oblige me as we are to have an important meeting att 5 this evening. I am Sir

Your most obedient servant,
Joseph Salvador

JOSEPH SALVADOR TO CHARLES JENKINSON

Add. MS. 38202, f. 148.

White Hart Court, March 7, 1764.

Sir,

I cannot get over the immense difficulty of forming a direction without which all our endeavours will prove abortive. I have desired Lord Clive, and Mr. Rouse [6] to wait on Mr. Grenville to form some plan. Nothing new on this subject can occurr till to morrow night. Friday morning you shall be informed what passes. I think we may be successful, but not without a head. I am Sir,

Your most obedient servant,
Joseph Salvador

1. £500 stock was the necessary qualification for a proprietor's vote in the election of Directors. In March 1764 the General Court passed resolutions against " splitting " immediately before elections, and in 1767 an Act was passed to make a year's possession of stock a necessary qualification for voting in the annual elections. See Miss L. Stuart Sutherland, " Lord Shelburne and East India Company Politics ", in *E.H.R.*, July 1934.
2. Robert Glover, a Lombard Street banker, or Richard Glover, M.P. for Weymouth, poet and merchant, about whom see *D.N.B.*
3. Robert Marsh.
4. Robert Jones, M.P., merchant and Government contractor. See p. 213.
5. Peregrine Cust, merchant and M.P. for Bishop's Castle. See p. 213. Jones and Cust were business partners.
6. Thomas Rous, merchant, was elected Chairman of the East India Company on April 12, 1764. He had been Chairman before (1762–63), but in 1763–64 was out of the Direction by rotation.

JOSEPH SALVADOR TO CHARLES JENKINSON

Add. MS. 38397, f. 78.

White Hart Court, March 8, 1764.

Dear Sir,

There was a meeting to night of the proprietors of India where there were several gentlemen of weight and a numerous meeting yet not such a one as that I think they can succeed unless Mr. Grenville gives us a head. I find Lord Clive has not chose to introduce Mr. Rous to Mr. Grenville. Whatever direction his Lordship with Mr. Grenville should appoint I will support, but with little hope, unless a full exertion of our strength is very speedily made. Then I think we shall succeed. Lord Temple is against us. The Duke of Devonshire as yet is neutral. This is all I know. I am so much indisposed I can't wait on you. Were Mr. Amyand, Mr. Jones or Mr. Fonnereau att our head all would do well. I am dear Sir

Your most obedient servant,

Joseph Salvador

JOSEPH SALVADOR TO CHARLES JENKINSON

in Parliament Street

Add. MS. 38202, f. 159.

White Hart Court, March 14, 1764.

Dear Sir,

I have taken all possible pains about trying peoples sentiments with regard to a direction. Mr. Rous will wait on Mr. Grenville, with my Lord Clive or myself whenever he pleases (I fear there is no prevailing on Mr. Amyand to stand) so he must be our chief man. Mr. Jones seems willing to aid us. I dare say he will do it on Lord Sandwich or Mr. Greenvilles request. I fear Mr. Bacon [1] is not qualified. Mr. Cust is critical having divided against us yet I will sound. There is no doubt of finding proper men but I would have some friends, I wish to know Mr. Fonnereau's [2] sentiments but dont know how to

---

1. Anthony Bacon. The qualification for a Director was £2000 of stock.
2. Thomas or Zachary Fonnereau. See p. 115.

sound him without going too far. Mr. Harley [1] is out of the question. Without this point we have done nothing, and I am very apprehensive of the bringing it about. I am with great regard, Sir,

Your most obedient servant,

Joseph Salvador

JOSEPH SALVADOR TO CHARLES JENKINSON

Add. MS. 38202, f. 168.

White Hart Court, March 16, 1764.

Dear Sir,

I received your favor while in close conference, with Mr. Amyand, Lord Clive, Mr. Rouse, and Mr. Boulton,[2] on the subject of the direction they chose an interview. Mr. Amyand remains fixed in his determination though we shook him and perhaps after Friday his sentiments may alter. I would not have him spoke to before, we turned our thoughts on other people. The most proper that offered were Mr. Harley, Mr. Jones or Mr. Stevenson.[3] The last may add weight to us but is not a man of business. Att length we determined trying the first. My cruel indisposition hinders me from exerting myself but I hope for success. The case is to find a head. I assure you the difficulty is immense. A hint from you would be gratefully received. I am with the greatest regard Sir,

Your most obedient servant,

Joseph Salvador

1. Thomas Harley, Alderman and M.P. for the City of London, younger son of Edward Harley, 3rd Earl of Oxford and Mortimer. He became Lord Mayor in 1768.

2. Henry Crabb Boulton, M.P. for Worcester 1754–73, was an East India Director and succeeded Sulivan as Deputy Chairman at this election. He had formerly been a supporter of Sulivan but his votes and splits in 1764 make it clear that he was then of Clive's party. Clive thought him " a great rogue ". See *Grenv. Pps.* ii, 46.

3. John Stephenson, merchant, M.P. for St. Michael in Cornwall 1761–80, and afterwards for Tregony and Plympton, was politically connected with Sandwich. See Namier, *Structure of Politics*, p. 355. In 1754 he and Robert Clive were returned together for St. Michael, but unseated on petition in favour of Simon Luttrell and Richard Hussey.

JAMES ROSSETER TO CHARLES JENKINSON

JAMES ROSSETER TO CHARLES JENKINSON

Add. MS. 38202, ff. 180-81.

James Rosseter, Alderman of Broad Street ward and Governor of Ticket Porters, was interested in the felt trade.

Nicholas Lane, Lombard Street,
Wednesday Evening, March 21, 1764.

Sir,

The Beaver Bill [1] was read the second time yesterday and committed, Mr. Nugent made no objection at the second Reading but intends to make his proposition to exempt Ireland from the new duty on Tuesday next in the Committee.[2] The manufacturers are apprehensive that Ireland will supplant us in the hat trade in foreign markets by the advantages they have in rabbits fur, provisions, and labour, and that Ireland will also be a channell to convey beaver to France and other country's in case they are permitted to have it duty-free, and it may be entered out for Ireland and carried elsewhere.[3] I have spoke to several Members of Parliament who are against Mr. Nugent's proposition, which gentleman yesterday proposed a compromise to some of my friends, for Ireland to pay part of the duty. Permit me Sir to beg the favor that you will make my most humble respects to Mr. Grenville and desire that he will be pleased to consider what is proper to be done on the occasion, and I will wait on Friday morning at the Treasury to know Mr. Grenville's pleasure herein, because I would by no means desire the members who have particularly appeared in support of the Bill to attend on Tuesday to oppose Mr. Nugent's proposition in case the Treasury should think Ireland ought to be favoured, but in case we had been aware of any such exemption we should not have solicited the measure at all, because we doubt it will defeat the intention of the Bill

1. See p. 231. This Bill received the Royal Assent on April 5, 1764.
2. Robert Nugent was joint Vice-Treasurer of Ireland. About him see p. 161.
3. Cf. Add. MS. 38337, f. 231, a memorial from Rosseter to Jenkinson on the state of the fur trade in Ireland, written in reply to the suggestion that Ireland should be exempted from the proposed duties on imported beaver skins. Rosseter claimed to have imported several thousand pounds' worth of rabbit skins from Ireland, and observed that the Irish hatters had an advantage over the English in cheaper rabbit's fur, labour and provisions, that they produced more hats than they needed, had imposed an import duty on foreign hats, and have " sent a great many hats to Portugal before any French hats were introduced there ". As in addition to this England paid a duty of 9d. per dozen skins on rabbit's fur from Ireland, Rosseter saw no reason why Ireland should be exempted from the duty. By the statute 4 George III, c. ix, no special terms were made for Ireland.

which is to encourage the hat trade in Great Britain : I have the honour to be with all due respect Sir

Your most obedient servant,

James Rosseter

P.S. In the debate about the money for the Bridge [1] when some gentlemen exulted at the spirit of the Common Council of London in the measures they have lately taken to oppose Administration I was sorry no notice was taken of the behaviour of the Minority in that Court, for addressing on the Peace was agitated, and strongly supported, though it could not be carried. And I am sure if the Committee had acquainted the Court with what Lord Bute said to the Town Clerk,[2] the King would not have been petitioned against the Cyder Bill, this they were aware off, and chose to conceal it. The question upon my motion to thank the Sheriffs after burning the North Briton was even upon a division and the Mayors casting vote gave the negative.[3] And the late question for thanking the City Members was opposed. Pray therefore don't let it be supposed the Corporation is unanimous in opposition, on the contrary the Ministry have many good friends in it, and if half a dozen noisy, inflammatory persons (who mislead many honest men) were not amongst us, I perswade myself the City would lend every aid, instead of endeavouring to clog the wheels of Government.

1. The debates on the City's petition for a grant to continue work on Black-friars Bridge came on in the House of Commons on March 16. As the Corporation had been a focus of opposition ever since the conclusion of peace, their demands were received with derision by some of the Government's supporters. Writing to Lord Hertford on March 18, Horace Walpole said of the City's petition : " It was refused, and into the accompt of contempt, Dr. Hay threw a good deal of abuse on the Common Council — a nest of hornets, that I do not see the prudence of attacking ". The question was raised again the next year when Grenville procured them a grant of £7000. See Walpole, *Memoirs*, ii, 61 ; and George Onslow to Newcastle, March 17, 1765, Add. MS. 32966, ff. 55-7.

2. Sir James Hodges, about whom see p. 70. On March 28, 1763, the City presented a petition to the House of Lords against the Cider Bill, and announced that if the Bill were not thrown out, they had another petition ready to present to the King. This so terrified Bute, who foresaw a recurrence of the Excise riots, that he is alleged to have sent word, first by Sir John Philips and then by Sir James Hodges, to the Common Council, that if they would drop their petition, he would undertake to have the Act repealed next session. When taxed with this in Parliament on March 30, he denied it, whereupon the City called a Court of Common Council to make enquiry whether Sir James Hodges " had not been too *officious* in his late conference with the Minister. . . . At this enquiry, which was upon oath, the above facts appeared to the entire satisfaction of all present ; which clearly showed who was the liar " (*History of the late Minority*, p. 115). See also Walpole, *Memoirs*, i, 200 seqq., and *Parliamentary History*, xv, 1309.

3. Cf. *Grenv. Pps.* ii, 237, and see p. 246 above.

THE EARL OF SANDWICH TO CHARLES JENKINSON
in Parliament Street

Add. MS. 38202, f. 191.

March 26, 1764.

Dear Sir,

The bearer of this, Mr. John Scott, is recommended by me to Mr. Grenville to be a Tidewaiter on the first vacancy, he has been the means of engaging a very material person at Cambridge in my favour, therefore let me beg of you to see him and to forward his business by every means in your power.

I am very sincerely yours,

Sandwich

FREDERICK STUART TO CHARLES JENKINSON
in Parliament Street, Westminster

Add. MS. 38469, f. 97.

Winton, March 27, 1764.

Dear Sir,

I received your kind letter last post, and am very glad to hear that you and your sister were well. I thank you very much for the franks you was so good as to send me, indeed they were very acceptable to me for this reason because I had promised a great many to my school fellows, and I was not then able to give it. We dined at Mrs. Jenkinsons the other day, she had had the rheumatism but was then much better. I must now conclude by desiring you to give my c⟨ompliments⟩ to Miss Jenkinson.

I am dear Sir, yours,

F. Stuart

SIR JOHN FIELDING TO CHARLES JENKINSON

Add. MS. 38202, f. 202.

Bow Street, March 28, 1764.

Sir John Fielding presents his respectful compliments to Mr. Jenkinson, and as Mr. Grenville's time must be extremely

(276)

ingrossed at this juncture, will not attempt to wait on him, but wishes that Mr. Jenkinson will be so obliging to obtain his leave to pay him his half years salary and favour him with a line when he may wait on him for that purpose.[1] Sir John Fielding will soon have an occasion to pay his respects to Mr. Grenville, and to acquaint him with the very good effects of the Horse Patrole he established this winter, and such has been the effects of his late spirit and resolution, that it is amazing as well as pleasing to see its happy influence amongst all orders and degress of people ; [2] if you think I irr in not going now to Downing Street, I am sure your friendship will set me right, I am

Your affectionate friend,

J. Fielding

MR. MORRIS TO CHARLES JENKINSON

in Parliament Street

Add. MS. 38202, f. 211.

Corbyn Morris, F.R.S., economist and Commissioner of Customs 1763–78, was " a gentleman well known in the literary world ". He wrote on problems of insurance and population. About him see D.N.B.

Peter How, Receiver-General for Cumberland, John Younger, and John Wilkinson were Whitehaven tobacco merchants (see their signatures to a " Petition of the Merchants of Whitehaven " on p. 107) who went bankrupt in December 1763, when the Crown, under a writ of immediate extent, seized some tobacco, the effect of Peter How, which was to be sold for the benefit of the creditors. How's assignees, John Gale, John Newthwaite, and Robert Wilkinson, applied to the Treasury to be invested in the Crown's rights to this tobacco, giving security that they would re-export it and pay off the Crown's debt. In December 1763 some of the creditors, headed by Anthony Bacon, applied first to have the assignment deferred and then to have the debt transferred to Sir James Lowther on similar terms. Lowther decided to accept the trust (see Robinson to Jenkinson, March 10, Add. MS. 38202, f. 149) for political motives, How's creditors being mostly Whitehaven merchants. The Treasury referred Bacon's petition to the Commissioners of Taxes, then to the Attorney- and Solicitor-General, and finally to the Board of Customs, who reported on April 9 that as the tobacco was perishing, it might be sold under a commission of Bankruptcy, but that if the assignees would consent to Sir James Lowther's being immediately invested in the Crown's rights, there would be no need to wait for a commission. The assignees, however, refused, and the case was brought up to the Court of Exchequer and finally

1. Fielding received £400 a year. Cf. Add. MS. 32862, f. 375.
2. See p. 234.

terminated in their favour on June 5.[1] The case is typical of local politics in the Lowther-Portland country. As soon as it became clear that Lowther would support the creditors, the Duke of Portland came forward to protect the assignees. Hence Lowther's fury when the case began to go against him. Every obstruction from the Treasury was attributed to Grenville's ill-will, though there is no evidence that Grenville favoured the assignees to spite him. Jenkinson afterwards wrote that he was employed by Grenville about this time to urge Bute to reason with his son-in-law, but whether it was over this case or over patronage disputes, he did not specify. In any case, Bute refused to interfere. See below, Jenkinson's " Memorandum on the Relations between Bute and Grenville ", p. 397.

Saturday Afternoon, Piccadilly.
Docketed " March 31, 1764 ".

Mr. Morris's compliments wait upon Mr. Jenkinson, and acquaints him, that the Petition of Mr. Bacon and other creditors of Mr. How, Younger, and Wilkinson, was this day read to the Board, being referred to them by an Order of the Treasury — praying that Sir James Lowther may be invested in the Crown's Right to the effects of these bankrupts, if he will please to accept the same, upon his giving security to pay the debt of the Crown, within two years, etc. But as it does not appear, that the assignees to the effects of these bankrupts agree to place Sir James Lowther in their right, nor, in case they shall doe so, that Sir James will accept the trust, the Board think it requisite to be previously informed of these two points, in an authentic manner, which Mr. M. is desired to suggest to Mr. Jenkinson.

Mr. Morris desires to wait upon Mr. Jenkinson either on Monday evening, or Tuesday morning, as either shall suit his pleasure, which he will be so good to signify.

CHARLES JENKINSON TO SIR JAMES LOWTHER

Add. MS. 38202, f. 218.

Parliament Street, April 4, 1764.

Mr. Jenkinson presents his compliments to Sir James Lowther ; he will transmit immediately Sir James's information

1. About this case see Add. MSS. 38337, ff. 264, 293, 294, and Treasury Minutes for December 15, 1763, January 30, April 9, and June 5, 1764, in P.R.O., T. 29/35. See also Namier, " Anthony Bacon ", in *Journal of Economic and Business History*, November 1929.

to the Commissioners of the Customs, directing them to take it into consideration and report what is fit to be done in consequence thereof; the Treasury cannot do more than this, till the Commissioners of the Customs have made their Report.

JOHN ROBINSON TO CHARLES JENKINSON

Add. MS. 38202, f. 269.

Wednesday Afternoon,[1] Past 4 o'Clock.
Docketed " April 1764 ".

Dear Sir,

I am extremely sorry to find that *particular people* at the board of Customs raise so many difficulties nay even seek about to find them against the request desired by Mr. Bacon's Memorial, which I am certain is not only founded on grounds of the utmost safety to the Revenue of the Crown, but realy of oeconomy and saving, as well as tenderness and humanity to the creditors of the poor unfortunate bankrupts. You will see this assertion is well founded by the inclosed Minute just now received which I could not omit a moments sending to you. Sir James goes out of town this afternoon but has desired me to speak very fully to you on this business, and some other things. You will hear from Mr. Morris, who I was with this morning and ⟨has⟩ been very civil on the occasion, further particulars, ⟨   ⟩ this last proceeding hath surprized Sir James very much after the account delivered to the Board this day by Mr. Morris, in answer to their first inquiries.

I realy feel more from the circumstances than I can express to you by letter, and my concern is heightened by the manner I find Sir James receives this treatment. Whenever it suits you I shall be glad to have the opportunity of waiting on you and I am dear Sir

Your most obedient humble servant,
J. Robinson

P.S. I am sure you will oblige Sir James by acquainting Mr. Grenville with the whole of this business and transaction.

1. Probably Wednesday, April 4. See preceding letter.

Thursday Morning [April 5 ?, 1764].

Mr. Robinson presents his compliments to Mr. Jenkinson. He hath just now received Mr. Jenkinson's note of last night. Sir James Lowther also received Mr. Jenkinson's note of yesterday afternoon with a copy of Mr. Jenkinson's letter to the Board of Customs just before he left town ; it is hoped that letter may have effect, but realy it is now become so serious a matter from the *opposition* raised to it *here*, and from the stories propagated about it, in the country, by the adherents of the Duke of Portland, who endeavour to cast great odium upon Sir James from not obtaining the Extent among the poor loosing creditors of the bankrupts, who in such a situation are apt to be influenced with every trifle that may prejudice the effects, that it is necessary something should be immediately done. The *gentlemen* here throw every difficulty in the way to retard the measure, and *their* friends in the country throw out that it is impossible Sir James can have seriously applied to put this business on an advantageous footing for the creditors for it is not *to be believed* that if he had, Mr. Grenville would have refused him such a request, a request not of favor, but in the common course of business and the usual lenity of the Crown and practised in many instances. Mr. Jenkinson may be assured these assertions have no little weight. Mr. Robinson therefore wished to see Mr. Jenkinson as early as possible, to have had something certain fixed, and he flatters himself, that if Mr. Jenkinson will inform Mr. Grenville of the whole of this transaction, Mr. Grenville will be pleased to send down orders to the Board that may be obeyed. Mr. Grenville told Sir James that he would send down orders to that Board to prevent the opposition he met with there about the little small places, and every day shews more and more the necessity of them, for it appears that in any thing where Sir James is concerned, not even the least indulgence will be shewn, but scarce the common course of business pursued. No little uneasiness also hath arose from nothing having been done about the other Memorial relating the Tobacco Duties desiring the same indulgence as the other ports have, and the merchants say that they will severally be obliged to bring actions against the Collector for their money due on Debentures, a step that Mr. Robinson wishes much to prevent as involving in much litigation and expence, and which might be very easily stopped. As Mr. Robinson can't have any time fixed for seeing Mr. Jenkinson before Saturday morning he must take the opportunity of speaking to Mr. Jenkinson at the House, and hopes then to know Mr. Grenville's resolution about this matter.

Mr. Robinson will then also mention the other business to Mr. Jenkinson, as Sir James desired Mr. Robinson would give him determinate answers about these things on his return.

JOSEPH SALVADOR TO CHARLES JENKINSON

in Parliament Street

Add. MS. 38202, f. 224.

The following letter is quoted by Miss L. Stuart Sutherland in her essay on "Lord Shelburne and East India Company Politics", in *E.H.R.*, July 1934, p. 452, as "particularly significant of the normal technique of Government intervention" in East India elections.

White Hart Court, April 8, 1764.

Dear Sir,

Our cause seems to me to promise success y⟨et⟩ not so strongly so as to be neglected. Our returns seem to foretell a majority yet we are not rightly acquainted with the state of your friends ; we have no advices from the Post Office, Custom House nor Excise. We now come near and should be able to determine our fate to a man, for on that knowledge may depend some essential measure. I am with great regard Sir

Your most obedient humble servant,

Joseph Salvador

BENJAMIN HALLOWELL JUNIOR TO CHARLES JENKINSON

Add. MS. 38202, f. 227.

Captain Benjamin Hallowell junior, son of Benjamin Hallowell of Boston, Massachusetts, and father of Admiral Sir Benjamin Hallowell Carew, about whom see *D.N.B.*, was Controller of Customs there in 1764. About 1770 he came to England without leave, and in 1771 was appointed one of the five Commissioners of the new American Board of Customs in succession to John Temple (see p. 230 and n. 1), who complained in a memorial to the Treasury, dated February 7, 1772, that " Mr. Hallowell (an inferior officer) had an allowance of a guinea a day for the most part of the time that he was in England, holding at the same time either the post of Comptroller at Boston or that of Collector at Piscataqua, and for some part of the time the emoluments of both ; besides an allowance from your Lordships of seventy odd pounds for his passage to and from Boston " (*The Bowdoin and Temple Papers*, Mass. Hist. Soc. Coll., 6th series, ix, 290). He died at York in Upper Canada in 1799, " The last surviving member of the late American Board of Customs ".

Suffolk Street, April 9, 1764.

Sir,

    Always having had an aversion to the illicit trade and being lately appointed Comptroller of his Majesty's Customs for the port of Boston I think it much my duty, to give every information in my power, where their is the least opening for that trade, and beg leave to inform you of a practice now carrying on in North America to evade paying his Majestys duties, by molasses being imported into the Colonies from the French and Dutch ports, by the way of Newfoundland ; in many parts of which there is no Custom house officer ; and where there is no officer they enter and clear with a Justice of the Peace who gives them a Certificate that admits them into any other port, this is a new method of carrying on the illicit trade. I am Sir,

    Your most obedient and very humble servant,

Benj Hallowell Jnr.

ANTHONY TODD TO CHARLES JENKINSON

Add. MS. 38202, f. 230.

General Post Office, April 9, 1764.

Dear Sir,

    Upon my return hither at 10 this evening, I received the note which you mentioned to me in the House, of two persons besides myself who have votes in the India House, but I am affraid there is a mistake in the names, as I know neither John Barker nor Richard Cotsford. We have one Clerk called William Cotsford who promised me his vote in favour of Lord Clive, and I shall certainly give mine for the same List, being

always happy in obeying your commands for I truly am dear
Sir

Your most obedient humble servant,

Anth. Todd

The East India elections took place on April 11 and resulted more or
less in a draw, for though Sulivan's party had a majority of 4 in the new
Direction, whose composition was 12 neutral, 8 for Sulivan and 4 for Clive,
yet when Sulivan was proposed for Chairman on April 12, the new Directors
voted equally pro and con, and Sulivan felt obliged to retire in favour of
Clive's friends Thomas Rous and Henry Crabb Boulton, who were elected
Chairman and Deputy Chairman respectively (Court Book 73). According
to the *Gentleman's Magazine*, Sulivan felt himself so much defeated that he
had to be restrained from selling out his stock so as to disqualify for a
Director.

The following letter refers to the Parliamentary management of Hastings.
Edward Milward had succeeded his father as Newcastle's election manager
for Hastings where he commanded a majority in the Corporation, but
when in February 1763 he found himself deprived of his surveyorship of
the riding officers for Kent, he remembered the vulnerability of his friends,
the freemen, sixteen of whom held places under the Government,[1] and
interceded with Bute to have them continued in their employments.
The request was granted, but Milward was " very uneasy being obliged
to act contrary to the opinion of my most worthy friend his Grace of Newcastle or stand the chance of losing my interest in Hastings (which I had
laboured to complete for many years at great expence) and subject my
friends to be ruined and support my interest against the Treasury at my
own expence and at the same time it did not appear to me to be in my
power to do his Grace any service for several years, as I had not a seat in
Parliament ".[2] In September 1763 he was frankly managing Hastings
for the Government,[3] while to Newcastle he kept up a pretence of serving
two masters. Newcastle was easily persuaded of his good faith and refused
to listen to the repeated allegations of W. H. Coppard,[4] but when in July
1764 Thomas Lamb, his faithful manager for Rye, informed him that
Milward had opposed his agency, Newcastle replied : " Nobody that has
given you any opposition in your affairs can be a friend of mine ".[5]

1. Their joint annual salary, including Milward's £250 a year, amounted to
£1580, and of the remaining 26 freemen " a good many were fathers, sons,
brothers, etc. to the men thus provided for " (Namier, *England etc.* p. 480).
2. Milward to William Michell, August 13, 1763, Add. MS. 32950, ff. 333-6.
Cf. Milward's letter to Newcastle of March 26, Add. MS. 32947, f. 325, quoted
in *England etc.* pp. 479-80.
3. See Add. MS. 38201, f. 125.
4. See his letters of April and December 1763 accusing Milward of treachery.
Add. MSS. 32948, f. 109, 33068, ff. 259, 269, 279.
5. Add. MS. 32960, f. 312.

Add. MS. 38304, f. 14.

April 11, 1764.

Sir,

I have had the favour of your letter of the 5th instant, I have shown it to Mr. Grenville who agrees with you that Mr. Thomas Evitt [1] is a very proper person to succeed you as Mayor. He approves also of your other sentiment with regard to the management of the borough. I had not forgot what I promised as to the £80 : 10s. The payment has only been prevented by the many other necessary occupations I have had of late, but you may depend upon it that it shall be paid into Mr. Hoares hands tomorrow morning. With respect to yourself I need say no more than that Mr. Grenville wants by no means inclination but only an opportunity to give you that credit among your friends and acquaintance you ought to have,

I am, etc.

C. Jenkinson

JOSEPH SALVADOR TO CHARLES JENKINSON
in Parliament Street

Add. MS. 38397, f. 77.

White Hart Court, April 12, 1764.

Dear Sir,

I see this perplexed affair in such a situation that if you could but be satisfied I should think it much for the Company's interest that a reconciliation for the present could be effected. If not contradicted in answer, I shall try the measure. I beg Mr. Grenville's orders and speedily for all must be settled by twelve o Clock. I am Sir,

Your most obedient humble servant,

Joseph Salvador

1. Thomas Evitt was Mayor of Hastings 1762-63, when Milward succeeded him. In March 1763 he recognised that Milward had "undeniably a clear majority of interest in this Corporation" and refused to back Newcastle against him. Add. MS. 32947, f. 323.

Docketed in Jenkinson's writing : "What am I to say in answer to this ? "

In another hand, unidentified : " Mr. G. has no objection to his Lordship doing just as is most agreeable to him ".

CHARLES JENKINSON TO JOSEPH SALVADOR

Add. MS. 38304, f. 14.

April 12, 1764.

Dear Sir,

I have shewed the letter I have just received from you to Mr. Grenville who bids me say that he shall have no objection to whatever is agreeable to Lord Clive and his friends.

I am etc.

C. Jenkinson

CHARLES JENKINSON TO SIR CHARLES TYNTE

Add. MS. 38304, f. 16.

Sir Charles Kemeys Tynte, 5th Bart. of Halswell, Somerset, was M.P., Tory, for Somersetshire 1747-74. He died in 1785, when the baronetcy became extinct.

April 21, 1764.

Mr. Jenkinson presents his compliments to Sir Charles Tynte, and acquaints him, that he has spoken by Mr. Grenville's order to Lord Clive in favor of Mr. Daniel ; Lord Clive informed him, that Mr. Sullivan had left so many officers upon their hands, that many of them could not go out with Commissions, but were to serve as Cadets only : that he would however speak to Mr. Rouse about it, and do all he could ; and that Mr. Jenkinson should hear further from him upon that subject.

JOSEPH SALVADOR TO CHARLES JENKINSON
in Parliament Street

Add. MS. 38202, f. 248.

The two months which elapsed between the East India elections on April 11 and Clive's departure for India on June 4, were spent in fierce wrangling with the Directors over the settlement of subordinate appointments and the eternal question of his jagghire. On April 19 Clive saw the Directors and proposed that the Company should allow him the quit-rents for ten years, promising to use his influence with Mir Jaffer to have them continued afterwards to the Company. He asked that John Spencer, second in council at Calcutta, should be sent back to Bombay, and outlined his ideas on military, commercial, and political reforms in Bengal. These he set down in a letter to the Directors on April 27, which was laid before the General Court on May 2. His main points were that the Nabob should be dependent on the Company, that the civil servants should forswear their private inland trade, and that a force of not less than 3000 troops should be kept in India with a reserve of 1000 more in England, ready to embark at a moment's notice. These points were rejected on a ballot by the General Court on May 17. Meanwhile on May 5 the Proprietors accepted Clive's terms for the jagghire by 583 votes to 396. Finally on May 25 the Directors granted Clive, and a committee of four, full powers until the restoration of peace, but recommended them to consult the Council at large whenever possible. Even so, eleven Directors, including Sulivan, voted against these extraordinary powers as unnecessary and dangerous. See Court Book 73. Clive wrote furiously to Grenville in May (the date is not given), that " the Directors, from timidity and want of capacity, refuse to give me those powers which they have already given and sent to Mr. Vansittart . . . and I am determined never to appear in India with less authority (when I ought if possible, to have much more) than my predecessor, Mr. Vansittart " (*Grenv. Pps.* ii, 310-11). How this difficulty was got over does not appear. On May 30 Clive took leave of the Directors.

Bath, April 22, 1764.

Dear Sir,

I delayed giving an answer to your favour of the 18th in hopes of seeing Mr. Grenville and receiving his commands on the present situation of affairs ; he being gone to my Lord Botetourt [1] it may be some days before I have the pleasure of seeing him and by my advices from London, I find there is no time to be lost. We are now come to the most difficult part of our task. Whatever my Lord Clive may tell you I foresee much difficulty in carrying his points. I therefore must beg your efficacious and speedy exertion for all depends on a nicety, and pray consider of some means either to secure success or bring about a reconciliation, for matters can never go on as they are.

I propose going up to attend the General Court and shall use my utmost endeavours to fix things on a solid basis for I

1. Norborne Berkeley, 4th Baron Botetourt. The barony had been in abeyance since 1406 ; this was terminated in his favour in 1763. He was a Gloucestershire magnate and Lord Lieutenant of the county. While staying with him Grenville received an angry letter from Bedford on the subject of Clive's appointment to the Order of the Bath. *Grenv. Pps.* ii, 501-2.

am apprehensive these disputes if not stopped will give the administration much trouble in future.

I am obliged to you for your kind wishes of my success in drinking the waters. They agree very well with me and my being taken from the use of them is very disagreeable to me. I am ever att your commands dear Sir,

Your most obedient humble servant,

Joseph Salvador

CHARLES LLOYD TO CHARLES JENKINSON

Add. MS. 38202, f. 251.

Bath, April 26, 1764.

My dear Sir,

I have no public intelligence of any sort to communicate to you except an invitation which will probably shine in the latest annals of this Kingdom, an *unanimous* invitation by the merchants and Corporation of Bristol to Mr. Grenville, to dine with them this day : this request he complies with, taking Bristol in his road from Lord Botetourt's hither. It is really amazing and no less diverting to see the shoals of letters dated from the metropolis, all with one consent denying Conway's being deprived of his *Regiment*,[1] a sign manual from you would not convince them I believe : I am sure whoever undertakes so hopeless a task, must have more confidence (and) more time to throw away than I have. Martin and Salvadore are here, the latter of whom returns to town on Monday next in order to be present at the next General Court for India affairs. I am dear Sir,

Your most sincere and faithful

C. Lloyd

1. On April 17 Conway was dismissed from his place of Groom of the Bedchamber and deprived of his regiment of dragoons for having voted in the minority when Government was hard pressed over General Warrants. This tampering with military commands for Parliamentary purposes was exceedingly unpopular and involved Grenville in complicated and disagreeable explanations. See his correspondence with Horace Walpole and Thomas Pitt, *Grenv. Pps.* ii, 320-27, 335-60 *passim*. See also Walpole, *Memoirs*, i, 320, and below, Jenkinson's Memorandum, p. 396 and n. 4.

Hastings, April 28, 1764.

Sir,

I take the liberty of acquainting you that agreeable to Mr. Grenville's commands, signifyed by your last favor, I called my friends the Jurats and freemen together the other night when Mr. Thomas Evitt was unanimously nominated for the succeeding Mayor which comes on the 13th May so there seems to be a total end of all opposition. I have the pleasure to inform you that we spent the evening very merrily, in drinking His Majesty's, Mr. Grenville's, your own, and many other loyal healths, and the whole concluded in a chearfull peaceable manner, and not only the Corporate Body, but the inhabitants in general are extremely pleased and satisfyed with the present measures. In order to shew a proper respect to the interest on this occasion, I believe it cost near £10, the particulars of which I shall lay before you when I come to town with my reason for so doing. In my last I took notice that several freemen had died in my Mayoralty and some others then dangerously ill, and that I had not replaced them, and I am pleased to find by yours in answer, that my management has been agreeable to Mr. Grenville. This morning James Bossom ⟨   ⟩ one of our Jurats who was Tide Surveyor and Commander of the Boat stationed here at £50 a year salary departed this life and I humbly beg leave to recomend Benjamin Stevens one other of our Jurats in his room which will be agreable to every body. As ours is not a port of trade or boarding I hope there is no occasion for the successor to Bossom to have any other instructions than usually given by the Surveyor General or Mr. Evitt our Collector of Customs, and Mr. Bossom never had any other instructions, as the business is only to command the Boat and act as all the other Boatmen do. I only mention this because I believe that Tide Surveyors in some ports of great trade have received regular instructions from London, but that never was the case here, neither is it in any respect necessary or usefull. I intreat the favor of you to present my humble duty to Mr. Grenville and believe me to be

A most faithfull and obedient servant,

Edwd. Milward

Add. MS. 38202, ff. 265-6.

Park Place, April 29, 1764.

Dear Sir,

The Mr. Hare mentioned in the inclosed note is a son of the late Bishop Hare.[1] Mr. Gee [2] is a gentleman of a considerable estate in Kent, and one always zealously attached to the Government. He is brother of Lady Isham, at whose request, and that of Sir Edmund's [3] her husband, I trouble you with the inclosed application to the Treasury, and desire your good offices in the affair.

Since I saw you at Mr. Grenville's I have been almost constantly confined to my chair by the stone. My journey into Lincolnshire is fixed for next Saturday, if I can bear a coach by that time. I shall endeavor if possible to embrace you before my departure. If not, I desire your acceptance of my hearty wishes for the increase of your prosperity. I will not now beg the continuance of your friendship, because your obliging repeated assurances have given me a right to claim it. I can indeed offer nothing in return which is worth your having for the reciprocal affection of a broken and useless implement of Administration can pretend to no value. I shall therefore shew a great opinion of the disinterestedness of yours, when I still ask favours of you.

One is that as I have failed in my endeavour to see my Lord Bute, to whom I have so many obligations, you will be so kind as to convey to his Lordship what I wished to have said myself, viz. that I shall always think of him with the most affectionate and truly grateful respect. The other, that you will take my poor nephew, whose disappointment of profiting by his Lordship's generous intention you know better than any body, into your protection, and endeavor with Mr. Grenville's favour to procure him, either some Custom House place to attend himself in the country, or some small thing

1. Francis, younger son of Francis Hare, Bishop of Chichester (died 1740), about whom see *D.N.B.* Francis Hare junior was one of the Council at Calcutta and died there in 1772. The note, Add. MS. 38202, f. 267, was a petition from Gee and Hare to the Treasury that Gee's son might be made their deputy as searcher at Gravesend for which place they owned a joint patent.

2. Richard Gee of Orpington in Kent, died 1791.

3. Sir Edmund Isham, 6th Bart. of Lamport, Northamptonshire, M.P. for the county 1737-72. He married as his second wife in 1751 Philippa, daughter of Richard Gee of Orpington.

here executable by deputy, which may remitt him £80 or £100 a year to feed his half starved numerous children. His name is *John Grant*, his direction *at the Whitehouse near Lostwithel in Cornwall*. If I take too much liberty in troubling you with his address, I shall not attone for it in adding my own, which is at *Sowerby near Brigg, Lincolnshire*.[1] But I cannot forget that I once had no need of an apology for such freedom, nor believe that you require it now of, my dear Jenkinson

Your very sincere friend, and humble servant,

E. Weston

John Grant of Whitehouse, Fowey, who died on April 8, 1767, was appointed Collector of Customs in the Isle of Man in June 1765. In December 1766 Weston made some enquiry about him to Jenkinson, who replied : " You have applied to the worst person in the world for the information you desire, for during the time I was secretary of the Treasury I interfered in the disposition of offices as little as possible, having been thoroughly tried with that branch of business while I acted as Secretary to Lord Bute. . . . I sent to Mr. Lloyd who did this business principally under Mr. Grenville " (Add. MS. 38305, f. 23). Apparently Grant's warrant " was made out by mistake in the name of James instead of John Grant, your nephew, as it was done just when we was leaving the Office and every thing was in hurry and confusion " (*ibid.* f. 23 b).

GEORGE GRENVILLE TO CHARLES JENKINSON

Add. MS. 38191, f. 80.

Bath, April 29, 1764.

Dear Jenkinson,

I write these few lines by Mr. Salvador who sends me word that he is to set out for London this evening, and that great opposition is threatened to Lord Clive at the General Court. I need not tell you how much I wish Lord Clive's success in every thing that is reasonable, and therefore desire you will inform such of our friends as are likely to attend to my recommendation, that I shall be obliged to them for any assistance which they can properly give to Lord Clive upon this occasion ; and that you will tell him that you have done

1. See a letter from Weston to Grenville, July 25, 1763, asking for a pension, as " the daily threatenings of the stone, with the increase of my other infirmities, which must and will very soon put an end to my political life, will, without doubt shorten the natural one too " (*Grenv. Pps.* ii, 80).

so, and that whatever the event may be (though I flatter myself that there is no likelyhood of its not being successfull) yet I hope he will take no definite step upon it but in concert with his friends. You will have heard from Mr. Charles Lloyd that as I propose to settle my boys at Eton in my way to London, and as the school does not meet till Wednesday, I shall defer my journey one day, and not be in town till that evening instead of Tuesday, as I at first proposed. I forgot to tell you in my last, that I entirely approve of your doing all you can to prevent any inconvenience, from what Mr. Long mentioned, to our trade with the Spaniards in America, and that I will talk to you upon that subject as soon as we meet. I have been most obligingly and kindly invited by the Mayor and Corporation and the Incorporated Society of Merchants at Bristol and have dined there, where I was as well received and every thing passed as well as was possible. I am always, dear Jenkinson, most faithfully and affectionately

Yours etc.

George Grenville

CHARLES JENKINSON TO GEORGE GRENVILLE[1]

London, May 1, 1764.

Dear Sir,
    I have this day had the honour of your kind letter of the 20th[2] ultimo. I have solicited such of our friends who are proprietors of East India Stock, in the manner you have desired, and I have acquainted Lord Clive of the directions you have given in this respect. I have tried to see his Lordship, that I might mention to him the advice you give him, that he should take no definitive step but in concert with his friends. I have not yet been able to see him, and I think it more prudent not to write it, lest it should be supposed to imply more than was intended.
    The enclosed note from Monsieur de Marmora[3] came to day, desiring that I would open it, if you was not in town ; I have done what is desired in it with respect to Monsieur

---

1. Printed in *Grenv. Pps.* ii, 309-10.
2. Almost certainly a mistake for the 29th. There is no letter of April 20 from Grenville in the Liverpool MSS.
3. Sardinian Envoy in London.

de la Perrier's [1] baggage, and I sent word that you would not be returned 'till tomorrow evening.

There is no news but what is lately arrived from the East Indies ; I know no more of that than what I read in the public papers ; it is affirmed that Monson has been defeated by one whom we have learnt the art of war, when he commanded the sepoys in our service, but who is now become a Prince of the country and turned against us.

Lord Clive's friends think that this event will be of use to them at the General Court tomorrow, as it makes Lord Clive's presence more necessary in India.

I rejoice to hear of the kind and polite reception you met with at Bristol. It will have a good effect ; the fame of it has reached here already.

                                         I have etc.

                                              C. Jenkinson

I hope that Colonel Draper [2] called on you at the Bath, and made suitable apologies. He assured Mr. Drummond that he would do so, and that he was in perfect good humour.

CHARLES JENKINSON TO EDWARD MILWARD

Add. MS. 38304, f. 20.

                                         May 4, 1764.

Sir,
    I have had the favour of your letter ; I am extremely glad to hear you have had so little trouble in the choice of your Mayor and that there appears to be an end of all opposition at Hastings. I do assure you that there is very little to fear from them anywhere. When you come to town, I shall be glad to see you and beg you would bring your account with you. Mr. Grenville has ordered Benjamin Stephens to be appointed tidesurveyor etc. in the room of Bossom.[3] I will

1. Baron de la Perrière, a son of Count Viry, succeeded La Marmora as Sardinian Envoy in London in 1766. In 1761 he married Thomas Gray's friend, Henrietta Speed, and a son of his afterwards sat in Parliament (1790–96) as Henry Speed. About him see Namier, *England etc.* p. 93 n.

2. Lieutenant-General William Draper (1721–87), the conqueror of Manila, for whom Bedford had obtained a promise of the K.B., which was given to Clive. He was very angry and wrote to Bedford from Clifton on April 28, 1764, " Whenever I am employed again, I will be a most dirty dog, rob and pillage wherever I can, deserve to be hanged, and then carry every point for myself and my associates " (*Bedford Corr.* iii, 262). See also *Grenv. Pps.* ii, 301-7, 501-2.

3. See p. 288.

endeavour to save him as much trouble as possible with respect to his instructions and everything shall be done that can be consistently with the established rules of the customs.

I am etc.

C. Jenkinson

HENRY KENNAN TO GEORGE GRENVILLE

Add. MS. 38202, f. 278.

Golden Ball, May's Buildings,
May 7, 1764.

Sir,

I had the honor some months ago, jointly with Mr. Reid to wait upon you with proposals for victualling His Majesty's troops at Augustine. You apprehended that a Contract was not necessary at that time, General Amherst having supplied the garrison with a quantity of provisions.

Being however now assured that a Contract will be made for both the Florida's, I again beg the liberty to offer my services for that purpose. Mr. Reid declines the engagement, but Mr. Witter Cummings informs me that he expects to be the Contractor : Mr. Cummings proposes to supply with salt provisions.[1] Permit me Sir, to observe to you, that in a country where it is practicable to supply the troops with fresh provisions, at least eight months in the year, without any additional expence to Government, the choice will undoubtedly be for the fresh provisions ; especially in a climate where it may be of such importance to the health of the garrison, and consequently to the service.

I do not hereby mean to supplant Mr. Cummings in obtaining a Contract, but as he must necessarily have some person joined with him who will reside upon the spot, if it be intended to supply fresh provisions, I should be glad, if you, Sir, approve of it, to be that person, being convinced there is no one now in Britain better knows how such a Contract must be conducted in those Colonies.

Permit me farther to say, that as I propose to settle a plantation in East Florida, I can be very instrumental in

1. See Treasury Minutes for May 17, 1764 (T. 29/35, f. 394). Witter Cummins proposed to victual the troops in East Florida at 4½d. per man a day and to remit at 2 per cent and the Treasury contracted with him and his partner, Mason, on these terms. See *ibid.* f. 451.

(293)

promoting, what I am well assured you have greatly at heart, the establishment of that Colony. I have the honor to be Sir, Your most obedient humble servant,

Henry Kennan

JOHN ROBINSON TO CHARLES JENKINSON

Add. MS. 38202, f. 316.

Tuesday morning, 3/4 past 11 o'Clock.
[May 8, 1764.]

Mr. Robinson is much obliged to Mr. Jenkinson for his notes of yesterday and to day. He had not the least doubt of Mr. Jenkinson's attention to the things Mr. Robinson mentioned to him from Sir James, but thought it could not be amiss Mr. Grenville should be acquainted with the necessity of an immediate appointment of Mr. Lutwidge [1] from the circumstances which required a survey, and therefore took the liberty to trouble Mr. Jenkinson with the note of yesterday. Mr. Robinson is extremely glad to find this morning that Mr. Grenville hath been so obliging as to appoint Mr. Lutwidge, and will immediately send to Mr. Lutwidge, that he may give his securities to the Custom House, resign his former Warrant and get out of town on his survey. Mr. Robinson hopes that Mr. Jenkinson will be so good as minute the appointment to be within Whitehaven in the port of Carlisle, the two places being now again consolidated. Mr. Robinson did give Mr. Jenkinson a memorandum of that before. Mr. Robinson will acquaint Sir James with this and Mr. Jenkinson's note relating the Surveyor General of Barbadoes as soon as ever he sees Sir James this morning and endeavour to get Sir James to fix a time for his waiting on Mr. Grenville as soon as he thinks he can be able, which Mr. Robinson hopes will be in a few days as Sir James recovers apace now.

1. Charles Lutwidge of Whitehaven, a Cumberland J.P., was an authority on the Isle of Man and on the smuggling trade on the West coast. He supplied the Treasury with information which was used when Grenville's Government bought the island from the Duke of Athol in 1765. See below, p. 315, and Add. MSS. 38462, which are papers on the Isle of Man including several reports from Lutwidge. On May 9, 1764, Jenkinson replied to Robinson's letter, saying that Grenville had appointed Lutwidge Surveyor-General and Supervisor of the Customs for the coasts of Cumberland and Westmorland and the Port of Lancaster, " as Sir James Lowther desired " (Add. MS. 38304, f. 18).

Add. MS. 38202, ff. 292-3.

Charles Street, May 12, 1764.

Dear Sir,

As you have been before acquainted with most of the particulars of the extraordinary behaviour that hath passed in the business of the Whitehaven Extents, I will not trouble you with laying the whole before you, but I hope you will approve my sending the inclosed papers which crowns all, and shews clearly for what intent the whole delay hath been made and the neglect to comply with the orders of the Board of Treasury. Sir James Lowther thinks he hath been extremely ill used, and desires me to say, that after such treatment he can only leave it to the Board of Treasury to support their own order, or concurr in the ill usage he hath received as they shall think proper, or to distress the tobacco trade of the town of Whitehaven, and no inconsiderable branch it was, though too much depressed at present, for to gratify the malice of two or three assignees and not above ten creditors, and banish that branch of the manufactory of tobacco out of the Kingdom, against the unanimous voice and application of above nine parts out of ten of the creditors in value and thirteen to one in number. He desires however that as you and Mr. Whateley together know every circumstance almost of this affair, since the orders of the Treasury were given you will take the trouble to lay the whole before Mr. Grenville, that whatever consequences arise from it, he may not be unacquainted with the affair ; and I assure you Sir James resents the treatment so much that though he is still ready to undertake the disagreeable task for the benefit of the creditors, and to oblige them, desirous as they are for it, yet he will not stir one step further to obtain it, finding his wishes and efforts have no effect, but leaves it entirely to Mr. Grenville and the Treasury Board.[1]

Is it not most strange, or can it be conceived, that the Officers of the Crown disobey the orders of the Crown in a thing both beneficial to the Revenue and equitable, and that

1. The case was eventually terminated in favour of the assignees, *i.e.* against Lowther. Petitions from both sides were read at the Treasury Board on May 23 and referred to the Court of Exchequer, and on June 5 Litchfield, the Solicitor to the Crown, reported that the assignees had paid the Crown's debt on Saturday last and were consequently to be invested with its rights to the effects (T. 29/35, ff. 402, 430).

Mr. Litchfield the Solicitor of the Crown, whose behaviour hath been very extraordinary in this business, should be the very man who is to find out means to delay and evade those orders of the Crown. But is it not more amazingly strange that to have the orders of Administration complied with you must court Opposition, and that Opposition can have an influence at a Board of the Revenue that friends to Government cannot, and this I fear in this case is too true. Surely there wants some what to rectify these things, which in the end must distress Government. I ask your pardon for being so prolix, but realy this seems some how so unaccountable to me that I have run on without intending it. I am dear Sir,

Your most obedient and faithful humble servant
J. Robinson

JAMES MARRIOTT TO CHARLES JENKINSON

Add. MS. 38202, ff. 299-300.

In May 1764 James Marriott (about whom see p. 110), after a temporary breach with Newcastle, was working in Hardwicke's interest at Cambridge, when the death, on May 20, of Sir Edward Simpson, M.P. for Dover, Dean of the Arches, etc. etc. (see *D.N.B.*), made a vacancy of King's Advocate and of the Mastership of Trinity Hall. On May 22 Newcastle, who knew that Marriott was a candidate for the Mastership, asked him notwithstanding to give his vote and interest to Peter Calvert, a man to whom Newcastle had fewer obligations than to Marriott, but who had two brothers in Parliament. Deeply hurt, Marriott told John Roberts he meant to leave no stone unturned that might procure him success in his canvass for the Mastership of Trinity Hall (Add. MS. 32959, ff. 34, 29). See D. A. Winstanley, *Cambridge in the Eighteenth Century*, pp. 283-4. Marriott had already applied on May 18 to the Administration for one of the places likely to be vacated by Simpson's death (see the following letter), and the quarrel with Newcastle doubtless decided him to connect himself with Sandwich, both politically and at Cambridge, where Sandwich supported him in his campaign for the Mastership. At the same time he disingenuously wrote to Charles Yorke on May 22, asking him for the Vicar-Generalship, one of Simpson's places in the gift of the Archbishop of Canterbury, who " may be pleased to leave that post to the recommendation of your family. . . . If such a thing takes place permit me in soliciting this office the honour of ranking myself under yours and your family's patronage, which I shall be proud to merit upon every occasion " (Add. MS. 35636, f. 461).

Doctors Commons, May 18, 1764.

Sir,

Your very friendly attentions always on my behalf demand from me the utmost gratitude and confidence, and I hope the same good nature and unmerited dispositions will grant me an excuse for the liberty I now take.

Sir Edward Simpson, whose health has been declining for several years is now thought to be in the utmost weakness and danger, and I imagine that Dr. Hay's [1] late exertions in Parliament must recommend him as a successor to the present Judge of the Arches and Prerogative, notwithstanding that I have been told, the Archbishop is rather averse to him.[2] But if instead of Dr. Hay Dr. Bettesworth [3] should be preferred to the Chair, the post of Advocate to the Admiralty will be vacant, and so it will be in case he succeeds Dr. Hay as Advocate to his Majesty.

I should have esteemed myself fortunate if a precedent could have been made *without inconvenience* in compliment to her Majesty by creating such a titular post for me (and indeed for the encouragement of this declining profession) as the Queen's Advocate ; and I fear it little becomes me to entertain the least hope now of following Dr. Hay as the King's Advocate although my zeal for his Majesty's service and a disposition to take pains might compensate for the great disparity of experience and abilities ; and although I believe the Earl of Mansfield would be so kind as to give me a character, if I were permitted to aspire to so honourable a title.

Whether the Vicar Generalship will be judged proper to be resigned by Dr. Hay I cannot guess. In this train of things however I hope I have an equal claim with Dr. Bettesworth or any other gentleman of this profession. Having had the honour to combat by your side and follow you *non passibus aequis* in the cause of our country against the Dutch, I shall rely much on your kind recommendation of that effort, of which you best understood the utility in the distress of Government, unnoticed and unrewarded by former ministers in a former reign.[4]

1. George Hay, M.P. for Sandwich 1761–68, Newcastle-under-Lyme 1768–78, knighted 1773, King's Advocate and a Lord of the Admiralty. In 1764 he succeeded Simpson as Dean of the Arches and Judge of the Prerogative Court and became Chancellor of the Diocese of London. See *D.N.B.*

2. The Dean of the Arches was in the gift of the Archbishop of Canterbury who had promised it to Newcastle. Secker and Newcastle both disliked Hay, but Charles Yorke was so importunate with Newcastle in Hay's behalf that Newcastle was afraid to disoblige him. See Add. MSS. 32959 *passim*.

3. John Bettesworth, Advocate to the Admiralty ; afterwards Chancellor of London. See *D.N.B.*

4. In 1758, the year in which Jenkinson published his *Discourse on the Conduct of Great Britain in respect to Neutral Nations*, Marriott published *The Case of the Dutch Ships Considered*, of which Jenkinson wrote to Grenville on December 26, 1758: " It is written in a dry, unentertaining manner, but it contains many good

I shall leave it to the fiercest enemies of the Earl of Bute to say whether my *Political Considerations,* the winter before last, which were unanswered, by the moderation and irony of that piece, did not more effectually hurt their cause than any other attacks which were violent. Mr. Roberts [1] complained to me heavily of it, as of a thing that ⟨had⟩ been felt very prejudicial to the Duke of Newcastle and was more regretted by him than any thing of *that sort* he had ever met with in his life. His Grace himself, who has been no stranger to my being the author of it, has applyed to me since in the most flattering and almost supplicating terms, begging " *that we may be friends* " " *that we may be always together* " " *that I may depend* on his gratitude etc., etc.*" He wants me to engage with him *envers et contre tous* : and I have been strongly prest to do for him and his part what a little habit of writing might enable a man capable of being independent, to do. [2]

But I can not easily reconcile such engagements with my determination to conduct myself as a man submissive to Government although I am at liberty, for any thing I wrote, before the Preliminaries appeared, to make objections (if I thought there were any) to the particular parts of the system since pursued. The only thing relative to myself which has

materials ; has hit off several new topics of argument, and has a good deal of merit " (*Grenv. Pps.* i, 284). Marriott was envious of Jenkinson's success, and in 1762 his sense of injury induced him to write his *Political Considerations,* in the hope that " Justice will be done me too in my turn by the persons who have promoted him " (Add. MS. 32921, f. 281). See also Add. MS. 32919, f. 342.

1. John Roberts, M.P. for Harwich 1761–72, Commissioner of Trade 1761–62, 1766–72, Newcastle's election agent, about whom see Namier, *Structure of Politics, passim.* On May 25, 1764, he wrote to Newcastle about Marriott : " I despised him for being a dupe of those apostates from you, who had prevailed upon him to father a pamphlet against you which I was sure he was not the author of, and I told him last summer when he came to bath at Harwich, that I thought he had acted ungratefully. That conversation produced his conversion and the offer I made from him to your Grace " (Add. MS. 32959, f. 79). The offer was probably to act as Newcastle's private secretary if Newcastle would bring him into Parliament. See n. 2, below, and Add. MS. 32916, f. 352.

2. The Newcastle MSS. tell a different story. On August 6, 1762, some months before the publication of his *Political Considerations,* Marriott applied to Newcastle for a reversion of Shallet Turner's chair of Modern History and also of a professorship of Law at Cambridge (Add. MS. 32941, f. 175). On September 10 he was surprised not to have received them, and hinted at overtures from " powerful friends of very different attachments ". He also hinted that if he had a seat in Parliament he could send Newcastle " constantly full abstracts of all that passed " (Add. MS. 32942, f. 217). Marriott's pamphlet against Newcastle appeared towards the end of 1762, but during the following summer John Roberts convinced him that Newcastle had really meant to bring him into Parliament with an " establishment ", and on November 8, 1763, Marriott wrote Newcastle an abject apology for his past infidelities (Add. MS. 32952, f. 298). See also Roberts's covering letter, *ibid.* f. 397. After this " conversion " Marriott worked consistently for Hardwicke's election as High Steward, at the same time as he was applying to Sandwich for his patronage. See below.

given me concern is that I have been informed that the little merit of the *Political Considerations* was taken from me, and that this occasioned my being in some degree overlooked by the Earl of Bute : although every line was written and conceived by myself unassisted and alone ; and flowing from a heart zealous for his Lordship's character and his Majesty's service. I can not help expressing that I feel the injury. I have some reason to be suspicious that a Right Reverend prelate [1] has done himself service at my expence, and as I well know the busy intercourse he had with the Earl of Bute through Mr. Mackenzie, I am much inclined to ask an eclaircisement of Mr. Mackenzie : but I would not willingly do it, without consulting yourself.

In pursuing the objects I mentioned, I hope it will be no prejudice to me, that as I gave my vote to Mr. Conyers in Essex,[2] so at Cambridge I gave it to the Earl of Hardwick on a *private family account*, with whose brothers I was intimate at the University, and not being personally applyed to by the Earl of Sandwich otherwise than by general letter and by no one great person in his behalf.

I was by no means active in that affair.[3] And ever since the Earl of Bute's resignation I have spent most of the intervals between the terms at my house at Twinsted Hall near Sudbury in great retirement intending to be out of the way of faction as much as possible, and to give no offence or even suspicion. I hope both you and his Lordship will approve of my conduct : and you will do me the favour to communicate to him this letter or not as you shall judge proper. In this and all other cases I request the honour of your friendship and submit my fame and interests to your kind care, which I shall be proud to merit. I am, Sir, with the most perfect respect and consideration possible,

Your obliged and obedient humble servant,
James Marriott

Sandwich supported Marriott for the place of King's Advocate, as well as for the Mastership of Trinity Hall. On June 30 Sandwich wrote to Grenville : " I prevented his being in question for it while it was likely to be sought after by anyone of consequence in the profession ; but as it now absolutely goes a-begging, I cannot help wishing you would give him your

1. Marriott probably refers to John Douglas, Lord Bath's hack writer, the author of *Seasonable Hints from an Honest Man*. He was a Canon of Windsor. See *D.N.B.*
2. See p. 163.
3. But see his letters to Newcastle, Add. MSS. 32955, f. 134 ; 32956, ff. 263, 354.

support ". Sandwich, though doubtless aware that Marriott had supported Hardwicke more actively than he professed, wrote of the other candidate for the Advocacy that his " demerits in our late Cambridge contests are so great that it would be absolute destruction to our cause if it was given to him " (*Grenv. Pps.* ii, 371). Marriott succeeded Hay as King's Advocate in 1764, and afterwards as Judge of the Admiralty when Hay committed suicide in 1778.

JAMES MARRIOTT TO CHARLES JENKINSON

Add. MS. 38202, ff. 305-6.

Doctors Commons, May 27, 1764.
Sunday Morning.

Dear Sir,

I was yesterday with Lord Sandwich near three hours. I spoke to him as I did to you, and I think we perfectly understand each other.[1] I am to remain without declaring myself : which will puzzle the Cabal in my profession, and *the less I am talked of the better*. I should like however, that whatever is done in regard to myself should not be the work only of Lord Sandwich, for Lord Halifax [2] and Mr. Grenville are men with whom it is a honour to be connected : and their support I look upon as a most solid guarantee of our reciprocal engagements which have a vast extent in my profession and the university, in their consequences, I hope for the King and the general service. I make it two rules to act as much as possible in concert with my friends, that we may move all together, and another that I may create no jealousies or difficulties by making my lines in life not intersect with theirs. There is more danger than ever of the Duke of Newcastle's possessing himself of the devolution at Trinity Hall : from an unlucky pique between two men who used to be inseparable, and it will depend on my good offices to reunite them : which is likely to be very difficult : as one is to blame, the pique arising from

1. Cf. Sandwich to Grenville, June 30, 1764 : " I hope his late behaviour and assurances for the time to come will incline you to think he deserves the preference on this occasion " (*Grenv. Pps.* ii, 371). In spite of his new engagements to the ministry, Marriott remained in correspondence with Newcastle, who was so little aware of his duplicity, or so indifferent to it, that he offered to bring him into Parliament for Sudbury in November 1765. Marriott refused, thinking himself safer with Bute (Marriott to Bute, November 3, 1765. Bute MSS.).
2. Cf. Sandwich to Grenville, July 6, 1764 : " Lord Halifax and I were with Lord Chancellor the night before last. He is in perfect good humour and I think will recommend Dr. Marriott to be the King's Advocate " (*Grenv. Pps.* ii, p. 346. The letter is dated June 6, but, on internal evidence, should be placed in July).

the inferior and the obliged party not first paying the compliment to the superior, before he urged for himself as principal candidate.[1] I am dear Sir, most truly

Your very much obliged and obedient humble servant,

James Marriott

P.S. As the less I appear in the affair, and the D. of N⟨ewcastle⟩ and the Cabal have hopes of me, so I wish that my conference with Mr. Grenville and Lord Halifax may be not public : because the moment the alarm is given that I confer with your friends, the Cabal at the Commons [2] will know where to make an attack and draw off a man from the 7. I am to confer with Lord Mansfield tonight. I wish I knew how far I might venture to open to him, and also what use may be made of Lord Hilsboro whose Lady [3] is my friend, as is Lady Charlotte Finch.[4]

At Mrs. Sayers [5] in Southampton Street Bloomsbury, 2 doors on the left hand side from the Linnen Drapers Holborn.

JOHN BINDLEY TO CHARLES JENKINSON

Add. MS. 38202, f. 340.

West Hatch, Fryday Evening.
Docketed " June 13, 1764 ".

Dear Sir,
    I could not receive the account you give me of your sister without assuring you that she has my wife's and my best

1. Of the 12 Fellows of Trinity Hall at least 5 were candidates for the Mastership, though all except Peter Calvert were determined not to let the election devolve on the Chancellor. When Calvert's hopes began to fade, Newcastle supported William Wynne, while Sandwich supported first William Ridlington and then Marriott. Mathew Robinson seems not to have counted on outside support, and Mr. Winstanley is of opinion that Sandwich's interference had little influence on the result. Marriott was elected on June 13 by the last-minute defection of Stanhope Pedley who wanted to prevent a devolution. See Winstanley, *Cambridge in the Eighteenth Century*, p. 295. Mathew Robinson and Ridlington were probably the friends whom Marriott had to reconcile. Ridlington, the junior Fellow, stood forward at the beginning of the campaign as Sandwich's protégé, and Robinson refused to vote for him because he was in orders. The Fellows of Trinity Hall were mostly lawyers of independent means, inclined to look down on the two " Professors " in the society.

2. Doctors' Commons.

3. Lord Hillsborough married on March 1, 1747/48, Margaretta, daughter of Robert Fitzgerald, 19th Earl of Kildare, and sister of James, 1st Duke of Leinster.

4. Charlotte, daughter of Daniel, 8th Earl of Winchelsea.

5. Marriott was the son of an attorney in Hatton Gardens " whose widow married a Mr. Sayer, a name well known in the law ". Her husband was possibly Everard Sayer, Proctor for the Admiralty, who died in 1745.

wishes for her happiness, and we hope the change of her name
and condition will not deprive us of the happiness of her
acquaintance.[1] She will not think we flatter her to tell her
that from Mrs. Bindley's and my first seeing, we conceived a
very great esteem and opinion of Miss Jenkinson. We should
be very sorry to loose so very agreeable an acquaintance.
When matters are all over, therefore you must see that my
wife and your sister ⟨are⟩ brought together at mine or your
cottage.

My friend Townshend is in perfect health. He is at
Adderbury. His letter of today says *I am a free man bound to
no party or system* : etc. etc. I hope therefore, dear Sir, Government will find some means to engage and employ his talents.[2]
I know you love him and I am sure you have always wished
it. I want very much to see you, and if you will give me a line
to the Office mentioning what mornings you are in town and
the time, I will endeavour to step from the office and call
upon you. I propose going to Adderbury in a few days and
for a few days, for it is so long since I have seen my friend, that
I am quite impatient. I want to know his hopes, his fears and
his plan. I hear on all sides that Minority is much displeased
with its leaders. He is abused ; Mr. Pitt is abused, C. York
is abused, and they tell me they all abuse one another, though
the town has put a fresh compliment of Mr. Pitt's to Mr.
Townshend on foot ; perhaps the town made it and not
Mr. P.

You cannot think how much I have improved West Hatch.
I am glad for your health's sake that you have got a place out
of town,[3] but I am sorry for my own, because otherwise I
might have hoped to have possessed you here now and then ;

1. Elizabeth Jenkinson married her cousin Charles Wolfran Cornwall, afterwards Speaker of the House of Commons, on August 17, 1764.
2. Since his *faux pas* over the Admiralty in August 1763, Charles Townshend
was out of office, though constantly manœuvring to return. In January 1764 he
made overtures through Bindley to Halifax and Grenville, of which Grenville was
first informed by the King. On January 11 Halifax repeated the message to
Grenville, and in the evening Jenkinson told Grenville that Bindley had brought an
express message from Townshend saying he should like to act with Grenville and
Halifax, though " he did not like the rest of the Administration ", and apologising
for his attacks on Grenville in the last session (Grenville's diary, *Grenv. Pps.* ii,
482). In spite of their imminent peril over General Warrants, the Administration
did nothing for Townshend in January 1764. These overtures in June are not
mentioned in the *Grenville Papers*, but in November Townshend was again
soliciting through Bindley. See Jenkinson to Grenville, November 20 (*ibid.* ii,
465) : " With respect to himself, Mr. Townshend said that the Pay Office, and
being a Cabinet Councillor (which he was, he said, before) would satisfy him ".
He had to wait for this place until May 1765, when he succeeded Lord Holland.
3. Jenkinson had bought a house at North End.

where I am always, always at home, and almost always alone. After the hurry of Paris we enjoy our own fields with greater *goût*. I am dear Sir, ever

Your faithful and obliged humble servant,

John Bindley

P.S. You will remember Mondays and Saturdays I do not attend the office.

CHARLES JENKINSON TO MR. WOLTERS

Add. MS. 38304, f. 28.

June 15, 1764.

Dear Sir,

I have had the favor of your letter of the 8th instant. I will represent to Mr. Grenville what Sir J. Yorke and you desire in favor of Madame Gentil ; [1] that an addition may be made to her pension so that she may receive a 100 clear of all taxes and deductions, though I own I despair of success as a precedent of this kind would lay upon the King too many other claims of the same nature and would bring the publick taxes as far as they now affect those who live by His Majesty's bounty upon the civil list revenues which are in too bad a condition at present to be able to bear any new burthens. I am obliged to you for the information you sent me of the number of persons who are going from Rotterdam to Pensilvania : [2] I agree with you in opinion that it would be more for the publick benefit that they should be induced to go to any other colonies particularly those to the southward, and I have taken care that the method you recommend for that purpose should be carried into execution. I want to know whether there have been any Collections published of the proceedings and representations of the Parliaments of France with respect to their taxes or money affairs. If any such Collection has been published I should be obliged to you if you would send it me, as I should like to see all that has passed on that subject in one view.

I am etc.,

C. Jenkinson

1. See p. 221.
2. German emigration to Pennsylvania had continued intermittently since the end of the Thirty Years' War. See J. T. Adams, *The Epic of America*, p. 64.

CHARLES LLOYD TO CHARLES JENKINSON

Add. MS. 38469, f. 103.

Wotton, June 30, 1764.

My dear Sir,

Perhaps you will imagine me so much of a rural esquire, as to be smelling of haycocks, looking at a hive of bees, or some such simple divertisement, and will expect my letter to be dated from the Barn Door, the Oat Hills, or the Octagon Seat at the End of the Lake. But I assure you I am as much in town as you are at No Man's Land, I mean as to thoughts ideas speculations contemplations and the like. You are not so barbarous as to expect news, I mean so easily pleased as to listen to the account of the untimely death of a Muscovite duck, or the languishing decay of a Newfoundland goose, for of these interesting particulars must my journal be composed. If you write any thing for my private ear make use of some other frank for yesterday on my coming hither Mr. G⟨renville⟩ put my letter into your [sic] hands desiring at the same time I would read it and expecting, I found, to be acquainted with the contents. If you think proper I should be much obliged for a *speedy* hint on my subject as to the place offer'd to Paterson, aiming at something being done upon this specifick occasion for me by an arrangement as to Mauduit or any one else.[1]

The weather was so very bad that I thought it was better to go to Oxford than to walk dripping under the trees at Stow. Barrington [2] desires to be remember'd to you. The sooner you write to Mr. G. — probably the more effectual.

Sunday Morning.

Surely these are the regions of sleep and repose not of action. For my own part I neither hope nor fear, contrive nor design any thing that relates to this mortal life but am as much at rest as the people that are sleeping in their sepulchres. I am in some doubt whether I belong to the Society of the Living or the Dead and am ready to ask myself ' Is this existence real or a dream ? ' If you mean to do a very acceptable thing you must dispatch a messenger if it were but to let us know what it

1. Paterson is unidentified. Israel Mauduit was Customer of Southampton and Lloyd was Receiver-General for Gibraltar, and Paymaster of the Band of Pensioners.
2. Shute Barrington.

is o'clock by St. Paul's. I have been twice asked today by Madam whether it is likely you would send one. Adieu.

Yours most faithfully,

C. L.

Be so good as to forward the letters under cover to you to their respective destinations.

On July 2, 1764, Jenkinson wrote to Grenville : " In the last session of Parliament you assigned as a reason for not going on with the Stamp Act, that you waited only for further information on that subject. This having been said, should not Government appear to take some step for that purpose ? I mentioned this to you soon after the Parliament was up. I remember your objections to it ; but I think the information may be procured in a manner to obviate those objections, and without it we may perhaps be accused of neglect " (*Grenv. Pps.* ii, 373). Possibly in consequence of this reminder, at the end of the Session the Colonial Agents were invited to a conference with Grenville on the subject of the proposed American taxation. An account of this conference was published by one of the participants. In 1776 Israel Mauduit, the Agent for Massachusetts, to a fourth edition of his *History of the New England Colonies*, appended " An Account of a Conference between the late Mr. Grenville and the Several Colony Agents in the Year 1764 ". The account is also printed in the Collections of the Mass. Hist. Soc., 1st series, ix, 268-71, where it is taken from his MS. notebook in the possession of the Society. It was written after Grenville's death to refute Edmund Burke's statement in his famous speech on American Taxation on April 9, 1774, that Grenville never gave the colonies any alternative to the Stamp Act. In justification of Grenville, Mauduit appended to his account of the conference the reply he received from the Speaker of the Massachusetts Assembly, dated Boston, June 14, 1764. Massachusetts rejected alike the proposals of a Stamp Act and a self-imposed tax, and instructed their agent " to remonstrate against these measures, and if possible to obtain a repeal of the Sugar Act, and prevent the imposition of any further duties or taxes on the Colonies ". After this Mauduit supposed that no one " will doubt, but that they had the offer of raising the money themselves ; and that they refused it. Which is all I am concerned to prove." A draft of this account in Mauduit's own hand is in the Liverpool MSS., Add. MS. 38337, ff. 259-60. It agrees with the published account statement by statement and only differs slightly in the wording. In the printed account, however, he concludes by calling to witness " Mr. Montagu, who was then agent for Virginia, and present at this conference with Mr. Grenville, I have his authority to say, that he entirely assents to every particular ". He also referred the reader to William Knox's statement in a *Review of the Controversy between Great Britain and the Colonies* (1769) (pp. 198-9). Knox did not mention a conference but wrote that Grenville desired the agents to tell the Colonies that he would consider another tax if they did not like a Stamp Duty and would not tax themselves. " But he warmly recommended to them the making grants by their own Assemblies, as the most expedient method for themselves upon several accounts."

Add. MS. 38337, ff. 259-60.

Docketed " My Account of the Optional Offer
about the Stamp Act ".

In March 1764, when the Plantation Bill, consisting of a
great number of regulations, was depending, a Resolution was
past, that it might be proper to lay a Stamp duty in America.[1]
At the end of the Sessions, the Agents waited on Mr. Grenville
in form to know if he really intended to bring in such a Bill.
He answered, he did ; and then repeated to us in form, what
I had before often heard him say in private, and in the House
of Commons ; and had wrote to the Assembly of Massachusetts
Bay. That the late war had found us sixty seven millions,[2] and
left us 140 millions in debt. That in these circumstances it was
his duty, as a steward for the publick, to use every just means
of improving the revenue. That however he never meant that
the Colonies should be charged with any part of the interest
of the National Debt. But beside the yearly interest of that
Debt, the nation had incurred a great annual expence in the
maintaining of the several new conquests which had been
made so much for the benefit of the Americans. That the
American Establishment, after the peace of Aix la Chapelle,
was only 70,000. It was now increased to 350,000. That this
was a heavy expence incurred upon an American account and
he thought that America ought to contribute towards it. He
did not expect that they should raise the whole. But some part
of it he thought they ought to raise and this Stamp Duty was
intended for that purpose. That he thought that method the
easiest and the most equitable, that it was a tax which fell only
upon property,[3] and would be equally spread over North
America and the West Indies so as that all would bear their
share of the public burthen. He then went on : I am not
however sett upon this tax, if the Americans dislike it and
preferr any other method of raising the money themselves, I

1. In the same hand, in red ink in the margin, is added " It was the 15th
Resolution ".
2. The printed account says seventy millions.
3. The printed account adds : " would be collected by the fewest officers ".

shall be content. Write therefore to your several Colonies and if they choos any other mode I shall be satisfied, provided the money be but raised.

(I don't recollect that he then mentioned the sum which he reckoned the Stamps would produce, but in private I well remember that he said to me when I asked him, that as far as he could conjecture it might probably raise from 80 to 100,000.) All these things I had heard him say before in the House of Commons and in private conversation, and had mentioned them in my letters and therefore did not think it necessary to repeat them over again.

The event shewed that it was not necessary, for the Assembly's refusal of the option which had been given them to raise the money themselves instead of having a Stamp Act was written and sent away before the arrival of any account of this Conference. It should also be remembered that the assemblys and the Agents mind was then much more employed about the Molasses duty than about this Stamp duty which was then only in embryo and had not then received any of that importance which the debates on its repeal and all the subsequent proceedings have since given it.

CHARLES LLOYD TO CHARLES JENKINSON

Add. MS. 38203, f. 6.

Wotton, July 3, 1764.

My dear Sir,

Walker brought me the favor of your letter of yesterday.[1] The next comfort to the hearing news, is the knowing that there is none : you have formed your idea of Wotton from the dead silence and repose of No Man's Land ; I can assure you however, that by the number of letters that were dispatched from hence yesterday Mr. Grenville might very well have imagined himself in Downing Street.[2] He is prevented from writing to you to day by an inflammation in his eyes and therefore bids me acknowledge the receipt of your letter : and he will take the several points of busyness you mention under consideration, and will talk to you on them as soon as he

1. John Walker, messenger to the Exchequer. A letter from Jenkinson to Grenville dated July 2 is in the *Grenv. Pps.* ii, 372-5.
2. Grenville went to Wotton for ten days on June 27. *Ibid.* p. 504.

comes to town. As to Mello's [1] request, he desires you will inquire whether Mello delivered in a list of the things belonging to his premiere entrée, and if he did whether the articles mentioned in his letter are comprized in that list, or if no such list was given in, if bona fide, those articles appear to be part of his first entries and equipage, what he wishes may be complyed with. But for the future Mr. Grenville desires that upon any Foreign Minister's arrival in England, the Secretary of the Customs do write to such Minister's Secretary, or agent, requiring a list of articles for his premiere entrée, and assuring him that none will be allowed of afterwards but such as have been comprized in that list. With regard to the Collectors in Florida, that matter is to remain as it does till Mr. Grenville comes. You are desired very much to press Dr. Campbell to go on with the papers you gave him and to finish them [2] — We have a good deal of discourse about the manner of announcing the birth of this literary production to the world, the advertising circulating extracting from it etc., etc., etc. Pray let him devise a catching title, the denomination of *An Answer to the*

1. Don Melloy Castro was Portuguese Ambassador in London. The foreign ambassadors were allowed six months from the time of their arrival in England to bring in their baggage duty free, and were expected to furnish the Treasury with a list of the dutiable articles they intended to bring in. The Custom House, spurred to unusual zeal by Grenville's campaign against smuggling, seems generally to have suspected the ambassadors of abusing their privilege. Cf. Guerchy's complaints about his allowance of wine in December 1763 (*Grenv. Pps.* ii, 188, 259). In June 1764 Grenville strained diplomatic relations by causing a retention at the Customs of Guerchy's *habit de gala* and some taffetas belonging to the Ambassadress. *Ibid.* p. 334, and P.R.O., S.P. 44/328, ff. 41, 42, 45, 46. See particularly the Treasury's reply to Halifax defining the rights of ambassadors, f. 46, a copy of which is in the Liverpool Papers, Add. MS. 38202, f. 312, and the Treasury Minute of May 31, T. 29/35.

2. John Campbell, LL.D. (1708–85), about whom see *D.N.B.*, formerly one of Bute's political writers, and the author of a *History of the New Sugar Islands* (1763). In May 1764 David Hartley published his broadside, *The Budget*, ridiculing Grenville's claim to have increased the sinking fund by £391,000 as a result of the new customs regulations. In July 1764 appeared *The Wallet : a supplement to the Budget*, of which Conway complained to Welbore Ellis on July 22, 1764. Ellis replied, " I know not that any papers are under the more immediate protection of Government, except the Gazette ; and as to that anonymous pamphlet, the *Wallet*, which I have not read, I have some good reasons to believe that it is neither avowed, approved, or protected by Government " (*Grenv. Pps.* ii, 405). *An Answer to the Budget, inscribed to the Coterie* also appeared in 1764. From references to the author of *Considerations on the German War* it may have been the work of Israel Mauduit. In December 1764 Thomas Whately published his *Remarks on the Budget*, the most effective Government retort, to which Hartley replied in *The State of the Nation* in 1765, and in the Liverpool Papers (Add. MS. 38338, ff. 198–271) is a MS. of a fourth, apparently unpublished Government pamphlet of which the title-page is missing. This or *The Wallet* may have been Campbell's work referred to here. Lloyd's letter confirms Walpole's and Almon's belief that Grenville was responsible for the pamphlets which appeared on his side : " Some were drawn up by Whately, his secretary ; others he penned himself or gave the materials " (Walpole, *Memoirs*, ii, 6 n. 2).

Budget has been already forestalled by a meer catchpenny published evidently by an enemy.[1] I wish somehow or other our auxiliaries would put themselves in motion. They put me in mind a little of the Russian army, who it is said are the most expensive body in Europe to get into the field. For my own part to carry on the allusion, I should be for trying whether a scarcity of forage might not force them to scour about.[2] Mr. Grenville desires you would send him a messenger on Thursday next, if none should be sent him from the Secretary's offices on that day. Be so good as to deliver the papers herewith sent to Broughton.[3] Adieu,

I am most assuredly yours,

C: L:

Upon second thoughts I send Broughton the papers without troubling you with them.

Wednesday, July 4.

Upon third thoughts, Walker having been detained here yesterday no messenger will be wanted to morrow as was before desired, except you should see cause to send one. Many thanks for your kind letter. Mr. G. will probably write by Maddox, he seems hurt at what has been done to Lord Fife.[4]

C: L:

1. Not apparently *An Answer to the Budget, inscribed to the Coterie*, which is on the Government side. If Campbell's pamphlet was *The Wallet*, the title was not happily chosen, for in the second edition the author was obliged to point out that the word *supplement* did not imply its being written on the same side as *The Budget*.

2. There was no lack of ministerial pamphlets in 1764. In addition to the answers to *The Budget* there appeared *A Letter to the Rt. Hon. George Grenville on the Conduct of the Late Opposition* which Walpole seems to attribute to Philip Lloyd (*Memoirs*, ii, 5). Charles Lloyd wrote an answer to Charles Townshend's *Defence of the Minority* on General Warrants, which was in turn answered by Sir William Meredith, and Will Guthrie wrote two pamphlets justifying Conway's dismissal, the first of which was answered by Walpole (*ibid.* p. 4). Walpole declared that the writers of the ministerial broadsides confided to him the secret of their authorship, but he did not know that Charles Lloyd had written the *Defence of the Majority* (*ibid.* p. 6).

3. Bryan Broughton, a clerk in the Secretary of State's office for the Northern Department, where he was placed by Grenville in July 1762. (See *Cal. H.O. Papers, 1760–65*, No. 620, Grenville to the Postmaster-General, July 16, 1762.)

4. James Duff, 2nd Earl Fife (Irish), M.P. for the family seat for Banffshire 1754–84, was disappointed in a recommendation for the place of Sheriff Depute of Banff. See below, Jenkinson's " Memorandum on the Relations between Bute and Grenville ", p. 397. In July 1764 Mackenzie, who was in charge of the patronage in Scotland, appointed John Erskine, Advocate, to be Sheriff Depute of Banff. All appointments in the county, however, were disputed between the rival Earls, Fife and Findlater, each of whom believed that a Sheriff had been appointed through the interest of the other, though in reality Erskine was recommended by neither. See Mackenzie to Grenville, July 15 ; *Grenv. Pps.* ii, 388–90. Lord Fife applied for redress to Grenville, and Lord Findlater to Mackenzie, with the result that Grenville thought Mackenzie was opposing him. Jenkinson endeavoured to smooth things over by insisting that it was now too late to change

CHARLES JENKINSON TO J. S. MACKENZIE

Add. MS. 38304, f. 30.

July 4, 1764.

Dear Sir,

I have long delayed writing for want of news to send you, and I have no other pretence at present, but that of wishing you joy on the wedding of Lady Anne ; this I do most sincerely as I am sure from the knowledge I have of Lord Warkworth whom I have long been acquainted with that this alliance will prove in every respect such as you and Lord Bute could wish.[1] There is no other publick news, except it be the conduct of the Spanish Governor on the coast of Honduras. I hope this is no more than a piece of etourderie of his own, and that his Court will never approve of it.[2] As no dispatches have however been received from Spain since we made our complaint, it is not yet known how it will be taken there. Lord Bath is recovered from a fever which might have been fatal, even to a young man. D'Eon endeavored this day by his Council to get his triall put off, assigning for the cause that Monsieur de Guerchy had sent away some of the witnesses, which it was necessary to have in his defence, but the King's Council proved that these men had left England three months before the fact of which he stood accused was committed, so that the Court would not allow of the plea and the trial will certainly come on

the appointment, that Grenville had himself ordered Sandwich to take Mackenzie's recommendations, and that in any case there was no question of personal hostility from Mackenzie to Grenville. In September the affair was reopened, when Erskine resigned the Sheriffdom to become Clerk of the Admission of Notaries (see p. 334). Mackenzie wrote to Mure on November 27 : " I have had one meeting with Mr. Grenville, and as we were in good humour and he showed facilities on his side, I thought it right to do the same on mine, and yielded to him the affair of the Banff Sheriff, which he was anxious to have ". Mackenzie asked Mure to apologise for him to Lord Findlater for taking Grenville's recommendation of Mr. Urquhart, Lord Fife's man : " The fact, between you and I, is really this : it was not a thing of moment enough to differ about, and thereby delay or prevent other matters of much greater consequence taking effect " (*Caldwell Papers*, Part 2, i, 275).

1. On July 2, 1764, Anne Stuart, Bute's third daughter, married Hughe Smithson (Percy), afterwards 4th Earl of Northumberland, styled Lord Warkworth, 1750–66.

2. The English merchants trading to Honduras accused the Spanish governor of Yucatan of interfering with the British logwood cutters whose rights had been established in the Treaty of Paris. See Walpole, *Memoirs*, ii, 10 ; *Grenv. Pps.* ii, 378, 380. Halifax sent a protest to the Spanish Government. See Miss Vera Lee Brown's article, " Anglo-Spanish Relations in America, 1763–74 ", in the *Hispanic-American Review*, v, No. 3, 351-68.

in about 10 days.[1] Your last request in favor of Mr. Oliphant [2] of Gask is referred today to the Barons of the Exchequer. Pray take care that there is returned a proper report upon it. My respects to Lady Betty and

I am etc.,

C. Jenkinson

THOMAS BRADSHAW TO CHARLES JENKINSON

Add. MS. 38203, f. 19.

Stenbury, Isle of Wight, July 7, 1764.

Dear Sir,

The last account of Lord Holmes, makes his recovery impossible ; and I dare say he will be dead before this reaches you.[3] Two of the Boroughs in this Island, require the attention of Government, and I am getting all the lights I can, in regard to their present situation, for your information.

I find it will not be in my power to attend you, at either of the Boards in the next week ; and I must request your excuse, and also that you will have the goodness to excuse me to Mr. Grenville. I am, with the truest attachment, dear Sir

Your most faithful and obliged servant,

Thos. Bradshaw

1. Cf. Jenkinson to Grenville, July 5, *Grenv. Pps.* ii, 382-3. The Chevalier d'Eon came to England in September 1762 as Secretary to the Duc de Nivernais, on whose return to France he was left in charge of the embassy until the arrival of the Comte de Guerchy, when he was recalled by his Court but refused to return, whereupon he was forbidden to appear at the Court of St. James's. On March 23, 1764, he published out of spite the *Lettres, mémoires, et négociations particuliers du Chevalier d'Eon*, containing some correspondence between the Ducs de Nivernais and Praslin in which they spoke contemptuously of Guerchy. At the instance of the Diplomatic Corps in London the British Government were obliged to file an information against him for libel, and his trial took place on July 10. He absconded before the trial, at which he was found guilty. W. J. Smith, editor of the *Grenville Papers*, says (ii, 124) : " Until the Revolution deprived him of it, he enjoyed a pension from the French Government ; and he spent the latter years of his life in England, passing for a woman, and always wearing the female costume. He died in 1810." See Walpole, *Memoirs*, i, 241-2, 312-14, ii, 10-11 ; and J. B. Telfer, *Strange Career of the Chevalier d'Eon de Beaumont* (1885).

2. Laurence Oliphant of Gask (1692–1767) was descended from a cadet branch of the Scottish Lords Oliphant. He was exiled for taking part in the rebellion of 1715, and on July 14, 1760, James III at Rome created him Lord Oliphant, but he resolved not to bear the title until the Stuarts were restored. See Mrs. M. E. Blair Oliphant, *The Oliphants of Gask* (1910).

3. Lord Holmes died on July 21, 1764. He was M.P. for Yarmouth. About him see p. 127.

P.S. Mr. Miller (son of Sir John [1]) who is now with me, desires his best compliments to you.

JOHN CAMPBELL TO CHARLES JENKINSON

Add. MS. 38203, f. 27.

Queen's Square, July 9, 1764.

Dear Sir,

If my head had not been so extreamly full of that piece of business, which you know occupies all my attention,[2] I think I might have answered your question upon the spot ; the Earl of Fyfe appears to me to have the greatest interest in Bamff-shire. It is true the Earl of Fynlater lives very near the Town of Bamff, and has a great estate in the neighbourhood,[3] but the Earl of Fyfe who is a Peer of Ireland, though a Scotch title, is knight of the Shire, and his family as I apprehend, were first created Lords Bracho, afterwards Viscount Macduff, and Earl of Fyfe merely in respect to that Parliamentary interest, as I have often heard from him that best knew it, and to whom they were indebted at least for the first of their titles.[4] However, I have sent to a gentleman who is a native of that County, and who of course must know that matter to the bottom, as in that part of the world there is little else to be known, and his account I will transmit as soon as I receive it. I propose waiting on you either Wednesday evening or Thursday morning, which is most convenient to you, that, having the whole in your hands, you may be the better able to alter, add, or leave out, as shall be necessary. The single point is to make it useful, and to that point if I can contribute, it will give the greatest satisfaction possible to him who is with the utmost esteem and respect,

Your faithfull friend and obedient humble servant,

John Campbell

1. Sir John Miller, 4th Bart. of Lavant, had two sons, one of whom, Thomas, was afterwards M.P. for Lewes 1774–78.
2. See p. 308.
3. James Ogilvy, 6th Earl of Findlater, had estates at Deskford in Banffshire.
4. William Duff, 1st Earl Fife, was M.P. for Banffshire 1727–34. He was created Baron Braco (in Banffshire) in 1734 and Viscount MacDuff and Earl Fife in 1759. He died on September 30, 1763. In 1790 his son, James Duff, 2nd Earl Fife, was created 1st Baron of Fife in the British Peerage.

Add. MS. 38458, f. 49.

John Eames succeeded Lord Holmes as M.P. for Yarmouth (Isle of Wight) in January 1765. He afterwards sat for Newport 1768–73, when he was appointed a Commissioner of Taxes. He was a Master in Chancery.

Tuesday Night, July 10, 1764.

Dear Sir,

I am sorry it is not in my power to obey your commands by waiting upon Mr. Jenkinson ; for as this is a matter wherein I have little or no concern, I would not chuse to interfere in it without receiving directions for that purpose. As I imagin'd you might have an inclination to be in Parliament yourself, I was willing to give you an intimation of what was then, and I believe is still the party's designs who has the direction of this borough. In a few days I shall probably be more fully informed of his intentions, and if I can then with any propriety talk with Mr. Jenkinson on the subject, I shall wait upon him with great pleasure. I am most truely Dear Sir

Your most obedient servant,

J. Eames

CHARLES WOLFRAN CORNWALL TO CHARLES JENKINSON
in Parliament Street

Add. MS. 38458, f. 47.

Wednesday Morning [July 11, 1764].[1]

You will see by the enclosed, that my friend Eames is cautious of stepping forward in this business, 'till he has received Mr. L's directions on the subject. And indeed I cannot disapprove of his conduct, as I know, he stands in a very delicate situation with the family and friends of Lord Holmes.

You may depend on the information I gave you from him, and may make any use of it.

I will see Eames at any time, and for any purpose you shall think expedient, I have not the smallest doubt of his com-

1. The letter is undated but incloses John Eames's of Tuesday, July 10.

municating with me very freely, from the same motive on his part which first engaged him to give me the intimation on this subject, and of which, I have not a view or wish of availing myself in any other degree, than the satisfaction I have, of disclosing to you, what may be of some little use to our friends in the future management of this affair.

Your's etc.

C. W. C.

CHAUNCY TOWNSEND [1] TO CHARLES JENKINSON

Add. MS. 38203, f. 62.

Lansamlet, July 30, 1764.

Sir,

As I have a large demand upon the Treasury for Warrants of a long standing and having occasion to make some payments, hope you will excuse this trouble to desire you'l as soon as convenient issue the mony for them which will add to the obligations laid upon Sir,

Your most obedient humble servant

Chauncy Townshend

If Mr. G: interferes in the county election in my neighbourhood I wish to know for whom or a hint some way to know his wishes.

J. S. MACKENZIE TO CHARLES JENKINSON

Add. MS. 38203, ff. 86-7.

Castle Menzies, August 13, 1764.

I received the favor of your several letters the last whereof is dated the 27 past. I had also a few days ago a letter from Mr. Grenville in answer to one I wrote him concerning the affair of the Sherif of Bamfshire ; by that letter, I find that he now sees the matter in a different light from what he did when he wrote me the former letter, though I don't think he

1. About him see p. 226.

takes it exactly right yet, however I return'd him an answer the next day after his reach'd me.[1]

I have wrote to Lord Cathcart, in consequence of what you inform'd me, concerning his sallary and pension being settled, with which he seems mighty well pleased.[2]

You say you are going to take very vigorous steps with respect to the Isle of Man and the proprietor of it. I should be much obliged to you if you would let me know everything you are doing in it ; Mr. Grenville once told me that he would lay the grant before the Attorney and Sollicitor General and that he apprehended they would declare it void as the Grantee had exceeded the powers given him by the Charter in imposing certain new duties in the Island. Mr. Grenville lent me a very ample Memorial on that subject last spring, and I gave him a copy of another which I had ; those two papers throw great light on the subject. has the Grant been laid before the Crown Lawyers ? If so, what do they say to it ? What sum do you think of offering for the purchase, etc., etc. ; do tell me all about it.[3]

What is Spain doing with us ? they seem to be out of humor I think. Drop me a line soon about all these matters.

As I shall probably have occasion to write again soon, I will detain you no longer at present. Adieu my dear Jenkinson. I am most sincerely

Yours

JOHN ROBINSON TO CHARLES JENKINSON

Add. MS. 38203, ff. 82-3.

August 13, 1764.

Dear Sir,

At this place [4] I find there is a likelihood of many changes in the Customs, and an addition of officers for the advantage

1. See p. 309. The only letter from this correspondence published in the *Grenville Papers* is that from Mackenzie to Grenville of July 15 (ii, 388-90), in which he explains the case and disculpates himself from "countenancing attacks on your friends, which God knows I never even dreamed of ".

2. Charles Schaw, 9th Baron Cathcart, was appointed First Commissioner of Police in January 1764 and the appointment carried with it a salary of £1200 a year payable at the Exchequer, and an additional pension of £300 a year paid by the Paymaster of Pensions. On June 8, 1764, Jenkinson wrote to Mackenzie, "I have often mentioned to Mr. Grenville Lord Cathcart's application for the additional £300 per annum " (Add. MS. 38304, f. 26).

3. Grenville's Bill to buy the Isle of Man from the Duke and Duchess of Athol was opened on January 21, 1765. See above, p. 294.

4. Whitehaven.

of the revenue, I therefore cou'd not omit immediately writing to you, to say that I hope you have agreeable to the assurances Mr. Grenville gave put the several places within this port and Carlisle on the establishment, that we may have to apply to him alone and not risque any advantages to be taken by the Board of Customs in the nomination. The Land Surveyor here I find hath been particularly negligent, if not incapable, having no book to produce to the Inspectors, and I was the more surprized to find he had acted a part in the party affairs here, inconsistent with his attachments to Government. He it is apprehended will certainly be discharged. As Sir James is at such a distance, he may not have it in his power to recommend immediately to Mr. Grenville the persons to succeed to the vacancies, but if you think Mr. Grenville wou'd in the meantime accept any letter of application from *me* on the part of Sir James to request his not appointing the officers till he hears from me, that I may venture and will readily do. In this I should be glad to have your sentiments, if writing to you is not sufficient. I have not heard from Sir James since he cou'd receive my letter from town. Since my return into the country I have been in almost every quarter of these two counties and it is with pleasure I can say to you that I don't find the Duke of Portland hath done Sir James any great hurt, or made any advantageous connexions in point of interest. Mr. Grenville hath sent us a prebend I find to Carlisle.[1] I have been here about two days, and hope we have got all the unhappy affairs here in a good way to be well finished for the peace and trade of the town, notwithstanding the *Attorney General* hath *consented* to the Assignees having the extents, and armed them with the power of Government which surprized me.[2] I am dear Sir with great truth

Your most obedient and ffaithful humble servant,

J. Robinson

P.S. Since writing the above I am desired to apply on the part of Mr. William Nicholson Jackson who is Chaplain to one of the Battalions of the Royal Americans, and who hath received a Letter from the Secretary at War ordering him to repair to his regiment or find a Deputy. He is very desirous that the Colonel Commandant should have such a Deputy as is agreeable to him, ⟨   ⟩ since General Stanwix[3] quited

1. Roger Baldwin was appointed Prebendary of Carlisle on August 1, in the place of Thomas Wilson who was made Dean. See p. 397.
2. See pp. 277, 295.   3. About him see p. 130 and n. 3.

the Battalion desired General Stanwix would apply for that purpose, and apprehend it had been settled by the General. If Sir James had been at home I am certain he would have wrote to Mr. Ellis [1] upon it, but as he is not and I am no how acquainted with Mr. Ellis than as you introduced me to him, I must desire you will please to speak to him on it and get Mr. Jackson excused attending which I am certain will be agreeable to Sir James.

Ever yours,

J. R.

CHARLES JENKINSON TO J. S. MACKENZIE

Add. MS. 38304, ff. 46-7.

August 14, 1764.

My dear Sir,

The Treasury having come to a resolution to have a survey made of all the ports of Scotland in the same manner as a survey of the like kind is now carrying on in the ports of England ; I thought you would like to have notice of it, and I send you inclosed for this purpose a letter I have this day written by order of the Lords of the Treasury to the Commissioners of the Customs in Scotland, which will shew you the plan upon which this book is to proceed. I have not added the instructions mentioned in my letter, as they relate only to the detail of this business, and are exactly the same as we have given to those employed on the survey in England ; if you should choose to have a copy of them, I will at any time send them to you.

I have just left the family in South Audley Street, who are perfectly well ; I go with them to-morrow to Luton.[2] Mr. Legge cannot live long : all are now satisfied of this and he expects his fate.[3] The Duke of Devonshire is going to the Spa in consequence of his fitt.[4] All the little talk we have about town is concerning two pamphlets the one in defense of General Conway said to be written by Horry Walpole,[5] the other in

1. Welbore Ellis, Secretary at War. About him see *D.N.B.*
2. Bute's family.
3. H. B. Legge died on August 23, 1764.
4. He died there on October 2, 1764.
5. In August 1764 Horace Walpole published *A Counter Address* in answer to Will Guthrie's *Address* on Conway's dismissal, which pamphlet Walpole then believed to have been written for Grenville by Edward Shebbeare. See Walpole to Hertford, August 4, 1764.

defense of the Minority ascribed to Mr. C. Townshend but which his friends deny.[1]

I beg my respects to Lady Betty and I have etc.

C. Jenkinson

CHARLES JENKINSON TO GEORGE GRENVILLE

Add. MS. 38304, ff. 47-8.

August 18, 1764.

Dear Sir,

I am just returned with Lord Bute and the Primate from Luton, after having spent there two days very agreeably ; I delivered your message to Lord Bute acquainting him that you would certainly comply with his request in favor of Mr. Smith whenever the vacancy happened ; he desired me to return you his thanks and to assure you that he is very much obliged to you for this favor : I can say with confidence that every thing I have heard or had occasion to observe has been as satisfactory as I could wish.

I find that there is a great clamour endeavoring to be stirred up concerning the new laws for imposing the 4 and a half per cent duty in the Granades etc., etc. I know the merchants give out that it was determined hastily in the Council upon an old opinion of Sir Edward Northey,[2] which related only to a country when held by conquest, and not by cession as the Granades are at present, that if the present Attorney and Sollicitor General had been applied to for their opinions, instead of being ordered to draw the law, they would have been against it ; that it is an exercise of the prerogative of the Crown which cannot be justified by law, and if it could be justified, extremely imprudent in the present hour, when there is so much noise already about improper exertions of the King's prerogative, and that the advantage to be derived from it would not compensate the difficulties and opposition it will bring on the Government. This and much more I heard from a quarter not otherwise indisposed. I found also that it had made some impression on others, and what most surprized me was the exact knowledge they had got of the state of the

1. Charles Townshend was the author of *A Defence of the Minority on the Question relating to General Warrants.*
2. Attorney-General 1701-7.

affair, and the positive assertion of what is the opinion of the Attorney and Sollicitor General. I thought therefore I would tell you all this, that you might judge whether you would stop any further proceedings in this business which I suppose it is still possible to do, as Governor Melville is not yet gone, but sails as I understand on Wednesday.

I send you a letter from the Custom House by which you will see that the Commissioners demur to the delivery of what Count Seilern [1] applied for : if you choose however to oblige the Count the omission he has been guilty of in not presenting his list in due time may be imputed to his not knowing the rule, and I really believe that this was the case. I trouble you with a letter I have received from Sir J. Lowther's friend Mr. Robinson,[2] and should be glad you would let me know what answer I should return to it.

I beg my best compts to Mrs. Grenville and I have etc.

C. Jenkinson

GEORGE GRENVILLE TO CHARLES JENKINSON

Add. MS. 38191, ff. 81-2.

Wotton, August 19, 1764.

Dear Jenkinson,

I am very glad that you passd your time so agreably at Luton, and that every thing you heard or observd there was so perfectly satisfactory to you. I have considered that part of your letter, which relates to the imposition of the $4\frac{1}{2}$ per cent duty on the Grenades and the other new ceded Islands in the same manner as it is payable in all our other Leeward and Windward Islands. I do not wonder that those who have purchasd any part of them, shoud wish to be exempt from the same burthens which the Brittish subjects in the neighbouring islands are liable to, but I shoud be much surprizd, if the latter would quietly submitt to a distinction in favor of the French proprietors of the new ceded Islands, against the English proprietors of the old dominions of the Crown which woud greatly lessen the value of the latter. As to the manner of imposing this duty, my sentiments will best appear from the

1. Count Seilern was the Imperial Ambassador in London.
2. See p. 315.

Memorial which the Treasury presented about it,[1] but I cannot believe that the Attorney and Sollicitor General have declard " that if their opinions had been askd about the legality of that measure, they woud have given them against it ", because if that were the case, it was certainly their duty to have represented against it, instead of drawing the instrument, and to have informed the Council that they were mistaken in the law, and that this was an exercise of the Prerogative of the Crown which coud not be justifyd by law. For these reasons and many others I am persuaded, however positive the assertion of it may be, that it is ill founded. Be that as it may, after this instrument has been prepared by them, approvd of by the Council, and established under the Great Seal, it is quite impossible for me to take upon myself to stop any farther proceedings upon it. I directed Mr. Loyd whilst you was at Luton to write to Mr. Freemantle [2] upon the demur made by the Commissioners of Customs about M. de Seilern's list not being deliverd soon enough, and to desire that what he asks in that list, may be immediately complyd with ; if it is not already done, I desire that you will take care that he may meet with no more trouble or delay, as his behaviour has been extremely fair and unexceptionable. With regard to what Mr. Robinson writes to you about, you know the footing upon which this was left, and that since that time I have done nothing farther in it, which is the only answer I can give, till I know what Sir James Lowther desires of me. I am, dear Jenkinson,

Most faithfully yours,

George Grenville

CHARLES LLOYD TO CHARLES JENKINSON

Add. MS. 38203, f. 96.

Wotton, Sunday Evening.
August 19, 1764.

Dear Jenkinson,

I hope you have had an agreable tour and that you found everything as favorably disposed as you had reason to

1. This seems to have been a memorial mentioned in the Treasury Minutes of December 23, 1763, recommending that 4½ per cent duties be imposed by an Order in Council on the new ceded islands. See P.R.O., T. 29/35, p. 246.
2. John Freemantle, about whom see p. 363 and n. 3.

expect. For my own part the very light of this house has so sunk my spirits that I have been considerably below par ever since my chaise stuck in the first gateway of the avenues. I have sent what you saw with all its imperfections on its head.[1] Indeed, indeed my dear Sir, one had need of all one's philosophy to digest the manner of treatment I here meet with. I am sometimes tempted with the Prodigal Son to say, make me as one of thy hired servants. Lord Chancellor goes from hence on Tuesday.[2] If any thing new be so good as to communicate. Pray was Daniel Baston appointed a Land carriage man, recommended by Savage Lloyd.[3] Lord Harcourt is expected to morrow. If I pick up any traits of Lord N.,[4] I shall not fail sending them to you.

Yours most sincerely, Adieu
C: Lloyd

I have looked over the Public Advertiser for this last week and find no care taken of inserting Government advertisements. Will you be so good when you can properly as to speak to Cockburne [5] and Wallace.[6]

CHARLES LLOYD TO CHARLES JENKINSON

Add. MS. 38203, f. 97.

[August 20, 1764.[7]]

Dear Jenkinson,

I fancy you will hardly hear from Mr. Grenville to day who has got a hoarseness and cold (without any fever) for which he has been blooded. Mr. Lloyd the second Master of Westminster School who has a living in this neighbourhood dined here yesterday. He mentioned to me that he had not received the £50 for last quarter, viz Midsummer. I shall be much obliged to you if you will by the return of the post or by Thurs-

1. Possibly the MS. of his *Defence of the Majority on the Question relating to General Warrants*, which was published in September 1764.
2. Cf. Grenville's diary, Saturday, August 18, 1764 : " Mr. Grenville returned to Wotton and brought my Lord Chancellor down with him, who professes the warmest attachment to Mr. Grenville. He went away on the Monday following " (*Grenv. Pps.* ii, 512). 3. Richard Savage Lloyd, M.P. for Totnes 1759–68.
4. Lord Nuneham ? See p. 354.
5. George Cockburne, Controller of the Navy 1756–70.
6. James Wallace, Secretary to the Treasurer of the Navy.
7. From internal evidence. The letter is undated.

days post acquaint me with the state of this matter whether the money is now receivable, or when it will be. This puts me in mind of the liberty you gave me some time ago of putting your name to the subscription to his sermons. But this is in no sort of hurry ; when I see you in town will be full time enough. I will only add that the large paper is only 10s. 6d. Your situation etc. will make a guinea very handsome.

Lord Chancellor went away to day. I shall see little or nothing of Mr. G. to day. As soon as I can form any observations on the answer from the other side of the water you shall know them. You received a letter of complaints from me on Sunday. I am now more resign'd and can compare my feelings to nothing more like than to those of a bird who upon being first caged flies and flutters about against the sides of his cage very outrageously but time brings him to bear the confinement and the solitude with patience.

I am very sincerely yours,

C. L.

CHARLES JENKINSON TO GEORGE GRENVILLE

Add. MS. 38304, f. 49.

North End, August 20, 1764.

Dear Sir,

I send you herewith as I promised, all the papers, I have as yet been able to collect relative to the Isle of Man, I should be much obliged to you if you would look them over, and enable me by your assistance to procure still further information on this subject ; the particular points on which the information I have hitherto obtained is defective, are first the ancient history of the Isle of Man before it came into the possession of the Earls of Derby ; secondly what is the nature of the tenure, by which this island is held. You will see that there have been two Grants of the Isle of Man, the one in Henry the 4th's reign and the other in that of James the 1st. And the latter was confirmed by a private Act of Parliament of the 7th of James the 1st.[1] I have not yet been able to procure this Act of Parliament ; it may possible [sic] contain something worthy attention. Among the papers I have got from the Council Office, you will find a reference to the

1. An Act for the assuring and establishing of the Isle of Man.

Attorney General in 1691 concerning the legal authority and powers of the proprietor of this island. But it does not appear by the Council Books that the Attorney ever made any report, if any such report could be found it would be very curious.

I add some papers relative to the Islands of Guernsey and Jersey. Parliament will take the state of these islands into consideration as well as that of the Isle of Man, so that it will be necessary to be informed of one as well as the other. I shall be glad that you would let me have my papers again as soon as you conveniently can as I have no copies of them.

I am etc.

C. Jenkinson

GEORGE GRENVILLE TO CHARLES JENKINSON

Add. MS. 38191, ff. 83-4.

Lieutenant Henry Prittie, in command of a cutter stationed at Deal, suspected that smuggling was being carried on from an East India ship, the *Falmouth*, anchored there, and on July 25 and August 7, 1764, ordered his men (illegally as the Solicitor to the Customs afterwards discovered) to search some Deal boats, in doing which the men from the cutter fired into the boats and wounded two men. As no action was taken by the civil magistrates in consequence of this incident, the Deal men in revenge launched their boats on August 9, surrounded one of the cutter's boats which was cruising near the shore, took it ashore and manhandled the crew of five. These eventually escaped and a riot took place outside the town where the civil powers were unable to stop it. An account of the riot, including letters from Prittie, was sent to the Treasury by the Secretary to the Admiralty on August 18 and 22. See P.R.O., Treasury Letters, General, T. 27/29, p. 57. A report by the Solicitor to the Customs dated September 11, 1764, and a letter from Jenkinson to the Secretary of the Admiralty inclosing reports and affidavits from the Collector of the Customs at Deal, dated September 15, are in the Admiralty Letters from the Treasury, Adm. 1/4286.

Wotton, August 22, 1764.

Dear Jenkinson,

The outrageous insult committed by the smugglers at Deal requires the most effectual and speedy remedy. I approve therefore of every step that can be taken for that purpose. There seems to me but three things to be done. The first is to have the offenders prosecuted and punished as severely as the law will allow. The 2nd is to reinforce the Lieutenant of the Cutter by a sloop and a Man of War who may be fully sufficient to keep that gang in order. The 3rd is to send some troops, particularly Dragoons, upon that part of the coast. Your letter to the Commissioners of the Customs is a proper one, but I would add to it the advertisement which you mention of a reward for discovering and apprehending the offenders, which shoud be put into the Gazette both by the Admiralty Office and the Commissioners of the Customs, that it may carry the more terror by both Offices taking it up, though I think the prosecution shoud be carried on, as it is for a smuggling offence, by the Commissioners of the Customs. Directions shoud be likewise given to them in your letter or otherwise, to enquire what the East India ship was, and who was the Captain, and to prosecute him likewise if it was an English East India ship, as I take for granted. The East India Company shoud likewise be applyd to that they may punish him by dismission if he had any part in this infamous transaction, which it seems impossible to me but that he and his officers must have been principally concerned in, and all who were, ought to share in the punishment. Shoud not the East India Directors be told that the breaking bulk in this notorious manner before the ship is deliverd into the care of the Custom house Officers incurs the penalty of forfeiture, and therefore, if that is the case, it is doubly incumbent upon them to punish the offenders with the utmost rigour. At all events I desire to know what the ship is, the name of the Captain and what steps can be taken in this business with the Directors of the East India Company. I askd Mr. Pitt [1] whether any orders had been sent by the Admiralty to reinforce Lieutenant Prittie, which most certainly shoud have been done immediately from any of the neighbouring stations, as the whole ship might otherwise be unloaded in a few days. Mr. Pitt did not know that any such orders had been given, but told me he woud write to Mr. Steevens [2] about it to day. I think the Commissioners of the Customs shoud be asked why they have sent us no account of this transaction and that they shoud be directed to write to Lieutenant Prittie to encourage him in the execution of his duty, to tell him that they have orders to prosecute the offenders with the utmost severity, and that he will be supported both by a land and sea force, and to desire him to give them an

1. Thomas Pitt, M.P. 1761–83, when he was created Baron Camelford, was a Lord of the Admiralty 1763–65. He was a nephew of William Pitt but supported Grenville.
2. Philip Stephens, First Secretary to the Admiralty 1763–95, previously Deputy Secretary; M.P. for Liskeard 1761–68, Sandwich 1768–1805. About him see D.N.B.

exact account of the farther proceedings of the East India ship's, and of the measures which he shall take with regard to her. I think you shoud write an answer to Mr. Steevens to inform the Admiralty of what we have done, to press them to strengthen the Sea Guard there and reinforce Lieutenant Prittie as soon as is possible, if it is not already done, and to let them know of the orders to march troops to the coast, which you should write to the Secretary at War to hasten with the greatest expedition. What I have traced out above will I hope be sufficient to restrain so daring an act of violence under our eyes, which it imports to repress effectually in the first instance, if we mean to preserve, much more if we mean to encrease, the revenue of Customs. I am much surprizd that we have not heard from the Commissioners upon this subject. I am, dear Jenkinson,

Most faithfully yours etc.

George Grenville

[Note in another hand :] Falmouth, Captain O'Hara.[1]

On August 23 Jenkinson wrote to Philip Stephens, Secretary to the Admiralty, to say that the Treasury had applied to the Secretary at War for troops to be sent to Deal and had ordered the Commissioners of the Customs to apprehend and prosecute the offenders and to advertise in the *Gazette* for information leading to their discovery; in the same letter the Admiralty were requested likewise to offer a reward in the *Gazette* and to reinforce Prittie. See P.R.O., Adm. 1/4286. This letter is transcribed in Treasury Out Letters, General, T. 27/29, p. 59, where the date is given as August 24 and where there is also a copy of Jenkinson's letter to the Secretary at War, also dated August 24. Two letters from Jenkinson to the Commissioners of Customs, written in consequence of this from Grenville and dated August 24, are in the Entry Book of Treasury Letters to the Customs and Excise, T. 11/27. In spite of the Treasury's instructions the *Gazette* for 1764 contains no advertisements from either the Customs Office or the Admiralty.

CHARLES JENKINSON TO JOHN ROBINSON

Add. MS. 38304, ff. 51-2.

August 22, 1764.

Dear Sir,

I should sooner have answered your letter, but it found me upon an excursion with Lord Bute : I prepared in the

1. In 1764 Captain James O'Hara was master of the *Peggy* sloop. He was a son of Lord Tyrawley, about whom see p. 37 and n. 4.

manner you and I settled the proper warrant for putting the officer you desired upon the Establishment, but upon my offering it to Mr. G. for his signature, he would not sign it ; he assigned no reason, but I suppose it was that he would not do this, till he had settled every thing else with Sir James. I shall apply to Mr. Grenville and do all I can that every thing may succeed as Sir James could wish ; but alas ! My dear Sir, I have but little influence where I am always considered as a party. You must have observed this, and the difficulties I have on this account been under ; I am clear therefore that your applying to me is not sufficient, and that you should write to Mr. Grenville himself, and indeed I can see no harm in this measure, and should therefore advise it, whatever the success of it may be. As to the offices upon Incidents, Mr. Pennington[1] who, by a letter I have received from him is I find apprized of this, will I suppose take care of them, and if my personal application is wanting, I will give it with all its force, for where I alone can act, I am always ready ; and I should be much obliged to you if you would take the proper opportunity to convince Sir James of this. I rejoice to hear that all the attempts of the Duke of Portland have had so little effect. I will take care that Mr. Jackson's business shall be properly settled. I wait for Mr. D'Oiley's[2] return to town who will manage this better than his principal. How has the Attorney General succeeded at Wigan.[3] I shall be happy to hear from you when you are at leisure and

I am etc.
C. Jenkinson

PHILIP LLOYD TO CHARLES JENKINSON

Add. MS. 38203, f. 106.

Piddletown near Blandford.
August 29, 1764.

Dear Charles,
    I who lived 3 years in the house easily believe that you may have many uncomfortable circumstances which it would

1. Joseph Pennington.
2. Christopher D'Oiley, Deputy Secretary at War to Welbore Ellis. He was afterwards M.P. for Wareham 1774–80, Seaford 1780 till his death in 1795. He was Under-Secretary of State for the Colonies 1776–78.
3. There was no re-election at Wigan in 1764.

be hard perhaps to explain,[1] but there are others very good ; what however strikes me as advantageous in it, is, that it will throw you still more into the Parliamentary tract where the opening is so very inviting, and where I have no doubt of your going very far.

I am much obliged to you for your expressions of readiness to serve me in my own way, which is what so few people will do.

In the mean time I shall return to London, about the middle of next month with a great desire to hear the present state of the scene. You gave me great pleasure by informing me that publick affairs go on well.

My brother's information strengthens the account I had before I left London of an entire change in Mr. Pitt's language.

Mrs. Lloyd and Miss Cade desire me to present their best compliments to you. I am dear Sir,

Yours most faithfully,

P. Ll.

I should be obliged to you if you would frank this letter to Miss Poole at Lewes in Sussex.

SHUTE BARRINGTON TO CHARLES JENKINSON

Add. MS. 38469, ff. 109-10.

In August 1764 Nathaniel Bliss, Astronomer Royal and Savilian Professor of Geometry, was dying, and on August 20 Joseph Betts asked Jenkinson to speak to Bute on his behalf (Add. MS. 38469, f. 107). Shute Barrington, who had another candidate to recommend, thought the honour of administration concerned in the appointment, and addressed himself therefore through Jenkinson to Grenville.

August 30, 1764.

Dear Sir!

Convinced by a variety of proofs of the abilities of Mr. Hornsby,[2] and supported in my opinion by the united testimonies of Doctors Bradley and Fanshawe,[3] I ventured to recommend him to Mr. Grenville's favour to succeed to the place of Astronomer Royal whenever it should be vacant ; I

1. Philip Lloyd had been tutor to Grenville's children. He seems to refer to Jenkinson's relations with Grenville.

2. Barrington recommended him to Jenkinson in July 1762 when he was chosen Savilian Professor of Astronomy. See p. 46.

3. John Fanshawe, D.D., Regius Professor of Greek 1735–41 and of Divinity 1741–63 at Oxford. He died in May 1768.

found him rather disposed to favour the pretensions of Mr. Maskelyne.[1] I at that time knew nothing of Mr. Maskelyne's character of which I have since learnt from undoubted authority the following circumstances and then submit it to your judgment whether they are not sufficient to prevent Mr. G.'s recommending him to an employment which will place him in so conspicuous a station in the astronomical world. When he went to St. Helena to observe the transit of Venus, he had been so negligent as not to look at his instruments before he set out on the voyage by which means when he arrived at the island he found them out of order, was incapable of remedying their defects, and therefore of making a single observation. In his late voyage to Barbadoes when one Green [2] who went on the same errand with himself declared the longitude of the island to be what it proved to be within an inch or two, Maskelyne erred no less than forty leagues. His moral character as a clergyman is infamous ; his intrigues with the black women were notorious to the whole island by his letters to them being publickly handed about. I write in the greatest hurry ; Bliss is probably by this time dead ; and if you think as I do that Mr. G's honour is concerned in the nomination you will be so good as to give him early information of these facts ; which I have been induced to communicate to you more from a regard to his credit than to the advantage of Mr. Hornsby. I am, dear Sir with unfeigned esteem

Yours
S. Barrington

Bliss died on September 2, and on September 8 Lord Morton, President of the Royal Society, sent Bute a *Memorial relating to the Royal Observatory at Greenwich*, urging that the new Astronomer " ought to have no other avocations which might divert him from the business of the Observatory . . . a Professorship in either of the Universities or any other employment which might oblige him to a residence elsewhere ought not to be conjoined with the Office of Royal Astronomer " (Fortescue, *Corr. of George III*, i, 69 ; see also Namier, *Additions and Corrections*, p. 22). Nevil Maskelyne was a brother-in-law of Clive, who tried to bring him into politics in 1761. See *Structure of Politics*, p. 387. Possibly through Clive's influence with Gren-

1. Nevil Maskelyne (1732–1811), D.D., F.R.S., Fellow of Catherine Hall, Cambridge, about whom see *D.N.B.* From 1755 he had been associated with Bradley, through whose influence he was sent by the Royal Society to observe the transit of Venus at St. Helena on June 6, 1761. According to the report in *Philosophical Transactions*, liv, 349 *et seq.*, the transit was concealed by clouds, while Maskelyne's zenith-sector was rendered practically useless by faulty suspension (see *D.N.B.*). In 1763 he was sent to Barbados by the Board of Longitude to try Harrison's time-keeper, see p. 166 n. 2.
2. Charles Green, astronomer, had been assistant both to Bradley and to Bliss.

ville, though Clive was now on his way out to India, Maskelyne was given the place of Astronomer Royal, which he kept for forty-six years. The Savilian chair of Geometry was not filled until December.[1]

RICHARD JACKSON TO CHARLES JENKINSON

Add. MS. 38203, f. 121.

Wearnham near Bougham, Norfolk,
September 4, 1764.

Dear Sir,

I send you in 2 packets (that it may not be overweight) the little piece we read together, incompleat enough, I am very sensible, but as compleat as I have had health or spirits to make it, having been plagued with a nervous headache, and what is worse, a great deal of company. You will perceive it is neither pointed, nor over accurately wrote, where it is legible ; which I fear it is not, in some places. In truth I never could prepare any thing for the press in any degree ; and must therefore beg you would dispose of it as you please, though perhaps if I should see it after it is wrote into some better shape, I might add something that may occur to me, and which has already happened without my being able in the confused state both of my paper and mind to find a place for it. I am sensible I might just as well have sent this paper 10 days ago, but then I thought while there remains any reason to fear an immediate rupture with France, it would be ridiculous to argue against the probability of it. I suppose this will be less uncertain in a few days. I am dear Sir
Your most obedient faithfull humble servant,
Rd. Jackson

September 12.

I have kept these papers 8 days longer in hopes I might have been able to have wrote over the calculations more accurately, but though they are sufficiently clear to me, yet I find it is impossible to write them in the form I would put them, to make the operation easy to others, without transcribing the whole which I cannot undertake and have no amanuensis here. If we should get into a War with France or Spain or

1. See p. 341.

both (forgive me if I provide against what you may know is utterly unlikely, for I am out of the way of all intelligence but newspapers), I will when I come to town endeavour to give the whole another turn. I should not have kept it so long but you said there was no hurry.

When I return to town I should be glad to have my foul copy because many of the obliterated parts are memorandums to me.[1]

CHARLES JENKINSON TO J. S. MACKENZIE

Add. MS. 38304, ff. 59-60.

September 11, 1764.

My dear Sir,

As you desired to receive an account of all that passed with respect to the Isle of Man and particularly to have a copy of the Duke of Athol's answer I send you a copy thereof inclosed, and I add the reply which the Lords of the Treasury have thought proper to make to it. I shall be curious to know what his Grace's next letter will be. You will be so kind as not to let any one know that I send you these copies as I have not the permission of my superiors, though God knows there is no occasion to make a secret of this business.

What you see in the papers of my sister's marriage is true, and I am much obliged to you for your congratulations upon it. She is married to a first cousin, several years younger than herself, and who has a very comfortable patrimonial fortune, and is bred besides to the Law, in which I think him likely to succeed ; so that I think she has a fair prospect of happiness.[2]

The answer of the French with respect to Monsieur D'Estain's conduct at Turk's Island is a most explicit disavowal of it with the strongest assurances of their desire to keep the peace.[3] I know nothing further of what relates to Prince Ivan.[4]

1. No pamphlet fitting this description seems to have been published in the autumn of 1764 or spring of 1765.

2. See p. 302.

3. Cf. Halifax to Grenville, September 9, 1764, *Grenv. Pps.* ii, 436. Marshal D'Estaing seized Turks Island in the West Indies in the early summer of 1764, but the French Government disavowed his action and paid damages. They refused, however, to punish him and during the American War he commanded the French fleet. He was guillotined during the Revolution in 1794.

4. In July 1764 there was a plot to release Ivan VI from prison in Schlüsselburg, but it was detected and he was murdered by his gaolers under orders.

I shall be glad to be indulged when you return to town with a perusal of the Papers you have collected concerning the Scotch Revenue ; I have endeavoured as far as I am able to make myself master of that subject. I have received lately from the Commissioners of Excise in Scotland some papers containing proposals for the improvement of the revenue under their management, part of which appear to me to be exceedingly reasonable, and proper, but as they have been offered to former Treasuries and were not carried into execution by them I am apprehensive that there is some latest [? latent] objection. I wish therefore you would talk with the Commissioners who will tell you what the several points are, that I may be favored with your sentiments upon them when we meet.

When the Board meets on Thursday I will lay before them the Report of the Commissioners of Stamps in favor of your Stamp Officers.

The point on which there is most talk at present is the domestick quarrel that has arisen between the Duke of Grafton and his Dutchess ; his Grace chooses to keep a mistress ; some say, she is the girl that Lord Shelborne and Mr. Nesbitt kept before him.[1] The Dutchess resents in the highest terms this as a want of affection or perhaps rather as a slight put upon her beauty ; the Duke however persists, and in consequence thereof the Dutchess has left him and is gone home to her father's ; it is not yet certain whether this separation will be permanent. It is said that his Grace intends to go abroad, but I believe this is not determined. If any of our friends had chosen to have been guilty of such a frolick, how would the papers have been stuffed with the scandalous story.

September 13. I was prevented sending this letter by the last post, as the clerk did not send me in time the copy of the Duke of Athols letter, I have thereby an opportunity of acquainting you that the Treasury have consented to the additional salary desired for the Stamp Officers, and that all the requests you last made to the Board are complied with,

1. Nancy Parsons, whom Walpole called "the Duke of Grafton's Mrs. Hoghton, the Duke of Dorset's Mrs. Hoghton, everybody's Mrs. Hoghton", began her quasi-marital career with a West Indian slave merchant called Houghton and eventually married Charles, 2nd Viscount Maynard, in 1776. In 1786 she became the mistress of Francis Russell, 5th Duke of Bedford, then twenty-one, who turned his grandmother, the formidable Gertrude, out of Woburn to make way for her. Walpole does not mention her connexion with Shelburne or Arnold Nesbitt. Much of his account of her is omitted from the published part of his memoirs. About her see *Grenv. Pps.* iv, 275-7. The marriage of the Duke and Duchess of Grafton was dissolved by Act of Parliament in 1769.

and sent already to Scotland. I tried to day to get them to consent to the additional allowance to be made to Mrs. Olyphant of Gask but without success.[1]

I received yesterday from your Commissioners of the Customs a letter containing an account of the survey made by Mr. Clerk Maxwell [2] and the Commissioner of Excise (I forget his name). I have laid it before the Board who were very much pleased with what has been done : and Mr. Whately will send by their order a Letter of Approbation and troops will be ordered to march for the assistance of the gentlemen of the country in the suppression of smuggling.

I have nothing to add but my respects to Lady Betty and that you would believe me to be

With great truth etc.

C. Jenkinson

PHILIP CARTERET WEBB TO CHARLES JENKINSON

Add. MS. 38203, f. 143.

Busbridge,
Friday, 14 September, 1764.

Dear Sir

On my return from a small excursion yesterday, I had the pleasure of receiving your letter, I have made some progress in the outline for the work we talked of when I last saw you, but I find it will require the perusal of many materials that are in London before I can give it the degree of perfection I would wish. I intend to leave the country in three weeks haveing many things to transact here; if I am wanted sooner, I will attend your sumons, and am with great truth

Your very obedient and affectionate servant

Philip Carteret Webb

Jenkinson wrote to Webb on September 29, " I am glad to hear that you proceed in finishing the work you have undertaken which will I am convinced be of great service in the present conjunction " (Add. MS. 38304, f. 64).

1. See p. 311.
2. George Clerk Maxwell was Commissioner of Customs for Scotland 1763–84.

SIR HARRY ERSKINE TO CHARLES JENKINSON

Add. MS. 38203, ff. 163-5.

Spa, September 23, 1764.

Dear Sir,

'Twas with great pleasure that I received a letter from you ; but I had not quite so much satisfaction in the perusal of it. I wish'd that your attempts for thorough conciliation had been attended with more success.[1] Time and accidents may produce, what friendship has fail'd in. Tis not one of the smallest misfortunes incident to human nature that we always see clearer into other people's affairs than we do into our own ; we have such a multitude of passions and prejudices always acting upon us, that our reason is certainly not a free agent.

Tis with regret that I perceive we are to open the next campaign [2] in the same situation in which we were the last. There has been much time for conciliation, tis pity that it has elapsed in so fruitless a manner. If we gain no ground before the meeting of Parliament, Opposition will. Charles Townshend's pamphlet I have seen ; and I think it but a very poor performance. I long to see Horace Walpole's.[3] When I hear of a domestic separation I am exceedingly sorry for the parties : but now that there is a separation which of the two shall we gain the Duke or the Duchess, I am inclined to wish for the latter, and to think her the more valuable acquisition.

You inquire about the Duke of Devonshire's health. When it was said that he was coming hither, it was foretold by Lord Spenser's physician that the waters would not be of service to him. When he first arrived I thought him much better, than I expected to see him from the accounts we had received.

But on tryal he could not bear a sufficient quantity of the waters to be of service to him. He has declined we are told very much since he came. The physical folks seem to entertain no hopes of his recovery ; he himself entertains none and wishes his distemper at an end. Some fluttering intervals he has had ; but if, as it is alledged his distemper lie in the mind, no waters and now especially at this time of year can be of service to him.[4]

1. Probably between Grenville and Mackenzie. See p. 397.
2. The word "campaign" is scratched out, but no other inserted in its place.
3. See p. 317.
4. See p. 317 and n. 4.

I am obliged to you for your friendly expressions with regard to me. I certainly have received great benefit from these fountains ; and hope to return to London in perfect health.

I presume you know that the Spa water drinkers are forbidden to use the pen. I wish you wou'd be so kind to acquaint your sister Mrs. Cornwall of this ; for otherwise she and Mr. Cornwall must think Lady Erskine and me very much to blame in not congratulating them sooner. You'll ask me perhaps why then I venture to write now : my answer must be that recovering patients take whiskis inspite of their doctors. You have perhaps seen Sir James Lowther in his passage to Westmoreland, and from him have learnt more about your Spa acquaintance than I can write. There is nothing worth writing about ; and every trifle may be agreeable matter of conversation. Lady Erskine I presume inform'd Mrs. Cornwall before her marriage that she received her commands and will execute them. She presents her compliments to you : and allow me to offer mine to your whole family and amongst the rest to your brother Whately.[1] Pray what is become of my sollicitation to Mr. Grenville. You make no mention of it in your letter. We hear that you are grown very strict folks in England ; and stop every traveler on the pier of Dover : but we hear also that you have mistaken the law and stretch your power beyond it. It is alledged that merchandise is the only object of the law. I am dear Sir,

Your most affectionate friend,

H. Erskine

CHARLES JENKINSON TO J. S. MACKENZIE

Add. MS. 38304, f. 66.

September 25, 1764.

My dear Sir,

Mr. Grenville has received a letter from Lord Fife informing him that Mr. Erskine the present Sheriff for the County of Bamff, has desired to be appointed Clerk to the Admission of Notaries in the room of Mr. Nasmyth lately deceased, and that he has been told that he was certainly

1. Thomas Whately, Jenkinson's colleague as Joint Secretary to the Treasury.

named for that Office ; and as in such case the Sheriffdom of Bamff must be vacant, he recommends his friend Mr. Keith Urquart to succeed Mr. Erskine ; I was desired by Mr. Grenville to acquaint you with this, and to express his wishes that you would defer taking any step towards the disposal of this office 'till he has had an opportunity of talking with you upon it. I write for no other purpose but to say to you what is above by Mr. Grenville's order.[1] We have nothing new ; I hope soon to have the pleasure of seeing you in town.

I beg my respects to Lady Betty and am etc.

C. Jenkinson

CHARLES JENKINSON TO J. S. MACKENZIE

Add. MS. 38304, f. 73.

October 9, 1764.

My dear Sir,

I received yesterday your letter of October 1st 1764.[2] I shewed it to Mr. Grenville who desires me to assure you how very sensible he is of your attention to him on this occasion. When you come to town, he will talk to you concerning Bamffshire and all that relates to it. I thank you for the little note I found in your letter ; I entirely agree with you in opinion, and I have long endeavored to persuade Mr. G[renville] to think with us on that subject ; he is half inclined ; perhaps you may succeed in making a convert of him. Our accounts of the Duke of Cumberland now are that he has got a swelling in his knee ; he thinks it himself to be the gout ; Ranby [3] thinks it is a humour, and says that there is at present no appearance of danger, that if it should break favorably it will do him good, but that if it should not, he cannot say what the consequences may be.

I am etc.

C. Jenkinson

1. See p. 309 n. 4.
2. Not in the Liverpool MSS.
3. John Ranby (1703–73), Sergeant-Surgeon to the King, about whom see D.N.B.

WILLIAM COURTENAY TO CHARLES JENKINSON

Add. MS. 38203, f. 208.

Captain William Courtenay, R.N., Commissary-General for Minorca, was a brother-in-law of Bute, having married Lady Jane Stuart, a daughter of James, 2nd Earl of Bute.

Bath, October 30, 1764.

Sir,

I beg leave to sollicit you, about an affair in which your friendship, can be of particular service to me, it is concerning the contract, for the salt provisions for the garrison of Minorca, to which His Majesty's commission to me, as Commissary General of that Island, entitles me ; the words being as follows :

"As well by taking under your care and charge all our said Stores of War as by providing provisions and other necessarys for our forces in garrison there",

by which it appears, that my department, is not confined to the article of bread only, but to provisions in general. I mentiond this to Lord Bute, in July last, and his Lordship agreed that I had a right to the salt provisions, as well as the bread, and desired me, to go to you about it, I went accordingly, to wait of you ; but was told, you was gone into the country ; being in town about a month ago, I went again to wait of you ; but had not the good luck to find you ; and now as I am certainly informed, that Messrs. Amyend and Linwood have applied for this contract, and expect to have it, in a few days, I must beg of you, to stand by me, in the affair, by laying it before the Lords of the Treasury ; in which case, I doubt not, but their Lordships will give me the preference, as the tenor of my commission entitles me to it, and that I am ready to undertake it, on as easy terms, as the before mentioned gentlemen, or any other person that can offer ; but if their Lordships have already enterd into any agreement with those gentlemen I hope they will at least be so good, to let me have some share in the contract with them, and should I be so unfortunate to be totally refused any part of it I must still, so far stand by my Deputy,[1] as to request the favour of you

---

1. Courtenay was unlucky in his deputies. One of them, a man called Wilson, who was dismissed about 1764 for speculating with the money for provisioning the troops, tried to get Courtenay into trouble with the Rockingham Administration, by suggesting to Conway that it was illegal for the Commissary or his deputy "to carry on any kind of merchandize". On August 14, 1765, Lady Jane

to have it so settled with whoever gets it that the salt provisions may be consigned to him in order to his issuing them out, to the troops ; which is his right, and has ever been the practice, since our first having possession of that Island ; nevertheless Messrs Amyend and Linwood, have lately acknowledged, to my Deputy that should they get the contract (which they seemed to have no doubt of) they would consign the provisions to Mr. Forbes, Deputy Paymaster of Minorca, who has no manner of right to it, nor indeed any person, whatever, but the Deputy Commissary. The favour of your answer will greatly oblige, Sir,

Your most obedient and most humble servant,

Wm. Courtenay

CHARLES JENKINSON TO J. S. MACKENZIE

Add. MS. 38304, f. 82.

November 3, 1764.

My dear Sir,

Not having heard from you since you revoked your orders of the 8 ultimo concerning the appointment of John Macgowan, I have taken no further step in that business.[1] I see by the public papers that you are come to Edinburgh, and they add that you are soon to set out for London. This being the case I thought proper to trouble you with one more letter before I have the pleasure of seeing you, and particularly as it may be right to apprize you before you leave Scotland that we shall probably want some evidence from thence to appear before the Bar of the House of Commons, with respect to the smuggling trade carried on from the Isle of Man ; the points to which we

Courtenay wrote an indignant letter to Jenkinson stating that she had seen the Order in Council quoted by Wilson which " seemed rather to be made in favour of the Commissary than otherwise, to prevent others from interfering with him, since of necessity he . . . must import corn for the use of the troops ". In the meantime Wilson's successor, one Fraser, was anxious to resign as he feared an enquiry. Jenkinson advised Courtenay to get the matter cleared up with the Treasury in view of his connexion with Bute. Add. MSS. 38204, f. 332 ; 38305, ff. 16, 18.

1. Mackenzie wrote to Jenkinson on October 10 to postpone the nomination of John Macgowan as Assistant Solicitor to the Customs and Excise lest the joint salary should be too large. The salary for the Excise was £80 a year. Mackenzie was uncertain if the salary for the Customs exceeded £20 a year. Add. MS. 38203, f. 183. In 1779 Macgowan appears in the Parliamentary Register, vol. 16, p. 560, as Solicitor both to the Excise and the Customs and the salary of the second place is given as £20.

shall wish to direct our evidence, first the extent and enormity of the smuggling trade, and the loss the revenue suffers by it, secondly, the actual importation of East India goods into the Isle of Man contrary to the provisions of the 7th of George the 1st with the privity of the Lord Proprietor, his Officers or Agents, and 3dly any ill treatment which the King's Officers may have met with in the execution of their duty either from the inhabitants of the Isle of Man, or from the Servants and Officers of the proprietor or from the Courts of Justice of that Island. We have not yet come to any determination as to our method of proceeding, but I think we shall certainly call for the evidence abovementioned. It may therefore be adviseable for you to talk on this subject with those you can confide in (for we should certainly keep our method of proceeding as secret as possible ;) and previously settle who it may be proper to send to town, if this evidence should be required. We have not the least news, and every thing here is as composed as we could wish.

I beg my compliments to Lady Betty and I have etc.

C. Jenkinson

CHARLES JENKINSON TO WILLIAM COURTENAY

Add. MS. 38304, ff. 83-4.

November 9, 1764.

Sir,

I have had the favor of your letter of the 30 of October. It is not the intention of the Lords of the Treasury to enter into any contract at present for supplying the garrison of Minorca with salt provisions. Their Lordships think it more expedient to carry on this supply by commission, and they have employed Messrs Sir George Amyand & Linwood for that purpose, and whenever they alter this method, I am inclined to think that they will treat with some merchants of London, as has always hitherto I believe been the case, provided they will do it upon as good terms as any one else, and that their Lordships will not think themselves bound by the article of your Commission which you mention in your letter, the Treasury having never I believe in any former period treated with the Commissary for the supply of provisions, notwithstanding that the same article has always been inserted in the Commissions of former Commissaries : I will state the other request you make in favor of your Deputy in as advantageous a light as I am able, that if the provisions can be assigned to him without raising the price of the contract your wishes in this respect may be complied with. I acquainted Lord Bute with the state of this affair yesterday, whom I had the pleasure of seeing in perfect health.

I am, etc.
C. Jenkinson

BENJAMIN HALLOWELL [1] TO CHARLES JENKINSON

Add. MS. 38203, f. 227.

Boston, New England, November 10, 1764.

Sir,

My last to you was the 8 and 26 October, in which with great submission I took the liberty to write you as particularly as I could to that time, since which the General Assembly of this province have addressed the Parliament of Great Britain to be presented by their agent, which should have sent you a copy of, had not I been assured that Mr. Mauduit would have shown you the original, which comes by this opportunity.[2]

I am very sorry, Sir, to inform you that every day convinces me that the duties to be collected on goods from Great Britain will fall far short of expectation ; nine sails of vessels have arrived here from London, since the first day of October — the duties raised are as follows for each particular vessel, vizt. £22-2-6 ; £3-13-3 ; £6-18- ; £7-2-4 ; £18-2-9 ; £95-9-6 ; £32-2-1½ ; £3-18- ; £0-0-0. The whole nine ships amounting to £189-8-5½ duties, and I believe next year will be less as many of the coarse goods pay the highest duty. As the sum that is to be collected from the present duties on goods from Great Britain to the colonies will fall so vastly short of expectation, I beg leave to remind you of the liberty I took in my former letters in saying that notwithstanding the duties imposed by the late act of Parliament are so much complained of in the Colonies, that if a duty of 4 or 5 per cent was laid on all

1. About him see p. 281.
2. The petition of the Massachusetts Council and House of Representatives, dated November 1, 1764, is printed in *The Bowdoin and Temple Papers*, Mass. Hist. Soc. Coll., 6th series, ix, 32-6.

goods whatsomever exported from Great Britain to the Colonies to be paid on exportation, that the people would be intirely satisfied, the exportation very little if anything lessened, and the revenue greatly benefitted. The people here are so little acquainted with paying of duties that they had rather be charged with a shilling on the exportation than ninepence on the importation here, they saying money is hard to be gott, and they can always find some kind of produce to send to market to be remitted to Great Britain, to pay for such goods as they may import from thence. They also say that money will be scarce as that all duties to be collected for the Crown is to be remitted into the Exchequer.[1]

Only twelve sail of vessels have arrived in this port from the foreign plantations with sugar and molasses, since the first day of October, the duties uncertain as they are not all unlaided yet. The trade to those islands at present seems to be dull. I have obtained one of the French permissions of which I send you a copy. There is only twenty five of them in all. This is a new method. They in Martinico and Guadeloup have come under some regulations different from but cannot say what they are.

The office which I have the honour to hold as Comptroller of His Majesty's Customs for this port, according to the instructions I received before I came from England, and those sent me be the Honourable Commissioners of His Majesty's Customs, is become an office of equal importance to the Collector and greatly added to the business of former Comptrollers and my whole time with an assistant is taken up in the execution of my office, without ten pound a year addition to what was paid when the office did little or no duty. When I was in England I took the liberty to memorial relative to the fees of this office with a list of fees now received, a copy of which list I beg leave now to inclose you,[2] to show the great

1. John Temple also believed that the duties would be " laying still in coffers for the Crown instead of circulating in the Colonies, already very much drained of cash ". See his letter to Thomas Whately, September 10, 1764, *Bowdoin and Temple Papers*, p. 26. On November 5, 1764, Whately wrote to reassure him that the money " is to be applied to the support of troops there and consequently will not be sent hither in order to be sent back "; and again on June 12, 1765 : " I find your people still alarmed with the idea of their country being drained of all their money by the new taxes. The fact is that no more will be remitted from thence hither, than will just be sufficient to pay the expence of office here, which will be very inconsiderable " (*ibid.* pp. 38, 59).

2. Add. MS. 38203, f. 228. For entering and clearing vessels from New York, the West Indies, and Europe, the collector received 15s. and the controller 3s. 9d., and for vessels from Connecticut, Rhode Island, and Nova Scotia, the collector got 9s. and the controller 2s. 3d. The other fees were all very small.

disproportion between the Collector and Comptrollers fees, which beg the favour of your assistance in settling as shall be thought proper. I am Sir, with the greatest respect,

Your most obedient and very much obliged humble servant,

Benj. Hallowell junr.

JOSEPH BETTS TO CHARLES JENKINSON

Add. MS. 38469, ff. 115-16.

November 29, 1764.

Dear Sir,

I must own I was greatly affected when I was with you last, to hear you speak with so much unconcernedness about my giving up my pretensions to Greenwich.[1]

It is true you observed, that were I consigned to the Professorship at Oxford, it would be made as good a place : but granting the income might be made the same, it by no means follows that it would be an equivalent. The place at Greenwich is tenable with any other preferment, that at Oxford with none. Besides the pension were it to take place, would not I am persuaded be continued long. By the reports sent to Lord Mansfield concerning poor Bliss, we may collect what would be the case of any other person ; and the times I think are not better ; or can there be any grounds to believe, that those that may be communicated concerning his successor would be more favourable or less pernicious. Many other reasons might be given to the same purpose.

But I must now tell you of a fact, which probably you have not been a stranger to for some time, that there is a new candidate for the Savilian Professorship, Dr. Smith[2] a physician of Oxford, who I thought was in great practice, and has ever since Dr. Alcock's[3] time read annually a course of anatomical or chemical lectures or both. He has been it seems with all the electors, and declared himself a candidate, if neither I or Maskelyne stand. I know Dr. Smith has great friends, and of

1. See p. 327.
2. John Smith, of Balliol, M.D., succeeded Betts as Savilian Professor of Geometry 1766–87.
3. Nathan Alcock, of Jesus, M.D., F.R.C.P., died in 1779 (?) The text suggests that Alcock was dead in 1764, but there seems to be no other doctor of that name.

course the best intelligence : and I know moreover that the Arch-bishop seemed inclined a month ago to bring on the election. If this be the case, my prospect which by your account was some time ago fair and promising, will soon unless Mr. G. heart is changed, be closed with disappointment and distress.

For these reasons let me beg of you in your future conversation with Mr. Grenville not to speak of it as a matter of indifference whether I go to Greenwich or Oxford — I make this request on supposition the above scheme does not take place, which you may believe has filled me with alarming apprehensions. Consider I have a very powerful body my enemies, some of whom I have heard are not content to use fair means to lessen my interest, but injuriously the dirtiest and lowest devices the meanest heart can invent. But to trouble you no longer, I know it is in your power to be of great service to me on this occasion. Let me not therefore I entreat you have reason hereafter to lament that you failed me in a point so essential to my happiness. I am with great truth and sincerity

Your most obliged humble servant,

Jo. Betts

Betts was appointed Savilian Professor of Geometry in January 1765. After so much persistence he only lived to enjoy it a year. He died on January 7, 1766.

PHILIP FRANCIS TO CHARLES JENKINSON
in Parliament Street

Philip Francis (1708?–73), father of Sir Philip Francis, the reputed author of *Junius*, was a pamphleteer under the protection of Lord Holland in whose family he was chaplain. In January 1764 Grenville obtained for him a Secret Service pension of £300 a year, in addition to the £600 annuity on the Irish Establishment which he enjoyed since September 16, 1762, probably as a reward for his attack on Pitt. See *Grenv. Pps.* ii, 250, 254-5, and *D.N.B.*

Add. MS. 38203, f. 288.

Downing Street, Wednesday Night.
Docketed " December 5, 1764 ".
Sir,
    I have this moment read the *Some Account of Mr. Legge's Character*, and as I really think it a most unjustifiable, invidious

attack on Lord Bute's reputation, I could wish to be employ'd in answering it ; [1] if indeed it be thought proper to answer it without injuring the gratitude which I hope I shall ever preserve to Mr. Grenville for the happiness, the perfect, unwishing happiness, I enjoy. I am well assur'd I am not meanly indebted for it to his Lordship.

I shall not give you the trouble of acknowledging the receipt of this note, unless I may have the honour of being employ'd. Your assistance then, your instructions will be most necessary. I am Sir with all truth and esteem

Your obliged obedient servant,

Phil: Francis

CHARLES JENKINSON TO PHILIP FRANCIS [2]

Add. MS. 38304, f. 97.

December 5, 1764.

Dear Sir,

I have just had the favor of your letter, I feel *myself* much obliged to you for this instance of your attention to those who have contributed to be of service to you. You may imagine that I can give no positive answer to what you so kindly propose 'till I have consulted the principal person concerned ; and he will not be in town 'till Saturday evening.

I am etc.

C. Jenkinson

1. On December 3, 1764, John Butler, afterwards Bishop of Hereford, about whom see an anonymous letter to Grenville (May 27, 1764, in *Grenv. Pps.* ii, 330), a pamphleteer who had attacked Bute in 1762, published in a *Character* of H. B. Legge, the correspondence between Legge and Bute on the Hampshire election of 1759, when Bute, through his agent Samuel Martin, " invited Legge to withdraw in favour of Simeon Stuart, and on Legge's refusal, asked him to undertake not to contest the county against the Prince of Wales's two candidates at the general election ". Legge died on August 23, 1764, and these letters were published posthumously at his desire, as he believed they explained his dismissal from the Chancellorship of the Exchequer in March 1761. See Walpole to Hertford, December 3 : " He showed the letters to me in the Spring, and I then did not think them so strong or important as he did. I am very clear it does no honour to his memory to have them printed now." An answer to Butler's pamphlet is printed in the *Gent. Mag.*, 1764, p. 555, but the letters " published partially and falsely, are not comprehended within these observations. They can be answered. Whether they will or not, I neither know nor care."

2. In Jenkinson's letter book this letter and the next one are addressed to Mr. F.

CHARLES JENKINSON TO PHILIP FRANCIS

Add. MS. 38304, f. 99.

December 10, 1764.

Dear Sir,

Since I wrote to you last I have seen the person whom I thought proper to consult on the subject of your letter. He is of opinion that what relates to him in the account of Mr. Legge deserves contempt and nothing else, and that the returning an answer to it might give it more weight than it seems to have at present in the opinion of mankind. He desires me however to assure you of the sense he has of your obliging attention to him on this occasion.

I am etc.

C. Jenkinson

R. WOLTERS TO CHARLES JENKINSON

Add. MS. 38204, ff. 20-21.

Rotterdam, January 11, 1765.

Dear Sir,

In obedience to the commands contained in the honour of your's of the 25 past I send you inclosed abstracts of two letters from New York ; and also the particulars of what has happened to the ships chartered by Mr. James Crawfurd [1] of this place, to carry setlers to America.

You are better than any body able to judge of the truth and importance of the facts sett down in these two papers.

If the encouraging setlers to go to America, is as material as most people think it to be, it is certainly to be wished that obstructions of this kind were removed ; as on the one hand they will greatly diminish the spirit of migration in the Germans, and on the other will discourage the merchants, notwithstanding the great profits which they make, from sending them to our settlements.

The anxiety of the Dutch upon the French Edict [2] is as great as can well be imagined, but as to disturbances, you know that their moneyed men are ever passive when the French are

1. ? John Crawford died at Rotterdam in 1766.
2. See p. 224 n. 2.

(344)

in the case ; besides they are in so very deep in the French stocks, that they are ashamed of their own imprudence : the majority flatter themselves with the ill grounded hopes of the Edict's being called in soon.

As to the Edict itself, I do not yet find that any body understands it perfectly. If any thing material occurs upon this head you may depend upon my transmitting it to you.

Poor Mrs. Renard is very anxious to have Mr. Grenville's decision upon her affair ; if once I have the satisfaction to hear from you that her cause is thought just and that her pension is restored, I make no doubt of my prevailing upon her to do something for her sister.[1]

I send you inclosed your account of £4–18–9 which if you will please pay to Mr. Stephens at the Admiralty, he will remit to me with some other small sums.

I have the honour to be with great truth and regard, dear Sir,

Your most humble and most obedient servant

R. Wolters

Note in Jenkinson's writing on the back of Wolters' letter :
" Mr. Nesbitt
    Mr. Carpenter
    Mr. Potinger."

CHARLES JENKINSON TO BENJAMIN HALLOWELL

Add. MS. 38304, ff. 111-13.

January 12, 1765.

Sir,

Since my letter to you of November 8, 1763,[2] I have received yours of the 8th and 28th of October and of the 10th of November. I am much obliged to you for the informa-

1. Jane van Segveld was the wife of Daniel Renard, who succeeded his father in 1746 as joint agent at Amsterdam for Great Britain and Hanover, with a salary of £200 and 200 rix-dollars a year. In 1746 Daniel Renard gave a legal undertaking to allow his sisters 300 francs a year, but as the Hanoverian part of his money was never forthcoming, he reduced this allowance to 200. In 1748 he became insane but continued to receive a pension of £200 a year until it was stopped in November 1764, apparently at the instance of one of his sisters, a spiteful woman who had lost two law-suits against him, and now meant to ruin the family. On November 13, 1764, Wolters sent Jenkinson a documented account of the case and strongly recommended Mrs. Renard for the restoration of her husband's pension. Add. MS. 38203, ff. 233-55.

2. A mistake for 1764 when Jenkinson wrote to Hallowell about the molasses fraud at Anguila. Add. MS. 38304, f. 84. This fraud is mentioned in the corre-

(345)

tion you have sent me. The people of the Colonies have done themselves much hurt by their resistance to the legislature of this kingdom in general, they have thrown thereby all serious men into the scale against them. The oeconomical spirit which has been introduced in consequence of the late law, if it should continue, would do no hurt to the public in general, though it might in a small degree diminish the revenue ; but I am convinced it will not last long. And as to the idea of people of the Colonies becoming manufacturers themselves, I see no reason to apprehend it at present. Whenever they can work cheaper than the manufacturers of this country, they will become so of course. This is not the case at present, nor likely to be so soon. The present act will not in any respect hasten this event for it lays no duty on British manufacturers and consequently cannot raise the price of these. I should think it indeed very inadvisable to take any measure of this kind which makes me disapprove of what you suggest in some of your letters of laying a duty of 5 per cent on all goods exported from Great Britain.

I am obliged to you for the several other things you suggest. The fraud committed by those who clear out in ballast and do not therefore give a bond will certainly be remedied. I see that the revenue must lose by the payments being made in silver at 5s and 6d per ounce, but this has always been the method of payment and if we were to alter it, it would operate as an additional duty which might not be liked. There can be no reason to apprehend that this revenue will deprive the country of money ; you yourself say that it will not amount to a great deal, and if it should amount to much more than is expected we shall always be forced to send from hence much larger sums for the payment of troops and establishments there. I am not surprized that the produce of those duties should not be great at present. You say that they had laid in great stores of goods previous to the commencement of it. This will prevent the receipt of any considerable sums for some time. I should think however it would gradually improve, and the smallness of it at present is at least a proof that it is not oppressive, and the price you mention of molasses convinces me of what I always thought, that the price of them would not rise greatly in the Colonies and that the French who have no other method

spondence between John Temple and Thomas Whately. See *The Bowdoin and Temple Papers, passim,* and a note by the editors, p. 26. Hallowell's letters of October 8 and 28 are not in the Liverpool MSS.

of disposing of them would be forced to pay the duty and not the people of the colonies who perchase them.[1]

I referred a great while ago the table of fees you gave me to the Commissioners of Customs ; I have yet received no answer, but I will write to them to hasten their report. I return you thanks for the candles you have sent me. They are not yet arrived. Mr. Grenville desires me to return you thanks for those which you have sent to him. I shall hope to hear further from you, and shall like to have explained what you mentioned in your last letter that the duties are highest on the coarsest goods, and I shall like particularly to know how much the price of the sugar and molasses at present exceeds what it was before the act passed. I rejoice to hear that all the officers of the customs are determined to discharge their duty. They cannot be too much commended for it.

I am with great truth and esteem etc.

C. Jenkinson

CHARLES JENKINSON TO R. WOLTERS

Add. MS. 38304, ff. 113-14.

January 18, 1765.

Dear Sir,

Your several letters have arrived in due time, I am much obliged to you for them, and particularly that of the 11. I am not surprized to hear that the Law passed last Session relating to America is complained of ;[2] the several Laws that had formerly been passed on this subject, tho' they had always been esteemed of the utmost importance to the commercial interests of this country, had been executed for some time in a most negligent and shamefull manner. The beginning to execute them afresh made them have the appearance of new Laws, tho' they had subsisted in reality for a great many years, and the adding new provisions to these for securing the effectual execution of them would necessarily cause great complaints among those who had long been free from any due restraint,

---

1. It was one of the points of the Massachusetts petition (see p. 339) that the duty on molasses would ruin their trade in " inferior " fish with the French, who permitted no fish " to be carried by foreigners to any of their islands unless it be bartered or exchanged for molasses ". Hallowell wrote to Jenkinson on May 3, 1765, that molasses had actually gone down in price since the Act, as quantities had been imported before September 29 and kept for the market, " which is now obliged to be sold " (Add. MS. 38339, ff. 118-19). 2. See p. 251.

thro' the negligence of the Officers of the Crown, and were very unwilling to be made again subject to them. The increase of our Colonies is certainly what we wish but they must increase in such a manner as will keep them usefull to the mother country ; and any regulations that are essential to this last object, tho' they may to a small degree prevent the increase of the Colonies, are founded on true policy and should be complied with. The late Law is formed on the principles of the Act of Navigation : The intention of it is to prevent all commerce between our Colonies and any part of Europe except Great Britain, unless in cases specially allowed, and to permit under certain regulations the commerce of our Continental Colonies with Foreign Islands so as to leave a clear and undoubted proof [? profit] to our own Islands. With this view all the provisions of it are formed ; and as far as it is necessary for this purpose to restrain the commerce of our Colonies, it is an evil to which I think they ought to submit for the good of the whole : If in the execution of these Laws any of our officers have behaved improperly the Law is open to such complaints and will not fail to inflict due punishment upon those who are found to be guilty.

I will renew my application with respect to Madame Renard and what you mention in your last letter of her making an allowance to her sister in law may perhaps enable me to bring this affair to a conclusion. I will take care to pay what I am indebted to you into Mr. Stevens's hands as you desire : I would have the Gazette de Commerce continued. I wish you most sincerely a happy year, and a long continuance of them,

And am with great truth and regard etc.

C. Jenkinson

JAMES MARRIOTT TO CHARLES JENKINSON

Add. MS. 38458, f. 58.

February 14, 1765. At Mrs. Sayers,
Southampton Street, Holborn.

Dear Sir,

The borough of Brackley is open : [1] If it is in the certain disposition of Government [2] and Mr. Grenville has not fixed

1. On the death of Alderman Marsh Dickinson, M.P. for Brackley 1754–65.
2. The Duke of Bridgwater was borough patron of Brackley. He was a nephew of the Duke of Bedford, belonged to the Bedford group, and accepted their recommendations.

on a man more useful to his own interests than it is very much
my wish to endeavour to be, I hope I shall have a place in
your thoughts and his.

I have been remarkably busy otherwise should have done
myself the pleasure of waiting on you before now, and indeed
wanted much to put into your hands for any half hour of
leisure a report or two I have made ex officio [1] to the Privy
Council on some extraordinary questions, on which I should
have begged your opinion, as I have differed from some great
Men of the Law : for though you have dropped the Civilian
for the character of the Financier, the world will not forget
that you first pleaded with success for your country to all
Europe, for measures Government had pursued but could not
justify.[2]

I am, with the utmost respect possible
Your most obedient obliged humble servant,
James Marriott

CHARLES JENKINSON TO JAMES MARRIOTT

Add. MS. 38304, f. 120.

February 14, 1765.

My dear Sir,
No man wishes more than I do to see you exercising your
abilities in Parliament as well as everywhere else. I am sorry
however that Brackley is disposed. Lord Sandwich's eldest son
Lord Hinchinbrook [3] is already I believe chosen there. I shall
be happy to have the pleasure of seeing you whenever your
business will permit, and I shall be still more happy to have
the perusal of your reports ; for I have still an affection for a

1. As King's Advocate.
2. What Marriott now called pleading " with success " thus appears in his
letter to Newcastle, dated February 28, 1761 : " I can not help thinking it hard
that Lord Holdernesse's interest should procure an establishment for Mr. Jenkinson
only . . . as that gentleman's history of the dispute relating to the Treaty of
1673/4 afforded no one argument to quiet the Dutch demands upon our Court
except their breach of treaty, but actually made against us by showing how the
treaty of 1673/4 was made on purpose to serve our own turn at the time ; of which
account of the treaty therefore all the Dutch writers availed themselves " (Add.
MS. 32919, f. 342).
3. John Montagu, Viscount Hinchingbrooke, was returned for Brackley on
February 15. He represented it until 1768, and afterwards sat for Huntingdonshire 1768–92, when he succeeded his father as 5th Earl of Sandwich.

science in which though I do not pretend to much merit, I once took some pains.

I am etc.

C. Jenkinson

EDWIN WARDROPER TO CHARLES JENKINSON

Add. MS. 38204, f. 79.

Rye, February 16, 1765.

Sir,

Observing by the votes that you are to bring in a bill for naming Commissioners of the land tax for the present year, I intreat the favour of you to insert the following names for the Town and Parish of Rye.

Walter Waters, Edwin Wardroper, and Richard Wardroper. As we all pay considerable land tax there, don't apprehend there can be any reasonable objection, but did not choose to apply to the Members for a reason you know.[1] I am already a Commissioner for the County of Essex but should be glad to have Mr Waters and my son named there likewise being both qualified to act, and am Sir,

Your most obedient servant,

E. Wardroper

Jenkinson replied on February 23 (Add. MS. 38304, f. 122) : " I will take care that the gentlemen you have recommended shall be appointed commissioners of the land tax ".

LORD NORTHUMBERLAND TO CHARLES JENKINSON

Add. MS. 38204, f. 170.

Northumberland House, March 27 [1765].

Dear Sir,

I take the earlies⟨t⟩ opportunity to inform you that His Majesty ⟨has⟩ been pleased this day to appoint your brot⟨her⟩ Captain of Dragoons in Colonel Carpenters Regiment on the

1. The two members, John Norris and John Bentinck, M.P.s for Rye 1762–74 and 1761–68 respectively, sat on Newcastle's interest.

Irish Establishment,[1] and I assure y⟨ou⟩ it gives me every sincere pleasure to h⟨ave⟩ had it in my power to contribute to his be⟨ing⟩ placed in a situation which I hope wil⟨l⟩ prove agreeable both to you and him, be⟨ing⟩ with very great truth and regard, dear Sir,

Your most obedient humble servant,

Northumberland

CHARLES JENKINSON TO LORD NORTHUMBERLAND

Add. MS. 38304, f. 127.

March 27, 1765.

My Lord,

I have this instant at my return from the House of Commons, received the honour of your Lordship's letter acquainting me with my brother's good fortune. The friendly and generous manner in which your Lordship has acted on this occasion, deserves my most grateful acknowledgements, and I hope I shall have opportunities, in the future parts of my life, to shew the sense I have of it. I esteem it as one of the happy consequences of Lord Bute's patronage of me, that it has introduced me to your Lordships acquaintance, and I flatter myself you will always find me (as I trust he has always done) truly and zealously attached to your interests.

I am etc.

C. Jenkinson

CHARLES JENKINSON TO THOMAS ROUS

Add. MS. 38304, f. 129.

Thomas Rous was Chairman of the East India Company April 1764–65. See p. 271.

March 31, 1765.

Dear Sir,

Some of Mr. Grenville's friends propose to meet at the King's Arms in Cornhill to-morrow evening at 7 o'Clock in

1. Captain John Jenkinson joined Colonel Benjamin Carpenter's regiment, the 12th, or Prince of Wales's Light Dragoons, on March 21, 1765. On December 20, 1764, Charles Jenkinson wrote to thank Northumberland for a promise to serve his brother " whenever a proper occasion offers " (Add. MS. 38304, f. 102).

(351)

order to sign a proposal for filling the subscription with money in case the little Bills that may be offered on or before the 5 of April next should not be sufficient for that purpose. I mention this to you that you may be at the Meeting if you think proper. You will find there Sir Samuel Fludyer, Sir G. Aymand, Mr. Salvadore, and several of your friends.

I am etc.

C. Jenkinson

JOSEPH SALVADOR TO CHARLES JENKINSON
in Parliament Street

Add. MS. 38204, f. 175.

Garraways Coffee House, 9 o'Clock.
Docketed "April 1, 1765".

Dear Sir,
    The meeting desird was held and the following gentlemen were present or desird their names to be inserted. They have agreed to all you can wish. Sir Samuel Fludyer will convey their sentiments to morrow. Their names are

Lord Catherlough [1]	Sir Samuel Fludyer [2]
Sir George Amyand [3]	Sir Thomas Fludyer [4]
Mr. Weyland [5]	Mr. Jackson [6]
Mr. Brown	Mr. Thornton & Co.[7]
Mr. Franks [8]	Mr. Jones [9]

1. Robert Knight, 1st Earl of Catherlough (Irish), 1st Baron Luxborough, M.P. for Grimsby 1734–47, 1762–68, Castle Rising 1747–54, Milborne Port 1770–72.
2. Sir Samuel Fludyer, 1st Bart., M.P. See p. 239. He was one of the Directors of the Bank.
3. Sir George Amyand, 1st Bart. (1720–66), M.P. for Barnstaple 1754–66, was a merchant-banker and East India Director, supposed to be worth £160,000 ; in spite of which he received help from the Treasury for his election in 1754. See Namier, Structure of Politics, p. 247 n. 5.
4. Sir Thomas Fludyer, knight, younger brother of Samuel Fludyer, M.P. for Great Bedwin 1767–68, Chippenham 1768–69.
5. John Weyland, Governor of the Bank April 1765–66. As the elections of Directors of the Bank took place in the first week of April, he may still have been Deputy Governor when this meeting was held.
6. Richard Jackson, M.P. See p. 191.
7. John Thornton was the biggest English banker connected with Russia. In 1784 he had three sons in Parliament. One of these, Henry Thornton, was the friend and collaborator of Wilberforce. See Structure of Politics, pp. 70, 421 n. 2.
8. Moses Franks, an American Jew, partner of Fludyer and Adam Drummond. See ibid. pp. 65-6.
9. Robert Jones, M.P., and Peregrine Cust, M.P., were partners. See p. 213.

Mr. Cust [1]	Mr. Prescott [2]
Mr. P. Fonnereau [3]	T. Fonnereau [4]
Major & Co. [5]	Burrell [6]
Bacon S. [7]	Salvador

I congratulate you on this success, it does us honour. I shall certainly wait on Mr. Grenville.

I have reflected on your scheme for £200,000 Exchequer Bills I think twill answer but let me caution you that tis too near to pass them att 3 per cent and I heartily wish you would consult the Bank before you do it.

I dont find the Bank has seen the draught of the Bill These matters are very nice as to form and an error has no remedy after Parliament is up. I would not have it brought to your charge. I am dear Sir,

Your most obedient servant,

Joseph Salvador

LORD NUNEHAM TO CHARLES JENKINSON

Add. MS. 38204, ff. 180–81.

Saturday Evening.
Docketed " April 6, 1765 ".

Sir,

It is the business of an honest man when he has injured a person, to endeavour to make all the amends in his power, and to entreat a pardon for it. I have injured you, and though you do not know it, I still think it equally incumbent on me to inform you of it and acknowledge my error. You may have perceived a great coolness in me towards you, and when I

1. See note 9 on facing page.
2. George Prescott, M.P. for Stockbridge 1761–68, Milborne Port (*vice* Lord Catherlough) 1772–74, originally a Leghorn merchant-banker ; he was helped to a seat in Parliament by Henry Fox. See Namier, *England etc.* p. 295 n. 3.
3. Philip Fonnereau, M.P. See p. 110.
4. Thomas Fonnereau, M.P., his brother. See p. 110.
5. John Major, M.P. See p. 116.
6. Merrick Burrell, one of the Directors of the Bank 1764–65, M.P. for Grampound 1754–68, about whom see *Structure of Politics*, pp. 261, 429.
7. Anthony Bacon, M.P. See p. 194. Of the eighteen men at this meeting twelve were in Parliament ; Thomas Fonnereau had a brother in Parliament whom he was afterwards to succeed in his seat ; John Thornton was later to have three sons in Parliament. Franks and Salvador as Jews were debarred from sitting in Parliament.

tell you that I had been informed that *on the night of my voting against the Ministry on the General Warrants,*[1] *you had immediately dispatched a messenger with a note to my father* you will not be surprized that a man with so warm a temper as mine, should be shocked at such treatment from one whom he esteemed as his friend and for whom he had a very great regard. The believing this I acknowledge to be wrong, very wrong, but I was the more hurt because I had an esteem and friendship for you ; for as to the nonsense of party, (however different my sentiments may be in politics from yours) I should never be mean enough to disregard you the more, or love you the less. I have now stated the fact, and again entreat your pardon for what I have done, which I most sincerely repent of, and will contradict what I formerly said concerning this affair to the few to whom I have mentioned it, (for mention it I will own I have). It is not for me now to ask a favour, if it were, it would be to express my wishes that you would not enquire into the authors of this cruel invention, for they are beneath your anger, and as they *were women* you cannot if you would, expect satisfaction.

It is not five minutes since this affair has by chance been cleared up to me, but I could not go out though engaged, without writing this letter, as it is a justice I owe to your character and my own. I am Sir,

Your very obedient servant,
Nuneham

CHARLES JENKINSON TO LORD NUNEHAM

Add. MS. 38304, f. 131.

North End, April 7, 1765.

My Lord,

The letter I have just received from you at this place, has, I own, surprized me. Your behavior to me of late I have thought not so friendly as I had reason to expect from you. The cause of it I never guessed ; it is clear now that I never could, for it never had any existence. I am much obliged to you for acknowledging your error now you have discovered it. If you had applied to me you should have known the truth before, whether it had been as the case now

1. On February 17, 1764. See p. 266.

appears, or even if it had been otherwise. I was so far from conveying to your father the information you supposed, that he was I believe the first person from whom I received any certain account of it. I trust to your justice that you will contradict what you have told to others concerning this affair ; I am not surprized that false stories are spread of me ; it is the common lot of such as are in my situation, and as you say they are women from whom you received this intelligence, I shall not make any further enquiry concerning it, but only hope that you will not for the future give credit to those who have in this instance deceived you.

I have etc.
C. Jenkinson

LORD NUNEHAM TO CHARLES JENKINSON
Add. MS. 38204, f. 225.

Docketed " April 1765 ".[1]

Sir,

Your letter has given me great satisfaction, and I shall take the first opportunity to thank you for it in person ; I flatterd myself indeed that the step I took would obtain my pardon for my former crime, for such it was, though a person less credulous than myself might have been deceived into such an error, by the means that were made use of to enflame my warm, and unsuspecting temper ; I thought it a justice due to you, and to my own character, to inform you myself of the affair, rather than that it should hereafter be reported to you by others, for I could not submit to be taxed with disingenuousness, a reproach I should have merited had I not acted as I have towards you. You need be under no apprehension as to my not contradicting this shocking report, I have already done it to some, and have employed a friend to do the same, and to relate the whole story, to every person that has ever heard of it. I shall take more pains to publish my error than I would the most laudable action, because I had rather be thought a dupe, than a rascal, which I should be, were I to let an honest man suffer through my means, when I have it in my power to prevent it. I have the honour to be Sir

Your most obedient Servant
Nuneham

1. Probably written as soon as he received Jenkinson's of April 7.

North End, April 8, 1765.

Dear Sir,

I have the honor to send you for your signature two warrants, the one for the distribution of the aggregate, the other of the general Fund. I had obtained the hands of two of the Lords [1] to blanks for this purpose before they left town, so that your signature will complete it. I hope you will return them as soon as you can, that the Bank may have the money to pay the annuitants.

I add a state of the Sinking Fund for this quarter, and also a state of the same Fund for the same quarter of last. You will thereby be enabled to compare them ; and I send also a short comparison of my own ; by which you will see that the excess of this quarter above the produce of the same quarter of last year after making every fair deduction is no less than £46,775 : 4 : 6 I sincerely congratulate you on all this. It more than confirms the truth of all that you stated to the House of Commons ; [2] and there are circumstances in the state of our revenue which convince me that their produce in the future quarters of this year will not be less favorable. I add also the best account I have yet been able to procure of the value of the messenger's places ; I cannot say I much depend upon it ; but I will endeavour to procure you a better.

I am under great difficulties about the subscription ; some of the possessors of the certificates for fractional parts have not brought them to the Bank, or paid into it the money necessary to make up their certificates £100 each, and the Treasurer of the Navy's Office has not taken an exact account of what they have granted of these fractional certificates. I am at a loss therefore to know the state of the subscription and what money to ask of our friends. Mr. Race [3] says that the possessors of fractional certificates who did not bring them and their money to the Bank, before the 5th of April ought not to be allowed to subscribe at all ; and he says that he will take it upon himself to refuse them. This removes all diffi-

1. Of the Treasury.
2. On March 29, when he opened the Budget.
3. Daniel Race was one of the Cashiers of the Bank of England.

culties, for the Bank can give us an exact account. Mr. Yeates [1] and I doubt whether the resolution of the House of Commons authorizes this, and yet I fear that there is no other method to be pursued for the subscription is to be closed on the 18th and the House does not meet till the 19th so that no new powers can be obtained. It is impossible to enter a long discussion on a subject of this nature by letter. I shall endeavour to act for the best and whenever it is possible reserve every thing for your ultimate direction.

I shall dispatch another messenger to morrow with the Post Office Bill and such observations as appear to me of any consequence.

I hear of no news and every thing seems to me to be in as tranquil a state as it is possible to wish it. The King continues well ; I beg my best compliments to Mrs. Grenville and I have the honor to be

With great truth and respect etc.

C. Jenkinson

CHARLES JENKINSON TO GEORGE GRENVILLE

Add. MS. 38304, f. 134.

North End, April 11, 1765.

Dear Sir,

I send a Warrant for your signature, directing the Bank to open Books for the subscription in pursuance of the last Resolution of the House of Commons. It is drawn according to the usual form ; when you have signed it I shall be glad to receive it back, that I may get the hands of two other Lords to it and send it to the Bank.

I trouble you also with the copy of a letter I have written to Mr. Weyland [2] concerning the money that is wanted to compleat the £1,500,000.

I send you also the Post Office Bill with a letter I have written to Lord Trevor on that subject. [3]

I add lastly the propositions made by the Commissioners of Salt for the improvement of their revenue. I have made in

1. Robert Yeates, about whom see p. 203.
2. John Weyland, Governor of the Bank. See p. 352.
3. Robert Hampden, 4th Baron Trevor, in 1776 created Viscount Hampden, was Postmaster - General 1759–65. He was an adherent of Grenville's. His daughter married Lord Suffolk, who led the Grenville party after Grenville's death.

the margin a few observations. If you have no objection I submit to your consideration whether you would not mark with your pencil such of the propositions as you choose to adopt, and then return the paper. I will then take care that the clauses shall be properly drawn, and that in wording them much of the rigour which Mr. Talbot [1] has instilled into them shall be softened.

I have been to town every day, but I hear of no news except that the world begin to say that Lord Northumberland does not go again to Ireland, and to enquire who is to be his successor.

I am afraid that you have had but bad weather since you have been in the country. I hope however that the quiet you have enjoyed has established your health.

I beg my best compliments to Mrs. Grenville,

And I have etc.

C. Jenkinson

CHARLES JENKINSON TO GEORGE GRENVILLE

Add. MS. 38304, f. 134.

North End, April 11, 1765.

Dear Sir,

I send you a very civil answer I have received from Mr. Weyland concerning the subscription.

I add the best account that can be procured though it is but conjectural, of the fractional certificates that were delivered out at the Navy Office, and have not been brought to the Bank ; they are more than Mr. Race imagined, but still of no great importance ; and the Bank are so very friendly that we shall easily now get over this difficulty.

I have talked with Governor Pownal concerning the clause for billeting soldiers in America. He will furnish me with the printed Bill which he passed at Boston for this purpose ; and he and Mr. Frankland [2] have been framing a clause on the

1. Henry Talbot was Chairman of the Salt Board 1763–84. About him and about the Salt Office see Edward Hughes, *Studies in Administration and Finance, 1558–1825*, pp. 277, 317, 319. He received a Secret Service pension of £300 a year from 1779 to 1782. See Add. MS. 37836, f. 139 and accounts, *passim*.

2. Vice-Admiral Thomas Frankland, M.P. for Thirsk 1747–80 and 1784, till his death on November 21. In 1768 he succeeded his brother Sir Charles Frankland as 5th Bart. He had American connexions, having married a daughter or granddaughter of Chief Justice Rhett of South Carolina.

same plan to be passed here ; this he has promised to give me, and I will send them both by the next messenger. If you choose to examine him I am sure he will have no objection but I own I should be unwilling to trust to his discretion as an evidence.

I send inclosed the report of the Secretary at War upon the Barbadoes demand ; and I have added a note at the back of it shewing the opinion of the Board when these papers were laid before them. I should think that the difficulties which occur in this affair from the greatness of the charge and the doubts of the Secretary at War may enable us to diminish part of the demand and that the people of Barbadoes ought to be contented.

Mr. Jackson called on me yesterday at the Treasury and desired me to acquaint you that the Legislature of the Colony of Massachusetts Bay had offered to make him their Agent, and that he was in doubt what to do ; his own inclination rather led him to decline it and yet if his acceptance of it would be of service to Government he was ready to take it. On this he desires to be favoured with your sentiments. He says that this proposition in his favour was carried by a majority of about 60 to 40. The person set up against him was the younger Mauduit,[1] but in case he should decline he does not think that Mauduit will be chosen but seems apprehensive it may be somebody recommended by Sir William Baker.[2] I beg you would let me know what answer I am to return to him.

I beg my best compliments to Mrs. Grenville and I have the honor to be etc.

C. Jenkinson

I have seen Lord Trevor this morning and settled all that relates to the Post Office Bill.

1. Richard Jackson, one of Grenville's private secretaries (see p. 191), succeeded Jaspar Mauduit as agent for Massachusetts in 1765. According to Governor Hutchinson's *History of Massachusetts Bay* (1828), p. 105 note, about 1764 the Assembly voted for Israel Mauduit to succeed his brother Jaspar on the grounds that Israel did all the work (he attended the conference of province agents in March 1764, see p. 305), but Governor Bernard " having a desire to introduce another person ", induced the Council to non-concur, and Jaspar continued in the agency until 1765. In 1766–67 the Assembly quarrelled with Richard Jackson (see below, Israel Mauduit's *Annus Pacificus*, p. 439) and he was dismissed from the agency. In 1770 he became agent for Connecticut.

2. Alderman Sir William Baker, M.P. for Plympton 1747–68, was one of the principal merchants trading to America, a friend and adherent of Newcastle's and one of his chief advisers on American affairs. In 1771 his son married a granddaughter of William Penn of Pennsylvania. See Namier, *England etc.* pp. 280–81.

CHARLES JENKINSON TO GEORGE GRENVILLE

Add. MS. 38304, f. 135.

April 13, 1765.

Dear Sir,

I received yesterday your letter by Walker and I rejoice to hear that by the assistance of the country air you have already got rid of your cold : I send by this messenger a large packet from Governor Pownall. It relates to the clause for quartering troops in America, I hope that you will find it of use to you, and that it will strike out some lights which may releive you from the difficulties of that affair.

You will receive likewise a Warrant, which is wanted at the Exchequer and which I should be obliged if you would sign and return to me.

I add also a Warrant appointing Arthur Savage Comptroller of the Customs at Falmouth in New England. This is the man whom Mr. Mauduit recommended to you as a person particularly qualified to watch and check the smuggling trade. The man wishes to go to his station by a ship now ready to sail, and would set out immediately if you thought proper to appoint him.

I send likewise an account of the vacancy of a little office in the Stamp Office.

I have settled a plan for remitting the American Revenue. It concerns no body but the Receiver General of the Customs, and the persons who have contracted to remit the pay of the troops. I have consulted Mr. Levinz's Deputy [1] and Mr. Hulton [2] and they approve of it. I have not been able to get a sight of the Remitters who are all flown into the country, but I do not think they can have any objection ; but as it relates to the payment of public money it is proper that it should be done by a Minute of the Board ; I send you the draught of such a Minute and to obviate any evil that may arise from this delay ; I have written the inclosed letter to the Commissioners of the Customs, that they may apprize their Collectors in America, and the West Indies of what the Treasury intend ; I did not care to order them expressly not to send

---

1. John Piggot was William Levinz's assistant as Receiver-General of the Customs. About Levinz see below, p. 382 n. 1.
2. Henry Hulton was the Plantation Clerk in the Custom House. In 1767 he was appointed one of the five Commissioners of the new American Board of Customs.

any money home ; I thought this was too delicate a point to be the subject of an express order ; but I have endeavoured to convey that meaning and I explained it more fully to Mr. Hulton. Besides it is too late to prevent any money coming home that may arise upon the settlement of the April Quarter ; and after the Board is met we shall have time enough to send instructions that will regulate the payments of the quarter ending the 5 of July.[1]

I have gone over the American Bill of this year, I do not send it to you, as there must be many amendments made in it before it is worthy of your perusal. The points on which I want your orders are the following.

1st. Whether we should not take off the whole of the last shilling duty from the Plantation coffee, and the half of it from the Asiatick. I think we should not in any instance take off more than the last shilling ; and yet a distinction should be made between our own coffee and that of foreign countries.

2dly. Whether you would provide any remedy to remove a difficulty, that has arisen upon that clause of the Bill of last year that relates to the distribution of seizures. I send you some papers that will explain the whole of the business and I have taken the liberty to add my own opinion on the case.

The Board of Trade have promised that I should have their sentiments on the granting a bounty on timber and iron on Monday. I understand that they will propose a small bounty on timber and with respect to iron, they will propose a duty on Swedish iron which may answer the charge of a bounty they wish to have given to American.

As to the anonymous letter you have received concerning the bonds to be given by the persons who import rice, the writer of it does not know the checks and restrictions with which the intended clause is guarded ; I send you a copy of it, that you may form some judgement thereof yourself. I know there is danger in every thing of this nature ; and in general the Commissioners of the Customs are against it, but if I do not mistake, this is a proposal of their own. I will send however to Mr. Morris[2] and talk to him further upon it.

I have troubled you enough with business and I hear no news of any kind. Every body indeed is out of town.

1. Cf. Whately's assurances to John Temple that the money collected from taxation in America would be used for the maintenance of the troops there and would not be sent home to England. See p. 340 n. 1.
2. Corbyn Morris, Commissioner of Customs, about whom see p. 277.

My compliments attend Mrs. Grenville and I have the
honor to be etc.

C. Jenkinson

GILBERT ELLIOT TO CHARLES JENKINSON

Add. MS. 38204, f. 241.

Docketed " May 19, 1765."

My dear Sir,

It would be a great comfort and satisfaction to me to be
able to pass a few hours with you in the country, but I really
cannot quit a moment my own house, as my poor wife wants
my support very much. I by no means lose hopes of my child
though her fever still continues unabated but with no particular
symtom of any kind, which always give hope of some crisis.
If you can call here, any time this afternoon, it will be a great
comfort to me, no body can be so inhuman as to suspect us
at present of caballing. For my own part I am in the most
profound ignorance, I have seen no body but Lord March,
and Lord Denbigh, who assur'd me yesterday he knew nothing
of what was going on, and said he had seen Lord Leichfield
who was equally ignorant. My physicians tell me that all the
Bedford family and friends go to court to day, saying openly
they are to be out, but that they are not to resign. I have heard
not a word either from Lord Bute, or Mr. Grenville.[1]

Yours ever,
G. E.

Whether from general views of things, or from the impression
of my present feelings I know not, but I have hardly a wish
as to myself, whether I am to continue in office or to be out
of it.

1. On May 19 a negotiation was in progress between the King and Pitt,
through the agency of Cumberland who was that day at Hayes. The negotiation
failed, and on May 22 the King came to terms with Grenville and the Bedfords.
See Gilbert Elliot's diary below, pp. 367 et seq.

CHARLES JENKINSON TO GEORGE GRENVILLE

Add. MS. 38305, ff. 10-11.

June 16, 1765.

Dear Sir,

I send you herewith Mr. Lutwidge's Commission [1] signed by His Majesty, and I add some instructions which I have prepared for his direction : these will be sufficient I should think for the present and will meet I hope with your approbation, I have also sent the Secretary at War an account of the difficulties and resistance which the officers of the Revenue meet with in the Isle of Man in carrying the laws into execution and desiring he would take His Majesty's pleasure for sending orders to the troops stationed there to give the officers of the Revenue all legal and proper assistance, I think therefore we have now finished all that is necessary for us to do in the business. I send also a Warrant for doing what Mr. Fane desires in favor of Lyme.[2] I add also a letter from Mr. Freemantle [3] concerning the effects of Monsieur de Blosset [4] that were seized which proves Monsieur de Blosset to be a great smuggler, and shews that our officers both at Dover and on the road must have connived. I intend to send Monsieur de Blosset a copy of the letter ; and I have written one myself to the Commissioner of the Customs ; a copy of which you will find inclosed and which you will I hope approve of, I trouble you also with a draft of a letter to the Commissioners of the Navy. They want some such authority as this for the payment of the Fractional Certificates, and Mr. Wallace [5] says they cannot pay them without it. I have drawn the letter so as to follow the intention of the Treasury with respect to the Certificates as expressed in their Minute. I see no objection to it, But I did not choose to sign it without your approbation. The state of the bounty List is as follows.

1. Charles Lutwidge, Surveyor-General for Cumberland and Lancaster, about whom see p. 294, was employed by Government in the administrative reforms carried out in the Isle of Man after its purchase from the Duke and Duchess of Athol.
2. Henry Fane, M.P. for the family borough of Lyme Regis 1757-77, for which he received £100 a year Secret Service money. See Namier, *Structure of Politics*, p. 255 and *passim*.
3. John Freemantle was appointed Assistant Secretary to the Commissioners of Customs in January 1765.
4. The Marquis de Blosset was French Resident in London.
5. James Wallace was Paymaster and Accountant under Lord Barrington, Treasurer of the Navy.

Vacancies to the amount of £60 per annum.
Cash in Hand to be given away £110.

If you would have any other messenger besides this sent to you during your absence except on urgent business you will be so kind as to let me know, and to what place. I beg my compliments to Mrs. Grenville

And I have the honor to be etc.

C. Jenkinson

PHILIP LLOYD TO CHARLES JENKINSON

Add. MS. 38204, f. 272.

Wotton, June 17, 1765.

Dear Sir,
Mr. Grenville this morning sets out for ⟨Stowe [1]⟩ and having some papers before him which it is necessary he ⟨giv⟩e answers to in his own hand, he has directed me ⟨to tel⟩l you that he entirely approves the instructions drawn ⟨for Lu⟩twidge, which you will receive inclosed and signed, as well ⟨as Lu⟩t-widge's Commission, and the Warrant desired by Mr. ⟨Wallace⟩.
Mr. Grenville has no objection to the draught of the letter to the ⟨Commissioners of the⟩ Navy. ⟨He stay⟩s at Stowe 'till Friday, and desires that a messenger ⟨be s⟩ent thither to him either on Wednesday or Thursday ⟨according⟩ to the business which arises ; but would have one certainly sent to him at Stowe on Thursday to receive any orders which Mr. Grenville may then have to give him. I am dear Sir,

Yours most faithfully,

Philip Lloyd

CHARLES JENKINSON TO GEORGE GRENVILLE

Add. MS. 38305, f. 11.

North End, June 19, 1765.

Dear Sir,
The messenger who brings this attends you in consequence of Dr. Lloyd's letter to me. I send you inclosed a letter I have received from Mr. Webb concerning the arguments etc.

1. Grenville was at Stowe from Monday, June 17, to Friday, June 21, when he returned to Wotton. While he was there, on June 19, Pitt had an interview with the King.

that have been had in the Court of Kings Bench and Common Pleas on the affair of the General Warrants. I am told on all hands that the Sollicitor General in the Court of King's Bench argued this point exceedingly well. It is said that this Court by giving the first decision in the manner they have done against the principle of a General Warrant have stole a march upon the Court of Common Pleas ; I am told that in giving their judgement they said that notwithstanding the number of precedents produced from their office whence these Warrants had usually issued, and that several of them had from time to time been before that Court, they were of opinion that they were illegal, and that they could not be argued a second time. I hear that both the Attorney General and Mr. Yorke equally plume themselves on this occasion : the Attorney says that an eminent lawyer and one whom Mr. Yorke acknowledges to be so has been found to argue this point which Mr. Yorke said in the House of Commons was impossible and Mr. Yorke says that the Court has determined this point according to the opinion he had already given. There is however an end of the question.

I trouble you with a letter from Mr. Hollowell [1] at Boston, which shews that our firmness here has got the better of the obstinacy of the Colonies and that all there will end well. I add a letter from Mr. Drummond Commissioner of the Excise in Scotland.[2] There are I beleive none of that Board at present absent, so that his request may with propriety be complied with, if you have no other objection.

I trouble you with a letter which Mr. Bradshaw has received from Mr. Stanhope the Receiver of the Land Tax for the County of York.

I heard to day at the Treasury that Mr. Pitt had been this morning with the King and had stayed with His Majesty 3 hours, but nothing of what passed there has as yet transpired. You will receive together with this a packet of letters and with it a knife for Mrs. Grenville. I beg my compliments to her and Lord Temple

And I am etc.

C. Jenkinson

I have just received a letter from the Commissioners appointed for the Sale of Land in the Ceded Islands by which

1. See p. 281.
2. George Drummond, Commissioner of Excise in Scotland 1761–66. Some of his accounts are in the Liverpool MSS., Add. MSS. 38337, ff. 253-6 ; 38338, f. 101.

I find, that the report of Mr. Young's [1] death is without foundation.

PHILIP LLOYD TO CHARLES JENKINSON

Add. MS. 38204, f. 289.

Wotton, June 23, 1765.

Dear Sir,

I return you the Comte de Guerchy's letter and Memorial which last Mr. Grenville desires you will send to the Custom house that he may at his return to town receive full information upon the subject.[2] He is much obliged to you for the reports upon the present state of things of the particulars of which nothing is here known.

This is the first moment I have had to acquaint you with what I am sure will give you the truest pleasure, that the joy in both parts of the family is as great as the reconciliation is cordial. The reception at Stowe was one continual scene of pleasure embellish'd with the circumstances of illuminations etc. The family from thence come hither to morrow.[3] I am dear Sir,

Yours sincerely,

P. Lloyd

I also return you Hammond's letter.

THE EARL OF SANDWICH TO CHARLES JENKINSON

Add. MS. 38204, f. 290.

Belvidere, June 25, 1765.

Dear Sir,

The enclosed letter is from a person who together with his father is joint Re⟨ceiver⟩ of the Land Tax for the County

1. William Young, Lieutenant-Governor of Dominica, about whom see p. 120, was one of the five Commissioners for the sale of lands in the ceded islands, and the Receiver of money arising out of these sales.

2. Several memorials from Guerchy in May and June 1765 are mentioned in the *Cal. H.O. Pps.*: the nearest in date is No. 1776, June 10, which asks for the restitution of a French boat laden with timber condemned by the Admiralty Court in Ireland.

3. The reconciliation between Grenville and Temple was celebrated by a visit from the Grenville family to Stowe. They went on June 17 and returned to Wotton on the 21st. According to Grenville's diary, on June 23 "Lady Temple, Lord Bristol, and Mr. James Grenville's two sons came to Wotton". Temple left Stowe that day to consult Pitt before seeing the King. *Grenv. Pps.* iii, 199-200.

of H⟨untingdon⟩.[1] The appointment to that office I ap⟨prehend⟩ is annual, and you will observe ⟨it has⟩ not passed this year.

Mr. Jackson is a person of great ⟨considerati⟩on in our county, and it extremely concer⟨ns⟩ both mine and Lord Carysforts [2] interest t⟨hat⟩ he should not be displaced, which if this matter should remain open may possibly happen ; as they are both father and son particularly ⟨obnox⟩ious to the Duke of Manchester.[3] ⟨I sh⟩all be much obliged to you if you ⟨wi⟩ll lay this matter before Mr. Grenville ⟨and⟩ beg him to order it to be dispatched ⟨to⟩morrow, which I fear will be his last day of acting as first Commissioner of the Treasury. I am very sincerely yours,

Sandwich

The following document is a copy of Gilbert Elliot's memorandum on the negotiations of May and June 1765, mentioned by G. F. S. Elliot in *The Border Elliots* (pp. 393-5), and quoted in the *Bedford Correspondence* (iii, 284, 290). The original is in the possession of the Earl of Minto. The wording of the Liverpool copy varies slightly from the text quoted in the *Bedford Correspondence*. It is neither in Jenkinson's hand nor Elliot's. The passages in brackets are inserted on the left-hand side, on the blank back of the preceding page. They appear to be in a different writing from the text. Some of them might be treated as insertions or additions, whilst others are more of the character of marginal notes. For some the place in the text is indicated, but not for all. They are all reproduced here in brackets. The paper is docketed in another hand : " 1763 [an obvious mistake for 1765] : The King, Lord Bute, Mr. Grenville, Duke of Bedford ".

Add. MS. 38335, ff. 120-33.

The King, Lord Bute, Mr. Grenville, Duke of Bedford.

Monday, May 13th.

The Silk Bill was rejected by the Lords. They seemed to be unanimous tho' the Duke of Bedford only spoke.

Tuesday the 14th.

Upon his way from the House of Lords His Grace was insulted by a body of weavers and even received a slight wound

1. H. Jackson wrote to Sandwich on June 24.
2. John Proby, 1st Baron Carysfort (Irish), M.P. for Huntingdonshire 1754-68. He was a Lord of the Admiralty 1763-65.
3. George Montagu, 4th Duke of Manchester, was M.P. for Huntingdonshire 1761-62, Lord Lieutenant 1762 to his death in 1788.

on his face. The same morning they had been at Richmond where the King then was. They clamoured loudly for redress and were dismissed with an answer rather favorable.[1]

Lord Northumberland had been that day with the Duke of Cumberland and by His Majesty's orders had acquainted him with the intention of changing the Administration.[2]

The Duke came to town, thought it advisable to act with the utmost dispatch and immediately sent to Stowe for Lord Temple.[3]

Wednesday the 15th.

A considerable mob assembled at the door of the House of Lords. They carried Colours flying, seemed to act under direction, applied to the Lords as they past, but committed no outrage.

Sir John Feilding and the other Westminster Justices were summoned, they appeared at the Bar of the House. Their answers were not satisfactory nor had they shown any great forwardness on this occasion, the mob for the present disperst. The Lords appointed a committee to inquire further into this business. The House of Commons adjourned till the Wednesday following, their business being now concluded.[4]

This evening there was a great riot at Bedford House and the Guards were sent for and continued to do duty for several days, His Grace was visited by the Ministers and many other persons of the first rank. The mob assembled from time to time. The troops were properly posted both Horse and Foot and every thing carried the appearance of a siege but little mischief was done.[5]

1. Cf. Walpole, *Memoirs*, ii, 110, 111; *Bedford Corr.* iii, 283; *Grenv. Pps.* iii, 163-4. The rejection, on May 13, of a Bill to protect the silk industry against foreign competition from which it had been automatically protected by the war, was the cause of riots, which lasted approximately from May 14 to 20.
2. Cf. the Duke of Cumberland's statement in Albemarle, *Memoirs of the Marquis of Rockingham*, i, 191 (the events in this part of the statement are antedated by a week); *Grenv. Pps.* iii, 224; *The Duke of Newcastle's Narrative*, edited by Mary Bateson, Camden Series (1898), p. 9, where the date of this visit, which took place on Monday, May 13, is wrongly given by Newcastle, as here by Elliot, Tuesday, May 14.
3. See Cumberland to Temple, May 14, and Temple's answer in *Grenv. Pps.* iii, 37-8.
4. Fielding was summoned on Friday, May 17. See Halifax to the King, May 18, 9 P.M., in Fortescue, *Corr. of George III*, No. 67; and Grenville's diary, *Grenv. Pps.* iii, 169. Cf. also Walpole, *Memoirs*, ii, 112.
5. See Welbore Ellis to the King, May 17 and 18, and Halifax to the King, May 17 and 18, Fortescue, *op. cit.* Nos. 62, 64-8; Namier, *Additions and Corrections*, pp. 26-8.

Thursday the 16th.

The Chancellor and Mr. Grenville went to the King in the morning produced the Speech they had prepared for closing the Session and proposed that Parliament might be prorogued the Tuesday following. The King acquainted them that it was his intention only to adjourn the Parliament for a few days, they represented that all publick business was now finished and prest for a further explanation, but they received none. They immediately declared that a change of Administration was intended, and this they declared very publicly.[1]

The Lords employed themselves in questioning the Westminster Justices and in hearing evidence with regard to the mob. The Secretaries of State expatiated upon the wickedness of those who could be capable of advising the King to change his Government, at a time when so respectable a Minister as the Duke of Bedford was exposed to the insults of a lawless mob and prevented from attending his duty in that House. The examination of the evidence was so directed as to fix if possible the imputation on Lord Northumberland of having encouraged the insurrection as it was now called, but the attempt proved ineffectual.[2]

Friday the 17th.

The committee of the Lords continued. The mob reassembled at Palace Yard. The Guards were placed at the door of the House but no violence was committed.[3]

Lord Temple had been at Hays with Mr. Pitt and now returned with his answer to the Duke of Cumberland's propositions which was general and by no means satisfactory to his Highness.[4]

1. Cf. Grenville's Diary, Grenv. Pps. iii, 165-6 ; Walpole, Memoirs, ii, 117-18, where the events of May 16 and 19 are telescoped and ascribed to May 18. Normally Parliament was prorogued at the end of the session. By adjourning it, the King indicated that he meant to keep it sitting in order to issue writs for the re-election of new ministers.

2. Elliot appears to have antedated, or at least telescoped events. The House of Lords considered the riots on May 17 and 20. On the second day Halifax and Sandwich insinuated that the riots " were a plot (of Lord Bute's) to get the Duke of Bedford destroyed ". See Egmont's notes, May 20, Fortescue, op. cit. No. 69. See Walpole's description of the manner in which the Earl and Countess of Northumberland were received at Bedford House on May 19, Memoirs, ii, 113. In Walpole's opinion " the mob was blown up by Humphrey Cotes and the friends of Wilkes ".

3. Cf. Welbore Ellis to the King, May 17, Fortescue, op. cit. No. 62 ; and Grenv. Pps. iii, 168. Elliot's date is correct.

4. Cf. Cumberland's statement, pp. 194-7, and Grenv. Pps. iii, 225. Temple went to Cumberland from Hayes on Thursday, May 16.

Sunday the 19th.

The Duke of Cumberland went himself to Hays and had a conference with Mr. Pitt which lasted several hours. He was desired to accept the Seals of Secretary of State and to name his colleague and to take the direction of the House of Commons. Lord Northumberland was suggested for the Treasury and several of the Duke of Newcastle's friends for other offices, but this conference also proved ineffectual.

[Mr. Pitt said he was surprised to see the spirit and alertness with which the Duke of Cumberland conversed and the perseverance with which he urged that Lord N⟨orthumberland⟩ should be at the head of the Treasury. Mr. Pitt said that Lord N. was a respectable person and fit for a great office but not to be head of the Treasury.[1]]

Monday the 20th and Tuesday the 21st.

[The plan of Administration which the Duke of C. proposed at this time was so ridiculous that the King could not help smiling at it. The Duke said that His Majesty's friends were the only men of abilities, that he could only lend him great names.]

The friends of the Duke of Newcastle now began to blame Mr. Pitt's impracticability, and the Duke of Cumberland attempted to form an administration consisting mostly of them. Lord Littleton and Charles Townshend were offered the Treasury and other arrangements were proposed but none could be found to accept the great responsable offices.[2] Reports were spread that the mob would even receive a great reinforcement from the great manufacturing towns in the country. The Ministers proposed that the Duke of Richmond, Lord Granby and Lord Waldegrave should be invested with the command of the troops. The King desired the Duke of Cumberland to act as Captain General if necessary, but this country mob never assembled.[3] A great body of troop however were ordered to march to London and the neighbourhood

1. Cf. Cumberland's statement, pp. 201-3, and other sources. Elliot's date is correct.

2. Egmont was to be Secretary of State; Lyttelton or Holdernesse, First Lord of the Treasury; Charles Townshend, Chancellor of the Exchequer. Newcastle objected to Egmont " as what I knew would make everything desperate with Mr. Pitt " (*Newcastle's Narrative*, p. 15), and Townshend refused, preferring to accept the Paymastership with Grenville on May 22. See Egmont's notes, Fortescue, No. 69; Grafton, *Autobiog.* p. 47.

3. See Halifax to the King, and the King to Halifax and to Cumberland, May 20, Fortescue, Nos. 72-4, and Namier, *Additions and Corrections*, p. 28.

of it. Alarm posts were fixed and Guards stationed upon the high road and in different quarters of the town. Hervey, Adjutant General had the command and every method was employed to excite a general apprehension. The Royal Family came from Richmond to town.[1]

Wednesday the 22d.

The Duke of Cumberland, the Chancellor and Lord Egmont advised the King to re-establish his former Ministers. They represented the impossibility of forming at that time any other Administration and His Majesty after expressing the utmost reluctance at length complied.

[The Chancellor said that the Duke of C was in the Closet with him and in his presence gave up his design and said he could do no more. The King then employed the Chancellor to speak to Mr. Grenville and his friends.[2]]

Thursday the 23rd.
Friday the 24th.

The Ministers resolved to start certain propositions to the King and if they should be rejected to quit their offices. Mr. Grenville went into the Closet and on his own part and in the name of the President of the Council and the two Secretaries of State proposed, that Lord Weymouth should be sent to Ireland, that the King should never discourse on politicks with Lord Bute, that Lord Holland should be dismissed from his office of Paymaster, and Mr. Steward McKenzy from that of Privy Seal for Scotland and from the direction of the affairs of that country. His Majesty agreed to the first condition, as to the 2d. said he had talked no politicks with Lord Bute since he retired to his house at Luton, August 1763, agreed that Charles Townshend should be named Paymaster. But as to the last article said he knew Mr. Mackenzie would have no objection to give up the direction of Scotch affairs which he had ever considered as a great load upon him but added that when he appointed that gentleman Privy Seal he had passed his Royal word that this office should continue for his life. Mr. Grenville persisted. The King complied using these expressions : You force me to break my word, and

1. See Fortescue, No. 73 ; *Grenv. Pps.* iii, 176. The King came to London on May 21.
2. Cf. Egmont's notes, May 22, Fortescue, No. 79, and Northington to the King, May 22, *ibid.* No. 81. The King had already spoken to Grenville on May 21, *Grenv. Pps.* iii, 177.

you must be responsible for the consequences.[1]

[What relates to Lord Holland was not one of the conditions proposed to the King but the fourth condition was that Lord Granby should be put at the head of the Army to which the King answered that in case he put any body there he had promised it to his uncle.

What relates to Lord Weymouth had long been in agitation. It was the Duke of Bedford's particular wish that he should go to Ireland. Mr. Grenville was evidently ashamed of the recommendation and only supported it as the Duke of Bedford's wish stating to the King that no person could be found more proper.[2]

The King employed the Chancellor to dissuade the Ministers from their intention of dismissing Mr. McKenzie from his office. The Chancellor did what he could at a meeting held on the Wednesday Morning but without success.[3] All the Ministers determined when the King made a difficulty of complying with this condition. Mr. Grenville said that then they could not continue to serve him to which the King replyed : No Sir, I will not by refusing this condition put my Kingdoms into a state of confusion but remember you force me etc.[4]]

He sent for McKinzie in the evening and a very affecting scene past between them.

He also on this and the following days repeated to many of his servants the conversation he had had with his Ministers and complained warmly of the force that had been put upon him.

Sunday the 26th.

Continued at Richmond his mind so agitated that he did not chuse to take the Sacrament that day nor was there any Drawing Room.[5]

1. Cf. passage from Elliot's diary quoted in *Bedford Corr.* iii, 284, from " His Majesty said that he had talked no politics " to " must be responsible for the consequences ". It was on May 22 that Grenville first laid these points before the King. See *Grenv. Pps.* iii, 41, 183-6, and the King to Egmont, May 23, Fortescue, No. 82. Both the points relating to Granby and Holland were included in the King's answer (*ibid.*) but in his memoranda (*ibid.* pp. 166, 172) the question of Cumberland's appointment is omitted.
2. Cf. *Grenv. Pps.* iii, 163. Weymouth wanted the Lord Lieutenancy because he was in debt, but though appointed he never went to Ireland.
3. This was on Thursday, May 23. See *Grenv. Pps.* iii, 186.
4. Cf. Grenville's diary, May 23, *ibid.* p. 187, and Egmont's notes, May 23, Fortescue, No. 82, and Namier, *Additions etc.* p. 30.
5. Cf. *Bedford Corr.* iii, 284. See Mackenzie's account of his dismissal in a letter to Will Mure, June 4, 1765, *Caldwell Papers*, part II, ii, 36-8.

Wednesday the 29th.

Distinguished Mr. Mackenzie at Court in a very particular manner hardly spoke to any of the Ministers; this public conduct he continued to observe all that week and the week following.

[The resolution the King took on this occasion was to give the Ministers no difficulty in carrying on his Government but at the same time to shew the world that they were not in his favour. For this reason he was easy to them in his Closet as they themselves allowed tho' he shewed them no civility either at his Levée or Drawing Room.]

Lord Weymouth kissed hands for Ireland and was admitted into the Privy Council, Lord Frederick Campbell brother to Lord Lorn was appointed Privy Seal for Scotland admited also into the Privy Council and the affairs of Scotland under certain limitations entrusted to him but without access to the Closet. The King spoke to neither of them. The Ministers had further intended to have exacted certain explanations from those whom they suspected to entertain any friendship for Lord Bute, as to their future conduct when the hour of difficulty should arrive. But they droped this design partly deterred from it by the imputation of Cabal which they saw it must fix upon them and partly by the manner in which a hint of this kind was received by one gentleman and by the voluntary declaration of another who said he would faithfully support the administration of which he was a part but that he would on no consideration combine with any body of subjects against the undoubted right of the Crown to name its own officers; improper measures he would oppose in a Parliamentary way if any such were adopted, but of this he saw no probability.[1]

[Mr. Grenville heated with the prospect of success was very violent on this occasion. He demanded an explanation of the person here alluded to in the most angry terms at the door of the King's Closet and was only prevented from receiving as angry an answer by the King opening the door and calling him in. He never ventured to demand an explanation in the same manner again. He touched the subject more gently and upon receiving an answer to the same purpose as

1. This paragraph from " the Ministers had further intended " is quoted by G. F. S. Elliot in *The Border Elliots*, pp. 394-5. The " voluntary declaration " seems to have come from Gilbert Elliot himself. The other gentleman was probably Jenkinson.

the voluntary declaration mentioned on the other side he replyed it was rather cold but proceeded no further.]

Tuesday [should read : Friday] the 31st.

The Queens Master of the Horse vacant by the promotion of Lord Weymouth was given to the Duke of Ancaster in opposition to the recommendation of the Ministers, this week also some military promotions took place which had been recommended by the Duke of Cumberland.

Tuesday, June the 4th.

The King's Birthday.

Wednesday, June the 12th.

The Duke of Bedford went into the Closet and read a paper to the King in which he declared that upon the Ministers agreeing to continue in Government they had all expected and particularly himself to receive some particular marks of His Majesty's favour but in this they had been greatly disappointed, that he was going into the country for a fortnight, perhaps for three weeks, perhaps for a month, that if upon his return they were not received with greater expressions of favour and confidence *he and his colleagues were determined to resign their offices.*[1]

[Instead of the words scored under the Duke of Bedford concluded his speech by saying that the King's Government could not go on and that he as well spoke this on the part of his colleagues as of himself. Mr. Grenville as well as the other Ministers deny that they meant by this a resignation and when Mr. G—— heard that Mr. Pit had been with the King, he wrote a letter from Stowe to the Chancellor saying that he did not mean to resign ; the Chancellor shewed the letter to the King but it was after His Majesty and Mr. Pit had agreed.[2] The Chancellor told the Ministers when they discoursed with him concerning their want of the King's affection that it was in vain to attempt to gain it by force, that if they had his

1. Cf. Bedford's minutes of this conversation, *Bedford Corr.* iii, 288-9 ; the King's letter to Northington, June 12, Fortescue, No. 85, and his memoranda, pp. 166, 172 ; also Grenville's diary, *Grenv. Pps.* iii, 194. The entry from Elliot's diary for June 12 (which of course does not comprise the part in brackets) is quoted in the *Bedford Corr.* p. 290.

2. Cf. Sandwich to Grenville, June 20 (the day after Pitt saw the King), and Grenville's answer, June 21, in *Grenv. Pps.* iii, 56-60. Grenville was at Stowe with Temple from June 17 to 21, *ibid.* pp. 196-9. There is no draft of any letter from Grenville to Northington in the *Grenv. Pps.*, nor any mention of one in Grenville's diary, nor is one preserved among the few extant papers of Northington.

authority, and for their having this he pledged himself, he thought it sufficient ; that the Duke of Newcastle long governed this country by having the authority of the Crown without the affection of his Sovereign. He disaproved also very much of the dismissing Mr. McKenzie from his office tho' he thought it right that he should not have the management of the Scotch affairs.]

The King replied that the confidence necessary for the conduct of the publick business he had given them that as to favour they had not taken the way to merit it. Next day or the next but one the Duke of Bedford Mr. Grenville and Lord Halifax went to their seats in the country.

Monday, June the 18th [17].

The Duke of Cumberland had canvassed such of his friends as he had met at Ascot Races but found among them no union nor agreement of sentiment. He now told the King that he was convinced his interposition had prevented Mr. Pitt from closing with His Majesty's propositions, and he advised him to see that gentleman personally.[1]

Tuesday the 19th [18].

The Duke of Grafton carried the message next day to Hays from the King, Mr. Pitt said he was now persuaded His Majesty was sincere, that hitherto the means of accepting had not been furnished him.[2]

Wednesday the 20th [19].

Mr. Pitt had a conference with the King at the Queen's house which lasted three hours, and turned mostly on foreign affairs.[3]

Saturday the 23rd [22].

Another conference was held at the Queen's House at the close of which Mr. Pitt declared himself perfectly satisfied both with the foreign and domestick plan settled in this conversation and added that the places His Majesty agreed to open afforded sufficient room for his friends. He only wanted

1. See Cumberland to Pitt, June 17, *Chatham Corr.* ii, 311-12. Monday was June 17.
2. Cf. Grafton's *Autobiog.* p. 52, and *Grenv. Pps.* iii, 197.
3. Pitt saw the King on June 19, 22, 25, and 26. See Grenville's diary, *ibid.* pp. 199-202. From Monday, June 24 to the end, Elliot has the dates correct.

to know Lord Temple's opinion without whose acceptance of office he himself could not come into administration.

[Mr. Pit was evidently gained by the King and has always spoken of these two conversations with the highest satisfaction. The King on his part seemed to be gained likewise and has said that he and Mr. Pit thought alike upon every subject. Mr. Pit's plan of foreign politicks was that an alliance should be made with Prussia but without a subsidy that if his Prussian Majesty did not consent to it a proposition of the same kind should be made to the Court of Vienna.]

Monday the 24th.

Lord Temple arrived at Hays that same morning. Mr. Grenville set out from Wotton to the Duke of Bedford at Wooburn and came late in the evening to London, Mr. Grenville had been some days at Stowe with his brother Lord Temple.

Tuesday the 25th.

Lord Temple and Mr. Pitt went to the Queen's House. Lord Temple first entered the Closet. He exprest himself respectfully but said that such was the state of men and things that he despaired of answering the publick expectations, that he would not therefore undertake the Treasury nor come into office. The King prest him by every private and publick consideration. He even attempted to pique him in point of honour by alledging that the greater the difficulty the more it became him to give his assistance to his King and country. His Lordship owned that he felt all the force of what His Majesty so kindly urged yet still he declined accepting office saying he would retire to Stowe and there hide his head for the rest of his life.

Mr. Pitt came next into the Closet. He regreted in the most pathetick terms the resolution which Lord Temple had so unhappily formed and to which he adhered with so much obstinacy : he lamented the miserable state of his own health and but for that consideration he said not even his engagement to Lord Temple should prevent him from sacrificing to His Majesty's service the few years he had yet to live ; but circumstanced as he was how could he undertake the direction of publick affairs deprive⟨d⟩ of the aid and comfort of his sole remaining friend. To Mr. Grenville he allowed the merit of an able and industrious Member of Parliament but intimated his apprehensions that the present Ministers were by no means equal to the forming and carrying into execution any liberal or statesman-like plan of Government. He concluded by saying he would publickly and every where declare that Lord Temple's resolution was the only obstacle to his acceptance of His Majesty's very gracious offers. He left the King disapointed at his refusal but not a little pleased with the frankness and respect of his declarations.

Wednesday the 26th.

Mr. Pitt again attended the King at the Queen's House by His Majesty's order. He was offered President of the Council and a peerage, desired to say whether if he could not accept he would support the measures or advise the new arrangement of Administration. He declined acceptance, eluded a positive answer with regard to the support of measures with which he could not yet be acquainted. He advised continuing Mr. Grenville at the head of the Treasury. This advice he protested flowed from no family purpose nor from any predilection to the man had he accepted he would have set him at defiance but as things now stood without him he saw nothing in that department either solid or substantial. In opposition too he might give great trouble, his knowledge in revenue matters was considerable and perhaps bitterness and rancour [1] were not the smallest ingredients which went to the composition of his character. The same day Mr. Grenville did his ordinary business with the King but entered not into the state of Administration.

CHARLES LLOYD TO CHARLES JENKINSON
Add. MS. 38204, f. 317.

Docketed " July 23, 1765 ".

The many obligations which I lay under to you, and which I assure you I am incapable of forgetting will not suffer me to remain an indifferent hearer of any event which concerns you. I do not enquire from what quarter this promotion [2]

1. Written b—tt—s and r—c—r.
2. Jenkinson, who resigned from the Secretaryship of the Treasury on July 12, was appointed Auditor of Accounts to the Princess Dowager.

has come to you. It is sufficient for me that it is agreable to you, and I would not omit the earliest opportunity of telling you the part I take in what has happen'd to you which I expect to be believed in the sooner even in these selfish times, because the patronage you introduced me to renders any other unnecessary. All I desire is to deserve your good opinion, and that you will believe I shall never be unmindful of the favors I have received from you. I am my dear Sir with the truest esteem and most affectionate regard

Your most obedient and most faithful servant,

Chas. Lloyd

TOM RAMSDEN TO CHARLES JENKINSON

Add. MS. 38204, f. 320

Pontefract, July 27, 1765. Saturday.

On Thursday night I received, my dear Jenkinson, the favor of your letter of the 22, which gave me very great satisfaction; for though there was no doubt of the kind inclination, yet there might not have been so soon an opportunity of giving you something; I heartily rejoice at it, though it is far short of your late income. If one could be surprized, I think there is room, at some things, that appear in the news papers, which is all the intelligence I have. But no more. I had a few lines from Todd, who does not tell me when we are to receive any salary. I do not know who he applys to, for he does not say more, than he has nothing else but his salary to depend on, which will make him exert all he can. I wish your successors would either of them forward the matter. We are already two quarters in arrear, and if there should be any difficulty, it will fall hard on me, as my place was granted to me for life. But I can't suppose, that there will be any long delay. Did you leave the warrants you had prepared relating to it? Poor Todd is also under anxiety for his wife, who, I fear, is too far reduced to expect any great good from Bristol water.[1] I hope you will be able to get into the country; you have been long enough confined to the town, and fatigued with business. When does our friend Lord Harcourt return to England? My brother (the Colonel) is in or near London, and intends to go

1. She died on August 7.

(378)

into waiting, next month, so that he can't come into these parts till September.

We want rain in these parts very much, and *all* things are *very* dear.

I conclude you do not want to be re-elected. Can't find in the Calendar, that there was any such officer as Auditor.

Do you know any thing of Sir James; where he is. He has been expected to go to Whitehaven, but is not passed by here.

I can't help repeating that I am much obliged to you for writing, and when you have time, shall be very glad to hear any good from you, being most truely yours.

J. S. MACKENZIE TO CHARLES JENKINSON

Add. MS. 38204, f. 327.

August 4, 1765.

Dear Sir,

I have just now received the favor of your letter of the 28 past which I suppose should have been dated the 29th, the London post mark upon the cover is dated the 30th so that if you did not neglect to send it on the 29th which was Monday, they have detain'd it at the Post Office till the Tuesday night, viz: the 30th, as possibly Potts [1] had not time to open it and read it sooner.

I thank you heartily for the news you have transmitted to me, and beg you'll continue to drop me a few lines on every occurrence, as there are many things which all the world on the spot knows, though they remain a secret to people at a distance. I think Lord Frederick Campbell [2] might have found out a better reason than he has assign'd for his resigning an office which had never been given him by the only person in the Kingdom who could legally bestow it on him. I fancy however, he is mistaken in its having been offer'd to some persons whom I heard before I left London it had been offer'd to, but since I came to this country, I have learn'd, that that report was not well founded.

1. In July 1765 Henry and Samuel Potts were restored to their former places of Secretary to the Inland Office and Controller in the Post Office.

2. Lord Frederick Campbell was appointed Privy Seal of Scotland in place of Mackenzie on May 29, 1765, and on November 5 was succeeded by Lord Breadalbane. According to Walpole he did not resign but was removed. *Memoirs*, ii, 142.

I pass'd a day on my way hither, with Lord and Lady Northumberland at Alnwick Castle. His Lordship approves greatly of the Kings friends connecting themselves together closely, and acting in a body as occurrences shall happen. This seems to be the opinion of every body who really loves the K. and desires to keep free from every Cabal whether in power or out of it.

I am yours, my dear Jenkinson most sincerely.

CHARLES LLOYD TO CHARLES JENKINSON

Add. MS. 38204, f. 340.

Salt Office, York Buildings,
August 24, 1765.

Dear Sir,

Brummell [1] has probably informed you of my being dismissed from the Receivership of Gibraltar,[2] I set out the next day after it had taken place for Mr. G—— who has promised to appoint me Deputy to his son, but as he means to do it in a civil manner to Mr. Hindley he proposes to talk to him about it and I shall not enter upon the office till next Michaelmas.[3] The very obliging offer you made me of being my Security, will be extremely necessary to me, and I have the less scruple of accepting your good offices on this occasion because though it is a money'd employment, the Checks are so many and so ⟨con⟩stant, and no sums ever lodged in the Deputies hands, that no ⟨ris⟩k is run except that of the Exchequers being robbed or burnt ⟨do⟩wn. The sum usually given to the Deputy Principal is £⟨⟩ooo security. What part of this will it suit you to give? ⟨ h⟩ad much political conversation the particulars of which I ⟨re⟩serve till I see you. No news.

1. William Brummell, father of the famous Beau Brummell, was a clerk in the Treasury from 1763. According to *D.N.B.* his father lived in a house in Bury Street where Jenkinson is alleged to have had rooms, and Brummell is supposed to have acted as his amanuensis. From 1770 to 1782 he was one of the chief clerks in the Treasury, and apparently North's private secretary. He died in 1794 worth £65,000. See *Gent. Mag.* p. 285.

2. Lloyd seems to have taken offence at the manner of his dismissal. See a letter to him from Edmund Burke, then private secretary to Rockingham, October 1, 1765, in *Grenv. Pps.* iii, 86.

3. Frederick Atherton Hindley was deputy to George Grenville junior, who succeeded Lord Macclesfield as one of the four Tellers of the Exchequer in 1764. Hindley had previously been deputy to Lord Macclesfield from 1757. Lloyd succeeded him in 1766.

Huske [1] is talked of to succeed Mellish [2] as Secretary to the Treasury. I am with the truest esteem and most affectionate regard, dear Sir,

Your most faithful

C. Lloyd

TOM RAMSDEN TO CHARLES JENKINSON

Add. MS. 38204, ff. 338-9.

Pontefract, August 24, 1765.

My dear Jenkinson,

Not having heard from Todd about our money matters, and the 1st Lord of Treasury being arrived in this country to attend races, I conclude nothing is done. I do not like being 3 quarters in arrear, which will be the case in October. [3] For my part I should have been very glad to have remained in the way we were ; but if that is found to be too great a burthen for the stock out of which it is issued, and the whole of the sum should also be found, to be impracticable to be charged on the Post Office by virtue of the act of the last session, why may not as much as possible of it be charged on the Post Office, and the remainder be paid, as it has hitherto been. Now, I think, as all expences relating to the management of the Post Office may be paid by that Office, that the Decypherers and Translators may very properly come under that head, for who can read cyphers or a foreign language, that they are not acquainted with, and why should not that Office be supposed to send their papers compleat ; and what farther shews it is that they have always been paid by the Post Office. These expences would take off above 2000 a year, that I know of. But I will not trouble you farther on this head, as you cannot do any thing at present towards settling it.

1. John Huske, about whom see p. 149 n. 1, was Charles Townshend's deputy as Treasurer of the Chambers.
2. William Mellish of Blythe, M.P. for East Retford 1741-51, was Commissioner of Excise 1751-60 and Receiver-General of the Customs 1760-63, when he was removed in favour of William Levinz. On July 12, 1765, he came back into office under the Rockingham Government as Joint Secretary to the Treasury with Charles Lowndes in succession to Jenkinson and Whately. On September 17, 1765, he was removed from the Treasury and restored to his old place of Receiver-General, which he kept until he resigned it in 1786 on succeeding to his family estate. He married Mrs. Villa Real, a daughter of Mendez da Costa, with a fortune of £35,000. His obituary notice in the Gent. Mag., 1791, p. 1166, is slightly inaccurate.
3. Ramsden's salary as Decipherer came out of the Post Office. See p. 21 n. 2.

I see in the Papers that Lord Harcourt is returned to England; I hope in perfect health, as also Lord Newnham, and ready for the assault, in which I truely wish him all joy and happiness. Do you know any thing of my brother Weston ? If you should happen to see him, pray tell him, I should be glad to hear from him.

Our last news papers mentions the death of Mr. Levinz,[1] if so, Mellish I dare say will be happy to have his old place, I wish you would succeed him.

I saw Lady Rockingham at my brother's, as she was setting out for York last Monday morning ; but my Lord did not stop in these parts. I fancy he has no *time* to lose. She said, that Mr. Yorke was Attorney General, which I suppose he has accepted on condition that the Chancellor shall not be removed for Prat. The news papers are odd ; stripes of truth and falsehood, so mixt, that it is very difficult to know any thing. Did Mr. P. write to Sir Fletcher, and in the stile they mention.[2] Are the rods in pip to las [lash(?)] the children ? And 3 per cents to be at par before Xmas, as our 1st Lord is said to have declared? I shall do nothing but ask questions, if I write more, so God bless you.

Ever yours,

T. R.

GILBERT ELLIOT TO CHARLES JENKINSON

Add. MS. 38204, ff. 342-3.

Paris, August 26, 1765.

I am extremely sensible, my dear Sir, to your kind remembrance of me, at this distance, and so totally unacquainted with the immediate scenes, which are dayly passing before your eyes, and yet your letter guarded as it was, brought me better information than I have received by any other means. I hope, your hours continue to glide on smoothly notwithstanding all that has happened, as to your own situation I

1. William Levinz was Commissioner of Customs 1747–63. On February 22, 1763, he was appointed Receiver-General of the Customs, a place worth £1000 a year, not £2000 as stated in his obituary notice in the *Gent. Mag.* (1765, p. 395). He died on August 17, 1765.

2. There was a rumour that Pitt had written to Fletcher Norton to say that he would not have dismissed him.

can never be uneasie about it, you are sure of success *tuum enim est illud curriculum*, you come fully prepared to it, you have youth and spirits to carry you through it, for though old in business you are as yet but young in political altercation, I am directly the reverse ; I think I love the publick, and I am sure I love my friends and shall ever do my best to serve both, but as for that partial spirit which gave so much energy to business, be it a bad or a good spirit, it is by me totally irrecoverable. I will never be angry with Ministers because they are incapable of a true confidential friendship, the misfortune is theirs, and it is a misfortune to be imputed not always to the heart, but often to the situation. They are not always capable, nor have they at all times leisure to distinguish, so perhaps they do wisely to distrust in the lump. But let us who are not Ministers, let us my dear Jenkinson continue the same simple and unbounded confidence, which we have hitherto maintain'd in spite of the jealousy, malignity or weakness with which we have been too often surrounded, I long to be ⟨in⟩ England again to participate with a few at least the feast of reason and the flow of soul. In the mean time the great *spectacle* of this country is not unamusing, manners so unlike and yet differing so little from our own ; yesterday was the day of St. Luis the great day of the French Academy, I was there, the Eloge of Decartes was read, poor Bacon and Newton, made but a second-hand figure, Monsieur Thomas,[1] and an other person were both crown'd, the Duke of Nivernois then read some fables in verse of his own composition. The Hall was very much crowded, and his Grace receiv'd great and deserv'd applause ; I make no doubt but that the Duke of Bedford employs his talents in the same elegant and unambitious manner.

In a visit I lately made in the country, I met with the old Duke of Richelieu,[2] and the young Dutchess of Choiseul, the one a very true sample of the vielle cour, the other the ornament of the new. The ladys drink tea in great quantitys, play at whist, and wear great English hats. They learn English and admire David Hume, they observe that France has given the *ton* of the world to Lady Hertford,[3] and England

1. Antonie-Léonard Thomas (1732–85) won the prize at the Académie in 1765 for his *Éloge de Descartes*. About him see *Nouvelle Biographie générale*.
2. Louis François Armand du Plessis, Duc de Richelieu (1696–1788), Marshal of France. He drove the English from Minorca in 1756.
3. Isabella, daughter of Charles Fitzroy, 2nd Duke of Grafton, wife of Francis Seymour Conway, 1st Earl of Hertford, British Ambassador to Paris.

to Madame Guerchy, they all agree Mr. Pitt will be Minister. One is flatter'd however to find, that England notwithstanding the late frolicks is still so much the object of admiration attention and imitation.

Yours ever, my dear Sir

G. E.

If you should think it necessary to write me any thing too particular for the post, it will come very safely by any courier for Dr. Hume. Is it possible that J. Ha⟨　　⟩ is gone to stand for poor Sir Harry Erskin's Buroughs.[1]

J. S. MACKENZIE TO CHARLES JENKINSON

Add. MS. 38204, f. 346.

Castle Menzies, September 16, 1765.

Dear Sir,

I delay'd answering the favor of your letter of the 13. past, as you therein told me that you were going to make a ⟨to⟩ur somewhere ; but as I have now had the pleasure of yours of the 10th instant by which I find you are return'd from ⟨your⟩ expedition, I shall take this opportunity to ⟨offer⟩ my thanks for both your obliging ⟨letters. You⟩ surprise me greatly, in telling me that Parliament will meet so early as the ⟨midd⟩le of November for the dispatch of business, ⟨I h⟩eard something of their meeting in ⟨　　⟩ for to issue the writs for the re-elections ; ⟨　　⟩ for God's sake ! what have we to do ⟨　　⟩ called together so soon for business ? ⟨I sh⟩ould not have thought our new Ministry would have been in such a hurry for a meeting of Parliament where, without the support of those whom they have not treated with much indulgence, ⟨　　　⟩ the Kings firmest friends, they must in all probability, make but a very indifferent appearance ; however, I beg to hear, something farther on this subject of the meeting of Parliament.[2] Meanwhile let it meet when it will, I shall certainly, if I am alive and well, be in London before that ⟨　　⟩ together with several more, I hope, ⟨Scotch ?⟩ Members. I have never yet seen Mr. ⟨Yorke's⟩ name in the

1. Sir Harry Erskine died on August 9, 1765. He was M.P. for Ayr Burghs 1749–54, and for Anstruther Easter Burghs 1754–65. He was succeeded in them by Sir John Anstruther, Bart. " J. Ha⟨　　⟩ " may stand for " Haldane ".
2. Parliament met on December 17. See p. 401.

Gazette (the only paper I ⟨ever⟩ look into) as having kiss'd His Majesty⟨'s hand⟩ on being appointed Attorney General ⟨   ⟩ or is he not in that Office?[1]   Do drop me a line when any thing occurrs, and ⟨believe⟩ me ever, my dear Jenkinson

Most cord⟨ially⟩ and sincerely yours, etc., etc.

My address is always *at Edinburgh.*

J. S. MACKENZIE TO CHARLES JENKINSON

Add. MS. 38204, f. 348.

Castle Menzies, September 18, 1765.

Dear Sir,

I wrote to you by last post, since which I have yours of *Wednesday* the 11 ⟨   ⟩ the only day in the week the post does not leave London to go to Edinburgh.   I a⟨   ⟩ extreamly the demand made you for ⟨the⟩ continuation of the payment of the £⟨120⟩ per annum allow'd to the woman at the Excise Off⟨ice⟩ when poor Miss Cockburn has been most cruelly turn'd out of that little office [2] notwithstanding the strongest representations to Lord Rockingham by two or three ladies of the first rank, some of them particularly connected with him and his family.   If the person employ'd by Mr. Bindley to pay the money has actually paid the quarter to last Midsummer out of gross stupidity, I would not let him be the loser, but I think it might be deferr'd till you see Mr. Bindley to know from him how the matter stands.   Out of charity and compassion I paid her that little pension and now her protectors turn out the person ⟨whom⟩ I espouse, after which, they expect my bounty should be still continued. I should expect some understanding between the woman and the man who paid her, by his ⟨being⟩ in such a hurry to pay her even ⟨before their⟩ protectors were again in power and displacing ⟨some⟩body to make room for their own ⟨frien⟩ds.

As to Lord Talbot's intelligence about their moving some question against my brother in Parliament I do not in the least doubt their good inclinations, but I should not imagine

1. After a good deal of hesitation Charles Yorke accepted the office of Attorney-General in September 1765.
2. She was appointed deputy Housekeeper at the Excise Office in 1763 and removed by Rockingham in 1765.

they would proceed so far as to suborn evidence, without which, they themselves know, they could not hurt my brother, do what they would ; endeavouring to asperse his character, after all that has passed to that effect already, would be of very little consequence. Adieu my dear Sir
                    I am most sincerely yours etc.

I ask'd you a question in my last about Mr. Yorke which I have since been inform'd of.

SIR JAMES LOWTHER TO CHARLES JENKINSON
in Parliament Street

Add. MS. 38204, f. 350.

Carlisle, September 23, 1765.

Dear Sir,
    Your letter I received here. Be so good as to let me have the little occurrences as they happen for I dont in the least understand what the great man [1] intends to do or aim att. I think the present Administration are endeavouring to prolong their life by delaying our meeting. We ought all to be in Town a fortnight or 3 weeks before the meeting in order to settle and fix our plan ; see who are our friends and who we may depend upon and to know what the other sides are doing and upon what ground we stand. I shall return to Lowther tomorrow and wish much I could remain there. I am sincerely
                                    Yours
                                    J. Lowther

CHARLES JENKINSON TO SIR JAMES LOWTHER

Add. MS. 38204, f. 354.

London, September 26, 1765.

Dear Sir,
    I find now for certain that the Parliament is not to meet till the 12th of December and then only for issuing of writts, and from thence they are to be adjourned till after the hollydays. It is expected that in the mean time the present Ministers will

1. Cumberland.

negotiate some where or other ; the world suppose that it will be with some of those that you and I wish well to ; but as for myself I see not the least symptom of it. Grey Cooper was to have been Secretary to the Treasury in the room of Mr. Mellish ; but some difficulties are started, which makes me doubt, whether this will now take place ; [1] it is commonly supposed that this promotion was oweing to Mr. C. Townshend, as Mr. Cooper has for some time been connected with him, but Charles has declared that this is not the case, that he is not connected with the present Ministers, but that his attachment is solely to the King. My best compliments to Lady Mary. I am ever dear Sir,

Yours faithfully
C. Jenkinson

SAMUEL MARTIN TO CHARLES JENKINSON

Add. MS. 38204, f. 355.

Harden, Sunday, September 28, 1765.

Dear Sir,

I am to be in town tomorrow by three o'clock ; being obliged to see to the preparation of the business, with which I wait upon the Princess, on the day before I attend her ; and that attendance is, on the first day of the month.[2]

I wish therefore it may suit you to dine tomorrow at your own house in Parliament Street : for if so, I would invite my self to dine with you. First I want to speak with you on some affairs of business, no way relating to our mistress the Princess ; and secondly I shall want a dinner, having no servant in town that ⟨can⟩ roast a shoulder of mutton. However I take it for granted you will not be ceremonious enough to set aside for this purpose any other plan you may have designed of passing your Monday. If I see you before I leave London, on Wednesday or even a little ⟨time⟩ hence at Luton Park,[3] my end may be answered ; but ⟨not as⟩ well at the last place, as at your own house. I am, dear Sir,

Faithfully yours
Samuel Martin

1. He was appointed Joint Secretary to the Treasury in October.
2. Martin was Treasurer to the Princess of Wales from 1761 and Jenkinson her Auditor of Accounts from July 1765. See p. 377 n. 2.
3. Bute's seat.

North End, October 3, 1765.

Dear Sir,

    I have had the favour of your letter from Carlisle ; before that I had written another letter to you acquainting you that the Parliament was not to meet even for the issueing of writts till the 12th of December. I hear now that it will not be till the 22d. of that month. Before this is received or very soon after you will see Lord B⟨ute⟩. He will tell you all that had happened before his departure from London ; I shall be therefore the shorter and only add that though some have thought that C. Townshend would treat separately with the present people, yet I have been assured from more than one quarter and such as can be depended on, that he will never join with the present people or come nearer to them unless they widen their present bottom ; they mean to try him and that immediately, but as I am assured it will be without success.[1] I understand that many of the present Ministers are inclined to treat, but the great person under whose banner they act,[2] not seeing any danger (as they do), is not at all inclined that way, and without him they can do nothing ; for as I am told they dare not take a step, but as he directs. I was told today in Town that Mr. Pitt had left Somersetshire and was not gone to Bath, but to what corner of the earth that meteor is flown is not known.[3] I have heard that Colonel Harvey [4] says that nothing satisfactory can be got from Mr. Pitt

    1. Cf. Augustus Hervey to Grenville, October 3, 1765 (*Grenv. Pps.* iii, 87-9) : " the report about was strong that Mr. Charles Townshend was to have Mr. Conway's seals, who was to be Pay-Master . . . it is said to have gone off with a negotiation that Charles Townshend undertook with Lord Holland, who refused to take any part in the Cabinet ". And October 12 : " I hear Mr. Charles Townshend declares aloud that he has now given his plan to the King, and that if Lord Bute will agree to stand out, and promise not to flinch, he will engage to carry on the Administration, himself at the Treasury, and says he will kiss the King's hand with Lord Bute if he pleases tomorrow, but Lord Holland must be a Cabinet Councillor. Lord Holland has refused, though I fear from good authority that he is to be in town on the 20th " (*ibid.* p. 90). And Whately to Grenville, October 17, " the lie of yesterday was, that Lord Bute, Lord Holland and Charles Townshend were to form an Administration " (*ibid.* p. 100).

    2. The Duke of Cumberland.

    3. Pitt was at Burton Pynsent in Somersetshire on October 29, and proposed going to Bath in November. See Pitt to Temple, *Grenv. Pps.* iii, 102.

    4. Edward Harvey, M.P. for Gatton 1761-68, Harwich 1768-78, Colonel of the 12th Dragoons. He was afterwards Major-General and " a personal military favourite of the King " (Walpole, *Memoirs*, iii, 249).

with respect to Lord Temple and Mr. G⟨renville⟩ ; and he
laments that he (Mr. Pitt) not being inclined to take power
himself, will not contribute to confer it on his family. The
Colonel is, you know, the very best authority in this case, I
rely therefore on his information. I set out tomorrow morning
for Oxfordshire where I shall stay about a fortnight. You
will not therefore hear again from me till my return from
thence. I beg my best respects to Lady Mary and all our
friends, and I am with the greatest truth and regard, dear Sir,
Yours faithfully,

This letter and all my future ones shall be directed in
another hand to mislead the gentlemen at the Post Office.

J. S. MACKENZIE TO CHARLES JENKINSON

Add. MS. 38204, f. 362.

Castle Menzies, October 9, 1765.

I have the favor of your letters, my dear Sir, of the 24 past
and 2 instant delayed answering the former having nothing
worth troubling you with, and for the same reason I should
still continue silent, had you not express'd in your last a desire
to hear from me. Had I heard the report you mention of a
friend of ⟨   ⟩ treating separately with the Minister⟨s for⟩
himself, even before you had contradicte⟨d that⟩ rumor to
me, I should not have ⟨given⟩ it the least credit, as I think
he ⟨will⟩ steadily pursue the right plan ; ⟨   ⟩ thoroughly
convinced of the propriety ⟨   ⟩ as indeed every mortal must
be, for ⟨it⟩ amounts almost to a mathematical dem⟨onstr⟩ation
that it is the only right one to follow. I have wrote to him and
pointed out the mer⟨it⟩ of doing ⟨wh⟩at, you say, he wanted
to be inform'd of. ⟨Th⟩ank you for your obliging attention
to ⟨   ⟩ Porter's request.

I hear that since Lord Kinnoull's refusal of the Privy Seal
of Scotland and the direction of affairs here, they have offer'd
the same to Lord Hopetoun,[1] who under a variety of conditions
(that will be difficult for him to comply with, if they mean to

1. John Hope, 2nd Earl of Hopetoun, refused the Privy Seal early in October.
See his correspondence with Newcastle, Add. MSS. 32969, ff. 86, 279 ; 32970,
ff. 110, 258.

pay ⟨any⟩ attention at all to the affairs of this ⟨part of⟩ the Kingdom) has, 'tis said, accepted. ⟨When⟩ you have a leisure half hour ⟨let⟩ me know what is passing. Adieu ⟨my dear⟩ Sir, Your's most sincerely.

CHARLES JENKINSON TO SAMUEL JOHNSON
Add. MS. 38305, f. 19.

Parliament Street, October 25, 1765.

Sir,

About 2 years ago I put into your hands some papers concerning the late negociations for the Peace.[1] If you have no further use for them I should be obliged to you if you would return them to me, as the leisure I now enjoy affords me an opportunity of looking back on the publick transactions in which I have been engaged, and of collecting and arranging the papers that relate to them.

Having quitted the office I held under His Majesty's Government I have no longer the payment of the Annual Stipend which you receive from the Crown,[2] and least you should not yet be informed to whom you are to apply; I think it proper to acquaint you, that Mr. Mellish I find is the person who is intrusted with this business.

Permit me, Sir, to take this opportunity of congratulating you on the great additional reputation you have acquired in ⟨the⟩ litterary world by the work which you have lately published: it has fully answered the high expectations which mankind had entertained concerning it. You have given us Shakespear in a better dress than he has hitherto worn, and have ably vindicated from many objections which pedantry and a false pretense to taste had imputed to him.[3]

I am etc.

C. Jenkinson

1. See p. 203. 2. See p. 203.
3. Johnson's edition of Shakespeare was published in October 1765.

Add. MS. 38204, f. 366.

October 26, 1765.

Sir,

You will find all your papers carefully preserved, and uncommunicated to any human being. I once hoped to have made better use of them, but shall be much delighted to see them employed for the same purpose by a man so much more versed in publick affairs.

I intended, Sir, to have applied to you for the intelligence which your kindness has given me without application.

If my Edition pleases you, and such as you, it will really produce that additional reputation on which you are pleased to congratulate me. To gain and to preserve the esteem of such men will always be the ambition of, Sir,

Your most obliged most obedient most humble servant

Sam: Johnson

CHARLES JENKINSON TO SIR JAMES LOWTHER [?]

Add. MS. 38205, f. 1.

London, November 16, 1765.

Dear Sir,

The Duke of Newcastle certainly sent to Mr. Pitt a proposal immediately after the death of the Duke of Cumberland [1] and as certainly received a rough denial. The Administration however were not to be repelled and have made a second trial by sending another proposal ; I believe the answer is not yet arrived, but I have no doubt that it will be the same as the former. There is much in agitation ; but nothing as yet come to light, from whence I can form any conjecture of what will be the state of things. I hear that the Duke of Grafton has asked for the Garter and has been refused it, and that he is in consequence very much out of humour.[2] If I

1. On October 31.
2. It was given to Albemarle immediately after Cumberland's death. On October 17 Whately wrote to Grenville : " Another story was, that there was a violent competition between the Duke of Grafton and Lord Albemarle for the vacant garter ; but I believe that both reports are equally without foundation " (*Grenv. Pps.* iii, 101).

should have occasion in a week or ten days to send you information of a confidential kind, pray send me word in what manner I should convey it. My respects attend Lady Mary.

I am ever yours etc.

TOM RAMSDEN TO CHARLES JENKINSON

Add. MS. 38205, f. 2.

Byram, November 30, 1765.

I am very much obliged to you, my dear Jenkinson, for your letter of the 26. You was not one in my debt, and therefore the more obliged to you. I intended to have wrote to you, but imagined you would not return to London, as long as you could well avoid it. The account you give of Mr. G⟨renville⟩ surprises me ; thought he had had some foundation or suspicion at least for his conduct towards Lord B., for I always understood, that he was under the greatest obligations to his Lordship, and therefore am not surprised that the King, who knows the truth, may not so easily forgive it.[1] No man sure ever had a harder fate, and been worse used than Lord Bute. But it is no wonder in the present age, when there seems to be very little regard paid to either reason or justice. No wonder that Mr. P⟨itt⟩ and his brother in law do not agree. That has happened before at the time of the late change. I hope the D. of C. departure will not be *any* loss to the King ; I cannot see it in that light at present. I never heard of a Bishop being made a Dean before his day : and the advancement of an Admiral would never have happened but by him, etc. etc.[2] I long to see you in the Treasury again,

1. Jenkinson had several conversations with Grenville at Bath in November 1765, when they discussed the question of Bute's influence with the King. See *Grenv. Pps.* iii, 220, and below, p. 399. Unfortunately there is no draft of his letter to Ramsden of November 26 in the Liverpool Papers.

2. Frederick and Augustus Keppel were greatly advanced through the influence of their brother Lord Albemarle, who since Fox's defection had been the Duke of Cumberland's chief political agent. Frederick Keppel, Bishop of Exeter, was made Dean of Windsor in October 1765 " malgré the Duke of Newcastle's earnest solicitations for another, Lord Barrington for his brother, and the Duke of Grafton and General Conway for Lord Francis Seymour " (Augustus Hervey to Grenville, *Grenv. Pps.* iii, 91). Grenville when in office had promised his influence for this place to Shute Barrington. See p. 197. Admiral Augustus Keppel, who was second in command at Havana, owed his election for Windsor in 1761 to Cumberland's influence. See L. B. Namier's note on Viscount Keppel in the new edition of the *Complete Peerage*.

and hope it will be brought about. What are these good people doing. Nothing as yet appears ; not so much as any preparation for sending troops to North America, to enforce the law ; and if it is given up, our superiority is at an end, and the being dilatory will encourage the rioters, and what appears to me to be down right rebellion, as it is not an act of the mob, but of the Assemblys. Can this be suffered ?

I shall be very glad to hear from you at your leisure, when things open a little more, which they must do soon, as the Parliament is near assembling. It will rejoice me highly, if things are settled to the King's ease and satisfaction ; but I am afraid of it, as we want men with hearts on the right side.

My brother the Colonel is at Pontefract, 3 miles off ; and is very well ; and if he knew of my writing, would send his best wishes. When you see Lord Harcourt, or Lord Newnham pray make my compliments to them. I hope your sister, in Golden Square, and her husband are well. Adieu, my dear Jenkinson and believe me most faithfully yours.

Memorandum on the Relations between Bute and Grenville

Add. MS. 38338, ff. 274-81.

The following memorandum on the relations between Bute and Grenville, though not in Jenkinson's handwriting, was obviously compiled by him. It would seem from the use of the present tense in the last paragraph, to have been written not long after the events described, while they were still being discussed. Two points contained in the memorandum, Jenkinson also made during his Bath conversations with Grenville in November, when he acquired lights on Grenville's attitude to Bute which surprised Tom Ramsden (see previous letter).

Lord B⟨ute⟩ was dissatisfied with Mr. G⟨renville's⟩ conduct immediately after August 1763 when the Administration of which Mr. G. was at the head was formed a second time. Lord B. had desired Mr. Jenkinson when Mr. Oswald was by to carry a message to Mr. G.[1] to this purpose, that Lord B. would retire into the country and not come near the Court for a certain time and would not in the least interfere with Government. Mr. Jenkinson declined carrying this message,

1. This was probably at Kew on August 28, when Bute saw Elliot and Jenkinson. See Grenville's diary (*Grenv. Pps.* ii, 197). Grenville says nothing of Oswald being there.

upon which said he would write the same to the King that he might shew it Mr. G. ; this was done. Mr. Jenkinson never saw this letter and cannot therefore say what the exact words were.[1] Mr. G. took advantage of this letter and the [sic] in the circular which he sent to his friends upon this occasion he stated as one of the points on which the present Government was founded that Lord B. had engaged not to come to Court etc. I believe the words were faithfully taken from the letter the King had shewn him. Sir John Philips to whom one of these circular letters was sent astonished at this condition sent a copy of it to Lord B. desiring to be informed whether he had given any authority for what was mentioned in it respecting himself. Lord B. was extreamly angry that a publick use was thus made of what he intended should have remained a secret and that the world should thus be made to believe that the King could not form his Government but on condition that he should leave the Court and it should be observed that Mr. G.'s conduct on his occasion appeared so very indiscreet to one of his friends to whom he shewed this circular that he asked him with some emotion whether he had the King's consent for what he had written concerning Lord B. Mr. G. replied that he had not. His friend then advised him to shew the letter to the King and to obtain his approbation of it, thinking this necessary to justify his conduct on this occasion, Mr. G. followed his friend's advise and the King approved of the letter.[2]

Lord B. continuing at Luton expressed to such of his friends

1. Cf. Grenville's diary, August 29 (*Grenv. Pps.* ii, 201) : " His Majesty . . . read part of a letter to him [Grenville] from Lord Bute, in which his Lordship speaks with the greatest regard imaginable of Mr. Grenville, advising the King to give his whole confidence to him ; showing the necessity of his own retreat, from the reasons of nationality, unpopularity, etc., etc."

2. Cf. Grenville's diary, September 3, 1763 (*Grenv. Pps.* ii, 203) : " Mr. Grenville read the letter to the King, which he had written to Lord Strange, and to many others ", and Walpole (*Memoirs*, i, 236), who says that Grenville sent " a very voluminous letter to Sir John Philipps . . . of which letter the King had seen and approved every paragraph ". The letter to Lord Strange, dated September 3, is in the *Grenville Papers* (ii, 104), and the editor describes a similar letter to Granby but supposed it to have been heard and " approved by His Majesty before it was sent ". Philipps himself in his reply, however, refers to Grenville's letter as of September 2 (*ibid.* p. 117), which confirms Jenkinson's evidence that the circulars were sent out before the King heard of them on September 3. Grenville's use of the pluperfect tense in the statement in his diary practically amounts to an admission that the letters had gone. The friend who advised him was probably Jenkinson, for the King's approval, mentioned here, was not sufficiently cordial to be recorded in Grenville's diary. Referring to this incident two years later Grenville ignored the order of events. On May 21, 1765, he told the King : " Your Majesty regulated yourself Lord Bute's situation, told it me, and authorised me to make it known. . . . The King said, I do not deny it " (*ibid.* iii, 180).

as came to visit him there [1] great resentment at this measure of Mr. G. Mr. Jenkinson to whom he shewed Sir John Philips's letter and to whom he said much on this subject used every argument he could possibly think of to appease him. In subsequent visits which Mr. J⟨enkinson⟩ made to Luton he found Lord B.'s mind extremely irritated against the Ministers, more against Lord Halifax and less against Mr. G. than the others. In several conversations on this subject in which Mr. J⟨enkinson⟩ endeavoured to discover the real cause of this resentment, he could not obtain any positive declaration or avowal of what it was but he had reason to conclude that all the Ministers except Mr. G., and particularly Lord H⟨alifax⟩, had talked to the King in an adverse and hostile manner concerning Lord B. This was confirmed to Mr. J. by what Lord Hilsborough, Lord H⟨alifax⟩'s particular friend, said afterwards to him that Lord H⟨alifax⟩ was indiscreet in his conversation and that he had hurt himself by the language he had held to the King concerning Lord B.[2] Mr. J. was persuaded also that the information Lord B. had on this subject came directly from the King, it could indeed come from no other quarter or if it had there was no occasion not to avow it. The little people about Lord B⟨ute⟩ were always indeed endeavouring to do mischief but information of the kind abovementioned was not such as they were likely to procure.

Great pains were taken to dissuade Lord B. from taking any measure in consequence of his resentment and the argument which on this occasion seemed to have the most weight evidently was that the King's authority and influence were so much diminished by the very frequent changes that had been made in his Government since he came to the Crown that any new alteration at present might render it impossible for him to carry on his Government by the assistance alone of those who were attached to himself and that he would be thereby obliged to put himself and his Government into the hands of some of those leaders of factions who meant to give him the law.

When Mr. Grenville and his friends had been successful in the questions against Mr. Wilkes, Lord B. sent through Mr. J. a compliment of congratulation on that occasion. Mr. J.

1. Bute went to Luton on October 5, 1763, and remained there until March 19, 1764, during which time there is evidence that he was visited by Beckford, Le Despencer, Mackenzie, and three times by Jenkinson, on October 29, January 1, and March 17. Beckford also attempted to see him again early in March, but was not admitted. Grenville's diary, *passim*.
2. Cf. the King's statement to Grenville on October 14, 1763 (*Grenv. Pps.* ii, 215), that " Lord Halifax was too eager, and believed reports too easily ".

returned an answer by Mr. G.'s direction. This answer Lord B. thought was too cold. It might savour perhaps of Mr. G.'s natural flegm but it is certain that no incivility was intended.[1] This was the only intercourse that passed between Lord B. and Mr. G. while the former was at Luton.

Lord B. returned from Luton in April of 1764.[2] He appeared immediately in publick and made a publick visit to Mr. G. He did not I believe visit the other Ministers. He certainly did not mean to have any intercourse or connection with them. Mr. G. returned his visit but did not find him at home. He afterwards contrived a meeting with him by means of Mr. J. in which he desired Lord B.'s influence with the King for a private favour to Mr. G. This he urged with the utmost earnestness and solicitude. Lord B. promised his assistance and as he assured Mr. J. he punctually performed his promise but the King would not comply.[3] The favour was indeed of little importance but it was what the King had determined never to grant. There was also some political conversation at this time between Lord B. and Mr. G. the latter mentioned to his Lordship the design of dismissing General Conway. Mr. G. in relating the conversation never made any mention of the favour he had asked but gave an account of what had passed concerning publick affairs and intimated Lord B.'s approbation of the intended dismission.[4]

1. See *Grenv. Pps.* ii, 232. On December 3 " Mr. Grenville wrote to desire Mr. Jenkinson to express his warmest thanks to Lord Bute for this ". The next sentence, which starts a new paragraph in the diary, begins " Mr. Grenville was in great haste, going to some appointments ", which may be an attempt to excuse his discourtesy to Bute.

2. See *Grenv. Pps.* ii, 498. He returned on March 19.

3. About these visits see Grenville's diary. The ministers agreed to call on Bute on March 21, but when Grenville came he was not received, though Sandwich was then in the house. The same day Jenkinson brought Grenville a note of apology and invitation from Bute, to which Grenville replied verbally through Jenkinson that he would call next day. Bute returned the visit on March 24 when nothing passed but compliments which " Mr. Grenville answered . . . with great civility but no overstrained professions " (*ibid.* p. 499). In his diary Grenville does not mention the favour, which was for leave to have a house in Richmond Park belonging to the King. George III had no desire to have him so near Richmond Lodge and wrote to Bute on March 28 refusing the request ; see Sedgwick, *Letters from George III to Lord Bute, 1756–1766* (1939), p. 237.

4. See p. 287 and n. 1. Conway was dismissed on April 17 from his place of Groom of the Bedchamber and deprived of his regiment of dragoons for voting against the Government on General Warrants. His dismissal was an unpopular act savouring of " prerogative ". Hence Grenville's disingenuous attempt to fasten it on to Bute. The attempt was on the whole successful, for Conway himself believed that " Lord Bute has at least a share in it " (Conway to Hertford in *Grenv. Pps.* ii, 298 n.), and Walpole, though never able to assign responsibility, inclined to Bute as the only suspect who ever bothered to deny the charge (*Memoirs*, i, 320). In reality the dismissal was the King's idea. Grenville opposed it as impolitic (see *Grenv. Pps.* ii, 320-27, 335-60 *passim*).

Lord B. and Mr. G. had no communication after this. In the spring 1764 a dispute ensued between Mr. G. and Sir James Lowther concerning the Deanery of Carlisle and some other provisions applied for by the latter.[1] Mr. G. employed Mr. Jenkinson to desire Lord B. to use his influence with Sir James so that this affair might be accommodated. Mr. J. did speak but without success. Lord B. thought that his son in law might be unreasonable but did not chuse to interfere. In August 1764 Lord B. applied through Mr. J. to Mr. G. for a Commission of the Hawkers and Pedlars. Lord B. displeased at Mr. G.'s common method of treating people by giving them doubtfull answers desired a positive answer. Mr. G. promised it should be done.

About September 1764 Mr. G. authorised Mr. J. to state to Lord B. a publick measure of some importance (Mr. J. forgets what it was). He took an opportunity of stating this to Lord B. who replied shortly that he desired to have no communication with the Ministers upon publick points. He would explain his reasons for this another time. After dinner of the same day Lord B. took Mr. J. into another room and repeated again that he desired to have no communication with the Ministers on publick affairs. I wish, says he, I had not previously known of Conway's dismission, for, says he, they have not failed to make use of my name to authorise that act. From this time to April 1765 Mr. J. does not recollect having any political conversation with Lord B. except that once in consequence of some complaint made by Lord B. of the state of things he said emphatically things must be worse before they could be better. But during all this time there happened frequent disputes between Mr. G. and Mr. Mackenzie concerning Scotch provisions. The two remarkable subjects of dispute were first the Sheriffdom for the County of Bamff,[2] secondly the office of secretary to the Thistle. The first of these Mr. G. wanted for a friend of Lord Fife's. Mr. M⟨ackenzie⟩ opposed this first from a dislike to Lord F⟨ife⟩ and secondly that Lord F⟨ife⟩'s man was not properly qualified which was true as Lord Cheif Baron Orde assured Mr. J.[3] The particulars of this transaction may be seen in Mr. J.'s letters to Mr. M⟨ackenzie⟩. Mr. M⟨ackenzie⟩ at last gave way and Lord Fife's man was

1. See *Grenv. Pps.* ii, 383, 385. Sir James Lowther's recommendation of Dr. Thomas Wilson to be Dean of Carlisle was successful. See also above, pp. 278, 295, 316 and *passim*, for Lowther's too frequent recommendations to small places in the Customs and Excise.

2. See p. 309 n. 4. 3. See *Grenv. Pps.* ii, 382-90 *passim*.

put in. Mr. G. wanted the office of secretary to the Thistle for a brother of Lord Fife's, Mr. M⟨ackenzie⟩ intended it for a relation of his own but finding there were many competitors he withdrew his relation. Mr. G. came to Mr. M. in the House of Commons and kept him in conversation with great earnestness for two hours. He first stated that as he confered favours on his friends he ought to receive the like from him in return. He then threatened him and after that he cajoled him by saying that he would acknowledge as a favour confered on himself the obtaining this office for Lord Fife's brother. Mr. M. said that he would give in the name of Lord Fife's brother amongst the other competitors and leave it to the King to comply with Mr. G.'s recommendation if he thought proper, or if Mr. G. pleased he would give him the list to carry to the King himself. Mr. G. desired Mr. M. to carry the list to the King and hoped to have his interest for Lord Fife's brother. Mr. M. said that he would tell the King that he did wish for Lord Fife's brother as he was agreable to Mr. G.[1] Mr. M. carried the list to the King and complied with what he had promised to Mr. G.[2] The King then spoke kindly of Sir Harry Erskine and the next morning appointed him notwithstanding a very earnest recommendation made by Mr. G. himself in favour of Lord F⟨ife⟩'s brother. When this was done as Sir H. Erskine informed Mr. J⟨enkinson⟩, Mr. G. made a representation to the King which brought on a very improper and passionate conversation between them.[3]

The change of Government which happened soon after this has been imputed to the influence of Lord B., but Lord B. assured Mr. J., and said he would give him any testimony of it he could desire, that he had never advised a measure or recommended a person since he went first to Luton. The King declared also to Mr. G. that Lord B. had never had any political conversation with him since the period above mentioned and that another time His Majesty said to Mr. G. that he must do Lord B. the justice to say that he had no concern

1. Cf. *Grenv. Pps.* iii, 124, 126-7. According to Grenville's diary this conversation took place on March 25, 1765. By this time Grenville's hostility to Mackenzie was intensified by his growing doubts of the King.

2. Grenville did not believe this at the time. See his diary for April 3 : " Mr. Grenville . . . named Mr. Duff to the King for the Secretary to the Order of the Thistle. His Majesty made no other answer than desiring to see the names of all the persons soliciting that office, which in all probability is to take Mr. Mackenzie's recommendation, and seemingly to make it his own choice " (*ibid.* p. 126).

3. *Ibid.* p. 127. April 4 : " Mr. Grenville argued and pressed strongly for Mr. Duff, but in vain ".

in this affair.[1]   Lord B. from the beginning disavowed his having any concern in this affair even when it was likely that the negociation with Mr. Pitt would succeed and there was no fact appeared upon which the supposition of Lord B.'s influence could be founded except that he had all along very good information of what was passing in the Closet.[2]   Mr. G. has always said that Lord B. took the opportunity of His Majesty's illness in the spring to prejudice His Majesty against him when he alone was with him and none of his Ministers admitted, but Lord B. declares that he never saw the King but twice during that illness.[3]

Lord B. once told Mr. J. that the original cause of the King's displeasure with Mr. G. was the violence he used in endeavouring to extort every thing from him, his threats to Mr. Worsley for speaking to the King on the business of his office [4] first broke the ground and upon every occasion when any point was under deliberation or any office was to be given away Mr. G. would urge that it was necessary for carrying on His Majesty's Government that it should be as he would have

1. Cf. Grenville's diary for May 21 and June 10, 1765, *Grenv. Pps.* iii, 180, 215 ; and George III's memorandum, Fortescue, *Corr. of George III*, No. 141.

2. Jenkinson believed that Bute and the King were in constant communication by letter.   See Grenville's account of their conversations at Bath in November 1765 (*Grenv. Pps.* iii, 220) : " Mr. Jenkinson . . . had several conversations with Mr. Grenville, all tending to the justification of Lord Bute's conduct, and particularly upon the late change of Ministry, which he endeavoured to persuade Mr. Grenville had not been brought about by Lord Bute's influence. . . . He owned, however, to Mr. Grenville that the intercourse in writing between His Majesty and Lord Bute always continued, telling him that he knew that the King wrote him a journal every day of what passed, and as minute a one as if, said he, ' your boy at school was directed by you to write his journal to you '." Very few letters from George III to Bute are extant for 1764–65, and for 1765–66 only three comprehensive letters each covering several months, which makes it impossible that he should have written regularly.

3. According to Grenville, in November 1765 Jenkinson told him that Bute " never had seen the King but twice during his illness in the spring, which fact Mr. Grenville could not be brought to believe " (*ibid.*).   The King's illness, a first attack of mental derangement, lasted, according to Grenville, from February 25 to March 25, during which time Grenville recorded only one visit from Bute on March 4, for a quarter of an hour (*ibid.* p. 121).   On March 25 he wrote, " The King's confinement makes a great deal of talk, as few people believe him to be as ill as is given out by Lord Bute's friends " (*ibid.* p. 124).

4. Cf. George III's memoranda (Fortescue, *Corr. of George III*, Nos. 139-42) : " To prove the height of Mr. Greenville's insolence it may not be improper to mention his language to Mr. Worstley on my determination of curtailing the office of painter ;   when the Surveyor reported to him my intentions, he [Grenville] say'd if people presum'd to speak to me on business without his previous consent, he would not serve an hour " (No. 141).   Practically, Grenville was right.   It was essential to Parliamentary management that patronage should be distributed from a single fountain-head, otherwise it tended to act as a disruptive instead of a cohesive force.   Secretaries of State might speak to the King on foreign affairs without consulting the Prime Minister, but " business " (*i.e.* patronage) must pass through the hands of the manager of the House of Commons.

it.[1] This the King could not bear, besides the Ministers were constantly abusing each other in the Closet, the Chancellor abused them all.[2] With respect to the Regency Bill they had greatly offended him by advising him to a measure which was dishonourable to his Mother and which was the cause of a very tender and affecting scene between them. His Majesty first opened his design of a change to Lord Mansfield who disaproved of it. Lord B. says he disaproved of it also and so says the Chancellor. The King at first did not intend to remove Mr. Grenville but when the Duke of C. was consulted there was no possibility of pursuing moderate measures especially in favour of one who was personally obnoxious to his R.H. Lord Northumberland declares that the Duke first proposed himself to him that he should be First Lord of the Treasury, and this is confirmed by what Mr. Pit relates of the Duke's earnestness with him to carry this point.[3]

LORD MACCLESFIELD TO CHARLES JENKINSON

Add. MS. 38205, f. 10.

Shirburn Castle, December 1, 1765.

Dear Sir,

I am much obliged to you for your letter. I can not but congratulate myself on being out of this hurry and bustle of politicks which I find by you is as great as ever. To say the truth I have no great opinion of the stability of the present ministry, though I think them quite in the right to carry a good countenance and to try what they can do. As to the King I heartily pity him. Have you seen Lord Harcourt lately ? What says his Lordship ? It was with great pleasure that I read in your letter that you designed seeing this place soon. I shall pass the Christmas here and shall be glad of

1. Cf. *Grenv. Pps.* iii, 213. On July 10, 1765, Grenville, in his last interview with the King, demanded a categorical explanation of how he had given offence. " The King said in general that he had found himself too much constrained, and that when he had anything proposed to him, it was no longer as counsel, but what he was to *obey*." Grenville shrewdly pointed out that the appearance of constraint in making appointments was due to the " little choice he had of proper subjects from various circumstances ".

2. But George III encouraged them to abuse each other. See Grenville's diary *passim*.

3. Cf. the Duke of Cumberland's statement in Albemarle's *Memoirs of the Marquis of Rockingham*, i, 191 *et seq.*

your company whenever you will let me have it. Such a rustication at this time puts a man out of the way ⟨of⟩ *explications* which are not always the most agreeable. Pray give your [*sic*] compliments to your brother and believe me to be dear Sir

Your most obedient humble servant,

Macclesfield

CHARLES JENKINSON TO SIR JAMES LOWTHER

Add. MS. 38205, f. 16.

December 15, 1765.

I have seen Mr. G⟨renville.⟩ I find that he is determined to propose an amendment to the Address in support of the Legislative Authority over the Colonies in case any Address whatever should be proposed. I shall be curious to know what passes between Sir Fletcher and Mr. Grenville. I don't find that Mr. G. yet knows what is to be the Address or the proceedings on Tuesday.

On Tuesday, December 17, Grenville proposed an amendment to the address to declare the colonies in rebellion. Fletcher Norton opposed this amendment. See Conway to the King, December 17, in Fortescue, *Corr. of George III*, No. 161 ; Walpole, *Memoirs*, ii, 166.

CHARLES JENKINSON TO SIR JAMES LOWTHER

Add. MS. 38205, f. 23.

Monday Night, December 16, 1765.[1]

My dear Sir,

Mr. Grenville did not tell me anything of importance ; he talked much against the Address, of which he had got an account ;[2] and I rather suspect that he would only abuse it,

1. This letter is merely docketed December 1765, but was obviously written on Monday, December 16, the day before the opening of Parliament.
2. He received a second-hand account of the Address from Jenkinson, who wrote to him at 10 o'clock on Sunday night, December 15 : " I have just heard in confidence what has passed at the meeting in my neighbourhood : it was very numerous, but many were at it who had no right to be there, and never used to

and drop all idea of an Amendment, if he knew that the King's friends would not stick by him. Are you sure Sir Fletcher last night left him convinced that he would not be with him on this occasion? I wish you would be so good as to call on me in your way to the House tomorrow.

I am ever with the greatest regard dear Sir,

Yours most faithfully

C. Jenkinson

On December 17, Grenville's motion, seconded by Whately, was opposed by Charles Townshend, Gilbert Elliot, Fletcher Norton, Wedderburn, Dyson, and Lord George Sackville. See Conway to the King, Fortescue, *op. cit.* No. 161. All of these, however, except Charles Townshend who cannot be classed as a " King's Friend ", are in Newcastle's list of those who voted against the Repeal of the Stamp Act on February 21, 1766 (Add. MS. 32974, f. 169). This list includes also Jenkinson, James Oswald, Samuel Martin, Edward Harvey, P. C. Webb, Sir James Lowther and his friends Robinson, John Upton, and Lord Warkworth. Grafton's statement in his *Autobiography* (pp. 68-9) that most of the " King's Friends " voted for the Repeal appears unfounded, as Newcastle's list contains all the most important names.

BENJAMIN HALLOWELL TO CHARLES JENKINSON
Add. MS. 38205, f. 18.

Boston, December 17, 1765.

Sir,

Since my last in which I acquainted you with the violent measures taken here, in which I was a great sharer in the fate of; I received your letter saying you was not in the office in the Treasury, which gives me great concern, but not so disagreeable to you, I hope, the change being general.

⟨No⟩thing but resolutions throughout the Continent of America respecting the Stamp Act, to a man seem resolved not ⟨to⟩ take them, some people are determined to die rather ⟨than⟩ submit. We this day followed the example of the Southern Governments in clearing vessels on unstamped paper. God knows whether we shall meet with approbation; every

be at such meetings before" (*Grenv. Pps.* iii, 110). Lord George Sackville, a " King's Friend ", was present, though this preliminary meeting to the one at the Cockpit was usually composed of the active friends of Administration in the House of Commons. See L. B. Namier's article on " The Circular Letters " in *E.H.R.*, October 1929.

danger attended a refusal, there being no alternative, this day being the first since the act took place.

The loss I sustained in the attack of my house was £486 : 13 : 4 sterling, on 26 August, and while this spirit prevails and an officer does his duty he will be subject to the same treatment. I hope some method will be fell upon to secure the officers in the execution of their office, and reparation made for the loss I sustained and injury received, to forward which beg leave to ask the favour of your interest.

Every endeavour is made use of to come at the knowledge of what the officer of the Crown does, and have wrote. No money is spaired at the publick offices for copies of what is sent them, as also all private letters. Copies of both have been sent here and much to the disadvantage of those who wrote them, and I am told that by some stratagem one of the letters sent to you are here, whether intercepted or how, I cannot tell, but it is like to appear as a charge against me.

I am Sir, with the greatest respect,

Your most obedient and very much obliged humble servant,

Benj. Hallowell junr.

CHARLES JENKINSON TO SIR JAMES LOWTHER

Add. MS. 38205, f. 21.

December 24, 1765.

Dear Sir,

I have just received a message from Mr. Grenville enquiring after my health and saying that he was going out of town for five days. This is all I know from himself, but I have heard from other quarters, and such as may I think be relied on, that he and Lord Temple are gone out of town together ; and they say that they are to go together as far as Missenden, which is a town in Buckinghamshire in the way both to Stow and Wotton. This is all I know ; whether there is any thing political in all this, I leave to you to judge ; the person who gave me this information, thinks there is ; but as I am not inclined to suspect plots, I am of a different opinion. I am with the greatest regard dear Sir,

Yours most faithfully,

C: J——n

" Observations on the probable dissolution of Lord Rockingham's [first] Administration " [1]

Add. MS. 38339, ff. 307-10.

The political setting of this paper has been explained by Professor Namier in his Ford Lectures in 1934. The death of the Duke of Cumberland deprived the Rockinghams of their real leader and of the one intimate link they had with the King. Newcastle told the King that there was " a chasm which has to be supplied ", and pressed the Rockinghams to gain Pitt. Thomas Townshend junior was sent to Pitt on January 2 and negotiations ensued with no result. It was obvious that the Government was in need of additional strength; but the King, although he was in no way intriguing against them, did not consider it incumbent upon himself to try and gain for them support. Least of all did he wish for a coalition of the Rockinghams with Pitt formed to the exclusion of the so-called " King's Friends ". In a letter which the King wrote to Bute on January 10 he explained that while he was in honour bound honestly to support the Administration so long as they were able to carry on, if they admitted their inability to do so he would be free to form a different government — the present ministers " must either go on or give up "; see Sedgwick, *Letters from George III to Lord Bute*, p. 244.

After the opening debate of January 14, which in Rockingham's own words showed once more " the amazing powers and influence which Mr. Pitt has, whenever he takes part in debate ", Rockingham again put it to the King that a further attempt had to be made " to get Mr. Pitt to take a cordial part ". This the King rightly interpreted as an admission on the part of the Administration of their inability to carry on; and he now engaged in an attempt to form a new government without the Rockinghams, Grenvilles, or Pitt. The story of this attempt emerges clearly from the documents in Sir John Fortescue's *Correspondence of King George III*, Nos. 178, 198, and 324, if placed in their proper context (see L. B. Namier, *Additions and Corrections*, pp. 45-6); further see notes dictated by Grafton to Stonehewer, *Autobiography*, pp. 64-6. It was presumably at this time when the question was canvassed whether any Administration could be formed from among the " King's Friends ", that the meeting must have taken place, of which the following paper supplies an account.

At a Meeting of Gentlemen who could discourse in confidence with each other on the present state of affairs, the following facts were stated.

1st. That there was likely soon to be a dissolution of the present Administration by the resignation of some Members of it, who would not continue to serve unless Mr. Pitt was brought to the head of affairs, and that in consequence of this Lord Rockingham and the rest (who did not approve of this measure) might resign likewise as not being themselves able

---

1. The word *first* has been added later. Handwriting of the document unidentified.

or not being willing to carry on the publick business, after having lost two of their colleagues.[1]

2dly. That Lord Temple and Mr. Pitt were supposed from recent informations to be now wholly divided in consequence of what the latter said in the House of Commons on Tuesday and that Mr. Pitt therefore stood alone at the head of that part of the administration who were desirous of forcing His Majesty to receive him into his service, and that Lord Temple, now separated from his brother in law, was supposed through the mediation of Mr. Grenville to have joined and put himself at the head of the Duke of Bedford and his party.[2]

3dly. That Mr. Grenville, though of this last party, was willing that Lord Temple should appear at the head of it, and that he began to hold a language very different from what he had hitherto done, saying that he would not in Parliament make any peevish motions or endeavours to force himself into the King's service. The persons above mentioned began upon this to consider what measures it may be proper for his Majesty to persue towards forming a new Administration, if the intended resignations should take place.

The end to be wished is that His Majesty should have the free choice of his own Servants and that he should not put the management of his affairs unconditionally into the hands of the leader of any party.

The parties at present may be thus stated.

1st. Those who have always hitherto acted upon the sole principle of attachment to the Crown. This is probably the

1. None except Conway, Grafton, and perhaps Newcastle, wanted Pitt to join them, but after his speech on January 14, they were afraid to go on without him. See Rockingham to the King, January 15, saying the Administration will be shaken if no attempt is made to gain Pitt, though there seemed little chance of his supporting them (*Rockingham Memoirs*, i, 270). It appears from a letter of Egmont to the King, that on January 16, and probably also on the 15th, Rockingham meant to resign if Conway and Grafton did (Fortescue, *op. cit.* p. 234), but on the evening of the 16th, Grafton reported a favourable answer from Pitt (*ibid.* No. 203) and on January 18 he and Rockingham together called on Pitt with a message from the King. As the " King's Friends " were unaware that Rockingham now favoured a negotiation with Pitt, it seems likely that their meeting took place before this visit, *i.e.* between January 16 and 18.

2. Cf. Rockingham to the King, January 15 (*Rockingham Memoirs*, i, p. 270), " the conduct of Lord Temple in the House of Lords, who was peevish, and who dissented to every assertion of Mr. Pitts, has made very many now believe that Mr. Pitt is more separated from G. Grenville and Lord Temple than could have been relied on some days ago ". See also Wilkes to Humphrey Cotes, February 15 (quoted in *Grenv. Pps.* iii, 227 n.), " I hear that Bedford, Sandwich, Halifax, etc., are united with Lord Temple and George Grenville ". On January 15 Temple, who had heard Grenville's defence in the Commons, gave him £1000, " in testimony of my joy and conviction ". See Temple to Grenville, and Grenville's answer, *ibid.* pp. 227-8.

most numerous body and would on trial be found sufficient to carry on the publick business themselves if there was any person to accept of a Ministerial office at the head of them, and this is all they want. This defect however makes it necessary that they should be joined if it be possible to some one of the other parties.

2dly. Lord Rockingham and his friends.

3dly. The D. of Bedfords party with Lord Temple at the head of them. We form a judgment of the strength of this from the divisions at the opening of this session.[1]

4thly. Mr. Pit at the head of those who on this occasion forsake Lord Rockingham and the Administration. The strength of this party is merely ideal. It rests on no settled attachment and will be of no importance if the Crown declares against them.

But whatever choice His Majesty may think proper to make out of these different parties it is of the utmost importance to his future ease and to the honour of his Crown that he should not submit his affairs to the sole direction of any of them.

It is therefore submitted whether it may not be proper to suspend the choice of an Administration, and whether His Majesty by calling to his assistance not only those who are particularly attached to him but the honest and disinterested of all parties may not be able to carry on the publick business till such time as the several factions are returned to their senses and are inclined to submit to his commands instead of expecting conditions from him.

Something of this kind was practised at the beginning of the last War when Lord Holderness was left the sole Secretary of State and Lord Granville President of the Council and yet these alone went on with the publick business even in the midst of the War, when there was no First Lord of the Treasury and none I think of the Admiralty and but one Secretary of State ; when the Exchequer seal was in the custody of Lord Mansfield, and the supplies were opened by Mr. Nugent for the Parliament still continued to sit. This country was then as much divided into factions as it is at present and yet by these

1. On December 17, Gower, Halifax, Sandwich, and Bedford spoke in support of Lord Suffolk's amendment to the Address, which was rejected by 80 votes to 24. See Fortescue, *op. cit.* No. 163 ; Namier, *Additions and Corrections*, p. 42. In the House of Commons on December 18 Rigby's motion to call for the American papers was rejected by 70 to 35, and on December 19 Grenville's motion to adjourn to January 9 instead of 14th was defeated by 77 to 35. See Fortescue, No. 165 ; Namier, *op. cit.* p. 42 ; Walpole, *Memoirs*, ii, 168.

means an Administration was formed by which the late King's honour was saved and which was to the satisfaction of all parties and permanent.[1]

On the present occasion there are fewer difficulties to contend with and more materials to work on ; if Lord Rockingham can be persuaded to hold his office after his colleagues have resigned till a new Administration can be formed it will be necessary only to find a person to hold the seals of Secretary of State ; for the Secretary at War (Lord Barrington) and the First Lord of the Admiralty (Lord Egmount) will continue beyond a doubt. These will be sufficient to keep the machine in motion ; and if His Majesty should at the same time send for the principal of those who are attached to him and particularly Lord Strange, Lord Granby, Mr. Stanley [2] and Sir Fletcher Norton [3] explaining to them the state of things and the ill usage which he had suffered, and at the same time assuring them of protection and they would probably give more support than ever under a settled Administration.

The management of the American affairs is certainly full of difficulties but the House is so divided on that subject that whatever sentiments are adopted, they will certainly find support from one side or the other, and wherever the Crown casts its influence there will be success and the measure is of that kind that Administration will have only to execute what the Parliament shall determine ; and the Lawyers who must

1. Cf. Walpole, *Memoirs of the Reign of George II*, iii, 11. From Pitt's dismissal on April 5, 1757, to the formation of the Newcastle-Pitt coalition on June 29, the Administration was in suspense, while Fox and Newcastle each tried to form a government without Pitt. Devonshire, however, remained First Lord of the Treasury until shortly after the death, on May 6, of the 2nd Duke of Grafton, whom he succeeded as Lord Chamberlain, and Lord Winchelsea succeeded Temple as First Lord of the Admiralty on April 6.

2. In Newcastle's lists of the minority on the repeal of the Stamp Act, Add. MS. 32974, ff. 167, 169, Lord Strange, Granby, and Hans Stanley are counted as Grenville's friends. Granby, however, annoyed the Grenville-Bedford party in July 1765 by failing " to abide by his first determination of quitting his employment ". He was Master-General of the Ordnance. See *Grenv. Pps.* iii, 70, 218. Though he professed attachment to Grenville on July 18, on July 19 Rockingham had used his name as bait for Charles Townshend and his brother. See *ibid.* p. 68 note. At the same time Stanley was removed from the Admiralty Board, but kept his governorship of the Isle of Wight. See a letter from him to Grenville, October 14, 1765, saying he has refused to be reinstated, and one from Augustus Hervey, October 29 : " I suppose you know how Lord Rockingham submitted to send over and over again to Mr. Stanley . . . begging of him to come in again, which I heard afterwards even another *personage* offered, and when Stanley would have resigned the Government of the Wight, he was desired to remain, in the same language that Lord Granby and others were " (*ibid.* 99, 104). Lord Strange (see p. 93 and n. 1) was described by Walpole in 1749 as " a busy Lord of a party by himself, yet voting generally with the Tories " (Walpole to Mann, March 4, 1749).

3. Sir Fletcher Norton was removed from the office of Attorney-General in July 1765, to make way for Charles Yorke.

decide ⟨the⟩ question are almost all on the side of the Crown.

If Lord Rockingham and the whole of his Board should resign some persons must be found to fill up that Commission. This would certainly increase the difficulty and yet any thing had better be attempted, even the giving the Treasurer's Staff to some great Peer or to some one of the Royal Family, if it should be necessary rather than submit to the other alternative.

This seems to be the last struggle which it will be in the power of the Crown to make for independence. It is highly important therefore that it should be managed well. With wisdom and vigour it seems possible to succeed. If the heads of the several parties once find that Government can go on even for a short time without them they will grow submissive and offer such terms as can be received : his Majesty will then have it in his power to bring those into his service to whom he is most inclined, and to make those to whom he is less inclined serve him on such conditions as he shall approve and he will be repaid for the trouble which this one act of vigour may require with future independence and case.

CHARLES LLOYD TO CHARLES JENKINSON

Add. MS. 38205, f. 35.

Sunday Morning.
Docketed " February 9, 1766 ".

Dear Sir,

I have looked over all of the books, and therefore send them you as this may be a leisure morning with you. I have gone through them in the idea as you will find of putting down a dozen immaterial things, rather than run the chance of missing one material article. The oftener you employ me I shall like it the better.

Mr. Bradshaw's complaint is settled ; I have owned his right which indeed I never disputed and he has said that he never intended to make use of the Imperial style. I am sure you do not approve of that imperative tone, because whenever your name is mentioned at the Treasury it is always with commendation for a conduct the very reverse of it. I take great parts on these occasions, as well as upon every subject

in which your credit is concerned, as an attempt to shew myself
not unworthy of the kindnesses which you have conferred on
dear Sir,

Your much obliged and most faithful humble servant,

Charles Lloyd

JOHN ROBINSON TO SIR JAMES LOWTHER
at Lowther, near Penrith

Add. MS. 38205, f. 49.

House of Commons, April 22, 1766.
past 9 o Clock at Night.

Sir,

I received your express here last night about ten, and
having been engaged all this day again here I have not yet had
your letter which you referr to therein, but I shall take care to
observe your directions. The House have sat so late last night
and to night [1] that I have not been able to send the Minutes
I promised you of their proceedings but I will the moment I
can. To day they have been on the militia clauses which I
mentioned to you that I had prepared and they have all passed
the committee. finished a little while ago, and now the House
are upon the general warrants on the motion of Sir William
Meredith and a likelihood of a late night, Sir William only
having just done speaking and Mr. Grenville got up.[2] Yesterday the House were upon the report in regard to the Window
Tax and divided ; for the Tax 179, against it 114. This day
hath hitherto been spent in much conversation on the militia
without any opposition to the clauses, but in that conversation
Mr. Pitt threw out that he would go to the farthest part of
England to oppose and overturn that Administration that
should attempt to destroy the militia.[3] I send you a copy of
the militia clauses as they have passed the committee, and
hope to write more correctly and more fully to morrow night

1. On Tuesday, April 22, the House " continued to sit, till half an hour past
two of the Clock on Wednesday morning " (*Journals of the House of Commons*).
2. On April 22, 1766, Meredith moved the illegality of general warrants.
His motion passed by 173 to 71, but Grenville's was rejected by the Lords on
May 14. See *Parliamentary History*, xvi, cols. 207-9.
3. Cf. Walpole, *Memoirs*, ii, 224. George Onslow proposed a Bill to economise
on the militia by suppressing one serjeant in each company and reducing the pay
of the militia clerks from £50 to £25 a year. Pitt spoke against it and it was
rejected.

(409)

and that you will in the meantime excuse me. It gives me the sincerest pleasure to find you are in so fair a way of recovery for your illness much alarmed us. I most heartily wish it may continue and soon be perfect and am with the greatest regard and respect. Sir,

Your most ffaithful and most obedient humble servant,

J. Robinson

P.S. If I can let you know to night how these general warrants go I certainly will.

CHARLES JENKINSON TO SIR ROBERT JENKINSON

Add. MS. 38305, ff. 21-2.

Jenkinson's cousin, Sir Robert Jenkinson, 5th Bart., about whom see p. v, died shortly after this letter was written, on August 12, 1766. He married Mary, daughter of Sir Jonathan Cope, 1st Bart. of Brewerne, Oxfordshire, by his father's sister, Mary Jenkinson.

London, May 25, 1766.

My dear Sir,

I returned a few days ago from a jaunt I took into Oxfordshire with the French Ambassador and his family. I had the pleasure to see Banks [1] at Oxford in perfect health. I set out for Normandy on Friday and Sir Charles Cope [2] goes with me. This I hope will be of great use to him whose misfortune it is to be too shy. I shall hope to hear from you while I am abroad, and if you will direct your letters to me in Parliament Street, they will be properly forwarded. You will have heard of the arrangements that have been made in Administration. Nothing can be more weak, more absurd, or less likely to last. Lord North after much hesitation has refused to join them and this is a strong proof of his Lordships idea of their instability, and I leave England lamenting indeed the state of publick affairs, but without any apprehension that some plan of Government more agreable to my wishes and interest must in a short time take place.

1. Banks Jenkinson succeeded his brother as 6th Bart. and, dying unmarried in 1789, was succeeded by Charles Jenkinson, then 1st Baron Hawkesbury. He was a Fellow of All Souls.
2. Sir Charles Cope, 2nd Bart., was Jenkinson's cousin and a nephew of Sir Robert Jenkinson's wife. In 1767 he married Catherine, daughter of Sir Cecil Bisshopp, 6th Bart., who in 1782, one year after the death of her husband, married Charles Jenkinson as his second wife.

Permit me now, my dear Sir to open to you a scheme, which I own I have very much at heart ; the day after I saw Banks at Oxford it was suggested to me by some friends, who came over to me at Newnham, that if I thought fit to try it, I might have some chance of representing the University in case of a vacancy either by the death of Sir Walter Baggot or by his declining to stand any more ; it was supposed I might very well stand upon the ground of having received the whole of my education there, and of some pretensions to publick merit, and that under this pretence my relations and friends of different denominations might unite the several parties in my favor ; I determined however not to take any step before I talked to Lord Litchfield,[1] the Bishop of Durham [2] and Lord Mansfield. Upon my return to London I saw the first and the last of these but the Bishop was out of Town ; they were both very kind to me and in consequence of what they said I resolved to keep the object in view ; and Lord Mansfield undertook to sound the Dean of Christ Church,[3] and to see what could be done in that quarter, but they both recommended the strictest secrecy ; and that any design of this kind should not be known publickly at present ; this is all my dear Sir that has passed on this subject, and here I shall leave it 'till I return from abroad ; I thought it proper to communicate this to you and I wish you would shew this letter to Banks when you see him. I am persuaded I shall have both your and his good wishes and assistance ; and I would submit whether without talking of any such design being actually on foot, you might not from time to time insinuate to your friends the propriety of such a measure and the satisfaction you should receive from my succeeding in it.[4]

Since writing the above I have received your letter of the 24th instant. There can be no hurry about the payment of the Bills ; I only ordered Martin to send them to your house-keeper as they had been left over. I am sorry to find that you have so much trouble in getting a country house. I will not fail to make your compliments to Sir Charles Cope in the manner you desire. He comes to Town to-morrow. I beg you

1. Lord Litchfield was Chancellor of Oxford.
2. Richard Trevor, son of Thomas Baron Trevor, Bishop of Durham 1752–71, was a Fellow of All Souls and a Canon of Christ Church.
3. David Gregory, about whom see p. 48 n. 3.
4. In 1767 on the death of Sir Walter Bagot, and again at the general election of 1768, Jenkinson intended to stand for Oxford, but was obliged to abandon the attempt in 1767, and was defeated on a poll at the general election. See Add. MSS. 38457.

would present my best respects to Lady Jenkinson and dont fail to let me hear from you.

I am etc.

C. Jenkinson

P.S. I hear that the Great Man has left[1] you and is gone to Pynsent.[2] Lord Howe has resigned because he was not brought into the Administration.[3]

THOMAS BRADSHAW TO CHARLES JENKINSON
Add. MS. 38205, f. 56.

Tuesday, June 10, 1766.

I thank you a thousand times, my dear Sir, for your obliging letter, which gave me the most sincere satisfaction; I believe I shall take your advice, and pay a visit to the distressed women of Dieppe,[4] for I am of no use at Whitehall, and very heartily disgusted: I will not say, I do not wish every body to think as favorably of me as you do, but I will say, with great truth, I had rather deserve your good opinion, than the opinions of all those with whom I am now connect'd. It is more flattering to my vanity, as well as more pleasing to my heart.

I wrote you a strange letter by the last post, since which nothing material has happened. My intelligencer is in low spirits; he says things will not do as they are at present, and he has advised for some days the calling your friend at Canewood to the Cabinet;[5] I know he has done so. The Southern Department remains as it did; and it is reported that the person who fills it at present is not disposed to part with what he has got.[6] I think his party is so strong, that it is very likely to disgust in time, the man for whom I have the most regard, and of whom I have the best opinion.[7]

1. Here the word Bath has been written in and then crossed out.
2. Pitt lived at Burton Pynsent.
3. Richard, 4th Viscount Howe, M.P. for Dartmouth 1757–82, afterwards Vice-Admiral (see *D.N.B.*), was a Lord of the Admiralty under Grenville 1763–65, and Treasurer of the Navy 1765–70, when he was appointed Commander-in-Chief in the Mediterranean. In May 1766 he resigned the Treasurership of the Navy but resumed it in August under Chatham.
4. Jenkinson went to France with his cousin Sir Charles Cope at the end of May 1766 and remained there until October or November.
5. Lord Mansfield. Bradshaw's "intelligencer" was presumably Charles Townshend.
6. Conway.   7. Presumably Grafton.

I shall write you by every post, and if my letters are dull, you must excuse them. I had rather shew you the weakness of my head, than by neglect give you reason to think I was not truly devoted to you. Adieu my dear friend.

What a K- speech. A friend of yours and mine says he is sure Burke wrote it, it is so impudent.[1] Will Burke comes in for Bedwyn by a compromise between Lords Verney and Bruce, the former is to have one seat for 9 years, and Lord Bruce the burrough ever after.[2]

THOMAS BRADSHAW TO CHARLES JENKINSON

Add. MS. 38205, f. 58.

June 24, 1766.

I have been silent, my dear Sir, for some posts, not only from a total ignorance of any circumstance, worth your knowledge, but from a violent headach, which has made me unfit to take up my pen. I now address my self to you, rather in hopes of your giving it an answer, than with any expectation of informing or amusing you ; the times being barren of events, and my headach still continuing.

By what I can learn, the Americans are less pleased with the repeal, than displeased by the declaration of right. I should however think, they will remain quiet for the present : all regulations with regard to them are at a stand ; the Quebec business remains as you left it, and the three great lawyers refused to come to Council.[3]

1. Edmund Burke was Rockingham's private secretary.
2. William Burke, M.P. for Great Bedwyn 1766 (returned June 16) to 1774, a cousin of Edmund Burke whom he preceded in politics, having worked for Bute and Fox during the session 1762–63. On November 12, 1763, Fox recommended him to Sandwich as " a very clever fellow, and I believe a very honest one. He has as great a sway with Lord Verney, as I ever knew one man to have with another. Lord Verney has another vote besides his own. I owed them both to Mr. Burke last sessions, and they were never absent" (see Namier, *England etc.* p. 214 n. 1). The letter is from the Sandwich MSS. at Hinchingbrooke. In 1768 Thomas Brudenell Bruce, 2nd Baron Bruce, brought in his brothers James and Robert Brudenell for Great Bedwyn, but Robert electing to serve for Marlborough, William Burke was returned in his place. Ralph, 2nd Earl Verney, M.P. for Carmarthen 1761–68, also brought Edmund Burke into Parliament for his borough of Wendover on December 23, 1765.
3. Cf. extracts from Lord Hardwicke's " Memorial " and the Duke of Richmond's Journal in *Rockingham Memoirs*, i, 350–55. On June 27 a plan for the civil government of Quebec prepared by the Attorney- and Solicitor-General was submitted to the Cabinet when Northington objected to it and refused to attend

I have this moment heard, I think from good authority, that the dismission of Mr. Dyson has been asked, and that a great personage desired time to consider of the demand : I am told, if this is refused, it will be looked upon as a decisive proof of the want of power and support, and will open a new scene immediately.[1] My best intelligencer is in the country, but I have reason to believe my information is well founded.

Adieu my dear Sir ; to detain you longer from the pleasures, in which you are engaged, would be unkind ; I shall therefore only add, that your friends wish to know that you are well, and among that number, no one is more sincerely devoted to you than myself.

I don't know whether I informed you that General Conway's Burke[2] is to come in for Great Bedwyn. Mr. and Mrs. Cornwall and the Captain[3] set out on Thursday : I wish I was of the party.

THOMAS WHATELY TO CHARLES JENKINSON

Add. MS. 38205, f. 60.

[Parliament ?] Street, July 11, 1766.

Dear Jenkinson,

We agreed at parting not to write upon common occurrences, but if any extraordinary event happened, you desired me to let you know it. If I did not think the present occasion extraordinary, I believe I should never have an opportunity to obey your commands : for it is no less than a change of Administration : so much I may say for certain : and all beyond are speculations not worth troubling you with, and as different as men's countenances, in which there is at present a very great variety. The only step hitherto taken is the sending for Mr. Pitt, who ⟨has n⟩ot yet arrived ; but is expected to

any more Cabinet meetings on the subject. Though Bradshaw's letter is dated in his own hand June 24, he would seem to refer to the events of June 27 and 28. It does not appear from Rockingham's letters to Charles Yorke (*ibid.* p. 357 *seqq.*) that either Yorke or De Grey refused to attend the Cabinet meetings on Canadian affairs.

1. On June 27, 1766, the Cabinet for the second time pressed the King to remove Jeremiah Dyson, a " King's Friend ", from the Board of Trade, for having obstructed their Bill to grant Princess Caroline's marriage portion. At a Cabinet meeting on the same day, the Duke of Richmond proposed that they should all resign if Dyson were not removed, but to this Newcastle objected. See *Newcastle's Narrative*, p. 73. The King wished to give the Rockinghams no active help and refused to remove Dyson on a personal question.

2. William Burke was Under-Secretary to Conway.

3. John Jenkinson ?

day or to morrow. In such a situation you will hold all prophecies cheap ⟨   ⟩ will wait till they are history. The business with which the Treasury end their Administration has been the settlem⟨ent⟩ of the German Office : [1] and they have this week given £3000 to Cornwall, as much to Cuthbert, nothing to Pownall, £10⟨00⟩ to West, £300 to each Clerk of the first Class, and £100 to each of the second. The news from America is not very interesting. It is little more than bonfires, illuminations, and healths : and at Boston, where the ascendancy of the popular Party still ⟨continues ?⟩ in the Assemblys, choosing Mr. Otis [2] for their Speaker excluding Lieutenant Governor Hutchinson,[3] Mr. Olivar,[4] and three or four ⟨others⟩ who were friends to Government from the Council ; Governor Bernard [5] has put a negative upon all who were ⟨chos⟩en in their places. This is all I know at present which I think you can wish to know ; you will probably hear from me soon again : but do not wait for a second letter before you give me the pleasure of hearing that you are well and happy in your tour, and wherever you wander believe that you are always accompanied with ⟨the⟩ best wishes of, dear Jenkinson

Your most faithful etc.

T. W.

THOMAS WHATELY TO CHARLES JENKINSON
chez Messieurs Robert Foley et Co., Banquiers à Paris

Add. MS. 38205, f. 99.

July 22, 1766.

Dear Jenkinson,
    You Paris politicians have acquired a vivacity which we want ; and those which you on the 16th Instant call'd the

1. See p. 201.
2. James Otis (1725–83), the American revolutionary, about whom see *D.A.B.* At this time Otis with Samuel Adams and Joseph Hawley controlled the General Court.
3. Lieutenant-Governor Thomas Hutchinson (1711–80), the author of a *History of Massachusetts Bay*, about whom see *D.A.B.*, and below, Israel Mauduit's *Annus Pacificus*, p. 440. In 1770 he succeeded Francis Bernard as Governor.
4. Andrew Oliver (1706–74), about whom see *D.A.B.*, was a member of a distinguished Boston family. His wife and Thomas Hutchinson's were sisters and the two men were connected politically. Oliver was secretary of Massachusetts 1756–71 and appointed a Stamp officer in 1765, when he was hanged in effigy by the mob. In 1770 he succeeded Hutchinson as Lieutenant-Governor.
5. Sir Francis Bernard (1712–79), about whom see *D.A.B.*, and below, p. 439 *et seq.*, was Governor of Massachusetts 1760–70, through the influence of Lord Barrington, who was a cousin of his wife, Amelia Offley.

late are still on this 22d July the present Ministry : how long or how many of them will continue so, I do not pretend to guess, but I believe the alterations will not be many.[1] Mr. Pitt's plan was himself Privy Seal, Lord Temple at the Treasury, the Duke of Grafton President of the Council, Lord Shelbourne and General Conway Secretaries of State, and no other change of men, nor any that I hear of measures. Lord Temple's idea was a comprehensive plan to unite parties and abilities, and to fix a permanent Administration on a broad bottom. For this purpose he mentioned Lord Lyttleton for a Cabinet Office and Lord Gower as Secretary of State : upon which they differed ; Lord Temple is gone out of town ; and Mr. Pitt is to proceed, but he has done nothing yet : the reason assigned for which delay is his being ill and it is true that he has been much out of order but is better. So that we are still in a state of absolute uncertainty and consequently liable to a variety of reports : the most prevalent have been that Mr. Pitt and Lord Temple differed about Mr. Grenville, Mr. Mackenzie, and Lord Bute : all which I can positively contradict as without the least foundation, and if you hear any stories with either of those names in them, you may safely disbelieve them. Lord Bute entirely disavows any knowledge of the transaction, and is all this time at Luton. God knows how this will end, but I doubt your service will not be immediately wanted and I wish you may continue to get health, information and amusement wherever you go.

Yours sincerely and in haste,

T. W.

GEORGE GRENVILLE TO CHARLES JENKINSON

Add. MS. 38191, ff. 85-6.

Wotton, July 27, 1766.

Dear Jenkinson,

Your letter of the 6th of this month [2] found me here about ten days ago, since which time it has been impossible for me to answer it from the great number of letters which I have been obligd to write in consequence of the late public trans-

1. The new Administration took office on July 30, when Pitt was created Earl of Chatham.
2. This letter, dated from Paris, is in the *Grenv. Pps.* iii, 258-60.

actions though I have taken no part whatever in them and am happy to be able to tell you that agreably to my earnest wishes and desires not to embarrass or clog any plan which should be opend to Lord Temple when he went to town in persuance of his Majestys orders he expressly declind stating me for any thing upon this occasion.[1] As to the other parts of this business, the propositions which were made to him, and his reasons for thinking them utterly inadmissible and therefore refusing to engage I refer you to the other accounts which you will receive of them and as they are no secrets they will come to you more properly where you are from other hands than from mine, nor will I at this distance make any comments upon what must and certainly will speak sufficiently for itself. I rejoice to hear so good an account of you and that you have passed your time so very agreably since you have been in France which I hope will be attended not only with pleasure but with health and strength likewise sufficient to go through those scenes of public busyness, and of public difficulty which seem to be preparing. If you see either M. de Nivernois or M. de Guerchy whilest you are in France I desire you will present my best compliments to them and assure them that I shall ever retain with the greatest pleasure the memory of the friendship and regard with which they honourd me. There is a report spread in England that the latter is not to return hither again which I should be sorry for as a public man as well as a private man because I allways thought M. de Guerchy disposd to maintain peace and good understanding between the two Kingdoms. I shall be very glad to receive a good account of you from time to time, as your leisure and amusements will allow you to give it me and am allways, dear Sir, very affectionately

Your most faithful, humble servant,
George Grenville

My wife I hope gets better than she was. She makes her compliments to you, and returns you thanks for your good wishes and enquiry after her.[2]

1. Cf. Grenville to Charles Lloyd, August 8, 1766 : " I desired Lord Temple not to clog or embarass this transaction in any shape by mentioning me " (*ibid.* p. 299).

2. Jenkinson's answer to this letter, dated from Paris, August 10, is in the *Grenv. Pps.* iii, 301.

LORD HILLSBOROUGH TO CHARLES JENKINSON

à l'Hotel de Luynes au Rue Colombier

Add. MS. 38205, f. 62.

Hanover Square, August 1, 1766.

Dear Sir,

You will have received the list of those who have kissed hands from others I doubt not; but should it happen otherwise I send it by this post to Sir J. Lambert.[1] I write you a line only to mention the very extraordinary reception of a visit from Mr. P⟨itt⟩. He went (I think last Friday) to wait upon Lord R⟨ockingham⟩. The porter let him in; his chair was brought into the hall; the servant out of livery acquainted his Lordship that Mr. P. was there, My Lord replied — *I can't see Mr. P.*; the other went away. Thus much is fact. *I have heard* that Mr. C⟨onway⟩ told Mr. P. that Lord R. wished to see him, which occasioned the visit. When Lord R. heard this he desired Mr. C. to let Mr. P. know that he never had expressed nor should express any such desire till it was explained to him how his friends were to be treated. People imagine it will be contrived some how or other to give the Chamberlayn's Staff to Lord B.[2] Mackenzie is certainly to be restored. As to the other persons to whom you think ——[3] stands pledged, I hear little of them. It has been slightly reported that Lord Despencer is to have something. Not a word is yet said about Ellis. One person told me he heard you were to be again Secretary. There was something particular in the great hurry to appoint the new Lord of the Treasury ⟨   ⟩ Persons have told me that I am to have an offer of the Board of Trade *upon the same foot as formerly*; but I do not believe it.[4] I am apt to think the new paymasters will be Dowdeswell and Lord North, but nothing is declard.[5] Thus I write you nothing only to shew that I would not neglect to write something if in my

1. Sir John Lambert, 2nd Bart., lived in Paris. His family had settled in the Isle of Rhee, and his mother was French.
2. It was given to Lord Hertford.
3. The King.
4. It was offered him on August 5 when he accepted it as a Board of reference only and without a seat in the Cabinet, though he had held it under Grenville with fuller powers. See his letter to Grenville dated August 6, *Grenv. Pps.* iii, 294-6.
5. See p. 420.

power, for I shall always be happy to give you every mark of the affectionate regard with which I am dear Sir

Your most faithfull humble servant,

Hillsborough

SIR FLETCHER NORTON TO CHARLES JENKINSON

Add. MS. 38205, ff. 64-5.

Grantley, August 1, 1766.

Dear Sir,

I am this moment favored with your kind letter of the 23. past, which I wish I had seen before I left London as I should have had an opportunity of communicating the contents of it to our friend,[1] on Saturday last, who I saw in my way to this place and you will be surpriz'd when I tell you, that then and, I believe now, he knows no more where or how, things are carrying on, than you do in Paris ; for be assured no advances had then been made to him, nor to any of his friends, with his privity ; but if any such shoud be made, and they shoud be of a sort that he coud attend to, I am persuaded you will soon hear from him : for I am sure he considers himself, and so all your friends, as too much interested in your welfare to take any step without a due attention to you, and indeed I am happy to be able to tell you that I am doing him no more than justice when I say these ⟨are⟩ our sentiments. I thought you regularly heard from Wedderburn or some other of our friends also I should certainly have wrote to you if I coud have procurd your address which I presumed might have been done at your house.

I understand the Cabinet is fixd, and that they kissed hands on Wednesday last and by my news of to day not much more is determined and I dare not venture to give you my own opinion of things, for fear of ⟨   ⟩ but this be assured of, that it will not be my fa⟨ult⟩ if we do not all share one common lott, and believe me to be as I truly am

Ever most sincerely yours,

Flr. Norton

1. Bute.

Add. MS. 38205, ff. 66-7.

August 8, 1766.

Since I wrote to you last post, I have dined with Mr. T⟨ownshend ;⟩ upon my mentioning your being stil at Paris, he spoke of you in the strongest terms of regard ; and of your abilities as they deserve ; he added that he had laboured to the utmost exertion of his influence, with the Duke of G⟨rafton⟩ and also with the K. for bringing you as a Lord, to the Board of Treasury, but *that it could not be, yet.* Such were his words ; I relate them exactly to you : I told him, what I feel ; that you would be the most material acquisition, which the Duke of G⟨rafton⟩ or himself could make, for their own ease, and assistance, and for the honor of the Board. I now continue my Gazette.

Lord Hilsborough accepts the Board of Trade, as a Board of Reference only ; Lord North has kissed hands for half the Pay Office : I called to wish him joy, and he told me, he did not much like things, but that his office had been offered him, in such a manner, that he could have no reason to refuse it. I am told George Cooke is to be his partner, and as he is famous for never paying his debts, it is said, that the King by virtue of his Royal prerogative has made him a *Paymaster.*[1] Lord Granby is to be Commander in Chief. Lord Ligonier has been applied to, to resign his patent, but the old soldier as yet refuses to do so, and it will be unpleasant to dismiss an ancient General of 95 years of age.

Boyd has got an Irish regiment ;[2] Lord Bristol's youngest brother, his company in the Guards ;[3] and Colonel Amherst[4] is made an extra Aid de Camp to the King. Adieu, my dear Sir, and believe me ever yours.

The clamour against Lord Chatham is beyond all discription, you will form a better idea of it, from the public

1. George Cooke, Protonotary of the Common Pleas, a City follower of Pitt, and M.P. for Middlesex 1749-68. On August 8, 1766, Grenville wrote to Charles Lloyd, " I am sorry to see Lord North in half an office, joined with that able statesman, Mr. George Cooke " (*Grenv. Pps.* iii, 299).

2. Colonel Robert Boyd was put in command of the 39th Foot in Ireland on August 6, 1766.

3. Captain William Hervey was given a company in the 1st Foot Guards on August 6, 1766.

4. William Amherst, brother of Jeffrey Amherst, was Colonel of the 32nd Foot.

papers than I can give you ; in the mean-time he keeps up his spirits ; is in good health, and has long audiences of the K. every day ; he kept the K. from Chappel the two last Sundays. The servility of the Court is beyond conception ; Lord C. has always a circle about him, much superior to that which surrounds his master, and he gives his orders, like an Adjutant General to the Regimental Adjutants ; this is the discription which a friend of yours and mine gave me of the present Levees. Adieu.

LORD HARCOURT TO CHARLES JENKINSON
Add. MS. 38205, f. 68.

Cavendish Square, August 8, 1766.

Dear Sir,

I came to town the last of July, time enough to present the new Ministry to her Majesty.[1] You must have heard at Paris the particulars of the late changes, and nothing new has happened for these last four or five days, except Mr. York's resignation, which has made way for de Grey, whose late employment has been given to Willes, for which he kissed her Majestys hand to day.[2] The vacancy by Lord Dartmouth's resignation is not yet filled up.[3] Some imagine that it will be given to Lord Hillsborough, and even go so far as to say, that he has asked for it, but of that fact I am not certain. It is said that there will be many alterations in several of the Boards, but I rather imagine that there wont be many changes : for though there are several people who expect and want to be provided for ; yet I am apt to think that they will be cautious in their proceedings that they may not increase the ill humour that in general seems to prevail, and will probably grow into no inconsiderable opposition. Mr. Pitts popularity seems to have deserted Lord Chatham. So fickle and uncertain is the opinion of the Vulgar ! which every body knows, and nobody believes in their own particular instance. Every body imagined that there would be great alterations some time b⟨efore⟩ they took place, but they neither knew the extent of them, nor

1. Harcourt was Chamberlain of the Queen's Household from April 1763.
2. On August 6 William de Grey succeeded Charles Yorke as Attorney-General and Edward Willes succeeded de Grey as Solicitor-General.
3. William, 2nd Earl of Dartmouth, was First Lord of Trade under Rockingham.

expected that Mr. Pitt would accept the peerage ; for which his good friends in the City now abuse him very grosly. The Monument was intended to have been lighted up, and addresses were prepared to have expressed their sense of his Majesty's measures ; but the peerage, the fatal peerage has damped their spirits, and most probably will determine them to postpone, if not totally to lay aside their intended rejoycings. You are too well acquainted with mankind to be surprized at any thing they do, nor will you wonder when I tell you, that the late great Comoner is lampooned in every news paper, and loaded with scurrility. It is said that the Duke of Newcastle is by no means pleased with the bed of roses which Lord Chatham has prepared for him.[1] He is retired to Claremont with very little prospect of being employed again, which ought to be no great mortification to a man of his age ; but may probably be so to a man of his restless disposition. His friends who followed him when he resigned about three years ago dont seem disposed to pay him the same compliment if one is to guess from some appearances, that are not apt to deceive one. I forgot to tell you that the City politicians say that Lord Bute has had a hand in the late alterations, and that he has outwitted Lord Chatham, and been the principal means of his taking the title. I am far from thinking that their surmizes are well grounded, more especially as I dont hear of any provision, that is intended to be made for any of his friends. They say that offers however have been made to Mackenzie, who is now in Scotland, but perhaps he may not be overhasty to accept them, unless some more of his brothers friends are also to be employed. I have not yet seen Lord Bute but I shall call upon him to morrow morning, if he comes to town, and I am not without hopes of prevailing upon him to favour me with his company to Nuneham.

Dowdeswell is retired into Worcester, little pleased with the late arrangements, it was reported that he was to have an employment, but I dont yet hear that any thing is done for him.[2] The Marquis seems to have quitted his high station

1. In March 1766 Thomas Nuthall reported to Pitt a hope expressed by Lord John Cavendish that if Newcastle was to be laid aside " it might be on a bed of roses, not on a bed of thorns " (*Chatham Corr.* ii, 408), and when, on July 23, the King told Newcastle that Pitt would require the Privy Seal from him, Newcastle replied, " Where is that bed of roses which Mr. Pitt promised me? " See *Newcastle's Narrative*, p. 90.

2. Cf. William Gerard Hamilton to Temple, August 3, 1766, " Dowdeswell is so much offended at his being removed for Mr. Townshend, that he has refused to accept of being Speaker, of being at the head of the Board of Trade, or of being Joint Paymaster " (*Grenv. Pps.* iii, 290).

not without some reluctance, and his countenance shews dejection. You know the caracters of all the principal actors so well, and the nature of the different parts that are allotted to them, that I am unwilling to make any observations upon their caracters, or even to say what I think the denouement of the piece will be. If the interest of the Crown, and the very existence of the country were not so essentially concerned in these late transactions, it might be matter of some amusement to you at Paris to hear the French *raisonments* upon the occasion. With regard to yourself, I have not been in the way of hearing any thing material, and for many reasons I have avoided being over inquisitive, least I might do harm, where I wished to do the greatest service. There are people who for want of abilities, stand greatly in need of their friends assistance ; but there are superior abilities that make their own way, more especially when they are possessed by a man of honour and steadyness. I am far from advising you to return to England in this very critical season, because I think it more adviseable for you to be absent.

Friday Evening August 9. I have heard that your friend the new Chancellor of the Exchequer [1] had thoughts of offering you the same post you enjoyed under Mr. Grenville ; if any overtures of that sort, (which I own I dont expect) should be made to me, I shall not hesitate one moment about giving such an answer as I am sure you will approve of : for it will be such a one, as shall not lessen you in the esteem of your friends, or in the opinion of mankind. I was at St. James's this morning, since I began the foregoing part of my letter, and nothing new passed there, except Lord Hillsborough kissing hands for the Board of Trade, which it is said he is to have with lesser powers, than were intended by the late Administration for Lord Dartmouth, who was disgusted at the disappointment which he met with, in not having the powers that were promised to him, which have been given to the new Secretary of State. Cook of Middlesex is to have the Pay Office jointly with Lord North, but I don't hear who is to succeed Lord George Sackville in the Vice Treasurership of Ireland, his Lordship has resigned it, and nobody seems sorry for it.[2] Colonel Boyde has got Aldercron's [3] regiment, which

1. Charles Townshend.
2. James Grenville succeeded Sackville as Joint Vice-Treasurer for Ireland.
3. Lieutenant-Colonel John Aldercron was Colonel of the 39th Foot.

it is supposed Mr. Pitt (I beg Lord Chatham's pardon) had procured for him. Upon the whole, the new Ministry does not seem to promise any great degree of permanency : unless personal attachments to the King, and a desire to prevent confusion should prove serviceable to them, how far that may go I wont say. If Lord Temple's arrangements had taken place I hear your late master G. G. was to have been left out notwithstanding which he was to have supported his brother's Administration, a *disinterestedness worthy imitation*. I left the Colonel [1] well in Ireland, fully intent upon his duty, and ambitious of qualifying himself one time or other for a higher command. He commands the prettiest Corps I ever saw, and is not a little proud of it. I am very glad I have seen Ireland, but shall not venture to give my opinion of the state of that country, till we meet in town. Pray remember me to Monsieur de Beuvron for whom I have really an affection, and give my compliments to any who do me the honor of enquiring after me. Adieu dear Sir, and believe me

Most truthfully and affectionately yours,

Harcourt

You will probably see Lord and Lady Nunham soon at Paris.

CHARLES JENKINSON TO CHARLES TOWNSHEND

Add. MS. 38305, f. 29.

Compeigne, August 14, 1766.

Dear Sir,
    I am informed by a letter from my friend Mr. Bradshaw that you had kindly exerted all your influence to bring me to the Board of Treasury,[2] though your endeavours were not attended with success, I am however greatly obliged to you for them as they afford me a fresh proof of the regard which you have constantly professed for me ; permit me at the same time to congratulate you on your appointment to the Office of Chancellor of Exchequer. In this important and active

---

1. Harcourt's second son, William, afterwards 3rd Earl Harcourt, M.P. for Oxford 1768–74, was Lieutenant-Colonel of the 4th Light Dragoons. In December 1766 he succeeded Admiral Keppel as Groom of the Bedchamber. See *Grenv. Pps.* iii, 393, 396.
2. See p. 420.

station your talents will have frequent opportunities of contributing greatly to the publick benefit, and to the increase of your own reputation. I have passed my time since I have been in France very pleasantly, but in the midst of amusements I have endeavoured to pick up some information which may be found perhaps to be useful ; I have also had the happiness to become acquainted with the Duke of Buccleugh and Mr. Scott, they are at present at the Camp at Soissons but they return here to night or to morrow ; I can assure you I hear commendations of them from every one here to whom they are known and my own observation convinces me that in this they do them but justice ; [1] I cannot conclude this letter without returning you thanks for having taken under your protection Mr. Brummell.[2] He acted under me as a clark for many years with great diligence, skill and fidelity, and I am perswaded that you will have the same reasons to be satisfied with him ; I beg my best compliments to Lady Dalkeith and to Lord Townshend when you see him.

I am etc.

C. Jenkinson

[Note in Jenkinson's letter-book : "This letter ought to have been entered farther back ". It appears between letters dated July 4 and 17, 1767.]

LORD HARCOURT TO CHARLES JENKINSON

Add. MS. 38205, ff. 82-3.

Cavendish Square, August 26, 1766.

Dear Sir,

I hear from more quarters than one, that Mr. Townshend was very desirous of having you at the Board, as the only person from whose abilities he could expect any assistance. In the light I now see things in, I am rather apt to think, that your not succeeding in this particular instance, may prove a favourable circumstance, as I should rather wish to see you stand upon your own basis, than to see you brought in, either

---

1. In December 1765, Henry Scott, 3rd Duke of Buccleuch, went to France with his brother Hughe Campbell Scott, who died at Paris in October 1766 in his nineteenth year. Walpole wrote from Paris of their " natural modesty, good nature and good breeding " (Walpole to Lady Mary Coke, March 3, 1766).

2. See p. 380 and n. 1.

by Charles Townshend's recommendation or by the assistance of any persons now in place, because you might have been under great embarrasments the very first dispute that arises between him and the present Ministry, which may soon happen.

It seems that Mr. Townshend was promised to be of the Cabinet, but he has met with a disappointment allready ; for it is now confidently said that he is not to have that honor, which is the more surprizing, as the want of it must render his services far less effectual, than they might otherwise be. I hear he takes it horribly in dudgeon, and I dare say it will be productive of no great cordiality between him and his new friends ; because he must be convinced, that as long as he is excluded the Cabinet, the Secretary (Mr. Conway) must take the lead.[1]

I am still of opinion that it is full as much for your advantage to be absent, as upon the spot, because I think it keeps you clear of all entanglements, and leaves you more at liberty to take your own ground, when a proper occasion shall present itself. Lord Bute came over with Lord Litchfield and Lord DeLeSpencer [*sic*] to pay me a visit at Nuneham last week, they staid with me all night. Your friend, for so I must call him, expressed great surprize that you had not been employed. When Lord Chatham came in, there was reason to think that some notice would have been taken of Lord Bute's friends, but whether it was really intended, or whether the spirit raised against Lord Chatham, and the abuse bestowed on him, might make him alter his plan ; it is very certain that hitherto no regard has been shewn to them : except in the instance of Mr. Mackenzie, to whom they sent an offer of the Privy Seal. He came up from Scotland in consequence of it, and was in with the King on Sunday, but I am uninformed of the result of the audience, as I am but just come to town from Lord Hyde's.[2] My stay here will be short, for as there is to be no more drawing Rooms till after the Queen is brought to bed, I shall set out for Darbyshire to morrow, and shall stay near a fortnight at Sudbury. The Admiralty was not settled on Sunday, though there were some appearances, that inclined one to think, that there was a favourable disposition towards

---

1. By the end of September Townshend had persuaded Chatham to let him into the Cabinet, but Conway was officially Leader of the House. See Grafton, *Autobiog.* p. 92.

2. Thomas Villiers, 1st Baron Hyde. His seat was at Hindon in Wiltshire.

Sir Charles Saunders, as first Lord, though those who know him, think him very unequal to that high station.[1]

If anything occurs worth communicating, you may depend upon hearing from

Your most sincere friend,

Harcourt

My compliments to your brother and sister, and to Mr. Cornwall.

THOMAS BRADSHAW TO CHARLES JENKINSON

chez Messieurs les Frères Lavergne et Fils à Lyon

Add. MS. 38205, f. 84.

Rickmansworth, September 2, 1766.

Received here this morning, my dear Sir, your letter from Compiegne of the 14 August, with a ⟨post⟩ script from Paris, dated the 27. A visit to Lord Barrington at Beckett, has prevented my writing to you for some posts, of which I beg'd ⟨Brum⟩mell to acquaint you, and I dare say he has informed you of every thing, which I should have known, had I been in town ; I am very glad Mr. Townshend has taken Brummell to be about him. Before I would speak, I desired him to ask Mr. Cooper [2] if it would be agreable to him, and to beg his recommendation ; he promised Brummell to mention him to Mr. T——, however, I recommended him, and Mr. T. immediately desired to see him, telling me he was very glad to do what was agreable to me, in favor of a person who ⟨was⟩ under your protection. Mr. Cooper then ⟨cam⟩e in, and when he left the room I presented Brummell, whom Mr. T. told, he was very glad I had mentioned him, for that Mr. Cooper had that moment recommen⟨ded⟩ Mr. Ramus [3] to him.

---

1. Admiral Sir Charles Saunders, K.B. (1713–75), about whom see *D.N.B.*, M.P. for Hedon 1754–75, was appointed First Lord of the Admiralty on September 16. He resigned on December 1. See below, p. 437.

2. Grey Cooper, M.P. for Rochester 1765–68, and afterwards successively for Grampound, Saltash, and Richmond, was Bradshaw's colleague as Joint Secretary to the Treasury, a place he held from 1765 to 1782. From April to December 1783 he was a Commissioner of the Treasury. In 1775 he assumed the baronetcy of Cooper of Gogar as 3rd Bart., before the Sheriff of Edinburgh. See *G.E.C.* There was some doubt as to whether this Scottish baronetcy had ever been properly conferred.

3. Edward Ramus was a clerk in the Treasury.

(427)

Our sentiments are exactly the s⟨ame⟩ with regard to your situation: I am sure you will always act with dignity and hon⟨our⟩ which ensures happiness to yourself, and to your friend. I am convinced Mr. T. knows your value, and is sincere in his present professions : he is at present at Atterbury, where I shall send your letter, when Brummell has sealed it ; in my opinion your letter is highly proper, and I meant by what I wrote you to give you an occasion to write such a one ; [1] he returns to town on Tuesday, when I shall lead him to this subject, and mention what you desire, in the manner you would wish me to do it.

The appointment of Sir Charles Saunders to the Admiralty, and *Sir George Younge* [2] and Lord Palmerstone [3] Lords ; Lord Bristol Lieutenant of Ireland and Lord Hertford Master of the Horse, is all that has happened since I wrote you last. Rigby carried the offer of the Admiralty to Lord Gower. (Dingly told me). He hinted to Lord Chatham ⟨that⟩ he believed it would be acceptable. ⟨If⟩ this is so, the Duke of Bedford will not ⟨lo⟩ng stand out. There certainly has been no new proposition made to Lord Temple.

Mr. Mackenzie has the Privy Seal, but without any power as Minister for Sco⟨tland⟩. I will write to you by the first safe hands I can find to carry my letters. Adieu I am ever
Most faithfully yours

THOMAS BRADSHAW TO CHARLES JENKINSON

Add. MS. 38205, f. 88.

Tuesday, September 9, 1766.

When I have thanked you, my dear Sir, for your obliging letter of the 31st which I received on Saturday, I will proceed to answer your queres, in the best manner I can. From the most diligent, and effectual enquiries I have been able to make, and from the solemn declaration of himself and his

1. See Jenkinson's letter to Townshend on p. 424.
2. Sir George Yonge, 5th Bart., M.P. for Honiton 1754–61, 1763–96, was a Lord of the Admiralty 1766–70. He was afterwards Secretary at War 1782–94. See *D.N.B.*
3. Henry Temple, 2nd Viscount Palmerston, M.P. for East Looe 1762–68, and subsequently for Boroughbridge, Hastings, and Winchester.

friends Lord B. has not seen the K. before, nor since the change. He told Lord Ligonier upon his honor that ⟨he⟩ was ignorant of every thing which had happened and had not seen the K. for twelve months : his brother, who has the Privy Seal of Scotland, declares that he owes his restoration *solely* to the K.[1]

The Duke of Bedford's party are courted by the present people ; you know the negociation with Lord Gower. It is began from some hints Rigby gave that it would be agreable, and if Rigby is hearty the great Duke will not long remain in opposition. Lord Gower's refusal was peremptory, but it is thought the negociation is not absolutely at an end. Lord Egmont's resignation proceeded I am told from the strong party that was against him at his own Board,[2] and from the little support he had reason to expect in the Cabinet : I need not tell you, that he was always upon the worst terms with the present Minister.

I know nothing of Welbore Ellis, but I should think from some things I have met with Lord Northumberland will have an honorable office. I hear of no other arrangements, and I lament that some people are not taken in. We will talk all these matters over, when we meet.

His Grace of R.[3] must have been very wrongheaded if he had not seen your behaviour in the most amiable light ; I dare say you will not find him in the most pleasant humor about the late transactions here.

I must add to the trouble I have given you and Mr. C. by requesting you will smuggle for your cousin at Hendon six ounces of the same gold. . . .

1. Cf. William Gerard Hamilton to Temple, August 25, 1766 : " Lord Bute, who affects at least to be much dissatisfied with everything which is going forward, had a meeting with Lord Ligonier at Lord Townshend's, where he declared that he had not been in the least instrumental in the *disgrace* which his Lordship had suffered by the promotion of Lord Granby, and added that upon his honour, he had not seen the king, even once, during the last twelvemonth " (*Grenv. Pps.* iii, 309). On the formation of the Chatham Administration Bute wrote a letter of reproach to the King " for not applying to me about my friends or intimating your intentions about my brother " (Add. MS. 36797, f. 59).

2. The Admiralty.

3. Possibly the Duc de Richelieu. Elliot called on him when he was at Compiègne, and Jenkinson may well have done so too.

Add. MS. 38205, ff. 89-90.

Cavendish Square, September 16, 1766.

Dear Sir,

The Parliament was this day prorogued to the 11th of November, which may possibly threaten your tour even through Flanders and Holland. I came to town last Saturday night from Buckinghamshire, where I passed some days with an old acquaintance, whom we visited together some years ago.[1] The breach between him and Lord C⟨hatham⟩ is so much wider, *if possible*, than it was before, and indeed seems so well grounded, that though I wont say it is impossible to bring about a reconciliation, yet I think it is of all unlikely things, the most unlikely ever to happen. The late arrangements at the Admiralty board seem by no means to be approved of, nor is the person who presides thought equal to that active Department. As Lord Gower was certainly offered the Seals, Lord Shelburne would have been placed at the head of that Board, if Lord Gower had accepted them ;[2] and I am even apt to think that they had some thoughts of putting C. Townshend at the Admiralty Board, because they wrote to Dowdeswell after his first dismission, to let him know that he might still have the Chancellorship of the Exchequer, notwithstanding which they afterwards bestowed it upon Charles Townshend, who I hear talks as a man of his turn may be supposed to talk, when he quits an employment of more than £5000 per ann. for one of £3000. The late Chancellor of the Exchequer is returned to Worcestershire, as I am informed very much out of humour, and indeed with reason after the treatment he has met with.

The Parliament it is supposed meets the sooner in order to put a more effectual stop to the exportation of grain, for it seems by some omission or blunder in the Act of last year, it is thought that the Crown has not sufficient power and authority to stop the exportation by Proclamation.[3] You will have

1. Grenville. See next letter.
2. Cf. Grafton, *Autobiog.* pp. 99-101.
3. In September 1766 there were riots over the high price of corn and an Order in Council was passed on September 26 laying a forty days' embargo on its exportation. When Parliament met on November 11, Grenville and some of the Opposition questioned the legality of this emergency measure and Administration were obliged to cover themselves by an Act of Indemnity, which was passed on December 10.

heard that Lord Hillsborough accepted the Board of Trade, but you will be surprised to hear that he has accepted with lesser powers than he held it before, for it is no longer to be a board of representation, but merely a board of report upon reference, which is just making it the most insignificant Board in the Kingdom, and puts those who hold employments there upon no better footing than that of pensioners, without the least prospect of being serviceable. Sir George Pococke [1] I hear has thrown up, and is very disgusted as are several others, who happen to be seniors to Mr. Saunders. I am going to a very disagreable dinner at the Imperial Ambassadors, but I shall keep my letter open, in case I should happen to pick up any thing worth sending you.

Though there were a good deal of company at the Ambassadors, there was no news stirring ; so that I must content myself with sending you a letter that can offer you no entertainment. But if any thing happens that is worth transmitting to you when I happen to be in town you may depend, dear Sir, upon hearing from

Your most sincere friend,

Harcourt

My compliments to Monsieur and Madame de Guerchy and to Monsieur de Beuvron and family. I intend writing to him next post.

THOMAS WHATELY TO CHARLES JENKINSON

Add. MS. 38205, ff. 93-4.

Nonsuch Park, September 18, 1766.

Dear Jenkinson,

I was favoured with yours from Compiegne while I was in Buckinghamshire, where there was no occasion for me to trumpet your feats in the chace, as your fame had already reached so far, and you are allowed to be the greatest sportsman out of England by all who have been in France this summer. I shewed Mr. G⟨renville⟩ the passage in your letter which related to him, and he expressed himself highly pleased with

---

1. Admiral Sir George Pocock, K.B. (1706–92), about whom see *D.N.B.*, M.P. for Plymouth 1760–68, resigned his flag on September 11, and his name was struck off the list of Admirals.

the sentiments you entertain of his conduct : Mrs. G. desires the favour of you, if you go to Montpelier, to buy for her some of the liquorice which they prepare there in a manner peculiar to that place, in little cylindrical black pieces of about a sixth of an inch in length : but I fear now that your tour to the South of France will be shortened by the meeting of Parliament the 11 November. My little schemes are entirely disconcerted by it, as I have hitherto been very little at home and I had promised myself three months leisure in the country : I shall however have the pleasure of meeting you and some other of my friends so much the sooner : at present I see none unless I go into their counties to look for them, except that Wedderburn sometimes crosses me in passing from one ramble to another, and now and then some man going in or out of place calls upon me for my compliments of congratulation or condolence. Just now the only removal talked of is that of the Duke of Portland : [1] and I suppose it has been delayed hitherto not from any difficulty in making the vacancy, but in filling it up. The offer has been made more than once I believe to Lord Gower : who will have the place at last I do not devise. I hear that at New York they have voted the compensation to the sufferers as a grant to his Majesty for *charitable uses*. At Boston their debates upon the Requisition ended in a committee to enquire into the authors of the late disturbances : and at Rhode Island the Assembly broke up without taking any notice of the Secretary of State's letter. The other events in our political world you see in the publick papers : I will not add to those *authentic and consistent* publications the idle and contradictory rumours of the day : few of them reach even this place before they are disbelieved in London, and would be forgot here by the time I could send them to Paris. Opinions and surmises fluctuate with them, but these will have formed themselves into some settled determinations against your return, and will furnish matter for our perepatetic speculations in Parliament Street. I am with great truth, dear Jenkinson,

Your most faithful and obedient servant

Thomas Whately

1. William Henry Cavendish Bentinck, 3rd Duke of Portland, remained Chamberlain of the Household until the crisis over Lord Edgcumbe's dismissal in December 1766 (see p. 436 n. 3), when the place was given to Lord Hertford, who resigned the Mastership of the Horse.

Add. MS. 38205, ff. 95-6.

Cavendish Square, September 22, 1766.

Dear Sir,

Had I known a little sooner that Mr. Selwyn [1] was to set out for Paris as to morrow morning I should have had more leisure than I have to collect some materials for a letter. As I came to town last night I have not had time to pick up any news nor do I believe there is any thing of great importance now stirring. Lord Chatham is gone to Bath to recruit for the opening of the Parliament, though it is generally thought that his attendance in our House will not be very constant. I am apt to think that he would be overfond of engaging his brother Temple, who it is said will keep no terms with him, but will attack him with all the virulence that their present enmity can suggest. Many people imagine that if Lord Chathams Administration meets with any rubs or difficulties, his Lord-ship will retire and leave the drudgery to others, he will not quit his place, but he may plead bad health, or perhaps have recourse to the old expedient, of laying the blame upon Lord Bute's influence. The new Ministry seems by no means easy in their present situation, nor is it the opinion of the world, that their power will be very durable. If one considers how oddly the machine is framed the prospect is not very flattering. Lord Chatham is supposed not to be insensible of the abuse that is bestowed upon him. They have indeed bespattered his Lordship very sufficiently, and in many instances very grossly. I beleive I told you in my last that I had been at Wootton, the master of which place seems more calm and *talks* more dispassionately than I ever heard him. The breach between him and his brother in law is (if possible) wider than ever, and in all appearance irreparable. The wheat proves but very light, though upon the whole the quantity is not inconsider-able, however the great exportation has raised the price so high as to be very alarming least some publick calamities should ensue between this and the meeting of the Parliament, when I flatter myself you will return to England. The world, (at least the uncandid, which I fear is no inconsiderable part of it) will still suppose that Lord Bute had a hand in the late

1. George Selwyn, or Charles Selwyn the banker at Paris.

alterations, but I am persuaded from the assurances he gave me, that he had no concern in them, for says he, what marks of friendship have these gentlemen shewed me? have they done any thing for my friends? Indeed Mackenzie I am told does not think himself beholden to the Ministers for being reinstated. I believe they would wish to make up to Lord Bute, but they have not spirit to do it in a proper manner. The Queen is not yet brought to bed, but expects to be every moment.[1] You will hear of it at Paris, and there will be notice enough for your brother to come over to make his appearance at the Christening, which I would not mention if I had not particular reasons for so doing. Lord and Lady Nuneham leave Spa on the 27th so that you will see them in a few days at Paris. My compliments to all friends who enquire after me and believe me dear Sir,

Most sincerely yours

Harcourt

LORD HARCOURT TO CHARLES JENKINSON

Add. MS. 38205, ff. 97-8.

Cavendish Square, September 27, 1766.

Dear Sir,

You will wonder to receive two letters of such different dates under the same cover. You must know Mr. Sellwyn undertook to carry some letters to France, he intended to have set out three or four days ago, but some busyness or perhaps accident made him alter his plan, and obliged him to defer his journey, and to send back the letters, that they might be conveyed by the post, in case they required immediate dispatch. But I prefer sending my letter by him, to the usual method of the post, and I should hope he would arrive at Paris about the time you return from Lyons. Lord Bristol was yesterday declared Lord Lieutenant of Ireland by His Majesty in Councill, and Lord Hertford kissed hands for the Mastership of the Horse. Lord Northumberland was at Court and seemed much out of humour. It is said (but with what authority I know not) that he expected to be appointed Lord Chamberlain but the Duke of Portland does not seem inclinable to resign his post, and Lord Chatham is supposed to be averse to dismissing of

1. The Princess Royal, afterwards Queen Charlotte of Württemberg, was born on September 29, 1766.

him.[1] The Cavendishes are said to be out of humour, but I am not sure of that fact. Hitherto nothing has been done for Lord Bute's friends, for it is now understood that Mackenzie's being reinstated in his Office, was owing to the King, and not the work of the new Ministry. I have not seen Lord Bute this fortnight, but I dont see much room for any great alteration in his Lordships politicks since I saw him last. He then expressed some concern that his friends were not taken notice of, and he will be still more uneasy, to see them so totally slighted.[2] I am apt to believe that there is no indisposition towards them but that there is not spirit enough among the Ministers to do what would be right from an apprehension of making themselves unpopular. It is no easy matter in these difficult times, for men who are the best disposed to know how to conduct themselves with prudence and integrity. In your particular case, the same prudence and circumspection that have carried you the many shoals you have been exposed to, will enable you to conduct yourself in such a manner as to support the character you have so justly acquired. And as your circumstances are fortunately such, as do not oblige you to accept any terms but such as may be agreable to you I think you will be able to take such a part this winter, as may set you very high in the estimation of mankind.

The great exportation of corn, for some time past, and the thinness of the late crop, which was very light have raised the price of wheat so high, that there have been riots in many places.[3] Yesterday an embargo was laid upon all corn ships, and a Proclamation will come out to prevent the distillers from using wheat in their stills. These cautions seem prudent, and will I hope tend to quiet people's minds, and make them easy. Lord and Lady Nuneham will probably be at Paris before you, and will scarce stay there above a week or ten days. I expect the Colonel every moment from Ireland, though the wind has lately been contrary and in the east. I am dear Sir

Yours most sincerely,

Harcourt

The Queen is not yet brought to bed.

1. Cf. the King's letter to Chatham, dated September 25, in *Chatham Corr.* iii, 74-6. On October 18, 1766, Northumberland was created Earl Percy and Duke of Northumberland on the understanding that " he never would be an applier for employments ".
2. Cf. Bute's letter to the King complaining of neglect (see pp. xxi, 429 n. 1).
3. Cf. Fortescue, *Corr. of George III*, i, Nos. 389, 392-5.

I find upon reading over my first letter, that I have said the same thing over and over again but you will excuse it.

CHARLES JENKINSON TO SIR JAMES LOWTHER

Add. MS. 38205, f. 110.

The following letter is docketed merely November 1766, but seems to have been written on November 19. On that day, according to Grenville's diary, Rigby had a conversation with him in the House of Commons in which he disclaimed any part in the negotiation between Chatham and the Bedfords, while on the previous night the Rockinghams met to consider resigning over Chatham's dismissal of Lord Edgcumbe from the Treasurer-ship of the Household. See *Grenv. Pps.* iii, pp. 387-9.

10 o'clock.

Dear Sir,
I am just come home ; all I have heard is that the Duke of Portland had no audience today of His Majesty and returned from Court with his Staff ; [1] and there were no other resigna-tions. The world however still say that there are to be changes. At the House of Commons Grenville and Rigby were long in very close conference ; I hear that Lord Chatham is very angry with Charles Townshend.[2] I am ever

Yours faithfully,
C. Jenkinson

CHARLES JENKINSON TO SIR JAMES LOWTHER

in Charles Street, Berkeley Square

Add. MS. 38205, f. 106.

Thursday 3 o'clock.
[November 27, 1766.]

My dear Sir,
The resignations are to be today ; I suppose that they are made already.[3] This I have from such information that unless

1. According to Rockingham, Portland told Conway on November 20 that he meant to resign his place of Chamberlain of the Household, but Conway persuaded him to defer his resignation for a few days. See Rockingham to Lord Scarborough, November 20, *Rockingham Memoirs*, ii, 23.
2. Charles Townshend disagreed with Chatham's policy with regard to the East India Company.
3. On Thursday November 27, the Duke of Portland and Lords Scarborough, Bessborough, and Monson resigned their places, and the next day three of the

all mankind are lyars, I cannot doubt of it. There is also to be a Council tonight when a quarrel which has arisen between Lord Chatham and Mr. C. Townshend on Indian affairs will be brought to its issue ; I know that the latter thinks it will end in his going to Adderbury ; I use his own expression.[1] I am perswaded from many circumstances that the Government is drawing to a conclusion. I hope to know the issue of what passes tonight soon after it is over, when you shall hear further from me. I am

Ever yours most faithfully

C. Jenkinson

CHARLES JENKINSON TO SIR JAMES LOWTHER

Add. MS. 38205, ff. 108-9.

Thursday night, 10 o'clock.
[November 27, 1766.]

My dear Sir,
      I have heard since I saw you, that the resignations are tomorrow to proceed further, and that among others Sir Charles Saunders and Kepple mean to give up their employments. I have heard also that the Bedfords will not accept.[2] This last is Lord Mansfield's news. I have again seen Sir Fletcher Norton : and we both of us join in wishing that you would send a servant to Lord B⟨ute⟩ and beg of him to come to town ; he will at most lose but one day in the country ; and he may otherwise miss an opportunity of the utmost con-

Admiralty Board, Sir Charles Saunders, the First Lord, Admiral Keppel, and Sir William Meredith, told Chatham they would resign on the following Monday. On Sunday November 30 Chatham offered one of these places to Jenkinson, who refused it, but on Tuesday December 2 he again saw Chatham and this time accepted. On December 3 Jenkinson wrote a letter of explanation to Grenville, who "returned no answer, and forbid his porter ever to let him into his house again ". Grenville was particularly hurt at this defection because, on November 29, Jenkinson had attended a meeting with him, Fletcher Norton, Wedderburn, "and others ". Harcourt afterwards tried unsuccessfully to smooth things over between them. See Grenville's diary, *Grenv. Pps.* iii, 390-95, and Harcourt to Grenville, December 7, *ibid.* pp. 350-51.

1. According to Walpole (*Memoirs*, ii, 279) there was a Cabinet meeting at Conway's about this time, when Chatham declared he would resign if Townshend were not removed.

2. When Gower came to Bedford on November 28 with an offer from Chatham of places for himself, Rigby, and Lord Weymouth, the Bedfords thought they were to be asked into Administration and meant to accept. But when, on December 1, Bedford presented his terms to Chatham, the King refused them. In the meantime Chatham had unaccountably filled up the three vacancies at the Admiralty without offering any of them to the Bedfords, and so the negotiation was dropped.

sequence to himself and friends. There are certainly the strongest symptoms that the Government is coming to a conclusion ; and the King not knowing where to have recourse and complaining of his friends that they will not stand forward, may send for Lord Temple as he did for Mr. Pitt, and put all into his hands, and we may be used as ill by the former, as we have been by the latter. I am ever with unalterable regard

Yours most faithfully,

C. Jenkinson

Though there should be nothing to be done there can be no harm in coming to town.

LORD MACCLESFIELD TO CHARLES JENKINSON

Add. MS. 38205, f. 112.

Shirburn Castle, December 7, 1766.

Dear Sir,

You gave me great pleasure by informing me of your appointment to be a Lord of the Admiralty. I am glad that these changes have been productive of advantage to you. Nothing sure can be so unsteady as the political winds have of late been which have since Lord Chatham's being at the head of affairs shifted to every point of the compass of politics. Who would have thought of this last turn ; Lord Chatham endeavouring a connexion with the Earl of B⟨ute⟩ as the only means of supporting himself. Does that connexion subsist or is it only wishd by Lord C—— ? [1] Whatever it is I think Lord C——'s fall must soon come. I should be sorry it should happen before he has had an opportunity of letting the world see that Lord Chatham in power is no more than another man in the same situation as has it not in his power to work those miracles for the benefit of the nation, which the infatuated multitude have been taught to expect from him. I can hardly think that Lord B—— can heartily join with Lord C. the man who has traduced him and render'd him odious to the people. Whatever may be the case, I wish every thing may turn out

1. The places given by Chatham to Jenkinson, Le Despencer, and William Harcourt were considered by Newcastle as evidence that " my Lord Chatham had thrown off the mask, and publicly owns and courts my Lord Bute's friendship and support " (Newcastle to Rockingham, *Rockingham Memoirs*, ii, 28). See also Horace Walpole to George Montagu, December 8.

for the best, and that we may at last have a Ministry a little more durable than Ministrys have lately been, which will be the only means of doing any thing for the good of the nation. I am dear Sir,

Your most obedient humble servant,

Macclesfield

Lords of the Admiralty not being obliged to so strict residence as Secretaries of the Treasury, I shall flatter myself with the hopes of seeing you at Shirburn this Christmas during the Recess of the Parliament.

ANNUS PACIFICUS

The following paper in Israel Mauduit's handwriting was probably written about the year 1769, when he published the first edition of his *History of the New England Colonies*, to justify the British colonial thesis, but as it deals with the events of 1766–67, it is placed here.

Add. MS. 38337, ff. 261-3.

In this era of gratitude the Assembly quarrelled with Mr. Jackson the province Agent, and first took up the factious measure of having a separate Agent of their own (a Mr. De Bert) in whom they placed their confidence, though Mr. Jackson still continued the province Agent till near the end of the Session, when they dismissed him, assigning this curious reason, that he was Agent for Connecticut; [1] and the general interest of the Colonies cannot be so effectually served by uniting the Agency of several of them in the same person, as by each having its separate Agent. Yet when Dr. Franklin [2] was chosen their Agent; he was Agent for Pensylvania.

During the interval of this Sessions a few soldiers belonging to the Artillery arrived at Boston. The Governor and Council made provision for them according to Act of Parliament in the barracks at Castle William. This, in this Era of Gratitude was a violation of their new priveliges, and made a fresh subject of angry messages. Though the Governor and Council shewed, that this had always been the usage; and that they acted only on the old act, and provided them with fuel and candle only; and not with the other necessaries ordered by the new act.

1. See p. 359.   2. Benjamin Franklin.

In this year also this same Assembly started a new pretence for picking a quarrel with the Governor [1] and Lieutenant Governor,[2] by demanding in a message to know whether it was by the Governor's authority or his own, that the Lieutenant Governor sat in the Council chamber the first day of opening the Session, which they voted to be unconstitutional ; though they were obliged to acknowledge that the former presidents [3] were all for it ; and that, when the Lieutenant Governor happened not to be of the Council, yet he had always sat in the Council chamber on such occasions, though without a vote, ready to answer any questions that they should want.

It is often said that immediately after the repeal of the Stamp Act the people of Massachusetts were all satisfied and the next year was a year of peace. The very first act of the Assembly immediately after the arrival of the news was at their Election in May, was to leave out of the Council the Lieutenant Governor and the Secretary, with every other person that had the least connection with Government and to choose in their room the most obnoxious men they could finde. This laid the Governor under the necessity of resorting to his last power, and rejecting six of the Councillors they had chosen. The Lieutenant Governor and the Secretary had always before been used to be of the Council ; and were men (as the Governor says) not only respectable in themselves for their integrity and ability, but also quite necessary to the Administration of Government *in the very station from whence you have displaced them.* Through the whole following Sessions it appears from their journals, that they sought every opportunity of quarreling with their Governor ; carping at every expression in his speeches ; boasting of their loyalty, and gratitude to his Majesty ; which they expressed by turning out all those of his servants, whom they could turn out, and in the most taunting manner insulting the Governor, whom they could not turn out.

In this pacific year the revenue off⟨icers⟩ [4] dare to exert themselves. B⟨ut   ⟩ smuggling so very flagrant ⟨   ⟩

1. Sir Francis Bernard. It was largely due to his vigorous administration of the Stamp Act that it aroused so much antagonism. See *D.N.B.*
2. Thomas Hutchinson who succeeded Bernard as Governor in 1769. He wrote a history of Massachusetts, part of which was damaged when the mob looted his house in revenge for his support of the Stamp Act. Afterwards, in consequence of the Vote of Compensation, he was awarded £2500 damages. See *D.N.B.*
3. Precedents.
4. A portion of the paper, half the width of the page, is torn off so that eight lines are incomplete on one side and seven on the other.

at it. A large quantity of wine ⟨   ⟩ lodged in a store without paym⟨   ⟩er and deputy Collector with a ⟨   ⟩ proper attendants, went to ⟨   ⟩ immediately raised, who insulte⟨d   ⟩ and would not suffer them to enter the store till the next day, after the wines had been carried off in the night to some other place. Justices are not easily to be found to take depositions on these occasions. The officers were therefore obliged to make their complaints to the Governor ; and some depositions were then taken (which I believe were sent home to the Treasury). Upon which the Assembly made this riot their own, by a message to the Governor and Council to know by whose authority the depositions were taken, and to demand a copy of them, in order that they might vindicate the loyalty and obedience to the town. And thus began the practice of supporting their rioters by voting themselves loyal, and that any man who takes notice of these riots, is an enemy to the country, and means to alienate the King's affections.

Soon after the opening of this pacific Assembly Mr. Secretary Conway's letter to the Governor was communicated to the Assembly for their making compensation to the several sufferers in the riots about the Stamp Act. Every word of the Governor's speech upon this occasion was carped at. The Assembly affectedly used every pretence to put off the making the compensation. They at length found, that this was not an act of *justice*, but of *generosity* ; and therefore desired a recess, that they might consult their constituents. ⟨   ⟩ found a 2d pretence, and de⟨   ⟩ thus after wrangling it off ⟨   ⟩ Assembly meets, 10 December, ⟨   ⟩eir bill of Compensation with an ⟨   ⟩ it. And even that was passed ⟨   oppr⟩obrious Resolutions.

[*Here, at the top of f. 263 of the text, three lines have been inserted later and then scratched out. They are in a different ink but in the same writing* : upon two of the foregoing heads, the turning out of the Lieutenant-Governor and Secretary, and refusing the Lieutenant-Governor seat without a voice, as well as the negativing six of the new Councillors, see Lord Shelburn's letter at the end of 1768.]

Long as is the foregoing Catalogue, there is yet one more instance of their pacific disposition during this year of gratitude for the repeal of the Stamp Act. Among the whalers on the coast of Labradore very great disorders had arisen ; and certain people of some of the New England Governments, had been guilty of acts of robbery, piracy, and murder. Governor Palliser upon this published a proclamation against these disorders, with regulations for preventing them, and punishments for the breach of them, and sent these Proclamations to the neighbouring Governments. Governor Barnard, as his duty required, published this proclamation in his province. For this the Assembly sent him a number of angry messages from which messages it appears the sole object with them was not to express their resentment against the perpetrators of these crimes ; not to deter them in future, or bring them to punishment ; but, in their usual cant, to charge the Governor with disgracing the province, and alienating the affections of his Majesty and his Ministers against them.

See the various messages that passed during the Sessions upon this subject, and all this quarrelsom and spitefull disposition against Government was shewn during the Ministry even of their friends, and in the honey months of their deliverance from the Stamp Act.

It is difficult to fix the date of the following paper which is in Jenkinson's own handwriting. It may have been drafted either when the Stamp Act or when its Repeal was under consideration.

Add. MS. 38339, f. 182.

People of the Colonies not taxable

State of Society.

> Farmers capable of being taxed though not so high as manufacturers.
> The subjects of this country taxed when they were only farmers, France and Spain.

Pay Taxes in other ways.

> Their commodities exported to foreign countries not subject to taxes.
> Their commodities here taxed high, but paid by the consumer, unless when the market is overstocked. This not the case and prevented by bounties on our and high duties or prohibitions on foreign commodities of the same kind.

(442)

Foreign commodities going to the Plantations pay one subsidy.

British commodites pay nothing.

Woolen ⎱
Iron ⎰ Nowhere else.

Linen has a bounty.

Additional freight a burthen. These not proportional to the burthens of this country.

Not possible to prevent manufacturing by any prohibitory Laws.

INDEX

THE END

PRINTED BY R. & R. CLARK, LTD., EDINBURGH